# The Classical Epic Tradition

# WISCONSIN STUDIES IN CLASSICS

*General Editors*

BARBARA HUGHES FOWLER *and* WARREN G. MOON

———

E. A. THOMPSON
*Romans and Barbarians: The Decline of the Western Empire*


JENNIFER TOLBERT ROBERTS
*Accountability in Athenian Government*


H. I. MARROU
*A History of Education in Antiquity*
*Histoire de l'Education dans l'Antiquité,* translated by George Lamb
(originally published in English by Sheed and Ward, 1956)


ERIKA SIMON
*Festivals of Attica: An Archaeological Commentary*


G. MICHAEL WOLOCH
*Roman Cities: Les villes romaines* by Pierre Grimal, translated
and edited by G. Michael Woloch, together with
A Descriptive Catalogue of Roman Cities
by G. Michael Woloch


WARREN G. MOON, *editor*
*Ancient Greek Art and Iconography*


KATHERINE DOHAN MORROW
*Greek Footwear and the Dating of Sculpture*


JOHN KEVIN NEWMAN
*The Classical Epic Tradition*

# The Classical Epic Tradition

John Kevin Newman

The University of Wisconsin Press

Published 1986

The University of Wisconsin Press
114 North Murray Street
Madison, Wisconsin 53715

The University of Wisconsin Press, Ltd.
1 Gower Street
London WC1E 6HA, England

First printing

Printed in the United States of America

Library of Congress Cataloging in Publication Data
Newman, John Kevin, 1928–
The classical epic tradition.
Bibliography: pp. 535–551.
Includes index.
1. Epic literature—History and criticism.
I. Title.
PN56.E65N49   1985      809.1′3      85–12460
ISBN 0-299-10510-5

UXORI AMANTISSIMAE

GRATIAS

# CONTENTS

## ILLUSTRATIONS

# PREFACE

D URING Michaelmas Term 1946 Maurice Bowra lectured at five in the afternoon in Wadham College Hall on the history of epic poetry. Europe was moving into a hard winter, and Oxford into night, but from the speaker's lectern light fell through the gathering gloom onto the open notebook of at least one listener.

In 1967, my *Augustus and the New Poetry* examined the pervasive influence of Alexandrian poetic doctrine even on the vatic masterpieces of Augustan Roman literature, even on the *Aeneid*. There was an obvious next step. If the classical epic tradition had been subject in this way to previously unrecognized Callimachean interference, it seemed logical to ask what a history of European literary epic would look like which acknowledged Alexandrian influence as legitimate instead of either ignoring it or scolding as deviant great writers in whom its presence was too obvious to be overlooked. If this clue were to be followed, could precision replace complacent vacuity in the tracing of literary inheritance? Could some common patterns of development be detected, for example, between Virgil, Dante, Ariosto, Milton? Could some theoretical kinship be suggested between Callimachus and Eisenstein? Bowra had always upheld the banner of Russian culture in an increasingly polarized world. What was the relevance to the interpretation of the Classics of the theories of the Russian Formalists, of Mikhail Bakhtin?

Scholars are naturally inclined to think of artists as if they too were scholars and, in the case of the Alexandrians, they are often right. But there is a non-discursive cognition available to the artist, as Kant long ago pointed out, which modifies questions about particular sources and derivations. If the Greeks, as a classical scholar at least must firmly believe, deserve the epithet "classical," it is because, thanks to their chronological priority, they defined certain classes. They established the boundaries within which imagination and creativity will tend to move among artists of the European and European-influenced family. Those who come after them, and even those who do not know too much about them in any formal sense, will find that they bump against the same mental furniture as they grope in the half-dark about the mind's room. This is what is meant by saying that the Greeks, and their successors the Romans, are the architects—and even at times the interior designers—of our particular version of civilization.

Whether a given writer may or may not have read Callimachus has not therefore been my first inquiry. If he read Ovid, he read Callimachus enough. My book is concerned with the imagination's contours, with pattern and convergence, with the genre that remembers, even if the artist does not. Its justification can only be retroactive. Do its perspectives enlarge the spirit in our cramping age? Is it a contribution to *literae humaniores*?

I would like to thank the Center for Advanced Study at the University of Illinois for a year's leave of absence from teaching duties during the preparation of the manuscript, and the Research Board of the Urbana Campus, and its Executive Secretary, Dr. Linda S. Wilson, for generous access to computer facilities. My student Dr. Patricia Bogue lent me the benefit of her acumen and wide learning during work on Apollonius and Thomas Mann. Professor Herbert Marshall, Director of the Center for Soviet and East European Studies at Southern Illinois University at Carbondale, and a former student of S. M. Eisenstein at the Moscow Film Institute, kindly read and criticized a first draft of Chapter IX.

Tangible help and, even more important, encouragement, were provided in various ways and at different times by Professor Hugh Lloyd-Jones, Regius Professor of Greek in the University of Oxford; Professor Robin Nisbet, Corpus Professor of Latin in the University of Oxford; and Professor John Dillon, Regius Professor of Greek at Trinity College, Dublin. To these distinguished scholars, and to all who aided me in any way, I offer sincerest gratitude. I would also like to thank the University of Wisconsin Press, its Acquisitions Editor, Mr. Peter Givler, and its Chief Editor, Mrs. Elizabeth Steinberg, for their welcome; and an anonymous Reader at the Press for valuable comments.

This apograph from an open notebook is dedicated to my wife Frances, as is all I do.

J. K. NEWMAN

*Urbana, 1985*

# The Classical Epic Tradition

# I

# A MAP OF THE TERRAIN

THE classical epic tradition begins for us with Homer, and there are times when the reader of Homer, confronted by the inexhaustible riches which the *Iliad* and the *Odyssey* contain, is tempted to believe that the rest of European literature is merely a commentary on the first of its masters. Such a feeling would not be new; already in the ancient world Homer had been compared to a spring from which all other poetry gushed.[1] The wealth and variety of language, the subject matter ranging from the battlefields of Troy to the lonely fight against the elements, the characters as diverse as Achilles and Penelope, the tones of solemn majesty, satire and every intervening nuance—these are the qualities offering to the reader even now that panorama of things human and divine which made its author to later Greeks simply "the poet."

## I

It is the destiny of such towering figures to compel others to come to terms with them. The sincerest flattery is imitation, and "Homer"

---

[1] Compare Ovid, *Amores* III. 9. 25–26 and Georgius Pisides, *Exp. Pers.* I. 66 ff. This was evidently a Byzantine *topos*: cf. Eustathius in A. B. Drachmann's edition of the *Scholia Vetera in Pindari Carmina*, vol. III (repr. Amsterdam 1966), p. 286. Further parallels are collected by T. B. L. Webster, *Hellenistic Poetry and Art* (London 1964), p. 145 and note 1, and by D. A. Russell, *'Longinus' On the Sublime* (Oxford 1964), p. 116. The far-reaching influence on medieval and Renaissance criticism of the *De Homeri Vita et Poesi* attributed to Plutarch should also be noted here. Cf. Quintilian XII. 11. 21; E. R. Curtius, *Europäische Literatur und lateinisches Mittelalter* (Bern 1948), p. 211.—The vast mass of modern Homeric scholarship is surveyed, for example, by A. Lesky, *A History of Greek Literature* (Eng. trans., London 1966), pp. 14 ff., and "Homeros" (*RE*, Supp. 11, 1968), cols. 687–846; and by G. S. Kirk, *The Songs of Homer* (Cambridge 1962). The most important contribution to the understanding of the *Iliad* in our time has been made by W. Schadewaldt: cf. his *Iliasstudien*, Des XLIII Bandes der Abhandlungen der philol.-hist. Klasse der sächsischen Akademie der Wissenschaften, nr. VI (Leipzig 1938). The distinction between the scholarly and the literary problem made by Johannes Th. Kakridis, *Homeric Researches* (Lund 1949), is essential. Among more recent work, the English-speaking student will particularly wish to consult Howard Clarke, *Homer's Readers* (Newark, London, Toronto 1981); Jasper Griffin, *Homer on Life and Death* (Oxford 1980); C. W. Macleod, *Homer, Iliad Book XXIV* (Cambridge 1982).

sometimes meant to the Greeks, not merely and cleanly the poems
we now know, but a broadly defined volume of epic poetry on varying
themes drawn from the legendary past. Reaction against the heroic
values lauded by this aristocratic poetry began as early as Archilochus,
who praised the kind of general that Homer's first audience would
have classed with Thersites. Xenophanes objected to the moral ideals
enshrined in the Homeric poems,[2] and found a later voice to support
him in Plato, who invented a theory of narrative technique to justify
his disapproval.[3] Cast forth from the ideal state as little more than a
liar, the "educator of Greece" was defended by Aristotle, but even
so, rather ambiguously. Were the *Iliad* and the *Odyssey* superior to
their imitations? Yes, said the *Poetics*. Was the epic genre the highest
kind of literature, as previously maintained at least implicitly by those
who thought the best poet must write the best sort of poetry?[4] No,
came the answer, and by a surprising paradox the best kind of poetry
was declared to be tragedy, a genre of recent Athenian invention
and one exported on a limited scale to the Greek world by comparison
with the all-prevailing recitation of Homer's epics.

Even so, Aristotle was ultimately on Homer's side. One of the
seminal texts of European criticism, the *Poetics* nowhere sowed more
fruitfully than in the brilliance with which its author distinguished,
among a mass of indeterminate epic writing, what could rightly be
attributed to Homer. Aristotle's canon of Homeric work was more
catholic than ours, and included the now lost *Margites*, a poem in
mixed meter with a comically stupid hero. The authenticity and
superiority of the *Iliad* and *Odyssey* were based on two chief considerations. The first was that those epics selected and organized their
material. The *Iliad* did not sing the whole of the siege of Troy, but
only the wrath of Achilles, though this episode could be thought of
as encapsulating the entire story of the war, and indeed of all wars.
The second was that, in their treatment of events, Homer's poems
anticipated and prepared the way for drama, which was, in this sense,
their culmination and perfection. The far-reaching implications of
this poetic program cut away the ground from the epic as it had
been revived in the late fifth or early fourth century by imitative
poets like Antimachus of Colophon and Choerilus of Samos who
fondly imagined that by prolix treatment of myth or by versifying

---

[2] For the early moralizing criticisms of Homer see R. Pfeiffer, *History of Classical
Scholarship* (Oxford 1968), pp. 8 ff., and 58; and for Aristotle's views *ibid.*, pp. 67 ff.,
and Curtius, *op. cit.*, pp. 208 ff.

[3] *Rep.* III. 392 c ff. See S. Koster, *Antike Epostheorien* (Wiesbaden 1970), pp. 39–41.

[4] Cf. Plato, *Laws* II. 658 d–e.

history they were treading in the steps of the master, and showed that the effective recovery of the genre in the modern age would be difficult and painful.

The challenge thus thrown down by Aristotle was taken up by Callimachus, a prolific scholar and poet, author of the epic *Hecale*.[5] Callimachus lived and worked, no longer in Greece itself, but at the Royal Library in Alexandria, the capital of the Ptolemies at the mouth of the Nile, during the first part of the third century before Christ. There, as he began surveying the poetic possibilities open after a century of ever-encroaching prose on the one side, and ever-more bombastic dithyramb on the other, he saw that the superficial imitation of Homer's mannerisms was no longer feasible for any poet who wished to address his audience in terms which they could comprehend. To expatiate like Antimachus of Colophon on the legends of Thebes was to ignore Aristotle's lesson about the merits of brevity: to turn to versification of contemporary deeds of prowess, following the example set by Choerilus of Samos and his later namesake from Iasos, was to ignore both brevity and the difference between poetry and history. It is surely a profound tribute to Callimachus' literary seriousness that he even concerned himself at such a time with the problems of epic narrative at all. Then and now the poet has reaped small thanks. Bitterly criticized from diverse quarters, he replied in his old age that his adversaries had never been friends of the Muse; otherwise they would not have measured poetry with a Persian chain, instead of by the canons of art. In this ancient battle of the books, we touch upon matters of vital importance for the whole subsequent history of classical epic.

To understand a tradition, we must know what is being handed

---

[5] The appreciation of Callimachus has been immeasurably deepened in this century by the recovery of many fragments of works previously hardly known: see the monumental edition with Latin commentary by R. Pfeiffer, *Callimachus*, vol. I (repr. Oxford 1965), and vol. II (Oxford n.d.), which even so does not include the *Victoria Berenices* (below, note 29). The specialist will consult for the latest assemblage of fragments *Supplementum Hellenisticum*, edd. Hugh Lloyd-Jones and Peter Parsons (Berlin–New York 1983), pp. 89–144 and pp. 319–20, no. 675. The non-specialist will find Pfeiffer's text of the most important fragments conveniently presented and translated by C. A. Trypanis, *Callimachus, Aetia, Iambi, Hecale and other Fragments*, Loeb Classical Library (repr., London and Cambridge, Mass. 1968). The Loeb Library also offers an older text and translation of the *Hymns and Epigrams* of Callimachus by A. W. Mair (revised and repr., London and Cambridge, Mass. 1960). The verdict of A. Hecker, *Commentationum Callimachearum capita duo* (Groningen 1842), still stands: "Epicorum Graecorum nemo, uno Homero excepto, tantam apud posteros nominis celebritatem adeptus est quantam Callimachus" (p. 79: "Of all Greek epic poets no one, with the single exception of Homer, enjoyed such posthumous fame as Callimachus").

down. What was it in the first instance that Callimachus could conceivably have censured in the simple continuation of the Homeric style with other themes, whether legendary or historical? Precisely the notion that Homer is simple. If we turn back to Homer's *Iliad*, to the book on which Virgil modeled the end of the *Aeneid*, we shall be able to form some estimate of the greatness and range of the epic paradigm.

Callimachus' Alexandrian contemporaries probably had to create Book XXII of the poem in a fairly literal sense. Though the epics were divided into sections by listeners and rhapsodes even in classical times, the "books" as we now know them appear to have originated only in the Hellenistic period, with Homer's editors in the Alexandrian Library. This Alexandrian feeling that the presentation of the poems needed halting at well-defined intervals if they were to be fully effective responded to something latent in Homer's art.[6]

Book XXII opens with the rout of the other Trojans—they are compared to fawns—and the isolation of Hector, kept back outside the safe protection of the city walls, outside the gates, by destructive fate. Achilles appears in all his terrifying grimness; he has been pursuing Apollo who, disguised as Agenor, has used this trick to lend some relief to his favorites in the struggle. The terms of the contest are set. The collectivity fades into the background. The human warrior, isolated, is at grips with a more than human destiny, and when he falls foul of the gods, he has no redress. Informed by Apollo of the deceit, Achilles turns away, disgusted, angry, but impotent. He moves towards Troy, compared as he goes to a prize-winning horse that speeds over the plain with the chariot behind it. There is the first hint of the funeral games of the next book. Troy itself is like a tomb, at the doors of which are now to be celebrated the rites of death.

Old Priam is the first to notice Achilles' reappearance. A most elaborate simile likens the hero to a baleful star, which rises in the heat of summer and threatens fever to unhappy mortals, a poetic manipulation of astronomy for subjective and psychological ends destined to set a long precedent. The king appeals to his son in a speech of nearly forty lines not to challenge Achilles alone. His biting hatred for the man who has slain so many of his children is mingled with sorrow for the dead and deep affection for Hector, whose

---

[6] It is just possible that the division of the Homeric epics into books antedates the Alexandrian period: cf. R. Pfeiffer, *History of Classical Scholarship*, pp. 115 ff. For the importance of books of poems to the Alexandrians see W. Kroll, *Studien zum Verständnis der römischen Literatur* (Stuttgart 1924), pp. 225 ff. Ephorus had been the first historian to concern himself with writing unified books in prose: cf. Diodorus Siculus XVI. 1. 1; R. Laqueur, "Ephoros," *Hermes* 46 (1911), 161 ff., 321 ff.

survival will lessen the mourning for those who are gone. In that prophetic vein which raises the utterances of the old and doomed to apocalyptic awareness, Priam speaks of the fate that will overtake Troy on Hector's death, and in particular of his own expected maltreatment by the housedogs at his front door.

The appeal is taken up by Hector's mother, Hecuba, who, in a gesture to be recalled in later art by Clytemnestra and Helen, points towards her exposed breast as the symbol of what her son owes her. Inspired like Priam, she directly foretells the savagery that Hector's corpse will meet by the Greek ships.

Hector remains unpersuaded. He is compared to a serpent on the mountainside, which has fed on evil herbs and now awaits its victim. But even Hector is not without forebodings. He debates with himself, about his own folly in not accepting the proposal made by Polydamas on the previous night to withdraw to the city under cover of darkness, instead of risking the loss of so many men. He thinks of the possibility of restoring Helen to Menelaus and Agamemnon, paying half the city's possessions as a recompense, and so inducing the Greeks to depart. But common sense tells him that Achilles will be in no mood to entertain these suggestions. Ruefully, he reflects that a conversation with such a hero cannot start from the airy trifles that suffice a man and a maiden for amorous discourse. He concludes his soliloquy with the firm decision that it is better to find out which of the pair, himself or Achilles, Zeus intends to favor.

During this long interlude of psychological preparation of the audience, Achilles has been left in a state of suspended animation. He now draws near, looking like the god of war himself, Ares. His armor flashes like blazing fire, or the rising sun. Hector cannot stand his ground. He turns to run, as a trembling dove flies before a mountain hawk. The pathos of his flight in deadly peril is emphasized by eleven lines describing the familiar landmarks outside Troy which he passes,[7] the sources of the Scamander, the washing places frequented by the women in those distant times of peace before the sons of the Achaeans came. A mocking, atavistic comparison, clearly linked with the earlier comparison of Achilles to a prize-winning horse, likens the two warriors to racehorses, in some contest held to honor a dead hero.

Three times the pair circle Troy, as later Achilles will circle the doomed city dragging Hector's corpse. The gods are witnesses of the scene. Zeus, conscious of Hector's piety, asks the other gods to advise him whether to save Hector or leave him to Achilles' mercy. Athene is their voice. She concedes that Zeus has the power to save, but

---

[7] Cf. Schadewaldt, *Iliasstudien*, pp. 51–52 on *Iliad* XI. 166–181.

reminds him that he cannot expect approval for his action in rescuing a mortal long marked down for doom. Zeus yields to his "dear daughter," granting her permission to do as she pleases.[8]

Achilles is still in hot pursuit. Now he is compared to a hound, which cannot be thrown off the scent by all the maneuvers of the fawn it is hunting. In a second simile, the pair become like men in a dream, the one unable to escape, the other to overtake.

Hector has eluded his adversary so far because Apollo has lent him aid, and Achilles has reserved the slaughter of so important an enemy to himself. At this moment Zeus again intervenes. He places the dooms of Hector and Achilles in his golden scales. The fated day of Hector sinks down to Hades. Apollo abandons his favorite.

The field is now clear for Athene to assist Achilles. She bids him rest, while she deludes Hector into stopping and facing his foe. Disguising herself as Deiphobus, she offers help to Hector, who is overjoyed to think that one of his brothers has plucked up enough courage to emerge from the shelter of the walls and come out to his defense. Athene enjoys herself. In the extremity of malice, she addresses Hector twice by terms of endearment, using ambiguous language which she knows her dupe will take only one way. Accordingly, Hector determines to face Achilles.

Once again the course of the action is anticipated. Hector attempts to bargain that the victor in their combat shall not disfigure the corpse of the vanquished. Achilles' terrifying and implacable reply ends with his defiant hurling of his spear. The spear misses, but is restored to its owner by the goddess. Unaware of this, Hector believes that his chance has come. With words of mockery he too lets fly. His spear is parried by Achilles' shield. In amazement he calls out to Deiphobus to supply him with another. Deiphobus is not there. Hector grasps suddenly that death is upon him, and that he can hope for no more protection from the gods. He resolves to die as gloriously as he may. Like an eagle he swoops upon his enemy. Achilles, once again compared in all the brilliance of his divinely wrought armor to a star, marks the spot where his foe is exposed to a mortal blow, just at the throat. His point sinks home, the combat is won.

A final exchange of words lends pathos. Achilles is exultant, as he contrasts the fates in store for the corpses of Hector and Patroclus. Hector appeals for mercy, to be met once again with a violent and venomous rejection. At the end, he prophesies that Achilles too is

---

[8] For echoes of this scene in Virgil, Dante and Chaucer, see below, p. 257 and note 26, and p. 357. K. Reinhardt has some fine remarks: *Die Ilias und ihr Dichter* (Göttingen 1961), pp. 457 ff.

destined to meet death in battle. Over the dead body Achilles states his readiness to meet that death when it comes.

The rest of the Greeks gather to view the fallen hero, making grim jokes about his defenselessness, and each striking his own blow at the corpse. Achilles, in a last speech, recalls his dead friend Patroclus, and decides to challenge the Trojans to come out and rescue their defeated champion. Fastening the body to his chariot by the ankles he drags it around the city walls. Homer emphasizes that Zeus is permitting this ugly treatment.

The Trojans are stricken with wild grief, which is led by Hecuba and Priam. It is as if the whole city were given over to the flames of destruction.[9] Priam can hardly be restrained from rushing out to appeal to Achilles to spare his son; after all, he too has an aged father, Peleus. Hecuba's reaction is less extreme, perhaps a sign that for her grief is exhausted.

The action is however about to leap into yet another dimension of tautness. Andromache, Hector's wife, has not yet heard the news. She is busy at her loom, embroidering. A hot bath is being made ready for her husband's return. At the sound of the lamentation and shrieking she guesses the worst, since she knows that Hector has never shrunk from risking himself in single combat. Rushing to the walls, she sees what is happening. She flings away the headdress and veil which she received from Aphrodite as a wedding gift, and collapses into the arms of her kinswomen. Recovering, she speaks of herself and Hector as equally ill-starred, but her longest thoughts are reserved for her son. Vividly she pictures the fate that awaits an orphan, robbed of status and even of enough to eat. The name of Astyanax, suddenly introduced, applies this general picture to him. From the son she moves back to the father, and from the ill-treatment of the father to the garments all stored away for him at home, for which he will have no more use. She determines to burn them, as a public token of respect. Her sorrow is echoed by the womenfolk, and with that the book of 515 lines ends.

No one could read this narrative without being moved. Its appeal lies firstly in its alternations of experiences that are basic to all human hearts—laughter and sorrow, fear, revenge, betrayal, love for friends and family, death. But these experiences must, for the Greek, be expressed, spoken. This explains why over half the book (about 300 lines) is filled with direct speech. Many of these "speeches" are of brief duration; even so, they give a glimpse into a character's motives.

[9] Which of course will not be long delayed. Virgil understood this brilliant use of anticipation: *Aen*. IV. 669–71, the death of Dido.

The three of greater dimensions—that by Priam, attempting to dissuade his son from facing Achilles, that by Hector to himself, and Andromache's long lamentation—have as their function to give the reaction of the victims to their conqueror. They bring before us therefore a poetry which is not the simple tale of good versus bad, but one in which the defeated receive status as human beings.

The realization of this status is aided by the use of similes,[10] which are far from being mere decoration. The Trojans, compared to fawns in their bewilderment (vv. 1 ff.), are hardly likely to arouse hostility in the hearer. The fever-bringing star that Achilles recalls (vv. 26 ff.) is not wholly sympathetic even to a Greek. Later, when Hector is described as a mountain snake that has fed on evil herbs (vv. 93 ff.), the picture he presents must suggest not only terror and formidable power, but also delusion and diminution.[11]

Hector has been much criticized for running away, an action as contrary to heroic ethics as to those of a later age. The defense made by a modern scholar is conclusive.[12] This is one of Homer's most daring strokes. Achilles, bearing down like the god of war in the armor wrought for him by Hephaestus (vv. 132 ff.), is no ordinary adversary, and precisely the panic-stricken reaction of so great a warrior as Hector illustrates the fearful nature of the occasion. The fire symbolism of the simile at vv. 134–35 both enhances the elemental power of Achilles and shows that he is in the ascendant. Hector is reduced to a trembling dove at the mercy of a hawk (vv. 139–42). Yet even this simile has nothing cruel or contemptuous of him in it.

With the comparison to racehorses (vv. 162 ff.), Hector recovers some of his heroic dignity, since now he is put on a par with Achilles (and of course both heroes are celebrating their own deaths). The gods intervene, and immediately Hector is again at a disadvantage. He becomes like a fawn (vv. 189 ff.), reminding us of the beginning of the book where his fellow Trojans were also fawns. Yet again he recovers with divine aid. The seemingly eternal flight and pursuit, which recalls some episode in a dream or nightmare, takes both

---

[10] On the Homeric simile the standard, and sometimes too little heeded, work (since one still reads jargon about the "tertium comparationis") remains H. Fränkel's *Die homerischen Gleichnisse* (Göttingen 1921). W. Schadewaldt however well remarks (*op. cit.*, p. 120 note 4) that even after the researches of Fränkel and Bowra an examination of the structural function of the Homeric similes is still demanded. On the simile at 26 ff. Fränkel notes that it gives Priam's point of view. See below, pp. 133 and 162 for Virgil's development of this subjective technique in the *Aeneid*.

[11] Cf. Fränkel, pp. 69 and 103 note 1; Lesky, "Homeros," col. 771.

[12] Cf. Aristotle, *Poetics* 1460 a 15 and 1460 b 23; W. Schadewaldt, *Von Homers Welt und Werk* (2nd ed., Leipzig 1944), esp. pp. 303–06.

heroes out of ordinary time and already fixes them in the eternal present of Keats' *Ode on a Grecian Urn*.

Grasping finally that death is inevitable, Hector becomes again the hero he is. A further simile makes the point clear. Now it is Hector who is the bird of prey, and this time an eagle, who swoops down upon some tender lamb or cowering hare (vv. 308 ff.). His new-found resolution is in vain. Achilles is again compared to a star, but this time the unhappy associations of the earlier comparison at vv. 26 ff. are lost, and we hear only of the evening star shining in all its beauty. The implication that for Hector night was coming could hardly be ignored. This is the phrase used to describe Andromache's faint (v. 466); she herself stresses the identity of her and her husband's destinies (v. 477).

The importance of the simile in epic narrative right from the start is clear. At its most elementary level, it opens a world of reference which contrasts with the action in hand to bring both relief and emphasis. But it also has important structural functions. Similes may be made to echo one another, giving unity to the narrative and a depth of meaning which might be missing if all syntheses were left to the reader's own reflections. When the images evoked by a simile recur in the story itself, we find not only unity, but a moral and aesthetic satisfaction in their repetition.

All these uses of the simile may be illustrated from *Iliad* XXII. Fawns and hunting dogs recall the days of peace, and a pastime that has continued over the centuries to beguile the noble in his hours of enjoyment. The thought that the roles are reversed for both the Trojans and their champion Hector can only drive home their plight. Achilles, bright yet death-bringing star, *shows* the contradictory aspects of heroism in a way that is worth any amount of explicit moralizing. The comparison of the heroes to horses racing at the funeral games of some dead warrior signposts the real-life events of the following book when, with Hector slain, Achilles is free to celebrate the obsequies of his dead friend, and to accept his own mortality.

The tight unity that is imposed on the poem by this method of composition has further ramifications. Although Homer's traditions may occasionally have offered him alternatives to the particular myths he chooses, it is clear that he could not rely on the element of surprise alone to keep the interest of his audience. Such a procedure would have been naive in the extreme. Our feeling that an epic is concerned with the working out of human destiny demands an emphasis upon precisely that; we have to be assured that what we are hearing is not a capricious series of adventures, but conceals within itself some deeper purpose and design.

At times, this poetic purpose may betray itself obscurely. When we first meet Andromache in this book, she is weaving a double cloak, presumably for her husband's use. When we leave her at the end of the book, it is with her promise to burn all the clothes her husband has left behind echoing in our ears. The contrast between the two scenes speaks the more eloquently because of the connected images.[13]

In weaving this cloak, Andromache was recalling the action of Helen earlier (III. 125 ff.), but while Helen was somewhat complacently taking as her theme the battles which the Greeks and Trojans had fought on her behalf, on her cloak Andromache was embroidering flowers. The ironic difference between the images of wife and mistress, peace and war, points to a patterned complexity within the poem whose interpretation eludes the simple answer. Yet at other times the poet may tell us openly that what we witness is the will of Zeus (cf. vv. 301 ff., 366 ff. in this book, and I. 5). His ability to confront us in this way with the essence of the religious dilemma, the "problem of evil" in old-fashioned language, makes his epic both intellectually and artistically more compelling. The oral style, what Russian critics have called the *skaz*, is able to make these confrontations because of its polyphonic structure. We no more know what Homer himself thought in any partisan way than we know Shakespeare's views on the religious controversies of his day. An epic or drama that came down off this fence, that sought merely to "glorify," would be denying its nature.

Repetition of language is inevitably implied by repetition of image.[14] In Homer, the problem of repeated phrases and even whole passages is complicated for the modern exegete by the formulaic method of composition employed by the poet for technical reasons. This modern problem must not disguise what is actually important, which is not what Homer may have intended (the "intentional fallacy"[15]), but what he may have been supposed to intend by great poets who looked to him for guidance. It may be true in some trivial sense that, when the poet uses the same line to describe the deaths of both Patroclus and Hector, he does so because that was his formula for such occasions.

[13] On key images in the *Iliad* see C. H. Whitman, *Homer and the Heroic Tradition* (Cambridge, Mass. 1958), pp. 128–153. Book III, with its anti-climactic duel between Paris and Menelaus, and its querulous sexuality, is in ironic counterpoint to XXII. The serpent simile occurs in both books (III. 33 and XXII. 93). These ironies are the sense of the "typical scenes" investigated for example in W. Arend's well-known book, *Die typischen Szenen bei Homer* (Berlin 1933).

[14] Cf. K. Reinhardt, *Die Ilias und ihr Dichter*, pp. 14 ff., "Wiederholungen."

[15] A work of art means what it is, and even the author's marginal glosses are marginal. Cf. Yu. Tynianov in *Théorie de la littérature*, ed. T. Todorov (Paris 1965), p. 132 (from an article written in Russia in 1927).

But the imagination of Virgil, working from the insights that artistic necessity may have first disclosed, saw here the paradigm of all human violence.[16]

In Book XXII, Hector's death is linked not only with that of Patroclus, but with that of Sarpedon in XVI. In both cases, Zeus debates whether he may save a favorite son (XVI. 441–42 = XXII. 179–81). Other language recalls IV, where Athene intervenes to spoil the truce between the Greeks and Trojans, and VIII, where Zeus weighs in his scales the fates of Trojans and Greeks, and hurls a blazing bolt against the Greeks. These rich associations add color and resonance to the poetry as they are recapitulated here. When we are confronted with this terrible and pitiful picture of the gods' dealings with men, how little it serves to enquire sedulously which is the "original" Homer!

One kind of repeated language was to prove particularly fruitful in later literature. This was the primitive device of so-called "ring-composition,"[17] by which the conclusion of a speech or digression and the return to the main flow of the narrative was indicated with some verbal reminiscence of its beginning. Such verbal and thematic echoes, reinforced by their effective employment in the influential poetry of the lyric poet Pindar, were developed over the centuries into a powerful means for securing both unity and intensity in narrative. Rhyme and symmetry are other lyrical devices found in this book.[18] The second word of the *Iliad* is "sing," and there is

---

[16] Cf. *Aeneid* XI. 831 and XII. 952. The comments made by C. M. Bowra in *A Companion to Homer*, ed. by Alan J. B. Wace and Frank H. Stubbings (London 1967), pp. 30 ff., are not quite so penetrating as one might wish. On the other hand, the skepticism of F. M. Combellack, "Milman Parry and Homeric Artistry," *Comparative Literature* XI (1959), 193 ff. is utterly pointless, since it assumes that our imaginations cannot have free rein in the presence of a masterpiece. See Lesky's "Homeros," col. 761, for the interesting suggestion that Achilles may be anticipating his own death at lines 385 ff. In that case, Homer would be prefiguring a characteristically Virgilian irony (and "learning")—which is only another way of saying that the tradition in which Virgil stood had recovered the real Homer, by contrast with "cyclic" imitations of him.

[17] On ring-composition see Eustathius 878, 59 ff., quoted by L. Adam, *Die aristotelische Theorie vom Epos nach ihrer Entwicklung bei Griechen und Römern* (Wiesbaden 1889), p. 42, and the references given by B. A. van Groningen, *La composition littéraire archaïque grecque* (Amsterdam 1960), pp. 51 ff.; L. Illig, *Zur Form der pindarischen Erzählung* (Berlin 1932), pp. 55 ff. Eustathius had some inkling of its importance in Pindar (A. B. Drachmann, *Scholia Vetera in Pindari Carmina* III, p. 289): cf. L. Dissen's "constructio rotunda" (*Pindari Carmina* [Gothae et Erfordiae MDCCCXXX], p. lxvi). The most effective instance of all is perhaps *Aen.* I. 92 and XII. 951.

[18] Rhyme: XXII. 6–7, 56–57–58, 82–83, 199–200 etc.; symmetry: 1–13, 25–37, 38–76, 77–89, 247–59, 260–72, 477–515 (all 13 lines or 3 × 13 = 39 lines). For ring-composition cf. the hapax legomenon *pureton*, 31, answered by *puri* at the end in 512.

already an important sense in which Homer's epic is lyricized from the start.

Because language is so important to the poet, it must remain one of the most difficult features of his art to convey in summary or translation. He uses a literary dialect, never spoken, employing many archaic forms and words which, by a long process at which we can now only guess, have become superbly adapted to the easy course of narration. There is nothing stilted about the Homeric manner. Enjambement and pauses of many kinds prevent monotony. It was the type of style that could be enjoyed for its own sake by the connoisseur of the well-turned or piquant expression, or of rare words. Though not without occasional hints of colloquialism, it invested the world of heroes with a romantic dignity that imposed new dimensions on the imagination of later generations. "Estrangement," for the Formalists the basic task of art, the dislocation of perceptions from the commonplace of everyday, is exploited by Homer in many ways. Here it enjoys one of its most gracious flowerings.

Yet these blossoms had deep roots in the primitive. The mockery of the victim marked for death is the religious prelude to his resurrection. Hector is, after all, to be the last hero named in the poem. The "weighing in the balance" by a supreme god is familiar from the Book of Daniel. The comparison of the heroes to animals is something that native tribes take quite literally. When Hector and Achilles are like racehorses at funeral games, memories are evoked of the earliest celebrations of death, and assertion of the agonistic principle which declares that death must not be the end. It is the principle that inspired the gladiatorial games at Rome. The witnessing of the scene by Hecuba and Priam and even by the gods contributes strongly, as on Greek vase-paintings, to this ritual concept, so important in the structure of both comedy and tragedy. The duel is conducted before a community. Yet this community, even in the case of the human spectators, is already something "out of this world." Priam and Hecuba watch as it were from *outre-tombe*.

There is doubling, masking: Apollo blends into and out of Agenor, and Athene into and out of Deiphobus. At one stage Hector, like Achilles, is a man in a dream, and then again he debates with himself (internal doubling).

One of the most extraordinary features of the story is its manipulation of time. The line is not horizontal, but vertical. Priam and Hecuba know that Hector is as good as dead even before his duel with Achilles begins. The end of Troy is, as Andromache senses, already now. Time is felt as space. Homer's imagination has civilized these primitive and pre-literary motifs. But their lurking presence lends depth and shadow to his story.

Greek myth is the single greatest contribution of the Greeks to our civilization. Inevitably, as time went by, the ancients became more sophisticated. Philosophy and theology tried to fill the gap between traditional belief and their new sensibilities. But because Homer had such a breadth of sympathy he exercised a spell even on those who were most in disagreement with him. Outside the ranks of the professional philosophers his reputation suffered no diminution, and allegorizing interpretation could reconcile even the philosophers. To have such a poetry at the beginning of one's literature was a priceless advantage.

When Homer was credited with the invention of tragedy as well as epic,[19] his critics divined something implicit in the structure of his work. He moves continually between polarities, whether of person or thought, and is here the true son of his people. Apollo/Achilles; Achilles/Hector; Priam/Hecuba; war/peace; hate/love; triumph/grief: these are the clashes that will generate Achilles' (and the listener's) ultimate leap into the new dimension of mature awareness of human fate. The end of the book we have been discussing shows how easily a tragic scene could be deduced from Homer's narrative. As the lifeless body of Hector is dragged around their walls, the Trojans step forward in turn, father, mother, wife, to express their grief, supported by a chorus of mourning townsfolk. The germ of fifth-century dramatic art is already quickening. It only remains for music to be added, and Homer's tendency towards the lyrical makes it clear that such an addition would be perfectly natural.

One short book can by no means exhaust the poet's range.[20] The *Odyssey*, which later became a particular favorite and was thought to have special kinship with comedy, has been left unanalyzed. In antiquity, a different side to the poet's genius was savored in the *Margites*, describing the adventures of some sort of Simple Simon or Till Eulenspiegel of his day. That this poem, now lost, is believed by modern scholars to have been spurious, does not affect the total impression that the Greek world had of the universality of the Homeric

[19] Plato, *Rep.* X. 595 c, 607 a; J. Vahlen on Aristotle, *Poetics* 1448 b 34; Isocr., *Ad Nic.* 48; L. Adam, *op. cit.*, pp. 15 ff., 31 ff: S. Koster, *Antike Epostheorien*, pp. 51 ff.; G. F. Else, *Aristotle's Poetics, The Argument* (Cambridge, Mass. 1957), pp. 572, 595. J. A. Notopoulos' discussion of early Greek poetics, *Harvard Stud. Class. Phil.* 68 (1964), 45 ff., begins by repudiating Aristotle only to smuggle him in later ("dramatic qualities" in Homer, p. 64). See G. S. Kirk, *Homer and the Oral Tradition* (Cambridge 1976), pp. 69 ff.

[20] Compare, for example, A. Severyns, *Homère l'artiste* (Brussels 1948), on Homer's gods: "Dans ces tableaux olympiens, la note humoristique se fait parfois presque tendre et le raffinement d'Homère annonce étonnamment celui d'un Callimaque" (p. 101: "In these scenes on Olympus the humor sometimes verges on the tender, and Homer's refinement astonishingly heralds that of a Callimachus").

achievement, and of the role played in it by the topsy-turvy of the carnival.[21]

## II

In coming to terms with this universality, later poets had various courses open to them. They could develop the genres at which Homer had hinted, or which his work presupposed, such as tragedy, comedy, lyric. They could supplement the lacunas left by his story. They could adapt his style to other cycles of legend, and even to the history of contemporary events. The brilliance of the model began to dazzle its imitators. Aristotle assayed the true gold.

When later still Callimachus encountered the Homeric challenge, it is not surprising that he felt the same need for re-assessment. Homer undoubtedly presented many facets which were capable of exploitation at a superficial level by the Hellenistic poets.[22] It was a period in the history of Greek civilization when the molds of previous development had been shattered beyond repair by the conquests of Alexander the Great. Greece had in any case never enjoyed the stable acquiescence in tradition dear to classicizing nostalgia. The "Hellenistic age" may have begun already in 350, less than a century after Pericles' death and, on the fringes of the Greek world, even earlier.

Inspired by a romantic view of Homer, Alexander had strained the old structures to breaking point. But the new Achilles could find to celebrate his prowess only the mediocre, money-grubbing Choerilus of Iasos. The real consequences for literature of Alexander's revolution would be drawn after his death—in Alexandria.

Founded by the conqueror of Egypt in 331 B.C. at the mouth of the Nile, Alexandria was a *polis* totally unlike anything that had earlier enjoyed that name in Greece itself. Here a tiny ruling class of Greeks, with one of Alexander's former generals at their head, lorded it over a population with whom they had almost nothing in common. The sprawling city had been laid out as an example of town planning by one of Alexander's own architects. Brilliantly successful as a trading and maritime center, it supported a court and

---

[21] On the *Margites* see H. Langerbeck, *Harvard Stud. Class. Phil.* 63 (1958), 33 ff. The carnival is discussed below, pp. 195 ff.

[22] Theocritus, *Idylls* XVI. 20: ἅλις πάντεσσιν Ὅμηρος ("Homer is enough for everybody"). K. Ziegler, *Das hellenistische Epos* (2nd ed., Leipzig 1966), illustrates the uses to which Homer was put in the service of flattery. A gallant effort to lend respectability to the historical epic is made by R. Häußler in his two volumes *Das historische Epos der Griechen und Römer bis Vergil* (Heidelberg 1976) and *Das historische Epos von Lucan bis Silius und seine Theorie* (Heidelberg 1978). But a tradition culminating in Silius Italicus hardly commands admiration!

palace of huge dimensions.[23] Attached to the Royal Palace, as later
the Palatine Library would be adjacent to the dwelling of Augustus,
was a vast Library, into which manuscripts of the classics were imported
from all over the Greek world. This Library gave support to distinguished scholars invited from elsewhere. They had no other task
except to busy themselves with their learned researches and contribute
to the edification or amusement of the royal family.

The members of this family, the Ptolemies, were ardent patrons
of literature and the arts. Competitions of every kind stimulated the
efforts of the talented. Festivals, at which no expense was spared,
were provided to amuse the populace. The "Grand Procession" of
Ptolemy Philadelphus, recorded by a late and ambiguous source,[24]
in which a phallus, 180 feet in length, was paraded, already shows a
carnival sense of the "grotesque body," and the kind of taste relished
by the Romans.

Beautified with gardens, and basking in the sun, the city presented
an impressive spectacle to the visitor from the homeland. But its
artificiality could not be disguised. No Pericles would ever pronounce
there a Funeral Oration, no Aristophanes ever guy its politicians on
the stage. We do not look for that kind of committed rapture or
outspoken humor in the Alexandrian age, though eulogy, wit and
irony are plentiful enough.[25]

Hellenistic kings, too uncertain of their positions to tolerate a
second Aristophanes, were eager to avail themselves of more com-
pliant Muses to bolster their insecurity. One obvious way in which
they could gain their ends was to try to reduce literature to the level
of propaganda, and here epic was in particular danger. The example
of honoring contemporary military achievements was first set for
heroic, hexametric poetry by Choerilus of Samos at the beginning of
the fourth century. This genre was still flourishing in the fifth century
after Christ, and we may take the fragments we have from that date
as fair specimens of what it became after it left Choerilus' hands,

---

[23] U. von Wilamowitz gives an imaginative characterization of Alexandria, *Hellen-
istische Dichtung* (repr. Berlin 1962), I, pp. 152 ff. See further Theocritus, *Idyll* XVII;
Herondas, *Mim.* I. 23 ff.; H. Bengtson, *Griechische Geschichte* (Munich 1950), pp. 374
ff.; P. M. Fraser, *Ptolemaic Alexandria* (Oxford 1972). The older account by
L. Friedlaender, *Darstellungen aus der Sittengeschichte Roms* (10th ed., Leipzig 1922),
I, pp. 431 ff., is still worth reading.

[24] E. E. Rice, *The Grand Procession of Ptolemy Philadelphus* (Oxford 1983).

[25] Sotades, who attempted some sort of political satire, is said to have been
drowned: F. Susemihl, *Geschichte der griechischen Literatur in der Alexandrinerzeit* (repr.
Hildesheim 1965), I, p. 245. Machon's comedies, to judge by their fragments, hardly
owed as much to Aristophanes as ancient commentators assert: cf. Susemihl, I, p.
265; A. S. F. Gow and D. L. Page, *The Greek Anthology, Hellenistic Epigrams* (Cambridge
1965), II, p. 257 (on Dioscorides).

simply because conservatism and traditionalism were its essence. Consideration of these pieces suggests that they were unlikely to commend themselves to any great poet, not because great poets of the Hellenistic age were against flattering their sovereigns, but because they gave too little scope for an original talent to make itself heard.[26]

What happened to poets of such talent who, while not wanting to engage in mere Homeric pastiche, still felt the desire to come before their patrons with something more impressive than the epigram? What happened if they felt all the beauty and elegance that the modern movement had brought to poetry, and yet still wanted to write epic? Clearly their dilemma called for a radical solution, one which would be a thorough test of their genius, and which only a poet of the highest ability would survive. Such a poet was Callimachus: this was his dilemma, and his solution of it became of prime importance in the whole of subsequent classically influenced poetry.

III

Callimachus realized that the straight imitation of Homeric manner-isms was unacceptable. If poetry was to have a life because it caught something of the fears and hopes in the minds of contemporaries, it had to have a firmer hold on their allegiance than the mere external appeal of flattering some great man who might have sprung from nowhere and might as quickly fade. But it also had to be broader in scope than the two- or even ten-line epigram. No one knew better than he how much could be packed into small compass. But Greek taste traditionally demanded something more substantial from those who sought to be remembered even away from the banqueting table, and Callimachus was enough of a traditionalist to agree.

A new epic poetry needed a new patron, one who would have equal respectability and venerable antiquity with Homer, yet one who would allow room for experimentation. This was not to be mere playing with words. Callimachus had in mind the genuine purpose of introducing a poetry which, without betraying the advances made by his contemporaries, would nevertheless be worthy to stand at the side of the best that the past had to offer. Ultimately, he wanted to find a fresh way of approaching Homer, whose style had been usurped

---

[26] This was the "cyclic" epic, perhaps originally so-called because its authors filled out the cycle of legend implied by the *Iliad* and *Odyssey*. Callimachus (*Epigr.* 28. 1), followed by Horace (*A. P.* 136), used the term as one of contempt for those poets who trailed along behind Homer, missing the essence and catching at the shadow; cf. his *Epigram* 6 on Creophylus. For this style in Greek see D. L. Page, *Greek Literary Papyri* (London and Cambridge, Mass. 1950), no. 142, and H. Lloyd-Jones and P. Parsons, *Supplementum Hellenisticum*, especially p. 362, no. 764. In late Latin Corippus and Flavius Merobaudes might be cited as examples.

and corrupted by poets like Choerilus of Iasos. He did it initially by talking about Hesiod. Boeotian Hesiod, and Boeotian Helicon, became part of the code in which subsequent Alexandrian literary declarations are written, and which must be learned by those who want to decipher its message.[27] When we hear of Hesiod in the later tradition, or of any of the motifs derived from him, it is one of the signs that we are in Callimachean terrain.

As he was known, Hesiod had been the author of a motley collection of hexameter poems, not all of which now survive. Their versification revealed a hand less urbane than that of the supremely polished Homer, though he was reputed by tradition to have been at least as old as Homer, and even his poetic rival. His subject matter however had not been at all Homeric. The *Works and Days* was a didactic poem in which, in the course of nearly a thousand lines, Hesiod took issue with his brother Perses, and reminded him that every man ought to work for his living. This reminder gave occasion to detail the principal events and dates of the farmer's year. The *Theogony* sought to bring order into some of the confusing and at times crude legends which surrounded the story of Creation and the origin of the Greek pantheon. The *Eoae* was a catalogue of famous heroines of myth. Other poems, an *Astronomy*, a *Shield*, were attributed to him with varying degrees of certainty. None of his poems was long in the Homeric sense.

For Callimachus, Hesiod was ideally suited as the patron of the new poetry. Though ancient, he sanctioned a fresh range of topics. He allowed the poet to be "personal," to speak of himself and his vocation. He displayed an interest in the feminine, a side of Homer that appears to have been rather ignored by his martial imitators. More than this, his craftsmanship, with its recurring patterns, pointed beyond itself.[28] Callimachus was an artist exquisitely sensitive to the

---

[27] See ALEXANDRIAN CODE in the *Glossary of Critical Terms*. On Hesiod in this role cf. especially M. Reitzenstein, *Festschrift Richard Reitzenstein* (Leipzig and Berlin 1931), pp. 41 ff. Of course this did not mean that Callimachus had no interest in utilizing Homer; cf. H. Herter, "Kallimachos und Homer," in *Xenia Bonnensia*, 1929, pp. 50 ff. (repr. in *Kallimachos*, ed. A. D. Skiadas [Darmstadt 1975], pp. 354 ff.). The liveliness of the Alexandrian resuscitation of Hesiod is seen in the episode of Hesiod's prophetic literary dream inserted by Madeleine de Scudéry, the seventeenth-century French novelist, in *Clélie*, IV, pp. 796 ff., which R.-C. Knight, *Racine et la Grèce* (Paris n.d.), p. 59, finds "curieux."

[28] See H. Schwabl, "Beispiele zur poetischen Technik des Hesiod," in *Hesiod*, ed. Ernst Heitsch (Darmstadt 1966), especially pp. 182 ff., 187 and 217 ff., where a musical analogy is used. For the music of Callimachus' verse cf. Pfeiffer's index, Vol. II, p. 140, s.v. *vocalium consecutio euphoniae causa*, and F. Lapp, *De Callimachi Cyrenaei Tropis et Figuris* (Bonn 1965). B. Snell discusses "Die Klangfiguren im 2. Epigramm des Kallimachos" in *Glotta* 37 (1958), 1 ff.

refinements of the Hellenistic epigram. But the epigram was in its turn the heir of Greek lyric. With the brilliance of genius, Callimachus realized that the way to revive the flagging fortunes of epic was to lyricize it, to try to build into the poetic treatment a music that would transform its meaning. This meant that the harmony and euphony of the line would receive prime consideration. But it also meant that the epic treatment of myth could be revolutionized by borrowing from a so far unexploited technique, that of the great lyric poets of the seventh to the fifth centuries, and notably from the greatest of them all, and like Hesiod a Boeotian, Pindar.[29]

The outlines of what we may suppose to have been Callimachus' poetic, normative even for the new epic, now become clearer. It would rest upon the following premises:

1. The lyrical analogy, which means ultimately an analogy with music, would be paramount, and would make itself felt both in formal devices such as balance and verbal repetition, and in musicality of language and mood.

2. Selection of detail would be essential, to avoid tedium and the repetitiousness of the pseudo-Homeric manner. In a sophisticated society, myth could still be made acceptable, by angling the narrative to bring out the unfamiliar and the unexpected, rather than the trite. Turning to myth would enable the poet to avoid the pitfall presented by themes drawn from history, since he was Aristotelian (and Greek) enough to understand the inferiority of history to poetry. A poem written in this manner will often leave the obvious to be deduced by the reader, while dwelling with apparent naiveté on the trivial. The naive tone itself is another borrowing from Hesiod.

3. The details that are selected must receive their overall unity from tone and feeling conjured up in the reader's mind by suggestion. Therefore they must aim at stirring (but not too crudely) his emotions. He must be vividly (ἐνάργεια) aware of

---

[29] Callimachus' debt to Pindar is discussed in my *Augustus and the New Poetry* (Brussels 1967), pp. 45–48, and in *Pindar's Art: Its Tradition and Aims* (Hildesheim–Munich–Zurich 1984) [with F. S. Newman], pp. 89 note 9, 151 note 12. There are overt imitations of Pindar in *Iambos* VIII and frr. 383, 384 Pf. The new fragment of the *Victoria Berenices* first published in 1976 is examined by P. J. Parsons, *Zeitschrift für Papyrologie und Epigraphik* 25 (1977), 1–50. Parsons remarks on p. 46: "In some sense, Callimachus' normal manner is Pindaric. . . . But here . . . he seems to outdo himself." His debt is indeed wider than these imitations of theme. Milton followed a long tradition in coupling the two poets: "Those magnifick Odes and Hymns, wherein Pindarus and Callimachus are in most things worthy . . ." (*The Reason of Church-Government urg'd against Prelaty*, 1641, repr. in *The Works of John Milton*, New York 1931, III, 1, p. 238).

being as it were present with the characters (ἦθος, προσωποποιΐα) and their reactions (πάθη). The use of direct speech, already prominent in Homer, will be developed, following the precedents of lyric and drama.

4. Style too will seek to play on the emotions. The reader must be swept along in some places, made the recipient of hammer blows of assertion in others; and in all places be so charmed by the music of the verse that he is not over-concerned with its logical significance.

5. A *persona* (mask) adopted by the poet, which at times may become a character in the story, must intrude between the reader and the narrative, so as to prevent him from taking a detached view. He must always see the story through the author's eyes, as he is required to see it.

6. The language of the poem must inhibit stereotyped reactions. Sometimes the poet will merely mimic the elaboration of the high style, without tying himself down to its clichés. Sometimes he will deliberately shock by his unexpected and "unpoetic" turns of phrase.

7. Not only music, but also painting will be called in to provide the extra dimension of sensibility required by this kind of poetry. Such a borrowing from the other arts illustrates the continual tendency of this style to move into fresh aesthetic dimensions.[30]

8. This poetry will avoid the confident statement and large generalization, both as inappropriate to the more human role taken up by the poet, and as a deliberate means of criticizing by implication the assumptions of the myths he handles. This criticism, which verges on the comic parody, again obtrudes the poet's personality and prevents a passive acquiescence on the part of the reader in a world of guarantees.

The allegiance of this program to the symbolic figure of Hesiod must not be over-interpreted, for in many ways its real goal was to recover Homer from his cheap modern ("cyclic") imitators. The program is of far-reaching importance in the whole history of European literature, and certain parts of it only make sense as extrapolations from positions merely adumbrated by Callimachus. Various

---

[30] See E. Norden on *metalēpsis aisthēseōs* at *Aeneid* VI. 256 ff.: Simonides quoted by Plutarch, *De Gloria Ath.* 346 f – 347 c; D. A. Russell on "Longinus" 17. 2 (p. 132). Already the scholia had found something similar in Homer: cf. M.-L. von Franz, *Die aesthetischen Anschauungen der Iliasscholien* (diss. Zürich 1943), p. 29. See also the brilliant remarks by F. Dornseiff, *Pindars Stil* (Berlin 1921), p. 57, and W. Schadewaldt, *Der Aufbau des Pindarischen Epinikion* (Halle 1928), p. 41 note 2.

questions are raised by its presentation here. It may be asked why
the handbooks of ancient literary criticism are so silent about its
terms. If we read the *Poetics* of Aristotle or the *Ars Poetica* of Horace,
for example, why did they appear to the sixteenth-century Italian
critics reconcilable with a far different kind of poetry? These two
works between them have given rise to innumerable discussions of
more or less authoritarian character telling the would-be poet how
to write, of which the principal feature is their utter uselessness for
the purpose they profess to serve. Such discussions have the further
disadvantage that they mislead the modern reader, who seeks in them
a key to the understanding of the poetry of their time, usually in
vain.

The source of the trouble is complex.[31] When the context vanishes
in which a given poetic was drawn up, its prescriptions look faded
and incomplete. *Brevitas* (selection of detail), for example, is a basic
concept of Callimachean doctrine. What we find in Horace's *Ars
Poetica* is a warning against allowing brevity to lead to obscurity, and
a eulogy of Homer for not telling the story of the Trojan War at
inordinate length.[32] It is from these passages that we have to deduce,
firstly that brevity was so essential as to need not so much recommendation as control, and secondly, that in distinguishing between
Homer and his imitators, Hellenistic critics, following Aristotle, had
pronounced Homer to be superior precisely on the grounds of his
brevity.[33] If we read Horace however without these background ideas
in mind, we might be tempted to believe that Horace deprecated
brevity (it leads to obscurity), and that he was an admirer of Homer's
run-of-the-mill imitators (since he lays down rules for the proper
imitation of Homer in epic). Both these ideas are contradicted by
the evidence and practice of the poet himself.[34] As the understanding
of the ancient critical tradition is so very difficult, what we need is
to reconstruct the Callimachean poetic from the pages of its practitioners. Only then will we have the key to the theories we encounter,
so often in tantalizingly fragmentary form. This means in essence
that criticism should be the handmaid and not the scourge of genius.

---

[31] Cf. B. Weinberg, "From Aristotle to Pseudo-Aristotle" in *Aristotle's Poetics and
English Literature*, ed. E. Olson (Chicago 1965), pp. 192 ff. The same author's *History
of Literary Criticism in the Italian Renaissance* (2 vols., Chicago 1961) sheds a dismal
light on critical percipience. See below, pp. 244 ff.

[32] *A. P.* 25 ff., 136 ff.; cf. also 42 ff., 335 ff.

[33] See Kiessling–Heinze and C. O. Brink on Horace, *A. P.* 148. Cicero, *De Orat.*
II. 311, shows that one school of rhetorical theory did make room for digressions
where emotional effect could be gained. Horace is therefore taking up a position
here (later pushed to mechanical absurdity: Curtius, *op. cit.*, pp. 481 ff.).

[34] E.g. *Sat.* I. 10. 9–10. See further R. G. M. Nisbet and Margaret Hubbard, *A
Commentary on Horace: Odes Book I* (Oxford 1970), p. xiv.

In Callimachus himself, his poetic program found expression in two major works, the *Aetia* and the *Hecale*. The former, written in four books of elegiacs, began by recalling a scene from the opening of Hesiod's *Theogony*, in which Hesiod had encountered the Muses "while he was shepherding his lambs under holy Helicon." There, the Muses had reminded Hesiod of their power to sing both of false things and true, and presented him with a shoot of sturdy olive, "breathing into him a divine voice to sing of things to come and things that were before." This was a canonization in one sense of the primitive concept of vertical time to which reference has already been made. The present becomes unimportant, under the load of the past and future. It was exactly the license for which Callimachus was looking, and in his poem, after echoing this passage, and apparently transmuting Hesiod's experience into a dream, he proceeded to question the Muses about the reasons for every kind of strange ceremony and legend to be found in the Greek world. The details of these were familiar to the poet from his learned researches in the Library. Yet this was not an idle display of erudition. It was also a way of recovering the past in the present, and a religious procedure at that, familiar from the continual *aetia* that are found in the Pentateuch.

In the last two books, which may have been composed separately from the first two and published at a later date, Callimachus' interest in lyric made itself decisively felt. Book III opened with the *Victory of Berenice*, celebrating a chariot victory of the queen at the Nemean games with an account of the original founding of the festival by Heracles very much in the manner of Pindar and Bacchylides. This is the story to which is now assigned the poet's brusque "Let [the reader] draw his own conclusions, and so cut length off the song." The programmatic remark will attract attention later.[35]

To the *Victory of Berenice* at the start of Book III corresponded the *Lock of Berenice* at the end of Book IV. This famous episode, translated into Latin by Catullus, related that a lock of the queen's hair, which had vanished from the shrine of Aphrodite where she had dedicated it in honor of her husband's safe return from the wars, had in fact been taken up to heaven, where it was now visible in a new constellation discovered recently by the court astronomer, Conon. The ring-composition came full circle in compliment.

In these last two books, by a device which Formalists would call a *dénudation du procédé*,[36] the Muses seem to have disappeared from their role as interlocutors, and the different stories were presented

[35] Below, p. 432.
[36] Cf. Todorov, *op. cit.*, p. 289 (B. Tomashevsky).

by the poet directly, even, as in the case of the story of Acontius and
Cydippe, with explicit mention of the source from which the material
was drawn.[37] This gambit too would find imitators in the tradition.
When the poet's sense of fantasy is sure enough, it is no interruption
of his magic that occasionally stagehands should actually appear
before the public gaze.

Though the *Aetia* as a whole was written in elegiacs rather than
in the traditional heroic hexameter, it must be noted that already it
provided a model for the epic *Argonautica* of Apollonius.

Towards the end of his life, Callimachus gave expression to an
angry altercation with his literary adversaries in a Preface placed
perhaps at the head of his collected poems, and certainly at the head
of the *Aetia*.[38] This Preface is not preserved in its entirety, but enough
survives to make it safe to say that, if we wish to understand the
classical epic tradition, this is a document of essential importance.
Many precautions must be exercised in its interpretation. It is not so
much a positive statement by the poet of his own outlook, as a
rejection, at least in the first instance, of the outlook of his enemies.
He does not begin by coolly and calmly telling us what he has actually
sought in his own life as a writer, but rather by crying out against
the dogmatism of men who refuse to concede that any other approach
to the Muse than their own exists. The Preface is fragmentary both
in breaking off before its conclusion, and in the damaged condition
of individual verses. It is accompanied by an equally fragmentary
commentary, the work of the so-called Florentine Scholiast, which
raises many problems. Even so, we cannot shirk the study of this
precious relic.

The Preface begins quite abruptly. The poet notes that the Telchines mutter against his song. In legend, the Telchines were malicious
dwarfs, often associated with the island of Rhodes. The second line
defines that aspect of them which is uppermost in Callimachus'
thought: they are ignoramuses, who have never been friends of the
Muse. What they have against Callimachus is that he has not accomplished, in many thousands of verses, one continuous song, which
would take as its theme the deeds of kings, or mighty heroes. Instead,
he unwinds his poetry in fits and starts, like a child, though the
number of his years is not small.

After this statement of the attack, the poet begins his reply. The

[37] Callimachus, frr. 67–75 Pf. Fr. 75. 77, *hēmeterēn . . . Kalliopēn* ("our . . . Calliope")
is interesting for its metamorphosis of Muse into poetry. The quoting of a prose
source parallels Ariosto's frequent references to his alleged source in Archbishop
Turpin, 'and perhaps even Eliot's notes to the *Waste Land*.

[38] Pfeiffer, fr. 1 with the scholia.

papyrus is indecipherable at important points, but the Florentine Scholiast explains that here Callimachus compared the short poems of Mimnermus of Colophon and Philetas of Cos with their long poems, and asserted that their shorter poems were better.

Scholarly controversy has raged over this passage. Taking advantage of a possible but improbable ambiguity in the Scholiast's paraphrase, commentators have suggested that Callimachus was not comparing the work of Mimnermus and Philetas with itself, but with poems by altogether different poets. The interpretation must be rejected. Callimachus' argument would not hold water for a moment if he had said that the short poems of his favorites were superior to the long poems of certain others for whom he had no liking. The obvious rejoinder would be that his favorites, if they were so talented, would have done even better if they had supplied their admirers with more to admire: and this is exactly the argument being used against Callimachus himself, that he had not lived up to his calling and claims by writing large-scale epic. Callimachus' only effective defense is to say that he need not personally write long poems on the scale advocated by his enemies in order to be a good poet, because the example of good poets who had been tempted into length shows that they would have done better to remain within the limits of their shorter compositions.

Listing the real-life adversaries concealed by Callimachus beneath the mask of the Telchines, the Florentine Scholiast concludes that they were all men who blamed the poet for the thinness (τὸ κάτισχνον) of his poems, and for not undertaking (this seems to be the sense of a partially preserved verb) length (μῆκος). The interpretation of the charge depends on an understanding of rhetorical theory. Callimachus evidently accepted for his poetry the canons of style which distinguished the *ischnos charactēr*, as they had perhaps been worked out in Aristotle's own school.[39] It was a style that rejected bombast and inflated language in favor of a simpler and more human appeal. But why should the poet have been in trouble for employing a literary style that was in fact perfectly legitimate according to the rhetoricians' rules? It cannot have been the style in itself that caused the complaint. The only explanation for the bitter criticism made by the Telchines

[39] On the *ischnos charactēr* see Demetrius, *De Eloc.* 190 ff.: Quintilian XII. 10. 58: E. Reitzenstein, *op. cit.*, pp. 25 ff.: M. Puelma Piwonka, *Lucilius und Kallimachos* (Frankfurt 1949), pp. 118, 165: W. Kroll in *RE* Supplementband VII, "Rhetorik," cols. 1039–1138 esp. col. 1074: F. Wehrli in *Phyllobolia für P. von der Mühll* (Basel 1946), pp. 9–34: F. Quadlbauer in *Wiener Studien* 71 (1958), 55–111. J. Stroux argues strongly in *De Theophrasti Virtutibus Dicendi* (Leipzig 1912) that the three styles did not originate with Aristotle, but in spite of his insistence, one still wonders.

must be that Callimachus had taken a style that was unobjectionable in itself, but misapplied it.

Where this wrong application had been made becomes clearer if we look at the second charge against him. He was attacked for not undertaking in his poetry "length." But once again, the writing of short poems was a perfectly legitimate occupation for a Greek poet, and rather curiously the learned Scholiast includes in his list of Callimachus' enemies two, Posidippus and Asclepiades, who are still admired for their exquisitely finished short poems.

Callimachus then adopted a "thin" style and refused to write at length in honor of kings and heroes, and yet both these strategies, quite acceptable on their own, were the subject of a furious quarrel. The explanation of the paradox must lie in the *union* of these two activities. Callimachus had intruded into one of the grand genres where it was traditional to write at stilted length with a particular exalted subject matter, and had written there in relatively brief compass with a different subject matter in the more down-to-earth style normally reserved for less ambitious works. Only a flouting of tradition to this degree could account for the venomous reaction of conservatives who had found their dearest prejudices challenged.

Callimachus illustrates his opposition to the long epic style by alluding to the long flight of the migrating cranes between Africa and Thrace, and the long bowshots of the Massagetae. The examples are not chosen at random. The Massagetae were a tribe described by Herodotus, and one of the efforts made to revive the epic at the end of the fifth century by Choerilus of Samos had been precisely a versification of Herodotus' *Histories*. Aristotle had rejected the poem. History and poetry, he had insisted, are not the same. Callimachus was of the same opinion. The story of the cranes, employed by Homer in one of his similes, is also found in Herodotus. What we really seem to be hearing from the Alexandrian poet therefore is that epic may *not* be continued by the simple device of "Homerizing" modern historical material. After all, Hesiod's Muses had inspired him to sing of the past and future only, and had told him that they knew how to say many false things that looked like true. How could such a program justify the versification of historical research? It was, as Aristotle had noted in the *Poetics*, an unphilosophical confusion of two different aims. It would eventually mislead so great a poet as Petrarch.

Renewed abuse of the Telchines signals a break in thought. They are "the destructive brood of envious slander," who, in a phrase borrowed from Hesiod, can only "waste their own hearts." They are told that they should judge poetry by art, and not by a Persian chain, that is, not by a length that might suit a versified Herodotus. This injunction has terrified interpreters who, perhaps under the influence of English or German Romanticism, are not sure what place art has in poetry at all. "Art for art's sake," "decadence," are terms that spring easily to the lips of such critics. But is not the poet's appeal for the exercise of intelligence in the writing of poetry of the most moral and honorable kind? The epic was in a bad way. It had to be re-created. Callimachus is suggesting that in the process of re-creation we should use our brains.

The poet goes on to repudiate a loudly roaring song. Thundering is not for him, but for Zeus.[40] How little he is concerned with mere cleverness is shown in the following lines, where at long last he describes his personal commitment to the god of his art, Apollo (Callimachus, *Aetia* I. 1. 21 ff. Pf., tr. C. A. Trypanis, modified):

> For, when I first placed a tablet on my knees, Lycian Apollo said to me: ". . . poet, feed the sacrificial victim to be as fat as possible, but, my friend, keep the Muse slender. This too I bid you: do not tread a path which carriages trample; do not drive your chariot upon the common tracks of others, nor along a wide road, but on unworn paths, though your course be more narrow. For we sing among those who love the shrill voice of the cicala and not the noise of the . . . asses." Let another bray just like the long-eared brute, but let me be the dainty, the winged one.

What "art" really meant to the poet we may see from the next lines, where the complex word order of the Greek is not a mere trick,[41] as perhaps in some poets with whom traditional criticism would have no quarrel. Rather, it is the expression of a deeply felt emotion (*loc. cit.* 33–38):

> Oh, yes indeed! that I may sing living on dew-drops, free sustenance from the divine air; that I may then shed old age, which weighs down upon me like the three-cornered island upon deadly Enceladus. But no regrets! for if the Muses have not looked askance at one in his childhood, they do not cast him from their friendship when he is grey.

In this quotation, the return to the idea of the child, for the Telchines a term of abuse, is noteworthy. This kind of poetic and moral humility shows that we cannot divorce Callimachus' thoughts

---

[40] Compare Dante's objections to poetic shouts: *Donne ch'avete*, 6 ff.: *Purg.* XXVI. 125.

[41] On the complex order at lines 33–35 see W. Wimmel, *Kallimachos in Rom* (Wiesbaden 1960), p. 113 note 4, and more generally "Longinus", *De Subl.* 22 and W. Kroll, *Studien*, p. 262, who anticipated Housman's remark about *Culex* 51, made on Lucan III. 295. See further F. Dornseiff, *Pindars Stil*, pp. 16–17, and C. J. Fordyce on Catullus 66. 18.

about his vocation from a sensitive awareness of what is necessary in human life if it is to be lived authentically.

The *Aetia* which followed this Preface, a work of profound humanity, was already felt by Apollonius Rhodius to be enough of an epic to supply him with many hints about both language and treatment, when he came to write the *Argonautica*. But in the *Hecale* Callimachus actually composed a modern epic in answer to those who mockingly accused him of not being able to write a big poem.[42] The work began, so far as may be judged, without any formal exordium. The theme was drawn from a prose source, a chronicle of the early days of Attica. The great hero of primitive Athens, Theseus, the subject of bombastic poems from the days of Aristotle and before to those of Juvenal, was seen through the wrong end of a telescope—depicted as still young, and under his father's tutelage. His safety was threatened by his stepmother, Medea, who tried to poison him, but in vain.

The father's precautions after this incident became stifling to the young man, who, feeling the call of his high destiny, one day slipped away from the palace about nightfall in order to deal with a wild bull that was tormenting the inhabitants of nearby Marathon. He had not gone far when a heavy rainstorm broke out, and he was forced to seek shelter for the night in the lowly cottage of old Hecale. She was delighted to have such an unexpected visitor, and entertained him to a hot bath, simple salad, and long gossip. True to type, Hecale was even able to reveal that she had not always been poor, and that she too had royal blood flowing in her veins. We may savor the embarrassment of the prince, chafing at his father's protectiveness, who found that his bold enterprise had in this way promoted him to the nursery, and admire the good manners that enabled him to endure his situation.

The general spirit of the story is clear. Though Theseus did in the end capture the marauding bull, politely returning next day to bring the news to Hecale, and joining in the general mourning on discovering that she had died since his departure, the emphasis was not at all on the expected phases of his adventure. Instead, exemplifying the religious pattern found in the *Aetia*, the legend was made an excuse for explaining the origin of certain Athenian festivals and names which recalled Hecale, and the treatment was such as to display the hero in his unheroic moments, young, caught in a rainstorm, forced to accept the ministrations of an old and motherly crone. His

[42] Cf. the scholiast's comment on *Hymn to Apollo* 106 (Pfeiffer, *Callimachus*, vol. II, p. 53).

ability to master the bull was assumed, and apparently passed over without much fuss.

The poem was decked out with digressions, notably a narration by a crow explaining why crows are never allowed by Athene to enter the Acropolis, and why ravens are black.

The best context in which to understand what Callimachus did in the *Hecale* may be that of the traditional fairy tale.[43] The young prince goes to find his father (Telemachus, Phaethon). There is a wicked stepmother, a monster, a lonely cottage, an old crone, speaking birds (the "twa corbies"). But all these motifs are twisted or frustrated in some way. The finding of his father is the beginning rather than the end of the hero's quest, and brings him immediately into fresh danger. The fight with the monster is muted. There is no beautiful princess. The old benefactress offers no talisman, and the speaking birds look as if they parody her loquacity.[44] The whole achievement is shadowed by Hecale's death, and the festival is founded in her honor, not in that of the hero.

Another Russian critical theory may shed light on all this parody, a term which is in order, provided we do not use it in too cruel a way. The ancient serio-comic manner, the *spoudogeloion*, has been traced back beyond its ostensible beginnings in the popular preaching of the Cynic philosophers. Even Callimachus' own patron in the *Iamboi*, Ion of Chios, has been enrolled among its ancestors.[45] For M. Bakhtin this style "carnivalizes" the staider productions of more sober authors. It is here that parody, laughter, mixed feelings, a particular kind of emotionally measured space and time, masking and unmasking, are at home. There are elements of this popular manner even in Homer. One thinks of the laughter and tears, serio-comedy, of Andromache, as Hector unmasks himself in the presence of his baby son by doffing his helmet. Certain other primitive elements of this kind were already noted in the discussion of *Iliad* XXII.

But the *Hecale* too comments on the human closeness of tears and laughter (fr. 298 Pf.), and the reduction of its traditional hero to adolescence is both a manipulation of time and a kind of unmasking,

---

[43] Cf. V. Propp, *Morfologiya Skazki* (Leningrad 1928: Eng. tr. Bloomington, Indiana 1958).

[44] This could be the significance of the fact that the oath at fr. 260. 52 Pf. looks as if it were uttered by the crow, but is quoted by the Suda as a saying of Hecale herself. See the discussion by H. Lloyd-Jones and J. Rea in *Harvard Stud. Class. Phil.* 72 (1968), 143–44.

[45] M. Bakhtin, *Problemy Poetiki Dostoevskogo* (Moscow 1963), especially ch. 4. For Ion of Chios see Bakhtin, p. 142 and Callimachus, *Iambos* XIII. Bakhtin develops his theory of carnival literature especially in *Tvorchestvo François Rabelais* (Moscow 1965). The older English translations of his books cannot be recommended.

especially when there is an underlying comparison with the grizzled Odysseus in Eumaeus' hut.[46] The ultimate triumph of the carnival in Ovid's *Metamorphoses*, a profoundly Alexandrian work, should alert the reader to its presence at the beginning of the Alexandrian epic experiment.

By suggesting that we can only come to terms with the heroic if it is reduced in this way, Callimachus is putting genuine heroism on a plane which takes it outside the range of our experience. Theseus eating salad at Hecale's table slims the gargantuan banquets of heroes, downsizes the heroic world, and compels it in the process to abandon what we really expect to be part of it. But the subtlety of this use of irony must not be lost. It is far too crude to take it as implying that Callimachus no longer believed in fairy stories, and so wanted to communicate this daring truth to a public that did. What the poet really asks his listeners to do is to enter consciously the world of make-believe. We suspend our enlightened incredulity, and imagine for a time what a hero in the modern world, with our modern knowledge of "la résistance des choses," might be like. The poet suggests that he might be young, because that is an age to which naive heroism is appropriate; that he might be overprotected, because that is the kind of thing that happens to princes, especially those whose mothers are dead; that he might slip away from home, because he is after all a boy; that he might be caught in a rainstorm, because that is the kind of nuisance that can happen to anybody; that he might be sheltered by an old country-woman, because that is typical of Greek hospitality; that he might be well-mannered enough to come through the experience with credit. He obscures the capture of the bull, because such an exploit is too conventional to be convincing, if set in the spotlight, for an audience tired by sensational stories. But if the reader is asked to do the author's work for him, by supplying the omissions from his own knowledge, the potential deficiency is made up to everyone's satisfaction. This literary gambit is as old as Homer's refusal to describe Helen's beauty.

In none of this narrative of course is Callimachus attempting crudely to *satirize* heroism. The satire, part of the epic amalgam since the days of Homer's Thersites, and even of his Paris, has been sublimated. What we may say is that he is *playing* with the concept, playing in an "if only" kind of way.[47] Could this Theseus ever grow up?

---

[46] Pfeiffer on *Hecale* fr. 239.

[47] Cf. J. Huizinga, *Homo Ludens* (4th ed., Haarlem 1952). The difficult concept of irony is brilliantly treated by S. Kierkegaard in his M.A. thesis, *The Concept of Irony* (Eng. tr. by Lee M. Capel, London 1966). One of the best short introductions is

With the *Hecale*, a revolution in classical poetry was accomplished. For intelligent and critical listeners the epic again became possible. Homer could be useful, no longer as respectfully echoed model, but as sounding board, ironically distanced from the action by felt incongruity. It was the restoration to the epic of a polyphony native to Homer's own repetitive manner. We may salute the sophistication and refinement of a court to which this type of epic was acceptable.

Yet this poem, admired and studied until at least the thirteenth century, has not been appreciated by modern historians of literature at its true value. Scholars have themselves contributed to its being ignored by inventing a new genre, the *epyllion*, to which it may safely be assigned and thereby prevented from being heard. The plain fact must be clearly stated that there is no such ancient literary genre as the *epyllion*, and this in a world where grammarians were just as inventive of jargon as their more recent counterparts.[48] Callimachus was not intending to write something which stood to one side of the epic tradition, which shrank, for example, from direct confrontation with the windy work of Antimachus. He meant that in sophisticated times his was the only way in which epic could still be made plausible. This was the challenge that outraged his critics. Nothing less explains their ferocity.

Callimachus had done other things that would be relevant to the epic tradition. One of the last poems of the *Iamboi* was the *Deification of Arsinoe*, in which, after an opening invocation to Apollo and the Muses which recalled Hesiod, the queen's younger sister Philotera, already dead and honored as a goddess, was described as observing a huge column of smoke rolling across the surface of the Aegean. She asked Charis ("Grace") to fly to the top of Mount Athos to find its origin. Charis obeyed, and told Philotera that the smoke came from the funeral pyre of her sister Arsinoe, who had just died, and that all the cities of Egypt were mourning the queen's death.[49] Though the papyrus which tells us so much tells us now no more, it is possible to see here the outline of a familiar epic scene. Some untoward event is reported by a lesser deity to a greater, so that appropriate comment

---

given by A. Körte–P. Händel in *Die hellenistische Dichtung* (Stuttgart 1960), pp. 70 ff. B. Snell's essay in *Die Entdeckung des Geistes* (3rd ed., Hamburg 1955), pp. 353 ff., is at a rather more superficial level, as is K. J. McKay's *The Poet at Play. Kallimachos, The Bath of Pallas* (Leiden 1962).

[48] W. Allen, Jr. was absolutely right to protest against the use of the term *epyllion* in his vitally important article in *Trans. Amer. Phil. Ass.* 71 (1940), 1–26. It is a term which begs the whole question of the Alexandrian contribution to epic. S. Koster, *op. cit.*, p. 126 note 9, is a good example of persistence in error because it suits preconceptions (what the Germans call *Systemzwang*).

[49] See Trypanis' summary, *op. cit.*, pp. 162 ff.

and action may follow.[50] The meter of this poem, anapaestic, teasingly verging on the dactylic, and yet not the dactylic hexameter of tradition, shows how close epic and lyric were becoming.

## IV

Callimachean influence on the epic is proved by those undeniable epics which have owed a debt both to the *Hecale* and his other poetry. Of these, one is itself just beginning to be appreciated in its full implications for the classical epic tradition, and that is the *Argonautica* of Apollonius. The *Aeneid* stands in the same succession. Virgil's poem has never lacked appreciation, but it has often been admired for the wrong reasons, in ignorance of its literary background, and has either been viewed as something unique, or else forced to fit a mold which suits the preconceptions of the critic. Most ludicrous of all perhaps has been the folly of those who, after defining the *Aeneid* as a heroic poem in the conventional sense, have then proceeded to scold Aeneas for not being a conventional hero.

Poems with less prestige to defend them than the *Aeneid* have been dismissed as disastrous failures because their readers were not prepared to make the necessary adjustments for their comprehension. This has led to the disappearance of once respected authors like Boccaccio, Ariosto, Tasso from the repertoire of the educated public. The incomprehension has been creeping further, and in our time has threatened to engulf even Milton.

Yet, although the epic has been eliminated from the imaginative range of contemporary poetry, the taste of the broad mass of the public for heroic action convincingly illustrated on a heroic scale has continued to be fed by the film and the novel. Clearly it has received here sustenance of differing nutritional content. But the anti-hero is familiar to many a modern who knows nothing of the *Hecale* or of Apollonius' Jason, but who has read his Raymond Chandler or Graham Greene, or studied the trend in Hollywood Westerns from black and white towards shades of grey. We have had in modern poetry, or at least in modern criticism, an Alexandrian situation without a Callimachus. There has been all the ancient concentration on the highly finished and esoteric production appealing only to a learned few and demanding for its understanding a knowledge of the "Atlas-load of the past"[51] (really, a knowledge of vertical time), but we have had no

[50] See below, p. 257 on Dante's *Donne ch'avete*, a mixture of the Callimachean *recusatio* (conventional deprecation by the poet of his ability to handle grand themes of epic) with this particular encomiastic *topos* of the report by one deity to another.

[51] The phrase is K. Allott's, *The Penguin Poets: Contemporary Verse* (London 1951), p. 16. Compare the characterization of Ezra Pound's work given by G. Moore in *The Penguin Book of Modern American Verse* (London 1954), p. 99.

towering genius who has been able to unite the demands of a refined and polished art with the requirements of a larger-scale poetry in such a way as to win universal recognition for his work.

There have of course been approximations in a number of literatures to a universally recognizable Alexandrian ideal. English-speaking readers might, for example, wish to find this ideal embodied in T. S. Eliot.[52] That Eliot's poetry is Alexandrian needs no emphasis. We have only to study the *Four Quartets* to find all the points of the Callimachean poetic. The title of the poem shows the musical analogy to be of primary importance. There is selection of vivid, painterly detail, which however never wholly clarifies the poet's memories. The overall unity of the poems lies in their emotional effect. The poet's personality is everywhere. The language swings from the solemn to the colloquial. Finally, even though Eliot committed himself to definite religious beliefs in a manner remote (though not entirely remote) from Callimachus, his poems are by no means confident assertions of these beliefs. Doubts and questionings fill them.

Eliot was aware of the limited appeal of modern poetry, and anxious to find a wider audience. He turned to the writing of plays,[53] and rose to new heights with *Murder in the Cathedral*, whatever may be thought of his subsequent experiments in this genre. In choosing tragedy rather than epic, the poet was accepting Aristotle's view of tragedy's superiority. But the deliberate break with the hackneyed "Shakespearean" manner in both versification and vocabulary, like the earlier rebellion against the influence of Milton, corresponds to Callimachus' quarrel with the writers of hackneyed Homeric pastiche intended to glorify kings and heroes, and efforts to find a better way of recovering the Homeric spirit. Callimachus would have sympathized also with Eliot's presentation of the hero in his moments of self-doubt and temptation; with the lyricism of the chorus; with the archaic, spare selection of detail, by contrast with Tennyson's treatment of the same theme. If the drama broke with Aristotle's veto on the use of historical material in poetry, it must be remembered that, with his usual common sense, Aristotle allowed an exception when history could be assimilated to myth, and that in any case, for modern spectators, the history was so remote as to be more or less legendary.

Callimachus too had tried his hand at drama. His epigrams suggest that his experience there had not been happy. We know that he disapproved of bombastic language in tragedy, so that it is fair to

---

[52] Cf. E. R. Curtius, "T. S. Eliot," in *Kritische Essays zur europäischen Literatur* (2nd ed., Bern 1954), pp. 318 ff.

[53] His lecture "Poetry and Drama" (*T. S. Eliot: Selected Prose*, ed. J. Hayward, London 1953, pp. 67 ff.) is especially illuminating.

suppose his own plays exploited the resources of simple and even colloquial vocabulary.[54] Eliot tells us that he tried to learn from Euripides, and that his attempts to borrow from Aeschylus were a failure. In the ancient world, Aeschylus was looked upon by traditionalists as a model of the grand style, while Euripides appeared as a precursor of the ironic and polished subtleties of the New Comedy. In the debate sponsored by Dionysus in Aristophanes' *Frogs* at the end of the fifth century between the two Athenian playwrights, Euripides had much of the critical language applied to him which would later be applied to Callimachus in Alexandria. Callimachus alludes to Euripides in the Preface to his *Aetia*. Can we doubt that both he and Eliot learned something for their dramas from the same source?

The impulse towards the epic has not vanished in our age. Some of its most successful practitioners have been Russian, and they have left us theoretical discussions of their method which must be called into evidence by anyone seeking to substitute for the partial and misleading poetics of the ancient critics and their self-appointed successors in more recent days the genuine experience of the creative artist, who is not seeking to take the intellect's revenge on art, but himself to contribute to it. S. Eisenstein and V. Pudovkin, knowing nothing of Callimachus, have found themselves forced by the Alexandrian spirit of our time into his attitudes. In their work too there appear the analogy with music, the insistence on "cutting," the claim that the spectator's memory and emotions will supply omissions, the aim of working on those emotions, the omnipresence of the director's personality shaping our reactions, the attempt to mimic the high style, the quite unexpected avoidance for such committed artists of the confident assertion and the bold generalization.

But even in literature the epic has gone on, although for the most part not in verse. This is one of the most difficult developments for the traditionalist to accept. When the conservative first hears the word "epic" applied to a novel,[55] his reaction is rather like that of the Hellenist who hears someone speak of a "marathon" wait to get tickets for a pop concert, or of an "armchair Odyssey."[56] But already Aristotle had argued that meter is not the distinguishing characteristic of imaginative writing. In a controversial passage at the end of the

---

[54] Cf. the comment by Porphyrio on Horace, *A. P.* 97 and Callimachus fr. 215 Pf. with *Epigrams* 7, 8, 59. Callimachus also experimented with satyr plays, which may explain why there is so much about this genre in the *Ars Poetica*.

[55] Cf. T. E. Maresca, *Epic to Novel* (Columbus, Ohio 1974).

[56] Fowler's *Modern English Usage* (2nd ed. revised by Sir Ernest Gowers, Oxford 1965) explodes s.v. "Epic," p. 161. But the authors evidently entertain a notion of epic which the present book totally rejects.

*Aetia*, Callimachus had declared that, having finished with that poem, he would pass on to the "prose pasture of the Muses." It seems that he meant his *Iamboi*, which the papyri suggest were published in a collection directly following the *Aetia*. If these more down-to-earth pieces can be described as "prose," and yet still remain poetry, imaginative writing, why could one not go all the way, though still in the company of the Muses, to prose itself? The later Greek writers of romances did exactly that. In any case, the amalgamation and confusion of what were earlier more clearly separable genres (though never so separable, even in Homer, as critics like to make out) is a feature of the Hellenistic period. The writing of an epic in prose only takes further a development which is present in embryo in the theories of Aristotle,[57] in the work of Callimachus, and even more mightily in the prose epic of so classical an author as Thucydides.

The Russians are the heirs of a Byzantine, Greco-Roman classical tradition which has been less carefully filtered for "impurities" than the one we know in the western half of the Empire. Their literature offers many examples of the epic in prose, even as early as *The Lay of Igor's Campaign*. At the start of the nineteenth century Gogol called *Dead Souls* a "poem," and imitated Homeric similes in *Taras Bulba*, a violent and tragic account of Cossack resistance to Polish might. But the supreme instance of such epic must surely be *War and Peace*. This immense novel, conceived on a vast scale, may be fruitfully analyzed with the help of the ancient tradition. Its use of an historical theme only appears to contradict Aristotle. Its anti-heroes, Pierre, Prince Andrei, Kutuzov, are aware of their own limitations, while the ostensibly heroic Napoleon and his minions are depicted as futile and pompous. These are characterizations that would have attracted Callimachus, and the Apollonius who showed a Jason out of his depth in the quest for the Golden Fleece. They suggest that even a work that strove to be an *Iliad* had to accept Alexandrian principles in order to acquire its real and lasting significance.

The Callimachean poetic as we have defined it set at its head an analogy with music. This is exactly what Thomas Mann declares he did in his own epic attempt to make sense of the horrifying debacle endured by Germany in our century. *Doktor Faustus*, ironically and learnedly commenting on the new relevance of old myths, ambiguously clouding its answers to simple questions of guilt or innocence, mixing autobiography with fiction, classical allusion with contempo-

---

[57] Its germ already lay in Aristotle's suggestion that verse is not the essential thing in imaginative writing, "poetry." See D. W. Lucas' note on p. 59 of his edition. On Callimachus' "prose pasture" see Pfeiffer's commentary to fr. 112, 9 and Puelma Piwonka, *op. cit.*, pp. 206 ff.

rary reality, shadowing the past with the future, is one of the most modern productions of our age, and yet one of the most Alexandrian. In a fresh way, this means that it stands with the *Aeneid* and the *Divine Comedy*, which also both describe a descent to hell.

Joyce and Proust are other major authors of our time who show an allegiance to Alexandria. The delicate world of the madeleine and the salon speaks, like the New Comedy of Athens, with only a muffled voice of the terrifying events that were then wrecking Europe. But it does construct a poetic world from these slender materials intended to defy the power of darkness with a dream. Joyce's *Ulysses*, looking back to the *Odyssey*, exploits, with Virgil, a technique drawn from the *Hecale*.[58]

The proper understanding of the classical epic tradition, and in particular of its double, Alexandrian nature, both Hesiodic and Homeric, is a thread that can draw together the most diverse creations of the European genius, and produce order in what seems like fertile chaos. In our day, when the creative tradition is threatened from every side, it is of more than academic importance that we should grasp what we inherit. Only so can we hope that at last poetry will unite its divided streams and find a community both to charm and instruct, to refine aesthetically and morally, to raise beyond the elegiac record of what man does and fails to do to what he may do if the gods' radiance strikes him.

[58] It is the technique by which two Homeric analogues are blended to form one modern character: cf. R. Ellmann (*TLS* no. 3838, Oct. 3, 1975, p. 1118): "But this is to misunderstand one of Joyce's cardinal principles, that Telemachus and Ulysses must be allowed to exchange and combine roles so as to make possible their eventual fusion." So in the *Hecale* young Theseus mingled in himself elements drawn from Homer's Telemachus and Odysseus.

# II

# ARISTOTLE, CALLIMACHUS
# AND THE
# ANCIENT CRITICAL TRADITION

THE incomplete state of Aristotle's *Poetics* has never hampered dogmatic interpretation of the master's teaching.[1] Sharing the fate of the rest of his work, it has become over the centuries a repository of authoritarian doctrine which has been more often used to bludgeon originality than encourage it. It seems consistent with this tradition that modern scholars too should advance the notion that the new poetry of Alexandria could not have drawn, in the first instance, any inspiration from the Peripatos.[2]

It is important here to ask what purpose Aristotle intended the *Poetics* to serve. We know that many of his other works bear the stamp of a practical intelligence well adapted to tutor Alexander the Great. His series of *Constitutions*, of which we now possess that on Athenian government, gave substance to his *Politics*, and this latter treatise has had wide repercussions throughout European and American history. In turn, the *Politics* found its essential basis in the personal problems of the *Ethics*. His books on *Metaphysics* react to and seek to progress beyond the theories of his teachers, especially Plato. It has been the achievement of our age to recognize in Aristotle a mind by

[1] The subtle interpretations of the "Chicago Aristotelians," based on the premise that the *Poetics* is a complete and rigorously logical text (cf. the introduction by E. Olson to *Aristotle's Poetics and English Literature* [Chicago 1965], and the concluding essay by R. McKeon) may be contrasted with *La Poétique d'Aristote: Texte primitif et additions ultérieures*, by D. de Montmollin (Neuchâtel 1951). The perennial novelty of the *Poetics* is illustrated by the renewed attraction which it has for the most modern criticism: cf. *Aristote, La Poétique*, edd. R. Dupont-Roc and J. Lallot (Paris 1980); *Die Poetik des Aristoteles. I. Interpretationen: II. Analysen*, by Ada B. Neschke (Frankfurt am Main 1980).

[2] So, for example, R. Pfeiffer, *History of Classical Scholarship* (1968), p. 137. But this view is rightly repudiated by S. Koster, *Antike Epostheorien*, pp. 120–22. It looks as if Pfeiffer is influenced by K. O. Brink's article "Callimachus and Aristotle," *Class. Quarterly* XL (1946), 11 ff., though he makes no mention of it.

no means static, but continually growing and reaching out to fresh problems—problems that were those of his society and time.[3]

Those who interpret the doctrines of the *Poetics* as purely conservative and backward-looking are therefore in danger of making the work an anomaly. They are aided to some degree by the fragmentary nature of the text, from which the promised discussion of comedy, presumably occurring in a second book, is missing.[4] Aristotle did express his views on poetry and poets in at least one other work, but this too is lost. His *Rhetoric* is perhaps the nearest surviving parallel, and yet this was certainly intended to guide the student and remind him of the most effective oratorical techniques.[5]

It seems right therefore to assume that the *Poetics* too had some practical significance, hard though it may be now to recover. Can we in fact read it as a key at least to some kinds of later literature?

I

It begins with a very unconservative notion, by admitting the possibility of imaginative ("mimetic") writing in prose, and so looking ahead to the modern novel. Aristotle had adopted the theory of *mimesis*, itself quite old in Greek thought, from his teacher Plato. It creates difficulties for him at the outset with the poetry of those who, like Empedocles, appeared to be using verse as the medium for scientific and metaphysical communication. Yet we should note that Aristotle, after raising this problem, left the question of Empedocles' exact place in critical theory unresolved, since later in the *Poetics* he clarifies an obscurity in Empedocles' poetry without suggesting that he is going outside his proper sphere, and in his *On Poets* (fr. 70) he both called Empedocles "Homeric" and attributed to him that ability with metaphor which he regarded as the poet's chief and unteachable gift. Another fragment tells us that Aristotle thought of Empedocles as the "founder of rhetoric."[6]

Like all good teachers, Aristotle evidently threw off queries to

---

[3] "[T]he *Rhetoric* and *Poetics* . . . both have a *practical* slant" (*Aristotle's Poetics*, by Humphry House [London 1967], p. 36). Modern interpretation of Aristotle as no Aristotelian is particularly indebted to W. Jaeger: cf. A. Lesky, *A History of Greek Literature*, p. 575.

[4] Richard Janko, *Aristotle on Comedy: Towards a Reconstruction of Poetics II* (London 1984), attempts to rehabilitate the *Tractatus Coislinianus* as the record of at least part of Aristotle's lost treatment. There is something in this: see below, pp. 420–21.

[5] W. Kroll, "Rhetorik," *RE* Supplementband VII, cols. 1058 ff., states that Aristotle's practical bent comes noticeably to the fore in a confusion made by the *Rhetoric* over orators' aims. A. Döring, *Die Kunstlehre des Aristoteles* (Jena 1876), summarizes on p. 79 his discussion of the practical intent of Aristotle's theories.

[6] Cf. Diogenes Laertius 8. 57.

which he himself had no answer, while proceeding to operate with existing answers as the best working hypotheses available. It is simplest not to exaggerate an incidental remark by him about the deficiencies of Greek literary terminology, and the awkwardness of fitting poetry like that of Empedocles into the mimetic category, until it becomes a point of contention between Aristotle and the Callimachean admirers of the Alexandrian didactic poet Aratus.[7]

Disliking *mimesis*, Plato had expelled as no better than lies all but the most crudely propagandistic genres of poetry from his ideal state.[8] Aristotle, by contrast, finds imitation natural to man. In defense of poetry's emotional and upsetting effect, he advances his famous theory of *catharsis*.[9] The feelings of pity and fear, for example, which a great tragic masterpiece induces can have a cleansing and purifying issue. The idea that poetry should work on the emotions is therefore central to his aesthetic; and for the audience the effect of this working will be drastic.

Homer, it can never be emphasized enough, was for Aristotle the author of the comic *Margites* as well as of the *Iliad* and *Odyssey*. In this book, where epic and tragedy are compared, he plays a leading and ambiguous role in the discussion. It is clear that Aristotle's own inclination is towards tragedy, but tragic drama is to be understood as in some sense the culmination of epic, and epic as in some sense the ancestor of tragedy. Accordingly, though Aristotle informs us that he is going to deal with tragedy first and epic later, we find that in the event Homer's epic is not excluded from the argument. When unity of plot is mentioned, Homer is cited as an excellent example of an author who knew how to select from a mass of material so as to find unity in what was left. Stories do not acquire unity by being about one person, simply because so much happens to an individual which has no internal coherence. Selection, dramatic effect, a unity other than that of using the same names throughout: these are criteria which will be of vital concern to the epic yet to come.

Something else emerges. If epic was in a way the preparation for drama, there will be times when the epic tradition is best sought in drama, and not in a formal adherence to some outmoded epic guise.

---

[7] So Körte–Händel, *Die hellenistische Dichtung*, p. 272, against Brink, *loc. cit.*

[8] *Rep.* II and III. 377 a – 392 b; X. 595 a – 608 b. Cf. *Laws* VII. 810 c – 811 b.

[9] Cf. D. W. Lucas' edition of the *Poetics* (Oxford 1968), Appendix II, pp. 273 ff. R. Heinze has some interesting remarks (*Virgils Epische Technik* [4th ed., repr. Stuttgart 1957], pp. 466–67), in which he suggests that Aristotle's original doctrine was trivialized after his death and made to accommodate grosser emotional effects. See also E. Norden on *Aeneid* VI. 14 ff. But the scholia on *Iliad* I still preserve some memory of *catharsis*: see below, p. 47.

We need look no further than Shakespeare or Racine—or Brecht—
to feel the truth of this observation.[10]

It is in this context that Aristotle makes a sharp distinction between
poetry and history. A poem that merely sets out to follow the facts
of a given life or event is prevented by this attention to detail from
soaring into the poet's proper realm. The facts may, in real life, reach
no very satisfying conclusion. The poet must have freedom to
manipulate and maneuver. If the work of Herodotus were to be put
into verse, it would remain a history for all that. There is a covert
allusion to Choerilus of Samos, who towards the end of the fifth
century had versified Herodotean material in his *Persica*. Precisely
the same illustration of how not to write epic would be used later by
Callimachus.[11] Only when the facts happen also to be aesthetically
rewarding may they be selected as they are for poetic treatment. For
Aristotle then the "historical" epic would suffer from a fundamental
defect right from the start. Its author would have confused his
mission.

When Aristotle finally turns to discuss epic in itself, he opens with
the remark that much of what has been said about tragedy applies
to this more ancient genre. Homer's selection of material again comes
in for praise. The criterion of length for tragedy is again repeated
for epic. The reader must be able to take in the whole as a unit.
Aristotle comments that this means the plots of modern epics must
be shorter than those of older epics. Here is clear proof of the
practical bias of his work.

But the most startling passage of the *Poetics* as we now have it is
found at the very end. After suggesting certain ways in which epic
might be thought to have the advantage over tragedy, Aristotle
suddenly turns round and reverses this judgment. Tragedy, we now
learn, contains all the elements of epic, including the ability to use
the epic meter, but on top of that it has the added effect of music
and spectacle. Moreover, "it fulfills the purpose of its imitation in
smaller compass, and what is more compact is more pleasing than

[10] On Brecht see, for example, M. Seidel and E. Mendelson, edd., *Homer to Brecht:
The European Epic and Dramatic Tradition* (New Haven 1976). The lively debate about
the literary status of Brecht's work to which modern studies bear witness, and the
distinction made by Brecht himself between his epic drama and Aristotelian drama,
must not obscure the extraordinary tribute which the very notion of epic drama pays
to Aristotle's insight into the dramatic tendencies of the Homeric *epos*.

[11] *Aetia*, fr. 1. 15 Pf. Cf. p. 26 above. Proust agreed with Aristotle: *À la recherche
du temps perdu*, Eng. tr. by C. K. Scott Moncrieff (London 1941), vol. 11, p. 334.
R. Häußler, *Das historische Epos von Lucan bis Silius und seine Theorie* (Heidelberg
1978), p. 9, thinks that Aristotle is referring here to Aeschylus' *Persae*. But in what
sense did Aeschylus versify Herodotus?

what is spread over a great length of time. . . . Epic has less unity."[12] Its writers are confronted with the dilemma that either they must choose a unified story, in which case a brief presentation comes to an abrupt end; or, if they seek to follow the length appropriate to their meter, the subject matter is watered down. Even though the *Iliad* and the *Odyssey* are constructed in the best possible way, and are the imitation of a single action so far as epic can be, they still have in them many parts with a substantial character of their own. Finally, the pleasure aroused by epic is more diverse and less predictable than that aroused by tragedy, and this too proves tragedy's superiority. Presumably Aristotle means that tragedy makes a more concentrated assault on the emotions, and so secures its cathartic effect more powerfully.

In the last analysis, poetry is a matter of words. Aristotle seems to have been in some perplexity in this matter. The *Poetics* attempts to take up a middle position. Diction has to be clear without being common, lucid yet not colloquial. To secure this aim, nouns may be used in metrically varied forms. But to replace rare words with common ones can be to rob a line of its effect. The point is illustrated with a quotation from Euripides, where a single change from the ordinary word used by Aeschylus makes all the difference. Ariphrades, a comic writer who ridiculed the out-of-the-way expressions employed by the tragedians, is taken to task for failing to understand that all these forms, precisely because they are not in everyday use, lift the language of poetry out of the ordinary. Formalist critics would say that Ariphrades had not understood the doctrine of estrangement.

But in Book III of his *Rhetoric*, Aristotle returns to the question of diction and of the vocabulary of tragedy, and he has changed his mind. Now we are told that modern tragedies have abandoned the adornment of their texts with unusual words. There is a naturalness which should be one's guide. Artifice escapes notice when the artist uses current speech. Euripides does this, and was the first to show how.[13]

In vacillating about the effectiveness of current speech in poetry, and using Euripides to prove two opposites, Aristotle opened the door to at least one way of rejuvenating outworn poetic vocabulary. The combination of the "gloss," the old-fashioned or poetic word recommended by the *Poetics*, with the modern language praised by the *Rhetoric*, could clearly bring both poem and reader to life. The

---

[12] *Poetics* 1462 a 18 – b 4.

[13] *Rhet.* III. 1404 b 25. There are some excellent notes on Euripides' prosaicisms in Wilamowitz's edition of the *Heracles* (repr. Darmstadt 1959), e.g. on 705, 728, 1000, 1001. See below, pp. 147–48, 247–51, 260–62, 283, 312.

epic writer of the future, understanding that either type of language can produce the required estrangement, would be faithful to both Aristotle's insights.

The extreme modernity of the *Poetics* is best revealed in those passages of which his traditional commentators have made least sense. Anticipating the close study that both Formalist and Structuralist critics have given to linguistic usage, Aristotle there sketches a theory of grammar and even of metrics. The Formalists were to argue that larger stylistic devices were an outgrowth of the same device in miniature, so that repetition could run all the way from alliteration to the leitmotif. But what else can Aristotle mean when he says that the unity of the *Iliad* is a variety of the unity of the word "man"? The Alexandrians have often been in trouble for their verbal experiments. But were they not sanctioned by this same section of the *Poetics?* A whole new area of such exploration was opened by such remarks both in the ancient world and our own.[14]

"Verisimilitude" is a term that has often been used to stifle imagination. A modern scholar has shown how a fateful, perhaps deliberate, mistranslation at a later period of Aristotle's text shifted the emphasis of this word from plausibility to propriety.[15] What Aristotle meant was that the writer should not strain credulity too far. Obviously the limits of credulity will vary from period to period, audience to audience, and principally with the imaginative dominance exercised by the artist. Aristotle has this much on his side, that an utterly implausible, surrealistic presentation stands in danger of losing all human appeal. But in no sense was the admirer of the *Oedipus Rex* binding the artist to a mediocre realism, so that only what the man on the Clapham omnibus thinks acceptable may be introduced into the imaginative construct. In restating this truth, the Formalists were returning to the classical tradition.

Aristotle's theory of composition has been found particularly puzzling. The tragic (and epic) poet is urged to keep the scene he is writing so far as possible before his eyes. This prevents awkward discrepancies when the time for production comes. Aristotle adds (*Poetics* 1455 a 29 ff.):

> He should also, so far as possible, complete his work by using the

---

[14] The Formalists were the theoreticians of the Futurist movement in poetry. The Alexandrians had their own Kruchënikhs and Khlebnikovs: cf. Heracleodorus and the *kritikoi* (C. Jensen, *Philodemos über die Gedichte fünftes Buch* [Berlin 1923], pp. 147–48). See also below, p. 470 note 53.

[15] R.-C. Knight, *Racine et la Grèce*, pp. 64 ff., citing Riccoboni, Victorius and Heinsius, who changed *Poetics* 1451 b 5 ("What could happen") into *qualia fieri debent* ("What should happen"). The Formalist B. Tomashevsky agrees with Aristotle: T. Todorov, *Théorie de la littérature*, p. 284.

gestures. For, if their natural powers are equal, those who are actually in the emotions are the most persuasive: he who is storm-tossed storms and the angry man rages with the maximum of conviction. And this is why poetry needs either a talented nature or a madman, the former being impressionable and the latter inventive.

Scholars have been divided. Is Aristotle talking about the actor here or about the writer? The answer is that he is making the actor's art the paradigm of the poet's. The powerful pressure of imagination on the mind of the creative writer conjures up no longer abstractions best suited to the arid pages of the social scientist, but particular details of what it must have been like to enter that room and commit that murder. It is by his selection of these particulars which are yet clues to the universal from his excited imagination that the writer re-creates the scene and its accompanying feelings in the mind of his audience, "imitates" how it felt to be there.

But how does the writer excite his imagination? An interesting sidelight is thrown on this theory of composition by two passages in Aristophanes. In the first, Euripides is shown dressed in the ragged garb of his lame and suffering heroes. In the second, it is Agathon who has got himself up as a woman in order to enter into the spirit of a female role. In the *Poetics* Aristotle describes Euripides as "the most tragic of poets." This seems to mean "the poet most able to exploit emotional effects," and now it may be seen how those emotional effects were thought to have been generated. Aristotle's theory was revived by Stanislavsky and Eisenstein in our time.[16]

This brief survey of some Aristotelian doctrines is intended to place a far different emphasis on his work than that assigned to it by classicizing criticism. The question of what Aristotle meant by "imitation," "verisimilitude," "episode" and by any number of technical terms dear to the hearts of exegetes has been divorced from the way great poetry has actually been written. Because they have read the work with abstract problems in mind (and sometimes with the small man's eagerness to punish genial deviants), scholars have been puzzled to discover that later literature does not share their concerns, and indeed have advanced the astonishing view that this means the work was without influence after Aristotle, and may even have disappeared from sight.[17] But perhaps the solution to the difficulty is that they

---

[16] See below, pp. 413 note 44 and 436–37.

[17] G. F. Else, *Aristotle's Poetics, The Argument* (Cambridge, Mass. 1957), p. 337, even suggests that after the dispersal of Aristotle's papers the work was not known again until the fourth century A.D. I find this impossible to believe: cf. my article "Callimachus and the Epic," in *Serta Turyniana*, ed. J. L. Heller with the assistance of J. K. Newman (Urbana 1974), p. 346 and note 18. This article supplements in detail the arguments presented here.

have put the wrong questions to the *Poetics*. The real question is: what did the *Poetics* say to poets? In our particular enquiry here, what did it say to Callimachus?

There are many points of contact between the *Poetics* and what we know about Callimachean teaching. Firstly, there is the dethronement of the cyclic epic by both writers, the hexameter poetry that filled up gaps in Homer's accounts of the heroic age, and all poetry written in a univocal, pseudo-Homeric manner. Aristotle went on to veto any attempt to revive epic by taking a theme from history. So did Callimachus, using the same Herodotean, and Choerilan, example.

The *Poetics* makes no allusion to another effort to revive the decaying epic, that made by Antimachus of Colophon at the end of the fifth century. This attempt to retell the story of Thebes met with applause from Plato, and a great deal of criticism from elsewhere. The extreme elaboration and prolixity for which Antimachus was notorious indicate that, when Aristotle leaves his *Thebaid* unmentioned, he cannot mean us to deduce praise. Callimachus rejected another work of Antimachus, the elegiac *Lyde*, as being "fat and unclear."[18] The terms of the condemnation are Aristotelian. It would have been impossible for Aristotle to demand brevity, selection, dramatic treatment, clarity from the modern epic writer, and then to have implicitly praised meandering Antimachus merely for the sake of his master, Plato.

These demands on the new epic are however calculated to appeal to Callimachus' innermost artistic convictions. Yet here an irrelevant distinction has been dragged into the argument. Aristotle wanted epic to be *eusynopton*, to have a clearly graspable unity. In the Preface to the *Aetia* Callimachus speaks angrily of critics who assail him for not writing "one continuous song," and the *Aetia* itself treated a number of themes that look as if they were only loosely associated (though we can see that ring-composition linked its first and last books, and probably its third and last as well). So the assertion has been made (Brink) that Callimachus, unlike Aristotle, was against the Homeric ideal of epic, "unified and grand in style and subject matter" (the *Margites*?). Happily, Horace shows that Callimachus' "one" was not understood as a technical term. His translation *unum* (*Odes* I. 7. 5) means "unimaginative," "uninspired." Callimachus then, like Aristotle, was not against unity. He was against poetry that was boring, and that went on too long for its own good. He knew, again like

---

[18] Fr. 398 Pf. Less polite than Aristotle, Callimachus expressed open skepticism about Plato's ability as a literary critic (fr. 589 Pf.).

Aristotle, that such unity was not to be secured by the simple device of using the same names throughout, or by Homeric pastiche.

The modern reader may discover with some amazement that the term "didactic," so frequently applied to a certain kind of epic with an air of authority, and an implied Greek pedigree, was not in fact used in the ancient world to distinguish a separate sub-genre of epic poetry.[19] Arguments about whether poetry had a didactic mission or not covered all poetry, not a section of it. Aristotle had shown that what we would call "didactic" epic, exemplified for him by Empedocles, was not easily assimilated into the traditional theory of imitation. In Alexandria there was a great controversy over the versified version of Eudoxus' astronomical lore made by the poet Aratus of Soli. Aratus was defended by Callimachus as "an excellent and learned poet," while Praxiphanes of Mytilene, a known Aristotelian, attacked him. Praxiphanes is presumed, as an orthodox follower of the master, to have known that "didactic" poetry was impermissible. Callimachus, in departing from this prescription, allegedly showed his break with Aristotelian doctrine.

The argument has at least one interesting corollary, and that is its assumption that Callimachus and Praxiphanes must have been aware of the doctrines of the *Poetics* in order to quarrel about them. But need Aristotle's hesitations be quite so firmly resolved? Aristotle certainly admired Empedocles as an artist[20] in spite of the difficulty he had in classifying his poetry.

In any case, the line of argument ignores the nature of Callimachus' defense of Aratus, couched in a famous epigram. He does not say there that such poetry is to be classed with that of Empedocles. He categorizes it instead as in the manner of Hesiod. Aristotle had not said anything about this venerable author. Callimachus, who had seen that, if the epic was to be revived, it would have to be under different auspices from those of Homer, since Homer was pre-empted as a patron by those who mechanically copied the externals of his style, rejoiced to find in Aratus an experiment in writing a relatively large-scale poem in a way that was not pseudo-Homeric. He pointed out to Aratus' critics that there was perfectly good precedent in Hesiod

---

[19] "Didascalic" is used by late grammarians, e.g. Diomedes, I. 482. 31 Keil, but the value of these late categorizations for the understanding of the classical poets is doubtful.

[20] Cf. Aristotle fr. 70 (Rose) from the *peri poiētōn*. Cicero and Lucretius alike (*De Oratore* I. 217; *Rer. Nat.* I. 731 ff.) agree on the excellence of Empedocles' poetry, yet Horace selects him as the example of the mad poet (*A. P.* 464 ff.). Apollonius Rhodius was interested in Empedocles (IV. 676 ff.). A controversial figure continued to arouse controversy, suggesting at least that Aristotle was not thought to have settled the matter once and for all.

for this kind of poetry. In none of this controversy is there any need to suppose that he was deliberately contradicting Aristotelian teaching.[21] The epic he did write, the *Hecale*, was not "didactic" and not, in any real sense, "Hesiodic."

More differences between Aristotle and Callimachus have been found in the matter of length. Once again, we have paraded before us the wearisome stereotype of Callimachus as the advocate of the short poem only (his literary remains fill two substantial volumes in Pfeiffer's edition), and of his allegedly Aristotelian adversaries as the supporters of the long epic in "many thousands" of verses. In both cases the stereotype fails to do justice to the living reality. Aristotle was not an admirer of length in itself. He advised the modern epic writer to confine his poem to the amount of material that could be got through in the time normally occupied by a day's dramatic performances, now often calculated at about 7000 lines. In all cases he insisted that the epic writer must not go beyond the limits of "synoptic" unity. He had even criticized the *Iliad* and the *Odyssey* for not matching the ideal demands of unity in brevity.[22] Callimachus, for his part, was certainly not the admirer of the short poem and nothing more. In the same Preface from which the evidence is derived for his opposition to the Homerizing long epic, he states that length is an *irrelevant* criterion, and that what matters about a poem is its art. He could hardly reconcile this contention with the belief that only the short poem counts.

The only reason why Callimachean poems are likely to be short, when compared with poetry such as that of Homer and his cyclic imitators, is that, given the new demands of art, and the repudiation of the temptation merely to coast along on the broad bosom of the grand manner, Callimachean poetry will be very hard to write. This does not preclude the theoretical possibility that, as the new style becomes more sure of itself, it will be able to expand its scope to dimensions beyond the reach of pioneers.

Aristotle clearly leaned towards a poetry which should be more than the elegant epigram, and which communicated a pleasure deeper than the satisfaction of a taste for the virtuoso performance. Callimachus, so bitterly criticized by poets who were masters at doing precisely that,[23] if we study the evidence of what he left, shared his inclination.

When therefore the *Poetics* was read by Callimachus in Alexandria (in its full form, including the now missing treatment of comedy),

---

[21] See my *Augustus and the New Poetry* (Brussels 1967), pp. 315 ff.

[22] *Poetics* 1462 b 7 with Lucas' note.

[23] E.g. *Anth. Pal.* XI. 321, 322.

we need not suppose that he was in violent disagreement with anything he found there. He would encounter a call for the reform of the epic, and a hint that the two efforts made to reform it so far (by Antimachus and Choerilus of Samos) were unsatisfactory. He would find a suggestion that language should aim at clarity, and yet explore the estranging resonance of the poetic gloss. He would find the implication that the epic would have to learn from the drama if it was going to survive, for had not Homer himself been "dramatic"? Length, he would learn, while certainly desirable in a poem that hoped to impress, was by no means a guarantee in itself of good poetry. Unity was more important, and that would entail limitation. The aim of serious poetry was to produce pleasure by effecting some sort of drastic emotional experience, although even there the "heart-rending" talent of a Euripides might touch the truest essence of tragedy. Drama's superiority in attaining its emotional effect lay in its openness to the other arts, painting, but above all music. Yet Homer was also, thanks to the *Margites*, the father of comedy, and comedy engendered laughter. All this was exciting and congenial enough. Not conservatism, but revolution, was the message.

Not all could be accomplished at once, or by one man. The astringent bittersweets of the *Hecale* were perhaps more akin to Prokofiev or Poulenc than to Bartok. But Callimachus shares enough with the iconoclasm of the *Poetics* (including the acceptance of the buffoonery of the *Margites* as Homeric) to justify us in speaking of critical kinship. If he did not put our questions to that Delphic volume, we must be large-hearted enough to acknowledge that perhaps, after all, he knew better.

## II

Aristotle's legacy to practical criticism after him, though no doubt with more influences than his at work, may be traced, for example, in the Homeric scholia. The study of these ancient marginalia, awkward, crabbed, pedantic, shows what a sophisticated poetic the greatest epic writer of all was believed to have followed.[24] Much of this material originated in Alexandria.

Both the *Iliad* and the *Odyssey* were looked upon as tragedies, though the notion was not lost that Homer was the founder of comedy too. The overwhelmingly important criterion of poetic art lay in its emotional appeal, and even the theory of *catharsis* has not entirely

---

[24] The following remarks are indebted to L. Adam, *Die aristotelische Theorie vom Epos nach ihrer Entwicklung bei Griechen und Römern* (Wiesbaden 1889); M.-L. von Franz, *Die aesthetischen Anschauungen der Iliasscholien* (diss. Zürich 1943); R. R. Schlunk, *The Homeric Scholia and the Aeneid* (Ann Arbor 1974).

vanished.[25] It was conceded that these emotions might at times be contradictory.

Homer's narrative was sharply contrasted with that of the historian, a clear proof of Aristotelian influence. Though the scholia do not doubt the historical truth of his tale, they regard the poet as its free manipulator. His technique is distinguished by the alternation of suspense and rest (what the Formalists were to call "staircase structure"), and by a non-linear presentation:

> The poet commonly turns his story topsy-turvy by bending back, and stuffs the beginning into the middle. Experts say that in longer narrative poems to proceed in orderly fashion from the beginning to the actual story makes for hard listening, while to start with something more drastic gives more pleasure and tension.[26]

Homer makes great use of anticipation and reminiscence, summing up in this way the whole story of Troy while only telling a part of it. He found a particular successor here in Euripides. His use of connected imagery for this purpose was understood.[27]

The school of Isocrates in the fourth century had demanded from the narrator clarity, brevity and "verisimilitude."[28] All three criteria are important to the scholiasts. Many of their explanations are based entirely on pointing out the persuasiveness of the given details, showing very clearly how the famous verisimilitude was understood by them. The poet's clarity is found in his heaping up of individual touches. His brevity (which means his ability to say much in little) is particularly assisted by his use of multi-sensory metaphors[29] and personifications that lend "emphasis" (another favorite word) to what is said so shortly.

"Fantasy" is another important term of varying nuance. It can be used of the purely imaginative flight, as when Zeus holds his hand protectively over Troy (*Iliad* IX. 420). But it can also be the vehicle that transports the auditor vividly into a particular scene, so that sometimes the scholiasts speak of Homer as himself the witness of what he describes. By a happy choice of expression, sometimes of the simplest kind, the poet's own fantasy can grip that of the reader. Dante would later pay homage to this doctrine.[30]

---

[25] Adam, p. 40, from the scholia on the opening of the *Iliad*.

[26] Eustathius 878, 59 ff., quoted by Adam, p. 30. Ariosto does not seem far away: see below, pp. 417–18 and note 56.

[27] Schlunk, p. 41.

[28] Quintilian IV. 2. 31. Cf. Philodemos, ed. Jensen, pp. 12 ff.

[29] Von Franz, p. 29. See below, p. 419.

[30] *Fantasia*, *Paradiso* XXIV. 24. It is noticeable that the poet continues with language drawn from that of the painter.

Homer's narrative is especially vivid because it shows such closeness to painting. When the mourning Priam veils himself (*Iliad* XXIV. 163), it is an anticipation of the veiled Agamemnon of Timanthes.[31] "Graphic" (= "painterly") is a frequent term of praise.

But the poet's mastery of acoustic effects, of onomatopoeia and rhythm, is equally praised. All these devices contribute to the impressiveness and pathos of his story.

Homer avoids the banal, but that does not mean that he writes in some monotonously "sublime" style. The very fact that ancient critics discovered in him the models of all three of the later *genera dicendi*[32] shows how little they believed the epic poet should confine himself to some artificial elevation. Briseis' lament over Patroclus (*Iliad* XIX. 282) is said, for example, to belong to the middle style. The scene is impressive in its narrative part, and "graphic," while working on our feelings of pity.

Yet such impressiveness is combined in the poems with variety. Here, the similes are particularly praised. They have a psychological as well as pictorial element.

Aristotle had commended Homer for his knowledge of when it was suitable to write in his own person. Such writing must be restricted, since that was not the kind of imitation proper to epic. The scholiasts find Homer engaged in his own poetry perhaps rather more than Aristotle would have liked. Sometimes he is showing covert sympathy with Greek fortunes; sometimes he is alluding to his own art. His Greek sympathies allow him nevertheless to admit the faults of Greek heroes like Achilles. The degree of "subjectivity" admitted by this kind of criticism is interesting even for the history of Greek elegy.

The scholia show what the classical epic tradition was: that mixture of Aristotelian and other ideas, some deriving from Aristotle's contemporaries and some from Alexandria, which scholars term "Hellenistic." They do not support the notion of unrelieved and monumental grandiosity which is often supposed to be classical.

### III

This is something we see even more clearly from ancient historiography. Dismayed by Aristotle's strictures on their art (which apparently they were able to read), later historians seem to have decided to fulfill in their work every demand he had made on the serious poet. What they have to say about their procedures constitutes

[31] Not "der Maler Sicyonios" (von Franz, p. 23), but "the Sicyonian painter." See below, pp. 430–31.

[32] Quintilian XII. 10. 64; Aul. Gell. VII. 14.

therefore another practical poetic, and in effect a theory of imaginative prose composition.[33]

Ephorus, the pupil of Isocrates, is praised by Polybius (XII. 28. 10) for his use of language, his handling of his material, and for his thought. "Handling of his material" looks like what the scholiasts praise in Homer as "economy," and proves that the ancients did have what is so often denied, a theory of overall, unified composition. Ephorus was the first historian, it was believed, consciously to employ book division. In asserting that such books had to be complete units, later historians were accepting for themselves the organic metaphor which Aristotle had applied to poetry.

Narrative had to be clear and easy to follow: more Aristotle here. But necessary digressions were allowed. The exception was broadly interpreted, and even Polybius excuses discontinuity in his own narrative by pleading the need for variety.[34]

The length allotted to a given topic should correspond to its importance, and topics of similar importance should therefore have similar length. Lucian was later to blame Alexandrian poets for ignoring common-sense proportions in their narratives. What he has not seen is that length has, by this procedure, become an artistic weapon. Tacitus draws from the same arsenal.

Speeches, including letters and descriptions, were areas where fidelity was particularly liable to clash with the historian's penchant for rhetorical display. Not surprisingly, rhetoric often won.

Clarity did not mean clinical objectivity. As Polybius reveals in his assault on Phylarchus (II. 56. 7), it was the handmaiden of emotional effect. But Polybius himself accepts the theory he castigates. He rejects the kind of history that is like false and lifeless painting done, not from life, but from stuffed dummies. Timaeus is accused of this bookish attitude. Even the temporal sequence of narrative may yield to the demands of emotional effect.[35] The historian's contradictions show that there was a dilemma. To manipulate the reader's feelings too clumsily was wrong and damaging. But the greatest historians will manipulate these feelings nevertheless, only they will do so by using the details selected from real life convincingly. We need look no further than Tolstoy for the dangers which attend the historian here, and which may lead him to be assailed by some, yet lauded by others as a master of realism. Thucydides has had the same experience.

Striking and impressive effect, requiring the use of telling detail vividly presented, could also require obscure and archaic language

[33] Cf. P. Scheller, *De hellenistica historiae conscribendae arte* (diss. Leipzig 1911).

[34] Scheller, p. 45.

[35] Scheller, pp. 59–61.

("estrangement" in Formalist terms). Thucydides again offered the model.[36] Praxiphanes, Callimachus' critic, wrote about history, and mentioned Thucydides' lack of fame in his own lifetime by contrast with his posthumous celebrity.[37] Perhaps he was pointing out that "Thucydides mythistoricus" had in fact anticipated the prescriptions laid down by the *Poetics* for tragedy. At any rate, it is interesting that Thucydides, the great master of epic history, should have been so early an object of theoretical discussion by an Aristotelian.

Evidence has been sought from other sources in an effort to illumine the Alexandrian tradition. There survives under the name of one "Demetrius" a treatise on style that has been dated as far back as the third century before Christ.[38] These arguments have been rejected as inconclusive, but if the book comes even from the Augustan age, it is not without some importance, since critical conservatism may have fossilized teachings drawn from a much earlier period.

The general standpoint of Demetrius' treatise is Aristotelian. The discussion of what he calls the *ischnos charactēr*[39] merits attention, since it was for *to katischnon*, according to the Florentine Scholiast, that Callimachus was in trouble with the Telchines.

The *ischnos charactēr*, the plain style, does not admit compound words. It aims particularly at clarity. It uses current vocabulary. It has parallels in drama, notably in Euripides. Its desire for brevity often leads to obscurity. It shuns length (*mēkos*) as a device of stylistic elaboration. Its employs signposts in its sentences. It aims at vividness and persuasiveness. It finds a model in the prose poet Ctesias. It follows Theophrastus, Aristotle's successor, in realizing that not every point must be made if tedium is to be avoided.

Several times in this list we catch the voice of Horace. He too warns against obscure brevity, deprecates length, talks about current vocabulary, notes the use of homely language by Euripidean heroes.[40] Augustan poets are abstemious with compound adjectives by comparison with their Republican predecessors. How fascinating to discover that it is a mark of their sympathies with the plain style![41] Virgil likes a triadic structure. It is the same tendency at work.[42] Interesting results might flow from a systematic application of De-

---

[36] Dion. Hal., *de Thuc.* 50. 13 ff.: Scheller, p. 62.

[37] Marcellinus, *Vit. Thuc.* 30.

[38] Cf. G. M. A. Grube, *Phoenix*, Suppl. 4 (1961), p. 56.

[39] *De Eloc.* 190 ff.

[40] *A. P.* 25–26, 234, 95 ff.

[41] *De Eloc.* 211 ff.

[42] Norden, *Aeneis VI*, pp. 376–77; *De Eloc.* 205.

metrius' principles for the plain style to the criticism of Latin poetry. We can only assume that their relevance ultimately stems from that advocate of the plain style in high places, Callimachus.

If Demetrius did indeed reflect the views prevailing in Callimachean circles, and if scholars had known this with certainty, the history of literary criticism might have been different. But his treatise has stood to one side in discussion. More exciting than the sober assessment of what his views could do to illuminate even the epic tradition has been the effort to recover from the charred fragments dug up in the eighteenth century at Herculaneum the outline of a work on poetry by the late Republican epigrammatist and friend of many literary figures, the Greek writer and philosopher Philodemus. The immense difficulty of the task that scholarship has set itself here must be emphasized. The papyri were not well handled by their first discoverers. Those dealing with Philodemus' views on poetry, read by the brilliant Jensen, were published at a time when rising costs made the full statement of the evidence impossible. Estimates of Philodemus' own sensitivity and intelligence have varied widely.[43]

It is possible that Philodemus discussed the opinions of his predecessors, in order to attack them from an Epicurean standpoint, in separate sections. Jensen thought at first that the treatment was more desultory, and even Brink admits that the same critic may be refuted more than once. Some recurring themes do seem to emerge. Is poetry educational ("didactic")? What degree of knowledge must the poet have? Does he aim at pleasure, usefulness, or both? Are clarity and brevity his main attributes? Can good poetry be written by someone who is not a good poet, and what is a good poet? Is form more important than content? Evidently some Greek Mallarmé had declared that in poetry finish matters more than impressive thoughts. Even Praxiphanes had distinguished between a good subject matter and a good poem, and had pointed out that the former does not necessarily guarantee the latter. Demetrius of Byzantium had been unconvinced.

Eventually, in all this welter of Greek critical opinion, we meet Neoptolemus of Parium. He is important. It is from a work by him that Horace is alleged by an ancient commentator to have drawn the doctrines we meet in the *Ars Poetica*.

It looks as if Neoptolemus separated the verbal composition of a poem from its thoughts, and set the poet side by side with both small-scale and large-scale poetry, much to Philodemus' annoyance. Small-scale poems came first in the literary genres, and they are concerned

---

[43] C. O. Brink, *Horace on Poetry*, Vol. I (Cambridge 1963), pp. 53 ff.

with verbal composition only. Thoughts, arrangement, actions, character all come into play only when the poet himself is engaged. Harmony will be found even in large poems. The perfect poet will aim both at powerful emotional effect and at being useful, following the model of Homer.

What can all this mean, and why was it so annoying? To separate the verbal composition of a poem from its thoughts means presumably to agree that poems are written with words, and not with ideas. Then again, the poet himself is set side by side with his work. Would not Kant later say something similar, in stating that the artist's natural endowment is his real, non-phenomenal self?[44] The artist is someone who has access to a world obscured to the rest of us by phenomena. All that has really happened is that Kant has transferred to the artist and poet what Plato reserved for the philosopher. It looks as if this transference had begun in the Hellenistic age, and hence Philodemus' chagrin at the rival claim of access to the useful truth made by Neoptolemus for the poet. When we think of the subjectivity this claim implies about poetry, we find a link with the scholiasts' insistence on the overwhelmingly emotional appeal of Homer's poetry, and on his personal involvement with his story. Can we be far from Alexandria?

Can we in fact be far from Callimachus? A modern commentator has found in Neoptolemus a man of compromise, one who allowed a place for the grand genres, but did not repudiate Callimachus' call for reform.[45] This may well have been Neoptolemus' position, and if it was, we must salute the ingenuity which has succeeded in tracing it among the ravages of time. But it was no compromise. It was an exact reflection of the opinions of Callimachus himself.

Of course Callimachus acknowledged the legitimacy of the grand genres as they had existed in the past. Why else did he spend his life cataloguing their records? He denied however that the simple imitation of the past was enough to make a man a serious poet any longer, and this was his quarrel with the authors of the Homeric pastiche aimed at flattering "kings and heroes" which too often passed for epic in his own time. As he had ultimately committed himself to the statement that length was irrelevant to the judgment of poetry, and that it was only art that counted, it seems perfectly consistent to make him say that he too would accept the grand genres, provided they met the new standards.

But would Callimachus' demand for the reform of traditional

---

[44] Theodore E. Uehling, Jr., *The Notion of Form in Kant's Critique of Aesthetic Judgment* (The Hague–Paris 1971), p. 105.

[45] Brink, *Horace on Poetry*, I, pp. 43 ff.

poetry be so imperious that the grand genres simply would not survive? Would the whole idea of drama or epic now have no meaning? His own practice gives the answer. If the poet had rejected the grand genres entirely, why would he have tried his hand at the drama? Why would he have written his *Hecale*, which, for all its novelty, was still recognizably an *epos*, and left its mark both on the *Aeneid* and on that self-confessed *carmen perpetuum*, the *Metamorphoses*?[46] Why would the *Aetia*, a work that also influenced the epic tradition, have been composed at such length? It looks as if, in their call for reform which should not be riddance, Neoptolemus and Callimachus were one.

When Neoptolemus urged that poetry had a double aim, to delight and to be useful, he was correcting the third head of the Alexandrian Library, Eratosthenes, who had said that poetry simply delighted. Obviously Callimachus accepted from Aristotle that poetry should delight. That is why the word "sweet" occurs so often in his own criticisms.[47] But the poet who did not exclude a certain moralizing from his *Iamboi* must not be thought to have had no feeling for the utility of poetry and, after all, it was Callimachus who, when Aratus was under attack, had *defended* the didactic poem.

Philodemus, like his fellow countryman from Gadara, the poet Meleager, and like all the philosophers and literary men whose arguments he criticizes so freely, lived in an age when the poetic personality, as the poet's endowment, had indeed become of prime importance. All the modern discussions opposing "subjectivity" to "objectivity" in the artistic construct must not hide this basic fact. The question was becoming: what *kind* of personality must the poet cultivate? The time was ripe at Rome, though as always under Greek inspiration, for the doctrine of the *vates*.

## IV

If the poet in his Roman surroundings were to adopt a public *persona*, would that mean that he would need a new poetic? When we consider what Alexandrianism had become in some of its minor practitioners, it would have been unsurprising if, impatient with the trivia of that virtuosity, the Augustans had demanded an entirely new poetic program. In fact, they did not. The greatest testimony to the astonishing paradox that the new, imperial poetry would start from evolved and complex Alexandrian premises is provided by Horace's *Ars Poetica*.

Now we can see why the poem insists so much on the nature of

---

[46] *Aen.* VIII. 175 ff.; *Met.* VIII. 639 ff.

[47] E.g. *Aetia* fr. 1. 11 Pf.; *Epigr.* 27. 2. Compare Horace's *dulcia, A. P.* 99; Quint. XII. 10. 33 *dulce carmen*.

the true poet, as opposed to his mimic. Horace has no intention of
denying this Hellenistic emphasis on the poetic personality. But in a
Roman way this poet will be engaged with the public weal.

The most important section therefore of the whole epistle, if we
are thinking of its Augustan context, begins at verse 391. The first
of poets is not Homer, but Orpheus, who raised men by his lyric art
from the primitive and brutal barbarism of the forest. Amphion
comes next, for by his song he founded civic life. In a passionate
outburst, whose kinship with a Ciceronian idiom is not always understood,[48] Horace notes that this primeval poetic wisdom, with its
themes, dear to the Roman heart, of the city as center of law, has
now vanished. Yet, in its time, this it was that gave honor to the
inspired *vates* of old. After them stands Homer's fame;[49] after them
come the other genres. In the circumstances of the Augustan age,
under a *princeps* whose achievements recall those of the early *vates*,[50]
fresh scope is given to ancient inspirations. No need then for the
elder Piso to be ashamed of his high vocation, exalted as it is by the
recent founding of the temple of Apollo, with its cult statue of Apollo
the Lyrist. No need to feel that poetry does not merit from a Roman
the serious and unremitting attention which Horace recommends.

This is a climactic passage. Within this dominant Augustan tonality,
Horace reads the demands of art in his day in terms which Callimachus
would have acknowledged. He begins by warning against the grotesque, the surrealist art produced by those whose claims to freedom
have been pushed too far. They admired the kind of carnival or
fairground metamorphosis which had a perennial fascination for the
Roman mind, and would find its supreme exponent in Ovid. Yet it
was not without attraction even for Virgil (Polydorus in *Aeneid* III).
It returns to haunt Horace himself in the shape of the bear/leech
with which this poem ends,[51] and it certainly disfigures a prominent
ode (II. 20) in which the *vates* is enswanned.

The remedy for such extravagances is Callimachean—strict atten-

---

[48] As in *Cat.* I. 3 and *Verrine* II. 5. 45, *fuit . . . quondam* (*A. P.* 396) calls for a revival
of the past, and does not merely note its disappearance, like Virgil's *fuimus Troes* or
*et campos ubi Troia fuit* (where no *quondam* is used).

[49] A comma must be placed after *Homerus* at 401. The linking of Homer and the
elegist Tyrtaeus would be absurd, quite apart from the vapidity of *insignis* as an
attributive adjective here. Horace explains his view of the lessons offered by the *Iliad*
in *Epp.* I. 2. It does not include war-mongering. Cf. *tristia bella, A. P.* 73.

[50] See below, p. 192 and note 10.

[51] On the significance of the grotesque see M. Bakhtin, *Tvorchestvo François Rabelais*,
pp. 37 ff., with reference to A. Dieterich, *Pulcinella: Pompejanische Wandbilder und
römische Satyrspiele* (Leipzig 1897), and pp. 329 ff. Classical readers will remember
the Silenus image applied to Socrates in the *Symposium*, popular in Renaissance writers
(as Bakhtin notes).

tion to art. The poet must weigh his own powers carefully. Then he will lack neither the free flow of inspiration nor clarity of presentation. Clear presentation means selection. Only what is relevant immediately has to be said immediately.

The second section of the discussion, beginning at line 46, turns to the question of vocabulary. The aspiring author should be both *tenuis* and *cautus*. *Tenuis* is an outright Alexandrian word.[52] Horace remarks that a brilliant effect may be obtained by using familiar language (which is what *tenuis* would imply) in unexpected contexts.[53] New words too will be acceptable within reason, provided they follow Greek analogy.[54] Words come and go like nature's own seasons. The usage of educated speakers must be our guide.

A brief review of the traditional meters begins with Homer's hexameter, appropriate to the deeds of kings and generals, and to gloomy wars. All the genres demand observation from anyone who claims the title of poet. Even so, a significant concession is made. Although tragedy and comedy are normally distinct, they can approximate at times, either when a comic character expresses violent emotion, or when, in seeking to touch the heart, some tragic hero resorts to the simple language of everyday life, abandoning the cumbersome and bombastic. The examples appear to be chosen from Euripides, and of course look forward to Shakespeare. The scholiast however reminds us that here we are especially close to Callimachus. He might have added Virgil.[55]

Poems, remarks Horace, should not simply be *pulchra*—noble and impressive. They have to be *dulcia*, moving and appealing, if they wish to strike home to the listener (*Ars Poetica* 99–100):

> Non satis est pulchra esse poemata; dulcia sunto,
> Et quocumque volent animum auditoris agunto.

It is not enough for poems to be beautiful. They should be sweet, and draw after them wherever they wish the reader's soul.

Matching example to precept (an old device), he uses rhyme as an

---

[52] Nisbet–Hubbard on Horace, *Odes* I. 6. 9; Prop. III. 1. 5 and 8.

[53] The traditional order of lines should be kept at vv. 45–46.—The strange reluctance on the part of some scholars to accept B. Axelson's conclusions about Horace's use of prosaic words (*Unpoetische Wörter* [Lund 1945], ch. IV) must yield before the doctrine of *callida iunctura* ("skillful combination"), which is of far-reaching importance in the tradition of European poetry, not least in Virgil.

[54] Cf. Dem., *De. Eloc.* 91 and 96. This is from Demetrius' discussion of the elevated style, and explains why the tone of Horace's poem rises at this point.

[55] E.g. *Aen.* II. 523; IV. 328, with R. G. Austin's notes.

example of what he means. But so had Homer. Petrarch, Milton and a host of others would note the lesson.[56]

Vocabulary must suit the characters' emotions if it hopes to be effective. It must also conform to their background and upbringing. The discussion glides naturally into an examination of the problems of character drawing in general. The writer has two alternatives: to follow tradition or, if he departs from it, to invent something consistent.

It is difficult to particularize general characteristics (the problem which Eisenstein and Pudovkin saw as basic to dramatic art). You personally, says Horace to his addressee, are doing better to escape this problem by turning the *Iliad* into drama (where the work of particularization has already been done by Homer), than if you tried to advance wholly new themes. Yet there is a way of handling hackneyed material even in epic so as to make it your own—that of avoiding the cyclic poem and looking directly to Homer himself. Homer sets the example of a modest beginning, which aims to bring light out of the confusing mass of material rather than to use what is already clear to create darkness. This does not prevent Homer from attaining impressive and romantic effects later in his poem, once the initial difficulties are solved. Homer always speeds towards his goal. He selects his material and abbreviates it. Anything that cannot make a brilliant effect is eliminated. Throughout his poetry, he never loses sight of the demands of unity.[57]

This break turns out to have been merely a digression. We return to the need for good character observation if plays are to be convincing. A series of remarks about differences of character concludes at line 178.

A motley collection of precepts about drama then glides into a further section, where we find ourselves (v. 202) discussing music. Simplicity (again we hear *tenuis*) is the key. It was only after victory in war had brought greater material prosperity that Greek taste lapsed, and eventually made the tragic chorus rival Delphi in its oracular ponderosity.

The invention of tragedy was later followed by that of the satyr play, because in festive mood the audience craved something new. Horace does not object to this development, provided the satyrs know their place. Their language must neither be too low nor too elevated, neither drawn merely from current vocabulary nor merely comic.

[56] *Africa* V. 638–39; *P. L.* IX. 781–82: above, ch. 1, note 18. The formal rhymes of the Italian vernacular epic are only the development of an already latent tendency.

[57] Cf. H. Fielding, *The History of Tom Jones*, Everyman Editions (repr. London 1962), I, p. 268, where Horace is interestingly combined with Callimachus.

Once again, the unexpected use of the familiar is recommended as an artistic, though difficult solution to the problem of poetic language. The association of the doctrine of the *callida iunctura*, so important in Virgil, with the satyr play in this way (*iunctura*, vv. 48 and 242) is highly revealing for the Augustan interaction of the comic with the serious. Callimachus had written satyr plays. Are we hearing in these prescriptions something of his voice? Do satyr play, tragedy, comedy and even epic meet at this point, in spite of Horace's own strictures?[58]

Greek precedent, we go on to learn, must be studied night and day to improve metrical technique. The modern must not be content with hoping that he is going to get away with his negligence. The new standard of the *lepidum* (v. 273), already for Catullus the polished perfection of the Alexandrians,[59] forbids such slovenliness.

The fatal flaw preventing Roman fame in literature from matching Roman fame in the field has been the refusal to see the need for revision and correction. Indeed, matters have gone from bad to worse. Relying on the doctrine of certain teachers who elevate genius above skill, many have assumed the status of poet by assuming its externals: long hair, long fingernails, no gregarious visits to the bath, solitude. Horace comments sarcastically that no one would be a better poet than he, were the title so easily earned. With his allusion to the role of melancholy in the artist's makeup, he touches upon a theme still resounding in our own age.[60]

Horace proposes to remedy this situation by laying down rules for the poet's nurture. The first thing the real poet must do is to study *Socraticae chartae*, not so much books of moral philosophy as the kind of dialogues, ultimately derived from the mimes of Sophron or the Sicilian comedy of Epicharmus, in which moral philosophy could be seen in action. Living language, the poet reminds us, will be drawn not from abstractions, but from the model of life itself.

Another section seems to open as we encounter a eulogy of the Greek genius. This looks back to the claim made by false poets that genius is superior to art. Horace reminds these *poseurs* that the greatest geniuses of all are exactly the ones acknowledged to have been the best artists.

What is the purpose of poetry? Some of it aims to be useful, some to give pleasure, some to do both. If the aspiring author does wish

---

[58] Racine seems especially relevant: see L. Spitzer, "Die klassische Dämpfung in Racines Stil," *Archivum Romanicum* 12 (1928), 361–472.

[59] Cf. Catullus' *lepidum novum libellum* ("smart new little book"). E. Norden, *Die römische Literatur* (repr. Leipzig 1954), pp. 33 ff., has an excellent introduction to the key vocabulary of Alexandrian terms.

[60] In Mann's *Doktor Faustus*, mediated by Dürer's *Melencolia I*. See below, p. 483 note 106.

to be useful, his moralizings should be brief. If he wishes only to produce delight, he should be guided by probability in his imaginings. The ideal compromise is to combine both instruction and amusement. This is the kind of poetry that both brings in cash for the publisher and secures worldwide repute for the artist.

Not all poetry can be flawless. Some defects are forgivable. But a mistake which recurs constantly, and so is proof of some basic misjudgment, runs the risk of classing its author with the notorious Choerilus of Iasos (the epic poet of whom his patron, Alexander the Great, said that he would sooner be Homer's Thersites than Choerilus' Achilles). Poetry, like painting, demands different perspectives for its judgment. Sometimes the critic has to stand close, sometimes to stand back.[61] But, in either case, it must be able to withstand the shrewd judgment of the connoisseur. This will mean nine years of maturation, says Horace. He is thinking of the epic *Zmyrna* of Catullus' friend, Cinna.

It is at this point that Horace inserts the passage we have already noted concerning the social and moral role to be fulfilled in the new circumstances of Augustan Rome by the *vates*, the heir of Orpheus and Amphion, the protégé of Apollo the Lyrist, the collaborator of the emperor, who is both rewarder and example. It is apparent from what Alexandrian bases the *vates* will start. Not repudiation of the achievements of the recent movement in literature, but development and culmination of those struggles is the program that the *Ars Poetica* proclaims.

Horace can now with perfect logic resume his attack on the false *poeta* with fresh energy. Certain pretenders at Rome have been taken in by the ideal that genius is superior to, and dispenses its possessor from, the claims of art. But both are necessary. In other walks of life—sport and music are the examples again chosen—long and arduous preparation is required. In poetry, everyone joins the fashion, and no one has the courage to admit his need for lessons. The disease is aggravated when the amateur author is rich. Then he is able to command an audience of flatterers whose last thought is to tell the truth. The serious poet however needs, not flattery, but the stern criticism of experienced scholars. Only in this way will otiose lines be removed, clumsiness be castigated, the unfinished be obelized, "fine writing" be pruned, obscurities be explained, ambiguities be brought to light. He will not be offended by such treatment from

---

[61] Heavy punctuation should be placed at the end of v. 363, and lighter at the end of v. 364. Horace's purpose is not to condemn impressionism, but to insist that every style must be able to endure critical scrutiny.

one he thought was a friend, because he will know that, if neglected, his self-delusion can have the gravest consequences.

Horace modulates into the close of his poem, with a passage whose irony cannot mask its heartfelt seriousness. Just as the patient with a contagious illness is shunned, so is the crazy *poeta*. On he goes, mockingly chased by little boys, spouting his verses, perhaps even falling into a well or a pit in his career. If sympathizers feel tempted to rescue him, Horace suggests they should ask themselves whether the man's fate was not deliberate. They should remember Empedocles who, in his eagerness to be thought a god, jumped into the crater of Etna. In any case, rescue is pointless. The malady will continue unabated. Its cause is unknown, but its victim is like a bear in a cage. He rattles his bars to attract attention. Anyone he manages to seize he keeps tight hold upon, until he has, leech-like, gorged himself with blood.

This little work, now numbering 476 lines, has been the subject of the deepest controversy, which has included the suggestion that it may not have survived in its entirety. Some have seen in it, not a formal treatise, although already Quintilian speaks of it as an *Ars Poetica*, but a letter, in which the author leaps around from topic to topic as fancy, and perhaps circumstances now unknown, dictate, and where it would be wrong to look for any very rigid principles of order. Others believe that there is a specific sequence to the development of the argument, based upon ancient "isagogic" or introductory treatises. In these, the theme moves from the individual detail to matters of broader structure and then finally to consideration of the writer in himself. A compromise suggests that we should apply the concept of the "gliding transition":[62] Horace, it is urged, did have a larger plan in mind, but disguises its skeleton by shifting imperceptibly from precept to precept, from section to section.

Letter or treatise? This is the dilemma into which scholars have been driven by their failure to set the *Ars Poetica* within the context of its tradition. The poem is both. A letter can be offered as a substitute for (and had already been so offered by Lucilius) an epic! And not as something inferior in the context of the time. Horace is after all writing in *epē*, hexameters. His poem is a didactic epic in the tradition of Aratus. Whatever the objections which a modern

---

[62] C. O. Brink uses this term on pp. 456 and 486 of *Horace on Poetry: The 'Ars Poetica'* (Cambridge 1971): cf. U. Knoche's "fließende Übergänge," *Philologus* 90 (1935), 372 ff. It seems no accident that precisely such transitions are discovered by scholars in Pindar (e.g. by L. Illig, *Zur Form der Pindarischen Erzählung* [Berlin 1932], p. 49 note 3: *gleitende Übergänge*), and bear witness to the lyrical technique found in the *A. P.*

literary sensibility may raise against the epic claim, they had been raised in exactly the same way in Alexandria, where it was Callimachus who championed Aratus as "an excellent and learned poet," and who made Hesiod, also didactic, the figurehead of a style alternative to the Homeric. Ancient definitions of epic are vague.[63] They are so because they have to accommodate poetry of such diverse nature. It is not for modern critics, who should be the interpreters rather than the reformers of tradition, to impose a terminology.

If therefore Horace was taking up a pro-Callimachean stance in presenting to contemporaries a versified treatise based upon the prose original of Neoptolemus of Parium, as Aratus had versified the prose of Eudoxus, or Lucretius that of Epicurus, we should expect the solution to the difficulties presented by the order and sequence of his poem to be Callimachean. The first item of the Callimachean poetic suggested above was that the analogy with music would be paramount.[64] Can this analogy help to explain the *Ars Poetica* also? It is after all the work of a lyric poet who derives the origins of poetry from the lyric of Orpheus and Amphion.

The epic tradition must be explained from within epic itself, and from the implicit criticism of practical poets. There is in fact another writer of epic who has also been in trouble with critics for his apparent inattention to *lucidus ordo*.[65] This is Ariosto, *anima naturaliter Horatiana*, at least if we consider his *Satire*. What is said about him appears strangely relevant to the charges made against Horace. Modern students of the *Orlando Furioso* now believe that Ariosto was inspired by the musical innovations of his time, such as polyphony and counterpoint.[66] It is telling to find the latest editor of the *Ars Poetica* invoking just such musical analogues in the work of Horace.[67]

Horace's poem, so full of precepts offered and commented on in minute detail, issues one precept so huge and obvious that it usually

---

[63] S. Koster concludes (*Antike Epostheorien*, pp. 159–61) that there was nothing quite so pedantically precise about ancient terms for epic as literary historians, with their talk of "didactic" and "epyllion," would like to assume.

[64] See above, pp. 20–21. Cf. Neoptolemus' "harmony," above, p. 53.

[65] "Dicono altresí che va per tutta l'opera saltando d'una cosa in un'altra intricando tutto il poema . . ." (G. B. Pigna on Ariosto: "They say further that he goes through the whole work leaping from one thing to another, complicating the entire poem"). Cf. Brink, *op. cit.* (above, note 62), pp. 445 ff. on Horace, and Eustathius (quoted above, p. 48) on Homer.

[66] C. Muscetta in *Orlando Furioso* a cura di Carlo Muscetta e Luca Lamberti (Turin 1962), p. XVIII, comments on the comparison of his work to music made by the poet himself at *O. F.* VIII. 29. See my paper "Orazio, Ariosto and Orazio Ariosto," *Acta Conventus Neo-Latini Amstelodamensis* (Munich 1979), pp. 820–34.

[67] Brink, *op. cit.*, p. 197 ("subject," "motif," "descant," "codas").

escapes attention,[68] and that is in its form. Presented through a structure which makes little sense by purely "logical" standards, the *Ars Poetica* instructs the budding poet that the unity after which he must strive is a musical creation, in which arrangement and correspondence, interlacing and arabesque, are to replace the dull and pedestrian sequences of elementary prose. This form will be exploitable at its fullest only by the writer who chooses a theme with the necessary scope and scale. Yet, although the music of Virgil, of Ariosto, of Tasso, may be vaster than Horace could command within the narrow keyboard of his Alexandrian verse, it is not different in kind.

When analogies with music are invoked, commentators may mean that they are at a loss to explain how a piece fits together, and that their impression of vagueness is akin to the other vagueness stirred by listening to a favorite prelude. This is to confuse art and emotion, end and beginning. The indefinable *non so che* communicated by the work of art is still the product of the application of certain defined rules and procedures. Even the most indeterminate composition of a Delius has, after all, a score. This is why modern scholarship must welcome, in the same breath as it welcomes analogies with music, the mathematical analyses which some commentators have applied to ancient poems.[69] It is a commonplace in art-criticism that the most familiar masterpieces command fresh attention when analysis points out the "intelletto d'amore," the concentrated and rational care which the artist has lavished on his composition.

*Ut pictura poesis.* A very simple analysis of the *Ars Poetica* might start from the following observation. There is no reason to doubt Porphyrion's statement that Horace depended on a lost work of Neoptolemus of Parium for the gist of his prescriptions. But it is clear that he occasionally departed from his source in order to add his own glosses. What could Neoptolemus have said, for example, about early Roman literature?

But what could he have said about the *vates*? The section in

---

[68] Although of course Professor Brink is an honorable exception. The fact that he should draw a parallel between the *A. P.* and the *Odes* seems particularly significant for later classical epic.

[69] Notably Duckworth and Le Grelle, but see also E. L. Brown, *Numeri Vergiliani* (Brussels 1963) and N. E. Collinge, *The Structure of Horace's Odes* (Oxford 1961). Cf. Douglas Brooks, *Number and Pattern in the Eighteenth Century Novel* (London 1973): Judith M. Kennedy and James A. Reither, edd., *A Theatre for Spenserians* (Manchester 1973), especially the papers presented by A. Kent Hieatt and Alastair Fowler: H. Kreuzer and R. Gunzenhäuser, edd., *Mathematik und Dichtung* (2nd ed., Munich 1967). The Virgil who put his references to Maecenas in the *Georgics* at lines 2, 41, 41, 2 of consecutive books was not indifferent to mathematical calculations. This could be one of the most fruitful areas to be explored by the use of computers.

question runs from vv. 391–407 and, if the 476 lines we have are all that Horace wrote, it thus occupies exactly one twenty-eighth of the entire poem. Professor Brink marks a new section at v. 119. This is exactly one quarter of the way through the poem. If the poem were divided into multiples of 17 (the length of the *vates* section), twenty-eight units would result. At eight places such units may have been in the poet's mind. Brink, who scolds previous editors for their failure to use paragraphing, indents, for example, at vv. 119, 153, 202, 220, 275, 309, 391 and 408 (these are, of course, not his only indentations). Actual multiples of 17 would be: 119, 153, 204, 221, 272, 306, 391 and 408.

Sometimes Brink's paragraphing (introduced presumably purely on grounds of sense) produces a stanzaic effect. The sequence 251–294 becomes 12, 12, 10, 10: 295–360 becomes 14, 24, 14, 14; 379–390 becomes 6, 6. There are three paragraphs of 15 lines, three of 13 (and one of 26), five of 10 (and one of 5).

The suggestion (which needs taking much further) that the *Ars Poetica* plays with some sort of musical arithmetic in this way (*numerosus Horatius*) hints at a far different interpretation of this precious document than was made by those Renaissance commentators who looked for logic and ended with dogma.[70] The poem illustrates, like the *De Sublimitate*, its own precepts. The classical epic tradition thus finds room for a devious, repetitive, allusive, symmetrical art which leaves a great deal to the cooperation of the reader, and which balances easily between the serious and the ironic.

How interesting, for instance, it is that Virgil and Varius are linked (vv. 54–55) with the comic playwrights Caecilius and Plautus! These poets are cited together in an early discussion of vocabulary. Horace returns to this topic, as we noted, when he discusses the proximity of the vocabulary of tragedy and comedy at times of great emotional stress. Finally, he renews his argument in a discussion of the satyr play, where he even uses the first person (the "preacher's I") to assert that, when he writes such plays, he will not confine his choice of words to those of everyday life, but will match Silenus' role as guardian and attendant of Bacchus with something verging on the dignity of tragedy (vv. 234–239). This passage is linked with the allusion to Virgil and Varius by a repetition of the doctrine of *iunctura* (vv. 47–48; 252), the transforming power that context may have on the commonplace.

Scholars have wondered if Horace here was simply taking over from Neoptolemus, for the sake of completeness, a number of

---

[70] See Marvin T. Herrick, *The Fusion of Horatian and Aristotelian Literary Criticism 1531–1555* (Urbana, Illinois 1946).

injunctions about the satyr play (apparently practiced by Callimachus) which could have little relevance to Roman conditions. Alternatively, they have speculated that a move to revive the satyr play in Latin was contemplated, and that Horace is dutifully laying down the rules of the game. But, on either view, the interesting thing is that the poet who began by warning against the grotesque hybrid now prescribes for a locus in which tragedy and farce will coalesce, and associates this coalition with the verbal experiments of Virgil, who had used Silenus as the mouthpiece of his epic ambitions in the sixth *Eclogue*. Of course there is a classicizing taste evident in the *Ars Poetica*. But one wonders if the classicism is not asserted against a pressure from the bizarre and "carnival" which lay not far beneath the surface, and molded the contours, of all Roman literature. Again we noted that Horace's poem, in spite of its classicizing severity, ends with a male bear which turns into a female leech.

Horace's direct remarks about epic include a eulogy of Homer's superiority to the cyclic poets, equally condemned by Callimachus. Homer's exordium, we learn, is best because it is specific (136 ff.). He strives to bring light out of smoke. Yet this is not an arid, Cartesian clarity. It is so that then he may produce his striking marvels such as Antiphates, Scylla, the Cyclops, Charybdis. Ariosto was later to be criticized for a narrative lacking in "verisimilitude." Horace does not mind that sort of romance.

Homer effects his aim, according to Horace, by selection, by hastening always towards a result and therefore plunging his reader into the middle of the action. These remarks must be understood against the background of the cyclic poetry already rejected. Antimachus, for example, was a byword for prolixity.[71] But because Homer has a total plan and architectonic organization for his material, he can write at length without being accused of the same fault.

Ariosto could have found support in some of Horace's more general remarks, about epic vocabulary,[72] about the need for emotional appeal that sanctions the use of rhyme. One of the most baffling features of the *Ars Poetica* is its continual use of cross-references. No topic is ever wholly exhausted in the section where it is first introduced. It was of Ariosto that Gherardini would say that the author had

---

[71] Plutarch, *de Garr.* 21; cf. Horace, *A. P.* 146.

[72] Giraldi defends Ariosto's use of *nuove voci* (*Storia della critica* 9, *Ariosto*, by A. Borlenghi [Palermo 1961], pp. 125–26, 129). Nisieli accuses the poet of lacking *locuzione epica* (*ibid.*, p. 138).

wonderful gifts, but that the form of his poem is a labyrinth that confuses and wearies.[73]

Horace's cross-references are particularly evident when actual verbal reminiscence occurs. "The author of a *promised poem*" is advised at line 45 to be selective in presenting his material. At line 138 Horace says of the cyclic writer: "What will this *promiser* produce worthy of his mouthing?" He seems to have coined a noun to make the connection with the previous passage.

In speaking of the poet's need to work upon feeling, Horace develops at length the Aristotelian theory of writing as acting, later to be rediscovered by Stanislavsky:

> As men's looks smile with those who smile, so they sympathize with those who weep. If you want me to weep, you must first feel grief yourself: then your misfortunes, Telephus or Peleus, will hurt me. If you have an ill-suited part to speak, I will either doze off or laugh. Gloomy words befit a sad expression; threats one that is angry; light words go with jest, grave with austerity. It is nature who first conditions us within to every sort of fortune; nature delights or else drives us to anger, or again bows us to the ground and tortures us with the weight of sorrow. Afterwards she proclaims our inner emotions with the tongue as interpreter. (*Ars Poetica* 101–111)

Can we doubt the influence of these theories on the Virgil who was famous for the wonderful harlotries of his voice, and for his *hypocrisis?*

The *Ars Poetica* does contain dead passages. A Roman and Augustan preoccupation with character seems at times to have paralyzed Horace's imagination, so that an emphasis on internal consistency hampers an understanding of the polar absence of consistency found in some of the greatest writing.[74] But taken as a whole, and especially when considered in the light of its form, and its concession to the serio-comic (*ita vertere seria ludo*, v. 226, of the satyr play), the treatise is a key to the most exciting possibilities in epic. Only such a complex work could have made any sense in the age that was to produce both the *Aeneid* and the *Metamorphoses*.

Together, Aristotle's *Poetics* and its later interpretations in Alexandria and Rome form a critical seedbed fertile enough to quicken

---

[73] Borlenghi, p. 153. Pindar too had been described as labyrinthine (by Eustathius: cited by A. B. Drachmann, *Scholia Vetera in Pindari Carmina*, repr. Amsterdam 1966, III, p. 289), and Tolstoy would discover a "labyrinth of interconnections" in his *Anna Karenina*.

[74] W. Kroll comments on p. 131 of his *Studien zum Verständnis der römischen Literatur* (Stuttgart 1924) on the hypothesis to Euripides' *Medea*, where we hear that Medea had been criticized for weeping. Contrast S. Eisenstein's comparison of the characters of Greek tragedy, with their internal contradictions, to those of Dostoevsky: *Izbrannye Proizvedeniya* (Moscow 1964), III, p. 136.

the most moving and even sublime creations. Beneath the rank weeds of commentary lurks the promise of a glorious harvest, if we will but look.

V

The word "sublime" inevitably introduces thoughts of another famous treatise, that attributed to Longinus.

There are two ways of taking what the *De Sublimitate* says. One is to seek there a series of precepts and judgments that may be used to belittle what has actually been done by poets. The other is to rescue from a rather limited analysis whatever may help us to be humble before the masterpieces of the past.

Limitations are immediately apparent when we read that, although emotion is important in the genesis of stylistic height, there can be both inferior emotions and height without emotion. The author's inferior emotions include pity and fear (8. 2). The flagrant contradiction of Aristotle threatens the devaluation of tragedy. On the other hand, height without emotion, one example of which is, according to "Longinus", eulogy, runs the risk of producing that stillborn Victorianism which deadens so many sermons and works of piety. Can either of these alternatives be relevant to the living record of achievement?

In his chosen writers, "Longinus" is eager to find "ecstasy" and "astonishment." As often, he is simplifying to the point of crudity an original insight of Aristotle. Astonishment (*ekplēxis*, literally "knockout") is one effect of powerful writing.[75] Can it be the only one? Ecstasy, a descendant of Aristotle's *catharsis*, needs broader definition if it is to be useful as a critical concept.[76]

An attempt to rescue what is worthwhile in all this might begin with "Longinus' " doctrine of *phantasia* or *eidolopoeia* (here translated "imagination"), significantly not his own invention.[77] He declares (15. 1):

> In general, imagination may be defined as any thought which in its occurrence produces speech. In this context the term is most common nowadays when, under the influence of enthusiasm and emotion, you seem to see what you are saying, and then communicate that vision to your hearers.

[75] E.g. *Poetics* 1455 a 17 ("knockout" in recognition).

[76] See below, pp.430–31, where it is suggested that Eisenstein's "ecstasy of pathos" is a modern version of Aristotle's *catharsis tōn pathēmatōn*.

[77] *Phantasia* is commonplace in the scholia (above, p. 48). For *eidolopoeia*, see Plutarch, *De Gloria Athen.* 347a. Both terms are ultimately Platonic. See above, pp. 42–43 (Aristotle's *Poetics*).

Diogenes Laertius helps us to understand the process implied (7. 49):[78]

> Imagination precedes, and then the mind, with its tendency towards speech, communicates in words its imaginative experience.

Quintilian (VI. 2. 29) had equally discussed the role of *phantasiai* in helping both poet and orator to bring scenes vividly before their audiences. The power of imagination can make us see what is absent. We can develop this faculty by exploiting our natural inclination to daydream.

"Under the influence of enthusiasm and emotion." Utterance not so inspired simply passes on bare facts, an impoverished, clinical notion of a given event or situation. But if the artist has an emotional relationship to what he is saying, the very act of putting his thoughts into words summons up recollections of what truly happened, constructs of what truly might have happened, with all the particular aspects and details of experience likely to trigger an emotional response. These details, selected on the basis of their ability to evoke feeling, form the compelling description which is then presented to the listener. Their presence explains why the work of art is effective.

This important theory, already adumbrated by Aristotle and repeated, as we saw, by Horace, has the widest implications. There are two stages: the perception, and then the re-creation, inspired by enthusiasm and emotion, of that perception for someone else. The student of English literature will immediately think of Coleridge's distinction between imagination and fancy. Fancy is the cold perception of objects ("I see, not feel," from *Dejection: An Ode*). The secondary or poetic imagination, aided by enthusiasm ("Joy" in the *Ode*, but elsewhere Coleridge uses "Longinus'" word), can rise to a sense of wholeness in its contemplation of the universe which in turn engenders an organically whole work of art.

For the Russian director Stanislavsky, the actor's chief need is to understand what has been called by Scotus and Hopkins the "thisness" of things. There is no generality in art. There is only this person doing this thing at this time. It is from precise depiction, aided by emotion, that the mind rises to the universal. The confusion of the two stages can only lead in art to vapid abstraction.[79]

"Longinus" comes closest to grasping the force of his own arguments when, somewhat unexpectedly for so austere a theorist, he finds an illustration in a famous poem of Sappho. He notes Sappho's

---

[78] This passage and that from Quintilian are adduced by D. A. Russell in his edition of *'Longinus' On the Sublime* (Oxford 1964), pp. 120–21.

[79] See below, pp. 436 ff. It is in this context of close observation of telling detail that, for example, the *Characters* of Theophrastus makes sense.

selection and combination of elements into an organic whole (again, one feels that Coleridge is not far away). He sees that she has first distanced her various sensations ("they have gone off as if they belonged to someone else"). He observes her polar use of opposites (the *coincidentia oppositorum* of Nicholas of Cusa which has had such modern repercussions). But the treatment of Sappho remains an isolated element in his discussion. It is not the sort of poetry he really likes.

We see this from the grudging praise afforded to another master of the pathetic style, Euripides. Aristotle had described Euripides as the "most tragic of poets," paying tribute to his unfailing ability to extract the maximum emotion from a given scene. "Longinus" is forced by his preconceptions to narrow Euripides' effects to knockout (ch. 15). The term may serve for the scene from the *Orestes* which he quotes. But it seems curious that one of the other plays selected to illustrate Euripidean knockout should be that *Fantasiestück*, the *Phaethon*. Accepting the critical orthodoxy of his time, "Longinus" contradicts Aristotle by believing that Euripides was a fundamentally non-tragic writer who forced himself into the tragic mold contrary to his real nature. Theory and appreciation are here violently at variance. If "Longinus" wanted to advocate a narrow view of sublimity with full logical rigor, he should have dismissed Euripides. His effort to ascribe what he considers the successes of the younger poet to imitation of Aeschylus[80] is one-sided and unfair. Both poets must be investigated in terms of their common roots in the carnival, and their common use of pathetic structure.

A similar unease attends the admission that Euripides can employ low vocabulary effectively (40. 3). This is an Aristotelian modification of the critic's earlier commendation of appropriate[81] and magnificent words. An example is drawn from the *Heracles*: "See, I have a full cargo of suffering, and there is no room to stow more" (1245). "Longinus" comments that the language is vulgar, but reaches the heights because "it bears a relationship to the structure." The remark is perceptive. At line 631, protectively rescuing his children, Heracles had declared: "I will take them in tow with my own hands, and draw

---

[80] Aristophanes shows that Aeschylus and Euripides were thought to be in opposite camps. This is not true (cf. O. Krausse, *De Euripide Aeschyli Instauratore* [Jena 1905]), but a correct assessment would demand the wiping out of the entire battlefield.

[81] *Kuriōn* (ch. 30) looks as if it has this un-Aristotelian meaning, though Dion. Hal. (*de Comp.* 21 and 24) and Horace (*A. P.* 234) still echo Aristotle. Cf. *le parole . . . splendide, signoreggianti* in Giacomini; Weinberg, *A History of Literary Criticism in the Italian Renaissance*, p. 1059 note 137, which is certainly a remarkable parallel to the *De Subl.* Could "Longinus" possibly have reversed the Aristotelian meaning of this technical word as early as the first century A.D.?

them on like a ship." At the end, it is the ruined hero himself who follows Theseus "in tow" (1424). The recurrence of the nautical image in Heracles' description of his "cargo of suffering" fits perfectly into the structure of the play.[82] But again, as with Sappho's ode, the insight does not induce revision of a point of view.

The prejudice which blinds the critic to the full range of Euripides' tragic palette makes itself felt once more in the famous comparison of the *Iliad* and the *Odyssey*. Again, "Longinus" starts from an Aristotelian position, repeating from the *Poetics* the adjective "dramatic" which Aristotle had perhaps invented to describe the distinctively Homeric manner. But Aristotle had not gone on from that insight to argue for the inferiority of the *Odyssey*. In attributing even the *Margites* to Homer, he had opened the door to epic comedy, and accepted Homer as the originator of that side of the tradition too. Yet for "Longinus" the *Odyssey* is inferior because it is a comedy of character (9. 15). This contempt for comedy denies one of his own better insights. He sees, for example, that hyperbole, though an aid to sublimity, has its comic aspect (38. 5). He allows a certain height to Aristophanes (40. 2). Laughter is defined as an emotion with pleasure, and emotion is an important element in the genesis of the sublime. But elsewhere (29. 2) "Longinus" wishes to associate comedy no longer with emotion, but with character. It is a confusion of terms which can only damage the total theory.

The narrowing of poetic effects by "Longinus" to knockout explains his insensitivity to irony. He misses it, for example, in the passage where Theopompus describes the lavish invasion preparations made by the Great King (43. 2). All he can see is incongruity. He misses the comic resonance, still echoing in Rabelais, in the descriptions of the microcosm of the body which he cites (32. 5) from Xenophon and Plato.[83] He quotes Cleobulus' epigram quite seriously (36. 2), without any reminder of the cutting rejoinder to these human pretensions which had been made by Simonides.[84] A critic with these blinkers was not likely to be sympathetic to the Alexandrians.

Nor is he. The ominous chapter (33) opens with a blunt rejection of the Callimachean doctrine of stylistic purity.[85] "Supergreat natures are the least pure." Callimachus would have rejoined that such supergreat natures are a critic's fiction, invented to excuse incomprehension of the total masterpiece. Purity is the intense fire of the

---

[82] See Wilamowitz's note on v. 631.

[83] Contrast M. Bakhtin, *Tvorchestvo François Rabelais*, chapter 5, especially pp. 386, 397.

[84] Denys Page, *Poetae Melici Graeci* (repr. Oxford 1967), no. 581.

[85] *Hymn. Ap.* 111, *Epigr.* 7. 1. Cf. Horace's *indignor, A. P.* 359.

artistic realization, which ideally burns without ash. If art is to be forgiven its defects for the sake of a single redeeming moment, its mighty stream will sweep down to the ocean such filth as to make it ecologically unacceptable. Really supergreat art does not allow itself the luxury of such complacency. That is why it costs its practitioners their sanity, or their lives.

Can there be any point of contact between such opposing views? Interestingly, if "Longinus" is annoyed with the artistic mediocrity of his contemporaries, it is because of their moral failings, their love of money and pleasure. But the theme of the "poor poet," the artist who refuses to compromise his honesty for the sake of easy rewards, is one of the Alexandrian commonplaces which have been repeated by the centuries.[86] Can it then be lack of moral fiber which prevents the Callimachean from attempting the "sublime"?

The chief answer which the Callimachean would make to "Longinus" is that the poetry he demands would be both monotonous and univocal, crudely unresponsive to the breadth of human experience, and indeed to the ambiguous origins of literature itself in the primitive, undifferentiated consciousness. How long can one go on knocking one's auditor out and still expect him to survive? On the critic's own admission, Homer himself "declined" from the *Iliad* to the *Odyssey*. But Shakespeare went from *King Lear* to *The Tempest*, even to a Greek romance like *Pericles, Prince of Tyre*. Beethoven followed the Fifth with the Sixth Symphony. Thomas Mann published *Felix Krull* after *Doktor Faustus*. If these later achievements are not knockouts, our sensibilities must be broad enough to allow for victories on points, and our theory broad enough to accommodate them. Otherwise, like the wheeltapper with the cracked hammer, we shall be continually sending the great engines of epic back for repairs, with never an inkling that our own puny instrument may be at fault.

"Longinus" clashes directly with Callimachus when he criticizes Ion of Chios, claimed as a literary predecessor by the Alexandrian in his thirteenth *Iambos*. Does not Callimachus prove his decadence by selecting such a minor figure as model from a century so prolific in great masterpieces? In answer we must invoke a Formalist theory of literary history. Literature is a sequence in which grandsons inherit, but not sons. It does not proceed in smooth transitions from one acknowledged master to his disciples, but in violence and repudiation of the immediate past, as each new voice struggles to make itself heard above the chorus of complacent uniformity generated by the

---

[86] Cf. Pfeiffer on Call. fr. 193. 17, and M. Puelma Piwonka, *Lucilius und Kallimachos* (Frankfurt 1949), pp. 249 ff. Pudovkin and Thomas Mann revive the theme: see below, pp. 434, 487 note 113.

timid imitativeness of the mediocre. Genres follow a cycle in which they submerge and re-emerge, and what sufficed in one period to carry the poetic message must later yield to an estranging alternative.[87] Callimachus could no more "imitate" Sophocles than Eliot could Milton. The less forceful, more diffuse genius of Ion, and his universality of interest, offered however a model for experiment. He was accessible to Callimachus just because he was less great. He left something to be done.

"Longinus" shares with other ancient authors, including Aristotle, the failing of haphazard quotation. This carelessness is unhappy when the quotation is adduced to support a particular theory of sublime effect. His adaptation of Homer's description of Poseidon (9. 8) has attracted the attention of a modern scholar sympathetic to his ideas:[88]

> Trembled the high mountains and the forest
> And peaks and the city of the Trojans and the ships of the Achaeans
> Beneath the immortal feet of Poseidon as he went.
> And he advanced to ride over the waves, and the sea creatures gambolled beneath him
> On all sides from their lairs, and well knew their lord:
> And in joy the sea parted, and on they [his horses] flew.

The passage does not occur as such in Homer. It has been compiled by the critic, with both conflation and omission. It reflects a taste on the level of "Great Tunes from the Old Masters," in which one might pass from *Tristan und Isolde* to *Parsifal* in the space of five minutes. This is the evidence that enables him to speak patronizingly of Apollonius!

But the Alexandrian poet has a similar passage, unconflated. Apollo appears at dawn to the Argonauts (*Argonautica* II. 669 ff., adapted from R. C. Seaton's translation):

> Now when the immortal light has not yet come, nor is it utter darkness, but a faint glimmer has spread over the night, when men wake and call it twilight, at that hour they ran into the harbor of the desert island Thynias, and with weary toil made their way to the land. And to them the son of Leto, as he passed from Lycia to the countless folk of the Hyperboreans, appeared; and about his cheeks on both sides his golden locks flowed in clusters as he moved; in his left hand he held a silver bow, and on his back was slung a quiver hanging from his shoulders; and beneath his feet all the island quaked, and the waves surged high on the shore. Helpless amazement seized them as

---

[87] Cf. V. Shklovsky in *O Teorii Prozy* (Moscow–Leningrad 1925), pp. 162 ff.; B. Tomashevsky in *Théorie de la Littérature*, ed. T. Todorov, pp. 302 ff.

[88] E. Auerbach, "Camilla, or The Rebirth of the Sublime" in *Literary Language and its Public* (Eng. tr. by R. Manheim, London 1965), pp. 181 ff.

they looked; and no one dared to gaze face to face into the fair eyes of the god. And they stood with heads bowed to the ground; but he, far off, passed on to the sea through the mist. . . .

This is an example of psychological intensity and religious revelation which will stand comparison with "Longinus' " Homeric fake. Apollonius is a master of this kind of suggestivity (IV. 1477 ff.):

> But on that day Lynceus thought he saw Heracles all alone, far off, over measureless land, as a man at the month's beginning sees, or thinks he sees, the moon through a bank of cloud.

This kind of art, with its "far off,"[89] impressed Virgil. Shall we be troubled that it did not impress "Longinus"?

The *De Sublimitate* is the product of a late age, eager for kicks. It quarrels with Aristotle, the greatest critic of antiquity, in order to make prescriptions which, fulfilled, would produce a literature consisting of nothing but sensations. But such a literature would not be a human communication about the world in which we live. The classical epic tradition, mediated through Alexandria, has not written for high-minded professors of rhetoric, but for contradictory humanity in all its kaleidoscopic richness, where comedy and pity, irony, grief, fear, yes, and even delicacy and charm, have their place as essential and civilizing concomitants of heroic grandeur. Apollo does not always stretch his bow. But he remains Apollo.

---

[89] *Aeneid* VI. 453–54. For Virgil's use of the indefinite *procul* see Heinze's note on Horace, *Satires* II. 6. 105; Norden on *Aeneid* VI. 10. Joyce's pun on "far" and "phare" (and "Pharphar," the river of Damascus in the Douai version) in the "Anna Livia Plurabelle" monologue of *Finnegans Wake* is in the same tradition. Compare also *De Subl.* 15. 7 and *Argonautica* II. 918 ff.

# III

# APOLLONIUS RHODIUS

THE three accounts we possess of Apollonius' life agree in making him the disciple of Callimachus. His epic *Argonautica* therefore acquires major significance as the first example, after Callimachus' own *Hecale*, of the direction that the new Alexandrian epic would follow.[1]

The first thing that strikes us on taking up the *Argonautica* is that it is a poem divided into books, deliberately by the author as a matter of literary judgment. Secondly, though these books are no doubt long—they anticipate the length of Lucretius' books—they do not, when added together, come anywhere near the length of the *Iliad* and *Odyssey*. This must have said something to contemporary readers, when we are assessing with whom Apollonius stood in that "battle of the books" to which the Preface to the *Aetia* bears such eloquent testimony. The *Argonautica* dealt with a heroic theme in the time taken by the tragedies exhibited at one showing; it echoed Homer's language without ever pedantically copying it; it selected its material even to the point of abruptness; it owed a debt to both music and painting; it depicted a "hero" who was often no hero at all. Can this work then have been greeted by Callimachus with indifference and contempt, as some literary historians have claimed?[2] And by Callimachus' enemies, the Telchines, who admired one continuous poem in many thousands of verses in honor of kings and heroes, as the

---

[1] The ancient biographical information is conveniently assembled, for example, in R. C. Seaton's old Oxford Text, and by G. W. Mooney on pp. 1–2 of his edition (*Apollonius Rhodius: Argonautica* [repr. Amsterdam 1965]), where the rewriting of evidence to suit prejudice may also be examined (p. 2 note 1). H. Fränkel's massive *Noten zu den Argonautika des Apollonios* (Munich 1968) marks a new era in the appreciation of the poem. Excellent modern treatments are also to be found in D. N. Levin's *Apollonius' Argonautica Re-examined: The Neglected First and Second Books* (Leiden 1971); E. Livrea's edition of Book IV (Florence 1973); and F. Vian's Budé edition (three vols., Paris 1974, 1980, 1981). See also M. Campbell, *Studies in the Third Book of Apollonius Rhodius' Argonautica* (Hildesheim 1983).

[2] E.g. K. Ziegler, *Das hellenistische Epos*, whose schematism forces him (pp. 37–38) to put Apollonius with Ennius in the same anti-Callimachean camp!

evidence of sympathy with their side of the feud? What in fact had Apollonius written?

The *Argonautica* is a poem about a naive young man who sets his heart on winning a golden prize and, bewitched by a girl, falls into deep waters—an archetypal version of the familiar *Bildungsroman*. Apollonius has estranged this tale by casting it into a mythical past, and by realizing literally the metaphor of witchery.[3] He has nonetheless made the moral significance of his story plain.

I

Firstly, the golden-red prize, whose polysemous color is shared even by the blushing cheek of love.[4] By omitting the end of his narrative,[5] Apollonius both suggests the illusory nature of all quests, which turn sour once they succeed, and sets his reader's imagination working. The Greek reader already knew from Euripides that the relationship between Jason and Medea would end in betrayal. This knowledge is played upon by the epic poet to lend depth and resonance to his poem.

In Book IV, pursued by Medea's brother Apsyrtus, Jason decides that trickery is his only way out of a tight corner. Medea will invite Apsyrtus to a tête-à-tête, on pretext of discussing terms for her return home. As a token of good will, she is to send her brother a cloak, which Jason will provide (IV. 421 ff.):

> So the two of them agreed, and made ready a mighty trick against Apsyrtus. They offered many gifts of friendship, and among them gave a sacred robe of Hypsipyle, crimson in color. The divine Graces had themselves toiled at it in sea-girt Dia for Dionysus, and he in turn had given it to his son Thoas. Thoas left it to Hypsipyle, and she gave it to Jason, as a prize with many other trinkets, a well-worked gift of friendship. Neither by handling it nor looking at it could you sate your sweet desire. From it there arose an immortal scent, from the time when the Nyseian lord himself lay upon it, tipsy with wine and nectar, holding the fair breasts of the maiden daughter of Minos, whom once Theseus, when she had followed him from Cnossus, left in the island of Dia.

The cloak which will disguise treachery is made to recall another

---

[3] What Eisenstein calls the "Aristophanes effect." See below, p. 415 note 50; p. 459 note 22.

[4] Ἔρευθος and ἐρευθαίνω and their cognates are leitmotifs in the poem: see, for example, I. 726–27, 778, 791, 1230; III. 122, 163, 298, 681, 963. See also IV. 1427, Ἐρυθηΐς.

[5] Apollonius is also showing that he thought the *Odyssey* ended at XXIII. 296, a very interesting aesthetic judgment by one who was poet as well as scholar.

treachery. Theseus had abandoned his helper Ariadne, as Jason had already abandoned his helper Hypsipyle, and would in turn abandon his helper Medea. He knew the story. Inducing Medea to help him, he had told her, with diplomatic omissions, exactly the same yarn (III. 997 ff.):

> Once upon a time the maiden daughter of Minos, Ariadne, out of kindness rescued Theseus from his grievous struggles, she whom Pasiphae, daughter of the Sun, bore. Even so, when Minos had stilled his anger, she went on board ship with him and left her fatherland. And her the immortals themselves loved, and in midair as proof a crown of stars, which men call Ariadne's Crown, turns all night long among the signs of heaven. Such thanks shall you also have, if you save so great a company of heroes. For by your appearance you seem to excel in gentle courtesies.

"Such thanks shall you also have": the irony is devastating.

So a surrogate for the golden-red fleece, Hypsipyle's crimson robe,[6] is now to be used as bait for a murder and, lured by his sister's promises, Apsyrtus comes to meet her on holy ground in the temple of Artemis. Jason is already concealed in ambush, and at the opportune moment he leaps out with drawn sword and strikes down his unsuspecting victim (IV. 468 ff.):

> And Jason struck him, as a butcher strikes down a mighty, strong-horned bull, having watched for him near the temple which once the Brygians built for Artemis, coming from their home on the mainland opposite. It was in the vestibule of this temple that Apsyrtus fell on his knees, and as the hero breathed his last, in both his hands he held up (ὑπόϊσχετο) the black blood from his wound; and though his sister avoided him, he reddened (ἐρύθηνεν) her silvery veil and robe.[7]

Now the blushing red (ἔρευθος) which describes the fleece mars the white robe and veil with a brother's blood, in spite of a sister's evasions. The language looks back to the moment when Jason had seized the fleece (IV. 167 ff.):

> And as when a maiden catches (ὑπόϊσχεται) on her fine robe the beam of the moon at the full that rises above her high-roofed chamber, and her heart rejoices when she sees its fair sheen: with such joy then Jason picked up[8] (ἐναείρατο) in his hands the mighty fleece: and on his blond cheeks and forehead from the gleaming of the wool a blush (ἔρευθος) like fire sat.

In both passages, one object is as it were dyed by another: the robe

---

[6] The identification is helped by ἀφασσόμενος, IV. 181; ἀφάσσων, IV. 428.

[7] For "silvery" see III. 835; IV. 1407.

[8] ᾽Αείρω and its compounds unite such scenes as III. 734 and 1010; IV. 65 and 746.

by the blood, and Jason's face and beard by the fleece. Jason, a girl in the earlier scene, becomes as he commits murder the cruel Amycus.[9] The price of success is a carnival disorientation.

Yet Jason pays this price quite willingly. In Book I, deciding, against Heracles' more conventionally heroic judgment, to visit Hypsipyle, Jason had clothed himself in another crimson cloak (I. 721 ff.):

> But he pinned around his shoulders a work of the Tritonian goddess, double, crimson. Pallas had given it to him when first she was laying the keel of the ship Argo, and gave instruction in measuring the benches with the rule. More easily would you cast your eyes on the *rising sun* than look at its *blushing red*. For *blushing red* was it in the middle, but its ends were crimson on all sides.

It is exactly the comparison which is to be used of the fleece (IV. 123 ff.):

> And the two of them arrived along the path at the sacred wood, seeking the mighty oak on which the fleece was hung, like a cloud which at *the rising of the sun blushes red* before the fiery beams.

In equipping himself also with Atalanta's spear for his encounter with Hypsipyle, Jason is unmistakably assuming his sexual role.[10] His heroism will smell of the boudoir. This is made quite clear at the start of Book III. The task that Jason faces in Colchis is enough to baffle even goddesses. Eventually, Hera and Athene appeal to Aphrodite, and she in turn to her spoiled young son, Eros. Eros has to be bribed before he will do what his mother wants, and the bribe is a symbolic ball (III. 131 ff.):

> Come, please grant me my request: then I will give you a fine toy of Zeus, the very one which his dear nurse Adrasteia[11] made for him when he was still a baby in the Idaean cave, a round ball: you will get no other better toy from the hands of Hephaestus. Its circles are made of gold, and round each one double seams revolve. Its stitches are concealed, and over all of them runs a dark blue spiral. If you throw it from your hands, like a star it sends a *flaming furrow* through the air.

"Flaming furrow" is an important image in a book where the hero is to be called upon to plow with fire-breathing bulls. When the supreme test comes (III. 1377 ff.):

---

[9] Βουτύπος, II. 91 and IV. 468.

[10] Cf. I. 1168 where Heracles breaks his oar just before he loses Hylas. See below, p. 325 (Ariosto).

[11] The name occurs in the *Prometheus Vinctus* 936. Apollonius' use of Prometheus is mentioned below, pp. 81 ff. It is telling that what belonged to Zeus is now the plaything of Eros: cf. Lucian, *Dial. Deor.* 6. 3.

As from heaven a *fiery* star shoots up, trailing a *furrow* of light, causing wonder to men who see it darting with its bright ray through the air, so the son of Aeson charged the earth-born warriors.

And later in the same passage (III. 1391 ff.):

... so then did he cut the crop of the Earth-born, and with blood *the furrows* were filled, as the channels of a spring with streams of water.

In the climax of heroic exaltation, Jason, a fiery star cutting a furrow of light, evokes the toy given to the boy god of love which determines his success.

The unity established in this way for the *Argonautica* is of the densest kind. Depending on the musical technique of recurrence and leitmotif, it permits us to observe, for example, that the Hypsipyle episode as a whole serves both as retardation and as signpost. Jason's woolen cloak is not only crimson/red, and a precursor of the fleece. It is embroidered. The first picture on it takes up exactly where Orpheus' song had concluded earlier (I. 151). The Cyclopes are busy manufacturing Zeus' thunderbolts. Just as Orpheus' reminder of Zeus' supreme power warned Idas previously of the fate that was one day to be his in grim reality, Jason's cloak warns, or ought to warn, its wearer of the dangers he will run in flouting the moral order during his quest. The Argonauts may think later in their journey that they see the "Thunder" Mountains only in the distance (IV. 575–76). But so long as they carry Medea with them, they have not escaped "the justice of Zeus." Jason will eventually pay the same penalty as Prometheus.[12]

The next scene on the cloak shows the building of Thebes by Amphion and Zethus, the sons of Antiope. The legend had formed the subject of a tragedy by Euripides, and was current in various versions. Apollonius himself alludes to one of them later.[13] Antiope was cruelly treated by Dirce, while her son Amphion married the Niobe who became all tears after her children were slain by Artemis and Apollo.[14] In this poem, Medea and Jason are Artemis and Apollo. Medea/Artemis would eventually slay her own children. Amphion/Jason will be left to lament the blasting of his hopes.

[12] This explains why Phaeacia is in the "Ceraunian" Sea (IV. 983), since here Jason and Medea seal their fates by marriage.

[13] IV. 1090 (Arete appeals to Alcinous to help Medea). Callimachus too used differing versions of the same legend (Pfeiffer on fr. 576). Amphion and Zethus may have been in Mann's mind when he called the twin protagonists of his *Doktor Faustus* Adrian and Zeitblom (A/Z). See below, p. 503 note 175.

[14] I. 307; III. 878.

Now Aphrodite is seen, carrying Ares' shield. Her tunic has gracefully slipped from one shoulder, and she is admiring her reflection (δείκηλον) in the shield's shining bronze surface. Nothing could seem to illustrate better the spirit of Alexandrian rococo. But there are depths and heights to this chiaroscuro. Jason will depend on Aphrodite for his triumph (the shield of this new Ares will be handed to him by Love), and it was a commonplace of amatory verse that love had its own warfare.[15] The cruelty of a woman scorned, no less formidable than that of the god of battles, is another thought which inevitably crosses the reader's mind.

The key words "reflection" and "bronze" here recur in fact in the terrifying scene of Book IV where Medea, by her baleful glance alone, drives the giant Talos to break his life-vein (IV. 1668 ff.):

> Imploring them [the Fates] thrice she summoned them with her spells, thrice with her prayers: and fixing her mind on mischief, with hostile eyes she bewitched the gaze of *brazen* Talos: and she gnashed at him her destructive rage, and sent forth invisible *reflections*, violently angry.

"Reflection" is found in the poem only in these two passages. Medea, a student of Democritus, like her aunt Circe, who is a student of Empedocles, shows that there are more things in heaven and earth than your philosophy dreams of.[16]

The mythical examples on the cloak come nearer now to Jason's more immediate future. The next picture is that of a cattle pasture, where a bloody struggle is taking place between Taphian raiders (λῃσταί, I. 750) and Mycenean defenders. The fight is not yet over, but the raiders have the advantage of numbers, and there is no doubt that the cattle will be lost. This was another myth with unhappy implications. Ultimately the Taphians paid for their aggression. Hesiod had related at the opening of his *Shield* (accepted as genuine by Apollonius) how Amphitryon, leader of the Myceneans, had slain his wife's father in anger over cattle. In spite of her beauty and devotion, his wife then refused to sleep with him until he had avenged the murder of her brothers and burned the Taphian settlements. In Apollonius' poem, the raider Jason causes his wife to lose her father in anger over cattle.[17] Reversing the more natural sentiments of Alcmene, Medea will connive at her brother's murder.

The word "raider" in this story is of basic importance in the

---

[15] The theme is already hinted at in the Greek lyric poets (H. W. Smyth, *Greek Melic Poets* [repr. New York 1963], p. 294): cf. Pindar, *Pythian* 4. 213; Plato, *Symposium* 196 c–d; Jebb on *Antigone* 781.

[16] Δείκηλον is Democritean. Cf. IV. 672 ff. (Empedocles).

[17] IV. 1036; III. 492 ff.

poem.[18] The women of Lemnos, whom Jason is about to visit, had committed terrible murder because they were provoked by their menfolk's attachment to women acquired in raids (I. 612). But eventually we shall find that Medea herself is described as just such a raid-victim (IV. 35). The image had already been suggested by Euripides. Jason will repeat the pattern of the Lemnian husbands.

The scene that follows is inspired by the theme of unfair trickery in love's service. The scholia explain the story.[19] Oenomaus had promised his daughter to any suitor who could defeat him in a chariot race. But Hippodameia fell in love with one of those suitors, Pelops, and persuaded the royal charioteer to substitute a lynchpin made of wax, so that when it broke Pelops would win. On the cloak, Oenomaus is shown in the very act of falling from his car. Aeetes too will be defeated by trickery because his daughter is in love.

But the correspondences are more precise than this. Aeetes' son, Apsyrtus, bears the alternative name of Phaethon (III. 245). Like the Phaethon of Euripides' play, he drives his father's chariot (III. 1236–37; cf. IV. 224–25). Now we can understand why the lamentation for the legendary Phaethon by his grieving sisters is so emphasized when the Argonauts, homeward bound after the murder of Apsyrtus, enter the river Eridanus (IV. 596 ff.):

> They struck into the inmost stream of Eridanus. Here once, hit in the breast by the smoking thunderbolt, half-burned Phaethon fell from the chariot of the Sun into the mouth of that deep water: and even now it sends up a noisome stench from his burning wound.

Phaethon's sisters, enclosed in slender poplars, let fall to the ground drops of amber, which are dried on the sand by the sun. But when the waters of the dark lake wash over the shore beneath the blast of the moaning wind, then all together these amber beads are swept into the river by the surging stream. What must be sister Medea's thoughts in this romantically evocative scene as she reflects on what she has done to her Phaethon?

The Heliads' tears are dried up by the sand. The verb ($\tau\epsilon\rho\sigma\alpha\acute{\iota}\nu\sigma\nu\tau\alpha\iota$) is picked up later. The Argonauts' quest for the golden fleece hanging on a tree guarded by a serpent has a double in Heracles' quest for the golden apples of the Hesperides, also hanging on a tree and guarded by a serpent. Apollonius takes us to the site of this latter exploit after the hero has gone his way, leaving havoc in his wake, so that we can see what heroism costs its victims. Flies have gathered around the dead serpent, but so drastic is the poison of Heracles'

---

[18] I. 695, 801, 818, 823, 1252, 1259; II. 167, 303; III. 589; IV. 36, 400; Euripides, *Medea* 256.

[19] C. Wendel, *Scholia in Apollonium Rhodium Vetera* (repr. Berlin 1958), pp. 64–65.

arrows that they dry up (τερσαίνοντο, 1405) around its suppurating wounds. Later in this passage, the Argonauts themselves are flies (IV. 1453). The poet is more than a romantic.

Apollonius has added something to his description of the Eridanus. A Celtic story has it that the tears are really those of Apollo, grieving for the death of his son. But Jason, we saw, is Apollo. He too will grieve for the death of his children.

Apollo is indeed the next to appear on the cloak. He is defending his mother Leto against the assaults of the giant Tityos. The god's power is seen in his mastery, young though he is, of his mighty adversary. So Jason will master Aeetes, who relies in vain on the earth-born strength of his warriors.

But things are never so simple. From Aeetes' point of view, it is Jason who is the intruder, the violator of a woman's honor. Jason has his own reliance on something earth-born, the anointing unguent which sprang from Prometheus' blood.[20] Pindar had already made the inhabitants of Iolcus specifically compare Jason and Tityos (*Pythian* 4. 90). In later moralizing, Tityos, devoured in Hades by winged creatures rather as Prometheus is devoured by his eagle, was the example of the erotic torments afflicting the human heart. They certainly afflict Medea in this poem.[21] They would afflict Jason in another way.

Homer had not explained the symbolism of Achilles' shield. Apollonius ends his symbolic ecphrasis, the model for many in the Alexandrian tradition, by refusing to spell out the intent of his cinema montage (*Arg.* I. 763 ff.):

> And on it was also Minyan Phrixus, as if he were really listening to the ram, while the ram looked as if it were speaking. Seeing them you would keep silent and cheat your heart, hoping to hear some wise counsel from them, and long would you gaze in hope of that.

Reminding us of the basic theme of his poem, the ram's golden fleece, in this way, the poet teases his readers by making them wonder what the ram could have been saying. Was it a warning against madness in the family? Against ignoring the overriding power of Zeus? Or just a commentary on human folly?

As Jason takes up Atalanta's spear and sets out wearing this cloak, Apollonius again loads his narrative (I. 774 ff.):

> He set off for the city, like a bright star, which maidens shut up in their newly-made chambers see rising above the house, and with its

---

[20] "Earth-born" is another leitmotif: I. 943; II. 39, 1209; IV. 151.

[21] Cf. Euripides, *Medea* 1360, 1370; E. Norden on *Aen.* VI. 595; E. J. Kenney on Lucretius III. 992–94.

fair *red blush* through the dark air it charms their eyes, while the young girl rejoices, longing for her bridegroom who is among foreign folk, the groom for whom her parents are keeping her betrothed.

Star images are of constant occurrence in the poem. The heroes were all stars at the beginning of their journey (I. 239–40), and so the scope of the allusion may now be fittingly narrowed to their chosen leader. The blushing red of this particular star again hints at the fleece, and at love.

The maidens who see it are being kept in "newly-made" chambers. The adjective sounds odd,[22] until we find that it recurs in the very scene where the fleece itself, along with Medea, is being taken on board the Argo (IV. 183 ff.):

Dawn was spreading over the land when they reached the company; the young heroes were amazed when they saw the mighty fleece shining like the lightning of Zeus. Each started up, hoping to touch it and to receive it in his hands, but Aeson's son restrained them, and threw over it a *newly-made* cloak.

The Hypsipyle episode therefore cannot be treated as something complete in itself. Wherever he takes his cloak and his spear, Jason advertises his problems and his doom. It is inevitable that he should leave Hypsipyle to fulfill his destiny as a raider, and inevitable that his preoccupation with his mission should lead to the horrors of fresh "Lemnian deeds."

The poem is not blind to horrors of the most macabre kind. In Book II the heroes receive directions for their journey from old Phineus, whom they have rescued from the foul Harpies. So it was that Odysseus received directions from Circe. Medea too will be a kind of Circe, and will take Jason to Circe.[23] But so also Io received directions from the tormented Prometheus, when she learned that she would travel (as the Argonauts did) to the Chalybes and the river Thermodon.[24] Tortured by ever-returning Harpy-birds, Phineus is a double of Prometheus, and the Cook's tour he outlines far more like the passage in Aeschylus than anything in Homer.

It cannot surprise us then in this signposting style that eventually Prometheus becomes spine-chillingly important to the narrative. As the Argonauts draw near to the river Phasis at Colchis, they sight an eagle (II. 1246 ff.):

And as they went forward, a gulf of the sea came into view. It was

[22] See Mooney's note on I. 775: ". . . it would seem that νηγάτεος elsewhere is always used of some texture." Precisely.
[23] *Od.* XII. 37 ff.; *Arg.* III. 883–84; IV. 662 ff. Apollonius' use of Homeric parallels to his characters recalls that of Callimachus and was immensely developed by Virgil.
[24] *P.V.* 707 ff.

the steep crags of the Caucasian range which towered up where, with his limbs wound about steep rocks in brazen fetters, Prometheus fed with his liver the eagle that ever flies back. The eagle they saw high above at evening, flying over the ship with a piercing whir, near the clouds. Yet even so it shook all their sails as it wafted past with its wings. It had not the shape of a bird of air, but moved its swift wings like well-polished oars. And not long after they heard the deep groans of Prometheus as his liver was ravaged. The air rang with his screaming, until once again they observed the ravening eagle rising from the peak on the same path. And at night by the advice of Argus they came to the broadly flowing Phasis and the utmost bounds of the sea.

"At night"—evidently a symbolic time.

Later, Medea prepares to help Jason (III. 844 ff.):

Meanwhile, she took from her hollow casket a drug, which they say is called Promethean. If a man were to placate with night sacrifices the Maiden only-born, and then anoint with it his body, surely he would not be vulnerable to the blows of the bronze, nor would he yield to blazing fire, but in both valor and strength alike for that day he would be superior. A first growth did that spring up when the ravening eagle dripped to the ground in the glens of Caucasus the bloody ichor of tortured Prometheus. Its blossom appeared as much as a cubit above, like in color to a Corycian crocus, and it was supported by twin stalks. Its root in the earth was like newly-cut flesh. . . . And the dark earth was shaken with moaning beneath as the Titanian root was cut; and the son of Iapetus himself groaned, his soul distraught with pain.

In this passage, the pathetic "for that day" is worthy of Shakespeare.

Later again, as we have seen, Jason tinkers with the story of Theseus and Ariadne in order to secure Medea's aid. As he ends his beguiling speech, and is about to remind her of the tale, he takes the opportunity to explain where he comes from (III. 1083 ff.):

And if it pleases you to know of my homeland, I will tell you. For indeed my own heart urgently bids me do so. There is a land encircled by steep mountains, rich in flocks and pastures, where Prometheus, son of Iapetus, begot noble Deucalion, who first made cities and built temples for the immortals . . . in it is my city, Iolcus.

Apollonius relates these events in the reverse order from that in which they will affect Jason. The poet describes first the torture of Prometheus, secondly the origin of the ointment to be supplied by Medea, and thirdly the hero's home. But chronologically the hero's home came first. Next will come his anointing. Finally for him will come what Apollonius has described first: the torture by the eagle/ship, a doublet of the Argo, as his enterprise turns to resentful ruin with the murder by Medea of his new bride and children, as he who was a Tityos now becomes one.[25]

A final image of Jason's fate may be traced in the story of the rape of Hylas. In Apollonius, the drowning takes place by moonlight. Verbal repetition tells all (I. 1226 ff.):

All the nymphs who dwell on the mountain tops or in the valleys were ranging afar, watching the forest. But she, a water nymph, was just rising from the fair-flowing spring. She saw Hylas close at hand, *blushing red* with beauty and sweet graces. For the *moon at the full* shining from the sky struck upon him, and in helplessness *she could scarcely catch her breath.*

So when Medea has spent a sleepless night, agitated by thoughts of Jason (III. 633–34):

And shaking she rose in fear, and *she could scarcely catch her breath* as before in her breast. . . .

So when Jason seizes the coveted fleece (IV. 165 ff.):

And as when a maiden catches on her fine robe the beam of *the moon at the full* that rises above her high-roofed chamber, and her heart rejoices when she sees its fair sheen: with such joy then Jason picked up in his hands the mighty fleece, and on his blond cheeks and forehead from the gleaming of the wool a *blush like fire* sat.

There has already been occasion to note this last passage, since its imagery of reflected color anticipates the red blood which dyes Medea's silvery robe and veil at her brother's murder. But the simile also refers us back to Lemnos, and to the girl in her "newly-made" chamber who was longing for her prince to come, while watching the fair *red blush* of a star (I. 774 ff.). This maiden was then ultimately Medea. But, in conforming to her love, Jason has become identified with the feminine. Like Hylas, also blushing, also at the full moon, Jason has been drawn by a lovesick girl into deep waters, where he will drown. Euripides' play had perhaps already suggested this development too.[26]

## II

Apollonius' similes have always been thought attractive. They fulfill an essential structural purpose.

The first simile of the whole poem (I. 239) compared the departing

---

[25] On the non-linear narrative see above, p. 48 and below, p. 417 note 56. The Argo eventually killed Jason: Euripides, *Medea* 1386–88.

[26] Cf. E. M. Blaiklock, "The Nautical Imagery of Euripides' *Medea,*" *Class. Phil.* 50 (1955), 233 ff.

heroes to stars. At 774 this image was particularized, and Jason
became a star watched by maidens in their newly-made chambers.
Later, it was Aphrodite's ball, offered as a bribe to Eros, which
became a star (III. 141). Jason's heroism is evidently being twisted
out of shape by a distorting erotic framework, and this is suggested
by another comparison used of him, to the baleful star Sirius (III.
957), already used by Homer to modify the heroism of Achilles. This
sinister development had earlier been signposted in Book II (vv. 40
and 45), where Polydeuces was first a star, and then a wild beast.
The interlocking of the two images in this way provides a link with
all the other wild beast comparisons in the poem.[27]

Two other examples from Book III confirm that stars may be
ambiguous symbols. At 1359 the earth-born warriors who are Jason's
deadliest enemies are stars seen on a frosty night. But Jason, anointed
with his "Promethean" drug, is also in his way an earth-born warrior.
When Apsyrtus goes to his doom at Jason's hands, he is a child trying
a wintry torrent (IV. 460). Evidently Jason's stardom is as cold as
theirs. The limitations imposed on his heroism by the erotic furrow
which his star plows at III. 1377 have already been noted.

If the sun and moon may also be treated as stars,[28] the poetic
horizon widens even further. Medea's fluttering heart, like a sunbeam
on water, anticipates the image of the dew around the rose which is
dispelled by sunlight (III. 756 and 1020), and of course, if this is a
red rose, recalls the blush of love and the blush of the fleece. Jason,
dispelling the dew on this rose, is Medea's dehydrating Apollo. The
Debussyesque vision of the distant Heracles, like the new *moon* seen
through a bank of clouds (IV. 1479), unites with the comparison of
the fleece handled by Jason for the first time to a robe catching the
*moonlight*. Aspects of the two images are combined when the fleece
is further compared to a cloud (itself a repeated image[29]) blushing
red under the rising sun. When the god Triton guides the Argo back
to the sea, his fins are like the horns of the *new moon* (IV. 1616). Can
they really escape their dilemmas so easily?

If the first simile of all was to provide a vast range of allusion
throughout the poem, the second (I. 269) is no less evocative. Jason's
aged mother, Alcimede, stricken with grief at her son's departure, is
compared to a young girl persecuted by her stepmother, who weeps
in her nurse's arms. The image is so curious that it cries out for
deeper understanding. A young girl, robbed of her natural protectors,
can only be the symbol of Medea. A widowed bride, a widowed

---

[27] I. 1243; II. 45, 123, 278; III. 1351; IV. 1393.
[28] Cf. Norden on *Aen.* VI. 725 and Nisbet–Hubbard on Horace, *Odes* I. 12. 48.
[29] II. 173, 566; IV. 397.

peasant woman trying to eke out a meager living (III. 291; IV. 1062) and, as we have seen, a raid victim, at the start of Euripides' play Medea had had a nurse to explain her plight.

The third simile (307) is closely connected with the fourth (536). Jason is like Apollo, as he goes from some fragrant shrine to Delos, Claros, Pytho and Lycia. The Argonauts are then described as like dancers in honor of Apollo. The feeling is unavoidable that art and life are too close, since in the action the heroes are often represented as honoring Apollo.[30] If Jason is like Apollo, it is not surprising that in due course (III. 876) Medea is like Artemis, of whom Orpheus prophetically sings at I. 571. In Homer, it was Nausicaa who was like Artemis (*Od.* VI. 102 ff.). This is a charming allusion, and corresponds to one of the poles of Medea's pathetically structured character, though we must always remember that it is in Artemis' temple that Jason murders Apsyrtus. Apollonius develops his simile however with language borrowed from Homer's description of Circe (*Od.* X. 215 ff.). This blending of two epic figures into one, pioneered by Callimachus' Theseus/Odysseus in the *Hecale*, and perhaps ultimately inspired by the parodies of comedy, becomes typical of Virgil. Dido, for example, will be Diana (*Aen.* I. 498 ff.); and Aeneas, Apollo (IV. 143 ff.). In Virgil, the comparisons evoke a larger pattern of hunter and hunted[31] which perhaps in the end sums up the Roman poet's vision of human relationships.

At *Argonautica* I. 536 ff. the heroes depart. The fish that follow in their wake are compared to sheep following a shepherd to the fold (575 ff.). There is already a Homeric pathos about this allusion, since the Argonauts are not, like the shepherd, going home at the end of the day. Exactly the same ironic pathos had been employed by Homer in the Circe scene of *Odyssey* X to which we have just referred.[32]

Apollonius reinforces his meaning with verbal repetition. The heroes' armor flashes in the sun *like flame*, as their ship speeds on (I. 544). In Book III, when Medea has been smitten by Eros, his arrow

---

[30] This phenomenon, of which the most striking examples are in Book II (71, 168, 580), is an interesting refutation of the view that epic similes are supposed to distract the reader from the work of art. They do not point outside the poem to a "real" world beyond. There is only the world created by the poet, and its illustrations are drawn from within itself: cf. H. Fränkel, *Die homerischen Gleichnisse*, esp. pp. 97 ff.

[31] Cf. IV. 12 where Medea is a fawn, and contrast III. 879 where she is Artemis pulled along by fawns. Medea is a dove (III. 541), but the Argonauts are hawks (I. 1049–50; II. 933; IV. 485).

[32] W. B. Stanford on *Odyssey* X. 215 (dogs greeting their master). In *Arg.* IV. 674–75 Circe is attended by a flock of strange creatures who are compared to sheep following a shepherd. The departure looks ahead to what heroism will cost in blood.

burns deep in her heart *like flame* (287). Later again, the red blush
of the fleece will settle on Jason *like flame* (IV. 173).

The fish of the departure anticipate a scene in Book IV (933).
There the Argo is aided on its way through the Sicilian Planctae by
Thetis and her nymphs. As they circle the ship, they are like dolphins.
But there are some characteristic reservations about this cheerful
picture. Thetis, the estranged wife of the Argonaut Peleus, is in some
degree like Medea.[33] She too has a knowledge of things supernatural
which leaves an unbridgeable gap between herself and her husband.
She helps him here as a temporary favor to other goddesses, but it
is obvious that there is to be no reconciliation with her human partner.

Apollonius' use of dream imagery provides a fine example of
thematic harmony. Alcimede had never *dreamed* that Phrixus' rescue
would cause so much trouble (I. 290). The sufferings of old Phineus
have made him into a lifeless *dream* (II. 197). Even when he is rescued,
he is still in a *dream* (II. 306). In the next book, it will be Medea
herself whose mind is like a *dream* (III. 446; cf. 691). When she is
tormented by the suspicion that Jason may surrender her, she prays
that the fleece may vanish into the darkness of hell like a *dream* (IV.
384). Circe has disturbing *dreams* (IV. 685). Thetis, vexed by her
husband's incomprehension of her treatment of Achilles, vanishes
like a *dream* (IV. 877).

All the similes merit close study. Apollonius' use of them is
threefold. They draw together disparate parts of the narrative, and
compel the reader to see one event in the light of another, as the
departure is seen in the light of Medea's passion ("like a flame") and
all that will bring in its train. They are used to recall passages of
Homer, whose contexts we are expected to know, as the song of
Orpheus about Artemis at the departure prepares us for Medea/
Artemis/Nausicaa, and then the departure itself suggests Circe.
Finally, they connect the world of comparison, not with some external
reality, but with other and ostensibly factual parts of the story. The
most striking example of this is perhaps to be found in Book II,
where Amycus is compared (71) to a wave avoided by ships, while
later in the same book (168, 580) exactly such a real wave is avoided
by the Argo.

Homer had juxtaposed contrasting characters, in the archetypal
fashion of pathetic structure. Helen in Book III of the *Iliad* was an
ironic foil to Andromache in Book XXII. Hector/Paris, Hector/
Achilles, Odysseus/Ajax, Achilles/Agamemnon are other examples
of the technique. Apollonius, heeding Aristotle's lesson that epic

---

[33] Her son Achilles would in fact eventually marry Medea. Achilles had been
shown to his father (I. 553 ff.) as the Argo sailed away.

should learn from tragedy, internalized some of these contrasts in his single Medea, who is at one and the same time virgin princess in the grip of her first sexual passion, and witch.

When Jason is a star watched by maidens whom their parents have shut away, the reader thinks of any girl more mature than her well-meaning parents like to imagine.[34] A mythical analogue would be Danae,[35] to whom Zeus appeared in a shower of gold, and in the context of the poem we are bound to hear the first stirrings of the Medea theme. When Medea first falls in love, the comparison to a poor spinster rouses sympathy for her (III. 291 ff.):

> And as a handworker, whose toil is over wool, spreads tinder around a blazing ember so that she may kindle a light at night beneath her roof, for she has risen very early: and from that small ember rising with amazing strength it consumes all the tinder: so destructive Love wound deep in her heart and burned there hidden. And she kept changing the color in her cheeks, now to pale, now to blushing red, in the distraction of her mind.[36]

Repeated words here ("a light beneath the roof," "blushing red,") already anticipate the winning of the fleece.[37] The same comparison will return at the moment when, having secured the fleece for Jason, Medea begins to be afraid for herself (IV. 1062 ff.):

> . . . just as when a spinster turns her spindle all night. Around her whine her orphan children, for she is widowed of her husband. A tear drips down her cheek as she thinks of him and of the dreary fate that has seized her. So Medea's cheeks were wet, pierced with sharp pains.

These dripping tears recall those of the Heliades, Phaethon's sisters. But this passion, writhing and winding like a snake, and burning more fiercely than expected, hints at something else. Medea too is a golden fleece, guarded by a jealous serpent. She has the fleece's blush. She has its gold (IV. 727–29):

> For all the children of the Sun were plain to view, since from their eyes they sent forth before them a gleam as it were of gold.

When she is afraid, these eyes of hers fill with fire (IV. 16–17). With them, she can even lay low the giant Talos.

But Jason too is a golden fleece, and Medea has fallen victim to a universal illusion. In Book I, a halcyon bird flies over the head of

---

[34] Cf. Callimachus fr. 401 Pf.

[35] Mentioned at IV. 1091 by Arete in reference to Medea's plight.

[36] For the polar colors here see below, pp. 345 note 17, 407 note 22.

[37] IV. 168, 170, 173.

the sleeping hero, blond, nestling on soft sheepskins (1084, 1090).
Later, when Medea falls in love (III. 1015 ff.):

> And now she would have drawn her whole soul out of her breast and
> entrusted it to him, glad at his need: so did Love from the blond
> head of Aeson's son flash forth a sweet flame: and he snatched the
> gleamings from her eyes.

"Gleamings" are a leitmotif of the fleece.[38] Jason, here too a raider,
has usurped a false glamour. Medea sees one whom she imagines to
be like herself. Circe will point out her niece's confusion (IV. 745–46):

> Be off from my halls, following your stranger, whoever this unknown
> is whom you have picked up without your father's consent.

"Picking up" is what Jason did with the fleece (IV. 171). Both
parties have the rest of their lives to find out their mutual error. It
is an old story.

## III

It would be possible to say of this technique of composition what
Thomas Mann wrote as early as *Buddenbrooks* about the *strenger Satz*,
describing Hanno's music-making before his last illness:

> The little melody he had invented was more harmonic than rhythmic
> in its structure: there was an extraordinary contrast between the
> simple primitive material which the child had at his command, and
> the impressive, impassioned, almost overrefined method with which
> that material was employed. . . . He gave every simple harmonic device
> a special and mysterious significance by means of retardation and
> accentuation.[39]

In *Doktor Faustus* these early aspirations acquire deeper undertones,
more majestic resonance:

> One must go further from here, and form from the twelve steps of
> the tempered semitone alphabet bigger words, words of twelve letters,
> definite combinations and interrelations of the twelve semitones, series
> from which the piece, be it individual movement or whole work of
> several movements, must be strictly derived. Every tone of the whole
> composition, melodically and harmonically, must give proof of its
> relationship to this predefined basic series. None must recur before
> all the others have made their appearance. None must appear which
> does not fulfill its function as motif in the whole structure. There

[38] IV. 178, 1146.
[39] *Buddenbrooks*, Eng. tr. by H. T. Lowe-Porter (New York 1936), Part Eight, p.
115.

would be no free note any more. That is what I would call "strict composition."[40]

When these musical analogies are applied to literature, as of course they were by Mann, they suggest a style of writing in which not continuous novelty but repetition is of the essence. Certain themes must be presented and then re-presented in ever varying forms. Yet this is not aimless embroidery, but a steadily deepening commentary on the human significance of what is being said. This is in fact the classical epic tradition of which these pages speak.

There is another resemblance between *Doktor Faustus* and the *Argonautica* which points to a neglected side of the Alexandrian contribution to epic, and that is the use of astronomy, once a liberal art and now another specialty.[41] Apollonius refers frequently in his poem to stars and constellations. An example is found in a scene that has already attracted our attention, the appeal by Jason to Medea for aid, and the censored story of Ariadne (III. 1003–1004):

> . . . a crown of stars, which men call Ariadne's Crown, turns all night long among the signs of heaven.

If this passage is interpreted strictly, it refers us to the last week in April and the first week in May,[42] the only time of year when the constellation of Ariadne's Crown could in fact be described as turning "all night." Can we assume that Apollonius is hinting at this date for the interview? The *Argonautica* contains a large number of such allusive passages. They appear in the order in which they would appear throughout the lunar (354 day) year, and include references to solstices, equinoxes, lunar phases and nodes, eclipses, rising times of fixed stars and the positions of all five of the remaining then known planets.

The allusion to Ariadne's Crown is one of the most useful of these astronomical references. It is found in a carefully dated section of Book III. Because Book I ends with a reference to the full moon, while Book IV begins with a similar reference,[43] and because the

---

[40] *Doktor Faustus* (Stockholmer Gesamtausgabe 1956), pp. 255–56: my translation.

[41] The following remarks about astronomy in Apollonius are taken from a paper read at the December 1975 Meeting in Washington of the American Philological Association by my former student Dr. P. Bogue, and are quoted here by permission. For fuller details see her dissertation, "Astronomy in the *Argonautica* of Apollonius Rhodius" (University of Illinois, Urbana 1977), available on microfilm. Quintilian (*I. O.* I. 4. 4) and Gervase of Melkley (*Ars Versificaria: Perfecto versificatori non hiemet et . . . non diescat sine astronomia*) knew the importance of this topic.

[42] The Julian calendar (borrowed from Egypt) is assumed for the third century B.C., and the observation point is Alexandria.

[43] Διχόμηνις I. 1231; IV. 167.

poet counts out the intervening period day by day for his readers, it is possible to establish a relative chronology for the whole period of the Argonauts' adventure. This chronology is based on the allusion to Ariadne's Crown, but is supported by other references, in order, to the zodiac sign Aquarius, the month Lenaeon, the Feast of Pitchers, the setting of the star Arcturus and the House of Venus.

The striking passage has already been noted in which the Argonauts cross the path of Apollo, who is on his way north to visit the Hyperboreans (II. 669 ff.). The time of day is dawn, and Orpheus sings a song to the god as slayer of the monster Delphyne. At dawn on March 25 in the third century B.C. the sun was at the equinox, going north, and the constellation Delphinus on the meridian overhead.

If the Argonauts were at Thynias on March 25 in this way, the full moons mentioned in Books I and IV must have fallen on February 5 and May 4. The previous autumn equinox would have occurred on September 25, and rather unusually the old moon would on that date have been in conjunction with the sun in what is called "the astronomical new moon." This curious coincidence of dates occurs only once every nineteen years, and it would be likely therefore that a poet interested in astronomy would mention it. This is what he does. At I. 308 ff. Jason is described as resembling Apollo passing towards various of his shrines, but ultimately heading south (Lycia). The hero is leaving his mother, who is compared to a young girl, and on his way he passes the old priestess of Artemis.

At the autumn equinox the sun is by definition leaving the sign of the Virgin, is going south, and that year it was also passing the old moon.

Other dates now fall into place. It looks as if the Argo was launched just in time for the twenty-seventh day of the lunar month, the day when Hesiod said ships should be launched.[44] The bad weather which dogged the Argonauts was the natural consequence of starting a journey so late in the year. But Alexandria began its New Year in the autumn, and the season was also symbolic, since at the time of the autumn equinox the constellation of Aries, the Ram, the Golden Fleece, was as far from the sun (= Jason) as it ever would be.

Pindar had led his Argonauts to Lemnos at the *end* of their voyage (*Pythian* 4. 249–52). Apollonius *started* with Lemnos, making his men arrive in time for the fall plowing, and thereby gaining a pun.[45] Hylas, the water-carrier, is lost from the company while the sun is in

---

[44] *Opera* 814–18.
[45] For Love as plowboy see Callimachus, *Epigr.* 45; Moschus, fr. IV (Gow).

Aquarius. Heracles, a descendant of the gadfly-crazed heifer Io, disappears as Taurus sinks out of sight (I. 1153–1279).

Book III shows a particularly close correspondence between events in the sky and events on the ground. The bulls of Aeetes thunder up from their underground lair (III. 1290) as the constellation Taurus rises above the horizon. The poet makes Jason late for his tryst with Medea so that the hero could be described as rising like Sirius (III. 957) at the hour when the star Sirius actually would be rising. Jason pours a libation of milk (III. 1199 and 1210) as the Milky Way passes over his head. The poet makes Jason wait briefly for the crop (*stachys*) of the Earth-born to rise (III. 1340, 1389), so that this event will coincide with the rising of the star Stachys. Jason could not collect the golden fleece from Aeetes immediately after his ordeal was over as promised (III. 419), since by that time the constellation Aries had already set, and would not be visible again until two hours before sunrise, when of course he does collect it (IV. 109).

Interpreters have noted the doublet Hypsipyle/Medea. The calendar confirms that the stars which shone over Hypsipyle by day in early October, when the Argonauts were at Lemnos,—the Virgin, the Crown and the Folding Doors—were the stars that shone over Medea after sunset in the following May, when they were in Colchis. The difference between the two women is literally the difference between day and night. A similar astronomical distinction is made between the stars which attend Heracles (day) and Jason (night). It is the typical polarity of pathetic structure.

The geography of the Argo's homeward voyage has occasioned adverse comment. Astronomy indicates that Apollonius was faced by a special problem. The constellation called the Argo disappeared from the sky in late May, not to reappear until mid-July. During this same period the constellation called the River Eridanus was prominent. Apollonius hides his sailors away on the terrestrial river Eridanus under the protection of the Dioscuri, Gemini, the Heavenly Twins (IV. 588–96), because of these astronomical considerations. The sun is in Gemini for much of this time. The poet allows the Argonauts to return to the Mediterranean when the constellation Argo is once more visible.

At this point Apollonius picks up again a day-by-day account, marking off his travelers' adventures until the end of the lunar year saw them back home. The astronomical parallels continue to the end. Jason roars like a lion at noon (IV. 1312–38) on a day when the constellation Leo was overhead at noon. A great horse is described as not about to vanish beneath the earth (IV. 1378) at a time of year when the constellation Pegasus shone all night, and would still be in the sky at dawn. Apollonius varied from Pindar in his description of the foundation of Thera[46] because he wished to refer to the Milky Way passing overhead.

## IV

Epic and astronomy have not become sisters again only in our lifetime, in Mann's *Doktor Faustus*.[47] The poems of Dante and Chaucer are obvious members of the same family. But here another and, to the Formalist literary historian, more significant piece of evidence may be called in.

The displacement of the epic device of an astronomical calendar to a less imposing genre is already found in Ovid. Not the epic *Metamorphoses*, but the elegiac *Fasti* take up the Alexandrian inheritance. The alternation of genres of which Formalists speak is making itself felt. Ovid's carnival epic demanded another concept of space and time.

A later poet was not so fortunate. Petrarch was celebrated in his lifetime as the coming author of the most famous epic Europe would witness since the close of antiquity, the *Africa*. His difficulties with this poem, eventually left unfinished, are catalogued below.[48] He was right to believe that he had the epic impulse. The finest pages of the *Africa* are inspired by the same brilliance which illumines the *Canzoniere*. The disaster is that critical theory undermined poetic instinct. Inspiration became divided. Its more serious ambitions stifled the *Africa*. Its lighter and less trammeled wit played itself out in the sonnets and lyrical songs.

The epic potential that was confused in all this shows itself precisely in the shift of the astronomical calendar from the *Africa*, where it might have been at home if Petrarch had been allowed to recognize the legitimacy of the Alexandrian epic,[49] to the *Canzoniere*. A modern scholar[50] has pointed out how the poems forming this collection, 366 in all, are strangely divided at poem 264, apparently in contradiction

---

[46] IV. 1731–64; *Pythian* 4. 17–43. Astronomy rather than literary rivalry also accounts for the discrepancy between Apollonius' and Theocritus' story of the rape of Hylas. R. Pfeiffer (*Callimachus* II, xlii–xliii) had already suggested that the two poets wrote independently. See also A. Köhnken, *Apollonios Rhodios und Theokrit* (Göttingen 1965).

[47] See below, pp. 501 ff.

[48] Pp. 282 ff.

[49] There was perhaps going to be something astronomical in the *Africa*: cf. III. 90 ff., which is what survives from a projected visit by Scipio to the Palace of Truth (so N. Festa in the introduction to his edition [Florence 1926], pp. lxv ff.).

[50] Thomas P. Roche, Jr. See his article, "The Calendrical Structure of Petrarch's *Canzoniere*," *Studies in Philology* 71 (1974), 152 ff., and cf. E. L. Brown's concluding remarks in *Numeri Vergiliani* on Spenser's *Epithalamion*.

with the ostensible division of the work into poems about Laura's life and poems about her death. Editors have been led to assume that a division previously determined was let stand even though it no longer tallied with biographical, and autobiographical, fact.

The solution to the incongruity is however that Petrarch had important calendrical considerations in mind when planning his book. Tradition reported that Christ had been crucified on April 6, and this was also believed to be the day both of Man's creation and of his fall. It was also the day, so Petrarch assures us, when he met Laura for the first time, and it was the day of her death.

Suppose we assume that the first poem of the entire collection corresponds to April 6. One symbolic suggestion of this could be that, as Petrarch encountered his earthly love, Christ died. But 264 days after this Good Friday, April 6, comes Christmas Day. Christ is born, and poem 264 fittingly begins the section of the *Canzoniere* which honors Laura's earthly death and rebirth into a higher dimension.

... This new dimension sets the *Canzoniere* firmly in the context of fourteenth-century Christian morality. The Good Friday–Christmas division of the *Canzoniere* sets up a pattern of parallels between the two parts. In Part I the two ballate (11 and 14) are meant to emphasize the Good Friday–Easter dates of 1327 and 1348 [i.e. the years and times when Petrarch first met Laura and when she died]. Part I ends with the two sestine (237 and 239) emphasizing the beginning of Advent followed by 24 sonnets in preparation for Christmas. In Part II 270 sets up the segment of 52 sonnets beginning on the first of January, which leads to the non-sonnet group 323–325, framed by the two counterpointed Ash Wednesdays of 1327 and 1341 [i.e. the year of Petrarch's laureation], which leads us into that symbolic Lent of the last forty poems, a parallel to the Advent segment of Part I. Thus the beginnings and the ends of each part would seem to be formally structured around four major events in the Christian year: Good Friday, Advent, Christmas and Lent. Against this annual cycle Petrarch counterpoints the agony of his earthly love and his growing awareness of the disparity between it and the heavenly love he ultimately sought.[51]

Like Petrarch, Dante and, in our own day, Thomas Mann, Apollonius "doubled" his narrative by setting it against the unrolling of a heavenly order, which both magnifies and diminishes. It was a use of the idea of time deeply embedded in the primitive consciousness, and leaving its mark on the comic tradition. In Alexandria itself, Callimachus, with his *Lock of Berenice*, translated into Latin by Catullus,

[51] Roche, *op. cit.*, pp. 171–72.

showed the same awareness of the sidereal. Perhaps this was why he had praised Aratus' astronomical poem. Hesiod too was believed to be the author of an *Astronomy*.

The epic poem thus presented to the learned public of Alexandria was a truly astonishing achievement in the context of its time. Quite apart from its technical merits, of which its skillful renewal of the epic dialect is one of the most amazing, it offered a commentary on life worthy of Aristotle's definition of epic as "the treatment in literature of the serious."[52] The author was very far from being lost in some sort of weak romanticism, unable to face the sterner stuff of life. He noted how heroism was diverted from its path by eroticism: but could there be a heroism that was not exposed to this danger? He saw how fine promise leads to sordid deed, how in the hour of danger baffled uncertainty is liable to replace confident assertion, except on the lips of naive fools. He knew the ambivalent attitude of the gods towards mortals, their cruel indifference to suffering. Hera, devoted to Jason because of the respectful service rendered when she was on earth, has no scruple about exploiting Medea. Rhea, jealous of her worship, cares nothing for the fated end of King Cyzicus, or the suicide of his young bride.[53]

The lesson for the modern epic poet to be drawn from this success was complex. It is natural that Rome turned, in the first flush of her victories, to the Homerizing tradition of the "cyclic" poets, as transformed by Ennius. After the rude shock of civil war and national disillusionment, it was equally natural that Apollonius should have found a fresh auditor and a greater disciple in Virgil.

Given that the *Argonautica* is more than the pretty piece of Alexandrian froth for which it has so often and so unfairly been mistaken, its entire status in the classical epic tradition is altered. For the first time, the attentive student understood that the day of the epic poem was not done, that it was possible to use myth to provide a relevant and convincing illustration of the human situation under its greatest stress, that the new canons of art established by Callimachus were not a limitation on the scope of the oldest of genres, except in the most crassly material sense, and that properly understood they could open new ranges of meaning and symbolic perspective. In these circumstances it seems right to ask where Apollonius may have looked for help in formulating his new techniques.

This question means more than simply pointing to Callimachus. Because the *Argonautica* is (at least relatively) complete, it enables us

---

[52] *Poetics* 1449 b 10: cf. τὰ σπουδαῖα μάλιστα ποιητής, 1448 b 34. Perhaps one should add that the treatment is σπουδογέλοιον.

[53] Fränkel, *Noten* etc., pp. 135 ff.

to look behind Hellenistic poetry for possible sources of the manner common to both Apollonius and Callimachus. Revolutionaries never repudiate the past. They simply interpret it differently from their fathers.

The obvious source is Hesiod, and he certainly inspired some of the Alexandrians' technical innovations, especially when we remember that more poems then passed under his name than now survive. The *Astronomy* has already been mentioned. Apollonius also thought he was the author of the *Shield*.[54] The spondaic fifth foot, the use of color contrasts, the few-word line, variation of subject matter, a strong feeling for the divine presence in nature, powerful description which seems to anticipate Ovid's *Metamorphoses*, abrupt beginnings and concealment of the motivation of the action to the end, *ecphrasis*, wit, even interconnection of similes: all these are tricks visible in Hesiod to the most casual reader, and are encountered again in the Alexandrians.[55]

The *Homeric Hymns* too look as though they supplied valuable hints to a poet eager for fresh approaches. The *Hymn to Demeter*, for example, contains far more that is redolent of "Hellenistic" epic than one might expect from compartmentalized histories of literature. The whole poem is a kind of *aetion*, and in its richness again calls Ovid to mind. The flowers, the golden chariot, the feeling for the child, the riot of proper names, the use of repetition are not so much "Hellenistic" as Ionian devices destined to enjoy a long history.

## V

Yet perhaps it is here that analysis needs deepening. When we observe the mannerisms usually thought to be characteristically Alexandrian in this early Ionian poetry, no doubt it is chastening to find once more that there is nothing new under the sun. But the fact that we so often catch the name of Ovid in the argument should give us pause. Ovid was more than a great comic poet, and it is revealing that his tragic side found expression precisely in a *Medea*. But the *Medea* disappeared from history, and on the evidence of what did survive, truncated as it is of his supreme achievement, Ovid is not surely the most disciplined model of the Alexandrian spirit. The

---

[54] *Hesiodi . . . Scutum*, ed. F. Solmsen (Oxford 1970), p. 86.

[55] Color contrasts: e.g. *Opera* 155, *Scutum* 249, 294. Spondaic fifth feet: e.g. *Opera* 1, 2, 10. Few-word line: e.g. *Opera* 383: cf. the four-word opening of the *Theogony*. Variation of subject matter: e.g. *Opera* 519–20, 564, 582 ff. Divine presence in nature: e.g. *Opera* 737. Powerful description: e.g. *Scutum* 139 ff. Abrupt beginning: e.g. *Scutum*. Concealment of motivation: e.g. *Scutum*. Ecphrasis: e.g. *Scutum* 139 ff. Wit: e.g. *Scutum* 303–04. Cf. Actaeon in Ovid, *Metamorphoses* III. 247. Interconnected similes: e.g. *Scutum* 402 ff., picked up by 426.

genius of European civilization is to push the comic into the tragic, and in doing that it goes beyond these externals, indicative though their presence may sometimes be. Apollonius, who thought seriously about the nature of the modern hero; Callimachus, who wrote the impassioned reply to critics and defense of his art which we now read in the Preface to the *Aetia*—are these poets to be brought into correlation only with Ovid? The real Hellenistic/Alexandrian manner is more concentrated, more emotional, more allusive and indeed more serious than the poetry of these Ionian forerunners, who at that stage of development diverted their sense of the tragic to form philosophy. The Alexandrians united these divergent strands, which explains the absence of philosophers in the Museum. That is why in the last resort Alexandrianism is more important than it became in Ovid's hands.

The suggestion that the Alexandrians drew some of their greater maturity and mastery from lyric technique is attractive, because only in that technique do we find an implied doctrine of connected narrative that is more than the traditionally epic. Clearly the Alexandrians needed some such estranging model, if they were to wrench epic from Homerizing poetasters and resurrect it with any degree of conviction. A lyrical parallel to Apollonius' *Argonautica* is provided by Pindar's fourth *Pythian* ode. When one of Pindar's editors tells us that "in this poem we have a whole incorporated theory of the lyric treatment of epic themes, the Argonautic expedition in points of light,"[56] analysis becomes imperative.

At the beginning of *Pythian* 4 we plunge into more than *medias res*. The Argonauts are actually returning! Medea's direct speech, occupying lines 13–56 of the ode, employs a device common in Pindar. By anticipating the course of what is to come, it enables a shortening of the main account to take place.[57] At v. 32 ἀλλὰ ... γάρ ("let us say no more of that, since . . ."), an idiom used only with negations by Homer, emphasizes the new technique's preoccupation with brevity. The vivid questions of vv. 70–71, the adaptation of

---

[56] B. L. Gildersleeve, *Pindar, Olympian and Pythian Odes* (repr. Amsterdam 1965), p. 278. His remark was evidently inspired by the analysis of *Pythian* 4 in L. Dissen's *Pindari Carmina* (Gothae et Erfordiae 1830), pp. LIV ff. The whole discussion (pp. XLVI ff., "De Tractatione Fabularum") is still worth reading.

[57] What Illig, *Zur Form der Pindarischen Erzählung*, p. 31, calls the *kephalaion*. For this in epic see Servius' introduction to the *Aeneid: nescientes hanc esse artem poeticam, ut a mediis incipientes per narrationem prima reddamus et nonnumquam futura praeoccupemus ut per vaticinationem, quod etiam Horatius praecipit in arte poetica* (43: "Failing to grasp that poetic art means to start from the middle and then to narrate what happened first, sometimes anticipating the future as by prophecy. This is also what Horace prescribes in the *Ars Poetica*"). "Per vaticinationem" is another name for what German scholars have called the "Zukunftsstil": see below, pp. 274 and 337.

another Homeric turn of phrase at v. 86, reveal in the lyric poet a style consciously epic in its ambition, while the use of the apostrophizing vocatives at vv. 59, 89, 175 points to a development beyond the Homeric use of the same device which was to enjoy enormous influence.[58]

Pindar is concerned with more than rhetoric however. He is interested in the characters of his heroes, Euphemus, Jason, Pelias, Aeetes, and of course Medea. He uses verbal echoes[59] to provide unity and significant contrast in his tale. The cleverly abrupt ending of the main myth (vv. 245–46) suggests, long after the event, the building of the Argo, without saying so. Apollonius avoids the same topic.

This main myth falls into seventeen sections:

1. Opening. Pelias was warned to beware of a one-sandalled stranger.
2. This stranger came. His dress and hair are described.
3. Reaction of the citizens of Iolcus to his appearance, including direct speech.
4. Pelias arrives. Direct speech betrays his character.
5. The stranger answers him. Direct speech shows his character. Only at the very end do we learn that he is Jason. Here too, at the end, he describes his fate as a baby.
6. Jason enters his father's house. He is welcomed emotionally by his father and uncles. There is geographical detail about their origins. He gives a banquet lasting five days.
7. They all go to challenge Pelias. Jason's direct speech again reveals his frank and generous character. Pelias replies, and since he lies about his age, his character too is revealed.
8. There is a catalogue of the Argonauts. Not all are mentioned, but there is some detail about those who are.[60]
9. They set off with a prayer to Zeus, who answers with thunder.
10. The journey out. They found an altar to Poseidon. They "kill" the Clashing Rocks.
11. At Colchis, Aphrodite intervenes on their behalf. Medea is

---

[58] Wilamowitz and Norden (*Aeneis VI*, pp. 122, 126) are surely wrong to separate this from the use of apostrophe so common in Latin poetry. See Euripides, *Bacchae* 1287 (rhetorical), 1308 (emotional). But Homer had led the way with his mixture of the highly charged (*Iliad* XX. 2) and conventional ("O swineherd Eumaeus" in the *Odyssey*).

[59] The use of φθίνω and its compounds in the ode repays study. See below, p. 99, for more examples of this device.

[60] Compare Chaucer's handling of the epic catalogue in the *Knight's Tale*: below, pp. 350–51.

> infatuated. She is introduced casually, and what she did for
> Jason is summarized quickly.
>
> 12. Aeetes plows. Direct speech again reveals his character.
> 13. Jason plows. Aeetes' reaction.
> 14. The Argonauts' reaction. Aeetes shows where the fleece is.
> 15. Pindar breaks off. He has no time to fare along the high road.
> 16. He resumes. Jason kills the serpent guarding the fleece, steals
>     Medea "with her own aid," and reaches Lemnos.
> 17. Conclusion. This led to the founding of the line from which
>     sprang the house of Euphemus and Cyrene.

In its allusiveness and selectivity, this style seems in essentials to
offer a basis for what scholars call Hellenistic narrative technique,
especially as it was later to be developed by the Roman epic writers,
notably Virgil. Homer had been praised by Aristotle for introducing,
after a short prologue, "a man or a woman or some other character,
and nothing without character, but rather with."[61] Pindar seems to
have anticipated Aristotle's prescription. The action of his story is
filled with dramatic suspense growing out of the clash of character
expressed in direct speech. There is even a hint of a chorus (the
citizens of Iolcus, the Argonauts).

To secure his effects, Pindar manipulates the expected and familiar
details of the legend with sovereign mastery. Who could believe that,
halfway through the allotted space, the heroes would not yet have
set off, or that the poet who has time to describe Jason's hair-style
has no time to describe the seizure of the Golden Fleece? The literary
construct, estranging the commonplace, does not yield to logical
interpretation.

It is nevertheless carefully calculated. The entire main myth
occupies 1206 words,[62] and interestingly divides at the point where
Pelias proposes to Jason the quest for the fleece. It does therefore
revolve around its theme. The story of the oracle that warned Pelias
to beware of a one-sandalled visitor takes 45 words. It is immediately
followed by another section of 45 words: the arrival of the one-
sandalled hero. The catalogue of heroes takes 121 words, and breaks
at the name of Orpheus into two parts of 53 and 68 words. These
proportions recur. The journey out is described in 53 words, as are
Aeetes' plowing and speech. Sixty-eight words were previously allotted
to Jason's welcome and subsequent banquet. The myth concludes
with a passage of 49 words. This triumph matches the 49 words in

---

[61] *Poetics* 1460 a 10–11.

[62] The text used is that of A. Turyn (repr. Oxford 1952). All words receive the
numerical value of one, except μέν, δέ, τε, γε and καί which are not counted.

which the Argonauts applauded Jason's exploit, and Aeetes showed the whereabouts of the fleece.

When Aeetes saw that Jason could perform the task he had set, he gave a cry of astonishment (ὔξεν, 237). But Jason had only been able to do it because of Aphrodite's aid, in the shape of the wryneck (ἴυγγα, 214).[63] Here is the kind of comic pun, concealing a deeper truth, which would have delighted the Alexandrians. We can see in fact that by a habitual technique Pindar loads even what look like plain descriptions.[64] Jason's dress and limbs anticipate the dress and limbs of the Argonauts' games (ἐσθάς, 79; γυίοις, 80: γυίων . . . ἐσθᾶτος, 253: cf. χρόνῳ, 78 and 258). The *one-sandalled* stranger threw down a *foundation* of wise words. Verbal reminiscence made the connection (μονοκρήπιδα, 75; κρηπῖδα, 138). In her earlier speech, though Euphemus had not *disobeyed* the god, Medea *learned* that the fated clod of earth had slipped overboard (ἀπίθησε, 36; πεύθομαι, 38). In his speech, Jason *learned* that Pelias had *obeyed* his foolish heart (πεύθομαι, 109; πιθήσαντα, also 109). The verbal parallels contrast the pious and the impious. Like that of Apollonius, Pindar's art sets up constant patterns of verbal echo, sounding boards on which his meaning reverberates to infinity.

Exponents of the rhetorical tradition made a habit of matching precept and example.[65] But what else is Pindar doing when, after leading his audience up to the very moment of confrontation with the serpent guarding the fleece, he breaks away to congratulate himself on his poetic mastery? He has carefully prepared his hearers for violence, by talking about the serpent's size and girth in terms of a ship fashioned with blows of iron. When he turns away, the imagination cannot help building on what it has already been given ("montage"). Because each listener will build to his own satisfaction, since he is doing the job himself, the poet has discharged his responsibilities perfectly. It is the technique by which Homer refused to describe Helen, given fresh life in the fifth century by Timanthes' muffled Agamemnon.[66] He has reason then to congratulate himself at this point.

Both Pindar and Apollonius presuppose an epic model on which they play continuous variations. This may have been embodied in the work of authors now lost to us, and there is clearly some debt

---

[63] See F. Mezger, *Pindars Siegeslieder* (Leipzig 1880), pp. 38–39.

[64] Compare Apollonius' loading of his account of Jason's visit to Hypsipyle: above, pp. 80 ff.

[65] As Horace, for example, rhymed *A. P.* 99–100. See D. A. Russell's note on *De Sublimitate*, ch. 18 (p. 133 of his edition). V. Shklovsky's "clumsy coinage" *ostranenie* ("estrangement") is part of this tradition.

[66] See below, pp. 430–31.

to Homer anyway. But it may also be a model which has only a notional existence, a mold which exists only to be broken, so that the masterpiece may emerge.[67] The error of so many critics has been to mistake the abstract idea of epic for an actual poem. But, whenever the abstract is particularized, it must lose its ideal status. The more individual examples of epic are considered, the more their divergences from the critics' prescriptions are revealed.

Pindar could have taught Apollonius many things. The first is selection, which implies brevity. Apollonius avoids circumstantial detail at the start of his poem.[68] What he does select is vivid enough to set a scene. The material must be manipulated ("deformed") for effect, since the poet is not interested in writing history.

Like Pindar, Apollonius describes the emotional reactions of his characters through speeches. This is especially frequent in the case of Medea.

Both poets paint word-pictures. Pindar's description of Jason's appearance in the marketplace of Iolcus matches Apollonius' posed Victorian still photograph of the Argonauts listening to their chief before they set out.[69]

Apollonius incorporates so much music into his poetry that we clearly miss a great deal by not hearing it recited. Like Pindar, he makes use of verbal echo and recurrent imagery to give both unity and depth to his narrative.

Apollonius humanizes his story. Antimachus had said[70] that Heracles was left behind because he was too heavy for the ship, evidently an anticipation of the weightiness which would one day betoken the hero's godhead. Posidippus, one of Callimachus' critics, according to the Florentine Scholiast, had followed Antimachus. Apollonius tells instead, to explain Heracles' disappearance, the beautiful and structurally important story of the rape of Hylas. Pindar, though impressed with Heracles' prowess, had "reduced" him to babyhood (*Nemean* 1) and had described him as "physically slight" (*Isthmian* 4. 71).

Both Pindar and Apollonius are "noble" writers, and may be compared in this respect to the sentiment of the eighteenth-century novelists. But this quality is consistent with a sense of the comic (or komic).[71] Pindar displays this sense, for example, by his use of doubles

---

[67] See V. Shklovsky on *War and Peace*: below, p. 471.

[68] L. Adam, *op. cit.*, pp. 92–93, cites some remarks by Weichert which are pertinent: see also H. Fränkel, *Noten* etc., p. 21.

[69] Fränkel, p. 64.

[70] See C. Wendel, *op. cit.* (above, note 19), p. 116. We should note that Callimachus did not like Antimachus, nor Posidippus Callimachus.

[71] This side of Pindar has been explored in *Pindar's Art: Its Tradition and Aims*, written jointly with F. S. Newman (Hildesheim–Munich–Zürich 1984).

and puns. He and Apollonius explore character in a way which later critics would regard as more appropriate to comedy.[72] Yet this comedy is serio-comic. It is still concerned with the last things.

Confronted with a prolix, Homerizing (not Homeric!) style in which Antimachus took twenty-four books even to get his heroes to the gates of Thebes, and which later would instigate Ennius to tell the story of the Second Punic War by going back to Romulus and Remus, Apollonius understood that the only way to attract interest was to cut out the verbiage and plunge immediately into the bare structure of a dramatic situation: a tyrant, an oracle, a young and handsome prince. Where all this happened did not matter too much. The listener could supply that for himself. For the rest of his story, the poet would continually vary the scene, continually assume that his auditor knew what was commonly said so that he could be intrigued by a different version, continually give unexpected proportions to the treatment of the action. Pindar could not be bothered to describe the seizure of the fleece. Apollonius crams Jason's plowing with the fiery bulls into the last 130 lines of a book, most of which has been taken up with a love affair reported from the girl's point of view. There is enough in the younger poet to confirm that the recurring need of the epic for lyric infusion had led him to siphon from Dirce.

In the new, Apollonian style, language, including prosaic language,[73] acquired a dominating importance. The theory that the poet could be excused from rephrasing because Homer had already put everything so much better became totally irrelevant to an art that was responding to new sensibilities. Because Apollonius understood the need for estrangement, he was bound to regard even the work of Antimachus, praised by Plato, as of little help. Antiquarian bombast could have no place in a poetry that wanted to make its voice heard in the world of its own time. Still less, of course, could Apollonius learn anything from the historical epic of the two Choeriluses.

In the last analysis therefore is this poetry, this revivification of the epic style, to be dissociated from the influence and example of Callimachus? A glance at the Callimachean poetic outlined in the first chapter[74] will show how much of that program is exemplified in the *Argonautica*. It may even be that consideration of the program will enlarge our appreciation of the poetry. The musical analyses of the poem which have been offered by a modern scholar[75] acquire more

[72] Russell on *De Sublimitate* 9. 15.

[73] See my article, "Callimachus and the Epic," in *Serta Turyniana* (Urbana 1974), p. 354 note 48 (written in 1969).

[74] Above, pp. 20–21.

[75] A. Hurst, *Apollonios de Rhodes: Manière et Cohérence* (Rome 1967).

inherent plausibility if it is true that musicality is the essence of Alexandrianism. And there is always Mann's *Doktor Faustus* to support the theory in our own day.

One concrete fact in the relationship between Apollonius and Callimachus is the undoubted literary imitation of one poet by the other.[76] Chronology is an uncertain witness, and it will remain open for the skeptic to insist upon Apollonius' priority. Even so, some cases of imitation are so odd that only the supposition that Apollonius was the imitator makes any sense.

Yet the literary historians tell us that Callimachus and Apollonius quarreled over the admissibility of the long epic. It will not do![77] The *Argonautica* is not a long epic, but in any case a grave error of method is committed by those who try to solve this problem by collecting external evidence about the two poets' feelings for each other. The "intentional fallacy" consists precisely in confusing what an artist says about his work with the significance of the work itself. The truth is that, once a work is composed, it stands there only to be understood in terms of itself. What the artist intended to do, as he may subsequently inform us in letters or commentaries, has varying relevance to what he has actually done. What the scholar may deduce about the genesis of the work from previous sources has limited relevance to its ontological status.

Even if evidence far more convincing than the tittle-tattle of Byzantine scholiasts were produced to show that Callimachus and Apollonius had quarreled bitterly, and quarreled furthermore over literary matters, this would be irrelevant to our judgment in the perspective of history that, like so many bitter antagonists, the two poets were in the end on the same side. Literary history must not be made into another version of the conspiratorial history so discredited in other spheres.[78]

The evidence of the *poetry* of Apollonius and Callimachus is that, though of course they were two different poets with two different personalities, they shared certain ideals. They both found poetry in

[76] Pfeiffer, *Callimachus*, I, p. 17 and his comments on fr. 18. 9 and 6–15: H. Lloyd-Jones and P. Parsons, *Supplementum Hellenisticum* (Berlin–New York 1983), p. 95, no. 250. On fr. 12. 6 (= *Arg.* I. 1309, repeated in a variant at *Arg.* IV. 1216) see my article mentioned above (note 73), pp. 351–52.

[77] See my article mentioned above. M. Lefkowitz, *The Lives of the Greek Poets* (Baltimore 1981), pp. 117 ff., has since concluded that no reliance is to be placed on the story of the quarrel.

[78] As it is by K. Ziegler, *op. cit.*, p. 12. How extraordinary that the authors of those grand and vigorous anti-Callimachean epics conjured out of thin air by Ziegler should have been so feeble in the arts of publicity, though that was indeed their métier!

their own time languishing. Callimachus, the more versatile genius, set about re-energizing it by a whole series of experiments which had necessarily to be on the (relatively) small scale in the first instance, but which did not entail the small scale for ever. His interest in lyric precedent, in the reform of literary language, in the mixing of genres, in estrangement, in the ambivalence which was both serious and playful in the same breath, called for response from any poet capable of accepting the challenge. Apollonius undertook the most demanding of all the tasks which Callimachus had proposed, that of giving new status to the epic. His brilliant explorations of feminine psychology, of masculine helplessness, set in counterpoint against the eternal and predetermined movement of the heavens, opened a fresh chapter in Greek and European literary art.

# IV

# VIRGIL

THE Alexandrian tradition passed to Rome, to a quite different civilization, more primitive and barbarous in many ways, more vigorous, more comic, more aware of manifest destiny. It was from this shadowed, refracted, often paradoxically elusive and imprecise culture that Europe, and more than Europe, would take a stamp which has proved indelible.

The literary voice of Rome has been Virgil. In this sense he is the founder-poet of Western civilization. He has suffered the fate of all who succeed, even in offering only an unrealizable ideal: to be taken for granted. Raised in the Middle Ages to the status of magician, depressed by the Romantics to the level of pallid imitator, praised and abused for the wrong reasons, pointedly ignored, Virgil has for twenty centuries simply been there and available, the Sphinx of epic in a too often waterless desert.[1] But even the desert has a history!

Virgil was in the first place a product of his own time. He was an Italian and a Roman, born in an age when all things Roman seemed on the verge of destruction by the greed and ambition of Romans themselves. Blinded by the ideals set before us by poets and writers anxious to disguise abuses, the student sometimes forgets the sordid financial facts that lay behind the Roman domination of the world. The vindictive outburst of a Christian visionary is a valuable corrective (Revelation 18:11–17, New English Bible):

> The merchants of the earth also will weep and mourn for her, because no one any longer buys their cargoes, cargoes of gold and silver, jewels and pearls, clothes of purple and scarlet, silks and fine linens; all kinds of scented woods, ivories, and every sort of thing made of

---

[1] Cf. D. Comparetti, *Virgilio nel medio evo* (repr. Florence 1937); K. Borinski, *Die Antike in Poetik und Kunsttheorie vom Ausgang des klassischen Altertums bis auf Goethe und Wilhelm von Humboldt*, Bd. 1–2 (Berlin 1914–1921); G. Voigt, *Die Wiederbelebung des classischen Altertums oder das erste Jahrhundert des Humanismus* (Berlin 1893); B. Weinberg, *History of Literary Criticism in the Italian Renaissance* (Chicago 1961); Ralph C. Williams, *The Theory of the Heroic Epic in Italian Criticism of the 16 C.* (diss. Johns Hopkins 1917); G. B. Townend, "Changing Views of Virgil's Greatness," *Classical Journal* LVI (1960–61), 67–77.

costly woods, bronze, iron, or marble; cinnamon and spice, incense, perfumes and frankincense; wine, oil, flour and wheat, sheep and cattle, horses, chariots, slaves, and the lives of men. 'The fruit you longed for,' they will say, 'is gone from you; all the glitter and the glamour are lost, never to be yours again!' The traders in all these wares, who gained their wealth from her, will stand at a distance from horror at her torment, weeping and mourning and saying, 'Alas, alas for the great city, that was clothed in fine linen and purple and scarlet, bedizened with gold and jewels and pearls! Alas that in one hour so much wealth should be laid waste!'

The modern historian hastens to confirm the apocalyptic dream.[2] The conquest of the Mediterranean, essentially completed with the destruction of Carthage in 146 B.C., had brought untold wealth to fill the coffers of Rome, large amounts of which, both in coin and artistic treasures, had been diverted to build or adorn the mansions of the powerful. Laboring under impositions and exactions of the most outrageous kind, the once-proud cities of the eastern Mediterranean were sunk in ruin and degradation. Even the agriculture of that region had decayed to such an extent that nations which once supplied oil and wine to the rest of mankind were now forced to import those commodities from Italy.

Within Italy itself, heartless confiscations from the free but poor farmers, ruthless exploitation of the slave gangs, lavish political bribery, cynicism, manipulation of religious beliefs for ulterior motives, bloody proscription and massacre, profiteering, disregard for the law, had become the norm. From such wrongs not only Virgil's own family and township, but Horace and Propertius too, had suffered.

Materialism wrought spiritual chaos. The ancient religion of Roman peasants, never meant to provide a rationale of empire, had shown its inadequacy as early as the days of the Second Punic War. Its gaps were filled by the wildest superstitions imported from the very East where Roman depredation had induced desolation and despair. Among the more educated, we find the astonishing paradox that, in an Italy for which imperial opportunity seemed limitless, the Epicurean philosophy, preaching withdrawal and quietism, made widespread converts. One of the most notable literary monuments of Virgil's youth was a poetic restatement of these tenets of austere tranquillity. One of his teachers was the Epicurean Siro.

There had been, when it all began, gleams of a different dawn.

---

[2] Cf. *Histoire Romaine*, vol. II, part 1, by Gustave Bloch and Jérôme Carcopino (3rd ed., Paris 1952), esp. ch. III; M. Rostovtzeff, *Rome* (repr. New York 1960), esp. pp. 146 ff.; K. Latte, *Römische Religionsgeschichte* (Munich 1960), pp. 264 ff.

The clash between Rome and Carthage was one of those elemental struggles, to be repeated at Tours or Vienna, where it may be said that more than self-interest was engaged. If Rome was to push its way into the Mediterranean world, it had to break the stranglehold of the Carthaginian trade state. The Sicilian Greeks had been only partially successful in this. The outbreak of the Second Punic War was a continuation of their struggle to assert different values, to set Zeus and Apollo against Moloch and Baal. For their victory, eventually the Romans paid dearly. But, in that first flush of triumph, when Hasdrubal's head was tossed brutally into his brother's camp, when the elephants were routed on the field of Zama, the possibilities suddenly appeared infinite.

Ennius, who had himself fought with distinction in Sardinia, showed genius in channeling the potential of the moment into epic.[3] Borrowing Greek rhetoric and Greek philosophy, he expelled the native Saturnian meter, which had already done duty in a previous generation for Naevius' poetic account of Roman history, culminating in the First Punic War. The Greek hexameter which replaced it was for Rome a new verse intended to symbolize a new age. Consuls and tribunes, elevated to the status of Homeric heroes, were to have dangled before them the prospect of divinity itself, if they would but serve their country like Scipio, the conqueror of Hannibal. This potential for mythic renewal, familiar to contemporary Greek sensibility, struck an answering chord deep in the Roman psyche. The poet did not see that, while rival vied with rival for power and glory, these battles of would-be gods were to crush the commonwealth he prized so highly, or that the boundless ambition which his promises would provoke could not fail to bring forth in due time a Caesar.

## I

Alexandrian Greek poetry, typified by Callimachus, had already found this bombast unpalatable. When Virgil was young, as social problems multiplied, Roman reaction against Ennius had already begun. The satirist Lucilius had pushed him into the category of the inimitable. Accius had impudently borrowed Ennius' title *Annales* for a work that looks suspiciously like a Roman version of Callimachus' *Aetia*.[4] Newer poetry was dominated by a school of Alexandrianizing writers who all tended to come from the same part of the world—North

[3] He also of course robbed Latin poetry of the critical stance it had assumed in Naevius, who ended his life in exile. Whether Roman society could afford to do without such criticism is another matter. Cf. "Ennius the Mystic—III," *Greece and Rome* XIV (March 1967), 50.

[4] C. Buechner, *Fragmenta Poetarum Latinorum* (2nd ed., Leipzig 1982), fr. 3, p. 47.

Italy or Cisalpine Gaul—and who owed some sort of literary allegiance to the critic P. Valerius Cato. So much of their writing has now vanished that our attempts to reconstruct their activities from a few pitiful fragments are inevitably incomplete and illusory. One slim volume does survive, the *libellus* of Catullus.

This is a poetry which speaks to us with so direct a voice at times that its total message is easily misunderstood. All the world loves a lover, and the heart that goes out to the young provincial exploited by the aristocratic harpy (in the usual reconstruction) may not take with it the reader's mind. Those pieces that stand at the center of the collection as it has come down to us, where clearly metrical and formal considerations have determined the arrangement, may be rather neglected as mere experiments.

It is fatal to this point of view that poem 68, one of the most artificial in its structure,[5] is one that treats the poet's love for both his mistress and his brother, matters of the most personal and pressing intimacy. But the poem also universalizes the personal. Greek myth is made to illustrate a Roman dilemma, the inability of the writer to enjoy anything except a borrowed *domus* and a make-believe *domina*. Poetry is the only escape.

The division so often made between the lover and the poet, between the love-poet and the Alexandrian, will not do. There is no reliable means of placing the poems in chronological sequence of composition. In such an art (one remembers Petrarch's *Canzoniere*) would such anatomy be in point? Catullus was the same writer when he was fascinated by Callimachus as he was when he was fascinated by his *puella*.

The effort to wean Catullus—or that part of Catullus that was arbitrarily defined as worth reading—away from Callimachus was based on a theory of poetry which is now itself seen to be, in its conscious anti-intellectualism, inadequate and ill-conceived.[6] Classical scholars who subscribed to it, and to a naive view of Rome, were eager to find a healthy style which could be contrasted with the

---

[5] This has often been noticed: see, for example, C. J. Fordyce's edition (repr. Oxford 1968), p. 344. The interesting point is that this technique is Pindaric: L. Illig, *Zur Form der Pindarischen Erzählung*, pp. 56 ff. W. Schadewaldt says (*Iliasstudien*, p. 84) that it is in all archaic poetry, including Hesiod. S. Eisenstein notes it in Leonardo: *The Film Sense*, tr. J. Leyda, pp. 24 ff.

[6] C. K. Stead's *The New Poetic* (London 1967), by reminding us of the atmosphere prevailing in English poetry at the turn of this century, has done a great deal to illumine the aesthetic background controlling the appreciation of the classical poets at that time. We must not forget either the public school ethos as it degenerated into the unrelieved and boorish snobbery against which there were so many rebels (the Sitwells, Orwell). There were *George Brown's Schooldays* (Bruce Marshall) as well as Tom Brown's.

stifling bookishness of Alexandria. Ennius they guessed rightly to
have been no Alexandrian.[7] He therefore was cast as the father of a
genuinely Roman, epic poetry, whose next legitimate exponent was
Lucretius. Catullus could be fitted into this scheme at the side, as
the author of a few beautiful love lyrics and not much else, whose
aberrancies could be excused by his youth.

The assumption that because Ennius was not Alexandrian (though
he flirted with Alexandrian language) he must have been wholly
Roman is staggeringly naive. Here was a poet who drove out whatever
patrons of verse earlier Rome had had, and replaced them with the
Muses, who were uncompromisingly set to dance on the Greek Mount
Olympus. The epic paraphernalia which his major poem deployed,
decked out with all the flowers of the most modern rhetoric, was
intended to serve a wholly Greek purpose of offering apotheosis to
the great. This apotheosis was conceived in Greek (Homeric/Hellen-
istic) terms, as admission to a pantheon. The blow to native Roman
religion, and to *mores antiqui*, was deadly.

From the revolutionary twist thus given to the essentially comic
genius of Rome we are expected to construct a conservative, "Roman"
style of poetry, which next found epic utterance in Lucretius. It is
true that Lucretius expresses admiration for Ennius (I. 117 ff.):

> Ennius ut noster cecinit, qui primus amoeno
> Detulit ex Helicone perenni fronde coronam,
> Per gentis Italas hominum quae clara clueret;
> Etsi praeterea tamen esse Acherusia templa
> Ennius aeternis exponit versibus edens,
> Quo neque permaneant animae neque corpora nostra,
> Sed quaedam simulacra modis pallentia miris;
> Unde sibi exortam semper florentis Homeri
> Commemorat speciem lacrimas effundere salsas
> Coepisse et rerum naturam expandere dictis.

So Ennius sang, who first brought down from lovely Helicon a garland
of undying leaves, to spread its bright fame through the peoples of
Italy. Yet Ennius goes on to relate in his immortal verses that there
is a realm of Acheron. Our spirits and bodies do not persist there,
but rather certain images mysteriously pale. From there he tells how
the ghost of ever-flourishing Homer rose up before him, and began
amid salty tears to expound the nature of the world.

[7] The poet was certainly Hellenistic (K. Ziegler, *Das hellenistische Epos*, pp. 53 ff.),
and he may have borrowed some Callimachean and Alexandrian flummery from the
poetic fashions of his time, but the basic conception of his work—the long epic in
many thousands of verses taking an admiring view of "kings and heroes" (consuls
and tribunes)—is anti-Callimachean.

But then so does Propertius, who claimed to be the Roman Callimachus (III. 3. 1 ff.):

> Visus eram molli recubans Heliconis in umbra,
> Bellerophontei qua fluit umor equi,
> Reges, Alba, tuos et regum facta tuorum,
> Tantum operis, nervis hiscere posse meis;
> Parvaque tam magnis admoram fontibus ora,
> Unde pater sitiens Ennius ante bibit;[8]
> Et cecinit Curios fratres et Horatia pila,
> Regiaque Aemilia vecta tropaea rate . . .

I lay in a dream in Helicon's soft shade, where the spring of Hippocrene
flows. It seemed as if I could utter on my strong strings so lofty a
theme as Alba's kings and their deeds. Yes, I had brought my feeble
lips close to such mighty founts, whence father Ennius slaked his thirst
of old, and sang of the brothers Curii, the javelins of the Horatii, and
the royal trophies borne away on Aemilius' ship.[9]

No hyperbole of conventional language would ever persuade the
reader that Propertius had the slightest intention of taking Ennius
as a literary model. Why then must we give any greater weight to
Lucretius' words?

The question just raised is important because it illustrates something
of great relevance to all discussion of ancient literature and its
tradition, but particularly perhaps to epic. Over the genuine belief
of the poet lies a conventional set of literary symbols, dictating his
method of expression. It is essential to understand some of the
polarities into which this inherited and sometimes rather inapposite
language may force discussion.

One such polarity pits love against (cyclic) epic.[10] This may ultimately be traced back to one of Callimachus' epigrams (28), and to
the Preface to the *Aetia*, with its contemptuous rejection of verses in
their thousands about kings and heroes in favor of the new inspiration

---

[8] Propertius makes Ennius drink water from Hippocrene, i.e. turns him into an
Alexandrian version of Hesiod. Contrast Horace, *Epp.* I. 19. 7–8 (*Numquam nisi
potus*). See below, note 44, and p. 371 and note 67.

[9] See HELICON, HESIODIC EPIC, RECUSATIO, WATER-DRINKERS in the *Glossary of Critical
Terms.*

[10] In speaking of literary convention, we should also observe the force of *orbem*
at Prop. III. 2. 1. Propertius pretends that his admiration for epic is so great as to
make his own poetry merely "routine." He does this by applying to himself the terms
of contempt (*orbis* = *kyklos*: cf. Horace, *A. P.* 132) which he would normally reserve
for his epic opponents. He has no thought of inventing any other literary terminology
beside the Alexandrian. These debates operate in fact with remarkably limited
vocabulary: cf. Ariosto, *O. F.* XXXIV. 77, where the cicada, for Callimachus the
Alexandrian ideal (*Aet.-Pref.* 1. 30), becomes the despised court poet.

from Apollo, and the humble, child-like style.[11] This formula may
lead the Alexandrian poet to pose as the unassuming author of trivia,
deferentially yielding the palm to his loud-mouthed rival, while he
himself courts a less clamant Muse. That it is dangerous to take this
pose seriously is proved by Dante's example.[12] A particular gambit
in this poetic chess has been called the *recusatio* or "refusal poem."
The Alexandrian author "refuses" to tackle the grand genre of epic
eulogy because of his alleged inability. "Meanwhile" he offers something else, a second best. But we must not mistake this politeness for
reality. One such "something else" is the *Georgics!*[13]

What then shall we make of Propertius, when he writes of "father
Ennius" and speaks with apparent nostalgia of the grand old themes
of history? He too is simply ringing changes on the *recusatio* topos,
and certainly not committing himself to the suggestion that Ennius
was his superior. He spells this out quite bluntly in his next book,
where he does take up certain themes which might be thought to
have something in common with Ennius (IV. 1. 61–64):

> Ennius hirsuta cingat sua dicta corona:
>   Mi folia ex hedera porrige, Bacche, tua,
> Ut nostris tumefacta superbiat Umbria libris,
>   Umbria Romani patria Callimachi!

Let Ennius garland his words with a shaggy crown! Give me, Bacchus,
leaves from your ivy! Then Umbria will swell with pride at my books,
Umbria, birthplace of the Roman Callimachus!

Lucretius, in whom the Alexandrian element is too often ignored
or underplayed, must be treated with something of the same caution.
Ennius is certainly complimented by him. But the compliment takes
a curious form. Lucretius tells us that Ennius was "the first to bring
down from lovely Helicon a garland of undying leaves, to spread its
bright fame through the peoples of Italy." This is only partially a
paraphrase of Ennius' own claims to fame, and to have superseded
the work of Naevius.[14] Where in Ennius do we find, for example,
any reference to Helicon? It was of Olympus that the old poet had

---

[11] Cf. Ovid, *Rem. Am.* 381–82 (*Achilles/Cydippe*), and 759 (*Callimachus/amor*).
Callimachus himself had contrasted kings and heroes with his own "infancy" (*Aet.-
pref.* fr. 1. 3–6, Pf.). See also epigram 28, where the allusion to cyclic poetry triggers
a theme of love.

[12] The poet develops this antithesis, for example, in *Donne ch'avete*: see below, p.
256.

[13] On the *recusatio* see W. Wimmel, *Kallimachos in Rom* (Wiesbaden 1960), pp. 167
ff. Lucilius seems already to have used the characteristic *interea*: Marx, frr. 1086–87.
Cf. also Marx 612, *veterem historiam*: M. Puelma Piwonka, *Lucilius und Kallimachos*,
pp. 145 ff.

[14] *Annales* I. frr. 1 ff.; VII. frr. 231–32 (Warmington).

spoken in his proem. Helicon was peculiarly associated, not with Homer, of whom Ennius claimed to be the reincarnation, but with Hesiod. This clue explains the origin of the garland, of which again there seems to have been nothing in Ennius himself. When the Muses had finished speaking to Hesiod on Mount Helicon in the *Theogony*, they presented him with a "staff, a shoot of evergreen laurel."[15] From laurel staff to laurel wreath is no long distance.[16]

The paradox arises that even the second Homer, Ennius, is lauded by Lucretius in Alexandrian, Hesiodic terms. In the same context of Book I, Ennius is praised for being *primus*. Whatever its other connotations,[17] this is also Alexandrian. Callimachus had been urged by Apollo to follow untrodden paths in the Preface to the *Aetia* (25 ff.).[18]

The wholly Alexandrian cast of Lucretius' remarks about epic may be illustrated further. Even Homer himself, according to a later book, possesses the same Hesiodic qualities as Ennius. The poet is pointing out that all must die (III. 1036–38):

> Adde repertores doctrinarum atque leporum,
> Adde[19] Heliconiadum comites, quorum unus Homerus
> Sceptra potitus eadem aliis sopitus quiete est.

> Consider further the inventors of learning and delight, yes, the companions of the Muses of Helicon, whose unique prince Homer, with his scepter, slumbers at rest like everyone else.

"The inventors of learning and delight"—could there be a more Alexandrian phrase for "scholar-poets," whether we think of the implications in this context of *doctrina, lepos*, or *repertor?*[20] "Companions of the *Heliconian* maidens" puts poets, and Homer among them, into Hesiodic company. When Homer is made to hold a scepter, the allusion to the *Theogony* is unmistakable. In Lucretius, Homer still enjoys pre-eminence. In the time of Quintus Smyrnaeus, Hesiod will have become the patron even of Homerizing epic.[21]

It is only to be expected therefore that, when Lucretius speaks of

---

[15] *Theogony* 30.

[16] Cf. A. Kambylis, *Die Dichterweihe und ihre Symbolik* (Heidelberg 1965), pp. 173 ff.

[17] Some of Lucretius' *primus*-language may have been directly Epicurean: K. Büchner, *Lukrez und Vorklassik* (Wiesbaden 1964), pp. 7 ff.

[18] Cf. the paraphrases in Oppian Apam., *Cynegetica* I. 20–21; Oppian Anazarb., *Halieutica* IV. 68; and compare Pindar, *Paean* VIIb. 11, Sn.–M.

[19] I take it that *adde* here is resumptive, and that the second clause defines and climaxes the first.

[20] Cf. Horace, *A. P.* 77–78.

[21] Cf. XII. 306 ff., where Quintus quotes *Aetia* 2. 1 Pf. Silius Italicus had already eulogized Ennius in Hesiodic terms: *Punica* XII. 408 ff.

his own poetic ambitions, he should use Alexandrian vocabulary. In Book IV, for example, he promises to discuss sleep (IV. 907 ff.: cf. IV. 182 ff.):

> Nunc quibus ille modis somnus per membra quietem
> Irriget atque animi curas e pectore solvat
> Suavidicis potius quam multis versibus edam;
> Parvus ut est cycni melior canor, ille gruum quam
> Clamor in aetherii dispersus nubibus austri.
> Tu mihi da tenuis aures. . . .

Now for an explanation of the ways in which rest sheds sleep over our limbs, driving torment of mind from our breasts. This I will expound in sweetly speaking rather than in many verses. The tiny song of the swan is better than the clamor of cranes echoing in the clouds brought on by the stormy south wind. Your task is to lend me responsive ears.

What he is doing is to paraphrase an epigram from the Greek Anthology in praise of the *Distaff* of Erinna. Her three hundred verses are compared with Homer, not to their discredit.[22] The thought itself is obviously owed to Callimachus' Preface to the *Aetia*. Lucretius' language here naturally teems with Alexandrian catchwords: *suavidicis*, coined perhaps for the occasion, contrasts with *multis*; the humble song of the swan with the noise of the cranes; even the *tenuis aures* are Callimachean.[23]

At the start of the same book, repeating a passage from Book I in a way that suggests interesting experimentation with the Homeric manner, he had used more Alexandrian phrases (IV. 1 ff.: cf. I. 926 ff.):

> Avia Pieridum peragro loca, nullius ante
> Trita solo. Iuvat integros accedere fontis
> Atque haurire, iuvatque novos decerpere flores
> Insignemque meo capiti petere inde coronam
> Unde prius nulli velarint tempora Musae.

Trackless are the haunts of the Muses that I traverse, trodden as yet by no man's foot. I long to approach untouched springs and drink from them, to pluck fresh flowers and to seek for my head a garland of fame whence the Muses have crowned no man's temples before.

"Trodden as yet by no man's foot" here is a direct echo of Calli-

---

[22] *The Greek Anthology: Hellenistic Epigrams*, ed. A. S. F. Gow and D. L. Page (Cambridge 1965), p. 30.

[23] Cf. "De verbis *canere* et *dicere* eorumque apud poetas latinos usque ad Augusti aetatem usu," *Latinitas* 2 (1965), 100–01, and "Pushkin and Horace," *Neohelicon* III (1975), p. 333 note 5.

machus' "untrodden." Once again, we have the claims to priority and novelty, which are ultimately Callimachean, and the garland, which is ultimately Hesiodic. The precise significance of the drinking from the fountain is obscured by a literary (and typically Roman) looseness of thought. Hesiod did not speak of himself as drinking from any fountain, and Callimachus may have referred merely to dreaming *by* the fountain of Hippocrene. As time passed, and as the Callimacheans acquired the older sobriquet of "water-drinkers" from their opponents, in allusion to the puritanical rigors of their stylistic and scholarly standards, the details of the poetic symbolism that had opened the *Aetia* faded in memory, and the obvious thing to do with the fountain that had appeared there was to let the poet drink from it. Clearly we cannot read any *anti*-Callimachean meaning into Lucretius' drinking. Propertius did exactly the same, and an epigram in the *Greek Anthology* makes Hesiod do it too.[24]

Is this then the evidence for that "Roman" tradition of epic, dear to the hearts of the old-fashioned, stemming from Ennius, expounded by Lucretius, and ultimately triumphing (though not for long!) in Virgil? Virgil's task would have been very much simpler if such a tradition had existed. He admired Lucretius and, in his way, Ennius, profoundly. But the relevance of those two poets to his task was extremely doubtful. Could he claim, as Ennius might have done, that Caesar, whether Julius or Octavian, had been a new Achilles? Could he take a naively optimistic view of ever-expanding conquest, presided over by a selfless Senate and people?

In the event, he did not. A particularly telling example of his difference from Ennius lies in his treatment of the murder of Remus by Romulus. Ovid, rushing in where angels might fear to tread, shifts the blame for the crime to some noble of the day (just as Livy made the miscreant an unknown member of the crowd), and puts into Romulus' mouth a tearful speech of regret. Virgil, more aware of human sins, accepting by implication the fratricide, insists on the need for reconciliation both in direct and indirect allusion to Ennius. He wants no repetition of the old pattern. "And you first . . . cast down the weapons from your hand, blood of mine!" is Anchises' anguished cry to Julius Caesar. It was hardly the triumphant celebration of might as right which we should expect from the *Annales*.[25]

For his part, Lucretius had performed an extraordinary paradox.

---

[24] E.g. *Anth. Pal.* VII. 55. 5–6: cf. Kambylis, *op. cit.*, pp. 191 ff. and Wimmel, *op. cit.*, pp. 222 ff.
[25] Cf. *Augustus and the New Poetry*, pp. 82 ff.

Starting from a philosophy that despised poetry,[26] and preached freedom from any disturbing influence, he had generated a charged, unquiet epic that grips attention by denying its own ideals. Interpreters have made much of the "anti-Lucretius in Lucretius." But the anti-Lucretius is not there by accident, by some poetic loss of control. It is Lucretius. The poet has fissured his own atomic world. On one side of the chasm rises the majestically unapproachable figure of Epicurus who, even if he was a god, has vanished now from the realms of light. On the other, the poet's own shaping personality, ambitious, martial, sensitive, sexually aware, displays all the imperfections of unconverted humanity. In the last book, the pathetic polarity is forced even more dramatically upon the reader, as Athens plunges from center and home of civilization to victim of gruesome disease.

In Alexandria, it had been Callimachus who had defended the expository epic against the attacks of Praxiphanes. Lucretius has transformed the genre illustrated by Aratus into the medium for his own pathos. He uses Epicurean doctrine as Pindar uses myth, or Dante uses the teachings of Christianity. It forms a sounding board against which his own music plays all the louder. It is clear why such a poetry would attract Virgil. But its value as a guide to an epic with a "positive hero" (to use the Soviet term) was small. Only slowly would the realization come that even an Aeneas must be a Jason, reluctant and confused, owing his success to a power outside himself.

Virgil's dilemma therefore, when he assessed the possibilities of epic right at the beginning of his career, was grave. It is interesting that he should have turned briefly at this time to the Ennian tradition.[27] The simplistic terms in which the Roman Alexandrianizing poets had viewed Callimachus' relationship to his enemies were clearly paramount in his thoughts. Callimachus himself had protested that the criterion by which poetry should be judged was not length but art. The corollary of this position was that an artistic short poem had a

[26] Epicurean anti-intellectualism is noted by J. F. D'Alton, *Roman Literary Theory and Criticism* (repr. New York 1962), pp. 159–60, and F. Copleston, *A History of Philosophy*: Volume I, Part II (repr. New York 1962), p. 146. Metrodorus, Epicurus' disciple, remarked that "It need not trouble anyone if he had never read a line of Homer, and did not know whether Hector was a Trojan or a Greek." The *De Morte* of Varius may have shown Epicurean influence (H. Bardon, *La littérature latine inconnue* [Paris 1956], II, pp. 28 ff.). In that case, its disappearance suggests how little such influence could help the would-be epic writer. Virgil had Epicurean beginnings (*Catal.* 5: Probus, *Vita* 11, Hardie), but he had to grow beyond them to show Dido's shortcomings.

[27] *Vit. Donat.* 19. See Wimmel, *op. cit.*, pp. 132 ff. on the opening of *Eclogue* 6. Dante, Ariosto and Milton, like Virgil, all took time to find their appropriate, and Alexandrian, epic medium.

better claim to fame than an inartistic long one. The Romans, less subtle, had twisted this to mean that only the short poem was worthy of mention.[28] They had the excuse that to write a really long poem with an acceptable degree of finished elegance (*arida modo pumice expolitum*—"freshly polished by the dry pumice stone" [Catullus]; *exactus tenui pumice*—"finely finished by the thin pumice stone" [Propertius]) was for them more or less impossible. It must have been the Aristotelian idea that length was in some way a necessary condition of great art which led the young and aspiring Virgil to conclude that, if he were to do justice to the ambitions stirring within him, he would have to turn against the prevailing literary tide of the late Republic and look back to the cyclic epic and Ennius. Perhaps he felt in the enthusiasm of that assertive discourse a source of energy that would dispel contemporary uncertainty and re-affirm the elemental truths of Roman mission. Perhaps it was the typical sequence of literary inheritance from grandsire rather than father. Perhaps it was the time-honored and obvious way of making himself useful to the new Caesar.

It was however one thing to admire Ennius' faith, and another to share it. Roman life, departing so plainly and so far from early ideals, Roman death, inflicted by fellow-Roman upon fellow-Roman and Italian alike, prevented any straight heroic account of the events of the last fifty years which might have paralleled the chronological narrative of the *Annales*. "Disgusted by his theme," Virgil passed instead to the *Bucolics*.

## II

In his account of Pope's development, Johnson writes that it is not surprising that the poet should have begun with the pastoral style, since it made so few demands upon experience.[29] But what is valuable about Virgil's experiments with the pastoral is precisely the poet's effort to come to terms with experience through it.

Two points are initially important. The *Eclogues*, as these poems have come to be commonly known, were not merely "imitations" of Theocritus; and they are not to be separated from the rest of Virgil's work.[30]

---

[28] Wimmel, *op. cit.*, pp. 128 ff. See NEOTERIC SIMPLIFICATION in the *Glossary of Critical Terms*.

[29] Cf. his verdict on Milton's *Lycidas*, "easy, vulgar and therefore disgusting." There are further remarks of the kind towards the end of the *Life* of Pope.

[30] Both points are made by F. Klingner, *Römische Geisteswelt* (4th ed., Munich 1961), pp. 274 ff. and in *L'influence grecque sur la poésie latine de Catulle à Ovide* (Entretiens Hardt, Geneva 1953), pp. 132 ff.

They are not merely imitations of Theocritus because this description misses the complexity of the Greek comic/bucolic tradition.
Especially do we fail to find in Virgil any of Theocritus' lively humor,
or indeed any of that supreme sense of long growth which gives such
security to Greek achievement. From Theocritus' rich variety, which
contains some of the most beautiful poetry in Greek, Virgil has made
a narrow choice. Partly this was because the Greek bucolic itself, as
it was transmuted in the hands of Bion and Moschus, limited both
its range and its tone. The distance preserved by Theocritus, essential
if the poet was to use his material rather than be used by it, began
to vanish. The theme of the lover's pangs and his forever unrequited
sufferings was treated with a mawkish sentimentality that recalls the
tone of Meleager's Heliodora epigrams. This was the "modern"
bucolic which Virgil knew. It is this lachrymosity that informs the
*Eclogues*, though we see their author's genius fighting to transform it.

Vital evidence for this battle has only recently been recovered
from the rubbish dump of Qaṣr Ibrîm.[31] The poet Cornelius Gallus,
author of four books of *Amores*, exercised an extraordinary fascination
upon the shy and reclusive Virgil. It was evidently the attraction of
opposite temperaments. Gallus was an engineer, a general, eventually,
in a dizzying promotion for one of humble family, Viceroy of Egypt.
There he proved unable to hold his tongue at the dinner-table, and
after he was summoned by Octavian to Rome to explain his language,
he committed suicide.

His flamboyant temperament, if we may judge by the fragment
now recovered, also made him a master of pathetic structure. The
lines recently found set up constant polarities: the poet/Lycoris; the
poet/Caesar; Lycoris/Caesar; sad/sweet; Roman history/part of Roman history. In striking assonance Gallus visualizes the temples of
many gods which Caesar will make richer with his spoils "after [his]
return." This concept of "return" is itself religious. Gallus' fate will
change from sad to sweet when it takes place. The paradox is violent,
the flattery worthy of Statius' *Silvae*.

In the fragment, Gallus makes two assertions. The first is that
history is something that must be left to the Caesar who will be the
greatest part of it. Gallus himself will not make history. Rather he

---

[31] On the new fragment, first published by Anderson, Parsons, Nisbet (*Journal of
Roman Studies* LXIX [1979], 140), see my articles in *Latinitas* XXVIII. 2 (1980),
83–94, and in *Illinois Classical Studies* IX. 1 (1984), 19–29. David O. Ross, *Backgrounds
to Augustan Poetry* (Cambridge 1975), offers a somewhat different interpretation of
Gallus' work from mine. Propertius happily confounds Virgil with Theocritus in II.
34. 67 ff., and this suggests the risks inherent in reconstructing Gallus from Virgil.

will "read" the temples which Caesar by his victories is to make richer.

The second is that he has indeed written something, "worthy of his mistress." It is on these poems that he asks to be judged.

This is the characteristic shape of what has earlier been noted as the ancient "refusal poem," first outlined by Callimachus. The Roman satirist Lucilius had already made on Callimachus' forthright rejection of Homerizing epic a typically Roman, typically fuzzing gloss. Grand epic was no longer inadmissible in itself. It was something to be held in reserve for a better poet, or a better day. Gallus brilliantly adapts the topos by referring "history," for Callimachus the subject matter of the despised Choerilus of Samos, to Caesar himself.

Caesar himself thus becomes a kind of author, and what he writes will be the inscriptions on the temples which commemorate his achievements. Gallus foresees that he will (admiringly) read these honorific claims. He certainly made them for himself when he was governor of Egypt, and "Caesar" (Octavian) certainly made them too.

What Gallus has written is not however contemptible. The Muses themselves have made his poems, for him to declare them worthy of his mistress. We seem to find in this last passage an excessively Alexandrian preoccupation by the poet with securing good reviews from the critics. One's impression is not so much of an irresistible passion pouring itself out in strains of unpremeditated art, as of calculation. Gallus lavishes flattery of a religious kind on the man who can make his career. The wantonness of his mistress is partly foil to this positive theme, and partly a method of displaying his own poetic art.

That poetic art shows Gallus to have been engrossed, not so much in his mistress, as in himself. Lycoris was a convenient excuse for harping on his own sorrows. He was too much in love with his own personal ambitions to have much time for the love of a woman, and even perhaps eventually for the love of the Muse. In this sense, his "subjectivity" ultimately negated rather than defined his art. It was useful for him to be able to disarm criticism by casting himself in the comic role of the frustrated lover. But this staged *hypocrisis* must not be mistaken for "true confession." Against Lycoris' *nequitia* (she was already politically tainted by her association with Mark Antony, and *nequitia* is a term of political condemnation here, as it is in Cicero) could be set the glorious promise of the new regime.

The new fragment is so illuminating that we wish we had more. Fruitful comparison between some of Gallus' other, less combative and self-seeking elegiac lamentations, inspired by his love for Lycoris, and Virgil's adaptations of them in the *Eclogues*, might have quickened our appreciation of the new voice in Latin poetry. What Quintilian meant by calling Gallus *durior* than the surviving Augustan elegists is not clear. "Harsher" perhaps in technique, more akin to the Lucilian satire out of which the Roman love elegy grew. Perhaps "heavier," more like Euphorion, the later Alexandrian poet whose tone Gallus was said to have particularly followed, in broad emotional coloring. If Servius is right in saying that Virgil has largely paraphrased some of the lost elegies in certain of his hexameters, they will contain an essential clue to Virgil's development into an epic poet.

There are two particular eclogues that pay tribute to the poet's friendship for Gallus. They frame the second half of the book. The tenth, which concludes, evokes a scene made familiar by Milton, and perhaps ultimately derived from the *Prometheus Bound*. The figure of Prometheus/Jason has already caught our attention in Apollonius' *Argonautica*. The suffering lover elicits the sympathy of a series of visitors. When Virgil writes: "Let us sing of Gallus' troubled passion" (*amores*, v. 6), we seem to have a reliable key to the kind of elegies Gallus wrote. In them, as the new fragment confirms, it is not Lycoris in herself, but Lycoris as she impinges upon the poet's psyche, who is important.

In that case, it is interesting that *Eclogue* 10 should be a tissue of Alexandrian themes.[32] All nature weeps to find Gallus perishing of love: the laurels, the tamarisks, the mountains of Arcadia. The very sheep stand around, with the shepherds and swineherds. Apollo, Silvanus and Pan remind the poet that Love cares nothing for such complaints as his.

Gallus sadly replies with the wish that one day the shepherds' pipe might sing of his love. If only he could be a shepherd or vinedresser himself! He could perhaps have found consolation with a rustic sweetheart. But it was not to be so. He is a soldier, and meanwhile his beloved has deserted him, going off to face the cold Alps and the icy Rhine. Perhaps he will join the shepherds after all; but then perhaps he won't, since it is all to no avail against Love. "Love conquers all things: let us too yield to Love."

The charm of such a piece is certainly not to be described as "knockout," dear to "Longinus". Yet it demands an appreciation that is fundamental to the study of Alexandrian poetry in certain of its forms. We are not to forget that "Gallus" here is a literary construct, a fantasy. Beautifully and melodiously he gives expression to emotions that are exploited within well-defined limits. In this kind of poetry, expression is more than thought. We could be listening to an operatic

---

[32] Cf. Bion's *Adonis* 31 ff., 87 ff., and E. R. Curtius, *Europäische Literatur und lateinisches Mittelalter*, p. 99.

aria from Gluck or Puccini, and we need the same sense of make-believe to enjoy it.[33]

*Eclogue* 10 makes use of typically elegiac themes. Lycoris has gone off with her lover to the cold north, just like Cynthia in Propertius. Gallus attempts to console himself in the countryside by carving his beloved's name on the trees, as does Acontius in Callimachus' *Aetia*. He has been foolish enough to enlist as a soldier. The contrast between the delights of peace and the horrors of war is another theme he shares with both Propertius and Tibullus. He wonders if hunting might help him to forget, and echoes ideas as old as those of the love-sick Phaedra in Euripides' *Hippolytus*. Eventually, he resigns himself to the all-mastery of Love. It was the elegant expression of a topos that had lost its power to surprise.[34]

The Formalist critics have pointed out the dangers of topos criticism.[35] In seeking the lowest common denominator between different literary creations, it tends to overlook the differing functions which the same material may fulfill inside differently structured entities. Virgil's eclogue is more than a mere paraphrase of Gallus' or others' elegiac clichés.

The poet begins and ends by *commenting* on his theme, as his meter, not elegiac, does anyway. He opens by reminding us of the artificiality of poetry, using Alexandrian terms. His eclogue is an *extremus labor*, "a supreme effort." The noun indicates the conscious creative energy without which the Alexandrians could not accept poetry's value.[36] The adjective suggests both culmination and finality. *Pauca* ("few things") is another Alexandrian code word of the same sort.[37]

The excuse for the poetry is that of friendship, but, like Dante in "Donne, ch'avete . . . ," Virgil has a feminine sensibility in mind. His verse is to be read by Lycoris. Evidently, here he is picking up a

[33] When we say this, we should remember how much lyricism is here combined with prosaic or colloquial elements: e.g. *cantare periti* in v. 32, a prosaic adjective with a Greek epexegetical infinitive. The use of parenthesis is noted as colloquial by J. B. Hofmann, *Lateinische Umgangssprache* (Heidelberg 1951), pp. 114 ff.

[34] "Elegant" because of the polyptoton, in love poetry at least as old an Anacreon (Page, *Poetae Melici Graeci*, p. 183). Curtius describes what became of the topos later: *op. cit.*, pp. 132 ff. P. Dronke, "Motifs and Images" in *Medieval Latin Love-Poetry* (Oxford 1968), pp. 599 ff., offers comparative material. Other precedents to "Gallus' " lament may be noted in Gow on Theocritus 18. 47; Prop. I. 8a; Prop. III. 4 and 5 and Tibullus I. 10; Euripides, *Hippolytus* 215 ff.; [Tib.] 4. 3; Ovid, *Rem. Am.* 199 ff.

[35] Cf. Yu. Tynianov in *Théorie de la littérature*, ed. Todorov, pp. 19, 136.

[36] Cf. πολλὰ μογήσας ("with much toil") in Philetas (J. U. Powell, *Collectanea Alexandrina*, p. 92, no. 10, 3–4): Herodas VIII. 71; M. Puelma Piwonka, *Lucilius und Kallimachos*, pp. 125 ff.; Gow on Theocritus VII. 51.

[37] Callimachus, fr. 1. 9 with Pfeiffer's notes; Puelma, p. 119.

theme from Gallus himself. Arethusa, nymph of a Syracusan spring, is asked for her aid. Fleeing from her watery lover, she might lose her identity—the characteristically Virgilian theme—in that of the embittered matron, Doris. A long and powerful verb, *intermisceat,* makes the point. Virgil prays that this will not happen.

The continual repetition of Gallus' name in this proem is certainly a rhetorical device. But it also serves to lend an air of naive insistence, reminding the reader of the style employed by another master of telling simplicity, St. John.[38] Virgil's eclogue begins to define itself, not as a poem about love, but as a poem about poetry. His audience however, in the first instance at least, is not the imposing list of visitors who came to sympathize with Gallus, but the humble trees of the forest.

The sonorous evocation of proper names in the body of the eclogue (vv. 9 ff.) provides a stately and distancing backdrop to the action. Present sufferings are a re-enactment of myth. We can see this from the allusion to Adonis. Virgil asks "Gallus" not to be ashamed of the lowly audience of sheep (10. 17–18):

> Nec te paeniteat pecoris, divine poeta:
> Et formosus ovis ad flumina pavit Adonis.

> You must not be ashamed of the flock, inspired poet: even the fair Adonis pastured sheep by the streams.

Propertius will imply the same comparison between Gallus and Adonis when he writes of Gallus' recent death, in a couplet that seems to echo a line of Euphorion (II. 34. 91–92). The spirit of Bion's *Adonis,* even that of the solo aria in Theocritus 15 (100 ff.), seems close. It is the typically Roman renewal of mythic *exemplum.* The modern sufferer is the old writ large.[39] The motif is already exploited by Plautus. Similarly, Caesar, in the new fragment, is the "greatest part" of Roman history—the typically Roman and carnival exaltation of the here and now.

*Eclogue* 10 ends with another reminiscence of Gallus. Virgil depicts himself as sitting and weaving a basket (a homely adaptation of an old metaphor for poetic composition). He will leave it to the Muses

---

[38] Compare, for example, the fourth chapter of his *First Epistle* with its elaborate counterpoint of repetition (*pneuma/agapē*). Repetition is noted as a device of the *ischnos charactēr* by Demetrius, *De Eloc.* 196–97, 211–14. It is in the recognition with the Church Fathers of what the Bible has in common with pagan canons of style rather than in sharp antithesis between them that mimesis will be understood.

[39] This is the theme of the opening chapter of E. Fraenkel's *Elementi plautini in Plauto* (Florence 1960), pp. 7 ff. See also "*Memini Me Fiere Pavum*: Ennius and the Quality of the Roman Aesthetic Imagination," *Illinois Classical Studies* VIII (1983), 173–93.

to raise his verses to a height that will satisfy Gallus. His phrase *vos haec facietis maxima Gallo* is an echo of *tandem fecerunt carmina Musae* in the new discovery.

The poet himself has to go, because the shadows are harmful to singers. In the concluding lines of this poem, and of the whole collection, the emphasis laid on *umbra* is extraordinary (10. 75–76):

> Surgamus: solet esse gravis cantantibus umbra,
> Iuniperi gravis umbra; nocent et frugibus umbrae.

We must go. The shade harms singers, the noxious shade of the juniper: even the fruits of the earth are harmed by shade.

*Umbras* will be the last word of the *Aeneid*.

Standing at the opening of the second half of the *Eclogues*, Eclogue 6 acquires unusual prominence from its position. It is interesting that it should be a poetic discussion of the possibilities of epic.

The discussion is placed at the outset firmly under the auspices of Callimachus. The Preface to the *Aetia* is quoted at the very beginning (6. 1–11):

> Prima Syracosio dignata est ludere versu
> Nostra neque erubuit silvas habitare Thalea.
> Cum canerem reges et proelia, Cynthius aurem
> Vellit et admonuit 'Pastorem, Tityre, pingues
> Pascere oportet oves, deductum dicere carmen.'
> Nunc ego (namque super tibi erunt qui dicere laudes,
> Vare, tuas cupiant et tristia condere bella)
> Agrestem tenui meditabor harundine Musam.
> Non iniussa cano. Si quis tamen haec quoque, si quis
> Captus amore leget, te nostrae, Vare, myricae,
> Te nemus omne canet . . .

It was my Muse that first deigned to play with Sicilian verse, and did not blush to dwell in the woods. When I was (for) singing of kings and their battles, Apollo plucked my ear and warned: "Tityrus, all right for the shepherd to feed fat sheep, but his song should be thin spun." Now I myself (for there will be no lack of poets eager to celebrate Varus' praise and his gloomy wars) will practice my country music on my thin pipe. My theme is commissioned. Yet, if it finds loving appreciation, my tamarisks and the whole forest shall sing of Varus.[40]

A poet who is "first" and who "plays," who is forbidden by Apollo to tackle themes of princely warfare with their fatty richness, and ordered instead to sing a thin-spun song, is the heir of Callimachus.

---

[40] See CROWD, ISCHNOS CHARACTER, PASTORAL, PLAY, PRIMUS-LANGUAGE, RECUSATIO, TENUIS in the *Glossary of Critical Terms*.

Yet, as scholars have pointed out,[41] there are essential differences here. Callimachus received the injunction to leave the hackneyed themes of conventional epic alone at the time when he first took his writing tablets on his knee, presumably therefore before he had himself expressed any preferences. Virgil is rebuked after he has already started, in thought if not in deed. His refusal to sing of Varus' achievements is not categorical, like of that of Lucilius to sing of Scipio. *Nunc ego* (= "meanwhile") carries with it the implication that "one day" there may be scope for such topics.

Yet this interpretation does not do justice to the whole subtlety of the passage. Virgil is put off singing Varus' military exploits because of the large numbers who will find there ample scope. The Alexandrian rejection of "the many" has been cleverly turned into a compliment.

Here we seem to feel the particularly close presence of Gallus. Gallus too had turned the rejected history of the un-Aristotelian, un-Callimachean Choerilus of Samos into a means of enhancing Caesar's glory. His own poetry was second best to the honorific inscriptions (the victor's rewriting of history) that would appear on the richer temples dedicated from Caesar's spoils. Even so, it was "made by the Muses," and had hopes of satisfying even the most stringent critics.

Virgil too, even if he cannot write now the eulogy which Varus would like, can say by way of compensation that even pastoral poetry can be "commissioned," can win fame for those it mentions. If therefore he does come in due course to tackle a different kind of poetry, it will not betray these earlier claims.

Even before we had the new fragment to prove how much Virgil, when he theorizes about epic, depends on Gallan approaches, Servius told us that once again in *Eclogue* 6 we have close imitation of the other poet.[42] As the story begins, we hear how Chromis and Mnasyllus, two rustics, chance upon old Silenus asleep in a cave, still drowsy from yesterday's wine. Helped by the nymph Aegle, they bind the god with his own garlands, and force him to pay the tribute of a song. Obligingly, he tells them first of the origin of the world from chaos, then of the early history of mankind. He passes to the story of the rape of Hylas, of the love of Pasiphae for her bull. Apostrophizing Pasiphae, he puts into her mouth the words she had used in seeking for her beloved. We hear next of Atalanta, of the sisters of

[41] Cf. Wimmel, *op. cit.*, pp. 132 ff.

[42] On 6. 72. Gallus' general neoteric affiliation is made clear by Propertius at II. 34. 91–92, where it is obvious how little Propertius knows of any other poetry except that about Lycoris, while Virgil is already the author of "something greater than the *Iliad*."

Phaethon changed into alders, then of Gallus' own consecration as a poet.

Gallus has been wandering by the streams of Permessus. But then he is led up to the Aonian mountains by one of the Muses, and presented by the mythical poet Linus with the very pipes on which Hesiod himself had played, who is here made by implication a second Orpheus. His theme was to be the Grynean wood.

Silenus descends from these heights, to tell the tale of Scylla, daughter of Nisus, turned into a sea-monster; to tell of Tereus, transformed into a bird, and the unhappy story of the murder of his son by Philomela in revenge for the fate of her sister. All these themes that the Eurotas once heard from the lips of Phoebus were sung by Silenus until the evening star brought a halt to the telling.

It is difficult to believe that this poetic program had been put into effect by Gallus alone.[43] The neoteric poet Calvus had described the fate of Io. The author of the *Ciris* and Propertius exploit some of the eclogue's other hints. A great deal reads like a sketch for Ovid's *Metamorphoses*.

And it is exactly here that we have a clue to Virgil's own epic imagination. He too, just as much as Ovid, wrote a metamorphosing epic. The *Aeneid* is precisely an exploration of shifting identities, in which the Homeric sounding board never returns single echoes. This awareness of blurring boundaries (Cicero's *senseram quam idem essent*— "I had realized how much they were the same"—raised from historical experience to metaphysical generalization) did not mature in a single instant. But *Eclogue* 6 shows this Roman fascination with interchangeable masks in play as soon as the poet thinks of moving to a higher genre. The mish-mash of neoteric material (including Lucretian themes, which shows how Virgil apprehended Lucretius) offered in that poem quickens the seed bed from which the *Aeneid* would grow.

In the course of Silenus' song, "Gallus" is dedicated as a poet. The language is written in the usual Alexandrian code. Gallus has been wandering by the streams of Permessus. The river Permessus, the site of Gallus' wanderings, was the source of the spring Aganippe,[44] first mentioned it appears by Callimachus, perhaps at the opening of the *Aetia*. Propertius later toys with the same symbols. If we may interpret Virgil in the light of the more explicit Propertius, the meaning seems to be that Gallus has been dallying with trifling themes when he might have turned to something more important. But we are to observe in Virgil that he is greeted respectfully, not rebuked,

---

[43] Although his mentor Parthenius did apparently write *Metamorphoses*: see H. Lloyd-Jones and P. Parsons, *Supplementum Hellenisticum*, p. 304, no. 636.

[44] Cf. Pfeiffer, *Callimachus*, II, p. 103; Propertius II. 10.

by the Muses. It is because he has perfected his art on these lesser topics that he is now empowered to go forward to higher things.

The pipes he receives from Linus are those of an Orphean Hesiod, not Homer. His treatment of these larger topics then will be in the "new" epic style, not that of the trite and hackneyed, pseudo-Homeric *kyklos*.

The wood of Grynean Apollo formed the subject of a famous poem by Euphorion,[45] who was Gallus' particular model. It is tempting to believe that we have in Virgil, not anything from Gallus' own elegies, or at least not anything that implied a serious commitment to large-scale poetry by him, but rather an adaptation of a scene from some lost passage in the Greek poet, reworked in turn by him from the beginning of the *Aetia*. Gallus may have spoken of plans, and even commissioned Parthenius to summarize for him the plots of suitable myths to be introduced into either elegies or epics. In the new fragment, he appears to have toyed with the "refusal" poem. But in the event, one has the impression that his poetic horizons were bounded by Lycoris. Virgil may ostensibly be complimenting his friend in urging him on to greater things. In reality, he is using his friend to talk about himself.

Any interpretation must avoid the conclusion that "Gallus' " ascent into the mountains meant a departure from Callimachean principles.[46] The call to the epic style may indeed be a call to a higher genre, but the model for this genre is the Hesiod set by Callimachus at the beginning of the *Aetia*. *Hesiod* in fact had been the title of one of Euphorion's poems. The end of his poem about Grynean Apollo, alluded to by Virgil here, in which the quarreling seers Calchas and Mopsus could not be reconciled even in death, recalled Callimachus' account of the funeral pyre of Eteocles and Polynices.[47]

Sliding between identities, the poet of *Eclogue* 6 needed to fix landmarks in his treacherous terrain before he could hope to progress. Evidently Callimachus was such a *point d'appui*.

Interestingly, the pre-epic of the *Eclogues* is most visible in a poem which makes no allusion to Gallus. The "Messianic" fourth takes the form of a prophecy about a child, and indulges the conscious make-

---

[45] J. U. Powell, *op. cit.*, p. 47; Schanz–Hosius, *Römische Literaturgeschichte*, II, p. 171, bottom.

[46] Catullus knows that the Muses dwell on a hill (105). It looks as if Ennius' *Musarum scopuli* (*Ann*. 233 Warmington) and stylistic preoccupations were a borrowing ultimately from Callimachus' "narrower path" (*Aet.-pref.* 26).

[47] Cf. Ovid, *Tristia* V. 5. 53 ff. and Powell, *op. cit.*, frr. 97–98, who also notes (p. 48): *Eadem historia est atque regiorum fratrum Thebanorum* ("The story is the same as that of the royal brothers at Thebes"). For borrowings from Callimachus by Euphorion see Pfeiffer, frr. 573, 607, 643, 657, 703, 709 and his index, s.v. *Euphorio*.

believe of a comic Utopia (*Saturnia regna*, v. 6: "the reign of Saturn," always for Virgil a telling phrase). There will be just enough sin left in the world to enable the young prince to prove his mettle. After that, peace, and idyllic rest from toil. If he lives long enough, and has enough inspiration, Virgil will be the poet of this new age, not to be outdone by Orpheus or Linus. The *recusatio* is here transposed into the positive, but the key is still minor. The element of pathetic longing, wry self-depreciation and humorous exaggeration in this piece, which is intended as a eulogy and a dialogue with Catullus 64, comes closest in the *Eclogues* to capturing Callimachus' serio-comic tone.

Coming to grips with the riot of Alexandrian material, some of it too congenial to the Roman spirit, attempting to impose mastery and discipline upon it with the aid of clear, musical, ordered, astringent, distancing language—are these activities which in some way separate Virgil from Alexandrianism, as the writer who comments on a bourgeois existence is removed from the category of the bourgeois by Proust? Rather, they show exactly the quality of Virgil's genius, and illustrate why he rises above the writers who preceded and followed him. If the literary movement developed in Alexandria was incredibly rich in its potential, and permitted endless variations on its basic concepts, the danger for lesser men was the threat of drowning in the ocean thus revealed to their thirsty eyes. If we study, for example, the remains of Laevius, we cannot help feeling that this is just what happened. A steady and substantial current of Greek achievement has been diverted by the comic bent of the Roman into a thousand shallow channels. The corollary of this diminution was that the deeper draught of the Alexandrian tide had been unplumbed. Varro of Atax was able to translate the *Argonautica* of Apollonius, and to write *Satires*, but his *Bellum Sequanicum* in honor of Julius Caesar's Gallic campaign looks like a complete surrender to the *reges et proelia* which gave Virgil's inspiration pause. Furius Bibaculus could praise Alexandrian teachers, and then in his epic let Jupiter spew snow like spittle over the wintry Alps. Buried beneath this avalanche of bombast, the Alexandrian opening towards epic was in danger of vanishing.

### III

The painful road that led towards the recovery of the epic potential in Alexandrianism, and its utilization for Roman purposes, passed next through the *Georgics*.[48] The poem is defined by Virgil himself as Hesiodic (II. 176):

> Ascraeumque cano Romana per oppida carmen.

And I sing a song of Ascra through towns loyal to Rome.[49]

In the literary context of its time, this was a clear statement of allegiance.

But once again, as with the *Eclogues*, the peculiar circumstances of the close connection preserved by the Romans with their land, which could have no parallel in Alexandria, meant that this poem could embody still powerful political and social ideals for all its make-believe. Here for the first time in Latin poetry, on a scale large enough to impress, an epic style that could satisfy every Callimachean demand was being exercised by a *vates* determined to push beyond Callimachus. The soaring mastery and majesty of the new Virgilian manner were clearly too great to be confined forever to details of vine-planting or cow plagues. The fact that these earthy topics were an essential stage on the way to the *Aeneid* is however of the greatest significance.[50]

The poem gave evidence of perfected technique on every page: of the Alexandrian technique of musicality and refinement of expression, exhibited in exquisite patterns of alliteration and assonance which build upon Roman modes, but tower airily above that strong foundation; of balance and fall; of the association of the commonplace with the unexpected; of the polar juxtaposition of contrasts; of romantically ironic learning. Rhetoric (isocolon, tricolon crescendo, anaphora in particular) here returns to its original home and purpose.

The verse technique displayed by the *Georgics* was neither dissociated from Alexandrianism nor bounded by neoteric limitations. There had been, even in two such masters of style as Cicero and Catullus, a turning away from accomplishment already found in the hexameters of Ennius, for example, in the wild rhythms in which Ilia reports her dream (*Annales* 40–43 V):

> ... ita sola
> postilla, germana soror, errare videbar,
> tardaque vestigare et quaerere te, neque posse
> corde capessere, semita nulla pedem stabilibat.

---

[48] Cf. F. Klingner, *Virgils Georgica* (Zurich–Stuttgart 1963); L. P. Wilkinson, *The Georgics of Virgil* (Cambridge 1969).

[49] See ASCRA in the *Glossary of Critical Terms*.

[50] Eisenstein had to direct his agricultural film *The Old and the New* before he could go on to *Ivan the Terrible*: cf. his *Izbrannye Proizvedeniya* (Moscow 1964), III, p. 421.

... so it was that alone after that, my own sister, I seemed to wander, and slowly to trace and seek you and yet not to be able to seize you in my heart: no path gave secure foothold.

Euphorion may have been responsible for some of this diminution. In his description of Cerberus, brilliant though it is, there is visible a tendency towards end-stopped lines, and lines without any finite verb.[51] This was probably the symptom of a lyricism which ultimately triumphed in Nonnus.

In recalling the Latin hexameter to a freer discipline, Virgil was not rebelling against Callimachus. If we take the longest surviving fragment of the *Hecale*, we discover:[52]

1. There is ample use of run-on lines. About 22 are punctuated at the end, 32 are not.
2. There is equally good use of internal pauses (about 27).
3. There is much exploitation of dactyls, including four wholly dactylic lines. There are only two spondaic fifth feet.
4. There are only about eight lines where no finite verb or infinitive occurs, and this in spite of the differing syntactic structures of Latin and Greek. The sentences are not on the whole periodic, although sometimes Callimachus lengthens them by means of interpolated parenthesis.[53]

A similar lesson may be derived from Apollonius. The description of Medea's sleeplessness (III. 744 ff.), for example, contains in its first forty lines the same use of pauses and enjambement, the same fondness for dactyls and tempered use of fifth-foot spondees, the same use of verbs: only four lines in this passage lack some kind of verb or infinitive. The same staccato use of short sentences characterizes the style.

If it was Euphorion who led astray some of the Roman Alexandrians, that supplies another reason why Virgil had to come to terms with him in the person of Gallus. Callimachus had been less extreme

---

[51] Page, *Greek Literary Papyri*, p. 492. Five lines, nearly half the brief passage preserved, have no verb. B. A. van Groningen, *La poésie verbale grecque*, pp. 221–22, says that Euphorion stresses nouns and adjectives rather than verbs, although the fragments now printed in Lloyd-Jones and Parsons, *Supplementum Hellenisticum*, pp. 196 ff., may not conform to this pattern. The preference is Pindaric, if we may believe F. Dornseiff, *Pindars Stil*, pp. 86, 92, 94 ff. At the other end of the Greek tradition, M. String notes the same feature in Nonnus: *Untersuchungen zum Stil der Dionysiaka des Nonnos von Panopolis* (diss. Hamburg 1966), pp. 90 ff. See below, p. 387 note 108.

[52] Pfeiffer, fr. 260, approximately 69 lines. For a new text, see Lloyd-Jones and Parsons, *op. cit.*, pp. 130–34, no. 288.

[53] G. Williams, *Tradition and Originality in Roman Poetry* (Oxford 1968), takes a somewhat different view of this question.

in form than his Greek disciple, and in content had not even shrunk from some sense of political involvement.[54] These twin demands of art and utility are still urging Virgil forward in the famous profession of faith which closes the second book of the *Georgics* (475 ff.). How easily there praise of the country passes into satire about the city; satire about the city into half-tearful, half-comic eulogy of the last vestiges of the rustic Golden Age!

The stage is thus set for a flight of Virgilian irony: not wholly fanciful, not wholly real, but a delicate balance of polar reservation between these extremes. The poet, we begin by hearing, would like to fulfill what Posidonius had defined as the role of the Gaulish *vates*, but he understands by the themes suitable to vatic poetry a didactic far removed from the realities of Roman life, and shared with both Propertius and Apollonius' Orpheus. This is the ideal, already sketched in *Eclogue* 6 (vv. 31 ff.). But even the country themes which are second best, and which his lack of talent for higher things may compel him to celebrate, are viewed here primarily in terms of escape. Virgil's early Rome, with its rustic beginnings, is removed from the Rome Virgil knew. In his Utopia the farmer finds no brothers treacherous to brothers, no foreign foes. He does not care for the fortunes of Rome on the one side, or kingdoms destined to perish on the other. The bounteous earth supplies his needs, and he never so much as sets eyes on law in action, the Forum, the House of Public Records (in other words, on the chief symbols of Roman civilization at work). Others plunge into danger and crime for the sake of gain, hoard their wealth, pursue political oratory, take note of the reception they receive in the theatre. It all ends in fratricide and exile.

Meanwhile, content at his toil, the farmer supports his country and family alike. Nature sheds its goodness on him and his children and chaste wife. In due season he keeps holiday with his fellows, athletic and festive both. Here is where true valor flourishes, a Remus who lives again at his brother's side; from such origins Rome became the most beautiful city on earth. This was the golden age of Saturn (a deepening of the theme of *Eclogue* 4), when there were no trumpet blasts of war, no swords yet hammered on the anvil.

The voice of this utopian passage, comic and satiric, is yet tinged with the sadness of unrealized and realizable possibility. Comedy and satire are the most Roman of genres. But the theme of fratricide,

---

[54] Cf. E. Howald, *Der Dichter Kallimachos von Kyrene* (Erlenbach–Zurich 1943), pp. 12 ff., 90 ff. Even Catullus shows an interest in politics. Some long-lived Alexandrian original lies behind Silius' description of the Cyreneans (Battiadae) as *pravos fidei* (*Punica* III. 253), which looks back to the treachery of Magas in the First Syrian War (H. Bengtson, *Griechische Geschichte*, pp. 380 ff.).

thrice echoing in these lines, strikes too close to the heart to be drowned by traditional Roman and comic optimism. Fratricide now, yes: but not then. . . . And cannot "then" be "now"? The poet ends his book, and dismisses us with that sting in our consciences.

The unsatisfactory nature in terms of strict logic of this antiquarian nostalgia is evident. The notion that Rome's pre-history could be separated from war and bloodshed may have been beautiful, but it was wrong.[55] But there was *rerum . . . pulcherrima Roma* after all to set against *res Romanae perituraque regna*. Could logic in such matters say all?

The exordium to Book III shows equal hesitation in accomplishment. The poet rejects with Alexandrian fastidiousness the hackneyed topics. He has to seek fame by another path. Here he adapts Ennius to his meaning, but that he is still working within an Alexandrian frame of reference is shown by the *primus* language that follows. Virgil visualizes himself as some sort of hero, returning to his native spot and founding a temple to Caesar. Gallus' vision of Caesar's *templa deorum* may have been in his mind. In Caesar's honor, games will be held to attract the athletes of Greece, and this Pindaric theme too had a contemporary ring, since Augustus in fact founded such games both at Actium and in Rome.

Virgil will bring offerings to this temple, and yet the whole vision is suddenly betrayed as theatrical. The backdrop turns, and the curtain rises to mark the end of a scene.

When the poet continues, we find that on the doors of his pictured temple will be carved Caesar's triumphs. Statues of marble and bronze will tell the story of the imperial house as far back as Troy and Troy's founder, Apollo. Envy will be expelled under the threat of the pains of hell. For the moment rustic themes may beckon, but "soon" (a more flattering variant of "one day") Caesar's battles and glory will be his song.

Games and theatre are a reprise of a theme just heard at the end of Book II, taken up now in a more magnificent and imposing dimension. Earlier, Tyrian purple (also perhaps a Gallan theme) was the prize of the avaricious traitor (II. 506). Now the poet himself wears it (III. 17) as he drives his hundred four-horse chariots to the stream of his native Mincius. The trappings are transmuted, but the tone persists. Just as the escapism and Utopian account of Rome's origins at the end of the previous book of the *Georgics* prevented us from separating Virgil's progress towards heroic epic from a deep-seated Alexandrianism which was more than one of mere form, so

[55] *Augustus and the New Poetry*, pp. 217 ff.

here the fantastic speculations about the shape that his epic will
ultimately take show how necessary it is to postulate something other
than the cyclic manner in order to explain what Virgil eventually
did.

The poet will not be pinned down to any of the accepted clichés
of the grand manner. He is going to found his temple at Mantua.
Eduard Fraenkel has explained for forgetful readers the importance
of such *Lokalpatriotismus*.[56] But can we suppose that, in the atmosphere
of imperial Rome, this suggestion made any sense? The humble
Mincius is to rival the sacred rivers of Greece, and notably the
Alpheus. Virgil will be some sort of priest at these games in honor
of what we can only call, by an oxymoron familiar to Hellenistic
Greeks, the Roman Zeus. But then the whole scene is discovered to
be exactly that, a *scaena* (v. 24), a make-believe, part of the trappings
of illusion which so delighted the Roman groundlings, and against
which the more serious spirits of the age, like Horace, protested.[57]

The aery pageant is on the point of fading, when the attention is
caught by *Invidia infelix* (v. 37). Argument has arisen over the meaning
of the phrase.[58] Could there really be a reference here to a literary
topos made famous by Callimachus, and echoed in a hundred passages
by his imitators, or must we not rather see some more profound
political meaning? The answer to the problem depends firstly on
noting the Alexandrian code in which the whole proem to this book
of the *Georgics* is written, so that *Invidia* can hardly be taken out of
the code at the whim of the critic. But this Alexandrian concept
trembles here (like all the Alexandrianism of the passage) on the
brink of new life. What had in Alexandria and in the Preface to the
*Aetia* been a personal quarrel between the poet and his detractors
now acquires larger significance when that poet is the eulogist of
Roman greatness. Identified with the patron he now serves (and
showing once again his need for such props), he is able to think of
his *invidia* as a threat to something bigger, and what threatens that
something bigger in turn threatens him.

"Meanwhile" (v. 40) Virgil turns back to the countryside. The
theme is both untouched and difficult, satisfying two of Callimachus'
requirements. The temporary dalliance with larger subjects has had
about it both a Callimachean irony—there has been the hint that the
whole thing is merely the work of conscious fantasy—and a Callimachean romanticism. Virgil pretended to be some combination of

    [56] *Horace* (Oxford 1957), pp. 304 ff.
    [57] *Epp.* II. 1. 187 ff. But the profound theatricality of the Roman aesthetic cannot
be dismissed so easily!
    [58] Wimmel, *op. cit.*, pp. 183 ff.

victorious hero (Heracles) founding a second Olympia, of priest at his own foundation, and all the time a poet who has created his own illusion out of nothing. It is the kind of self-conscious virtuosity which distinguished the author of the *Hymns*, whose narrator may also be some mixture of priest, master of ceremonies and commentator on the action he describes.[59] But Callimachus had learned the trick of the mobile ego from Greek lyric, and its master Pindar, whom he had imitated in more than one poem. The elusive, punning, musical art of the great Theban has a relevance to more epic than that of Apollonius.

The *Georgics* then were certainly a preparation for heroic epic, but an Alexandrian preparation. The poem was long enough to give scope for some of the traditional epic apparatus, notably the division into books and the use of the simile. That there is some sort of intended polarity between the "optimistic" even books and the "pessimistic" odd books has long been noted. Similar contrasts pervade the *Aeneid*.

Conscious of the links uniting his own poetry, Virgil did not scruple to borrow from the *Georgics* in the similes of the *Aeneid*. There are notable examples in the culminating Book XII.

In his eagerness to confront Aeneas, Turnus arms, feverish and frenzied. Sparks flash from his face, fire gleams in his eyes (*Aen.* XII. 103–06):

> Mugitus veluti cum prima in proelia taurus
> Terrificos ciet atque irasci in cornua temptat
> Arboris obnixus trunco, ventosque lacessit
> Ictibus aut sparsa ad pugnam proludit harena.

Just as when for his first battle a bull summons his terrifying bellow and tries to vent his anger through his horns, pushing against a tree trunk: he challenges the winds with his blows or kicks up the sand as a prelude to the fray.

Later, when he and Aeneas eventually meet, they are again compared to two bulls in combat (XII. 715 ff.):

> Ac velut ingenti Sila summove Taburno
> Cum duo conversis inimica in proelia tauri
> Frontibus incurrunt, pavidi cessere magistri,
> Stat pecus omne metu mutum, mussantque iuvencae
> Quis nemori imperitet, quem tota armenta sequantur;
> Illi inter sese multa vi vulnera miscent,
> Cornuaque obnixi infigunt et sanguine largo
> Colla armosque lavant, gemitu nemus omne remugit.

[59] Cf. Dornseiff, *op. cit.*, p. 85; Wilamowitz, *Hellenistische Dichtung*, II, pp. 282 ff.

And just as when on mighty Sila or the top of Taburnus two bulls
rush to lock heads in the fray: the panic-stricken herdsmen withdraw,
the whole herd stands dumb with fear, the heifers mumble—who is
to be lord of the pasture, leader of all the herds? With might and
main the bulls plant rival wounds. With all their weight they plunge
in their horns, while streams of blood bathe their necks and shoulders,
and the whole forest echoes to their bellowing.

These passages demand reference to the *Georgics* for their elucidation.
In Book III of this poem, Virgil describes the dire effects of love on
the animal kingdom, and indeed on the whole of creation, including
men (v. 242). Horses and bulls have to be kept away from love's
influence, if the farmer is to get any good out of them. (We may
contrast the bees in the "optimistic" Book IV, who make do without
sex.) The argument is illustrated by the case of bulls, whose strength
is weakened and "scorched" by the sight of the female. Quotation
shows best what the poet was later to borrow from himself (*Georgics*
III. 219 ff.):

> Pascitur in magna Sila formosa iuvenca:
> Illi alternantes multa vi proelia miscent
> Vulneribus crebris; lavit ater corpora sanguis,
> Versaque in obnixos urgentur cornua vasto
> Cum gemitu; reboant silvaeque et longus Olympus.
> Nec mos bellantis una stabulare, sed alter
> Victus abit longeque ignotis exsulat oris,
> Multa gemens ignominiam plagasque superbi
> Victoris, tum quos amisit inultus amores,
> Et stabula aspectans regnis excessit avitis.
> Ergo omni cura viris exercet et inter
> Dura iacet pernox instrato saxa cubili
> Frondibus hirsutis et carice pastus acuta,
> Et temptat sese atque irasci in cornua discit
> Arboris obnixus trunco, ventosque lacessit
> Ictibus, et sparsa ad pugnam proludit harena.

A fair heifer grazes on mighty Sila. The bulls, turn and turn about,
with might and main join battle, exchanging many a wound. The
dark blood bathes their bodies. They push against each other their
interlocked horns, with far-heard bellows, echoed by the forest and
the deep sky. The rivals cannot share the same byre. Off goes the
loser into distant exile, with many a groan for his disgrace and the
blows of the proud conqueror, for the love he has lost unavenged.
And looking back at the byres he departs from the kingdoms of his
ancestors. So with all due care he trains his strength, and lies all night
among the hard rocks where he has made his bed. He feeds on
unkempt grasses and sharp sedge; he tests himself and learns to vent
his anger through his horns, pushing against a tree trunk. He chal-

lenges the winds with his blows and kicks up the sand as a prelude to the fray.

The description given here is plainly anthropomorphic. The normal procedure of the traditional epic has been reversed. It is the emphasis on the other pole which is always permitted in pathetic structure.[60] Instead of the world of animals being called in to illumine the world of men, the world of men is made to illumine that of animals. Virgil's never absent (comic) sense of shifting identities, which is also Aristotle's "metaphor," the greatest poetic gift, is at work. Man suddenly sees himself for what he is, a creature pulled about by appetites, and in this context the bravado of Leander, swimming the Hellespont, is the symbol of a universal, cosmic, *amor* (vv. 244, 258–63).

The attempt to master "Alexandrian" material (really, Alexandrian material that had been allowed to proliferate too far into the sentimental), noted in the *Eclogues*, is particularly visible in this refusal of the *Georgics* to accept the conventions of love-poetry, that love is of concern only to humans, and in them requires no deeper comprehension or justification. Apollonius had made this critique, and Callimachus had distanced and reduced romantic love in his story of Acontius and Cydippe.[61] Virgil subjects it to a biologist's, or farmer's, perspective. It is a critique that will be exercised by the *Aeneid*.

This similarity of outlook means that the comparisons developed in the *Georgics* are easily transferable to the *Aeneid*. Relying on our knowledge of what he had already written, Virgil in the later poem can afford to abbreviate and divide his material. It was merely the application to his own work of the method he had used with the poetry of others. In the first passage cited above from Book XII of the *Aeneid* (81 ff.), Turnus arms hastily and restlessly for his duel with Aeneas. The time when he does so is left rather vague. It looks as if Virgil implies that the hero prepared himself the night before, and editors have been worried by the lack of realism.[62] But, if we take a clue from the *Georgics*, we see that it is just the bull who fears he may lose again who robs himself of sleep and tosses on a hard couch in some sort of desperate self-punishment. The whole difficulty of the later passage vanishes in the light of the single word *pernox* in the earlier.

The *Georgics* explained at length the issues in the fight. The defeated must go into distant exile "with many a sigh" for his disgrace, and for the blows he has suffered from the proud victor, and for the love

---

[60] See below, p. 414.

[61] Frr. 67–75 Pf.

[62] W. S. Maguinness on *Aeneid* XII (London 1953), vv. 87 ff. J. W. Mackail, *The Aeneid* (Oxford 1930), has a sensitive note, p. 468.

he has lost unavenged. "Looking back at the byres, he departs from the kingdoms of his ancestors." These are exactly the thoughts which must pass through Turnus' mind, and which explain his wild, irrational state. All this resonance can be given to the four lines of the first bull simile of *Aeneid* XII by the "learned" technique of asking the reader to remember what the poet has already described while wearing his Hesiodic mantle in the *Georgics*. When subsequently the second part of the *Georgics* material occurs in Book XII, we are able to link the two similes because of their unity in the earlier poem (and to know that the poet wants them to be linked), and observe how they fit into an inevitable pattern of defeat.

Yet Virgil's intimate preoccupation with unity went further than this. As the *Georgics* are talking about bulls on their first level of discourse, it is legitimate for the poet to employ a second level, a simile, to assist our imaginations. The bull which eventually screws its courage to the sticking point and falls unexpectedly on its forgetful foe is like a wave, which whitens out on the deep and gradually rises and grows until, when it breaks on the shore, it is as big as a mountain.

In Book VII of the *Aeneid*, the peaceful relationships between the Trojans and Latins are ruptured by Ascanius' chance slaying of a pet deer. (He is of course here the true heir of his father's values, as the hunting imagery of I and IV makes clear.) Resentment is fanned by Juno, and at last serious fighting breaks out between the two sides. It is just like a small wave, growing to be a huge breaker (*Aen.* VII. 528–30):

> Fluctus uti primo coepit cum albescere vento
> Paulatim sese tollit mare et altius undas
> Erigit, inde imo consurgit ad aethera fundo.

As when a wave begins to grow white before the first puff of wind: gradually the sea swells, the waves increase. Then it surges from its low depths to high heaven.

Here again, the reader may be inclined to think that the poet has underplayed his effects in allotting only three lines to his simile. But the weakness[63] vanishes immediately when we think back to the far more impressive description of the *Georgics* (III. 237–41):

> Fluctus uti medio coepit cum albescere ponto,
> Longius ex altoque sinum trahit, utque volutus
> Ad terras immane sonat per saxa neque ipso
> Monte minor procumbit, at ima exaestuat unda
> Verticibus nigramque alte subiectat harenam.

---

[63] Yet contrast Worstbrock, *Elemente einer Poetik der Aeneis* (Munster 1963), pp. 138 ff.

As when a wave out at sea begins to grow white: far out on the deep
it ruffles the surface, then rolling ashore crashes on the rocks, and is
as tall as a mountain when it falls. It boils up from the depths as it
crests and tosses high the black sand.

In Book VII we have the beginning of the process that is to
culminate in the single combat of Aeneas and Turnus in XII. Already
we know that one of the combatants will die. Can we doubt the
conscious art, spanning the entire second half of the poem in this
way, by which the poet has used the *Georgics* to sound and resound
within the *Aeneid*? In the light of this back-reference, it is dangerous
to distinguish a "mature" epic style from the not yet perfected
manner of the *Georgics* (an absurd judgment anyway).[64] The poet is
only able to abbreviate later because he has expanded earlier. His
attitude to his poetry shows us a deeper sense of the word *brevitas*.
It is not a mechanical snipping. It depends on remembered tradition
to convey its dense meaning, even where the poet has had to create
that tradition himself. This is the essence of "learning" in literature.

Though the Alexandrian epic certainly gave much scope for similes,
it is interesting that Virgil worked into their use only gradually. The
first book of the *Georgics* has three. The inevitable regress of history
is like a boat swept downstream (201 ff.). The winter good cheer of
the farmers is like that of sailors who have reached port safely
(303–04). The headlong flight of the world to war is like a chariot
out of control (512 ff.)—a simile which may be intended to recall
Ennius and which, in a manner seen in Apollonius, anticipates what
is to be ordinary narrative at a later stage.[65]

The second book has two. At 279, the ordered vines are compared
to a legion drawn up on the field of battle, and at 336 spring is
compared to the days which must have been at the creation of the
world.

It is in Book III that the poet's imagination begins to take wing.
The vision of a temple commemorating Octavian's victories is like a
stage (24). At 89, the famous racehorses of myth are evoked, ending
with an allusion to Saturn himself, metamorphosed as he sought to
elude his spouse. The horse that is too old is like a blaze of straw,
hot but lacking force (99). The future racehorse, by contrast, is like
the north wind, rushing down on land and sea from its freezing
shores (196). The bull that returns to the fray after defeat is a wave,

---

[64] Cf. W. F. Jackson Knight, *Roman Vergil* (rev. ed., Harmondsworth 1968), p. 331.

[65] Cf. III. 103 ff., and II. 541–42; Ennius, *Annales* 88 ff. (Warmington). For
Apollonius, see pp. 85–86, above. Ships and chariots are associated by Varro of Atax
(fr. 2, Buechner, p. 122), though the comparison was much older (e.g. Bacchylides
5. 47).

slowly growing in power (237). The traveling herdsman in Africa is
like the laden Roman legionary (346). At 391, the farmer who
produces fine wool is reminded of the fleece with which Pan seduced
the moon. At 470, the whirlwind can bring no more storms than
there are plagues to attack the herd.

In Book IV similes really proliferate. The warring bees are compared to hail or acorns falling (80). The inferior bee is like a dusty,
parched traveler (96). The bees' labors over their honey are like the
massive struggles of the Cyclopes to forge Jupiter's thunderbolts
(170). Their use of pebbles as ballast is like that of boats (195). The
sign of illness in the hive, a deep and drawn-out buzzing, is like the
south wind in the forests, the sea in turmoil or the fire in a furnace
(261–63). At 312 another multiple simile is found. The bees that
emerge from the carcass of the slain ox are like a summer rainstorm,
or arrows shot by Parthians in the opening skirmish of a fight.

The concluding legend is distinguished by four similes. Proteus,
as he arrives at the cave for his siesta, is like a herdsman in the
evening safely folding his flock (433). On his journey to the underworld, Orpheus by his music arouses the shades, numberless as the
birds that hide in the leaves at night-time, or before a winter storm
(473). Weeping for his lost Eurydice, who vanishes like smoke (499),
Orpheus is like the nightingale, lamenting her brood, which has been
torn from the nest by the rude plowman (511).

It is evident that these similes lead into an ambivalent world.
Things are out of control, at the mercy of elemental forces, of the
god of war (I. 201, 512). But there is a way out. The farmer has
reached a safe harbor; the bees know how to use ballast (I. 303; IV.
195). War may be disciplined, as the Roman legionary is disciplined
(II. 279; III. 346) and the vine-dresser/herdsman knows the secret.
Spring in the countryside offers the chance of a fresh start to creation
(II. 336). But there is always the threat of winter from the malevolent
forces of nature (III. 470; IV. 473), and it was Jupiter himself who
deliberately made the sea stormy (I. 130). The very product of the
horse breeder's toil may threaten destruction (III. 91, *Martis equi
biiuges*; III. 197, *hiemes*). The sea/racing-chariot imagery of the first
book is united in this last comparison and points, for example, to
III. 473, where the storms of winter are the symbol of cosmic
harshness.

The bees labor like the Cyclopes, producing the thunderbolts that
are hurled by Jupiter in his anger (IV. 170). How is it then that the
roaring of fire in a furnace is a symptom of *illness* in the hive (IV.
263)? The ambiguity continues at IV. 213. The keeper is glad to
renew his swarms; but what if they are like a summer rainstorm (cf.
I. 259; IV. 312), or Parthian arrows before a battle? The warring

bees fall like destructive hail, and then again like the acorns which may still serve the farmer's purpose (IV. 80–81: cf. I. 305). The herdsman traveling across the African plain was admired; but the bee who is like him is doomed (III. 346; IV. 96). A fine fleece is well enough, but what if it can be used to seduce the chaste Diana (III. 391)? Proteus is a conscientious herdsman, looking after his flock, but he is not safe from attack for all that (IV. 433). Orpheus sings beautifully, like the nightingale, but both may lose all they hold dear (IV. 511). Yet can we blame the *durus arator* ("hardy plowboy": cf. I. 160) at his work? Burning the stubble left in the fields was so useful that four separate reasons were advanced to justify the practice (I. 84 ff.). But when the old racehorse is too weary for battle, his last efforts receive no such palliation (III. 99).

The continual refusal by Virgil to commit himself to any easy, simplistic view of human endeavor is profoundly faithful to the serio-comic spirit of the primitive mentality. It is reiterated and elevated to epic dignity in the story that he selected to conclude the whole poem, that of Aristaeus and his lost bees.[66]

This section of 244 lines is not, of course, to be described as an "epyllion," as if it were somehow detachable from the rest of the poem. Like Pindar's (or Plato's) excursions into myth, it sums up and recapitulates all that we have heard, lending to it a mythical, timeless dimension of validity.

The story is an *aetion*, as it explains in its first lines. Making an internal appeal to the Muses, it clearly intends to deploy the whole epic apparatus.[67] All the more surprising therefore after the invocation of the Muses must be the line that follows (316):

> Unde nova ingressus hominum experientia cepit?

> Whence did this new experience of men take its beginning?

*Ingressus, experientia*: these are words with a fundamentally prosaic ring. The let-down which the ancient reader must have felt warns that we are to expect here no ordinary epic.

The story plunges straight into *medias res*. *Ut fama* shows the dependence of the learned poet on tradition. Like Homer's Achilles, the grieving Aristaeus stands by the water and complains to his divine mother (cf. *Iliad* I. 348 ff., XVIII. 35 ff.). But Achilles did not ask for his mother's help by challenging her to prove her relationship to

---

[66] The episode has become the subject of an enormous literature. A particularly stimulating treatment is given by C. Hardie, *The Georgics: A Transitional Poem* (Abingdon 1971), pp. 11 ff. Once again, Virgil's imagination slides towards metamorphosis (Proteus).

[67] Cf. *Iliad* II. 484; T. Mann, *Doktor Faustus* (Stockholm 1956), p. 204.

him. That motif is to be found in the *Odyssey* (IX. 529), where the Cyclops, blinded and frustrated by the wily Odysseus, appeals to his father Poseidon in desperation. Thetis and Poseidon, both sea deities, easily blend. The story of Aristaeus therefore, although it is told in an "optimistic" book and ostensibly narrates a remedy for loss, has in fact an ominous background. Achilles found no remedy for the loss of either Briseis or Patroclus in the *Iliad*, except one that cost dearly in human suffering, and the Cyclops of the *Odyssey* no remedy for his lost sight. Ultimately we are to learn that Orpheus was eternally parted from Eurydice.[68] As in some musical overture, this discord is already heard by the attentive listener to Aristaeus.

In Homer, visiting Thetis is accompanied by a retinue of nymphs, whose names are also to be found in Hesiod. Recalling these nymphs, Virgil transforms them into Hellenistic ladies, spinning and listening to love poetry as they surround Aristaeus' mother, Cyrene. The particular tale they are hearing had been a favorite since the days of the *Odyssey*, where Demodocus sang a variant of it at the court of Alcinous (VIII. 266 ff.). Since Cyrene is a Hellenistic queen, she evidently cannot act like Thetis and deign herself to go ashore to find out her son's troubles. The royal party indeed is so busy that Aristaeus has to call a second time, whereupon it is Arethusa who decides to take a look. Cyrene, struck with maternal solicitude, tells Arethusa to invite her son to court to explain his troubles. The waters part to receive him.[69] The mechanics of this submarine journey are not further explained, and the whole underwater scene contrasts vividly with those in the *Iliad*. Aristaeus has entered a carnival *monde à l'envers*.

The fairground booth may profess to cater to scientific curiosity. Delighted by his vision of the working of the earth's river systems, Aristaeus appears to forget his troubles. When at last he reaches his mother's presence, she quickly discovers that his weeping is *inanis* (375: cf. 345 above). This adjective, whose usage in Virgil repays study, seems to combine the two meanings of both "groundless" and "pointless." Aristaeus' tears are groundless, because his situation is not really so bad. They are pointless, because he himself can really do nothing to improve matters.

Brevity permits Cyrene to know what is troubling her son without

[68] Orpheus eventually becomes Achilles and Odysseus: see below, p. 153.

[69] Cf. *Odyssey* XI. 243 and Bacchylides 17. 97 ff. The sexual allusion to the *Odyssey*'s story of Tyro should not surprise us in Hellenistic poetry. What differentiates Virgil from the Augustan elegists (and Gallus) is not ignorance of "love," but his critical attitude towards its manifestations, evident as early as the *Eclogues*, but particularly noticeable in the *Georgics* and the *Aeneid*.

repetition of his tale of woe.[70] Playing the role of the perfect mother, she treats him to a splendid meal, described in elaborate language,[71] whose elaboration is the clue to its humor. Afterwards, fortified by favorable omens, Cyrene refers him to the *vates* Proteus, who will explain to him the source of his troubles. The picture of the god is not without its amusing traits (394–95).

A note from the *Odyssey* had already been heard in the prayer of Aristaeus/Polyphemus. The borrowings from the *Odyssey* (IV. 351 ff.) in the story of Proteus are remarkable. To match the taste of a later age, Virgil ennobles his narrative. In Homer, Eidothea, helping Menelaus to entrap her father, applies ambrosia to the nostrils of the hero and his men to counter the stench of the sealskins in which they are disguised. In Virgil, ambrosia is applied to Aristaeus merely to make him look handsome and fit (mother's boy).

Homer's story is of the clearest kind. Menelaus and his crew are held up for twenty days on Pharos, at the mouth of the Nile. They do not realize that they have offended the gods. As Menelaus roams along the shore, Eidothea, Proteus' daughter, espies him and feels moved. She explains to him that he must lie in wait for her father, hold on to him in spite of all his changes of shape, and then question him about the reasons for the delay. The best time for this is when Proteus arrives at midday to take his rest after counting his herd of seals. Menelaus and three companions are shown how to disguise themselves with sealskins.

The plan is carried out like clockwork. Not only does Menelaus learn the cause of his own troubles, but he also hears about his brother Agamemnon, and even about Odysseus. There are a number of those repetitions, naive to us but satisfying to the unsophisticated listener, and deeply embedded in more than the Indo-European tradition, which indicate that the whole story is proceeding exactly according to expectation.

Virgil makes some characteristic changes to his model. We have already seen that he frames the episode with a borrowing, not from the *Odyssey*, but from the *Iliad*. He uses the technique, noted in Pindar's *Pythian* 4, of an introductory speech which permits shortening of the main narrative. Cyrene already explains to her son in detail the shapes which Proteus is likely to assume, combining what Eidothea says with what really happens in Homer. When therefore we reach the actual scene of the capture, a different emphasis from the Homeric is available to the Roman poet. The difference clearly owes something

[70] Cf. Accius, fr. 10 (Buechner, *op. cit.*, p. 48), for the problems sometimes raised by the Hellenistic search for brevity (Callimachus, fr. 57. 1 Pf.).

[71] See Norden's edition of *Aeneid* VI, p. 115.

to Callimachean descriptions of high noon and its devastating heat.[72] It is a dangerous, magical time in popular belief. Virgil's sun seems to be assaulting both men and nature (IV. 425–28).

> Iam rapidus torrens sitientis Sirius Indos
> Ardebat caelo et medium sol igneus orbem
> Hauserat; arebant herbae, et cava flumina siccis
> Faucibus ad limum radii tepefacta coquebant.

Already devouring Sirius who scorches the thirsty Indies was burning in the sky, and the fiery sun had consumed half his course. The grasses were parched, and the rays baked the hot streams in their courses so that, their throats dry, they turned to mud.

These four lines, with their insistent repetition,[73] are substituted for Homer's plain "at noon." In Homer, Proteus and his seals arrive separately. In Virgil, they arrive together, and Proteus' flock leaps and shakes spray around him. Homer describes Proteus' counting of his seals in a matter-of-fact manner. Virgil is preoccupied with the "psychological moment." Expanding a short half-line hint given in Eidothea's speech, he devotes three whole lines to his simile of the herdsman bringing his calves and lambs home, and the prowling wolves excited by the bleating from the fold.

Virgil also selects a different approach from Homer to the attack. First we are shown a charming picture of the old god seated (436). But this is followed by a line of such devastatingly prosaic character (*cuius Aristaeo quoniam est oblata facultas*, 437: "since Aristaeus was offered this chance at him") that we must assume a deliberate effort to jar the reader's sensibilities. Aristaeus charges in as Proteus is settling down (this has to be deduced from *iacentem*, 439) and fastens fetters on his victim. This takes three lines and one word, *occupat*, which is placed emphatically in the first foot. Menelaus attacks after the god has already lain down, and Homer disposes of the business in one line, plus one similarly placed emphatic verb. Virgil however can describe Proteus' metamorphoses in only two lines, since we have already had four lines about them in Cyrene's introductory speech. Now he needs only to set our imaginations working with a hint.

Three lines, marked by colloquialism,[74] give Aristaeus' question to Proteus. In Homer, the god answers Menelaus without more ado. Virgil takes time for a dramatic picture. The *vates* speaks only under strong compulsion. He turns eyes that burn with shining light, and

---

[72] Cf. *Hymn* V. 70 ff.; *Hecale* fr. 238. 15 ff.

[73] The view that *Sirius* here means "the sun," has the support of Lycophron, 397; cf. *Argonautica* II. 517 with the scholia (Wendel, pp. 170–71).

[74] Cf. R. G. Austin on *Aen.* II. 739, 786.

he gnashes his teeth mightily before he unlocks his lips to reveal the fates.[75]

Homer's Proteus and Menelaus actually communicate. When he has found out what is keeping him at Pharos, Menelaus seizes the opportunity to enquire what has happened to the rest of the Greeks on their way home from Troy. He and Proteus have a long exchange, in which Menelaus even learns what is to be his own eventual destiny. All this vanishes in Virgil. As in the *Aeneid*, his characters, like those of classical French tragedy, do not so much converse as soliloquize. In his Hellenistic/Roman version, Proteus speaks uninterruptedly to Aristaeus and then disappears before any further questions can be put to him.

What Virgil's Proteus says is not communication, because the answer bears such a disproportion to the (three-line) question. Fifty-eight lines recount the death of Eurydice, and Orpheus' vain attempt to recover her. It is the kind of story within a story enjoyed by the Greeks at all periods, but notably liked by Hellenistic authors.[76] It begins impressively with heavy spondees (453 ff.):

> 'Non te nullius exercent numinis irae;
> Magna luis commissa: tibi has miserabilis Orpheus
> Haudquaquam ob meritum poenas, ni fata resistant,
> Suscitat, et rapta graviter pro coniuge saevit.'

"Not from no power comes the anger that harasses you. You are paying for a grave offense. Unhappy Orpheus rouses this punishment against you, which by no means matches your deserts—did not the fates oppose. So profound is his wild sorrow for the rape of his wife."

*Non . . . nullius*, with the lingering on the second word demanded by the lengthening of *-us* before the caesura, again makes the hearer do the poet's work for him. What can these negatives mean in positive content? A second clause is introduced by the equally vague, equally emotive *magna*. Finally, a clause of two-and-a-half lines, introducing the name of Orpheus with the long epithet *miserabilis*, particularizes and clinches the meaning, with the ominous verb *saevit* kept to the end. The subordinate clause *ni fata resistant* again implies more than is stated. Bad as this punishment is, it is on the verge of being even worse. The syllable count is interesting:

| | | |
|---|---|---|
| non . . . irae | 13 syllables ⎫ | |
| magna . . . commissa | 7 syllables ⎭ | 20 |

---

[75] Proteus is like Charon, *Aen.* VI. 298–304. Once again, we are prepared for something more than an entertaining tale.

[76] Cf. Callimachus, frr. 178–84 Pf.; Catullus 64. 50 ff.; Ovid, *Metamorphoses, passim*; Petronius, *Satyricon* 111 ff.; Apuleius, *Metamorphoses* VII ff.

| tibi . . . suscitat | 26 scanned syllables | |
|---|---|---|
| et . . . saevit | 12 syllables | 38 |

The opening 13 is doubled by the 26 of the third clause of the crescendo, and the following 7 nearly doubled by the clinching 12. The 20/38 ratio will recur in the 20/37 of the next sentence but one.

This opening verdict is now succeeded by a three-line period that explains Eurydice's fate:

| illa . . . praeceps | 15 syllables | |
|---|---|---|
| immanem . . . herba | 28 syllables | 43 |

The next sentence but one will contain 42 syllables, dividing at the emphatic *te* (465) into 15 and 27.

The sentence *at . . . Orithyia* (20/37 syllables) is organized chiastically (*implevit/flerunt*), and its second section is especially distinguished by the use of Greek proper names and Greek hiatus. The names are arranged in tricolon crescendo that repeats itself (461–63). In the sentence *ipse . . . canebat* (464–66) there is hyperbaton of subject and verb, this time with use of apostrophe and fourfold anaphora. And so the use of crescendo and balance, of chiasmus, of alternating and contrasting rhythms goes on in a display of effortless virtuosity, of the *parola ornata*.

This music makes sense. Eurydice has died because she was bitten by a snake that she failed to see in her headlong flight from the attentions of Aristaeus. This is related in an entirely "subjective" way (IV. 457–59):

> Illa quidem, dum te fugeret per flumina praeceps,
> Immanem ante pedes hydrum moritura puella
> Servantem ripas alta non vidit in herba.

> She for her part, in her headlong haste to escape you at the riverside, poor maiden doomed to die, did not see in the deep grass the huge water snake before her feet as it lurked on the bank.

We are not told that it bit her, since that would suggest too much the outside observer. The mere collocation of *hydrum* and *moritura* (she felt "moriar!") is enough.[77]

Immediately, we pass to the emotional reaction roused by her death, since in this poetry everything turns on *Affekt*. First there is the company of her friends. Then there is Nature, and the *Getae*, the representatives of the wild north. Then there is her husband,

---

[77] The context suggests that *fugeret* (457) should be allowed to keep its full "subjective" meaning, and not be reduced to a colorless substitute for the indicative.

whose sorrow, by the intervening delay, has thus been given vast dimensions.[78]

Orpheus decides to seek his wife back from Hades, though no more precise explanation of this primitive recollection of the shaman is offered. Hell is described in emotive terms: *nigra formidine* ("with black fear"), *regem tremendum* ("fearful king"), *nesciaque humanis precibus mansuescere corda* ("hearts unyielding to human prayers"). Orpheus' arrival and his music stirs even the insubstantial ghosts.

At this point Virgil lavishes art on the pathos of the dead in a sentence lasting ten lines, adorned with a comparison of the departed spirits to birds huddling in the leaves at evening, or before a winter storm (IV. 478–80).[79]

> Quos circum limus niger et deformis harundo
> Cocyti tardaque palus inamabilis unda
> Alligat et novies Styx interfusa coercet.

They are all imprisoned and bound by the black mud and foul reeds of the river of lamentation: the ugly marsh with its sluggish waters enchains them, and the hateful river with its ninefold channels holds them in.

Translation gives the flavor of a rhetorical tradition of writing which must be bafflingly novel to a generation not trained in the literature of the past.

The place of punishment, even the torturers and the tortured, are astonished. The reversal of the religious motif of wonderment here which makes the human more than the divine pays extraordinary tribute to Orpheus' music. But the reader is to be even more astonished (IV. 485–86):

> Iamque pedem referens casus evaserat omnis,
> Redditaque Eurydice superas veniebat ad auras . . .

And now in her return she had escaped all mischance, and the restored Eurydice was coming towards the upper air . . .

But how? How after the terrifying description of the ninefold, binding channels? Virgil completely omits any account of how Eurydice and Orpheus gained this privilege from the grim gods of the underworld![80] It is also the first time that he has used the name Eurydice.[81] It has been kept in reserve until a dramatically effective moment. The

---

[78] Cf. *Verrine* V. 171 for a parallel to *Georgics* IV. 460 ff.; Curtius, *op. cit.*, pp. 167 ff.

[79] Cf. Norden on *Aen.* VI. 309–12.

[80] Contrast Boethius, *De Consol. Phil.*, III. m. XII. 40 ff.

[81] Illig notes this trick in Pindar: *Zur Form der Pindarischen Erzählung*, pp. 27, 30, 34 note 6; cf. J. E. Sandys on *Bacchae* 1113.

"restoration" in fact is a cruel deception, and she is about to be lost again, this time forever. The "upper air" is mentioned only to enhance the sense of loss.

The use of present participles in the subsequent description of the decisive happening (which we now see is *not* the illusory recovery) recalls Cicero's prose, as does that of the inverted *cum* clause (485):

> Iamque pedem referens casus evaserat omnes.

And already on her way back she had escaped every mischance.

Compare from *Verrine* V. 88:

> Evolarat iam e conspectu fere fugiens quadriremis, . . .

Already the fleeing quadrireme had practically disappeared from sight.

Virgil continues (488):

> Cum subita incautum dementia cepit amantem.

. . . when suddenly madness seized her careless lover.

Compare in Cicero (*loc. cit.*):

> cum etiam tum ceterae naves uno in loco moliebantur.

when even so the rest of the ships were still struggling in one spot.

It is obvious that Cicero and Virgil had received the same kind of rhetorical training.

Cicero, the master of vivid prose, seemed unable to transfer his gift to poetry, and a watery looseness betrays there the amateur.[82] Virgil knew the art of compressed particularization (*Georgics* IV. 490–93):

> Restitit, Eurydicenque suam iam luce sub ipsa
> Immemor heu! victusque animi respexit. Ibi omnis
> Effusus labor atque immitis rupta tyranni
> Foedera, terque fragor stagnis auditus Averni.

He halted, and on the very verge of light, forgetful, alas! and overcome in mind he looked back at his Eurydice. There all his toil was spilled. The truce made with the ungentle tyrant was broken, and thrice a crash was heard among Avernus' pools.

Orpheus' hard work is "spilled": the "terms" (of which we hear only

---

[82] Buechner prints a fragment (*op. cit.*, p. 87) from the *Marius*, which displays end-stopped lines and present participles. Only 7 out of 13 lines have a finite verb. When Virgil borrowed from the *De Consulatu Suo* for the *Eclogues* (Buechner, p. 82, no. 5) he seems to have enlivened what he took with colloquialisms: *Bonum sit!* in final position, *credimus, nescio quid.*

now, when they come into effect) are "torn apart": the echoing thunder is heard by the (barrier) pools of Avernus.

In this style, Eurydice must speak before she vanishes (494–503):

> Illa 'quis et me' inquit 'miseram et te perdidit, Orpheu,
> Quis tantus furor? En iterum crudelia retro
> Fata vocant, conditque natantia lumina somnus.
> Iamque vale: feror ingenti circumdata nocte
> Invalidasque tibi tendens, heu non tua, palmas.'
> Dixit et ex oculis subito, ceu fumus in auras
> Commixtus tenuis, fugit diversa, neque illum
> Prensantem nequiquam umbras et multa volentem
> Dicere praeterea vidit; nec portitor Orci
> Amplius obiectam passus transire paludem.

"Who," she cried, "has ruined me, poor wretch, and you, Orpheus? What is this great madness? See, once again the cruel fates call me back, and sleep hides my swimming eyes. And now, farewell! I am carried away, in the grip of huge night, and stretching out my weak hands to you, though I am no longer yours." With that she suddenly vanished away from his sight, like smoke dispersing in the thin air. He grasped in vain at shadows and would have said so much: but she never saw him again. The ferryman of Hell would not let her once more pass the barrier of the marsh.

She begins with evocative polarities: cruel fates/me; call me back/ (but not you); here/back. She continues with the pathetic "Sleep hides my swimming eyes," and "I am carried away, in the grip of huge night, stretching out to you—though I am not yours—my weak hands."[83] She vanishes "like smoke into thin air," and in spite of all his futile gropings, she never sees him again. This substitution for the expected "he never saw her again" sustains the scene at her point of view. *Umbras* (501) is characteristic.

The same interplay between overall and detailed balance that was noted before marks the series of rhetorical questions (504–05) that now shift the emphasis to the abandoned Orpheus. There is tricolon crescendo in the actual questions, which are marked by fourfold anaphora. Then a single line ("She for her part, already cold, was being ferried across the Styx"), aided by internal rhyme, hammers home the ineluctability of Eurydice's doom. We have:

| | | |
|---|---|---|
| quid faceret | 4 syllables | |
| quo . . . ferret | 10 syllables | 14 |
| quo . . . Manis | 5 syllables | |
| quae . . . moveret | 9 syllables | 14 |

[83] Medea uses this gesture in Apollonius, *Argonautica* IV. 107, perhaps the original of *Aen.* VI. 314.

illa . . . cumba                           15 syllables

The imbalance between questions and final statement must be supplied by the reader's own thought.

The section that now describes Orpheus' grief and fate occupies 21 lines (507–27). In them we learn three facts: Orpheus bewailed his wife; he refused the consolations of any other woman and as a result was torn to pieces by the *Ciconum matres* during their Bacchic revels; his shorn-off head continued to call on Eurydice even as it was swept downstream. Evidently the poet did not despise the kind of carnival motif ("the grotesque body") which delighted Ovid. The rest of the lines are given over to extracting the last tear from the tragic scene.

"Tragic scene" indeed, but this is not the technique of Greek tragic narrative. The "most tragic of poets" has left us an account of just such another Bacchic murder. Like Virgil, Euripides uses anaphora. The polarities implied are suggestive (silence/speech; the dove/aggressive madness), but far too much attention is paid by the Athenian to the realistic description of what is going on (*Bacchae* 1084 ff.):

> The air fell silent, in silence the wooded glen held its leaves, and you could not have heard the cry of animals. But the Bacchants, who had not heard the god's cry distinctly, rose to their feet and cast their eyes around. He called to them again, and when the daughters of Cadmus heard Bacchus' command clearly, on they rushed, no less speedy than the dove, so eagerly did their feet course along—mother Agave, her own sisters, and all the Bacchants. Over the dry river bed and the broken ground they leapt, maddened by the god's breath. When they saw my master seated on the fir tree, first they began to hurl at him boulders with all their might, climbing to a rock that towered opposite. . . .

Euripides is deploying the technique so often noted in Defoe and Swift, and sanctioned by Aristotle,[84] by which the plausible and telling detail persuades the reader into accepting the rest of the story. But in itself his description is far too lucid and orderly to have provided a model for Virgil's death of Orpheus.

A better parallel may be discovered in Greek lyric, including the lyric of tragedy. It was already noted that Pindar, for example, relates his myth, not as something emotionally neutral or simply ornamental, but as a dramatic exposition portraying the characters of sharply opposed antagonists, for the sake of which expected norms may be strikingly violated. His series of cameos (or "stills") so often appears

---

[84] *Poetics* 1455 a 13; 1460 a 19 ff.

abandoned at the climactic moment precisely because there the poet turns away to ponder the religious and moral meaning of the picture he has offered to our imagination.[85] Pindar would not have written the story of Orpheus with Virgil's fluidity. But he would have recognized what Virgil was doing.

In this context, the fragment surviving from Simonides' *Danae* is instructive. It is of this poem that Dionysius of Halicarnassus remarks that, if a piece of lyric poetry is written out as prose, it will be impossible to grasp the rhythm, or to distinguish strophe, antistrophe or epode.[86] In his previous chapter he had pointed out the resemblance between rhythmical prose and poetry, and in the earlier part of this chapter he had quoted from the *Odyssey*, and from the *Telephus* of Euripides, to show how close they are to prose. Young Horace, in talking about Ennius, had confidently taken the opposite view, asserting that a real poet like Ennius could be recognized anywhere. It is clear that the controversy first raised by Aristotle was still alive in the schools.[87]

Simonides, who is known from other evidence to have been looked upon as a model of the *ischnos charactēr*,[88] is enrolled by Dionysius on the side of the un-Ennian prose poets. When the *Danae* fragment is actually examined, it is not at all obvious that a modern critic at least would class it as prose, even if he were to meet it written out as such. There are in it accumulated adjectives, unusual epithets, other rare words. They may be contrasted with certain expressions reminiscent of Demosthenes.[89] With all this, the piece is undeniably aimed at squeezing the last tear out of the sentimental reader.[90]

Exactly the same criticisms may be made of Virgil's story of Orpheus and Eurydice. There, evocative Greek names jostle side by side with the prosaic *portans*.[91] The general tone of domestic pathos is enough to associate what Virgil has written with the tradition of lyrical narrative exemplified by Simonides, and not with the anti-Callima-

[85] Illig, *op. cit.*, pp. 20 ff. Dornseiff, *op. cit.*, p. 35, sees in Pindar "ein Artverwandter Virgils." Dissen's analysis of the myth of *Pythian* 4 (above, p. 96) is again relevant.

[86] *De Comp. Verb.* 26; D. Page, *Poetae Melici Graeci*, p. 38, no. 284.

[87] Cf. Hor. *Sat.* I. 4. 56 ff. Axelson is able to say about Horace's lyric what Dionysius had said about Simonides' (*Unpoetische Wörter*, p. 111).

[88] *Vita Aeschyli* 8. This is the implication of *leptotes*.

[89] E.g. compare lines 18–20 of the *Danae* with Dem. VIII. 30 and with other similar idioms (see J. E. Sandys *ad loc.*). Demosthenes also uses a verbal phrase with the construction of the simple verb: cf. E. R. Dodds on *Bacchae* 1288 and Simonides, *loc. cit.*, v. 20.

[90] The *Vita Aeschyli* has the word *sympathes* (8): cf. Catullus' *maestius lacrimis Simonideis*, 38. 8.

[91] Axelson, *op. cit.*, pp. 30 ff.

chean, Hellenistic epic, "grand in style and subject matter," as it has been reconstructed by its most sympathetic critic.[92]

The adaptation of the lyric *ischnon* to hexameter narrative had been made in Alexandria. A few lines from Moschus' *Europē* will illustrate the argument (95 ff.):

> And she began to fondle him, and with her own hands she gently wiped away the foam that was thick upon his mouth, and then she kissed the bull. And he lowed softly: you would think you were hearing the sweet sound of a Mygdonian flute calling. He knelt before her feet, and started looking at Europē, turning his neck, and showing her his broad back.
>
> And she spoke up among the long-tressed maidens: "Come, dear companions and friends, let us sit on this bull and take our pleasure: for see! he will spread out his back beneath and find room for us all, so meek and mild does he look, and not at all like other bulls: he has a fitting understanding in him, like that of a man. All he lacks is a voice."
>
> With these words, she sat down smiling on his back, and the other girls were on the point of doing the same thing. But the bull leapt up forthwith, having seized the one he wanted. And swiftly he reached the ocean. She turned round, and kept calling to her dear companions, stretching out her hands, but they could not reach her. Having got to the shore, the bull ran on forward like a dolphin, with unsodden hooves traveling over the broad waves.

The Greek of this poem is marked by a prevailing tone of subjectivity. Everything is done that language can do to draw the reader into the lush eroticism of the rape, although the author does season his sweets with a certain astringent irony. Given that this is an inferior talent, there is still a preoccupation with emotional reaction characteristic of Virgil's Orpheus episode. The adverbs *ērema* (softly) and *meilikhion* (sweetly), describing the bull's lowing, and the flute comparison, where the vowel alternations so cunningly echo the sound; even the apparently straightforward adjective *platu* of line 100, which shows us the bull's broad back as Europē was intended to see it; the tone of Europē's description of the bull in direct (and therefore subjective) speech; the scene as she is carried off, stretching out her arms in vain to her companions and turning round as the bull had turned round to her: all this reveals a determination to extract the maximum of pathos. What a pretty scene it makes!

It may seem far-fetched to compare Moschus with Virgil. Perhaps an analogy with the history of Renaissance painting will help. Schooled, like contemporary poets, in principles adopted from Aristotle, the

---

[92] Ziegler, *op. cit.*, pp. 43 ff.

artists of the sixteenth century (Cinquecento) set out to rescue their medium from the trivialization towards which the delight in every aspect of the world around them had drawn some of their predecessors. H. Wölfflin has been discussing Benozzo Gozzoli's *The Drunkenness of Noah*:

> Such a narrative does not occur after 1500, when the story is told with a minimum of figures, concisely, and without any by-play, giving only the dramatic kernel of the story without any descriptions. The subject is taken seriously and genre-like embroideries are not tolerated, for the aim is to grip the spectator, not to amuse him. The emotions are the main preoccupation, and the interest in humanity swallows up all the other things in the world.[93]

Wölfflin shows in his great book how the Cinquecento painters dramatize, concentrate, simplify, balance, unify, humanize. How well they understood the classical tradition!

Naturally, things could go too far in the wrong hands. An engraving by Marcantonio Raimondi, *Five Saints*, finds a parallel to its overdone pathos in Sannazaro's *De Partu Virginis* (1526), where the Biblical simplicity of Mary's *Fiat mihi secundum verbum tuum* ("Be it done unto me according to Thy word") is replaced by a long speech:

> oculos ad sidera tollens
> Adnuit et tales emisit pectore voces:
> Iam iam vince fides, vince obsequiosa voluntas:
> En adsum: accipio venerans tua iussa tuumque
> Dulce sacrum, pater omnipotens. . . .

Raising her eyes to the stars she nodded assent, and then uttered these words from her heart: "Faith must prevail, prevail the obedient will. See, I am here! In awe I accept your orders and your sweet command, Almighty Father!"

The room is flooded with light. She conceives. Thunder is heard from a cloudless sky

> ut omnes
> Audirent late populi, quos maximus ambit
> Oceanus Tethysque et raucisona Amphitrite.

The peoples heard far and wide, all that mighty Ocean surrounds, and Tethys, and hoarse-echoing Amphitrite.[94]

In our analogy, Gozzoli might represent the "Ionian" prettiness which was found in some of the Homeric *Hymns*. Sannazaro shows how Ionian lubricity may be tempered by Aristotelian, Alexandrian

---

[93] H. Wölfflin, *Classic Art* (Eng. tr., London 1952), p. 208.
[94] Wölfflin, *loc. cit.*, p. 211. I have corrected a misspelling.

discipline. He may have been lacking in imagination and intellectual force, but he is exploiting the same tradition as Virgil.[95]

Moschus' *Europē* for its part is too clever, too charming, too knowing. But it does contain the germ from which the art of Virgil's Orpheus story, embodied, we must remember, within an Aristaeus story, could spring. When Virgil, like the Cinquecento painters, sought in Aristotle for a new classicism, he had been nurtured on an Alexandrian art which already owed a debt to Aristotelian principles. A criticism that seeks to dissociate him from Alexandrian sensibility must remember the charged emotionality of his tale, and that Ovidian severed head floating, still with Eurydice's name on its lips, down the swift Hebrus.

With the disappearance of Proteus, who has taken so much time to communicate the one piece of information that it is Orpheus who is responsible for the death of Aristaeus' bees, we return to Cyrene. Amazingly, we find that it is not after all Orpheus who is the direct cause of the trouble, but the Nymphs. The language takes on a grave, liturgical tone (*tu munera supplex tende petens pacem*: "It is for you humbly to offer gifts, praying for reconciliation"). Virgil affects the naiveté of old epic when he repeats, in describing the behavior of Aristaeus, four lines from Cyrene's instructions. It can be seen that the repetitions here bear out the picture already formed of Aristaeus as essentially mother's boy.[96] The actual end of the whole process occurs quite abruptly, and is dismissed in five lines. Anticipation (281 ff.) enables this to be done without difficulty.

The 244 lines of the narrative, within a book of 566 lines, are distributed as follows:

| | | | |
|---|---|---|---|
| 315–316 | Introductory question | 2 lines | |
| 317–320 | Aristaeus loses his bees and appeals to his mother | 4 lines | 6 lines |
| | | | |
| 321–332 | His speech of complaint | 12 lines | |
| 333–347 | The underwater scene | 14 lines | 26 lines |
| | | | |
| 348–356 | Arethusa reports | 9 lines | |
| 357–362 | Cyrene reacts | 6 lines | 26 lines |
| 363–373 | Aristaeus' journey: the rivers of earth | 11 lines | |
| | | | |
| 374–386 | He is entertained: his mother takes the omens | 13 lines | |

[95] J. Burckhardt has a more enthusiastic evaluation: *The Civilization of the Renaissance in Italy* (Eng. tr. Oxford and London 1945), pp. 155–56.

[96] Aeneas would follow him here. What can we think when Venus appears to her son as a reincarnation of Nausicaa (*Aen.* I. 326 ff.) and leaves him as Aphrodite left her amour with Ares (*Aen.* I. 415 = *Od.* VIII. 362–63)?

| 387–414 | She explains what he is to do | 28 lines | |
|---|---|---|---|
| 415–424 | They go to Proteus' cave | 10 lines | |
| 425–444 | Proteus arrives: the struggle | 20 lines | } 28 lines |
| 445–452 | Proteus and Aristaeus converse | 8 lines | |
| 453–527 | Story of Orpheus and Eurydice | 75 lines | |
| 453–470 | Losing Eurydice, the mourning | 18 lines | } 28 lines |
| 471–480 | Orpheus enters Hades  Reaction of dead spirits | 10 lines | |
| 481–484 | Innermost Hades | 4 lines | } 13 lines |
| 485–493 | Orpheus returns, but breaks the  condition | 9 lines | |
| 494–503 | Eurydice vanishes | 10 lines | } 13 lines |
| 504–506 | Questions and reality | 3 lines | |
| 507–515 | Orpheus mourns | 9 lines | |
| 516–527 | His death | 12 lines | |
| 528–529 | Proteus disappears | 2 lines | |
| 530 | Cyrene speaks | 1 line | |
| 531–547 | She tells Aristaeus what to do | 17 lines | } 28 lines |
| 548–558 | He does it successfully | 11 lines | |

The episode begins in rapid style, with a question to the Muses and appeal to Cyrene for action. But then it slows down considerably, as we enter a carefully balanced section of 26 + 26 lines, which finds space for an ample report of divine insouciance about love and its troubles. Aristaeus seems to fall in with this spirit as he admires the underwater world, and is entertained by his mother at leisure. She accompanies him to Proteus' cave, and remains to watch over his efforts. When we note that her explanation of what to do and the struggle and subsequent conversation with the god both occupy 28 lines, we can be sure that everything is going to work out satisfactorily. Twenty-eight lines will in fact be allotted to the final interchange between mother and son (531–58) that solves all Aristaeus' problems.

Orpheus, who depends on the power of song, is not so fortunate. By his descent, he enters, not a charming underwater world, but a realm of darkness and cruelty. The 28 lines in which he braves hell and astonishes the dead, ultimately in vain, and the 26 lines in which he loses Eurydice through excess of love, stand in ironic contrast with those same symmetries in the framing story of Aristaeus. The 9 and 12 lines of his mourning and death echo the 12 and 9 lines of his enemy's speech of complaint and heard lament.

Smaller units balance within the larger wholes. Between 450 and 470, for example, we find the sequence 3, 4, 3, 4, 3, 4. Between

481 and 527 we have 4, 5, 4, 5, 5, 7, 5, 7, 5. Can the stanzaic composition of the Italian epic, or even terza rima, be so far away?

A "natural" way of telling this story might have been to omit a large part of the myth of Orpheus (what *is* its relevance to Aristaeus' problem?), and to cut down the underwater scenes with Aristaeus. A simple tale could have made a simple point. The space saved could have been given to further material about apiculture, or to the topic of gardening which Virgil had to leave to Columella because he himself was "too pressed for time."[97] It is evident that it is not enough in this art to speak of *brevitas*. Brevity is a psychologically useful convention. There is ample space available if the poet so chooses. But he chooses the picturesque, the unexpected, the emotion-filled. It is the lesson which the study of Pindar, and of Apollonius' *Argonautica*, has already revealed. The poet's aim is to work on feeling by a musical technique of recapitulation and intensification. What will not serve this purpose is ignored. The Aristaeus episode is there because it condenses and exalts the message of the poem.

Even the most superficial observer sees that the outer and inner aspects of the whole story are in conscious contrast.[98] The gloomy and tragic tale of Orpheus' irreparable loss and violent death, with its emphasis on the cruelty and inexorability of fate,[99] and the impotence of art, is juxtaposed to that of the easy-going Nymphs.[100] Orpheus' woe has no lighter moments, and everything in it implies that "take-it-or-leave-it" attitude on the part of the gods which is expressed in Apollonius' account of the death of Cyzicus. The role of the inevitable lover/loser seems to be a Gallan type.

Aristaeus' difficulties on the other hand are relieved by humor. His problem is not to be taken very seriously, and his willingness to be distracted from it by the rivers he sees is the proof. He is clearly mother's darling, and as mother is a goddess, it seems fair to assume that all will be well. His adventure is related in a balanced series of episodes, in which the six lines of his actual fight with Proteus fade into insignificance.

The epic ambition of the narrative is shown by its effort to come to terms with Homer. The way in which this was to be done by Alexandrian epic had already been indicated by Callimachus and Apollonius. Not simple imitation, but the use of the Homeric poems as an ironically commented background, was the way to revival.

The Homeric background to the Aristaeus episode is quite plain.

[97] IV. 116 ff. It is the manipulation of time which is found in *Aen.* VI (539).
[98] The technique of Catullus 64.
[99] Cf. lines 453 ff., 467 ff., 495 ff., 502 ff.
[100] Cf. 533 ff., *facilis, dabunt veniam.*

Aristaeus is Menelaus, though with touches borrowed from the inhuman Cyclops, and from the Achilles of the *Iliad*. Catabatic Orpheus too is Achilles, and of course Odysseus. It is the technique of blending (metamorphosis) which in the *Aeneid*, in all its full orchestration and perfection, lends such depth of resonance to the poem.[101]

The similes however are only in one instance borrowed directly from Book IV of the *Odyssey*. The simple comparison of Proteus to a herdsman (*Od*. IV. 413) is worked up by Virgil into a picture of the safely folded animals surrounded by hungry but baffled wolves.[102]

*Ceu fumus in auras* (499: "like smoke into the air") is indeed taken from Homer, but from the *Iliad*. The ghost of Patroclus appears to Achilles, who is lying exhausted by grief for his friend's death on the shore, and urges that he should be buried without more ado. The pathetic speech, which reminds its hearer of a childhood spent together, and asks that, when death overtakes Achilles in his turn, their bones should lie side by side, brings home all the awful finality of death. Achilles reaches out to embrace his dearly-loved friend, for what he has been told is the last time of greeting. But even this last time is denied him, and the ghost vanishes from his grip. "His spirit went off beneath the earth like smoke, shrieking" (*Il*. XXIII. 100–01).

For the moment then, as Orpheus loses Eurydice, he becomes Homer's Achilles losing Patroclus. But when Virgil's story opened, it was Aristaeus who was Achilles, standing on the shore and appealing for comfort to his goddess-mother.[103] The characteristic Virgilian ambivalence unites the two as victims of a common fate, even though their ultimate destinies are so different. It is the basic insight of the *Aeneid*.[104]

The final comparison of the weeping Orpheus to a nightingale whose brood has been torn from its nest by a *durus arator* ("hardy plowboy") has parallels in both Callimachus and Moschus.[105] But it is also a fusion of two Homeric images. The first of these is to be found in the scene where Telemachus and Odysseus are at long last reunited (*Od*. XVI. 216–18). Naturally, it is an occasion for tears of happy relief. "They wept shrilly, more intensely than birds, vultures

---

[101] As in the *Aeneid* (cf. G. N. Knauer, *Die Aeneis und Homer*, p. 337 note 1), Virgil also seems to bear in mind certain Homeric proportions. His story takes 244 to Homer's 236 lines: his Proteus speaks for 75+ lines to the 76+ lines of Homer's Proteus.

[102] Cf. *Aeneid* IX. 59 ff.

[103] Above, p. 137. Cf. also *Iliad* XVIII. 203 ff. and *Geo*. IV. 415 ff.

[104] See *Augustus and the New Poetry*, pp. 249 ff.

[105] Callimachus, *Hymn* V. 93–95: Moschus, *Megara* 21.

or eagles with crooked talons, whose nestlings the countrymen have taken before they were fledged."

The second is also from the *Odyssey* (XIX. 518–23). Odysseus is already in his own palace, has been recognized by his old serving-maid, but is still unknown to Penelope, with whom he converses in the guise of a traveler from Crete. In a burst of confidence, Penelope describes her plight. She is like the brown nightingale, singing beautifully at the beginning of spring, and lamenting her dead son Itylus, "whom once in folly she slew with the blade of bronze." Just as the nightingale's song changes, so she is in a constant turmoil of anxiety about her own position.

Finding the Homeric similes in contexts where reunion was in question, Virgil has evidently adapted them to another context where separation is ordained. Was he perhaps moved by the desire to tidy up Homer's disorder? Editors point out that the *reunion* of Odysseus and Telemachus has not much to do with the *loss* by a bird of its nestlings, and that in the second simile the resemblance lies more in the variation of the bird's notes and Penelope's thoughts than in anything else.[106] By putting his composite simile into a more nearly matching situation, Virgil may have intended to adapt the old epic style to the demands of a more sophisticated age.

Perhaps. But perhaps we also need to look deeper. What moves Telemachus and Odysseus is the unspoken thought that Odysseus did come so close to losing his son. It is the sudden ability to face this now averted threat which triggers the floods of relieving tears. The comparison speaks of birds of prey, because that is how the suitors will experience the avenging Odysseus.[107] In the context, Homer's *agrotai* ("men of the fields") is telling, since it suggests in Greek *agrios* ("savage"), and all the uncivilized behavior from which Odysseus and his family have suffered so much.

So with the second simile. Penelope has perhaps been tempted to compromise with the suitors and put an end to her wearying ordeal. She has been restrained so far by thoughts of her son. If she had yielded earlier, she might very well have been like the daughter of Pandareos, who slew her own son in a moment of folly.

But there is here a reminiscence of tragedy also. In the *Agamemnon* (48 ff.), Aeschylus compares the avenging expedition conducted to Troy by Menelaus and Agamemnon in search of Helen to the anguished search of vultures for their young. Their cry is heard by the gods, who send a Fury to punish the transgressors. Remembering

---

[106] W. B. Stanford notes this *ad loc.* in his edition of *Odyssey Books XIII–XXIV* (London 1965), pp. 336–37.

[107] *Odyssey* XXII. 302 ff.

from Aristotle that epic had to learn from tragedy, Virgil has given
to his adapted simile some sense of the persistence in sorrow, demanding divine satisfaction, which Aeschylus had expressed. It is of
course for Orpheus a frustrated persistence. He does not recover his
Helen.

For the Alexandrian tradition, this simile had stood in danger of
becoming a mere cliché. Virgil renews and toughens it. In this regard,
his phrase *durus arator* deserves attention. It replaces Homer's *agrotai*
who, in the mind of Odysseus, can hardly be sympathetic figures.
But Virgil is writing about the toils and endurance of just such men.
It is exactly the hardy plowboy who labors long in the fields, and
who is held up in the *Georgics* as the model of the good life, who is
guilty of this natural impiety towards the innocent birds. What we
are to think of this ambiguity is uncertain. It resembles a thousand
other things in this poetry, which stand for a thousand irreconcilable
facets of the experienced world. But it was Callimachus who had
taught poets to see again with such Argus eyes.

Is there, in these similes of the Aristaeus episode, any linking unity?
The herdsman protects his animals against the threatening wolves;
but Proteus, watched by Aristaeus who is about to fall on him and
take him prisoner, is himself in need of protection. The dead souls
are like birds sheltering from night and winter—but there is no
shelter in the lower world from the decrees of fate which have
brought those souls to where they are. Eurydice vanishes like smoke
into the insubstantial air; she is one of the souls to whom the previous
simile referred, as Orpheus will shortly be one of the birds. Robbed
of his wife, Orpheus may threaten like the vultures of Homer or
Aeschylus[108] but, unlike them, he is impotent. The gods intervene
against him, whatever the provisional victory which his music may
have won. A poet counts for nothing. He himself in due course will
be threatened and murdered.

It is fair to say that there is a common thread here. The fragile
world of men is projected onto a world whose characters are ostensibly
heroic and divine, and both are shown to be terrifyingly exposed
and insecure. Arbitrarily the gods select their favorites, and those
not selected must suffer what they must. Identities shift between
characters as their Homeric analogues briefly match. The *vates* Proteus
(not Orpheus!) fittingly symbolizes such a kaleidoscopic perception.
It is as if the redefinition of *vates* as "poet" adumbrated by the

---

[108] There is an ambiguity in the use of *numinis* at *Georgics* IV. 453. Some scholars
interpret it as referring to the Nymphs, who are however only mentioned later (532).
Orpheus looks terrible to begin with, but then his terrors fade.

*Eclogues* had proved too risky to be developed, and had to be left with a herdsman for safe-keeping.

Nevertheless, Virgil was not a herdsman, and not a farmer. The very act of commenting in this way releases him from the constraints which chafe his imagination. The poetic (literary-historical) lesson that the *Georgics* teach is in fact the same as that already taught by the *Eclogues*. All the time the poet has been striving to master the techniques of Alexandrian poetry in order not to be their slave. Obviously this cannot mean that he was *repudiating* Alexandrianism. Looking back on his early development, we can now see that he was presented in the Rome of his day, and by the Greece of his day, with a poetic tradition that was sadly diminished. The essential distance from his material that is needed by the virtuoso artist who is to be wholly an artist had been lost (even to some degree by so great a poet as Catullus), and there had crept in a facile exploitation of emotion for its own sake.[109] The other side of the coin was that poetry had lowered its ambitions, since no one can weep for 24 books. Lucretius had explored the possibilities of a retreat towards didactic.

Virgil understood that a return to the cool and ironic genius of Callimachus was necessary in order to widen scope. Gallus had been artistically useful to him for precisely this reason, that in his work Virgil had a ready-made example of the latest Greek techniques, expounded by a *cantor Euphorionis* ("singer of Euphorion"), on which he could comment, and so find a means of escape from the confining narrowness of the neoterics. Some of his contemporaries had sought this escape into epic by breaking away from the Alexandrians altogether, and going over to the cyclic manner. Whatever Greek precedent there may have been for this temporizing (Rhianus?), in the Roman context it showed that the restrictions of the neoteric simplification[110] were proving too much for poetic evolution. Those who did not wish to continue with the endless round of *paegnia* ("playthings") felt the need to extricate themselves, and, like Romans, do something big.

Even those who stayed within an Alexandrian allegiance were moving in a similar direction (Cinna, Catullus 64, even perhaps Gallus). Yet Catullus' poem mentioned here, the *Peleus and Thetis*, had driven Latin epic into a lyrical impasse from which only an anti-Catullan revolution could rescue it. Virgil decided to go back to Alexandrian first principles. In the *Georgics* he revived the Callima-

---

[109] Compare Gow and Page on Meleager: *Hellenistic Epigrams*, Vol. II, pp. 591 ff.

[110] The term is Wimmel's: cf. his "Stichwortindex" to *Kallimachos in Rom*, s.v. "vereinfachte Gebrauchsform des Rechtfertigungsgedichts." See above, note 28.

chean sense of distance and make-believe, the Callimachean detachment and comic seriousness, already visible in *Eclogue* 4, and combined them with the powerful Roman sense of monumentality, theatre, games, carnival. This was particularly visible in the "epic" proem to Book III. Even his attenuation of the role of the *vates* was a necessary withdrawal before the leap.

But this theatre, consistent with the experiments of other poets of the day, had a tragic slant. Back in *Eclogue* 6, Gallus had been offered the pipes of an Orphean Hesiod. Now his death evidently lent to the epic poet some dimension of personal feeling which, embodied in the story of Orpheus and Eurydice, would also deepen the story of Dido and Aeneas.[111]

## IV

Virgil's immense labors on the *Aeneid* undermined his health and ultimately killed him before the poem was completed. He himself was so dissatisfied with the work as to leave instructions for it to be burned in the event of his premature death. *Tanta incohata res est ut paene vitio mentis tantum opus ingressus mihi videar* was his comment in answer to the emperor's enquiry about his progress.[112]

It is necessary to stress this point (which is really the re-assertion of the Alexandrian poetic *ponos*-ideal) because there have been unhappy fluctuations in the history of European criticism which have tended to wash out the poem's significance. There have been the most naive objections brought against its author's skill. There has been impatient condemnation of bloodless Aeneas, boredom with the entire second half of the epic. But the real judges of poetry, as the first Alexandrians knew, are primarily poets. And the truth rather is that, in the eyes of *poets*, Virgil has set an indelible stamp on the European epic tradition, and that, unless we appreciate his achievement, we shall fail to appreciate the ideals of a whole civilization. If we do fail, if we really think that the poet's influence was for ill, was, for example, a naive laudation of public faces in private places, or

---

[111] Servius' statement that the Aristaeus episode was substituted for an original *laudes Galli* is not without some plausibility. Virgil needed Gallus as a prop for his vaults. The Aristaeus theme had been touched upon by both Callimachus and Apollonius (cf. Pfeiffer on Callimachus fr. 75, 33), and so the substitute is still serving the purpose of enabling the poet to come to terms with his predecessors. As the episode we have contains three of the four uses of *vates* found in the entire *Georgics*, it is tempting to suppose that it was conceived at a time when Virgil was already thinking of his vatic *Aeneid*. *Experientia* (I. 4; IV. 316) and other verbal reminiscences of the rest of the poem recommend caution!

[112] "So great is the task I have begun that I believe I was mad to start so great a work": Macrobius, *Sat.* I. 24. 11.

even of *raisons d'état*, we would do better to turn away from Europe altogether, and seek in some sanitized Utopia for a more congenial, less troubled citizenship.

Virgil composed very slowly, using a method similar to that employed by Menander and Racine. Apparently he first sketched out in prose the theme of a particular section, and then put the different sections into verse at random, taking up each one as he pleased and sometimes, if in the heat of the moment he was unable to think out a suitable continuation, inserting "props" that he would replace later. The text he left bears in its half lines some of the marks of this fragmentary style of writing. Study of the epic tradition suggests that the half lines, which were eventually to be removed, have nothing in common with the repetitions and parallelisms, which were to stay.[113]

Neither Menander nor Racine lacked an interest in the morals of his day. For Virgil, the opportunities were even greater. His age cried out for moral leadership, and his emperor was determined to answer the call. Recent speculation offered exactly the antiquarian justification for reviving the old notion of the poet as priest and teacher which was needed. We do not understand the *Aeneid* unless we see that it is in the first instance a *vatic* epic.[114] Yet paradoxically, this vatic poem displays an Alexandrian allegiance.

In Apollonius' *Argonautica*, the golden-red fleece is everywhere: in the cloak worn by Jason as he visits Hypsipyle; in the star watched by a maiden in her "newly-built" chambers; in the blushing cheek of love; in the silvery dress reddened by a murdered brother's blood.[115] In the *Aeneid*, Dido is everywhere, exactly as she promises (IV. 384–86):

> . . . sequar atris ignibus absens,
> Et, cum frigida mors anima seduxerit artus
> Omnibus umbra locis adero. . . .

Even when I am not there, I shall pursue you with my dark fires: and when cold death shall have separated limbs and breath, my shade will be everywhere.

The characteristic *umbra* will be noted. But by this device the poet/ *vates* is no longer commenting on private illusion and greed, like

---

[113] Menander: E. W. Handley, in his edition of the *Dyscolus* (London 1965), p. 10 and note 2, citing Plutarch, *De Glor. Ath.* 347 e; Racine: R.-C. Knight, *Racine et la Grèce*, pp. 206 and 376. Cf. *hypographa*, *Vit. Verg. Don.* 31. Handley points out the Aristotelian reason for this practice, unity of composition. The idea that repetitions are a flaw misses the whole musical essence of this art.

[114] *Augustus and the New Poetry*, especially pp. 115 ff., 207 ff.

[115] Above, pp. 74 ff.

Apollonius, but on the life and death struggle of nations. Dido is after all queen of Carthage, and Aeneas the ancestor of Rome.

Of such structural importance, *Aeneid* IV contains a number of lines repeated elsewhere in the poem. The study of some of these repetitions and subtexts illumines both Virgil's technique and his purpose.

Time in the *Aeneid* (it is one of its many carnival features) never has much to do with the clock. When Book IV opens, it is dawn (6–7):

> Postera Phoebea lustrabat lampade terras
> Umentemque Aurora polo dimoverat umbram.

The next dawn was shedding pure sunlight on the earth and had dispelled from the sky the dank shade.

The phrase echoes III. 588–89:

> Postera iamque dies primo surgebat Eoo
> Umentemque Aurora polo dimoverat umbram.

And now the next day was rising in the early east, and dawn had dispelled from the sky the dank shade.

In Book III, the Trojans are just about to meet Achaemenides, a Greek abandoned in Sicily to his fate. Trojan sympathy for him nearly leads to the loss of Aeneas' ships.

The moral symbolism which is never far below the surface of this vatic poem here puts us on the track of Ulysses, the treacherous and wily adversary of Troy already known from Book II. Achaemenides is an invented figure, and he is so clearly a doublet of Sinon in that earlier book that the poet must have wanted to convey something by the resemblance.[116]

The convincing explanation of Sinon offered by Heinze is that the whole scene in which he appears in Book II illustrates the *euētheia* (naiveté) of the Trojans.[117] Their moral gullibility leads them, out of sympathy, to take to their hearts a traitor, simply because he tells a long and circumstantial tale about how his life was threatened by a plot organized by Ulysses. Achaemenides' life too is threatened in similar conditions. He has taken part in the war at Troy, he has followed Ulysses and endured the horror of the Cyclops' cannibalism; he has shared in the famous plot that led to the blinding of the single eye and, in return for all this, he has been left out and left behind. The Trojans do not hesitate to take him on board, and Virgil wastes

---

[116] J. W. Mackail presents a fine example of the dilemmas faced even by the best older criticism in his edition of the *Aeneid*, Appendix B, pp. 516–17.

[117] *Virgils epische Technik*, pp. 8 ff.

no words on their decision. *Merito* (667) tells all. With this, Achaemenides, having served his purpose, disappears from the action,
except for brief mention as an anachronistic guide to the landmarks
of the Sicilian coastline.

It would be unlike Virgil however to offer a narrative at one level
of significance only. He has so closely imitated the external form of
the *Odyssey* at this point that it looks as if he is inviting us to examine
the structure of that poem in order to understand his own meaning.

The first "flashback" book of the *Odyssey*, in which Odysseus recalls
to an audience of Phaeacians his previous adventures, is Book IX.
The first lengthy episode in his tale is precisely the adventure with
the Cyclops, and it fills almost all that book. But Virgil has switched
his counter-episode to nearly the end of Aeneas' story. The end of
Odysseus' tale concludes, by contrast, with the slaughter of the Sun's
cattle, the subsequent storm and loss of all Odysseus' crew, followed
by Odysseus' avoidance of Charybdis and arrival at Calypso's island.
This is the last thing he tells the Phaeacians.[118]

If we compare this sequence with the *Aeneid*, interesting parallels
emerge. At the end of his narrative, Aeneas too has reached his
Calypso's island after a storm. Like Odysseus, he has had two
encounters with Scylla and Charybdis. Odysseus lost his crew. Aeneas
has lost his moral mentor, Anchises. But what Virgil has done is to
reverse the episodes of the eating of the cattle and the Cyclops. The
cattle were encountered at a comparatively early stage of Aeneas'
wanderings, where the Odyssean material was used to form the
*Aeneid*'s vatic Harpy scene (III. 209 ff.). The Cyclops has been shifted
to the end.

What deadly importance has the Cyclops adventure for Aeneas
which makes it comparable with the eating of the cattle for Odysseus?
In *Aeneid* III, the Cyclops poses only a limited threat. Aeneas and
his men are not locked up in the cave. They merely hear that story
from someone else. Even the blinded Cyclops, with his pastoral pipe
hung about his neck, cuts a pathetic figure,[119] and reminds us of the
impotence of all brute force when confronted with inspired intelligence. Enceladus under Etna taught the same lesson to Horace.[120]

In Book II of the *Aeneid*, the sympathy expended by the Trojans
on Sinon was not enough to induce the gods to save their city.
Doomed as they were, they failed to look beneath the surface, even
though portents made what was happening clear enough in hindsight.

[118] G. N. Knauer, *Die Aeneis und Homer* (Göttingen 1964), pp. 181 ff., 192 ff.

[119] The pastoral touch of v. 661 is not at all irrelevant. This is the kind of
Alexandrian prettiness which Virgil is now magnifying into epic dimensions.

[120] *Odes* III. 4. 75–76.

Here too the sympathy that the Trojans feel so instinctively for Achaemenides is not without some danger. Their delay gives the other Cyclopes time to assemble on the shore and threaten Aeneas' fleet. The risk is that, in their hasty escape, which reduces the narrating Aeneas almost to incoherence, they may again run into Scylla and Charybdis. Their plight is indeed to be taken seriously. They are rescued only by a providential change of wind at the last moment.

Is Virgil saying that human sympathy is historically irrelevant? If we think of the context in which Aeneas is speaking, and look at his behavior through Dido's eyes, it is Aeneas who is now Achaemenides and will become Sinon. Like Achaemenides, he is the lost and stranded adventurer taken in by Dido, as she bitterly points out to him in Book IV (373 ff.). Like Sinon, he told what she now considers a pack of lies (*aiunt*, 598).[121] She too was full of instinctive sympathy (I. 630), and forgot that she ran the risk of offending her own moral standards (IV. 24 ff.). She pays the penalty that Troy paid (IV. 669–71).

The poet's commentary on his own meaning is quite clear. The lesson of Enceladus under Etna, that love/lust and its fires are sins against the divine order, will be repeated at Carthage, where Aeneas too arrives, like Achaemenides, after encountering the Cyclops, and like Sinon, with a mission to destroy his too sympathetic hosts by treachery and fire.

But suppose that we then switch our perspective to that of Aeneas himself. For him, Scylla and Charybdis[122] were already the allegorical affirmation of a moral danger yet to be faced. At Carthage, he is still, on one level of meaning, in Thrinacria, in Sicily.[123] Can therefore the radiant Hellenistic queen and her splendid court conceal so horrible a threat as the man-eating Cyclops or the fires of Etna? But what was the Roman experience of Carthage? Dido could at least threaten Aeneas and his descendants with the one-eyed Hannibal and

---

[121] An investigation of the use of *fides* and *perfidus* by Dido in her relationship with Aeneas in the light of E. Fraenkel's article (repr. in *Kleine Beiträge zur klassischen Philologie*, vol. I [Rome 1964], pp. 15 ff.) would be rewarding.

[122] *Quanta laborabas Charybdi*, Hor. *Odes* I. 27. 19: see Nisbet–Hubbard *ad loc*. R. D. Williams in his edition of *Aeneid III* (Oxford 1962) compares *barathrum* (v. 421) with Catullus 68. 107–08: *tanto te absorbens vertice amoris/Aestus in abruptum detulerat barathrum*. Slowly we begin to understand why Aeneas quotes Catullus to Dido at VI. 460.

[123] Because the storm of *Aen*. V. 8 ff., as the Trojans leave Carthage, is imitated from *Odyssey* XII. 403–06, where Odysseus is leaving Thrinacria.

the fires of his marauding armies.[124] She could threaten the Trojan
fleet with fire (IV. 604–06):

> Quem metui moritura? faces in castra tulissem
> Implessemque foros flammis natumque patremque
> Cum genere exstinxem, memet super ipsa dedissem.

Doomed to die, whom did I fear? I should have carried torches into
his camp, filled his gangways with fire and wiped out father and son
with the whole brood, and then piled myself on top.

She could, in her avatar as Cleopatra, threaten the Roman fleet—
and Neptune and Venus—with the fires of her strange gods (VIII.
694–96):

> Stuppea flamma manu telisque volatile ferrum
> Spargitur, arva nova Neptunia caede rubescunt.
> Regina in mediis patrio vocat agmina sistro.

Flaming pitch and flying spears tipped with steel are hurled, the level
seas grow red with unexpected blood. The queen in the center
summons her forces with her Egyptian rattle.

Not simply Scylla and Charybdis, but also Etna has erotically
symbolic importance in the story. "My love is like the fires of Etna"
was a neoteric cliché destined to have a long history.[125] What Virgil
has done in Book III is exactly what Aristophanes does with the
"King's Eye." The metaphor is *realized*, so that we can understand
what it actually means. The queen, on fire with love, is listening
breathlessly to Aeneas' every word as he speaks at her table. Virgil
wants us to know what this implies on an apocalyptic, epic scale.
Here we can truly say that Alexandrian rococo is sublimed into heroic
intensity.

It is the *symbolic* importance of the last episode of Book III then
which explains why, at the beginning of the Achaemenides adventure,

[124] Livy describes Hannibal's loss of an eye (XXII. 2. 11), and Horace says (*Odes*
IV. 4. 42–44) that he passed through the cities of Italy like a flame through pines,
or the east wind through the waters of Sicily. The *ultor* of IV. 625 ff. is therefore
the climax of long, almost subliminal, suggestion.

[125] Cf. Hor., *Epod.* 17. 30 ff.; Ovid, *Rem. Am.* 491, *Her.* 15. 2, *Met.* XIII. 868;
Seneca, *Hipp.* 102–03; Petrarch, *Africa* V. 399 and 405; J. Sannazaro, *Epigrammaton
liber primus, Opera omnia latine scripta*, Aldine ed., 1535, p. 43, v. 3; A. S. F. Gow on
Theocritus II. 135 and XI. 51 ff. The allusions to Etna in VII (786) and VIII (419,
440) show that the mountain also signposts what is to be the fate of the Trojans in
Italy. The more general topos, that the flames of passion may have destructive
consequences in public fires, already occurs in Greek lyric (Page, *Poetae Melici Graeci*,
p. 525, no. 71) and was developed by Lucretius (I. 473) and Horace (*Epod.* 14.
13–14). Cicero was sufficiently familiar with the conceit to make a joke of it (*Verrine*
V §92).

we have the same indication of time as in Book IV, where Dido
wrestles with her scruples before throwing them to the winds at her
sister's instigation, and why the description of the Cyclops anticipates
that of Fama, Enceladus' sister.[126] Neither Achaemenides nor Etna
inspires a self-indulgent purple patch. Still less is the Achaemenides
passage a hastily tacked on afterthought, or something ultimately
intended to be substituted for the Sinon episode of Book II. In Dido's
eyes, Aeneas must move from one character to the other, dissolve,
like so many of the figures in the poem, into his carnival twins. The
Roman reader, with Aeneas, must eventually see Carthage for what
it really was.

But this said cannot yet say all. The Cyclops episode in the *Aeneid*
overlies that of the eating of the Sun's cattle, whose position in the
story-line of the *Odyssey* it has usurped.[127] There is already eating in
it, as the "grotesque body" of the carnival giant regurgitates the
gobbets mingled with bloody wine which formed his cannibal meal.
The eating by Odysseus' crew of the cattle of the Sun was a deadly
offense. Aeneas' eating at Dido's banquet-table is a deadly offense,
or at least would be if Jupiter would let him get away with it. He
would be devouring his own future, destroying his own son, like
Saturn, in a futile effort to preserve a Golden Age. Yet his abandonment of Dido is an offense too. It is the illustration of an old religious
problem. Man lies under a moral imperative to act, and yet his
"moral" action must itself be sinful. Orestes had exemplified the
dilemma, and Dido had visualized Aeneas as Orestes (IV. 471).

But the indication of time at the start of *Aeneid* IV also looks
forward to Book VII:

Postera Phoebea lustrabat lampade terras (IV. 6)

Postera cum prima lustrabat lampade terras (VII. 148)

Here, the Trojans are cheerfully celebrating their arrival in Italy,
and on one level this is already the prophetic sign of Dido's short-
lived happiness. Even as she talks to her sister, the reader knows that
for her this is a false dawn, a dead end. But the structure of Books
I and VII of the *Aeneid* is drawn in very close parallel. In both books
Juno implacably pursues her enmity, in both books she makes a similar
speech expressing her hatred for the Trojans, and appeals to another
divine power to help her: there, Aeolus; here, Allecto. The happy
relief of the Trojans in Italy too is to be short-lived. The attentive
reader knows this also. Burning Dido will be replaced by burning
Amata, and burning Turnus, and these fires will eventually burn

---

[126] R. D. Williams on III. 619–20 compares *Aen.* IV. 177.

[127] G. N. Knauer, *op. cit.*, pp. 229–33.

Trojan and Italian dead, Latinus' city, and even Aeneas himself: *furiis accensus* (XII. 946: "fired by the Furies"). Before Book VII is over, Aeneas' son, Ascanius, will, like his father outside Carthage, have shot a stag and begun a war.

Love and hunting are associated as early as Euripides' *Hippolytus*,[128] and the lover as huntsman was a Hellenistic topos. Once again, Virgil *realizes* the metaphor. The significance of hunting in his epic is illustrated by another indication of time repeated from Book IV at the opening of Book XI. In the earlier book, the Carthaginians and Trojans sally forth together on what must have been for Dido the most wonderful day of her life (IV. 129):

> Oceanum interea surgens Aurora reliquit.
> It portis iubare exorto delecta iuventus . . .

Meanwhile dawn rose above the ocean. Forth from the gates as the light springs goes the chosen company of youth.

Exactly the same line introduces Book XI:

> Oceanum interea surgens Aurora reliquit:
> Aeneas, quamquam et sociis dare tempus humandis
> Praecipitant curae turbataque funere mens est . . .

Meanwhile dawn rose above the ocean. Aeneas, even though his anxious thoughts pressed him to find time for the burial of his comrades, though his mind was troubled by death . . .

At the start of XI, Aeneas has just killed Lausus and Mezentius, and lost Pallas. The Trojans are victorious, but at terrible cost. There are many pyres to be lit. When the body of Pallas arrives home, the streets are lined with funeral torches. The mourning women "kindle the city with their cries" (XI. 142–47). *Fama*, also at work in *Aeneid* IV, is at work here too (139). Dido is not perhaps hunting Aeneas so much as haunting him, spoiling and frustrating his efforts, forever re-enacting her own fiery death.

Aeneas brings out one of two robes that Dido had made for him, to be put on Pallas' corpse (XI. 72–77):

> Tum geminas vestis auroque ostroque rigentis
> Extulit Aeneas, quas illi laeta laborum
> Ipsa suis quondam manibus Sidonia Dido
> Fecerat et tenui telas discreverat auro.
> Harum unam iuveni supremum maestus honorem
> Induit arsurasque comas obnubit amictu.

---

[128] See above, p. 119 and note 34. Cf. Callimachus, *Epigr.* XXXI, Pf.; Hor. *Sat.* I. 2. 105 ff.; Ovid, *Am.* II. 9. 9–10. Plato, *Protagoras* 309 a, shows that the metaphor was already current in fashionable Athens.

Then Aeneas brought out two robes, stiff with gold and purple, which Dido had once made for him with her own hands, smiling at her task. She had separated the threads with fine gold. One of these sadly he placed over the young man as a last mark of respect, and veiled with that covering the hair destined for the fire.

Old Acoetes, sent by Pallas' father in vain to act as armor-bearer and guardian, has to be guided behind the bier, so worn out is he by grief and age (85–86):

> Ducitur infelix aevo confectus Acoetes,
> Pectora nunc foedans pugnis, nunc unguibus ora.

Ill-starred Acoetes, worn out with age, is guided in the procession, disfiguring his breast with his fists and then his cheeks with his nails.

It is exactly the behavior of Anna, when she hears of Dido's suicide (IV. 673):

> Unguibus ora soror foedans et pectora pugnis . . .

A sister disfiguring her cheeks with her nails and her breast with her fists . . .

Evidently the Aeneas who killed Dido in the service of his imperial ambitions has now killed Pallas. He had in Book X killed the young Lausus, and there for the first time (813) been gripped by *sae-vae . . . irae* ("savage angers"),[129] which would eventually burn him (*furiis accensus et ira/Terribilis*: "fired by the Furies and terrible in his anger," XII. 946–47). Now he indulges in human sacrifice (81–82):

> Vinxerat et post terga manus, quos mitteret umbris
> Inferias, caeso sparsurus sanguine flammas.

He had bound the hands of some behind their backs, so that he could send them as offerings to the shades. He intended to sprinkle the flames with the blood of the slaughtered.

He is showing himself like Achilles (*Il.* XXIII. 175–76). But, in *Aeneid* VI. 89, it was *Turnus* who was to be Achilles! Turnus' dark fires (which are Dido's) have evidently spread.

These associations with Dido explain the beautiful simile that is used to describe Pallas as he lies on his bier.[130] He is like "a flower cut down by a maiden's thumb, a flower of soft violet or drooping hyacinth, no longer radiant, but still beautiful, no longer nourished and strengthened by mother earth" (XI. 68–71). There is Homeric parallel to this, notably in the deaths of Gorgythion and Euphorbus.

---

[129] Mackail has a sensitive note on this passage.
[130] Cf. Homer, *Il.* VIII. 306 ff., XVII. 53–58; Sappho, 105c, Lobel–Page; Catullus 11. 22–24; cf. 62. 39 ff.; Ovid, *Met.* X. 209 ff., XIII. 395–96.

But "hyacinth" is not Homeric. The name refers us to Sappho, Catullus, Ovid. Catullus had spoken of his love for his *puella* as like a flower at the edge of the meadow, touched by the passing plow. In his poem 62, his chorus of maidens had sung of virginity, whose loss is like the plucking of a flower. In both instances, he was perhaps thinking of a fragment of Sappho, describing the hyacinth trampled underfoot on the mountainside by shepherds. Her meter and dialect in these two brief lines are epic. Ovid was to relate the accidental murder of the beautiful Spartan youth beloved by Apollo, and the hyacinth, "inscrib'd with woe," which sprang from his blood.

It is not then the pathos of Homer only that is recalled by the dead Pallas. His flowerlike and perished beauty is lost virginity, lost love. The feminine sensibility evinced by the comparison makes it inevitable that Aeneas should bring out something of Dido's for him to wear at the last. Aeneas too was an unheeding shepherd (IV. 71) as he hunted Dido to her death.

But is Dido wholly innocent? This flower was cut down, after all, by a *maiden's* thumb. The burning of human victims is indeed Homeric. But even Homer condemns it. Is the action repeated by Aeneas merely because Virgil wants to make him like Achilles? Ennius knew that the Carthaginians were in the habit of sacrificing their own children to the gods.[131] Has "father Aeneas" (184) as he burns Italian captives studied a Carthaginian example too well?

A last instance of "dark fires" (cf. V. 666) may be sought from the very end of Book IV. Dido is in her death agony, and Juno must send her messenger Iris to clip the lock of hair that will give her release. The rainbow goddess descends on saffron wings

Mille trahens varios adverso sole colores . . . (IV. 701)

Trailing a thousand motley colors as she caught the sunlight . . .

In Book V, the Trojans are again in Sicily. Aeneas is reminded that exactly one year has gone by since his father's death, and libation is offered at Anchises' tomb. While he prays, a serpent glides from the shrine. The colors on its scales are like those of the rainbow, that

Mille iacit varios adverso sole colores. (V. 89)

. . . throws a thousand motley colors as it catches the sunlight.

There is indeed already an irony in the fact that, although it is Dido whose pyre the Trojans have glimpsed in their last sighting of Africa, it is Anchises whose obsequies they now celebrate. Aeneas had told Dido that one reason for his desertion of her was the warnings he

---

[131] *Poeni suos soliti dis sacrificare puellos*, Ennius, *Ann.* 237, Warmington.

was constantly receiving from his father's ghost. Now we can see the truth of his words. Even the last rites that the poor queen might receive from her pretend husband are diverted to Anchises.

But this is not the end of the story. The Trojan men are distracted by the funeral games at which Aeneas is presiding, and their womenfolk, left to their own devices, are downcast and weary. Juno seizes her chance, and sends Iris to stir up trouble (V. 609–10):

> Illa viam celerans per mille coloribus arcum
> Nulli visa cito decurrit tramite virgo.

Invisibly along her swift path the maiden sped downward, hastening her way along her bow of a thousand colors.

Iris disguises herself as old Beroe, and urges the women to burn the Trojan fleet. She snatches up the first brand from the altars of Neptune herself, and hurls it onto the ships. It will be another apparition of Anchises that prevents the despairing Aeneas from deciding to settle in Sicily after all. Dido cannot win against that kind of divine opposition. But at least she can try!

An historian contemporary with Virgil, writing in Greek, has left us an account of Aeneas' wanderings through the Mediterranean from which it is possible to deduce the compression practiced by the poet in selecting from traditional material[132] during the composition of Book III. Those portions of the journey that survived this process of sifting must clearly have seemed indispensable. It looks only natural that the first stage of all should have been retained. But, when we have said this, we are astonished at the way in which what has been kept has been treated.

Tradition related that, when Aeneas first left Troy, he attempted a settlement in Thrace. There was actually a town Aenus which may have inspired this story. Virgil has to show that this plan was impossible. When Aeneas is engaged in sacrificing to his mother and Jupiter, he catches sight of a myrtle and cornel clump on a nearby hillock. Approaching to pull off a branch to adorn his altar, he is horrified to find blood pouring down the torn tree. His further efforts produce the same result, until at last a voice emerges from the copse, and tells him that here lies buried Polydorus. Sent away from Troy by his father Priam with a large sum of gold to the safe keeping of the Thracian king, the boy had been slain by his treacherous host once it became clear that Troy was doomed. From the spears thrust into his gashed body the clump of trees has grown up.

This grotesque conceit, drawn from the deep wells of folklore,

---

[132] R. D. Williams has an interesting table, "Introduction," p. 10.

borrowed by Dante and Ariosto, would attract no attention if it were found in such carnival authors as Ovid or Lucan.[133] In Virgil, it seems absurdly out of place. To make matters worse, it looks as if the poet himself was the inventor of the story. The vivid feeling for nature's life, which could identify a tree with flesh and blood, has of course parallels.[134] But the traditional account of Polydorus' death knew nothing of this metamorphosis.

And this last word, touching something fundamental in Virgil's whole apprehension of the epic world right from the days of *Eclogues* 4 and 6, is the clue to what is happening here. The grotesque story is intended in the first instance to tell us something about men's appreciation of the workings of destiny. Just as our first experience of the *vates* in the *Aeneid* (II. 122: Sinon's story) is misleading and doubtful, so our first experience of the voice of God can be fearful and horrible. The divine is an acquired taste, like music. What we get from it depends on our ability to listen, and our capacity for reception. Aeneas, setting off from Troy in an atmosphere of death and destruction, sees in the will of the gods what he is conditioned to see. The grotesque is a carnival mask imposed on the supernatural world by his distorted senses.

The meaning is layered more deeply. Aeneas is playing to an audience. He knew that Dido had unhappy experience of the depths of human greed. Dido's own husband had been murdered by her brother Pygmalion in his lust for gold. His account of the similar fate of Polydorus is colored by the rich tones he knows will please the Hellenistic taste of his listener.[135]

Because we are constantly seeing new experience in terms of and by analogy with the old, we are justified in recalling that Aeneas has other occasions in the course of the poem to pluck, or see plucked, as it were branches from trees. In Book VI, he plucks the golden bough (of which we will shortly hear an anticipation).[136] There, joy and relief shape his feelings. The whole episode has lost the macabre horror of this, though this was in its way a rehearsal for it. In Book XII (786–87) his spear is plucked from the olive stock in which Faunus has imprisoned it and restored to him by his mother Venus at a critical moment in his duel with Turnus. In these later episodes, he has a juster perception of what destiny is to mean to him. Here,

---

[133] *Inferno* XIII. 31 ff.; *Orlando Furioso* VI. 51 ff. Cf. Ovid, *Met.* IX. 344 ff.

[134] Callimachus, *Hymns* IV. 82–85; VI. 39. Cf. Apollonius on the Hesperides, *Argon.* IV. 1406 ff. Ovid, Statius, Boccaccio, Chaucer, Tolstoy (in his short story *Tri Smerti*) would share this sympathy. See below, p. 363.

[135] Servius (cited by R. D. Williams on vv. 49–57) had already pointed out that Polydorus' fate resembled that of Sychaeus.

[136] *Lenis crepitans*, III. 70; *leni crepitabat brattea vento*, VI. 209.

he can see only the horror and the blood (which is what his destiny will mean to others).

It should not surprise us that, is seeking to communicate Aeneas' imperfect understanding of his fate, Virgil should have had recourse to Hellenistic art. We are only entitled to be surprised if we believe that there was an alternative poetic tradition open to him. But was not the lesson of the Aristaeus episode precisely this, that the new epic had to start from Alexandrian bases? Virgil is crossing Alexandrianism with the grosser taste of the circus and carnival, but the resulting hybrid is still that of his own age. The episode of the metamorphosed ships in two later books proves how persistent was this bias in his imagination.[137]

The subsequent journey of Aeneas and his followers to Crete however in Book III was not part of the traditional wanderings. The island belonged to Jupiter, and if the Trojans are to be driven on again, it is important that they should have their mission confirmed by a god even greater than Delian Apollo (cf. III. 251). They imagine that here they can settle in a home abandoned by one of their Greek enemies, like Andromache and Helenus: a king expelled by plague for sacrificing his own son in return for his safety. Aeneas too is to be expelled by plague. His staying would have been the sacrifice of his own son.[138]

Yet, whatever the vague legendary associations of Crete to which allusion may be intended here, we must remember that for Virgil Crete is not primarily the symbol of majestic power and justice which might have been conjured up by memories of Jupiter and Minos. Once again we are forced to look from one vatic book to another.[139] On the doors of the Cumaean temple in VI, Crete appears in rather more sinister guise. On those doors, Daedalus, fleeing from the kingdom of Minos, had depicted the death of Androgeos, the son of Minos and Queen Pasiphae, slain in Attica out of jealousy provoked by his athletic prowess. The story on the doors was continued with a picture of the yearly tribute of young men and maidens paid by the Athenians to expiate their offense; of the Minotaur, fruit of the guilty passion between Pasiphae and a bull; of Theseus, who, helped by Minos' daughter Ariadne, found his way through the labyrinth where it was kept and at last slew the monster. All these associations must crowd in on the memory when we rescrutinize, in the light of later developments, the Trojan plan to settle in Crete. When Aeneas comes to view these pictures in Book VI, they represent in some

[137] IX. 77 ff.; X. 219 ff.
[138] Cf. IV. 234.
[139] Cf. III. 131 and VI. 2. Compare IV. 70, *nemora inter Cresia* and IV. 73, *Dictaeos*. These names look like mere Alexandrian display, but serve a structural and epic purpose characteristic of the poet.

degree the pattern of his own experience, summed up for him before the prophetic, vatic doors swing open upon another destiny (although that too will be a destiny of repetitions). But already we can sense that Carthage is his Crete, Dido his Ariadne/Pasiphae. Ascanius might have been Androgeos. Metamorphosis is at work here too.

Because of a plague and a vision, Aeneas does not settle in Crete (III. 137 ff.). The Penates, solemnly handed to him earlier by Hector, appear and remind him that the original oracle from Delos has been misinterpreted. It is Italy that is meant by "the ancient motherland" of the Trojans. Anchises recalls that this is supported by unheeded prophecies once made by the *vates* Cassandra.

But, on leaving Crete, the Trojans are greeted by a violent storm. The language that describes it is almost exactly repeated at the beginning of Book V, where they are leaving Africa after escaping from Dido. Carthage, where also Aeneas is tempted to settle down, would have been, like Crete, another betrayal of destiny.

It is a sign of Virgil's close dependence on Homer that a similar storm passage is repeated in the *Odyssey*. When it occurs there for the first time (XII. 403–06), Odysseus and his crew are leaving Thrinacria where, against the warning of their leader, his companions have killed and eaten some of the Sun's cattle. In the storm they are all to be drowned, and only Odysseus is to survive, eventually to end up in the clutches of Calypso and from there at the court of Alcinous where, like Aeneas at the court of Dido, he is telling his story. Evidently, unlike Odysseus, Aeneas is also in Calypso's cave still.[140]

At the second appearance of the storm (XIV. 301–04), Odysseus has arrived safely on Ithaca. He is disguised, and telling an elaborate fiction to his own swineherd Eumaeus, making out that he is a *Cretan* merchant, and that this storm shipwrecked him.

Callimachus and St. Paul alike were impressed by the Cretan reputation in antiquity for lying,[141] which Odysseus is doing his best to sustain. But so was Virgil. The direct Homeric parallel to the storm in Book III of the *Aeneid* is the *false* storm in the *Odyssey*, since that allegedly happened as Odysseus was, like Aeneas after him, leaving Crete. Do we deduce that Aeneas is lying as he talks about his adventure to Dido, as Odysseus certainly was when he told this story to Eumaeus? Impossible? But she at least will certainly think of him as a treacherous liar in Book IV![142]

---

[140] For Dido/Calypso see Knauer, *op. cit.*, pp. 209 ff.
[141] Callimachus, *Hymns* I. 8, with Pfeiffer's note: NT *Ep. Tit.* 1:12.
[142] Above, p. 161 with note 121.

The *real* storm of the *Odyssey* happens when Odysseus' crew are leaving the scene of a terrible and impious offense against the Sun god, committed on the island of Thrinacria, later identified with Sicily. We can see how the Trojans would have committed such an offense, if they had stayed in Crete, against their Sun god, Apollo.

But if in fact they committed neither of these offenses, why do they deserve the storms of either *Aeneid* III or *Aeneid* V? Partly because they flirted with temptation and have to be warned. But partly because in the opening books of the *Aeneid* they do commit a terrible offense, one that sets the pattern of their history for centuries to come in cruelty and exploitation. They bring about Dido's suicide. The storm of Book I, which greets them as they leave Sicily, is a larger version of the storm in Book III. What happens to Aeneas in Sicily (Achaemenides, Etna, the Cyclops) is a prefiguration of what happens at Carthage. What happens at Carthage is reinterpreted for us at Cumae. Guided by Homer's repetitions, Virgil's metamorphosing imagination sees all these events in terms of one another, in terms of "Crete."

The heinous offense committed by the Trojans at Carthage corresponds to the eating of the Sun god's cattle in the *Odyssey*. This is a reminiscence that is still with the reader in the next episode in *Aeneid* III, the encounter with the Harpies. The eating of cattle that did not belong to them is precisely the offense committed here by the Trojans.[143]

Homer had certainly referred to the Harpies, but Virgil's allusion to the "house of Phineus" (III. 212) suggests that Apollonius was more prominent in his mind. Yet in the *Argonautica*, the Harpies, after being driven away from plaguing Phineus by the sons of Boreas, had made their home, not in the Strophades, to which Aeneas' men are now coming, but in Crete (II. 299)! The symbolic importance of the island is emphasized once more. "Crete" is the ever-present temptation in life to be content with a false solution to what the gods want. Only at the end will these associations vanish, when Venus plucks a herb from "Cretan Ida"[144] which restores Aeneas' strength for his last fight with Turnus. Yet since this episode recalls the herb given by Hermes to Odysseus that enables him to face Circe, even there we are not to be free of Dido.

The structural importance of the Harpy scene in the *Argonautica* has already been noted. Tormented by winged creatures, Phineus

---

[143] Knauer (*op. cit.*, p. 186) compares *Aen.* III. 192–95 with *Odyssey* XII. 403–06. We may also compare the way in which an anticipation of the golden bough occurs *after* the Polydorus episode: above, note 136.

[144] XII. 412: cf. *Od.* X. 302 ff.

offered the first hint of the Prometheus theme, which would find its climax as Jason anointed himself with the Promethean herb and so assumed his dreadful destiny with all its remorseful pangs. The Harpies play the same anticipatory role in the *Aeneid*. Their curse is a foretaste of Dido's (IV. 381 ff.). *Infelix vates* (III. 246) must be given its full, Virgilian force.

Virgil has used Apollonius' Phineus also for his later scene with Helenus in Book III. Himself a Trojan and the king of a tiny Troy, a *vates* (358), Helenus explains that he can reveal only so much of the future in his predictions and no more. It is exactly the apology that Phineus makes to the Argonauts in Apollonius.[145]

Aeneas himself subsequently comments on the inadequacy of what Helenus had to tell him (712–13). The principal danger, missing from both his prophecy and that of the Harpy Celaeno, is obviously Dido. For Aeneas, Dido and his treatment of her, her threat to his purpose, constitute the offense that parallels the eating of the Sun's cattle in the *Odyssey*. But it is too late for prophecy. The offense is going on even while Aeneas speaks.

In his Harpy scene, Virgil uses a familiar narrative trick of mystification. Celaeno prophesies something that the reader will find laughably innocuous, that the Trojans will eat their own tables. Yet she fills her prophecy with such dire foreboding that commentators rightly find in it terrifying hostility and gloom. There is a contrast here between form and content which must be explored. What situation could actually justify the threats and hints of impending disaster that otherwise seem so empty? The answer to the question can only be given by remembering where Aeneas is as he speaks, eating at Dido's table, devouring his own future.

Virgil has signposted his meaning by repeating a line. In order to entice the Harpies to their retribution, the Trojans set up tables (III. 229–31):

> Rursum in secessu longo sub rupe cavata
> Arboribus clausa circum atque horrentibus umbris
> Instruimus mensas arisque reponimus ignem.

Once again in a deep inlet under a hollow cliff hemmed in on all sides by the bristling shadow of trees we set up tables and put fire back on the altars.

The association of *umbrae* and *ignis* is notable. But this is where Aeneas will hide his ships when he has landed in Africa (I. 310–12):

---

[145] *Odyssey* XII. 127 ff.; *Argon.* II. 311 ff. The parallels between what Circe says in *Odyssey* XII and what Teiresias says in Book XI (XII. 137 = XI. 110) may have suggested the combination Circe/Phineus to Virgil.

Classem in convexo nemorum sub rupe cavata
Arboribus clausam circum atque horrentibus umbris
Occulit.

He hides his fleet within the vaulting forest under a hollow cliff where
it was hemmed in on all sides by the bristling shadow of trees.

This time, we only have *umbrae*. Dido will supply the fires.

This explains why the storm at the beginning of *Aeneid* V is, in
one of its Homeric antecedents, the storm that beset Odysseus and
his men as they left Thrinacria. It is in Africa, which thus becomes
a second Sicily ("my love burns like the fires of Etna") as well as a
second Crete ("the Cretans are always liars"), that Aeneas and his
Trojans will have committed their major sin.

In the light of all this, we can see once more why Dido never
leaves the poem; why, for example, her presence is so strongly felt
even in its last book. Certainly Dido appears as far from innocent.
But the poet also exercises a profound moral criticism of his hero
and, by implication, of the people whom that hero represents. There
was an original sin at the root of Rome's greatness, the hunting down
of Dido, the looting of what should have been left untouched. The
reader who looks back to the worm's eye view of the Roman *imperium*
cited at the beginning of this chapter will understand that Virgil had
looked around him too.[146]

This must not be seen through modern blinkers as some sort of
*covert* protest. Criticism of morals was institutionalized at Rome. The
first faltering utterances of Roman literature in the *satura* described
by Livy (VII. 2) were directed towards warding off a public plague,
and plagues, in the primitive mentality (as in Pharaoh's Egypt, and
in Virgil's Crete), are the consequence of public sin. The role of the
satirist as it was subsequently defined was still to denounce public
sin, and confess personal weakness as a particular *exemplum* of public
fault (the "preacher's—and psalmist's—I"). Virgil is still Roman
enough to share the satirist's pulpit. His vatic sermon does not make
him the enemy of an emperor who was himself *censor morum*, and
the stern protector of Rome's provincial subjects.

In the whole of the *Aeneid* only Venus and Aeneas have sons
destined for life. The poet shows indeed an extraordinary preoccupation with virginal heroines (the Sybil, Allecto, Camilla, Juturna).
It is because a virgin is out of the normal calculus of primitive society,

---

[146] Scholars comment complacently on Aeneas as founder of cities, by contrast
with Odysseus, their destroyer. But Virgil spells out quite clearly what Aeneas did to
Carthage (IV. 86 ff., 669 ff.). He is still doing it to Latinus' city (XII. 567 ff., 654
ff.).

someone close to the supernatural. Creusa, who might have offered the portrait of a wife and mother, vanishes mysteriously, though her son will live. Astyanax is mentioned only as a figure of the past. Lausus and Pallas are killed. Turnus dies childless. Lavinia is still a virgin. Dido pathetically wishes she had a baby Aeneas.

Juno, the goddess of marriage, plays in the action a rather unfruitful role. She can indeed promise a nubile nymph to Aeolus by way of bribe. But one of the most shocking of her cruelties shows her in quite an opposite light. Juturna, bereft of her virginity by Jupiter (though still childless) and recompensed with an immortality she does not want, clings to her brother Turnus, whom she knows to be doomed. Juno persuades her that Turnus will best be rescued if he is prevented from accepting Aeneas' challenge to single combat. The agreement made to that effect must be aborted (XII. 158):

> Aut tu bella cie conceptumque excute foedus . . .

> Either you must stir up war and get rid of this embryo treaty . . .

Literally, the "conceived" treaty must be "shaken out."

Dido is in her way a doublet of Andromache (and Pasiphae), robbed by murder of a son. When we meet Andromache in Book III, she is offering libations to dead Hector at an empty tomb. She cannot see that Hector is not dead, but living in the person of Aeneas. She is locked by grief into a past that in reality is not there (*falsi Simoentis, inanem*). It is in this context that we must interpret *si lux alma recessit* at v. 311 ("if the kindly light has gone"). Andromache says to Aeneas: "Are you alive? Or, if we are both dead, where is Hector?" When Aeneas replies and says "Of course I am alive" he is tactfully refraining from any comment upon her state of mind. Andromache is so taken up with the past that she is as good as dead. She is now what Dido will become after Aeneas has finished with her (IV. 692):[147]

> Quaesivit caelo lucem ingemuitque reperta.

> She sought light in the sky and sighed when it was found.

In her last words, after Aeneas has received the vatic prophecy of Helenus, Andromache thinks especially of her own dead son Astyanax, for whom Ascanius is some kind of substitute. The principle of legitimacy is safeguarded here also. Astyanax/Ascanius is the rightful heir apparent to dead Priam, as Hector/Aeneas is the rightful successor. But the complexities that attend this simple farewell reveal

---

[147] *Quibus est fortuna peracta/Iam sua* (493–94) must be noted. With *furenti* (313) we hear a major theme of Book IV. *Furiis agitatus Orestes* (331) equally anticipates Dido (IV. 471).

Virgil at his deepest point of sympathy with human feeling. Dido loses, by Aeneas' treachery (*perfide*, IV. 366), the son she might have had, and the gifts that Andromache offers to Ascanius anticipate those of Dido to Aeneas, of which we hear in the rest of the poem, not least at Pallas' death. In the *Odyssey* it is Helen who makes a similar gift to Telemachus.[148] She too has no son of her own, and Telemachus is just about to return to Ithaca to be reunited with his father.

Virgil suggests the parallel by a Homeric reminiscence. Andromache pathetically comments on the resemblance of Ascanius to her murdered son (III. 490–91). It means of course that her son is still alive, though she cannot see this. She echoes Helen's words from an earlier part of the *Odyssey* (IV. 143 ff.) remarking on the resemblance of Telemachus to his father, Odysseus.

Yet it is clear from other evidence in the *Aeneid* that the manifold sources for the character of Dido include Homer's Helen.[149] In Virgil's Helen/Andromache then we have an anticipation of Helen/Dido, and Dido is Aeneas' chief listener at this moment.

The whole hidden symbolism of Helenus' insistent warning against Scylla and Charybdis is against falling foul of eros. Horace exploits the topos at the dinner-table, sympotic level, and Virgil is raising it, *more suo*, to epic intensity. Cicero associates Scylla, Charybdis and the Cyclops with Phalaris and Dionysius as examples[150] of the kind of cruelty for which Sicily was notorious. Prophesying Helenus himself has undertones of Homer's guiding Circe. Yet, even though we feel the threat posed by Dido to Aeneas so keenly in these mythical and historical analogues, Dido is seen here to the most favorable advantage, as a double of the grief-stricken, childless, widowed queen Andromache. This is the *commented* use of Homeric material which was pioneered by the *Hecale*, but what a transformation has been wrought by the national genius of Rome!

The extraordinary unity of the *Aeneid* means that the poet is continually able to signpost his meaning. But his scenes never lack emotional justification in their own right. The maternal instinct that leads Andromache to linger over Ascanius is the most natural thing in the world, and it had been through this same instinct that Juno had worked on Dido in the cruel deception of Book I (683 ff.). This is the humanity that robs Virgil's poetry, carefully wrought though it is, of any taint of mechanical contrivance.

The Andromache/Helenus episode illustrates very well the poet's

[148] Cf. *Odyssey* XV. 125 ff.; IV. 141 ff.
[149] I. 650. So when Aeneas becomes Paris (IV. 215), Dido must become Helen.
[150] *Verrine* V §146.

subtle and complex views on religion. Ostensibly, there could be no quarrel with a hero who received prophetic help to guide him along his way. But the nature of the guidance here shows that for Virgil man's relationship to the gods was far from simple or easily comprehensible. Helenus can give only a partial glimpse of the truth, and he is still caught up in the naive idea that the important dangers are physical. When he refers Aeneas for further information to the *insana vates* (443), by which he means the Cumaean Sibyl, he sounds just as purblind as the most enlightened Lucretian Epicurean. When Aeneas, in response to this illumination, ends with his warm promise to make Hesperia and Epirus "one Troy" (504–05), he clearly has a long road to travel before he grasps the real truth of what the change to Italy is to mean to himself and his people. He is ignoring the whole lesson of his own words at vv. 493–94, declaring that the fortune of Andromache and Helenus is already worked out. He is certainly contradicting Virgil's interpretation of the pathetic and futile attempt to reconstruct the past at Buthrotum. Nevertheless Virgil, seeing further than the clever skeptics of his own and other days, does not believe that this half knowledge proves that religion must be an illusion. *Nos alia ex aliis in fata vocamur* cries Aeneas (494: "We are summoned from one destiny to another"). It is proof of his worthiness, in spite of all, to be the instrument of the divine purpose.[151]

The angling of the narrative at Dido's court towards its principal listener, visible in Book III of the *Aeneid*, enables us to see its second book with new eyes. Once again, the first thing to remember is where we are. It is not Virgil who is directly recounting the fall of Troy. The poet is employing the device of the "intruded narrator," made familiar by Plato's dialogues, and by the Christian Gospels. This narrator is Aeneas, and not we but Dido and her court are his prime audience. We are merely privileged to eavesdrop.

Aeneas describes the taking of Troy as a fierce struggle in the streets and houses of the city, against a backdrop of fire. Commentators have long noted the theatricality of this *mise-en-scène*, so improbable in itself. Neither Greeks nor Trojans would have had any real motive for burning their homes or their prize. Tradition set the burning of the city at the time of the Greek departure, when the conquerors had no further use for it. This was evidently not on the night of its capture.

But there was a famous city in Roman history that had been captured after a long siege, and whose inhabitants knew that the invading armies meant the end. In their despair, they had fired their

---

[151] Cf. III. 374–76, 475–76 and *pietate*, 480.

own buildings, and days of street fighting were needed to subdue their frantic resistance. As the city perished, the Roman general, a man of great personal culture, had recited from Homer:

> The day will come when sacred Troy shall perish, and Priam, and the people of Priam, with his stout ashen spear.

This general was of course Scipio Africanus Minor, and the city was Carthage.[152] The deadly pathos of *Aeneid* II for Dido is that, as she sits listening to the story of the dying night of a city in which the gods had no further interest, she is listening to her own city's doom. She could not know this. Virgil's readers, students of Polybius, who told the famous tale about the Younger Scipio, could; and know too that already the divinely set flames were spreading to the queen herself. The modern historical occurrence is projected onto the ancient myth, and both derive tension and excitement from the superimposition. Such was Virgil's brilliantly simple method of rescuing the historical epic without offending Aristotle's veto. He seized the universal in the particular, and made it the stuff of poetry.

If Troy was destroyed like Carthage, then Troy must have sinned like Carthage. This is another important lesson of the poem, and a lesson of Book II (622–23):

> Apparent dirae facies inimicaque Troiae
> Numina magna deum . . .

> Dreadful sights become visible, the mighty powers of the gods warring against Troy . . .

At this moment, Aeneas is furthest away from any possible understanding of the divine purpose which is to culminate in Latium. He can see only the horror. But even in Book XII (821 ff.), the terms for Aeneas' victory over Turnus are that it is to be a victory of one chieftain over another only. Italy will still triumph over and absorb Troy. It is almost the last metamorphosis of the poem.

The sinfulness of Troy is a theme that occurs even in the *Georgics*, as a bitter explanation of the civil wars that have threatened Rome's very existence (I. 501–02):

> Satis iam pridem sanguine nostro
> Laomedonteae luimus periuria Troiae . . .

> For too long now with our own blood we have been atoning for the bad faith of Laomedon's Troy . . .

An allusion to cheating Laomedon is found in the *Aeneid*, in a passage whose reminiscence of Dido is clear (VIII. 18–26):

---

[152] Polybius XXXIX. 4 ff.; Diod. Sic. XXXII. 23 ff.; Appian, *Pun.* 127 ff.; Zonaras 9. 30.

Talia per Latium. quae Laomedontius heros
Cuncta videns magno curarum fluctuat aestu,
Atque animum nunc huc celerem, nunc dividit illuc,
In partisque rapit varias perque omnia versat,
Sicut aquae tremulum labris ubi lumen aenis
Sole repercussum aut radiantis imagine lunae
Omnia pervolitat late loca, iamque sub auras
Erigitur summique ferit laquearia tecti.
Nox erat, et terras animalia fessa per omnis . . .

These were the events in Latium. The hero-son of Laomedon saw
them all, and tossed on a mighty tide of anxieties. He turned his swift
thoughts now this way and now that, darting in many directions, and
revolving everything, just as when the flickering light of water is
reflected by the sun from a bronze cauldron or by the image of the
shining moon, it flits through every place, rising high in the air and
striking the fretted ceiling of the room. It was night, and throughout
all the earth the weary creatures . . .

The beautiful simile is borrowed from Apollonius (*Arg.* III. 756 ff.),
who used it to describe the sleepless night spent by Medea when she
was debating whether to help Jason or not. Its inapposite use here
forces us to think of Dido, the obvious successor of Medea. *Nox erat*
looks back to a passage of *Aeneid* IV (522) that clearly begins with a
reminiscence of the *Argonautica*. *Fluctuat aestu* is also an echo of IV.
532.

But Dido had also assailed Aeneas as the true descendant of the
race of Laomedon, precisely in the same passage of IV (541–42):

nescis heu, perdita, necdum
Laomedonteae sentis periuria gentis?

Are you still ignorant, alas, and lost? Do you not yet feel the bad faith
of Laomedon's line?

As Aeneas tosses on his anxious couch in Latium, we see him suffering
what he did to Dido, even becoming Dido.

The immediate difference is that he is rescued by the apparition
of Father Tiber, who advises him to seek help from the Arcadian
settlers at the site of Rome. But it is here that we learn for the first
time the name of Pallas, ancestor of the Arcadians, and it was young
Pallas who would receive Dido's robe as his shroud. Virgil makes the
connection Dido/Pallas by more repetition. The god requests Aeneas'
close attention (VIII. 49–51):

nunc qua ratione quod instat
Expedias victor, paucis (adverte) docebo.
Arcades his oris, genus a Pallante profectum . . .

Now pay attention, and in a few words I shall explain how you may successfully achieve the present enterprise. To these shores the Arcadians, a line descended from Pallas . . .

So it was that Juno had requested attention from Venus, when Dido was to be used as a weapon in their struggle in IV. 115–17:

> nunc qua ratione quod instat
> Confieri possit, paucis (adverte) docebo.
> Venatum Aeneas unaque miserrima Dido . . .

Now pay attention, and in a few words I shall explain how the present enterprise may be fulfilled. Aeneas and with him ill-starred Dido to the hunt . . .

Bacchic themes provide a powerful link between Dido, Pallas and Turnus. Bacchus is first mentioned in Book I, where the Trojans have landed in Africa, and are taking some refreshment after their toils (215). But already a more sinister note is struck, for it is at a banquet with its freely flowing wine that Dido drinks in the flames of her infatuation with Aeneas and his possibility of a future (I. 686, 734). Another false hope had already been nourished at Buthrotum (III. 354).

But in Book IV the queen's Bacchic frenzy bursts out unrestrained (300–03):

> Saevit inops animi totamque incensa per urbem
> Bacchatur, qualis commotis excita sacris
> Thyias, ubi audito stimulant trieterica Baccho
> Orgia nocturnusque vocat clamore Cithaeron.

Helplessly she rages, and on fire raves through the entire city. She was like a Bacchant roused by the brandishing of the sacred emblems. She hears the god, and the celebrations goad her to frenzy; Cithaeron echoes at night with cries.

From now on, the association of Bacchus and Dido is constant. In Book V, as the Trojans take their ease in Sicily, the iridescent serpent bodes well for their fortunes. But in Italy Bacchus and the serpent mean something rather different. Allecto tosses one of the serpents from her own snaky locks into Amata's heart, and the queen's assumed Bacchic *furor* spreads to the other women, and ends in the call for war (VII. 346, 385, 580).

When in the last book of the poem Turnus is compared to a bull in a simile that borrows from Euripides' *Bacchae* (743 = *Aen*. XII. 104) to recall the futile struggle of Pentheus against the power of the god, the external allusion meshes with a web of internal allusions to form yet another link in the "myriad interconnections" (Tolstoy) that constitute the tight unity of the poem.

One of these allusions is to Turnus' laughter (VII. 435). The nightmarish figure of Allecto as she reveals her true shape and nature in the sequel lifts us into a realm of caricature that evokes the monsters of the carnival, survivals of the primitive imagination. Pentheus had laughed at Dionysus in Euripides' play, and discovered his mistake. Turnus' laughter loses a dimension if we do not see it in its Bacchic context.

Even in the most innocent presence of Bacchus danger lurks. We see this in retrospect, when we think what the first mention in Book I at the Trojans' African picnic will generate. At the site of Rome, equal peril. Evander welcomes the Trojans and pledges their first real alliance on Italian soil (VIII. 179–81):

> Tum lecti iuvenes certatim araeque sacerdos
> Viscera tosta ferunt taurorum, onerantque canistris
> Dona laboratae Cereris, Bacchumque ministrant.

Then in eager emulation chosen young men with the priest of the altar carry the roasted meat of bulls. They heap high in baskets the welcome bread, and serve the wine.

But Evander has a son, Pallas, and Pallas is to die. The king senses this. His emotional farewell awakens fresh echoes of Dido (VIII. 583–84):

> . . . haec genitor digressu dicta supremo
> Fundebat; famuli conlapsum in tecta ferebant.

These words the father poured out at the last parting. He fainted, and his attendants carried him to his palace.

Compare the fainting Dido, at her last interview with Aeneas (IV. 391–92):

> . . . suscipiunt famulae conlapsaque membra
> Marmoreo referunt thalamo stratisque reponunt.

Her attendants raised her up and carried her fainting limbs back to her marble chamber and set her on the couch.

But already this note had been struck as Evander greeted Aeneas for the first time (VIII. 152–53):

> Dixerat Aeneas. ille os oculosque loquentis
> Iamdudum et totum lustrabat lumine corpus.

So said Aeneas. Evander had long been scanning his face and eyes as he spoke, indeed his whole body.

So at the start of Dido's last speech to Aeneas, just cited (IV. 362–64):

> Talia dicentem iamdudum aversa tuetur

Huc illuc volvens oculos totumque pererrat
Luminibus tacitis . . .

As he said these things she had long been looking at him askance,
rolling her eyes this way and that, and scanning his whole body with
speechless gaze . . .

Dido's presence in and at Pallas' death cannot then surprise.

If Pallas shares in Dido, a different light is shed on the end of the
whole poem, where scholars seem unable to resist their moralizing
bias towards *raisons d'état* (XII. 945–49):

Ille, oculis postquam saevi monimenta doloris
Exuviasque hausit, furiis accensus et ira
Terribilis: 'tune hinc spoliis indute meorum
Eripiare mihi? Pallas te hoc vulnere, Pallas
Immolat et poenam scelerato ex sanguine sumit.'

Aeneas, after drinking in the reminder of his savage grief offered by
these spoils, fired by the furies and terrible in his anger: "Clad in the
spoils of my friends, are you to be snatched from my grasp? It is
Pallas, Pallas who sacrifices you with this wound and takes satisfaction
from your guilty blood."

*Monimenta* (IV. 498), like *exuvias* (IV. 651), is one of Dido's words.
So is *hausit* (IV. 661). So is *furiis*. *Accensa, ira, vulnus, poena, sceleratus,
sanguis* belong to the same complex. But if we write here

. . . *Dido* te hoc vulnere, *Dido*
Immolat et poenam scelerato ex sanguine sumit . . .

it means that Aeneas has become Dido. And in him, Dido is committing
suicide again, and this time a metamorphosed Aeneas is dying with
her. *Immolat* was used of him at X. 541, when he killed *Phoebi
Triviaeque sacerdos*. On the belt Turnus had taken from Pallas was
impressed the murderous crime of the Danaids, wives who slew their
own husbands (X. 496–98). And when Aeneas said farewell to
Ascanius (XII. 435–36), he had echoed the language of Sophocles'
suicidal Ajax (*Ajax* 550–51).

## V

The *Aeneid* is therefore a continuous commentary on itself. No part
is independent within a total harmony of meaning. Dido recurs
insistently throughout, not least in Book XII, where she is visible not
merely in the minor figure of Queen Amata, but even more largely
in the major hero, Turnus, also juxtaposed with a sister, also the
victim of Aeneas the huntsman, and even the African lion for which

young Ascanius had prayed (IV. 159: cf. *Poenorum . . . in arvis/. . . leo*, XII. 4 and 6). The poem's art may be compared with the cinematic technique of superimposition.[153] One scene, one transparency, is laid over another, and this montage produces extra dimensions of both feeling and significance.

Virgil is also continually overlaying his scenes on those of the *Iliad* and *Odyssey*—and of Apollonius' *Argonautica*. Dido is the *Odyssey*'s Calypso, Circe, Nausicaa, Arete, the *Iliad*'s Helen and Andromache. But her closest parallel is Apollonius' Hypsipyle. Only Hypsipyle is a queen in her own right, looking for a husband and able to offer him a kingdom. Aeneas is therefore Jason, as well as Odysseus, and Ajax, and many other heroes of the *Iliad*, Paris, Hector, Agamemnon, Achilles.

This art is certainly Alexandrian. Callimachus' Theseus in the *Hecale* had overlain some piquant reminiscences of Odysseus in the swineherd Eumaeus' hut. But it is also Roman. To understand this we have to remind ourselves of the incalculable influence of the circus on Roman aesthetics. Just as the Theatre of Dionysus stood at the center of Athenian artistic creativity, and constituted the framework for its most characteristic and lasting achievements, so the circus and amphitheatre stand at the center of Roman aesthetic expression, crudely brutal, yet at the same time lavishly spectacular: primitive and refined, and of the profoundest interest to the student of the real focus of Roman aesthetic originality. Juvenal sneers at Statius' need to eke out his poetic living by writing mimes.[154] But the mime left traces on Statius' more serious art. Lucan had written mimes too. The Christian bishop Sidonius gives us some impression of these performances in his day.

Interestingly, Lucian relates that one mime-dancer, in his depiction of the child-devouring Cronus, strayed into that of the cannibal supper of Thyestes. Another confounded the fiery death of Semele with that of Medea's victim, Glauce. It is this Roman addiction to *contaminatio* which both inspires the mixing we find in the Roman comedies of Plautus and Terence, and that in Seneca's tragedies. Seneca's Hippolytus is like Pentheus; his Phaedra like Pasiphae; his

[153] See below, p. 404. The slaying of Penthesilea by Achilles with its latent eroticism (shown, for example, on the Exekias vase: K. Schefold, *Götter- und Heldensagen der Griechen* [Munich 1978], p. 239) may be in Virgil's mind in the last scene of the *Aeneid*, and Penthesilea was one of the models for Dido (I. 491: see G. N. Knauer, *Die Aeneis und Homer*, p. 309).

[154] Juvenal, 7. 86. Lucan's *XIV salticae fabulae* are mentioned in the *Life* by Vacca. Cf. Sid. Apoll., *Carm.* XXIII. 272 ff.; Nonnus, *Dion.* XXX. 109–16; Lucian, *De Salt.* 80; in general, "Memini Me Fiere Pavum: Ennius and the Quality of the Roman Aesthetic Imagination" (above, note 39).

Medea like Orestes. The Greeks themselves had sometimes seen one myth in terms of another. What is exceptional for them because it is comic and lyric is set by Virgil at the very heart of Roman epic: not as an innovation made for its own sake, but simply as the essence of the Roman lyrical and comic perception of the world, already at work in Ennius and Plautus.

This kind of interpretation of the *Aeneid* does not give a clear picture of the poet's meaning. The reason is that the poem cannot in principle have a clear meaning. Classicizing criticism has erected the model of an ancient world in which everything had a defined place. When this model collapses, "decadence" may be diagnosed. Alas, how frequent these "decadences" were!

Least of all may Roman aesthetics be compressed upon a Procrustes bed of ordered clarity. The Roman imagination was disordered, unclear, inclined to blur and blend the incompatible, essentially comic ("satiric"), emotional rather than logical, imprecise, elemental. The *Aeneid* exploits these qualities to build a tragic vision of man's helplessness in the face of the gods' *inclementia* ("ruthlessness"), a word Virgil seems to have invented. *Tantaene animis caelestibus irae?* ("Can there be such fits of anger in divine hearts?") is an extraordinary insertion by the poet at the start of his epic. It signals the unanswered questions that he will leave in our minds when his voice is stilled at the end.

Yet if the poet had done no more than this, he would merely have translated Apollonius' Hellenistic sensibility onto Roman ground. What he adds is something at which Apollonius might have smiled, and that is a Roman and Augustan sense of national destiny, summed up in the *vates* ideal. *Inclementia* is not the whole story. The paradox of his poem is that it takes the art of a disillusioned Alexandrian world, and uses it to project an image of divine providence at work in history.

This was not in fact to prove an easy task for some of his epic successors. But Virgil's genius was aided both by the imprecisions native to his civilization, and by the obscurities that inevitably attend any authentic leap of faith. A simple eulogy of Augustus, a simple tale of an always infallible Aeneas, would have been unworthy of his talent and incredible to his audience, and by this time have become a literary curiosity. A genuinely religious epic was bound to be an epic which left questions. Here we can see even the "intruded narrator" of Books II and III in a fresh perspective. The serio-comic device recurs in the "messenger" of tragedy, and of Menander's *Dyscolus*, in the "prophet" of *Nemean* 1, the Er of Plato's *Republic* and the Apollodorus of his *Symposium*, in the evangelist writing in Greek about an Aramaic-speaking rabbi who also became a carnival

king, in Thomas Mann's Zeitblom from *Doktor Faustus*. It serves to
lend an air of remoteness to what is reported, even in the assertion
of its "Gospel truth." We must always make up our own minds when
all is said and done. And when Virgil was the reporter about a
mythical past to a contemporary audience, can this feeling of make-
believe have been diminished?

Two considerations help to illumine these paradoxes. The first
derives from Aristotle's declaration in the *Poetics* that Homer's superiority lies in his being "dramatic." Drama, the interplay of sharply
opposed characters and points of view, inevitably leaves questions,
and we need look no further than Shakespeare to feel the truth of
that. As epic grows towards its truest development therefore (what
Aristotle calls its *physis*), it will necessarily raise more questions than
it answers. Here Virgil, dramatic, like Homer, is the most faithful
exponent of the classical tradition.

The second consideration requires us to accept that "oral" epic
in the ancient world did not end with Homer. The same romanticism
that leads certain critics to idealize Homer (later epic is of course
"secondary," if not "decadent") leads them also to condemn the
*recitatio* at Rome. But the *recitatio* made epic oral again, or rather,
confirmed a "dramatic" feature that epic had always had. Virgil in
particular was famous for his *recitationes*, and on one occasion even
caused Octavia, the mother of Marcellus, to faint.[155] The *Life* by
Donatus, which narrates this episode, also refers to the "sweetness
and marvelous harlotries" of his voice, and tells the story found in
Seneca of the poet Iulius Montanus, who would have plagiarized
from Virgil if he could also have taken "voice and expression and
acting power." For the same verses, he went on, when their master
uttered them had a fine sound: without him they were empty and
dumb.

"Acting power" (*hypocrisis*) here reiterates Aristotle's point about
the essentially dramatic nature of all great epic. But it also refers us
to the Formalist theory of the *skaz*, the oral narrative which is assisted
by the actor/author with all the modulations and inflections and
even gestures that we would expect in a formal piece for the stage.
Obviously, such a text, when presented to a silent reader who views
it as a self-sufficient act of communication, is bound to lose most of
its meaning. When it is brought alive by a trained performer (someone
like Plato's Ion),[156] it acquires dimensions of which we never dreamed.
But these dimensions are dimensions of ambiguity, precisely because
the fusion and resolution of the whole must be the work of the

---

[155] *Vit. Verg. Don.* 28–30.
[156] *Ion*, esp. 535 b – 536 d.

individual, unique, unrepeatable performance, to which the auditor makes his own indispensable contribution.

This is why we should attend to Virgil's *cano*, the third word of the poem. Of course this is at one level a homage to the *Iliad*, but that already says something at more than one level. The *Iliad*'s repetitions and contrasts lend a dimension of ambiguity to it also. Hector dies like Achilles' friend Patroclus, and, over a meal, Achilles and Priam learn an accommodation with death. A funeral meal will conclude the poem.

In Roman poetry, *cano* was a word with a chequered history.[157] Ennius had rejected it, along with the mumbo-jumbo of the *vates* who used it. The Roman Alexandrians had remodeled the word on the analogy of the Greek *aeidō*, because they sensed the great debt that Alexandrian poetry owed to lyric. Virgil, though he certainly uses *cano* because he, unlike Ennius, is proud to be a *vates*, does not repudiate this Alexandrian nuance. His poem exploits repetition in every book, at every turn. Repetition, we are told by a modern authority, is music's most characteristic procedure. And music, we are told by a modern artist of the prose epic, is "systematic ambiguity."

The historian of literature will note that exactly the same lyrical ambiguity attends many of Pindar's images. The fire, water and night of the proem to *Olympian* 1 develop into the fire and water of the cauldron from which Poseidon rescues Pelops, into the night in which the luminous god appears from the sea to answer his favorite's prayer. Baby Heracles blends, as he handles the snakes sent to kill him in *Nemean* 1, into the mature warrior who will one day fight for the gods against the snake-limbed Giants. The horsemen over whom Hiero rules with so sure and yet gentle a hand at the start of *Pythian* 2 have doubles in the horse/men Centaurs, contrasting symbols of rebellion against the divine order. In *Olympian* 3, the pillars of Heracles suddenly find themselves, not at the end of the Mediterranean, but at the end of the Olympic racecourse.[158]

This plasticity of allusion, the supreme example of what Aristotle meant by "metaphor," the poet's chief and unteachable gift, awakens both in Virgil and Pindar echoes and vibrations that can never be wholly sounded at one hearing. In both poets, scholars have been aware of a religious dimension.

That the *Aeneid* should be like some great tragedy or symphony— perhaps, if we combine its two aspects, like Wagner's *Ring*—greatly alters our perception of the "classical epic tradition." Those writers

---

[157] Cf. my article in *Latinitas* XIII (April 1965), mentioned above, note 23.

[158] These facets of Pindar are reflected at greater length in *Pindar's Art: Its Tradition and Aims* (Hildesheim–Munich–Zurich 1984) [with F. S. Newman].

who have also been aware of musical ambiguity, like Tasso, fit much more easily than their critics believed into the classical mold. But we can more easily find room even for Ovid's comic masterpiece in the tradition in this way. The Roman sensibility was essentially comic, and though Virgil exploits comic devices with tragic intent and effect in the *Aeneid*, not least in some of his vocabulary, they remain comic in their origins. He is still the poet of a "circus" or "carnival" civilization, whose greatest monument of art is the Colosseum. For Virgil, metamorphosis, which had fascinated him right from the days of *Eclogue* 6, is downbeat and deadly. We need only think back to the Polydorus episode, which he apparently invented, at the start of *Aeneid* III. All Ovid had to do (here as so often the follower of the beaten path) was to lighten the mood.

His *Metamorphoses* therefore, a supreme achievement of carnival fun, takes its place as a typically Roman work at the side of the *Aeneid*. If the literary critic has been sometimes reluctant to paint this diptych, literary artists have never shrunk from doing so. These artists have included Shakespeare and Dante. What they saw in the *Metamorphoses* was imitable, because it was the work of a less intense genius. But they still saw it as the essence of the Roman literary legacy.

The *Aeneid* is not a cyclic epic, and a historical epic only by indirection. Schooled in the first instance by Aristotle, Virgil understood that an epic that merely hung a collection of adventures about a single name could not exploit to the full the dramatic potential of the genre. The mere addition of adventure to adventure did not in itself justify the writing of a long poem. Length could only be made acceptable if it was governed by, and made dependent on, art. Here we may suppose that Callimachus served to show how the comic technique of looking to Homer to provide an already existing pattern would, at one stroke, lend to a modern epic a depth and a resonance, a shape and a design, which were incomparably adapted to answer Aristotle's demands. Apollonius showed how this quest for dramatic and ironic unity could be further aided by the use of echoing similes and repeated language.

Ennius' imitation of Homer in the *Annales* had already revealed the bent of the national genius. But Ennius could still urge the superiority of his consuls and tribunes to their heroic and Homeric counterparts. Virgil's high tragedy *reduces* the implied laughter and optimism of his great predecessor. It is the typical refinement of sensibility in a society becoming more sophisticated, more troubled.

But Virgil remained a Roman! The techniques sampled above all show the Roman poet's *metamorphosing* mind. The blending into one

Virgilian character of many Homeric, indicated by the use of different Homeric parallels; the blending of images into one another as the poem progresses; the splitting of one Homeric character into more than one Virgilian descendant, are all evidence of this. Often there is something deeper still in the poet's imagination. The carnival concept of "vertical time" (deliberate anachronism) is brought into play. What is narrated ostensibly about one past is vatically colored by another: by what is yet to happen in the fictional story (and what the reader knows did happen) at Carthage; by what historically had happened between Carthage and Rome. In Book III, Polydorus, murdered for gold, was Dido's husband (and might-have-been son?). Widowed Andromache, fixed in the past, her son dead, was another Dido. Sicily, with its pastoral Cyclops and volcanic fires, would symbolize the love/hate of a more than Catullan passion. The story of that book, like the story of Book II, continually gains psychological intensity from being heard by a special auditor in a special place. Even its list of cities at the end, their glory a thing of the past for Virgil's listeners, for Aeneas an unrealized dream, encapsulates the ambiguity of the whole story. And is the tragedy of errors which defines the Trojan behavior to the peoples of Italy not a prefiguration of the Romans' behavior to their neighbors?

As he studied his Alexandrian inheritance, Virgil's own contribution was to raise what otherwise might have degenerated into a clever manipulation of devices and procedures to vatic stature. In the last analysis, poetry is not an affair of technique. Perhaps we should rather say that only under the pressure of emotion will the sensitive artist be able to discover the full possibilities of his art. In Virgil's Rome, as in that of Catullus and Lucretius, the need was not for cleverness, but for insight into human predicaments. The theory of the *vates*, legitimizing the groping quest to understand the ways of God towards man, was ideally suited to provide the vehicle for a new kind of poetry, one in which the heroic again became a fit topic for mature consideration.

Because however this new expression of the heroic was laden with all the reservations that history forced upon the attention of a self-conscious age, it offered for the first time to the classical epic the chance of reconciling ideal with reality, of acknowledging all the failures and compromises that go to make up the human lot, all the cruelties that go to form man's experience of God, without losing some faith in an ultimate, publicly realized order of right. Vibrant with the tension between this Augustan sense and Alexandrian sensibility, between faith and irony, Virgil's *Aeneid* claims primacy among the epics of European civilization. It first taught us how fragile is the virtue which, arbitrarily graced by heaven, masters the world, and upon its peace imposes a faltering morality.

# V

# THE LATIN EPIC AFTER VIRGIL:
# OVID TO STATIUS

THE age that followed that of Augustus was preoccupied with its literary status, and usually convinced that it had come down in the world. In Rome itself, the *causae corruptae eloquentiae* were one of the burning questions of the day, as the works dedicated to them by Tacitus and Quintilian, as well as the remarks of the Elder Seneca or which conclude the *De Sublimitate*, bear witness. Modern literary historians have been willing to accept this judgment, but the grounds for it are less unanimously agreed. Varying answers have been given to the inherited and assumed problem. One points to the political circumstances that developed as Augustus' carefully constructed façade of government collapsed. Free and soaring eloquence is the natural offshoot of unhampered debate and argument. Curtail the one, and the other withers.[1]

This explanation is presented in altogether too naive a fashion. In the first place, it takes far too narrow a view of the Roman achievement, whether imperial or aesthetic. It is absurd to pretend that everything came to an end with Augustus. The glories of the second century, even those of Constantine, were still to come. The Colosseum, central to the understanding of the Roman imagination, was yet to be built. In the second place it takes far too narrow a view of literature. There may indeed be grounds for supposing that the absence of political liberty throttles frankness in the debating chamber. But literature is more than political speeches! The situation in which writers found themselves in post-Augustan Rome did not differ radically from that which had prevailed at the court of the Ptolemies— or of many of the Greek tyrants who had been the most lavish patrons of a poetry still treasured—or even from the situation that had existed in Augustan Rome itself. Ovid paid with years of exile for offending the *princeps*, and part of his offense, on his own admission, was a

---

[1] Cf. A. Rostagni, *Storia della letteratura latina* (Turin 1955), II, pp. 236 ff., and D. A. Russell on 'Longinus', *De Sublimitate*, 44.

*carmen.*[2] The success of his *Medea* however hints that he might have been a better poet if he had known how to bow gracefully to this kind of pressure; and on the other side, it is just as possible that Virgil would never have attained the fullest development of his genius without it.

Dissatisfied with this political approach to literature, other scholars have pointed out that in many ways authors have never enjoyed better prospects than under the very emperors who are accused of stifling them. Tiberius, Augustus' immediate successor, was well known for his interest in Hellenistic poets, including the Euphorion at whom Cicero had sneered, and whose poems we miss so sorely. Caligula was the author of one of the most up-to-date criticisms of Livy to have survived, a judgment which shows that the atmosphere of his day was by no means alien to an historian who might wish to break away from the conventions of Hellenistic writing. Claudius was a scholar and antiquarian, steeped in Etruscan lore. Nero, the heir of Augustus, was passionately devoted to all the arts. The Flavians were no less concerned about letters. Vespasian appointed Quintilian to a chair. Interestingly, it was the same parsimonious emperor who built the Colosseum. Domitian rewarded Statius. Both these emperors promoted Tacitus. Hadrian founded the Athenaeum, and has come down to us as the author of an indispensable anthology piece.[3]

# I

There is in fact a basic mistake of method in all this debate. The literary historian is not, in the first instance, called upon to express judgment about the "decadence" or otherwise of the post-Augustan period. His task is to understand why Roman writers said the things they did. Here, two comparisons may help. The appreciation of the literature of Periclean Athens would not be greatly advanced by a student who took every gibe in Aristophanes literally, and a Russian scholar has pointed out that, in the age of Alexander the Great, Theophrastus, the successor of Aristotle, can find nothing but eccentrics for his *Characters*.[4] To see Athens or Greece only through the

---

[2] *Tristia* II. 211. Gallus' poems were allegedly removed from the public libraries after his disgrace. In Alexandria, Sotades is said to have been ultimately drowned by one of Ptolemy's admirals.

[3] See H. E. Butler, *Post-Augustan Poetry* (Oxford 1909), pp. 1 ff.; Schanz–Hosius, *Geschichte der römischen Literatur*, II (repr. Munich 1959), pp. 419 ff. H. Bardon, *Les empereurs et les lettres latines d'Auguste à Hadrien* (Paris 1940), takes (pp. 162 ff.) a more pessimistic view (though it is difficult to see how a French scholar writing at that date could have been in a position to throw stones!).

[4] Cf. O. Freudenberg, *Poetika Syuzheta i Zhanra* (Leningrad 1936), p. 317.

eyes of satirists would be an absurd distortion. Why is it not a distortion when we arrive in Rome?

Similarly, the reader of Dante's *Inferno* smiles to learn that the majority of the souls in hell are Florentine contemporaries of the poet, and the historian who deduced that thirteenth- and fourteenth-century Florence was decadent, and that its literature was decadent, would be thought of as relying on uncertain evidence. We take Dante's strictures as a function of the comic genre, not as a guide to literary and social realities. Why do we not do this with Juvenal and Martial?

It is not a judgment therefore but a question which the literary historian must advance in his first approach to post-Augustan poetry. Whether it was "decadent" is not the point. What matters is *why* the Romans moralized in the way they did about their literature and society.

Even at the most superficial level it may be seen that, when published artists complain that society is philistine and unreceptive, we cannot take them too seriously for, if their complaints were wholly true, we would never have heard them. Petronius amuses by his portrait of the upstart millionaire, as does Seneca with his description of a real-life Trimalchio in Calvisius Sabinus. The attractive thing about both men satirized is that they paid the best compliment they could—imitation—to literary culture. There is not the slightest proof that public misconduct was any worse under the emperors than on the eve of the Social War, when Lucilius wrote, and a great deal of evidence that, for ordinary people, life was vastly improved.[5] When Trimalchio and his fellow freedmen rose to prominence and wealth, they were continuing a trend already visible in the time of the Republic,[6] and can we do anything except applaud the mobility in Roman society which allowed at least some talented slaves to escape from their degrading condition?

What then was, and is, behind the still lingering sentiment that, in spite of its general benevolence towards literature, the post-Augustan age was nevertheless "silver," "decadent"? The ancient writers themselves who pronounced this verdict seem in some cases to have felt that literature ought to offer a cure for moral and social abuses, and that its failure to do this proved its degeneracy. This may explain why political eloquence was so suddenly elevated to be the paradigm genre—surely an otherwise curious choice, even for ancient

---

[5] M. Rostovtzeff, *Rome* (repr. New York 1960), p. 177; E. Kornemann, *Römische Geschichte* (4th ed., Stuttgart 1959), II, pp. 179, 208 ff.

[6] Cicero, *Verrine* V. 154, *conlibertos*. The tendency had already begun in classical Greece (Pasion).

Athens. There runs throughout the so-called Silver period the consciousness that something is wrong with society, and that, if literature is not addressing itself to this wrong, it is failing in its duty.[7] Hence the strange paradox that, in an age when we are told that free speech was menaced by the informer and the blackmailer, so much literature is made up precisely of satire, which depends for its effect on something like freedom of speech. Were the satirists toying with a *persona*, a mask, grown too big for them?

If however there is anything in the claim that literature is concerned with "sincerity," we may attempt to reformulate in a way intelligible now the Roman belief that things were not what they should be. A sincere fool is still a fool. Nevertheless, if sincerity means "moral honesty," an artist must cherish some sort of sincerity, as a necessary though insufficient condition of achievement. *Talis hominibus fuit oratio qualis vita* ("Men's style reflects their lives").[8] The whole argument of Seneca's 114th Letter (which interestingly takes Augustus' own minister Maecenas as the example of decadent style) is that, if men live wrongly, they will express themselves wrongly. As it stands, this is crude generalization. But the grain of truth in it may be that, if the artist does not live up to his calling to look at men's life in society honestly, his dishonesty will result in a preoccupation with the secondary that will soon decline into the second-rate.

Where then, in the circumstances of first-century Rome, did the calling for the artist to live up to his responsibilities come from? The primitive impulse towards conformity, which later becomes an impulse towards morality, was deeply layered in the Roman psyche. It was embedded in the office of censor, and in the concept of the *lustrum*. In another guise, it survived in the circus, where emperors were drawn willy-nilly into bantering dialogue with their subjects, into some sort of implicit accountability. *Libera lingua loquemur ludis Liberalibus* ("Liberal will be our language at Libera's games") had got Naevius into trouble. But it was a sentiment that would not die out for centuries. This social dimension may even explain the Augustan interest in reviving tragedy, where Ovid's genius, at least in the judgment of Quintilian, best showed its potential. Yet the tragic experiment failed.

The answer to our question therefore is to be sought, if we are thinking of literature, not so much from the theatre, as from that other Augustan poetic experiment, which had been to adapt the technical resources of Alexandrian poetry to a Roman conception of

---

[7] Martial remarks, in a poem criticizing preoccupation with Callimachus and the Theban legends, among others: *Hoc lege, quod possit dicere vita 'Meum est'* (X. 4. 8).

[8] Seneca, *Epp.* 114. 2.

the poet's role as the moral interpreter of society to itself. This concept of the *vates*, exemplified practically by the writer of the *Aeneid*, had been theoretically stated by Horace in a passage of the *Ars Poetica* which has not always attracted the attention it should. Taking Orpheus and Amphion as the ancestors of poetry, Horace defines their achievement as civilization itself—the refinement of morals and the building of cities. He goes on to call for a revival of this old idea (396–407):

> Fuit haec sapientia quondam,
> Publica privatis secernere, sacra profanis,
> Concubitu prohibere vago, dare iura maritis,
> Oppida moliri, leges incidere ligno.
> Sic honor et nomen divinis vatibus atque
> Carminibus venit. Post hos insignis Homerus,
> Tyrtaeusque mares animos in Martia bella
> Versibus exacuit: dictae per carmina sortes,
> Et vitae monstrata via est, et gratia regum
> Pieriis temptata modis, ludusque repertus
> Et longorum operum finis: ne forte pudori
> Sit tibi Musa lyrae sollers et cantor Apollo.

Yes, that wisdom did flourish once, which could distinguish public from private, sacred from secular, forbid sexual license, give legal sanction to marriage, build up cities, inscribe laws on wooden tablets. So it was that respect and honor came to divinely inspired *vates* and their poems. After them came Homer's repute, after them Tyrtaeus whetted warrior hearts for battle with his poetry. After them oracles were given in verse, the road of life was pointed out, the favor of kings wooed in the Muses' measures, playful verse invented to put an end to long labors. No need then for you to be ashamed of the Muse skilled in the lyre, and of Apollo the singer.

The essentially public function which the Augustan poet is to fulfill is shown by two things in this passage.[9] Firstly, the role of the poet is defined in terms which are colored by the activity of the emperor Augustus himself.[10] Secondly, the conclusion of the whole passage,

---

[9] See the earlier discussion, above, p. 55. "Octavian gave encouragement to the legend [i.e. that he was the son of Apollo] by allowing a colossal bronze statue of Apollo with his own features to be erected in one of the porticoes attached to the temple [of the Palatine Apollo]": L. R. Taylor, *The Divinity of the Roman Emperor* (Middletown 1931), p. 154.

[10] That Augustus himself was the supreme *vates* is suggested by a comparison of Horace's vatic program here and what is said about Augustus elsewhere: e.g. *Res Gestae* 34 and Suet. *Aug.* 31 (= *publica privatis secernere, sacra profanis*); *Res Gestae* 28

with its emphatic positioning of *cantor Apollo*, refers unmistakably to the temple of the Palatine Apollo, where the meetings of the Augustan *vates* were held, and where, if they behaved, their books were on view. This temple was the center and showpiece of Augustus' cultural legislation.

Nothing is ever wholly new, and least of all in periods of revolution. The *vates* has much in common with the satirist, the exponent of the most characteristically Roman genre. The first *satura* at Rome had been introduced from Etruria, when actors (*histriones*: the noun already contains the *str-* root) performed to flute accompaniment to dispel a public plague. The association of satiric and lyric in this way would be long-lasting. It has of course parallels in two other comic artists, Pindar and Aristophanes. And behind both of these looms Archilochus.

At Rome, the old, undifferentiated concept, with its ambivalent laughter, sacred and profane in one, could give rise both to the impromptu farce, and ultimately to Plautine comedy on the one side, and indeed to the whole history of the theatre. On the other, it could inspire the wide-ranging reflections of Lucilius, with all their awareness of the most recent Hellenistic currents and trends. Not least among its peculiarities was the display of the poetic ego, the "preacher's I," the confessional play with a Protean first person who is never wholly to be separated from the community, or from a patron advanced as the community's ideal.

The satirical *persona* had been subsumed by Virgil into both the *Georgics* and the *Aeneid*: the idealization of the farmer implied a critique of the city and its corruption; and the "Arcadian" origins of Rome in Book VIII, the brusque instruction to Julius to drop his weapons in Book VI, the reconciliation of Romulus and Remus prophesied in Book I, the condemnation of Dido's erotic (but more than erotic) *furor*, were tokens of a continuing interest in the morals of Roman society even in the story of Trojan migration.

---

(= *oppida moliri*); Tacitus, *Ann.* I. 2, *munia . . . legum in se trahere* (= *leges incidere ligno*: Horace's more sympathetic phrase makes the *vates* into a second Solon, which can only be relevant to Augustus); Suet. *Aug.* 34 and Prop. II. 7 (= *concubitu prohibere vago, dare iura maritis*). Cf. E. Fraenkel, *Horace*, p. 385 on *Epp.* II. 1. 5 ff. and pp. 376–77 on the *Carmen Saeculare*, quoting Cicero, *Pro Marcello* 23; my *Augustus and the New Poetry*, pp. 36 ff. The vatic ideals set out by Horace in 22 B.C. in the *A. P.* look back to the heady days of six years before when the temple of the Palatine Apollo was opened, and Octavian promulgated marriage laws of great strictness, rebuilt 82 temples and then restored power to the Senate and People. The emperor/poet topos was to last long: Origenes, apud Porphyry, *Vit. Plot.* 3; E. R. Curtius, *Europäische Literatur und lateinisches Mittelalter*, pp. 183–84. Stalin, here as so often the heir of the Byzantines, was regularly held up as Soviet Russia's greatest stylist.

It follows that the prime criterion for judging the post-Virgilian epic poets in the context of their times must be to ask: what was their attitude to the *vates*-concept? If they believed that poetry had to offer a criticism of life (which is what the Roman satirical bent implied and their contemporaries urged) what did they think about the Augustan attempt to answer this demand? And, if they were dissatisfied with the Augustan answer, what substitute did they provide, and how far was it acceptable? The unease with literature and its role which we find time and time again evinced by ancient Roman critics suggests that both they and writers generally acknowledged a high standard of literary "relevance." How did they meet this standard?

At the same time, it must be remembered that we are dealing here with a concept of the artist's function which is really extra- or pre-literary. If an author has the notion that his task is to offer or imply some ideal of human behavior, we may applaud. But this notion in itself will not tell him how to carry out his aim. Looking at the precedent set by Virgil, and at the precepts and practice of Horace's Alexandrian (because didactic) epic, the *Ars Poetica*, we can see that, whatever literary gambits, such as metamorphosis, were fostered by the Roman tradition, the technical execution by poets writing in Latin of the *vates*-concept had in the event been greatly indebted to resources accumulated by the modern Greek poetry of their day. This was in the nature of things. "Classicism" is already a betrayal, in its self-consciousness, of the classical, and any effort to revert to the conditions of the Greek city-state, where "classical" Greek literature had flourished, would have made no sense. The subtleties of a complex civilization like that of Rome required in the artistic response a rich, perhaps too rich, sensibility.[11]

Thus the Augustan legacy called for a delicate balance. The aspiring epic poet was to use the methods of Alexandria without being only an Alexandrian. He had to achieve the *os magna sonaturum* ("lips destined for mighty utterance") without falling into the vapidities of

---

[11] To make analysis of the differences between Augustan and post-Augustan epic center around the use of the word *vates* solves two difficulties in the assessment of the poetry of the early empire. It enables us to admit that there are changes of attitude and emphasis. But it remains possible to avoid looking too closely for "Silver" peculiarities in purely literary matters of technique and expression. The "Silver" and "Golden" distinction may correspond to something, but it has been grossly exaggerated by literary historians who have felt obliged to prove that because there were "bad" emperors there must have been "bad" poets. These are dangerous simplifications. For Aimeric in the eleventh century Cicero was "Silver" while Lucan and Statius were "Golden" (Curtius, *op. cit.*, pp. 460–61).—The reader will wish to compare with this whole chapter G. Williams, *Change and Decline* (Berkeley 1978).

the historical epic, with its lack of inner cohesion and, in the last analysis, its absence of genuine moral criticism. How did the writers of such poetry tread their tightrope?

## II

The first post-Virgilian and the longest Augustan epic that survives seizes, as we might expect from its author, upon an old trick and makes it new. Many times in the discussion of the *Aeneid* (but even in Homer, and certainly in Pindar, Callimachus and Apollonius) there was occasion to note poetry's tendency towards metaphor, towards seeing one character or thing as another. Helen and Paris were a parody of Andromache and Hector; the golden-red fleece became Medea's blood-stained robe and veil. With his technique of repeated lines and close, ironic imitation of Homer, Virgil was a master of what film-makers call "dissolve" and "superimposition." Dido haunts Aeneas, as she promised, as Camilla, as Lavinia, as Pallas, and finally as Turnus. That the Roman poet thought of himself as consciously exploiting a Hellenistic device is suggested both by the stories of metamorphosis he sketches in *Eclogue* 6, with which we may compare that of Proteus in the fourth book of the *Georgics*, and by the more obvious uses of the same trick—what Formalists call *la dénudation du procédé*—which he is prepared to exhibit in the *Aeneid* itself (Polydorus, the metamorphosis of Aeneas' ships).

Metamorphosis, the carnival spirit of the masque, has in fact a long history in Greco-Roman culture.[12] Its modern interpreter has described its typical features.[13] The carnival sets up a comic double of the world of everyday, where for a time the ideal and the mundane coalesce. Suddenly, all the world's a stage: *Circus noster eccum adest* ("Here's our circus!") as Plautus puts it. The laughable and the grotesque make fun of, parody, the sacred and the formally severe. Masking and unmasking, *mésalliances*, puns, profanities, ambivalences of every kind abound. Life is reaffirmed by feasting, drunkenness, sex. The grave loses its finality and sting, the old smiles to find itself pregnant with new birth.[14]

The carnival occurs in a special space and time. In the frenzied whirl of activity, the mechanical time of the clock ceases to count.

---

[12] Cf. H. Reich, *Der Mimus* (Berlin 1903), a long but unjustly neglected book.

[13] M. Bakhtin, *Problemy Poetiki Dostoevskogo* (Moscow 1963), especially ch. 4; *idem*, *Tvorchestvo François Rabelais i Narodnaya Kul'tura Srednevekov'ya i Rennesansa* (Moscow 1965).

[14] Bakhtin calls attention here to certain Kerch terra-cotta figurines which show a laughing, pregnant old woman (*Rabelais*, p. 31: cf. Reich, pp. 507–08).

There is only the subjective apprehension of change, in which a day may pass like five minutes, and five minutes be as long as ten years (Bergson). The space is that of the public square, the corridor, threshold, height, depth, heaven, hell, anywhere that dislocates the individual from his settled routine. This explains why the wheel is a recurring carnival and fairground symbol. It moves, and yet stays in the same spot, elevates and just as surely depresses. It is also at a deeper level the symbol of human fortune, already familiar to Herodotus.

As the ambivalence holyday/holiday indicates, carnival fun is not empty. It directs itself at the sacred because it has something sacred to affirm, at the old and outworn because it is bursting with new growth. The serio-comic style described by ancient critics and still alive today, not least in the pulpit, understands this double aspect of itself.

It is evident how much of all this is found in Ovid's *Metamorphoses*: the "grotesque body," for example, of a girl turning into a tree[15] or a bird, the sexual adventures, the breathless pace, the unrelenting wit, the neologisms. Ovid took up a thematic complex profoundly attractive to Virgil, and not without its fascination for Horace.[16] Eminently Roman, it must have corresponded to something in the ambience of the time, where perhaps the greatest metamorphosis of all was that of proscribing Octavian into clement Augustus.

It may well be that, as the Augustan court aged and ossified into conservatism,[17] the best function that a poet could perform was to loosen the hard and fast, call into question the rigid dogma, give rein to the spirit of fun. It was unfortunate that the emperor was unwilling to concede to Ovid the right (and rite) he accorded to others of circus freedom.

In his epic, posing the maximum contrast with the *Aeneid*, Ovid poked fun at the *vates*-concept. The sacred figure of Orpheus became there the vehicle for all the risqué stories which the poet ostensibly shrank from relating in his own person. It might just have been possible in another poet, or with another emperor, to excuse this as the necessary dethronement or uncrowning of the carnival king. But Ovid had been using this freedom ever since the *Amores*.[18] The carnival ideally asserts its freedom to serve some sort of purpose.

[15] Bernini's "Apollo and Daphne" will spring to everyone's mind: see R. Wittkower, *Gian Lorenzo Bernini, the Sculptor of the Roman Baroque* (London 1955), plate 14.

[16] *Odes* II. 20; *A. P.* 1. ff., 472 ff.

[17] "Les temps nouveaux ne sont pas favorables aux esprits originaux et hardis. Les arts eux-mêmes souffrent de cet affadissement" (A. Piganiol, *Histoire de Rome* [5th ed., Paris 1962], p. 230).

[18] Cf. *Augustus and the New Poetry*, pp. 182 ff.

The record seemed to show that Ovid's only purpose was facetious and worse. Augustus was intolerant and provoked. The response was not a smile, but Tomi.

Nevertheless, as the reign of Augustus and its particular problems faded from memory, Ovid's comic epic was able to take on a larger life. It could now be seen as part of the perpetual Alexandrian and carnival response to the stereotyping of the poetic tradition. The relevance of the *Metamorphoses* to post-Augustan epic is not primarily that it carried forward Virgil's new definition of the poet's role. It illustrates very well however one feature of the epic tradition which will be of continual importance for its correct interpretation in many centuries and many authors.

Virgil's epoch-making discovery was that it was possible to use Alexandrian methods to compose a large-scale, heroic poem without sacrificing art to public purpose. Now the relevance of the hackneyed manner, that of the eulogizing cyclic poets with their more straight-forward and uncritical imitation of Homer, was greatly diminished. Adherents of the really vital ("Hesiodic") tradition would hencefor-ward start from Alexandrian premises, and in many cases they would not get far beyond their starting point. This explains why Ovid had such an unexpected influence on epic after him.[19] For those who could not rise to Virgilian heights, perhaps who did not comprehend what those heights were, there was always the other half of the equation, Alexandrianism. And Alexandrianism was brilliantly ex-emplified in its Roman guise in the meter and language of the *Metamorphoses*, with their swiftness and clarity, their receptivity to neologism but feeling for the value of the common word. Even when a poet, like Dante, had sublimity in his comedy, Ovid could still offer a handy compendium of Alexandrian and carnival techniques, acces-sible because their author was less awe-inspiring than Virgil. For Shakespeare, Ovid could serve the function which for Virgil himself had been served by Gallus.

Ovid has been criticized for, in essence, trusting to natural talent, *ingenium*, instead of to the Callimachean principle of *ars*.[20] Certainly, like his predecessors, he stood under the influence of Callimachus, but Callimachus had been the great champion of *art*. Ovid, by contrast, exalts in his programmatic declarations not art, but the other side of

[19] E. Auerbach, *Literary Language and its Public* (Eng. tr., London 1965), p. 190 note 3, completely fails to understand this point. His distinction between the "sublime" and the "rhetorical" styles forgets that in this tradition rhetoric is essential to sublimity.

[20] E. Norden, *Die römische Literatur* (repr. Leipzig 1954), p. 73.

the old dichotomy, *ingenium*.[21] The unexpected preference still echoes in Meres' "sweet, *witty* soul of Ovid."

The reason for the paradox is that Ovid caught from Propertius a distortion of the *vates*-concept, with its elevation to prominence of the Pindaric and komic (comic) notion of the poet as priest and prophet, and borrowed that idea without realizing its commitment. In spite of his brilliant *Medea*, he too often forgot that the Comic Muse is the sister of the Tragic, and that both have a common mother in the human heart.

Ovid's other major work, the *Fasti*, stood clearly in the Callimachean camp, and it is exactly in accordance with our suggested analysis of Augustan poetry (its governing equation is Alexandrian technique + vatic ideals) that at the same time this should be the work where Ovid is most respectful to *vates*. Seeking in his disgrace palliation for his offense, Ovid naturally turned to the still-valid ideal of poetry which he had so much mocked in more carefree days.[22] He perhaps recognized that, with the *Metamorphoses*, he had misjudged the temper of the court. But charming though it may be, and in spite of its use of a calendar, the *Fasti* was hardly an epic, though Apollonius' borrowings from the *Aetia* show that for him Ovid's model at least had epic scope.[23] The conclusion cannot be avoided that this particular poem's Alexandrianism represents a retreat.

If, throughout his poetic career, Ovid was treading, amusingly of course, a beaten path, by his clowning and playing to the gallery, he was directly contravening the advice given to Callimachus by Apollo, that the poet should choose a narrower road, even if that meant more effort. This is why in the last analysis the glib parallels so often drawn between Ovid and Callimachus are unacceptable. When we think of the long nights and laborious days spent by the devoted cataloguer of the Alexandrian Library in lovingly reviewing the great achievements of the past, in prose discussions of literary problems, in editions of earlier authors, in research, we marvel that he ever had time to write his poetry. When we think of the poetry, with its brilliant accomplishment in the present and promise for the future, we realize that this in itself would have been more than enough to make its author's name secure. If we compare this record with Ovid's naive admission of his own disinclination for hard work, and reliance

---

[21] *Quamvis ingenio non valet, arte valet* he had brazenly said of Callimachus (*Amores* I. 15. 14). See the discussion in *Augustus and the New Poetry*, pp. 395 ff.

[22] This explains why the revision of the *Fasti* dedicated to Germanicus makes such flattering allusion to the *vates* (I. 25: *vates cape vatis habenas*). This is also a variant of the topos mentioned above, note 10.

[23] *Callimachus*, ed. R. Pfeiffer, II, pp. xli ff.

on his natural fluency,[24] only one deduction can be made. He was not the Roman Callimachus. This title cannot even go to Propertius, a more intense, more densely textured poet. The true successor to Callimachus in Augustan Rome is Virgil, since only he accepted the challenge implicit in the *Hecale*, already accepted in Alexandria by Callimachus' disciple Apollonius, to recover the heroic epic for modern literature in a form that, among the shifting uncertainties of modern morals, would make sense.

In saying that Virgil's epic was Callimachean, we acknowledge a certain inevitable unsatisfactoriness about it. The hero of such a poetry cannot be the romantic figure alone with his personal destiny presented by Achilles, and still less the tough, swashbuckling braggart of certain types of martial fantasy.[25] He cannot be a "hero" in the conventional fashion at all, and Virgil made this very clear when he introduced Aeneas at the start of his poem as terrified out of his wits and numb with cold. There is in Augustan poetry a clouding of the heroic which, springing from the ambiguities of the age, made the task of its heirs peculiarly obscure. Just as Augustus' own political settlement depended on its author and soon gave way after his death, so the Augustan poetry that tried to embody the heroic ideal depended on Virgil's unique ability to evade commitment in the very act of apparently bold assertion. This "irony," whose ancestor was the irony of Callimachus' *Hymns*, or of the *Hecale*, was too subtle a creation even for the immensely gifted Ovid, who too often relapses into simple parody or, on the other side, sentiment.[26] Its evanescent flavor was too refined for any poet of real ability until we reach Lucan. So long did it take for Virgilian example and fascination to stimulate a worthy successor.

## III

Students of modern literature are familiar with the disheartening influence that a great masterpiece can have on posterity.[27] A resounding and idiosyncratic success can seemingly exhaust the potential of

---

[24] *Tristia* IV. 10. 25, 37. *Nec mens fuit apta labori* seems to have inspired Milton's allusion to Shakespeare's "easie numbers" (below, p. 380). Such is the potency of these old formulas. Of course some of this in Ovid is literary pretense: cf. Horace *Epp.* II. 2. 124: *ludentis speciem dabit et torquebitur*. But one feels that the verdicts of the Roman critics (Seneca Rhetor, Quintilian) have something in them.

[25] Apollonius' Idas, Plautus' Pyrgopolinices, Statius' Menoeceus are all variants on this theme, which would be taken up by Tolstoy in *War and Peace*: below, p. 450.

[26] Parody: e.g. *Met.* I. 671–72 (contrast *Aen.* IV. 239 ff.). Sentiment: e.g. *Met.* VIII. 515 ff. (contrast Bacchylides 5. 136 ff.).

[27] T. S. Eliot's discussion of Milton (*Selected Prose* [London 1953], p. 137) is relevant.

a particular genre for generations afterwards. This is why, in the reigns of Tiberius, Gaius and Claudius, we have to be content to leaf through Phaedrus and Manilius, or to search in histories of literature for lists of vanished productions that have said nothing to other men. It is a mark of the new era represented by Nero that then at long last a fresh look at the heroic became possible.

Persius has given us a valuable glimpse into the poetic background of the time. Evidently the satiric and lyrical impulses have temporarily parted company. It is telling that the last satire is addressed to the lyric poet Caesius Bassus, and immediately follows a satire noting the excesses of the *vates*.

His first *Satire* shows us a band of poets essentially Alexandrian in inspiration, content to be used by that tradition (I. 63–71):[28]

> 'Quis populi sermo est? Quis enim nisi carmina molli
> Nunc demum numero fluere, ut per leve severos
> Effundat iunctura unguis? Scit tendere versum
> Non secus ac si oculo rubricam derigat uno.'
> Sive opus in mores, in luxum, in prandia regum
> Dicere, res grandes nostro dat Musa poetae.
> Ecce modo heroas sensus adferre docemus
> Nugari solitos Graece, nec ponere lucum
> Artifices nec rus saturum laudare. . . .

'What do the philistine critics say? What indeed, except that only in our time do poems have a flowing rhythm, so that their joins allow even the most sensitive nails to touch nothing but smooth surfaces. The modern poet knows how to make taut his line as if he were a squint-eyed builder letting fall the plumbline.' The task may vary: to speak against morals, luxurious living, millionaires' banquets, but the poet today has mighty themes. But we, while lacking the art to describe a wood or to praise the fullness of the countryside, teach our epic heroes to produce epigrams, with their usual Greek emptiness.

After noting the contempt felt by such poets for the past, Persius goes on to deal with the claim that at least modern poetry shows refinement (I. 92–102):

> 'Sed numeris decor est et iunctura addita crudis.
> Cludere sic versum didicit, "Berecyntius Attis,"
> Et "qui caeruleum dirimebat Nerea delphin,"
> Sic "costam longo subduximus Appennino."
> "Arma virum,"—nonne hoc spumosum et cortice pingui,
> Ut ramale vetus vegrandi subere coctum?'

---

[28] The Roman Alexandrian use of *populus* = "the philistines" is catalogued on p. 256. This is what Seneca meant by *Ennianus populus*: cf. Gellius, *Noctes Atticae* XII. 2. 10.

> Quidnam igitur tenerum et laxa cervice legendum?
> 'Torva Mimalloneis implerunt cornua bombis,
> Et raptum vitulo caput ablatura superbo
> Bassaris et lyncem Maenas flexura corymbis
> Euhion ingeminat, reparabilis adsonat Echo.'

'But beauty and coherence have been added to uncouth measures. The modern poet has learned to round off a line like this: "Berecyntian Attis," and "the dolphin which parted sea-blue Nereus," and "we took a rib from Appenine's long slopes." "Arms and the man"—isn't that full of froth and spongy bark, like old branches whose pith swells in the heat?' What then is supple enough to be read with head thrown back? 'They filled their rasping horns with Mimallonean booms, and the Bacchant, on the point of carrying off the head torn from a proud bullock, the Maenad just reining the lynx with her clustering ivy, redoubles her cry of "Evoe," which the ever-renewed echo takes up.'

The poet sarcastically comments (I. 103–04):

> Haec fierent, si testiculi vena ulla paterni
> Viveret in nobis?

Would all this be happening, if any drop of our fathers' spunk were still alive in us?

The lyrical and the satiric have fallen apart, always dangerous for Roman poetry since its inception. The essence of Persius' criticism seems to be that modern poetry, displaying total allegiance to Alexandrian doctrine, puts all its emphasis on polished, musical technique. It has lost its satiric bite. There are important themes to be tackled. There is need to attack morals, decadence, millionaires' dinners, and for that the Muse gives mighty scope to the modern poet. Instead, all we do is teach our heroes to show off their epigrams. We do this even though we are not yet able to describe a wood or praise the abundance of the countryside. We have not, in other words, learned to write an *Eclogues* or a *Georgics*. No wonder our *Aeneid* is so paltry!

Persius is therefore holding up Virgil's own poetic development as a still-valid pattern (a pattern accepted by Lucan).[29] He is certainly not saying that the remedy for current ills in poetry is to abandon Alexandrianism. His view is exactly that of Horace in the *Ars Poetica*. What is needed is harder work.

Persius does not seem to be so set against the past as some literary

---

[29] That Virgil's poetic career was felt to be the example for others is seen from Lucan's *Et quantum mihi restat ad Culicem!* (quoted in Suetonius' *Life* of the poet: Schanz–Hosius II, p. 495; cf. Statius, *Silvae* II. 7. 73–74). So it was that Dante resorted to an *Eclogue* in his own defense (below, p. 259) and Eisenstein directed a *Georgic* on his way to *Ivan the Terrible* (below, pp. 408–09).

histories have made out. His interest in the undoubted achievements of Republican literature resembles the eulogizing of the English Metaphysical poets or of G. M. Hopkins by a generation anxious to evade the influence of Tennyson or Milton. Authors are always looking for a springboard into estrangement. But hunting for precious gems (glosses) like *aerumnis* and *luctificabile* was pointless unless it was inspired by more than mere antiquarianism. With his ambivalent attitude to the *vates* (*Prologus* 7; *Sat.* 5. 1), the poet himself proved how hard the recovery of the past would be.

Modern poetry is finally defended by Persius' interlocutor on the grounds of its polish. There is no reason to deny the effectiveness of the lines that Persius quotes.[30] But a poetry made up of only such lines would be like a diet containing nothing but strawberries and cream. Yet again these modern poets realize that technique is not the whole story. They are led on in their dissatisfaction to criticize even the *Aeneid*. In the interpretation of a dense metaphor, *pingui* gives an essential clue.[31] The *Aeneid* is being rejected on Alexandrian grounds. *Vegrandi* is also significant. The poem is too big. It contains too much dead wood. What the critic ultimately appears to mean is that the *Aeneid* is like old branches, which swell up and sweat in the heat. There is need for the pruner's knife.

Persius' satire shows us then a poetry that is still receptive to the notion of epic, still interested in heroes. But a sensitivity to Alexandrian lyricism has run to extremes. The sharp, satiric edge has become blunted and soft.

In the course of trying to come to terms with itself, this poetry is forced to criticize the *Aeneid*. This may be both impudent and imprudent, but we should remember the constant need for the Alexandrian tradition to repudiate its own masterpieces whenever they threaten to deaden the poetic response. However, neither Persius nor his interlocutor suggests that the general Alexandrian assumptions underlying their whole discussion are misconceived. When Persius calls for some touch of the old Roman virility, this is not a new poetic program. It is a demand for a return to the vatic combination of lyric (music) and satire already found in the *Aeneid*.

## IV

It is in this light that we have to judge the most Roman epic that survives from the first century of our era, the *Pharsalia* of Lucan.

[30] Cf. H. Bardon, *La littérature latine inconnue* (Paris 1956), II, p. 132.

[31] *Pingui nil mihi cum populo, Appendix Vergiliana, Catalepton* 9. 64. In his reference to *vegrandi subere coctum*, Persius seems to be paraphrasing the Greek critical term φλοιώδης meaning "bombastic," "pretentious": cf. D. A. Russell on *De Subl.* 3. 2.

There can be no question of viewing Lucan as in some way insulated against Alexandrian influences and preconceptions,[32] and no question of being surprised by the recurrence in him of the Roman satiric impulse. But, unless we want to make Lucan the inventor of a wholly new sub-genre in Latin literature, the burlesque epic, we must find more in him than simple satire, and indeed it may be a mistake to think of any Roman satire as simple. The poet's satire in fact is to be seen as the legacy of the Augustans. Living in such close intimacy with Nero, himself a second Augustus,[33] Lucan could hardly have avoided the theory that poetry at Rome was meant for a positive, public, religious purpose. Here, he was the true successor of Virgil, and even of the Horace whose vatic odes mingle lyric and satire in a characteristically Roman alloy.

This is why, like the *Aeneid* and the first collection of *Odes*, Lucan's epic contains no use of the word *poeta*. The author is a *vates*, as he reminds us both at the beginning and end (as we have it) of his work.[34] Because he is a *vates*, of course he must take up the role of satirist and moralist. How much of the sort do we read between the lines of the *Aeneid*, which implies the most damning criticism of Roman attitudes! But shall we suppose that such censure was unwel-

[32] The all too brief remarks by O. Schönberger, *Untersuchungen zur Wiederholungstechnik Lucans* (2nd ed., Munich 1968), pp. 22 ff. and his comparisons with Wagner and Mann (pp. 5, 12 ff.) are illuminating, but what work of these two modern authors is inspired by the single-minded hate which Schönberger finds in Lucan? The Alexandrian and musical style is polyphonic. A valuable corrective to such views is offered by W. D. Lebek, *Lucans Pharsalia* (Göttingen 1976).

[33] The evidence of coins is particularly important for showing that, from the outset of his reign, Nero consciously aped Augustus. Augustus in a ceremonial chariot appears on the reverse of a coin displaying the 17-year-old Nero with Agrippina on the obverse. In 64, the unprecedentedly magnificent brass and copper coinage illustrated Roma and Apollo Citharoedus (cf. *Me quoque facundo comitatus Apolline Caesar/Respiciat*, Calp. Sic. IV. 87–88). This latter image, so important to both Horace and Propertius, had appeared only once before, on the coins of Augustus, with the inscription ACT (Actium). Augustus' interest in athletics of this Greek type, which extended to the foundation of games at Rome itself, is another feature shared with Nero, which perhaps explains some of the imagery in the proem to *Georgics* III. It was in Augustus' ceremonial chariot that Nero entered Rome after his artistic successes in the Greek competitions. Like Augustus, Nero boasted on his coins of his victorious career, of his closing of the temple of Janus, of the Ara Pacis, of his restoration of temples. A commentary by M. Grant on and reproductions of many of these coins, all preserved in the Ashmolean at Oxford, are to be found in *History Today* 4 (1954), pp. 319–25.

[34] I. 63; IX. 980 (cf. *invidia*, 982); VII. 553. IX. 359–60 and 963 show an Alexandrian consciousness of the power of art to modify mere "facts." Some interesting remarks on Lucan as *vates* are found in R. Häußler, *Das historische Epos von Lucan bis Silius und seine Theorie* (Heidelberg 1978), pp. 45 ff. But inevitably, because of the author's thesis, they lack the Alexandrian perspective.

come to Augustus, the *censor*, charged with *cura legum et morum*, and the protector of the peoples of the Empire? How much of the sort do we read or deduce in "Pompeian" Livy, whose loyalty to Augustus is nevertheless beyond question![35]

The interest of Nero's regime for literature lies in its openness to experiment with many Augustan ideas which had become moribund.[36] What we must not do is read back into Lucan's writings our own idea of Nero as a fiend in human shape (a poor fiend in our age of iron!), and our own admiration for those Roman authors whose satirical pessimism matches our personal disenchantments. Satire, a version of circus freedom—in the theological language being developed by Christian writers contemporary with Lucan, *parrhēsia*—is part of the Roman amalgam. The other part is lyricism. As satire split off from the epic in Martial and Juvenal, it would be in the first instance lyricism that was left, and this explains much in the *Thebaid*. But in the *Pharsalia*, in spite of Persius' worries, this split has not yet occurred, or else has been temporarily healed. To ignore the music therefore is to be deaf to the poem, and to its inherent, polyphonic ambiguity.

Lucan's aim in writing his epic was to do what he himself says: to bring Rome, through literature, face to face with the issues of the Civil War, and to show that, in spite of everything, the gods had been at work, the ultimate decision had been theirs. This is Virgil's theme (and Horace's), and it may be traced back at least as far as Pindar's *Pythian* 2.

It is this philosophical and religious reason then which explains why Lucan chose what at first sight looks like a theme alien to the Aristotelian and Alexandrian tradition, with its taboo on versified history.[37] Simple inspection shows that in fact the *Pharsalia* is not versified history—which is why it must not be called the *De Bello Civili*, and still less the *Bellum Civile*, which begs all questions by associating the poem with the Hellenistic eulogistic epic. It is a long serio-comic meditation on what happened at the beginning of the imperial system. Like the *Aeneid*, it does not blink the harsh facts of human weakness. It is not a straightforward glorification of the mighty, and it certainly does not lack art. Here at least it meets two of Callimachus' criteria.

The opening of the poem explains the author's intentions. He is to sing of wars that were more than civil. The *Überbietungsformel* is

[35] *Titus Livius . . . Cn. Pompeium tantis laudibus tulit ut Pompeianum eum Augustus appellaret*, Tac. *Ann.* IV. 34; cf. Seneca, *Nat. Quaest.* V. 18.

[36] Bardon has some sympathetic remarks: *La littérature latine inconnue*, II, p. 138.

[37] *Poetics* ch. IX; *Aet.-Pref.* 13–16.

typically Roman, and typically carnival ("the greatest show on earth"). The horror of these wars is *commune nefas* (6). Their only justification can be that they prepared the way for Nero's rule (*nefas* again, 37). The statement of the Roman crime is just barely overtopped by its palliation (32/34 lines), and the balancing device shows that these are the terms on which the argument is to rest.

Dedicating his poem to Nero, Lucan was forced to indulge in hyperbolic language by the very equation he had chosen. It is interesting to note how this language is nevertheless still in debt to Callimachus. As the poet contemplates the apotheosis that will inevitably follow Nero's death (just as it had followed that of Augustus) he declares that for him Nero is already a god.[38] If the young emperor is ready to inspire the poem, Lucan, the *vates*, will not wish to trouble Apollo or disturb Bacchus. The poetic fastidiousness that these lines imply is ultimately descended from Callimachus' rejection of the conventional thunder of the hackneyed epic.[39] The kinship must be recognized beneath the Roman and estranging dress; indeed the study of Lucan's use of topoi must be basic to any serious large-scale investigation of the poem. The alliance of the vatic ideal with Callimachean doctrine is in the purest Augustan tradition.

In the study of the *Aeneid* it is impossible in the last analysis to explain why Aeneas triumphs and Turnus goes down except to say "the gods willed it so."[40] This is exactly the lesson of Lucan's exordium (I. 126–27):

> Quis iustius induit arma
> Scire nefas: magno se iudice quisque tuetur;
> Victrix causa deis placuit, sed victa Catoni.

Who more justly put on arms is beyond man's power to know: each may appeal to a mighty judge; the conquering cause found favor with the gods, the conquered with Cato.

Basically, the civil war sprang from the immoral condition of society in the late Republic. This is an Augustan theme.[41] The poet's outraged protest is certainly satirical (I. 158 ff.). But this satire is part of his public, vatic role.

---

[38] The hyperbole had already been anticipated by the Augustan poets: Virgil, *Eclogues* 1. 6–7; *Georgics* IV. 562; Prop. III. 4. 1; Horace, *Odes* III. 3. 12; 5. 2. The convention is as old as Sappho.

[39] The *Hecale* began without an appeal to the Muses: Pfeiffer, Vol. I, p. 229.

[40] This is particularly evident in the blending of Turnus/Aeneas into Hector/Achilles, and then again into Achilles/Hector, and in the repetition of *solvuntur frigore membra* at I. 92 and XII. 951, first of Aeneas and then of Turnus.

[41] Lucan revives the *suis et ipsa Roma viribus ruit* motif (Horace, *Epodes* 16. 2, echoed by Propertius, for example, at III. 13. 60) at I. 72.

It is this same vatic, Virgilian function that enables him to speak quite openly from the very first about Caesar's ambition. Just as the gods chose Aeneas to be their instrument, so Caesar, determined to carry out his plans in spite of their illegality by normal standards, is testing whether he too is the chosen instrument of destiny. It follows that, in Caesar's remarks after the crossing of the Rubicon, the traditional reading *credidimus fatis* (I. 227: "My trust is in fate") must be retained. Caesar has deliberately put himself outside all ordinary terms of existence in order to discover the will of heaven.[42] It is an important definition of heroism. If he nevertheless comes through in spite of his undeserving behavior in human eyes, lesser mortals must bow to the will of the gods. This alone can excuse the methods by which he triumphed, and concede a sympathy in the human scale to his opponents.

A similar interpretation must be given to the scene in Book V of the poem in which Caesar proposes to cross the Adriatic to Italy in a fishing smack in the teeth of the most violent storm that the elements can contrive (an incident of no historical importance whatsoever). His pilot is terrified. Caesar explains his understanding of the workings of Fortune (V. 578–83):

> "Despise the angry sea," he cried, "and spread your sail to the raging wind. If you refuse to make for Italy when Heaven forbids, then make for it when I command. The only fair cause for your fear is that you cannot know your passenger, of whom Fortune deserves badly only when she comes *after* his prayers."

At about the same date, three Christian evangelists were using the same argument to prove the divinity of Christ:

> Jesus then got into the boat, and his disciples followed. All at once a great storm arose on the lake, till the waves were breaking right over the boat; but he went on sleeping. So they came and woke him up, crying: 'Save us, Lord; we are sinking!' 'Why are you such cowards?' he said; 'how little faith you have!' Then he stood up and rebuked the wind and the sea, and there was a dead calm. The men were astonished at what had happened, and exclaimed, 'What sort of man is this? Even the wind and the sea obey him.'
> (Matthew 8:23–27: *The New English Bible*; cf. Mark 4:37–41; Luke 8:22–25).

The sea was peculiarly the element where man was exposed to

---

[42] V. 301 ff.; VII. 333; VIII. 486, 568. At X. 21 (*felix praedo*) Lucan is taking up the same position. Plutarch asked whether Alexander's successes were owed to Fortune or virtue, and Lucan is answering this Stoic question beforehand in terms borrowed from his uncle (*felix temeritas: De Ben.* I. 13. 3). The caprice of Fortune is of course a peculiarly "carnival" theme.

divine vengeance, as both the Greeks and Hebrews knew. Caesar cannot control the storm, like Christ. But, like Jonah, he is spared because of his special relationship to the suprahuman. The Roman poet works up this simple scene to a length of nearly 200 lines. But his cleverness proves the same religious point.

It is because Caesar's victory is not defended as the triumph of right in human eyes[43] that Lucan can both idealize Pompey and satirize the senators who are his allies.[44] The freedom of range secured by this view of events enabled the poet to deploy, like Virgil, the technique of drama, the technique of what Formalist critics call the *skaz* or oral narrative. There cannot be one level of meaning in such a performance. Examining for example Gogol's *Overcoat*, Boris Eichenbaum pointed out how a story often thought to be a simple social protest, inexplicably marred at the end by a note of fantasy, is in fact all of a piece.[45] The disparate elements of fantasy and realism are held together by the ever-changing voice of the narrator/actor. The story must be taken as a whole, as something in the strict sense polyphonic, where no one interpretation, no one note, may be allowed to drown out its fellows without destroying the harmony. In an argument conducted by the Protean author with himself, every opinion is heard. Dante knew what this meant.[46] Can we doubt that those who heard Virgil's voice knew what it meant for the *Aeneid*?[47]

Classical scholars have dwelt on the evil consequences for "Silver" literature of the public reading. But should English readers familiar with accounts of Dickens' *recitationes* have isolated the Roman practice from its European background? Thomas Mann was still giving public readings of his work in our century. And, even worse, should they

---

[43] A similar attitude inspires Tolstoy's picture of Kutuzov in *War and Peace*. His laziness does not matter, since he is still the fated victor over Napoleon.

[44] I. 158 ff., 311 ff.; II. 242 ff.

[45] Cf. "Kak sdelana *Shinel'* Gogolya" (Petrograd 1919, reprinted in *Skvoz' Literaturu* [The Hague 1962], and translated into French as "Comment est fait le 'Manteau' de Gogol" in *Théorie de la littérature*, ed. T. Todorov, pp. 212–33). See further E. M. Thompson, *Russian Formalism and Anglo-American New Criticism* (The Hague–Paris 1971), pp. 119 ff. In assimilating Gogol's story to an oral narrative (*skaz*) Eichenbaum argues for the importance of what he calls "sound gesture," the music of what is said. There cannot be one level of meaning in such a performance. Thomas Mann's definition of music as "systematic ambiguity" must be remembered, and also his own interest in the *recitatio*: cf. the passage from *Joseph in Egypt* quoted at the opening of the essay by V. Žmegač in *Thomas Mann und die Tradition*, ed. P. Pütz (Frankfurt am Main 1971), p. 1.

[46] "Dicemo bello il canto, quando le voci di quello, secondo il debito dell' arte, sono intra sè rispondenti": *Convivio* I. 5.

[47] The remark attributed to Iulius Montanus by Seneca (*Vit. Verg. Don.* 28–29) is telling, especially the allusion to *vocem . . . et os . . . et hypocrisin*. Cf. Plato, *Ion* 536 a: *hypocrites*.

have ignored its literary significance, and this in an age when we have heard so much about the "oral epic"? If the poet is an actor, as Aristotle believed,[48] if polarity is essential to all pathetic structure, as Eisenstein maintains,[49] shall we flatten Lucan into a one-dimensional, univocal subversive because, in hindsight, we dislike Nero? That would be an incredible diminution of his range, and ignore completely the religious and philosophical aspects of his argument. A satirical epic that was nothing but satirical would be a monstrosity. Satire is part of the orchestral color, not the whole symphony, just as the Acclamations and their forerunners in the Circus/Hippodrome are part of the occasion, and not the whole show.

Lucan's poem draws its reader powerfully into the atmosphere of the public recitation, even declamation. We must picture the young poet, with youth's portentous solemnity, and not without some justified awareness of his own genius, taking his place amid the marble, pillared pomp of some Roman *aula*, perhaps that of the Palatine library itself, with the golden, red-veined columns of its portico, surrounded perhaps by the *imagines* of the great statesmen, generals and lawyers of the past—and those of the *vates*—to treat in his polished, nervous, stabbing lines themes of battle, political power, destiny, which were essentially Roman. Such a poetry, commanding an official audience, must have about it in Rome an air of the circus and carnival, of the *munus* which is also an *agon*, for that is where Roman aesthetics are most truly at home. Of course it is too desperately emotive, too feverish, for the quiet of the study. But that is not its intended ambience, and one might as well make the same complaint about the libretto of one of the mimes which the poet is also recorded as composing for the arena.

Even so, Lucan's epic is guided by a basic religious theme, that *fatum* or *Fortuna* was at work in all the carnage, and for this attempt at philosophical/religious explanation, far more plausible and convincing in that time and in that place, even the most disaffected Romans could feel grateful.

The *skaz* depends on harmony, not monotony. As Lucan's *skaz* progressed, did increasing hostility between him and Nero lead to a loss of balance (which would be a literary defect), to excessive partisanship towards Pompey and corresponding harshness towards Caesar?[50] The answer must be that there is a critical error of the first magnitude in such interpretations. Book VII, in a poem called

---

[48] Above, pp. 42–43.
[49] Below, pp. 415 ff.
[50] So especially A. Rostagni, *Storia della letteratura latina*, II, pp. 403 ff., and F. Ahl, *Lucan, An Introduction* (Cornell 1976).

*Pharsalia*, is the decisive book. Does it provide evidence of a change of heart on the poet's part, and the abandonment which that would mean of his attempt to bring the Romans to terms with their destiny?

If we look in this book however, we find that the gods are not with Pompey (85–86). *Vincis apud superos votis me, Caesar, iniquis* is his cry (113: "With your outmatching prayers, Caesar, you defeat me in heaven"). His mistake is to believe that Caesar is actually wasting his time on prayers (*nil opus est votis*, 252: "There is no need of prayers": cf. *cum post vota venit*, V. 583, cited above). Caesar has a much clearer idea of the terms of the contest (*haec, fato quae teste probet, quis iustius arma/sumpserit*, 259–60: "This is the day which, on the evidence of fate, will show who took up arms with greater right": the echo of I. 126–27 is audible). His realism, his refusal to judge by conventional standards, are well exemplified in all his speech.

Pompey, resolutely putting his faith in himself and in outworn concepts of personal loyalty;[51] Caesar, the favorite of Fortune and Fate, who sees that new values are demanded by the new age: these are the polar champions of this pathetically structured epic. Yet Lucan, *magis oratoribus quam poetis imitandus* ("more a model for lawyers than poets") in Quintilian's shrewd and often mistranslated phrase, appears to be more bitterly involved than this cool assessment may suggest. In a long passage of reflection which occupies the center of the book (385–459) he speculates on the meaning of Pharsalia for Rome's future. Both sides are *equally* carried away by anger (385–86, a significant concession at the start for Hellenistic ethics). What will be the effect of their yielding to such a passion?

In the first place, it will destroy Romans, Latins, Italians, the heart of Rome's manpower. Lucan's complaint is that of a contemporary of the satirist Lucilius, Ti. Gracchus, as he returned from Numantia, and witnessed the encroaching *latifundia*, and the arrogant treatment of the Italian peasantry by Roman magistrates. But, apart from this damage to Rome's force of arms, and hence to her civilizing mission in the world (cf. 429 ff.), Pharsalia has had even graver consequences. It has banished liberty forever beyond the confines of the Roman empire, rendering the whole history of the Republic pointless, and worse than pointless, since now the memory of freedom serves to make the yoke of slavery gall more painfully.

Lucan presses his argument further, inevitable in a style that cultivates "threshold" situations. There cannot be a providence at work in human affairs at all. Otherwise, why would Jupiter waste his thunderbolts on mountain tops, while leaving it to Cassius to strike down Caesar? The only revenge that the human race has against the

---

[51] Cf. VII. 377 ff., IX. 227 ff.

gods is that it produces rivals to them in the emperors it deifies. *Inque deum templis iurabit Roma per umbras* (459: "And in the temples of the gods, Rome will swear by ghosts").

The denial of divine providence in this passage has been noted as unique in a poet who normally makes such a parade of Stoic allegiance,[52] and this must make us careful about giving too much importance to it here. The random fall of the thunderbolt is in fact a commonplace of antireligious sentiment at least as old as Aristophanes,[53] and shall we suppose that either Lucan or his audience did not know this? The whole outburst is that of a particularly loud voice in the serio-comic polyphony. The harmony, the context, remains.

In that context, the references throughout are to Julius Caesar and his suppression of liberty, his victory in a battle where an ancestor of Nero is shown as dying nobly on Pompey's side in defense of freedom (659 ff.). If the scope of the allusion is wider, it nevertheless starts from this premise. It was true that Julius had affronted Roman feeling gravely, and it was easy to associate the bad government which the city had suffered since his assassination with his example. But there was an alternative, even for a Julio-Claudian emperor, as Augustus' own "Pompeian" leanings made clear, and this was the alternative that the young Nero had proposed to take. Just as Augustus had reacted against the excesses of Julius by his carefully displayed respect for Republican sentiment, so the second Augustus, Nero, sought respectability for his regime by reacting against the excesses of Claudius, who had thus to become, in this propaganda pattern, a second Julius. Claudius lent himself only too easily to the comparison. Like Julius, he had invaded Britain. He had extended the franchise and even put Gauls in the Senate. He believed in centralizing government, which bypassed cumbersome and traditional channels, and flouted the claims of the old families. Judged by Augustan standards, he was an abject failure, and this is exactly why Seneca, recalled from exile to be Nero's tutor, puts his condemnation into Augustus' own mouth. How could Claudius be admitted to heaven? *Dum tales deos facitis, nemo vos deos esse credet!* ("If you are going to

[52] See the introduction to O. A. W. Dilke's edition of Book VII (Cambridge 1965), pp. 40–41.

[53] *Clouds* 398 ff.: cf. Nisbet–Hubbard on Hor. *Odes* I. 2. 2; *Aeneid* IV. 208 ff.; Lucretius VI. 387 ff. There were of course perfectly well-known rejoinders to this brand of skepticism. Elsewhere Caesar quells a mutiny among his troops with language ultimately going back to that of Strepsiades in the same play of Aristophanes (Lucan V. 336 ff.; *Clouds* 1290 ff.: cf. Lucretius VI. 608 ff.; Claudian, *In Ruf.* I. 183 ff.). The manipulation of comic topoi must not be taken too one-sidedly.

make gods like that, no one will believe you are gods!'")[54] Seneca's comic dialogue, written to serve the public relations needs of the new regime, makes, like the comedy of Aristophanes already noted, the same point as Lucan's tirade in Book VII of the epic. That too then is comic, a mask assumed for a time to make a dramatic impact, part of the lawyer's pro and con.

Given the existence of this polarity *within* the imperial tradition, there is no need to assume that a criticism of Julius (even when he is called "Caesar") is necessarily a criticism of Nero. There was indeed the constant possibility, too often realized in the past, that the emperors would betray their trust. There was the reluctance of men in high position to find the courage to speak out. Tiberius had already impatiently complained of the Senate's readiness for slavery. Reflecting upon the cost of such betrayals, Lucan for a moment allows one of his voices to be carried away by anti-Stoic sentiment. Using the freedom of the Circus, which is also religious freedom, he puts the case against himself, secure in his faith that the divine purpose will ultimately triumph in history. Virgil had done exactly the same.

Eduard Fraenkel has spoken of Lucan's importance as the mediator to later ages of the ancient concept of *pathos*,[55] the vivid representation of human feeling of the serious kind. There are some astonishing things in the poem. The tone ranges from the melancholy of Pompey's departure from Italy to the macabre magic of necromancy, from horrible carnage to the description of an Egyptian banquet. The poet's many voices are heard, sometimes in direct apostrophe, sometimes in Roman indignation at what he has to report.

One of the most difficult things for the modern reader is to gauge his response to all he hears. This is because, although our literary histories have trained us to expect seriousness in epic, we are unsure about comedy. At the sea battle off Marseilles, for example, a good illustration of the carnival "sea-on-land" motif found also in the Roman *naumachia*,[56] already popular under Augustus, every kind of

---

[54] *Apocol.* 11. 4. Interpreters of Lucan's poem avidly collect any possible hits at Nero by the poet, while ignoring the question of hits at Claudius: e.g. IV. 824 (Claudius was the first to give a *donativum* to the Praetorians): VII. 540 ff. (Claudius was generous in extending Roman citizenship). Nero boasted on his coins of his success at feeding the Roman populace: cf. Lucan III. 56 ff. and Grant's article (above, note 33), but he had inherited this chore from his predecessors, and Claudius had made special arrangements for it (Piganiol, *Histoire de Rome*, pp. 251 and 256).

[55] *Kleine Beiträge zur klassischen Philologie* (Rome 1964), II, pp. 233 ff.

[56] The Panathenaic procession, with its peplos/sail, and the modern use of "float" in carnival parades, attest the same point: cf. Freudenberg, *Poetika Syuzheta i Zhanra*, pp. 208-09.

wildly improbable death is elaborated in gory detail. Catus was pierced from front and back at the same time (III. 587–91: trans. J. D. Duff):

> ... the weapons met in his body, and the blood stayed, uncertain through which wound to flow; at last the torrent from his veins drove out both javelins at once, parting his life in two and distributing his death between the wounds.

A twin loses his right hand (615–17: trans. J. D. Duff):

> Fiercely he renews the fight with his left hand and leans forward over the water to rescue his right hand; the left hand also and the whole arm were cut off.

At the end, a mere trunk, he sinks a Roman ship by jumping on board, and adding his weight to the cargo of carnage already there!

This is nothing to the death of Lycidas. He was pierced by a grappling iron (636–46: trans. J. D. Duff):

> He would have sunk in the sea, but for his comrades who seized his legs as they swung in air. He was torn asunder, and his blood gushed out, not trickling as from a wound, but raining on all sides from his severed arteries; and the free play of the life coursing through the different limbs was cut off by the water. No other victim's life escaped through so wide a channel. The lower half of his body resigned to death the limbs that contain no vital organs; but where the lungs were full of air and the heart of heat, there death was long baffled and struggled hard with this part of the man, till with difficulty it mastered the whole body.

Of course, these extraordinary deaths provoke extraordinary re-actions. One father, determined not to outlive his dying son, both wounds himself and jumps into the sea, so as to make assurance of a quick end for himself doubly sure. When the Greek vessels return to Marseilles, several of the dead are unrecognizable because of wounds (758–61: trans. J. D. Duff):

> Many a wife clasped a Roman corpse, mistaking the face, with features disfigured by the sea, for her husband's; beside lighted pyres hapless father strove with father for possession of a headless body.

We could be reading Ovid's *Metamorphoses*. But this was a real war, and this battle happened!

In Book IX, Cato is crossing the Libyan desert. Other generals had preceded him in order to consult the famous oracle of Zeus Ammon. Cato wishes to demonstrate his Stoic superiority to this idle curiosity by *not* consulting the oracle.[57] His withdrawal is beset with

---

[57] Cf. Diod. Sic. XVII. 49. 3 ff.

serpents, who wreak hilarious havoc with his men (IX. 763–76: trans. J. D. Duff):

> When a tiny *seps* stuck in the leg of hapless Sabellus and clung there with barbed fang, he tore it off and pinned it to the sand with his javelin. Though this reptile is small in size, no other possesses such deadly powers. For the skin nearest the wound broke and shrank all round, revealing the white bone, until, as the opening widened, there was one gaping wound and no body. The limbs are soaked with corrupted blood; the calves of the legs melted away, the knees were stripped of covering, all the muscles of the thighs rotted, and a black discharge issued from the groin. The membrane that confines the belly snapped asunder, and the bowels gushed out. The man trickles into the ground, but there is less of him than an entire body should supply; for the fell poison boils down the limbs, and the manner of death reduces the whole man to a little pool of corruption.

This is not the writing of a poet whose primary concern is to denounce Caesarism, or to protest against the excesses of a particular despot. It is utterly irrelevant to that aim. Lucan is *carnivalizing* his story, and his aesthetics are already exemplified by so classical an author (and one so sensitive to the theatre) as Lucretius, who concluded his exposition of the serene doctrines of Epicureanism with a horrible account of the Athenian plague. Lucan and Lucretius, diametrically opposed as philosophers, agree as Romans on the aesthetics of the carnival. But if Lucan is manifesting the carnival spirit ("Grand Guignol"), he must also be manifesting carnival ambivalence. Nothing there is ever quite what it seems. The black comedy at least hints that death will somehow be compensated by resurrection.

Lucan's interconnected similes, to be investigated below, show an organizing purpose which does not fail in the last books of the poem as we now have it. They are evidence both of an effort at universalizing the historical in myth, and of a serious intellectual intent. Lucan is helped here by the long history of Stoicism, with its many brilliant thinkers, which offered ready-made categories to his thought. The work of Seneca shows that Stoicism was not at all incompatible with monarchy. It all turned on the nature of the monarch.

But why does the poet disguise this seriousness with such macabre episodes as those of Cato's desert journey, or the comedy of the sea battle off Marseilles? The first part of the answer depends on remembering that the question is too narrowly put. The macabre did not have a fascination for Lucan alone. Even in "Silver" Latin, we need look no further than the tragedies of Seneca or, later, the work of Tacitus, for a similar preoccupation with the ghastly and exotic. Virgil showed us Orpheus' torn-off head, still mouthing the name of

Eurydice as it floated downstream. In an earlier book of the *Georgics* he had imitated Lucretius' horrible description of the Athenian plague.

Greek tragedy had detailed the dismemberment of Pentheus, and even Homer had not spared a certain grotesque realism in some of his wound descriptions.[58] Scholars have sometimes explained Roman excesses by referring to the experiences of the gladiatorial combats. There is in fact some kind of ritualized folk-memory of the primeval hunt and kill in all this, accompanied as it must have been by scenes of laughter and celebration, when the tribe knew that it would eat again, or that it had slain its demon/god. The absurdity of Euripides' account of the slaughter of Pentheus, when the women, in their Dionysiac frenzy, play ball with the king's remains, indicates where we are to seek an explanation of Virgil's and Lucan's absurdity.

The reference to the circus/arena then as the reason for Lucan's serio-comedy is correct enough, but the corollary is that the morals of the arena, when transferred to literature, cannot be interpreted univocally, unambiguously. Primitive laughter is the token of an unending cycle, where life and death interchange, blend, re-emerge. There can be no final statements here, only arbitrary interruptions of a process that continues even as the observer draws his static, and hence unfaithful, conclusions.

Lucan perhaps pushes the essential balance between the serious and the comic too much towards the serious, rather as Ovid pushes it too much towards the comic. It is an example of a phenomenon that has been called "reduced laughter." The author continues to deploy the comic apparatus, even when he reduces or suppresses his expectation of a smile. Throughout the reading of the *Pharsalia* one feels a nervous tension that is constantly distorting the vision of life which might have been held by a more "normal" writer. Lucan's grim determination to be a *vates*, to speak of Roman themes, tends to shut out all else that might make for grace or beauty. He knows that his system of values, which are Roman, public values, is threatened, and the over-reaction which this knowledge produces, deeper than any merely intellectual conviction, generates a fixed and fierce resolve to hammer home the reality of another style of living, with different ideals and values from those visible in the Rome around him. But it is interesting that he compares the moral struggle he perceives to a continuous gladiatorial match in the arena, *par quod*

---

[58] E. Burck, *Die Erzählungskunst des Titus Livius*, notes this kind of thing in the Hellenistic historians (pp. 205 ff.): cf. E. R. Curtius, *op. cit.*, p. 487. M. Bakhtin, *Rabelais*, p. 385, quotes Ronsard's preface to the *Franciade*. The outlandish wounds inflicted in Ovid's *Metamorphoses* (e.g. XII. 210 ff.) are also relevant.

*semper habemus* ("a never-ending duel," VII. 695). He does not expect a resolution.

Interrelated similes were a feature of the epic tradition particularly developed in Alexandria. Lucan makes obvious use of the device. His illustrations drawn from the sea and ships are (like those in another carnival author, Pindar) especially remarkable,[59] and now we may see the structural relevance of the scene with the fisherman Amyclas in Book V. Both Caesar and Pompey are mariners, literally and metaphorically. The changing favor of the people is an ocean on which they are embarked (II. 453), but while Caesar despises all that wind and waves can do, because he is the darling of heaven (V. 597 ff.), and is able to exploit with expert ease a flood (IV. 134 ff.), Pompey is a Sicilian or Briton (the historical allusion to Caesar's invasion and Sex. Pompeius' defeat is evident), ignorant of the water (VI. 65). Eventually, he becomes a sailor carried away by the wind (VII. 125). Earlier, one of Pompey's generals was seen as a sailor furling his sail before the wind of Caesar's onslaught (VI. 286). The lesson for Pompey and his army is clear.

There is more direct contact with the literary tradition than this playing with the "ship of state" topos. When Pompey's fleet sails away from Italy for the last time, it loses two ships (II. 715). So it was that the Argo lost its stern as it passed through the Clashing Rocks. Pompey then is a version of Jason. Can it surprise us to discover later that Caesar is Medea (X. 464)? It was from Pagasae that Jason sailed, and to Pagasae that he brought Medea back. But Pagasae is in Thessaly, the home of Pharsalia, laden with doom therefore for Pompey and Caesar also (VI. 400 and 441). During his flight, Cornelia urges her husband Pompey to scatter her over the sea if that will improve his prospects of escape (VIII. 100). Now therefore it is Pompey who is being invited to behave as Medea in one version of the legend had done with Apsyrtus. Naturally, he refuses. But at IV. 553, Vulteius, one of Caesar's men, had no scruples about imitating the earth-born warriors of Colchis in his desperate loyalty to his master.

Book I of the epic ends with the dire prophecies of a Roman matron, compared to a Bacchant (674). The Theban legends conveyed reminiscences of fratricide and murder which were in harmony with Lucan's story (I. 552, 574), as later they would be with Statius'. Vulteius unites Thebes and Colchis (IV. 549 ff.). The Theban story even has its associations with dread Thessaly (VI. 336 ff.). After this

[59] Apart from those mentioned in the text there are I. 100, 260, 498; II. 187, 665; III. 549; V. 217; VI. 265; IX. 799.

preparation, the assertion that Caesar's guilty dreams were like the madness of Pentheus or the waking horror of Agave acquires extra resonance (VII. 779–80).

Pompey is a doomed figure from the very start. Famous lines (I. 136 ff.) compare him to an ancient oak. The next simile (151) compares Caesar to a lightning bolt. At I. 327 Pompey is a tiger. But at V. 405 Caesar is *swifter* than the lightning or than a pregnant tigress. In the boldness of his engineering feats Caesar rivals Xerxes (II. 672). Pompey is like Cyrus—but his eminence merely serves to emphasize Fortune's kindness to Caesar, and to enhance his own funeral train (III. 284 ff.).

Pharsalia is a battle of the gods and giants (I. 35–36; VII. 143). The poet alludes several times to the giants' fate (V. 101; VI. 92, 293: cf. 410). When at this battle Caesar becomes Bellona or Mars (VII. 568–70), he is clearly enjoying the better part.

The first simile of all in the poem (I. 72) alludes to the end of the world, the Stoic *ecpyrosis* from which a new order would emerge. Similar allusions frame the battle of Pharsalia (VII. 134 and 812). The conscious art is apparent, and the inadequacy of regarding the poem as if it were a denunciation of Nero. After all, the conquering cause pleased the gods.

A direct reminiscence of Virgil is provided by a comparison of Pompey to a bull worsted in its first fight (II. 601).[60] The thought is unexpected, since Pompey does not in fact find any opportunity, like the bull in the simile, to return to the fray in Italy. But neither did Turnus in Virgil. Both can carry on the struggle only in the person of their followers and descendants.[61] Caesar indeed needs opposition if he is to flourish (II. 362).

Perhaps we are offered here a clue to the final interpretation of a poem which, in its unfinished state, has proved so baffling. The tensions must continue, with no hope of defeating the imperial system willed by the gods, but at least with the chance of changing and humanizing it. Cato's final importance in the epic was perhaps to have been that of Greek chorus. He would have prophesied, it may be guessed, Caesar's death and drawn out its moral, as he had with Pompey's (IX. 190 ff.). His suicide, admired by the Augustan poets too, could not however have been the last word. Stoicism was too optimistic—and too interested in good government—for that.

Yet although Cato might have been exalted in a final book as the

---

[60] Above, pp. 131 ff. on *Georgics* III. 219 ff. and *Aen.* XII. 103 ff. and 715 ff.

[61] Caesar, dallying at the end in Egypt with his Helen (X. 60) needs as much reminding of the difference between Eastern and Roman virtues as Aeneas (*Aen.* IV. 215 ff. with R. G. Austin's note).

of Cumae's vatic sibyl, if my laurel shines green on a deserving
brow. . . .[70]

and to the emperor (I. 7–10):

> Tuque, o pelagi cui maior aperti
> Fama, Caledonius postquam tua carbasa vexit
> Oceanus, Phrygios prius indignatus Iulos,
> Eripe me populis et habenti nubila terrae.

And you, whose fame the explored sea makes even greater, after the
Scottish Ocean bore your sails, that earlier would not bear the Trojan
Iulii, rescue me from the common herd, from the earth and its clouds.

Yet, as the proem advances, we find that public themes are to be
left to another, imperial poet. For the moment (*nunc*, 20), Valerius
offers his imperial patron a different poem. With this variation of
the "meanwhile" topos, he has cleverly gone back to the point from
which the *vates* began, back to the beginning of the third book of
the *Georgics*, back perhaps even to Gallus. His compromise would
echo even in Tasso's *Gerusalemme Liberata*.

But his "provisional" poem is not a mere translation of Apollonius.
The Alexandrian poet had, for example, deliberately turned away
from battle scenes in order to proclaim his indifference to the trite
notion of *reges et proelia*. In Book VI Valerius, at his distance, and
after the example set by Virgil and Lucan, is able to recover this
theme and color it with the experience of imperial Rome.

Standing as it does between Lucan and Statius, the *Argonautica* is
clearly an important poem. In assessing its achievement, it is necessary
to take account of the remarkable appreciation made by F. Mehmel.[71]

Mehmel regards the poem as explicable only in terms of the
Virgilian tradition, and in fact he forbids us to try to unite it, behind
the Augustan age, with the work of the Republican poets or with
the *Argonautica* of Apollonius. For him, Valerius is an author who,
seeing in Virgil two things, atmosphere (*Stimmung*) and ordered,
classical meaning, abandoned the meaning and concentrated entirely
on the generation of atmosphere. His work therefore may be compared to a series of happenings, aimed at stirring the maximum

---

[70] J. A. Wagner is right to remark on vv. 5 and 6 of his edition of the *Argonautica*
(Göttingen 1805) that Valerius' words are not to be taken too literally. Did the XVviri
Sacris Faciundis keep a *cortina* at home? Did they wear laurel wreaths? Is it anything
but literal-minded inference from this passage that Valerius belonged to their number?
What the poet says in his proem is figurative, guaranteeing his vatic status. At line
10, the Alexandrian *populus* (above, note 31) is noteworthy. This prepares us for the
*recusatio* of 12 ff.

[71] *Valerius Flaccus* (diss. Hamburg 1934).

emotion, of the grimmest and most tragic kind, regardless of unity or coherent, shaping purpose.

Mehmel contrasts this style with that of Ovid, Lucan or Seneca. Ovid he finds occupied simply in presenting a series of distanced, "interesting" pictures. Lucan he interprets as gluing ideas about the Civil War and Caesar's behavior onto historical facts for which he has no relish, and which he often abbreviates to the point of unintelligibility. Seneca, with deadly seriousness, offers in his dramas a series of non-actions, where we see the characters reacting in speeches that betray their utter disillusionment with the normal scale of values, and where their masochistic self-lacerations are their last means of asserting their outraged contempt for the world.

Valerius' epic, by contrast, seems to represent, according to Mehmel, some sort of renaissance. He has both action and atmosphere. He is enabled by his choice of mythical material to manipulate details to suit himself, with a freedom Lucan sacrificed. He has more involvement than Ovid, who merely skates over the surface of his stories. He avoid the static presentation to which Seneca falls victim. But he has none of Virgil's overriding sense of destiny. In Valerius, man is the feeble instrument of the gods, incapable of free will, yet liable to be punished as if he were free. The gods themselves lack all providence.[72] They act out of caprice. All the epic poet can do in his effort to delineate heroic characters is to put them in situations where the maximum emotional pressure is generated. But ultimately these situations are pointless, and life's tragedy is absurd.

Mehmel's thesis has attractive features, but much of the fault he finds in Valerius may be defended by a very Callimachean idea, the analogy with music. The poem reads like a series of operatic arias. Mehmel does not deny their effectiveness. What irks him is their monotony, and their lack of concern with unity. But could there be any feature more characteristic of this whole tradition than its belief that all arts aspire to the condition of music? That this encroachment of music on the Hellenistic poetic worked very powerfully on the minds of Romans already attuned to it by their national proclivities to the carnival may be seen very easily by comparing the plays of Plautus with those of the Greek New Comedy.

Opera, like other music, secures its unity through repetition. In literature, such repetition takes the form of recurrent language and images, and here Valerius certainly shows concern with unity. The

---

[72] This is not entirely fair: see I. 531 ff. In any case, the religious outlook for which Mehmel blames Valerius is as old as Greek tragedy (A. Lesky, *Die tragische Dichtung der Hellenen*, Göttingen 1956, pp. 95 ff.), and is certainly found in other epic (e.g. in Boccaccio's *Teseida*: below, pp. 296–98).

*ecphrasis* in Book I (130 ff.) clearly points to the future development of the action. Argus has painted on one side of the Argo Thetis, borne towards the bridal chamber of Peleus. Her escort includes the sea-nymph Galatea, who is abandoning her suitor Cyclops. Another scene shows Thetis and her husband, listening to Chiron's lyre. They are at a peaceful banquet.

On the other side of the ship is depicted the battle of the Centaurs and Lapiths, an example famous since the *Odyssey* (XXI. 295 ff.) of the power of drunken lust to destroy civilized order.[73] This scene is deliberately linked with the first by the inclusion of the same hero, Peleus; and Chiron, it must be remembered, was a Centaur.

It would be extraordinary if the student of Virgil had neglected to signpost here the future development of his poem. The marriage of Peleus and Thetis, famous in Alexandrian poetry, was unhappily ambiguous in its outcome. The couple were soon parted, and Thetis bore such a grudge that she is described by Apollonius as reluctant so much as to speak to her former spouse.[74] Valerius hints that she is disappointed to be fobbed off with a second best to Jupiter, her first suitor.

In the context of the *Argonautica*, all these allusions, including that to Galatea and her snubbed Cyclops, show what is to be expected from the marriage of Jason and Medea. Yet for the moment Valerius has chosen to depict Peleus and Thetis peacefully together, listening to Chiron's music. This departure from tradition (Apollo plays in Pindar), which yet places the listener dramatically in the marriage-banquet, is contrasted with another marriage-banquet, one that degenerated into bloody and drunken massacre, when the Centaurs and Lapiths rioted. The power of wine for good or ill (the undifferentiated primitive) seems to be the lesson (*post pocula*, "after the cups," 139: *multoque insanus Iaccho*, "mad with deep draughts of Bacchus," 140).

The polarity thus established is of constant recurrence throughout the poem. Among the many references to Bacchus may be noted that at I. 726, where Pelias, threatening vengeance because of his son's departure on the dangerous voyage, is compared to Lycurgus, turning against his own family when driven mad by Bacchus. By contrast, Hypsipyle saves her father Thoas by letting him take refuge

---

[73] There could be allusions now lost, if Valerius' Actor (I. 146) is the same as that of Euphorion (Page, *Greek Literary Papyri*, p. 494), who also seems to have been unhappy in his choice of partner.

[74] *Arg.* IV. 856 ff. Marine deities practice an abrupt manner: Virgil, *Georgics* IV. 528–29; Horace, *Odes* I. 15.

in Bacchus' shrine, whence he subsequently emerges disguised as the god, and is led to safety by his daughter (II. 255).

The symbolism of the drunken battle between the Centaurs and Lapiths is recalled when we hear that, as they part, the Argonauts and Cyzicus exchange gifts which include wine and "Thessalian bridles," *Thessala frena* (III. 5, 13). Later (III. 65), this battle is explicitly evoked as one of the comparisons which illustrate the erroneous and unreasoning fight between Cyzicus and his former guests.[75] When at long last the heroes realize their mistake, their spokesman, Tiphys, is compared to a Bacchant recognizing that her victim has been—Pentheus (III. 264)!

In the same book (538), when Juno is scheming to rob Hercules of Hylas, it is to Bacchus (and Phoebus) that she likens him in order to rouse the desire of the nymph who is to drown him. The comparison is perhaps in mind again when (IV. 23) Hylas appears to the sorrowing Heracles wearing *croceae frondes*, "saffron leaves." Saffron was Bacchus' garb.[76]

Book IV contains Valerius' account of the boxing match between Amycus and Pollux. As the fierce and barbarous king surveys his boyish opponent, he feels like the giant Typhoeus, confronted by Bacchus and Pallas (236–37). The fight between the pair compels a respite for both. It is just as when on the battlefield Mars refreshes the *Lapiths* or the Paeonians (280).

A more sinister aspect of Bacchus is visible in Book V (73 ff.). The Argonauts sail forward, and pass Callichorus, famous for the nightly revels of the god. It was in these waters that he washed clean the hands that dripped with Eastern blood. Here he refreshed the spirits of his worshippers, in such guise as the Theban Maenad and unhappy Cithaeron would wish to see him. The poet is reiterating his emphasis on the intimate connection between Bacchic frenzy and human death. The interpretation is explicitly confirmed by Jason's coupling of "bold Bacchus" and Perseus at 497. It was Perseus who had cut off the Gorgon's head (III. 54; IV. 605; VI. 176).

At V. 511, the hero offers gifts as part of his vain efforts to secure the golden fleece from Aeetes peacefully. Among these gifts was a bridle which the horseman *Lapithes* had been in the habit of using (cf. III. 13). Later (651–52), furious that the Argonauts may escape too easily with their prize, and that his temple may be robbed of its fleece, Mars challenges Minerva to single combat. The goddess

---

[75] Cf. the allusions to Athamas, III. 68; I. 280; VIII. 23.

[76] W. B. Stanford on Aristophanes *Frogs* 46–47. He also refers to Lucian, *Hist. Conscr.* 10, who says that Heracles himself had worn such a robe when under love's yoke. Cf. further Valerius III. 234, at the wedding of Medea.

reminds him that he has no Aloids or *Lapiths* to terrify in her. The allusion to this particular myth is insistent.

Bacchus' potential for violence is again emphasized in Book VI. His power is felt in Perses' army (137). A further allusion is reserved to the very end. As Medea leaves the wall from which she has been viewing the fighting (she is momentarily identified with Euripides' Antigone, *Phoen.* 88 ff.), she is compared to the worshippers of Bacchus who at first resist the god, but who soon yield, and then are ready for any deed. So Medea is now ready for the action of the next book.

Poetic expectation is fulfilled. There, when Medea has a further visit from a goddess (VII. 301 ff.), this time Venus, to compel her to help Jason, she is compared to Pentheus, led forth by savage Bacchus in women's clothes.

A better side of all this complex of legend occurs when Jason, mastering the fiery bulls, is compared to *Lapithes*, father of the Lapiths, riding the first horse (VII. 604 ff.). Lapithes has already been encountered (V. 511).

The last reference to Bacchus in the uncompleted poem comes at VIII. 446 ff. Medea, afraid that she may be abandoned by the Argonauts, is like a Bacchant ranging in madness over the Theban hills.

This chain of images suggests that the poet, contrary to Mehmel's assertion, was not indifferent to unity. The *Aeneid* too uses Bacchic allusions to connect its narrative. Valerius pushes this technique to the point of contrivance. But even in Euripides Bacchus was peculiarly a circus god, and Roman aesthetic bias may be showing itself here once more.

These are not the only images which the poem repeats.[77] Obviously Valerius was quite conscious of the need for unity. More than that of mere names, condemned by Aristotle, it turned upon the musical devices of recurrence and leitmotif.

It is this link with the Alexandrian tradition (extending even to the borrowing of the device of an astronomical calendar[78]) which

---

[77] Cf. II. 43 and VII. 560; II. 227; VII. 635; and VIII. 239. At II. 408 ff. Hypsipyle gives Jason a tunic embroidered with the rape of Ganymede, symbolic of what he is to do to Medea. The disinterested rescue of Hesione by Hercules contrasts with Jason's seizure of Medea when Jason is specifically compared to Hercules (VIII. 125, 230). At III. 82, Jason enters battle against Cyzicus looking like Mars among the Bistones. This recalls the Lemnian husbands (II. 107 ff.) and looks forward to VII. 648, where the allusion to the Cyclops refers us back to II. 95 ff. and IV. 104, 286 ff. The repeated (carnival) imagery of storms and winds, volcanoes, giants, animals, birds and much else needs deeper study than there is space for here.

[78] See P. Bogue's dissertation (above, p. 89 note 41), pp. 7–12.

provides the essential base for the judgment of Valerius' accomplishment. The problem confronting first-century writers was how to repeat Virgil's dazzling success in combining Alexandrian refinement with Roman breadth. Taking up again the theme of the Argonauts, handled with such fastidious delicacy by Apollonius, Valerius realized that he could not offer a mere translation. In his day, with the year of the four emperors behind them, and the accession to power of a new dynasty, the Romans were able to feel that some kind of a future was still possible. No one will read, for example, the catalogue of Perses' allies (VI. 42 ff.)[79] without being made aware of an imperial destiny still potent. But there could be no easy optimism. The Flavian *vates*, who had grimmer experience than Virgil of the hollowness of imperial pretenses, had to fall back on the power of wholly Greek myth to convey a truth larger than history. Nevertheless he still offers the ambiguous, carnival hope of a tempered *furor*, of a Bacchus who washes clean, of a Centaur who sings peacefully at a wedding-banquet and a Lapithes who knows what a bridle is for.

## VI

The *Punica* of Silius Italicus, in 17 books, is normally regarded as the example of all that is unendurable in first-century epic. In reality, the verse is always accomplished and even musical, as we should expect from so fervent a disciple of Virgil. Silius even perhaps lent to Dante the idea for a river of tears in hell.[80]

Taking up an unquestionably historical theme, Silius might be thought to be turning his back on the whole Virgilian experiment, choosing against the "Hesiodic" (Callimachean) in favor of the cyclic manner. That this simple explanation will not do is shown by a most telling passage where Ennius himself, on the point of being attacked in the fray, is preserved by Apollo for higher things (XII. 390–92):

> Sed vos, Calliope, nostro donate labori
> Nota parum magni longo tradantur ut aevo
> Facta viri, et meritum vati sacremus honorem.

With your sisters, Calliope, grant to my labor that the deeds of this mighty hero, too little known, may be entrusted to time. Let us hallow a worthy tribute to the bard.

---

[79] VI. 42 ff.: cf. VI. 55, 402.

[80] Cf. *Punica* XIII. 577 and *Inferno* XIV. 112 ff., and contrast no. 111 in *Medieval and Modern Greek Poetry: An Anthology*, ed. C. A. Trypanis (repr. Oxford 1968), with the note on p. 263. It is not clear whether Dante knew Silius, but there is some quality of imagination shared by the two poets.—An interesting modern discussion is offered by M. von Albrecht, *Silius Italicus* (Amsterdam 1964). See also R. Häußler, *op. cit.*, chapters 4 and 5.

First of all, Silius appeals to the Muses to allow him a digression in return for his *labor*. We are back with the *Eclogues*.[81] The point of the digression is to glorify the *vates* Ennius, the poet who historically had overwhelmed *vates* with utter contempt! Ennius' military prowess is compared (v. 398) to that of the *vates Thracius* Orpheus who, as a member of the Argonauts, joined the battle against Cyzicus. The unhappy associations of the battle are typical of the hamfisted style of the whole passage. Orpheus is brought in as an archetypal *vates* at all costs, even that of good taste.[82]

When Apollo does succeed in rescuing Ennius[83] he describes him as *sacer vates* and says that he will sing (*canet*, 410) the wars of Italy in famous verse, and will be the first to do so. The passage is written in the usual Alexandrian code (XII. 410–13):

> Hic canet illustri primus bella Itala versu
> Attolletque duces caelo; resonare docebit
> Hic Latiis Helicona modis nec cedet honore
> Ascraeo famave seni.

He first shall sing in famous lines the wars of Italy, and raise her generals to the sky. He shall teach Helicon to echo with Latin measures, and will not yield in honor or fame to the old poet of Ascra.

Some of this may be justified by Ennius' own *nos ausi reserare* ("we dared to fling open").[84] But *primus* language comes dangerously close to Alexandrianism, especially as it had developed at Rome, and of course *canet*, the *mot juste* for the despised *vates*, is quite untypical of Ennius.[85] It is certainly not true that Ennius "taught Helicon to echo with Latin measures." Helicon was the preserve of Hesiod, who is mentioned more directly in the next clause.[86]

So even the Roman Homer, as he once was, now comes before us disguised by Silius in Hesiodic dress, and to drive home the lesson,

---

[81] 10. 1, *Extremum hunc, Arethusa, mihi concede laborem*: cf. p. 119, above.

[82] When Horace had exalted Orpheus and the *vates*, he had correspondingly diminished the status of Homer (*post hos insignis Homerus, A. P.* 401). Contrast Ennius' proud *visus Homerus adesse poeta* (*Ann.* fr. 5, Warmington).

[83] The epic cliché (*Iliad* XX. 443) had already been guyed by Lucilius (fr. 231 Marx) and Horace (*Sat.* I. 9. 78).

[84] *Ann.* fr. 235, Warmington.

[85] W. Wimmel, *Kallimachos in Rom*, pp. 109 ff., 177 ff.; W. Kroll, *Studien zum Verständnis der römischen Literatur*, pp. 12 ff.; my article "De verbis *canere* et *dicere*," *Latinitas* XIII (1965), pp. 86 ff.

[86] *Theogony* 1, with M. L. West's note.

*resonare docebit* and *Ascraeus senex* are borrowed from the most Alexandrian of all Virgil's creations, the *Eclogues*.[87]

Yet this new Ennius is also a *vates*. The confusion is clear evidence of the powerful twist (*sdvig*) given to the Roman epic tradition by Virgil. In assuming the title *vates* and deploying Alexandrian technique to give his religious insights expression, he had in fact quite repudiated Ennius' explicit view of his poetic mission, whatever deeper continuities may still have linked Roman with Roman. Silius' naiveté in reclothing Ennius in complete Virgilian, vatic garb carries the revealing implication that, in his eyes, Ennius had no clothes of his own.

Silius' confused literary symbolism is proof of a confused literary purpose. If he really intended to seize the anti-Callimachean, Ennian, cyclic horn of the epic dilemma, and write poetry to the glory of kings and heroes in many thousands of verses, he should have realized that he could have nothing to do with the Hesiodic, Callimachean, anti-cyclic tradition. If he wanted to continue in Virgil's footsteps, he should have asked himself very carefully what it was that made young Virgil turn away from *res Romanae* to the *Eclogues*, quoted here so freely.[88] Perhaps he might then have been directed to myth, or to that subtle combination of myth and history developed by Virgil and again by Lucan, ultimately perhaps owed to Pindar and the Attic tragedians. Instead, what we have in the *Punica* is a long display of the externals of Virgilian technique devoted to a historical theme. But since they are externals, inevitably the heart is missing.

The interesting clue to the missing heart is that Silius can find no scope for the *vates*. He borrows vatic trappings, nowhere more blatantly than in the Proteus episode of Book VII (409 ff.). The return to the *Georgics*, the springboard from which Virgil launched into epic, is telling.

The point is reinforced by a later episode. In Book XIII (400 ff.), like Aeneas, young Scipio goes to consult the Cumaean *vates*. The poet strains for effect, and the present incumbent of the shrine is made to summon up her more famous predecessor. Amid scenes of the most blood-curdling horror the ghost of Appius Claudius eventually appears. He then enters with Scipio into a discussion of the varying funeral customs of the world!

---

[87] *Eclogue* 1. 5; 6. 70. The complex web of allusion here, which demands the recognition of a double strand in ancient epic, both Homeric and Hesiodic, for its unravelling, prevents the easy and misleading alteration of *Ascraeo* considered by W. Suerbaum in *Ennius* (Fondation Hardt XVII, 1972), p. 338 note 1. Quintus Smyrnaeus (XII. 310) actually quotes from Hesiod and Callimachus in setting out his poetic credentials as a writer of Homerizing epic.

[88] Above, pp. 115 ff.

Critics have been vexed. But all this offers an exact confirmation of the nature of the epic tradition as we have already understood it from the description of Ennius by Silius as Hesiod's disciple. Uncertain of his vatic role (and unable to return to an Ennianism that was artistically bankrupt), Silius offers only one half of the Augustan equation, Alexandrianism.[89] Here, Alexandrianism is seen in particular as Hesiodic, didactic. What Virgil and Lucan had subsumed into their epics is now made the stuff of epic itself.

That it was still possible to rise from this base to some sort of height seems proved by those few occasions when the poet does show signs of grasping the potential of his medium. During the long and tedious review of the illustrious dead in this scene there emerges the shade of Hamilcar. Scipio is able to challenge Carthaginian perfidy directly. He finds no repentance, and Hamilcar prays that his son Hannibal may regain Carthage's lost glory. Silius comments: "Then, with head held high, Hamilcar departed in haste, and his ghost seemed taller as it went away" (750–51). We could be reading Dante.[90]

Silius had picked up from the Callimachean tradition the useful hint that brevity could involve the reader in the narrative.[91] Sometimes the device is pushed to absurdity. In Book XVI (557 ff.), compression has reduced what might have been an exciting passage modeled on Virgil's account of the funeral games for Anchises, to total blank. Five compete, and the first three receive prizes of various kinds. The circumstances of the competition are simply omitted.

But elsewhere Silius was not so crude. In Book XVII (236 ff.), as the Carthaginian fleet approaches Africa, carrying Hannibal to his last fight, a storm arises which recalls, by a fine stroke of historical perspective, the scene that accompanies Aeneas' landing in Africa in the first book of the *Aeneid* (81 ff.). Venus appeals to Neptune not to destroy the Carthaginians utterly, lest the Romans be robbed of victory on land (Lucan's "Let me say the opposite!"). The waves sink, and the next line (291) describes how the two armies draw close to each other. The striking example of *brevitas* shows what is possible within these means.[92]

Silius is aware of the unity needed in epic. He does not regard the historical unity of the well-known story as sufficient to dispense with cross-references in his similes. At X. 321, for example, the

---

[89] Lucan's didactic episodes may be adduced, and R. G. Austin on *Aen.* I. 742 ff.

[90] His remark about Brunetto Latini may be compared (*Inferno* XV, end). Other Dantesque touches are *Pun.* V. 24 ff.; XII. 647; XIII. 531.

[91] *Aetia* fr. 57. 1 Pf. See below, p. 411.

[92] Though of course a lacuna has been supposed, as it has, for example, by P. Graindor at Callimachus, fr. 75. 40–41. Yet film montage teaches us that "lacunae" are of the essence: below, pp. 406, 410.

Roman army in bloody defeat is compared to an Alexandrian mer-
chantman, looking so mighty on the sea, and yet so vast in wreck.
In the same book (608 ff.), the defeated general, Varro, is sighted
approaching Rome. The citizens are at first uncertain what reception
to give him. It is just like the wreck of a ship. If the captain is saved
and swims to shore alone, men cannot bear that he should survive
when all his vessel is lost.

At XII. 6, the Carthaginians burst out of Capua to ravage the
countryside. They are like a serpent emerging from its lair after a
cold winter, with all the new energy of springtime. They turn towards
Naples, find their attack frustrated, and retire. It is as if a serpent
had attacked an eagle's nest, and been driven off by the talons fit to
carry thunderbolts (55 ff.).

These similes are so contrived that we are forced to believe in
their calculated relationship. In Book VII, as he flaunts a consul's
captured helmet, Cleadas is described as like Lucifer, the morning
star, when, refreshed by the waters of Ocean, he is approved by
Venus and outshines the greater stars (639). At XII. 247, the dying
Cinyps, famous for his beauty, is like the same star obscured by a
sudden cloud. Here also the details are similar enough to encourage
a search for the connection of thought. It is perhaps enough that
both youths are soldiers of doomed Carthage.

In an often quoted judgment, the Younger Pliny remarked of his
friend Silius that he wrote *maiore cura quam ingenio* ("with more pains
than genius").[93] Yet there is *ingenium* in the poem. Silius' talent is
proved by individual lines, as well as by continuous passages. Book
V, for example, ends strikingly. After Trasimene, like Tolstoy's
Napoleon after Smolensk, Hannibal visits the battlefield. He notes
the bravery of the Roman dead, and wonders if even yet Rome may
be destined for empire. He is overtaken by nightfall (V. 677–78):

> Sic fatus cessit nocti, finemque dedere
> Caedibus infusae, subducto sole, tenebrae.

With these words, he gave place to night. Darkness flooded in and,
taking away the sun, put an end to the slaughter.

In his moment of triumph, Hannibal "gives place to night."

Book VI immediately opens with the dawn of a new day, evoked
in the most elaborate terms of the *Stundenbild*. The beautiful and
exotic picture of the world's return to work[94] is sharply contrasted
with the scene of carnage on the battlefield. Yet the passage ends

---

[93] *Epp.* III. 7.
[94] Cf. *Aetia* fr. 177 with Pfeiffer's comment, and *Hecale* 260. 64 ff.

with an echo (*summo/ponto*, VI. 12–13) of the wider perspective of nature with which it began. Man's alienation from his background, one of the basic themes of twentieth-century literature, is here given forceful expression by the first-century poet.

Even so, in spite of Silius' obvious gifts, Pliny missed *ingenium*. Was he suggesting that Silius had fallen short of the Ennius he admired, and who is praised by Ovid, for example, for precisely that quality? Was he showing impatience with the allegedly Callimachean belief that "in art, art is all that matters"? Is he accusing Silius of being in the Callimachean camp in spite of his ostensibly historical theme? These were genuine alternatives in ancient literary theory, and the literary historian must not fudge his answers.

Pliny clearly believed that *cura* alone was not enough to make an epic. But could a recommendation from him to imitate Ennius more closely have made sense? The *Annales* were a description of Roman history, with particular emphasis on the Second Punic War, which did not scruple to employ all the tricks of the latest Greek rhetoric in the attempt to put Roman consuls and tribunes on a par with Homeric heroes. For Silius, such an enterprise would have been futile. We saw that he redefines Ennius in "Hesiodic" and Alexandrian language. It would be curious if Pliny, with his own literary penchant for writing occasional verses in the Alexandrian manner, had found this blameworthy.

What then was the quality of *ingenium* which Pliny missed? Every modern reader of the poem instinctively feels the same deficiency. Silius lacks what Lucan possesses so abundantly, and that is intellectual force and apocalyptic vision. Art, *cura*, is a means to an end. In the final masterpiece, art and intelligence are indissolubly fused into a whole transparent to reality. When Callimachus urged that *sophia*, poetic skill, should be judged by *technē*, art,[95] can he have meant anything other than this? The alchemy which reacts to produce the perfect work leaves no residue. As everything becomes art, art disappears (Hegel). So far then from urging Silius towards the cyclic epic, Pliny is saying that he should have fused more carefully the elements of Alexandrianism he has taken from the shelf in the crucible of creativity.

If Silius lacked *ingenium*, what could have inspired him to acquire it, to push such *ingenium* as he did enjoy to its fullest height? It could

---

[95] *Aet.-Pref.* 18. The antithesis *technē/sophia* here forms Callimachus' theory of the *ars/ingenium* polarity, dear to ancient criticism, and surviving into Byzantine times. It is not true that Callimachus sets no store by anything except art. A man's ability to use art at a certain level proves his genius. Thomas Mann's *Doktor Faustus* provides further insights into the resolution of this scholastic problem.

only have been a larger vision, a more intense feeling of the relevance of his poetry to his own time. The epic author is necessarily committed to some theory of what constitutes praiseworthy action. How does he show to his contemporaries the truth of his vision?

What we are really saying is that the epic poet at Rome must be a *vates*. Here is where Pliny's criticism strikes home.[96] Silius dwells on concepts which could be vatic: on Fides, on Hercules, on Scipio's choice between Pleasure and Virtue. He is aware of a philosophical background to his heroes' life. But the reader feels, to use Mehmel's unfair term about Lucan, that it is all "glued on." There is no deep thought inspiring the poet's notion of his task. Like the Younger Pliny himself, Silius, in his mellow old age, offers the picture of a kindly Roman amateur of letters, busy with trivialities, not unaffected by materialism, his heart sometimes in the right place, and always in his head a vacuum.

## VII

The Tchaikovsky among the first-century epic poets wrote under Domitian, a fact which in itself should be enough to refute the view that despotism necessarily strangles art. His major work, the *Thebaid*, was brought to completion, and indeed the poet had moved on to an *Achilleid*, suggesting that no excuses are needed here such as beset the reader in judging so many other Latin epics, even the *Aeneid*. Statius was a great poet. There should be no confusion on this point. His influence on the European tradition has been enormous, and deservedly so. Our only concern here is to ask about his place within and attitude towards that tradition.

Statius is unique among the first-century writers in that we possess more than epic by him. Here he resembles Virgil, enabling us to see him in other guises, and as master of techniques other than the sublime.[97] Of key importance for the understanding of the larger work is that these smaller pieces, making up the *Silvae*, are *lyric* in mood and theme. They contain the only surviving challenges from their period to Horatian alcaics and sapphics, and yet even their end-stopped stanzas surrender the verve of Horace's enjambements. As the vatic element drops away, or is taken back by the satirists, Alexandrian lyricism is what is left.

---

[96] One of Varro's etymologies for *vates* had been *a vi mentis*: Servius auctus ad *Aen.* III. 443; Isidor., *Orig.* VIII. 7. 3.

[97] One particularly regrets the loss of Lucan's minor works in this regard. *Saturnalia, salticae fabulae, Silvae* (Schanz–Hosius, *op. cit.*, p. 495) look attractive titles.

A modern analysis of the *Silvae*[98] develops an analogy between what Statius was doing and Mannerist art. Its author rejects the condemnation of the poems as "rhetorical exercises" which has tripped too easily off certain tongues. The Mannerist and "pointed" style has a perfectly valid place in literature. Most interestingly, Statius' mythology in these poems is not a conventional or boring interlude, but an essential part of the often triadic structure of his verse.[99]

"Mannerist" in style: what does that mean? In modern (post-Renaissance) art, Mannerism has often been thought most visible in the paintings of Parmigianino; for example, in his "Madonna with the Long Neck."[100] The artist has taken a theme consecrated by the masters of an earlier generation, and allowed his fantasy to play with it, in such a way that we concentrate, in viewing it, just as much on the technique, the self-consciousness of art, as on the vision which such a subject might once have been intended to convey of the woman who was the Mother of Christ. Parmigianino has *carnivalized* his picture. The Madonna's long neck finds a parallel in that of Alice in *Alice in Wonderland*. Both are examples of the *grotesque body*.

Cancik writes that certain realms of the imagination are characteristic of the Mannerist artist. Remembrance, fear, hope, anticipation are his states of mind. Shadow, mirror (Parmigianino's youthful self-portrait), echo, twilight, moon, mist, bat, are his symbols. Expectation, hesitation, dreams, wanderings, are his scenes. The whole background to this poetry may be described as "unreality."[101]

This is fascinating and challenging criticism, though perhaps it plunges us more into the world of Edgar Allan Poe than into that of classical Italy. One must always bear in mind that sunlight and those trees—and those feasts, games and circuses, about which we read in Statius, Martial and Juvenal, and to celebrate which the Flavian Amphitheatre had been recently constructed at the far end of the Forum. What is striking here is the analogy with the dream-world which critics have also found in the *Eclogues*. The analogy is

---

[98] H. Cancik, *Untersuchungen zur lyrischen Kunst des P. Papinius Statius* (*Spudasmata* XIII, Hildesheim 1965). Cf. H. Friedrich, "Über die Silvae des Statius (insbesondere V. 4, Somnus) und die Frage des literarischen Manierismus," in *Wort und Text. Festschrift für Fritz Schalk* (Frankfurt 1963), pp. 34–56.

[99] Cancik, pp. 29 ff.

[100] Reproduced by E. Gombrich in *The Story of Art* (London 1950), p. 226. See also P. Barolsky, *Infinite Jest: Wit and Humor in Italian Renaissance Art* (Columbia [Missouri] and London 1978), pp. 124 ff.

[101] *Op. cit.*, p. 40. This does not imply that Statius was inattentive to calculation and symmetry (e.g. pp. 17, 49). "Mannerism" is also discussed by E. R. Curtius, *Eur. Lit. und lat. Mittelalter*, pp. 275 ff., and "Zahlenkomposition" is noted on pp. 493 ff.

even more pressing when we note, among Cancik's parallels, certain poems composed by Moorish poets in Spain, as Arab culture there was on the verge of collapsing. Their preoccupation with the symbolism of reflection reminds us powerfully of Virgil's artificial landscapes, reflections as it were in verse of the wall-paintings or false windows of his day, composed when another civilization appeared to be crumbling.

The mirror, for example, exploited by Pindar, condemned by Plato, revived daringly for the *Odyssey* by Alcidamas, suggested for the Shield of Aeneas by Virgil,[102] is a typical symbol of the carnival double world, also familiar to English readers (like Alice's long neck) from Lewis Carroll. If such is the tradition into which the *Silvae* fit, how could they prepare a poet to write about heroic themes? Virgil too displays an omnipresent tendency to fall back into the world of unreality (*umbra*) of which Cancik speaks.[103] He rescued himself from passing wholly through the looking glass by developing a poetic philosophy which could utilize the doubts and hesitations he felt about the Roman mission in the world to give a truer picture of the heroic character. But he was able to do this only because he had some sort of religious belief in the ultimate benevolence of the gods, as expressed in the workings of the Roman Empire. This was precisely the point to which Lucan had to address himself in his effort to revive epic after the mad rule of Caligula and the let-down of Julius' ape, Claudius.

Statius marks a new departure in the post-Virgilian epic. Lucan, Valerius and Silius had all celebrated the public pomp of war and, in their different ways, suggested that there might be in empire a divinely sanctioned order. Lucan and Valerius indeed had both claimed to be *vates*. Statius is respectful enough to *vates* as priests in the *Thebaid*, but he no longer claims that title for himself. He denies the value of war. He can take from Virgil his redeeming humanity. He can no longer accept the imperial idea.

The poet makes his meaning clear by a simple device taken from the tradition as he encountered it even as late as Valerius, and that is the interconnection of similes. At one stroke, his poem acquires a unity and coherence which makes nonsense of all the criticisms heaped on his head by modern connoisseurs.[104]

His elegiac, serio-comic, "downbeat," minor mood is well in evi-

---

[102] *Nem.* 7. 14; *Republic* 596 d; Aristotle, *Rhetoric* III. 3. 1406 b 12; *Aeneid* VIII. 730. Cf. Lucretius III. 974.

[103] Cf. my *Augustus and the New Poetry*, pp. 214 ff.

[104] See further my article "De Statio epico animadversiones," *Latomus* XXXIV (1975), 80–89, and review of D. Vessey, *Statius and The Thebaid* (Cambridge 1973) in *The Classical World* 69 (1975), pp. 83–84.

dence in his first book. On his way to Argos, Polynices enjoys a
moonlit night, which gradually passes into a storm. In the darkness
he finds shelter in the porch of King Adrastus' palace, where he is
challenged by Tydeus, also looking for a place out of the rain.
Polynices is like a sailor in a tempest. The duel at the door is an old
motif. It breaks out here again and, when Polynices fights, he and
his rival are like Olympic athletes. When they are reconciled by the
king, whom they have roused from his bed, they are like winds at
sea, whose fury dies away (I. 312 ff.).

Yet Eteocles too is both a helmsman who ignores a coming storm
(II. 105), and the helmsman caught by that storm when it comes (III.
22). The quarreling brothers were compared to battling winds before
ever Polynices set out (I. 193). The fight between Polynices and
Tydeus as Olympic athletes looks forward to the funeral games of
Archemorus at the beginning of Book VI, which are themselves
illustrated by a nautical simile (19). The moon which Polynices had
enjoyed at first had already illumined the arrival on earth of Tisiphone
(I. 105), the instrument of the divine purpose in bringing down both
Thebes and Argos.

The rival brothers, who have their own relevance to Roman
history, were also rival bulls (I. 131). At the end of Book I, Adrastus
calls upon Apollo/Mithras, in a passage clearly positioned for dramatic
effect. Mithras is described as the bull-tamer (720: *indignata sequi
torquentem cornua*, "wrenching the horns that shame to yield"). Irony
about human pretensions is made explicit. Whatever the two brothers
may propose with a view to their own puny interests, whatever
Adrastus may devise with paternal solicitude about a good match for
his daughters, all must yield before the omnipotence—and caprice—
of the gods.

Tisiphone arrived on earth with a head crowned by serpents.
Serpents are a recurring motif of great importance in the poem. The
Thebans are unable to live peaceably precisely because there is some
sort of original sin in their lineage, the "Martial serpent" which gave
them birth. The tangible presence of a serpent destroys the innocent
Archemorus (V. 539). Statius' careful planning of his poem in the
light of Euripides' *Hypsipyle* is strikingly evident. The Greek poet,
punning on the boy's name, had taken his death as the omen of all
that was yet to happen in the war of the Seven, where the good seer
Amphiaraus, who had rescued Hypsipyle from death, would himself
fall victim to his wife's greed.[105] The thought that childhood and

---

[105] Page, *Greek Literary Papyri*, pp. 92, 102. On Bacchylides, *Epinic.* 9. 12 ff., H.
Maehler notes (p. 28): "δράκων Thebanos indicat." The hint given in whatever
common source Euripides and Bacchylides were following was probably of the most
laconic.

innocence are the first casualties of strife well suits the contemporary of the Peloponnesian War, traditional though it may have been. Statius develops the same insight, and in his whole Hypsipyle episode allows his readers to see what war is like in reality, so that when it happens in the epic they may have in their minds the necessary foil to the ostensibly heroic background.

What Statius thought of war in its conventionally heroic guise is brought out in a series of similes associated with Menoeceus, Creon's son, who perhaps comes nearest to being the clean-cut, ardent young warrior beloved of certain romantics. They occur in Book X. Creon take the omens to discover the future course of the war. The flame of augury is tellingly compared to a serpent (601: cf. *Martius anguis*, 612). Creon grasps that the sacrifice of his own son will be demanded. He is like a man receiving a spear-thrust, or a blow from lightning (618). In another, nautical, image, he is like Sicily, buffeted by the waves (622). Meanwhile, Virtue has disguised herself as Manto, Teiresias' assistant, the better to inspire Menoeceus for what is to come. She is like Hercules, when he was got up as a woman by Omphale (646). The sexual and sympotic lubricity of the comparison shows what we are to think of Virtue's pretensions here.[106]

When Virtue has done her work, and Menoeceus is nobly kindled for the fray in which he is to die, Statius remarks that he was like a cypress lit by a thunderbolt (674). The image recalls Cleon's initial reaction to the idea of his son's death (*fulminis* 618 and 674), and anticipates Jupiter's thunderbolt (*fulmen*, 927), which in this very book is to destroy Capaneus. The funereal associations of the cypress are plain (cf. VI. 99). In modern jargon, Menoeceus has a death-wish, which is being used by the gods to destroy him. Ultimately, when his mother learns of her son's fate, she is like a tigress who laments the loss of her cubs (820). Statius had already prepared for this picture too.[107]

In the welter of senseless carnage, which is what the war against Thebes turns out to be, all the poet can do is insist on the preservation of some memory of common humanity.[108] In Book XII (553–54), the wife of Capaneus appeals to Thebes to secure the burial of the fallen Argives. They were after all men, not Cyclopes, Giants or Centaurs. Yet the constant coupling of Adrastus, king of Argos, with his horse

---

[106] At IV. 550, Manto = Circe. Statius exploits the sympotic/carnival motif of transvestism particularly in the *Achilleid* (I. 260 ff.). Ovid had preceded: *Fasti* II. 318 ff.; *Heroides* IX. 57 ff. Changing clothes in general is also a religious motif ("Sunday best," "Go to meeting" clothes). Cf. the "wedding garment" of Matthew 22:11–12.

[107] Cf. II. 128; IV. 316; VII. 564; VIII. 474; IX. 15–16; X. 288; and XII. 169.

[108] Again a Euripidean theme, as shown, for example, by the speeches of Theseus in the *Supplices*.

throughout the poem has turned him into a kind of Centaur.[109] The appeal by an Argive against the Argive system of values is patent. At the end, Statius grimly comments that if he had a hundred tongues he could not list the number of dead on the field (XII. 797). He wants us to remember that Homer had used the topos of an army *mustering* for war,[110] before war's consequences weighed so much on the human spirit.

The *Thebaid* is, in the last analysis, what Bowra said of the *Aeneid*, an epic about failure written from the point of view of the failed. Direct comparison with the *Aeneid* will illustrate the argument.

In Book IX of the *Aeneid* the Trojans are confined to camp by the Rutulians during Aeneas' absence at Pallanteum. Two friends, Nisus and Euryalus, volunteer to make their way through the enemy ring to seek help. The whole lesson of the episode is that it degenerates from such brave beginnings into pointless slaughter, and ends with the frustration of the mission so nobly undertaken by the pair. Though Virgil admires the self-sacrifice that causes one friend to die with and for the other, which he allusively contrasts with the murder of Remus by Romulus, we may wonder if in his poem the episode does not fulfill something of the same function as the story of Paolo and Francesca in the *Inferno*. It may be intended to communicate, when all is said and done, how *not* to make love or war, and how the Romans, whose army knew nothing of the spirit that informed the Theban "Sacred Band" or Spartan companies, did not in fact go about either.

In Book X of the *Thebaid* Hopleus and Dymas are troubled, like Antigone later, by the thought of the unburied corpses of their slaughtered leaders. The military motives inspiring Nisus and Euryalus have been suppressed in favor of this signposting of the familiar myth. They set off, and after a prayer to the Moon (!) they come across the body of Tydeus—so much for the fine promise of Book I. They are carrying him back to their camp, when they are accosted by Amphion, who is patrolling with a squadron of Theban cavalry. Hopleus is killed. Dymas tries to make a fight of it. He is like a lioness, unable to deploy her full wrath against the hunting Numidians because of fear for her cubs. Compelled to surrender, he implores his enemies to grant honorable burial to his friend, even though they may deny it to himself. Amphion offers to grant his request, provided that Dymas betrays the plans of the Argive chiefs. In answer, Dymas

[109] Cf. especially X. 228 with IV. 139; V. 261; VII. 638; IX. 220; XI. 234. The Centaur theme was well developed in Valerius Flaccus (above, pp. 223–25), and had a long history in Greek poetry.

[110] Norden on *Aen*. VI. 625 ff.

falls on his sword, embracing Hopleus as the only burial he can give him. Statius ends by hoping that, though his skill is inferior, his heroes will nevertheless find a place beside Virgil's Nisus and Euryalus.

Though Virgil made his Nisus and Euryalus fail, their failure was not without either a vatic moral or a role in the total economy of the poem.[111] In Statius, there is no compelling motivation, or at least no motivation that might have advanced the course of the war. The open avowal of a literary model is astonishing in an epic writer.[112] The lioness simile shows in fact what interpretation we are to put on the scene as Statius has recreated it.[113] It is another example of the old curse at work, forever driving men to their destruction, forever rendering them unable to exercise rational control over their lives. The final motif is linked by irony to the original nature of the errand. Those who sought to give their leader burial are obliged to do without it themselves.

As Statius diminished the vatic element of the Augustan equation, so he enhanced the lyrical and painterly aspects of his verse ("sound gesture"), to an extent which has only rarely received its due.[114] The scene is made up as follows:

| 347–350 | Introductory. | 3½ lines |
|---------|---------------|----------|
| 350–359 | Hopleus proposes his plan to Dymas | 9½ lines |
| 360–375 | Dymas accepts and leads the way. He prays to the Moon. The Moon answers his prayer. Simile. | 16 lines |
| 376–383 | They catch sight of Tydeus' body and set off with it. | 8 lines |
| 384–385 | Maxim. Bold enterprises are rarely successful. | 1½ lines |
| 385–398 | Amphion appears and threatens them. | 13½ lines |
| 399–404 | Aepytus is not content to threaten and kills Hopleus. | 6 lines |

[111] G. N. Knauer, *Die Aeneis und Homer*, pp. 266 ff.

[112] Ennius' proclamation of his identification with Homer and quarrel with Naevius may have offered a parallel, but it was a parallel *not* followed in the admired *Aeneid*. It is akin both to Roman satire, and to the spirit of Callimachus' Preface to the *Aetia* and *Iamboi*. See below, p. 263.

[113] Oedipus is a lion at XI. 741: cf. II. 675; IV. 494; V. 203; VI. 598; VII. 529, 670; VIII. 124, 572, 593; IX. 15–16, 189, 739; XI. 27; XII. 356, 739. Statius' use of the Moon/Tisiphone motif looks ahead to the story of Antigone, who also died for burying a fallen leader.

[114] The one-sided development of the lyrical is already foreshadowed in Persius: above, p. 200. Statius' Pindaric studies may have influenced him: cf. *qua lege recurrat/ Pindaricae vox flexa lyrae* (*Silvae* V. 3. 151–52), and contrast Horace's defensive *numeris . . . lege solutis* of Pindar (*Odes* IV. 2. 11–12).

| 405–419 | Dymas does not know what to do. He fights. Simile. | 15 lines |
| 420–430 | He is defeated, dragged before Amphion, and appeals for honorable burial for Hopleus. | 11 lines |
| 431–434 | Amphion bargains burial against treachery. | 4 lines |
| 435–441 | Dymas kills himself, rejecting treachery and bidding farewell to Hopleus. | 7 lines |
| 442–444 | So they died. | 3 lines |
| 445–448 | Statius apostrophizes the dead pair. | 4 lines |

It will be seen that many stages of the narrative here are contained in paragraphs that are either the same as, or make up a simple numerical relationship with, their neighbors.[115] The two longest sections (360–75; 405–19) are in ironic symmetry (16/15 lines), and these are the two sections that are distinguished by similes.

Dymas does not know what to do. It is this absence of any decisiveness which is the issue of Virgilian, vatic leadings, and forms Statius' commentary on the *Aeneid* in the light of his own time. Whether, like our European ancestors, we find such perplexity tolerable in epic will depend on our own maturity, and our receptivity to lyricism, to the picturesque, to dramatic humanism.

Even the *Aeneid* ends with an irresolution. Aeneas, slaughtering Turnus in a paroxysm of fury and rage, could have been revealing his conversion to his enemies' system of values, or he could have been yielding to a momentary aberration (although its position at the end of the poem gives the momentary in that case an unexpected resonance). In either instance, he offered a vatic lesson to his hearers. Statius climaxes his epic with a duel which does not offer even the possibility of hope.

The religious symbolism which might have given it depth is denied in the words where Jupiter turns away (XI. 122 ff.). The almighty father (134) refuses to take any kind of responsibility. His behavior has some parallel in the epic tradition. But whereas in the *Iliad*, for example, a temporary withdrawal of divine interest provides a retarding effect in the action, without prejudicing its eventual outcome, in the *Thebaid* this is the outcome, about which Jupiter should at

---

[115] Cf. pp. 60–63 above, on the structure of Horace's *Ars Poetica*. The *Thebaid*'s relatively straightforward balances ultimately prepare the way for the stanzas of Italian epic, which are not therefore such a break with tradition as might appear. How right Curtius is to trace this device back to Latin Alexandrianism (*op. cit.*, p. 494). But it, and rhyme, originated in Greek lyric.

least have something to say.[116] Deserted by any sense of larger purpose, Eteocles and Polynices inevitably diminish in heroic stature.

If Jupiter will not interfere, King Adrastus will. He appears on the field of battle, and makes a futile speech of reconciliation. His words are as vain as the attempt of Scythian Pontus to halt the onset of the Clashing Rocks (XI. 437–38). Now we understand the relevance to the poem of the Hypsipyle episode, itself incidental to the adventure of the Argonauts. What was ostensibly past history as it was heard from Hypsipyle's lips (V. 28 ff.) was in fact the paradigm of all heroic endeavor. Statius had already made this plain when he described the loss of Amphiaraus by the Argive host as like the Argonauts' loss of their helmsman, Tiphys (VIII. 212).

Adrastus withdraws, with his horse, Arion, from the whole enterprise, like Pluto descending to the lower world. He had also been Apollo, allowing Phaethon to enter upon his deadly course (VI. 320 ff.), and some of his associations were with Centaurs.[117] Yet he can back out of his irrational folly. The sons of Oedipus cannot.

Jupiter is silent, but two lesser deities do make speeches, Pietas and Tisiphone. All they can do is affirm the working out of an irrevocable curse (*Martius serpens*, XI. 489). In order to extract the maximum in low-keyed agony from his orchestration, Statius prolongs his theme to nerve-wracking length.

The details of the duel have a Pindaric vagueness, though there are some touches borrowed from Euripides.[118] There is much interruption by speeches. Eteocles is the first to hurl his spear, in vain. Polynices responds with a prayer (XI. 504–08):

> 'Di, quos effosso non inritus ore rogavit
> Oedipodes, flammate nefas. Non improba posco
> Vota: piabo manus et eodem pectora ferro
> Rescindam, dum me moriens hic sceptra tenentem
> Linquat et hunc secum portet minor umbra dolorem.'

"Ye gods, whom Oedipus with blinded face did not invoke in vain, lend your fires to this crime:[119] my pleas are not wicked. I will cleanse my hands and open my breast with the same sword, provided that my

---

[116] Contrast Silius' borrowing from *Aen.* XII. 791 ff. at *Punica* XVII. 341 ff. (*Omnipotens* at 385).

[117] Cf. X. 227. Argos is the home of the Centaurs: II. 563; IV. 139; IX. 220.

[118] Cf. *Theb.* XI. 530 ff. and *Phoenissae* 1380 ff.

[119] *Flammate nefas* means "Strengthen my cause": cf. 541–42: *cui . . . nefas iustius.* There may be a deliberately perverted echo of Lucan's *quis iustius induit arma / scire nefas.* Heinsius' conjecture *flammare*, adopted by Garrod, robs the oxymoron of its distorted force. The amoral world of Boccaccio's *Teseida*, the paradoxes of Dostoevsky do not seem far away.

enemy leaves me to be king as he dies, and carries off with himself, a ghost of lesser rank, this sense of humiliation."

The motivation of such a prayer is operatic, ridiculous, carnival. It seems to anticipate the twisted mentality of Milton's Satan.

The fight progresses, and the brothers' anger and dislike increases. They are like wild boars, fighting to the death in a forest. All that even the huntsman can do is stand in amazement looking on, commanding his hounds to be silent.[120] Statius comments that now there is no need of the Furies. They too look on in astonishment and admiration, sorry that the madness of men has more power than their own. Watched in this way by spectators (a motif from Greek painting), the duel acquires both theatricality and distance.

Eventually, Polynices inflicts a deadly wound with his sword. Eteocles falls. Polynices cries that the gods have heard his prayer. He calls for the royal finery to be brought onto the very field of combat, so that his brother can see him wearing it while he can still see at all. He does not realize that with this request he is fulfilling the second part of his prayer, which had stipulated that he was willing to purchase the kingship at the cost of his own life. His brother is not quite dead. Incautiously drawing too close, Polynices also is fatally pierced. As he dies, he persists in declaring that they will take their quarrel to be prosecuted further in the lawcourts of hell.

Tradition allowed the epic poet to speak in his own person when confronted with some particularly striking event. Here Statius remarks (574–79):

> Ite truces animae funestaque Tartara leto
> Polluite et cunctas Erebi consumite poenas!
> Vosque malis hominum, Stygiae, iam parcite, divae:
> Omnibus in terris scelus hoc omnique sub aevo
> Viderit una dies, monstrumque infame futuris
> Excidat et soli memorent haec proelia reges.

Go, savage spirits, and stain gloomy hell with your deaths. Exhaust all the penalties which the world of darkness has to offer. And you, goddesses of Styx, now spare the sufferings of mankind. Throughout all space and time may one day alone have witnessed this crime! Let the ill-reputed horror be forgotten by posterity, and only kings speak of this combat.

The paradox is violent. If the story is really so terrible as not to deserve a place in memory, why select it for a twelve-book epic? The

---

[120] Tydeus was like the Calydonian boar at II. 469, where also there was an audience (480). So also Priam and Hecuba had watched the duel between Hector and Achilles in *Iliad* XXII: above, p. 14. K. Schefold notes the concept of the *Zuschauer*: *Götter- und Heldensagen der Griechen in der spätarchaischen Kunst*, p. 272.

punning *infame* actually acknowledges that the events of the myth are so well known that the poet has no power to obliterate them. These self-defeating hopes (a good example of "Let me say the opposite!") are capped by the supreme irony of the final wish, peculiarly relevant to the history of Rome. But the irony is secured at the expense of denying any cathartic influence to literature at all. The days when a poet-*vates* could hope to warn about the temptations of public office are apparently over. Statius did not believe that kings—or emperors—would be held back from civil strife by recalling what happened at Thebes. The whole history of the Principate, now a Dominate, proved the contrary.

Statius abandoned the vatic title, and, except in the most negative sense, the vatic function. His lack of expectation about the audience his poem might command led him, following a hint given by Valerius Flaccus, to revive the Callimachean *recusatio* in the proem to his epic in a way that paradoxically became topical for the tradition.

At the beginning of Book III of his *Georgics* Virgil, conscious that in his own development greater things were yet to come, had sketched an airy, Pindaric, theatrical fantasy of what these greater things might be before turning back—"meanwhile"—to his immediate farmyard theme. It did make sense for the future poet of the *Aeneid* to treat his earlier work as a preliminary to that colossal achievement. In the *Aeneid* itself there is no *recusatio*, no "meanwhile" offering of a second-best.

Lucan told Nero that under his patronage the *Pharsalia* would have no need of conventional epic thunder. Here, the *recusatio*, though now transferred to a large-scale epic, still makes sense. There is no suggestion that the rejected epic would be better. But Valerius Flaccus, in declaring that his patron's son will celebrate Roman triumphs, cannot mean that this epic alternative is *inferior* to his own. Statius goes the whole way. The *Thebaid* is only a second-best to the epic he will write one day about Domitian's conquests. He certainly wrote a poem on that very theme. But could even Statius really have thought it superior to or more relevant than the *Thebaid*?[121]

Both Dante and Petrarch will ultimately pretend that their major poems are only temporary substitutes for the real thing,[122] although not quite in the same way. Callimachus had vigorously rejected this

---

[121] If the *Thebaid*'s critique of war represents the poet's own conclusions, can he have accepted the values of the historical epic, in which criticism was necessarily abandoned for flattery? Can he have supposed that such epic was compatible with the achievement of Virgil, Apollonius, Callimachus, even Homer?

[122] *Paradiso* I. 34–36; *Africa* I. 40 ff. Cf. the discussion of Tasso's exordium, below, p. 329.

"real thing" as proof of his critics' insensitivity. Virgil had offered his temporary substitute on his way to the *Aeneid*. Statius is forced to disguise his "real thing" as a temporary substitute. Behind the conventions lies a world of change.

If the first-century epics are "Silver," it is because they represent the gradual failing and fading of the vatic ideal, a dialogue with Horace and Virgil which becomes more and more muffled. In our analysis, it is not enough to view poetry as merely the exploitation of technique. There have been epics which have done this, but they betray their inferiority in the long perspective of history. Technique is the servant of, and in a real sense depends for its existence on, an overriding vision of what "things divine, heroic and human" imply. The failure of vision which we have traced was not sudden, and it was not uniform. But there was a failure to link these two realms, to see the cities of man and God together. It would be long before a poet—interestingly, a comic poet—had need of both peaks of Parnassus.

# VI

# THE CRITICAL FAILURE:
# DANTE AND PETRARCH

THE role of the literary critic is to maintain awareness of the resources of the literary tradition, and this function was well enough understood in Alexandria,[1] especially in those early days when critic and creative artist were one. Unfortunately, the critic too often divorces himself from any practice of the art he professes to judge, and bolsters his sense of inadequacy by arguing that even those who do continue to practice are wasting their time.[2] This deadly development was also known in Alexandria and made, for example, the concept of "envy" one of the key ideas in Callimachus' thought.[3]

One of the most powerful weapons in the armory of the envious is the contention that the moderns are utterly inferior to the masters of the past, and have completely mistaken the nature of true poetry. It is sobering to reflect that the influence of these small minds on the classical epic and its successors has been such as to hamper and even destroy the work of genius.

## I

The critical failure is attested in Rome by the chorus of blame that

[1] The practical criticism exemplified in the Homeric scholia is described above, pp. 47 ff. The history of criticism is obviously a specialized study: cf. G. Saintsbury, *A History of Criticism*, 3 vols. (London and New York 1900–04); J. E. Spingarn, *La critica letteraria nel Rinascimento*, tr. A. Fusco (Bari 1905); the English original has most recently been reissued as *A History of Literary Criticism in the Renaissance* (Westport, Conn. 1976); R. Wellek, *A History of Modern Criticism 1750–1950*, 4 vols. (New Haven 1955–); B. Weinberg, *A History of Literary Criticism in the Italian Renaissance*, 2 vols. (Chicago 1963).

[2] Callimachus' critics, according to the Florentine Scholiast (Pfeiffer, *Callimachus*, vol. I, p. 3), included a number of whom we know nothing as poets: "the two Dionysii," "...]yrippus the rhetor" and Praxiphanes.

[3] E.g. *Hymn. Ap.* 107; *Epigr.* XXI. 4; *Aet.-Pref.* 17. In the Roman tradition, *Invidia* takes on a new life, for example, in Petrarch, *Africa* I. 36, 78; II. 173; III. 430; IV. 367; V. 86, 315, 655; VI. 440; VII. 545, 552; VIII. 577, 1033; IX. 34 ff. Cf. Dante, *Inferno* I. 111; M. W. Dickie, *Am. Journ. Philol.* 96 (1975), pp. 378–90.

greeted the *Aeneid*.[4] Virgil had fused Alexandrian "learning," which means knowledge of his Greek epic predecessors and what commentators had said about them,[5] with the Roman and Augustan awareness of national destiny. His epic was colored by a Dionysiac sense of carnival shared with the Greco-Roman world of his day.[6] The curious amalgam that resulted was, like all new masterpieces, shocking and disconcerting. Even so, it typified Roman taste for the bizarre and blurred, and its very uncertainties accorded well with the doubts of an age unsure of its own future in history. Its Augustan counterparts, Ovid's *Metamorphoses* and Manilius' didactic *Astronomica*, indicate from what kind of literary soil Virgil's epic sprang, and where investigation of its genesis and intent is most likely to prove fruitful.

Virgil had refreshed epic language as well as epic thought. Donatus tells us that a distinguished contemporary—interestingly, an enemy of Gallus, Virgil's admired friend—responded by calling him "the inventor of an unexpected type of bad style, not bombastic and not jejune, but drawn from common words, and therefore inobtrusive." Scholars have noted that the examples of prosaic language multiply in the second, "Italian" half of the poem. Horace, with his doctrine of the *callida iunctura*, the surprising juxtaposition of ordinary words which lends new life to the everyday, had provided the theoretical justification for this procedure. Aristotle had praised Euripides' use of terms drawn from what he calls "normal conversation."[7] Yet later, a medieval critic, the true successor of Agrippa, would disapprove the use of *sincategoreumata* in high poetry, prosaic particles like *porro*, *autem*, *quoque*.[8] Alas, there are 28 examples of *autem* in the *Aeneid*, and three in Catullus 64.[9]

The Roman critics, Perellius Faustus and Q. Octavius Avitus, collected instances of Virgil's plagiarisms or "resemblances" (if the corrupted text of Donatus is rightly restored).[10] In Avitus' case, the collection extended to eight volumes! Asconius Pedianus responded with a monograph in the poet's defense, which admitted the borrowings from Homer, but quoted Virgil himself in justification. "It was

---

[4] *Vit. Verg. Donati* 44 ff.; C. Hardie, *Vit. Verg. Antiquae* (Oxford 1967), praef., p. xiv.

[5] R. R. Schlunk, *The Homeric Scholia and the Aeneid* (Ann Arbor 1974).

[6] E. E. Rice, *The Grand Procession of Ptolemy Philadelphus* (Oxford 1983), illustrates these themes even in the age of Callimachus. Cf. Quintilian's *Alexandrinis . . . deliciis*, I. 2. 7. For Bacchic and carnival themes in the *Aeneid*, see above, p. 180.

[7] Above, pp. 41–42.

[8] Matthew of Vendôme, in E. Faral, *Les arts poétiques du XIIe et du XIIIe siècle* (Paris 1924), p. 167.

[9] B. Axelson, *Unpoetische Wörter* (Lund 1945), pp. 85–86.

[10] *Vit. Verg. Donati*, end.

easier," the poet was reported to have said, "to steal Hercules' club from him than a single line from Homer." Even so, Asconius felt it prudent to go on to plead that Virgil had, before his death, planned to withdraw from society so as to prune everything to his critics' satisfaction. "The unfinished state of the poem" has been a useful argument to all sides in the continuing debate about what it means.

The so-called plagiarisms from Homer and Apollonius however were not likely to have been removed wherever the poet might have withdrawn, since they are essential to the whole "ironic" method of composition. Nor could the *communia verba* have been deleted without serious loss to the total, astringent effect. But the poet was no longer there to speak except through his work, and his work demanded more than an "academic" response.

His defenders often sinned as badly as his enemies. Aulus Gellius in the second century A.D. shows the way to the canonization/ magnification of Virgil familiar to the Middle Ages. Instead of any attempt to appreciate the work as a whole, there is the constant analysis of individual turns of phrase, often marked by an irrationality that sacrifices intelligibility to archaism. The perpetual willingness to palm off "glosses" on Virgil invests his text with the approved distance from any real discourse, and means that it may be treated as some kind of incantation. The music of the Alexandrian poetic is allowed to outweigh everything else. The process is already traceable even in so sober a critic as Quintilian, and modern editors do ill to be influenced by the remarks of this kind of commentary when they have not adequately understood the psychology that inspires them.[11]

The school tradition of criticism, found at its best in Servius, was clearly limited. No volumes appear to have been available which

---

[11] Cf. Gellius I. 21 on *Georgics* II. 247 (*amaror* rejected by Mynors); I. 7 on *Verrine* V. 167 (*futurum* rejected by Peterson); IX. 14 on *Aen.* I. 636 (*dii* rejected by Austin, who remarks on p. 194 of his edition: "The learning of Gellius and his friends . . . has bedevilled the passage"). For the same reason one cannot believe that Virgil wrote anything except *cui non risere parentes* at *Eclogue* 4. 63. What paltry evidence is assembled by so fine a scholar as Norden to justify *qui*! Cf. *Die Geburt des Kindes, Studien der Bibliothek Warburg*, III (Leipzig–Berlin 1924), pp. 62 ff. and note 2. Virgil is perhaps alluding to the phenomenon described by Mary Goldring in *The Listener*, vol. 98, no. 2524 (September 1, 1977): the baby smiles first (= *incipe, parve puer*), and is then copied by his parents. The idea of the poet as *magus* is a concomitant of the exaltation of the "sublime," especially when assisted by a powerful nostalgia for the past and reaction against modern "decadence." On it see Horace, *Epp.* II. 1. 213; Gorgias, *Helena* 82, B 10 (Diels, *Fragmente der Vorsokratiker* [6th ed., Berlin 1951], II, p. 291); and F. Wehrli, "Der erhabene und der schlichte Stil in der poetisch-rhetorischen Theorie der Antike," *Phyllobolia für P. von der Mühll* (Basle 1946), pp. 9–34. Thomas Mann, whom his family used to call "the magician," experienced and explored the dangers of this view of art in our own time, notably in *Doktor Faustus*.

discussed Virgil's meaning as a totality, or which explored the unity and ultimate, vatic message of the poetry. Vatic now meant, not public pulpit, but private mumbo-jumbo (the *sortes Vergilianae*). Ennius' rationalism had triumphed.

Agrippa had remarked that Virgil's novel type of bad style was neither bombastic nor jejune. In the literary criticism of the day, this means that the *Aeneid* did not exemplify either the high or the low style. Its "common words" assigned it to the middle level.

Vocabulary in itself is an uncertain guide to total poetic effect, which is what Horace was trying to say in his doctrine of the *callida iunctura*. To overlook this elementary truth was not a promising start. In the course of the centuries a development occurred which had the effect of further stultifying what Virgil had actually done. Memories of the "three styles" persisted in treatises on rhetoric. Coincidentally, Virgil had written three major works. It seemed only natural to the orderly, academic mind that he should have written the *Eclogues* as an example of the plain manner, the *Georgics* as an example of the middle style, and the *Aeneid* no longer now as the model of the middle, but of the grand style. There are signs of this doctrine in late antiquity, though Macrobius, for example, is still aware of the real truth.[12]

For the *Aeneid* this fateful misunderstanding meant that the reader was now rendered deaf to the colloquialisms that Virgil, following Callimachus and Apollonius, had introduced there. All was accepted as on one uniformly "sublime" level. It followed that this stilted style clearly could not condescend to be humorous or ironical, and still less of course be indebted to the carnival and its masks. A whole dimension was thus lost from the *Aeneid*, as the epic was compressed into a stereotype of uniformly exalted narrative that made no allowance for its involuted contours. Under the strain, the constituent parts of the original creation fell asunder. On the one side, there was the literal-minded treatment of Aeneas as a conventional hero, which meant either dismissing him as an odious tyrant or closing one's eyes to all that so obviously was unheroic about him. On the other was the mystical belief that the poem was more than a poem, was, in fact, some kind of "vatic" revelation, which fitted its author to foretell private destinies. The synthesis presented by Virgil, that the vatic

---

[12] Macrobius, *Sat.* V. 1. 18 ff., argues that Virgil's mixture of styles is like the *concordia dissonorum* in music. Against this may be offset the statement in Donatus' *Life* of Virgil, ed. I. Brummer (Leipzig 1912) that the poet developed from the *tenuis* style of the *Eclogues* to the *validus* style of the *Aeneid* (p. 14).

revelation consisted precisely in the study of the interplay between human weakness and divine necessity, was lost.[13]

The origins of the doctrine of the three styles are bitterly contested. In Greek, they are presumed in the *De Elocutione* of Demetrius, which unfortunately has no agreed date. For the Romans, they were set out in the treatise *Ad Herennium*, known to the Middle Ages as a Ciceronian work and usually simply called the *Rhetorica Nova*. They are implied, as we have seen, in the criticism of the *Aeneid*'s bad new style already cited from Agrippa, where however the poem is judged to be in the *middle* manner, "not bombastic and not jejune."

In itself, the recognition of a multiplicity of good styles represented progress beyond Aristotle's theory that there was one norm of good style. A speaker aware of all the possibilities of his medium will demand a more subtle response from the critic, and be harder to pin down. Quintilian knew this (*Inst. Or.* XII. 10. 69):

> Utetur enim [orator], ut res exiget, omnibus, nec pro causa modo, sed pro partibus causae.

> The pleader will use all the styles, as circumstances require, and not only in different cases, but in different parts of the same case.

So too Macrobius in the fifth century notes that his admired Virgil is a master of all styles. In fact, he attributes *four* styles to the poet, and makes him excel in every one (*Sat.* V. I. 6):

> Quattuor sunt, inquit Eusebius, genera dicendi: copiosum, in quo Cicero dominatur: breve, in quo Sallustius regnat: siccum, quod Frontoni ascribitur: pingue et floridum, in quo Plinius Secundus et nunc nullo veterum minor noster Symmachus luxuriatur. Sed apud unum Maronem haec quattuor genera reperies.

> According to Eusebius, there are four levels of style: the full, exemplified at its best by Cicero; the terse, where Sallust is supreme; the plain, attributed to Fronto; the rich and adorned, where Pliny the Younger and in recent days Symmachus, a match for any of the ancients, show their abundance. These four styles will be found in the one Virgil.

All the individual examples that Macrobius now adduces are drawn from the *Aeneid*, and an example of all four combined to create a *pulcherrimum temperamentum* is taken from the *Georgics* (I. 84 ff.).

---

[13] For Dante, Aeneas is important as the bearer of destiny, and his personal qualities count for nothing. For Konrad of Hirsau (first half of the twelfth century) Aeneas made himself hated by his cruelty after his victory over Turnus, and was eventually struck by lightning (Curtius, *Europ. Lit. und lat. Mittelalter*, p. 462. Turnus on the other hand receives rather a good press). The epic had clearly dissolved into its elements.

Macrobius is not wrong to treat the poet as an orator, since poetry is an oral art. Quintilian's feeling for Lucan as an *orator* (lawyer) defined an important aspect of the *Pharsalia*'s art, its kinship with the *skaz*. In the Middle Ages only Geoffroi de Vinsauf appears to have recognized this truth, when he discusses *pronuntiatio*.[14] But even as the notion of the orality and polyphony of Virgilian epic faded, the rhetorical doctrine of the three styles became irrevocably and fatefully attached to the interpretation of what Virgil had done. John of Garland drew the logical conclusion from the theory of the three styles when he invented the *Rota Virgilii*, "Virgil's Wheel," which, with an ordered symmetry pleasing to the medieval heart, so conveniently sets out the misleading (and misunderstood) analysis.[15] It has been suggested that this ascription of different topics, implements, plants, and even names to the different genres exemplified by Virgil is the product of the medieval sense of caste. But already in Petronius Lucan is criticized by implication for his use of unsuitable vocabulary. As so often, new error was building on old.

Language is one facet of a total response to the world. When Virgil used words like *mussare, praesidium, mulier, interesse, gladius*, he was indicating a certain attitude, inspired by a Roman toughness, to the high-flown and stilted. This attitude was something that the Middle Ages could have easily accommodated. Evidently, medieval authors dearly loved a joke, and had a keen sense of satire. Medieval theorists however discuss comedy reluctantly. Geoffroi de Vinsauf tells a silly anecdote about "How I got my own back on a surly pot seller."[16] Its opening use of rhyme is noticeable:

> Tres sumus expensae socii pueroque caremus.
> Hoc pro lege damus, ut prandia nostra paremus. . . .

Three of us were going dutch, and had no servant. We laid down that we should make our own suppers. . . .

But he pulls himself up with a call to seriousness:

> Seria si tractes, sit sermo serius et mens
> Seria, maturus animus maturaque verba,
> Praescriptisque modis et res et verba colora. . . .

If your theme is serious, your language must be serious and so must your whole attitude, your mind adult, your vocabulary the same. Both topic and words must be handled in the appointed way. . . .

---

[14] Faral, pp. 259–60, 318.

[15] Faral, p. 87; G. Mari, *Romanische Forschungen* XIII (1902), 920; John M. Steadman, in *Chaucer und seine Zeit*, ed. Arno Esch (Tübingen 1968), pp. 1–33. Cf. Faral, p. 312 (Geoffroi de Vinsauf).

[16] Faral, pp. 255–56. Cf. p. 317.

# Virgil's Wheel

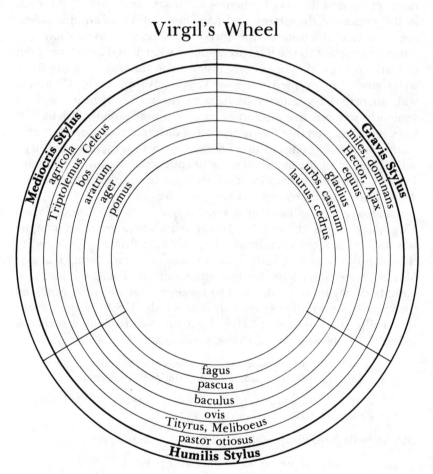

In the names given as appropriate to the "Mediocris Stylus," I have replaced the meaningless *Coelius* printed by editors with *Celeus,* father of Triptolemus: cf. Virgil, *Georgics* I. 165 with Servius' note.

In the verses cited here, Geoffroi has been paraphrasing Horace (*A. P.* 86–87), though *praescriptis* for *descriptas* betrays the authoritarian:

> Descriptas servare vices operumque colores
> Cur ego si nequeo ignoroque poeta salutor?

> If inability and ignorance stop me from keeping to the established genres and literary styles, why do I claim the title of poet?

But at what cost to the subtlety of his master! Horace had gone on in the same passage to modify his severity by admitting that plain vocabulary could sometimes be useful to the tragic writer, just as the comic writer could raise his tone in certain scenes. It has already been noted that, according to an ancient commentator on this passage, the modification was inspired by Callimachus. And it will be seen below[17] that this is exactly the passage of Horace which is quoted by Dante in his Letter to Can Grande to justify his own choice of vocabulary in the *Commedia*. Dante read the tradition with the penetrating eye of genius. All this refinement is missing from the academic doctrine.

Geoffroi notes a point of contact between comedy and the *Aeneid* in the use of *praecisio*, what is nowadays known as aposiopesis. But he distinguishes Virgil's use from the comic by saying that in Virgil it is a sign of *ira* or *indignatio*. It never occurs to him that comic *ira* is exactly the jumping-off point that allows Horace, the classical critic, to associate tragedy and comedy!

In his prose *Documentum* the same author declares:

> Si materiam ergo iocosam habemus prae manibus, per totum corpus materiae verbis utamur levibus et communibus. . . .

> If then we have humorous material in hand, throughout the entire work we must use light and ordinary vocabulary. . . .

In recommending *communia verba* to the writer of *comedy*, he cannot have known that Agrippa had accused Virgil of using *communia verba* in the *Aeneid*. Dante broke through to the insight that sublime poetry may be written with *comica verba*. Evidently he was not helped here by the critics. In a later age, Voltaire will still poke fun at Shakespeare for speaking in tragedy of a "mouchoir."

By the time of the Renaissance, the craving for simple rules at the cost of fidelity to the complexities of authorial experience spread to the interpretation of Aristotle also. It was now that the famous unities were elevated into demands that the modern dramatist had to observe or perish.

---

[17] P. 262, with note 37. See Horace, *A. P.* 97, and C. O. Brink, *ad loc.*

One of the most flagrant instances of the way in which traditionalist criticism is able unblushingly to trample down tradition concerns the Aristotelian theory of the epic. Aristotle had had grave reservations about what was happening to the epic in his own time, and he obliquely rejected the effort made to revive it with themes drawn from history by Choerilus of Samos in his *Persica*. He had not spared certain criticisms even of Homer. Eventually, in his final remarks, he had made the astonishing decision that after all tragedy is superior to epic, notably because of its concentration and its ability to use more than words in order to secure its effects. Who could believe that after this broadside some of the most influential Renaissance critics were still able to place epic at the top of their literary hierarchies?[18]

The Renaissance was following here the medieval tradition, which in its turn derived from late antiquity. As the grandest of all genres, epic demanded the grandest of all language. The same high style must be maintained regardless of the speaker. It is indeed the ordinary which will be elevated by the poet's language, since the aim of his poetry is to excite *admiratio*. The debt to the *ekplēxis* of "Longinus" is apparent.

The elder Scaliger gave these theories classic formulation. Comparing Homer and Virgil, he acknowledged in Homer the presence of *ingenium*, but it was for Virgil that he reserved *ars*; it is another example of the sometimes malevolent potency of these ultimately Greek formulas. The display by Homer of *humilitas, simplicitas, loquacitas* and *ruditas* in his style must make him inferior to Virgil. By epic style, Scaliger understands only the adaptation of language to the expression of heroic majesty. At every comparison, Homer for him must yield to Virgil's *magnificentia, splendor, grandiloquentia, ardor, affectus dictionis et numerorum*.[19]

In the course of time, with the rise in Europe of the Romantic Movement, these verdicts were reversed. Now it became Homer's apparent artlessness (!) which recommended him as better than his Roman successor. The inadequacy of these antitheses is obvious. Nothing is gained for civilization by making Virgil and Homer mutually exclusive rivals. Yet the most that Scaliger can do on observing that Virgil has taken the details of *Fama* in Book IV of the *Aeneid* from Homer's picture of Strife is to load Homer with abuse.[20] He does not see that the borrowing is the clue to the meaning.

---

[18] E.g. G. Strozzi, G. Vida, G. P. Capriano, G. Viperano.

[19] Cf. F. J. Worstbrock, *Elemente einer Poetik der Aeneis*, p. 20; B. Weinberg, *A History of Literary Criticism in the Italian Renaissance*, pp. 467, 745, 747; J. Cottaz, *Le Tasse et la conception épique* (Paris 1942), p. 330 (Robortello), and p. 337 (Minturno).

[20] On *Aen.* IV. 173 ff.

Because the relationship between Homer and Virgil was misunderstood, the entire structure of the *Aeneid* was misunderstood, depending as it does for its comprehension on the constant shadowing (a version of carnival "doubling") of its scenes and characters by their Homeric or Apollonian counterparts. Ancient theory in any case had come to neglect the question of unified structure. Scaliger denied it both for the *Iliad* and the *Odyssey*. That of the *Aeneid*, while duly admitted, was never analyzed in detail. The whole Alexandrian, ironic revival of the Homeric epic by the Roman was therefore ignored. The notion of tradition was replaced by that of annihilation.

## II

The Virgilian tradition was evidently read quite differently by the poet Dante. How differently, we may judge by our own sense of unfamiliarity when we first open the pages of his incomparable masterpiece.

Poet of European stature though Dante is, and ardent follower of Virgil though he professed himself, can there be any of his students who have not felt puzzled by the framework in which his mighty poem is cast? And how is the actual title *Comedy* to be explained? If we take our standard of what constitutes normal and acceptable epic from the classicizing critics, even from our memories of Milton's *Preface* to *Paradise Lost*, does it not seem peculiar to find a poem making such large claims which actually rhymes, and then again which proceeds in cantos, "songs," of relatively short duration? And when we peruse those cantos, do we not also find that the slow and deliberate pace of the poetry is at variance with the majestic sweep of eloquence we regard as proper? No doubt we are soon converted to the new style. But why is any conversion needed?

The answer to these questions again faces us with the central problem of recovering the classical epic tradition. It is this tradition which was instinctively seized by Dante in the face of contemporary misconceptions, and which alone can explain why his epic deserves the stature conferred on it by the judgment of posterity.

But was it an epic? Renaissance critics liked to deny this truth,[21] even though the *Comedy* so easily jibes with the ancient definition of epic made by Aristotle's pupil and successor as head of the Lyceum, Theophrastus, as the poetry that "embraces divine, heroic and human affairs." It should be noted that Dante himself claimed to have been made the sixth of a famous company of five ancient poets: Homer,

---

[21] The arguments about the literary status of the *Comedy* are chronicled, for example, by B. Weinberg, pp. 819 ff. The Theophrastean definition of epic mentioned is noted by S. Koster, *Antike Epostheorien*, p. 89.

Virgil, Horace, Ovid and Lucan (*Inferno* IV. 79 ff.). Only one of these is not "epic" in the traditional sense, *Orazio satiro*, and of course even Horace's *Satires* are written in the epic meter, the hexameter. The exception then to the epic company is most revealing. The satiric, moralizing, denunciatory/prophetic element present even in Horace's *Odes* is a sign of what the Augustans knew as the vatic aspect of their public poetry, and this is the element now being taken back into the epic tradition (from which it had been divided as early as Persius) by Dante. The poet's profession of collegiality is already a fine commentary on his understanding of the ancient tradition: on its awareness of large concerns, its interest in behavior, its metamorphoses, its orality, its public nature, its adaptations of history to poetic discourse.

In examining the work of Virgil, we discovered that it was advisable not to neglect his beginnings, since there was an important sense in which he remained loyal to them right to the end. The same is true of Dante, as he himself attests at the very opening of the *Inferno*. There, as he encounters Virgil for the first time, he declares in famous words (I. 79–87):

> "Or se' tu quel Virgilio e quella fonte
> che spandi di parlar sì largo fiume?",
> rispuos' io lui con vergognosa fronte.
> "O de li altri poeti onore e lume,
> vagliami 'l lungo studio e 'l grande amore
> che m'ha fatto cercar lo tuo volume.
> Tu se' lo mio maestro e 'l mio autore,
> tu se' solo[22] colui da cu' io tolsi
> lo bello stilo che m'ha fatto onore."

"Are you then that Virgil and that spring from which so rich a stream of eloquence is spread?" I answered him shamefaced. "Oh glory and light of other poets, may there avail for me the long study and the great love which has made me search your book. You are my master and my authority. You alone are he from whom I took the beautiful style that has made me honored."

Dante states that Virgil alone is the one from whom he took the beautiful style that has made him honored. He is very far then from thinking that the writing of the *Comedy* marked such a violent break in his work that what he had done earlier became irrelevant.[23] Instead, there is the arresting paradox that Virgil is acknowledged to have

---

[22] Dante here picks up a long tradition: cf. *qui* **solus** *legit et facit poetas* of P. Valerius Cato, Buechner, *Fragmenta Poetarum Latinorum*, p. 105. See further E. Norden, *Agnostos Theos* (Leipzig–Berlin 1913), p. 245 note 1; O. Weinreich, *Menekrates Zeus und Salmoneus* (Stuttgart 1933), pp. 6–8.

[23] Contrast the skepticism of Foster and Boyde, *Dante's Lyric Poetry* (Oxford 1967), I, pp. xxx ff.

inspired even the poet's other than epic writings. At once this makes clear the breadth of Dante's appreciation of Virgil. Instead of reducing him to the authorship of the *Aeneid*—which really means to misunderstand even the *Aeneid*—he was able to see him in the total context of what he had done, and grasp his relationship to kinds of poetry which were certainly both parts of Virgil's achievement and subsumed in the *Aeneid* itself, but which, because of the stifling impact of rhetorical theory, it had become fatally easy to ignore.

What facets of Virgilian art could have been relevant to *lo bello stilo che m'ha fatto onore?* The *bello stilo* was the work of the *stilnovisti* of Dante's generation. In his own *Vita Nuova* the poet had given fresh life to a lyrical tradition, stemming ultimately from the troubadours, which was in danger of being choked by its own ingenuity. He explains in the *Purgatorio* what he thinks he has done. The difference between his previous poetry and that of Bonagiunta of Lucca has been that he himself has adhered closely to the "dictatorship" of love, *dittare* being the regular term for poetic composition (*Purg.* XXIV. 52–54):

> E io a lui: "I' mi son un che, quando
> Amor mi spira, noto, e a quel modo
> ch'e' ditta dentro vo significando."

I answered him: "I am one who, when Love breathes on me, take note, and as he dictates within adapt my meaning."

What Dante is saying is that, instead of deploying a technique for its own sake, he and his friends have looked again into the immediacy of living experience, and allowed that to control their poetic responses. There could be no better indication of the inadequacy of tradition alone as a guide. Dante had done exactly what Virgil had done with the Alexandrian tradition of love poetry, as it was practiced in Greek by Meleager, for example, and in Latin by Gallus. He had both distanced and enlarged its vistas.

The poem with which Dante had risen to fame, and which he makes Bonagiunta quote, was the *prima canzone* of the *Vita Nuova*. It begins (1–14):

> Donne ch'avete intelletto d'amore,
>    i' vo' con voi de la mia donna dire,
>    non perch'io creda sua laude finire,
>    ma ragionar per isfogar la mente.
> Io dico che pensando il suo valore,
> Amor sì dolce mi si fa sentire,
>    che s'io allora non perdessi ardire,
>    farei parlando innamorar la gente.
> E io non vo' parlar sì altamente,

ch'io divenisse per temenza vile;
ma tratterò del suo stato gentile
a respetto di lei leggeramente,
donne e donzelle amorose, con vui,
chè non è cosa da parlarne altrui.

Ladies, who have intelligence of love, I wish to speak with you of my lady; not because I believe I can set limits to her praises, but simply to talk in order to relieve my feelings. I say that, as I think of her worth, such sweet love makes itself felt by me that, if I did not then lose courage, I should by talking make the whole world fall in love. And I do not wish to speak in such a lofty style that through fear I would become faint-hearted. Rather I will treat of her gentle estate in a meager style, compared with what she is, amorous ladies and girls, with you, since there is no reason to speak of her to others.

The complex rhyme scheme cannot mask in these verses an extreme simplicity of address. The vocabulary is of the most ordinary. The *callida iunctura* at the start, *intelletto d'amore*, uniting two concepts normally thought to be at variance, is the only attempt to rise. The poem takes for granted the woman's point of view, that love is the whole of existence, and proposes on that premise to reason about a particular woman. The poet is concerned with the personal problem of clearing his own mind. How close this is to the attitude found, for example, in Horatian satire, even to the limitation of the audience! The public, confessional *persona* of the satirist is next door to the public, confessional *persona* of the elegiac lover. Both eschew the grand and imposing. We see this in Lucilius.

When Dante thinks of his beloved, it is only his lack of courage which stops him from making the whole world fall in love with her by what he has to say. Yet he does not wish to talk of her so loudly as to frighten himself.[24] He proposes therefore to limit his confidences to amorous ladies and girls. There is no point in seeking a wider audience.[25]

Surface simplicity is deceptive. This *canzone* is inspired by Virgil in both literary attitude and content: in the first, because it is using a minor genre to rethink problems of major poetry; in the second, because it is borrowing epic material. Study of the tradition reveals

[24] For *vile* here cf. Boccaccio, *Teseida* V. 81. 3: *per maraviglia era invilita*. It will be remembered that in the *De Vulgari Eloquentia* (II. 7. 67 ff.) Dante cites this *canzone* as an example of what *cantio* should be. Once again, simplicity of language (the *genus tenue*) and lyricism were, as in Virgil's *Eclogues*, an essential stage on the road to epic.

[25] The rejection of the "common crowd" is however as old as Callimachus' *Epigr.* XXVIII. 4. *Populus* is an Alexandrian catchword in Latin poetry: cf. Catullus 95. 10; Horace, *Odes* I. 1. 29 ff.; Prop. II. 13. 13–14. Compare Petrarch, *Rime* 1. 9, *popol*, in a Propertian passage (III. 25). Seneca's *Ennianus populus* is in the same tradition.

that Dante is, in this poem, estranging and reducing devices of epic, in particular of the eulogy. The second stanza shows an especial debt. A divine being notices something unusual on earth, and appeals to another, superior god, even to the king of the gods, to adjudicate. The trick is already found in Claudian. In Sidonius Apollinaris it has become a mannerism. It goes back to Callimachus, even to Homer himself.[26]

Similarly, the thought that human excellence arouses the jealousy of the gods, familiar to the Greeks, had been adapted by the Augustan poets to flattery. It is developed in an inspired passage at the end of the first book of the *Georgics* (503–04):

> Iam pridem nobis caeli te regia, Caesar,
> Invidet atque hominum queritur curare triumphos.

> For long now, Caesar, heaven's palace has begrudged you to us,
> and complains that you trouble yourself with human triumphs.

It is also taken up into vatic lyric by Horace.[27]

The ennobling effect of love is a poetic commonplace, and the eyes as the tokens of love are well known to the elegists.[28] Dante has done his work well in reviving "in a meager style" (i.e. in the *ischnos charactēr*) these and other old gambits. But old they are, and they substantiate completely his claim to have learned from Virgil, and all the tradition for which "Virgil" was a shorthand compendium, already in the *Rime*.

The hidden learning of this *canzone*, the mixture of directness, simple—even colloquial—vocabulary with self-depreciation and rejection of the loud-mouthed, the limitation of the audience, the sensibility towards the feminine, are typical of Alexandrianism. Once again, just as in Virgil's own *Eclogue* 6, a tradition is being renewed from within itself. The lyrical achievement of Provence and Sicily, whatever may have been the original experiential insights which gave it birth, had in the course of time become overlaid with preciosity

[26] Cf. Claudian, *Prob. Olyb.* 73 ff.; Sidonius, *Pan. Anth.* II. 318 ff., *Pan. Maioriani* 53 ff., *Pan. Aviti* 45 ff.; Callimachus, fr. 228 Pf.; and M. Puelma Piwonka's discussion in *Lucilius und Kallimachos* (Frankfurt 1949), pp. 300 ff. Dante's use of the abstract Pietà (line 22) is a particular give-away; Pietas makes a speech in Statius, *Thebaid* XI. 458 ff. Venus' appeal to Jupiter (*Aen.* I. 227 ff.) is a variant of the topos which found many imitators (e.g. Chaucer, below, p. 355 note 40) and it is quoted by Dante at *Convivio* IV. 4. 115. The Homeric original of all this is the appeal of Thetis to Zeus: *Iliad* I. 493 ff.

[27] See further Nisbet–Hubbard on Horace, *Odes* I. 2. 45.

[28] K. F. Smith on Tibullus IV. 2. 5–6. P. Dronke, *Medieval Latin and the Rise of European Love-Lyric* (2nd ed., Oxford 1968), notes on pp. 12–13 some striking parallels to the angel/beloved idea in popular Byzantine poetry, though it is evident that the distinction popular/literary is not to be overworked.

and artificiality. There was need to summon such poetry to critical evaluation. The method that Dante used to do this recalls Callimachus' reaction against the formulas and stereotypes of his own day, particularly when it is noted that Dante too, like Callimachus in the *Iamboi*, was interested in rendering manageable once again devices of epic.

The Greek poet and the Italian are not of course the same, but neither *at this level* lacks the qualities of the other. Yet Dante has told us that Virgil alone was the one from whom he took all that brought honor to his beautiful style. This is certainly in one aspect a piece of Roman flattery. But in another way we may believe that Dante of all poets was able to scan Virgil's text with eyes of genius to discover the principles that guided its composition. It was precisely by such a return to a musical, Alexandrian tradition of love-poetry that Virgil had begun the task of preparing himself for the *Aeneid*. The *Eclogues*, with their numbers, their perfection of the hexameter, their exploration of psychology, fantasy, metamorphosis, didactic,[29] were the school in which Virgil learned his art. Dante, in forming *lo bello stilo* of his *Rime*, experimented under the patronage of Love with all these Alexandrian devices. His genius even led him to break through Latin Alexandrianism to the spirit of its Greek originals. Will any account of the *Rime* be complete which overlooks the *Greek Anthology*, where the same analytical refinement of language is applied to emotional complexities?

The suggestion that it was Alexandrianism which Dante began by taking from Virgil is borne out both by the *Comedy* itself, and by Dante's exchange with Giovanni del Virgilio, an academic and critic of his day. After Dante had begun work on his poem, he caused a certain disappointment among the more orthodox, the same disappointment which we ourselves feel if we have been brought up on the assumptions about the epic which they bequeathed to their heirs such as Scaliger. Famous for his mastery of the Roman poet's work, Giovanni del Virgilio remonstrated with Dante for choosing to write in Italian (15–24):

> Clerus vulgaria temnit,
> Etsi non varient, quum sint idiomata mille.
> Praeterea nullus, quos inter es agmine sextus,
> Nec quem consequeris caelo, sermone forensi
> Descripsit: quare, censor liberrime vatum,
> Fabor, si fandi paulum concedis habenas.

---

[29] *Eclogue* 6 offers an extraordinary mixture. It paraphrases the *Aet.-Pref.* at vv. 3 ff. The didactic element of vv. 31 ff. would eventually flower into the *Georgics*. Dante and Virgil share the claim to be Lucretius' greatest disciples, and what a tribute that is to the literary status of Lucretius' poem!

Nec margaritas profliga prodigus apris,
Nec preme Castalias indigna veste sorores.
At precor ora cie, quae te distinguere possint,
Carmine vatisono sorti communis utrique.

Educated people despise the common tongues, even if they do not themselves speak something else, since there are a thousand dialects. Besides, none of the other poets in that company of which you are the sixth, not even the poet you find in Purgatory [Statius], used the language of the market place. So then, since you a most frank critic of other poets, I will speak out, if you grant me just so much freedom to speak. Do not lavish your pearls upon swine, and do not embarrass the Muses with an unworthy garb. Rather, I beg, summon utterance that can win you fame, and with your vatic song be generous to both high and low alike.

He urges Dante to abandon a language that will make him unintelligible to those of his countrymen who do not happen to understand the Florentine dialect, and to turn instead to the universally understood Latin, more consistent with the dignity of the Muse.[30]

Dante, himself no mean connoisseur of Latin, did not reply to this academic challenge with a "straight" Latin poem of the type he had received. Instead, and most significantly for our argument, he answered in a Virgilian (and Alexandrian) *eclogue*. Masked as the shepherd Tityrus, he pleads old age and the need to finish the *Paradiso* as excuses for not accepting the invitation from "Mopsus" (Giovanni) to take up a more lucrative position in Bologna. For the first time since antiquity, we have a *recusatio* here which is more than a ploy.

His friend Meliboeus is not so sure anyway that Mopsus will be as impressed as Tityrus believes with the kind of poetry contained in the *Paradiso* (*Ecloga* I. 51–54):

Mopsus, tunc ille, quid? inquit.
Comica nonne vides ipsum reprehendere verba,
Tum quia foemineo resonant ut trita labello,
Tum quia Castalias pudet acceptare sorores?

"But what about Mopsus?" he said. "Don't you see that the master castigates comic language, not only because such words sound as if they had been worn down on the lips of women, but also because it embarrasses the Muses to entertain them?"

The whole scene is conceived in distinctly Callimachean terms. When refusing the invitation to abandon the vernacular for the high style of Latin poetry (as the critics had come to think of it), Dante

---

[30] On the Giovanni del Virgilio/Dante correspondence see J. D. Sinclair's note on *Paradiso* XXV (p. 367 of his edition, London 1946); cf. G. Albini and G. B. Pighi, *La corrispondenza poetica di Dante e Giovanni del Virgilio*, etc. (Bologna 1965).

instinctively turns to the Alexandrian genre of the pastoral, hallowed by Theocritus, a sympathizer with Callimachus' opposition to the traditional, long epic.[31] The choice of the pastoral is even more striking when we recall that Virgil himself, after an initial attempt to write an epic about Roman history along something like Ennian lines, had turned away, *offensus materia*, to the Alexandrian *Eclogues*.[32] We shall find this pattern repeated in Milton.

Giovanni's appeal to Dante is to move into the mainstream of literature, to seek fame and fortune. Dante's greatness is revealed by the complexity of his answer to this simple challenge. He confesses that he has put into his *Paradiso* comic words, *comica verba*, which "sound as if they have been worn down on the lips of women" (there is a covert allusion to Virgil's *Eclogues*[33]), the kind of words that threaten to embarrass the Muses. The fact that he should acknowledge this about his epic makes him truly the disciple of the Callimachus who wrote the *Hecale* and the Virgil who wrote *Aeneid* IV. What is surprising is Dante's ability to rediscover that tradition in the face of critical misunderstanding of the type evinced both by Giovanni's letter and by "Virgil's Wheel," and even in spite of his own theoretical writings.[34]

In the *De Vulgari Eloquentia*, for example, Dante is still feeling his way. To a large extent he remains under the influence of orthodox rhetorical theory.[35] He writes (II. 7):

Intuearis ergo, lector; attende quantum ad exaceranda egregia verba te cribrare oportet: nam si vulgare illustre considere, quo tragice debent uti poetae vulgares, ut superius dictum est, quos informare intendimus, sola vocabula nobilissima in cribro tuo residere curabis. In quorum numero, nec puerilia propter sui simplicitatem, ut *mamma* et *babbo*, *mate* et *pate*; nec muliebria propter sui mollitiem, ut *dolciada* et *placevole*; nec silvestria, propter austeritatem, ut *greggia*, et caetera; nec urbana lubrica et reburra, ut *femina* et *corpo*, ullo modo poteris conlocare. Sola etenim pexa irsutaque urbana tibi restare videbis quae nobilissima sunt, et membra vulgaris illustris.

[31] A. S. F. Gow on Theocritus VII. 47–48 (pp. 144 and 591 of his commentary).
[32] *Vit. Verg. Donati*, 19. On *Eclogue* 6. 3 Servius says that the poet was put off *nominum asperitate*. Quintilian takes the opposite view of Greek names in verse (XII. 10. 33).
[33] Cf. *Eclogue* 2. 34. There is also an echo of Cicero on the pure style of women's speech: *De Orat.* III. 45; *Brutus* 210–11. Laelia reminded him of Plautus and Naevius in her avoidance of all bombast and affectation.
[34] E. Auerbach has some excellent remarks in *Mimesis* (Eng. tr., New York 1957), pp. 159 ff.
[35] Yet there is quite an Alexandrian element in the critical vocabulary of the *De Vulg. Eloq.*, especially marked in II. 4.

Please take note then, reader: observe how much sieving is needed so that you may refine words of distinction. For if you think of the elevated vernacular, which poets writing tragedy in the common tongue should use, as has been remarked above, those whom it is our aim to instruct, then you will take care to see that only the noblest words are left behind in your sieve. In their number you will not be able to include the following: nursery words, on account of their naiveté, such as *mamma* and *babbo, mate* and *pate*; womanish words, because of their softness, such as *dolciada* and *placevole*; rustic words, because of their uncouthness, such as *greggia* and so on; nor the slick, unkempt words of the city, such as *femina* and *corpo*. You will see that all you have left are city words, but combed and luxuriant. These are the noblest, and form part of the elevated vernacular.

This was before Dante wrote his *Comedy*. But in the *Epistle* to Can Grande, explaining the title of his work, he states (Paragraph 10):[36]

> . . . Comoedia vero inchoat asperitatem alicuius rei, sed eius materia prospere terminatur, ut patet per Terentium in suis Comoediis. Et hinc consueverunt dictatores quidam in suis salutationibus dicere loco salutis, 'tragicum principium et comicum finem.' Similiter differunt in modo loquendi: elate et sublime tragoedia; comoedia vero remisse et humiliter; sicut vult Horatius in sua *Poetica*, ubi licentiat aliquando comicos ut tragoedos loqui, et sic e converso:
>
> > 'Interdum tamen et vocem comoedia tollit,
> > Iratusque Chremes tumido delitigat ore;
> > Et tragicus plerumque dolet sermone pedestri.'
>
> Et per hoc patet, quod Comoedia dicitur praesens opus. Nam si ad materiam respiciamus, a principio horribilis et foetida est, quia *Infernus*; in fine prospera, desiderabilis et grata, quia *Paradisus*. Si ad modum loquendi, remissus est modus et humilis, quia loquutio vulgaris, in qua et mulierculae communicant.

Comedy for its part begins with unruly circumstances, but its theme ends happily, as may be seen from the Comedies of Terence. This explains why some poets are in the habit of saying by way of greeting, instead of the usual good wishes, "a tragic beginning and a comic end." Likewise comedy and tragedy use different vocabulary. Tragedy speaks loftily and sublimely, comedy in relaxed and low tones. This is what Horace prefers in his *Ars Poetica*, where he grants comedians occasional leave to speak like tragedians, and *vice versa*: "Sometimes however even Comedy raises her voice, and in a temper Chremes gives full vent to his spleen in swelling utterance. The tragedian too often sorrows in the language of common life" [*A. P.* 93–95]. This shows why my present work is called a Comedy. So far as the theme is concerned, in the beginning it is fearful and noisome, because *Hell*.

---

[36] The quotation is taken from p. 416 of *Tutte le opere di Dante Alighieri*, ed. E. Moore (Oxford 1904).

At the end, it is happy, desirable and pleasing, because *Paradise*. So far as the style is concerned, it is relaxed and low, because its language is that of common life, used even by women.

The passage cited earlier from the *De Vulgari Eloquentia* is an expression of the accepted doctrine of the schools, with their customary insistence on *grandiosa vocabula* and avoidance of anything which smacked of the earthy and colloquial. Particularly noteworthy are the instructions to avoid nursery words and those that have a feminine ring. But, in the apologetic *Eclogue* written to Giovanni del Virgilio, it will be recalled that Dante was afraid the *Paradiso* would be censured just because it had used feminine words. It uses even nursery words,[37] an admission also made in the Letter to Can Grande. It is as if the poet had to learn an artistic humility, of which the critic, standing outside the struggle with the medium, knows nothing, before he could proceed to his final masterpiece. He shares this spiritual development with many of the exponents of the classical tradition, but notably with the Callimachus who represented his enemies as "muttering against my song because, . . . like a child, I roll out my epic in fits and starts, even though the count of my years is not small."

The poet of the *Comedy* was as faithful to his Alexandrian beginnings as the poet of the *Aeneid*. We see this if we turn to that passage in the *Purgatorio* where Dante meets Guido Guinicelli and Arnaut Daniel. The first encounter starts with a typically learned allusion in the Alexandrian manner (*Purg.* XXVI. 94–99):

> Quali ne la tristizia di Ligurgo
> si fer due figli a riveder la madre,
> tal mi fec' io, ma non a tanto insurgo,
> quand' io odo nomar sé stesso il padre
> mio e de li altri miei miglior che mai
> rime d'amor usar dolci e leggiadre.

Such as those two sons became during Lycurgus' sadness at seeing their mother again, so I became, without rising to such heights, when I heard my father speak his name, and the father of all those better than myself who ever used sweet and graceful rhymes of love.

The reservation in the third line ("without rising to such heights") reminds one of the rejection of the loud-mouthed in *Donne, ch'avete*. Again, Dante goes out of his way to reassert his loyalty to the "sweet

---

[37] Cf. XXXIII. 106 ff. with Callimachus' παῖς ἄτε, *Aet.-Pref.* 6. If in the Letter to Can Grande the poet had proceeded with his quotation from Horace, he would have come to a line (97) on which the ancient commentator Porphyrio expressly cites Callimachus.

and graceful rhymes of love" which he practiced in younger years. They are described in terms with which Callimachus could have picked no quarrel. *Dolci* ("sweet") was acknowledged as an Alexandrian criterion, while *leggiadre* may easily be paralleled in such Alexandrian catchwords as *leptos, gracilis, tenuis*. The preoccupation with love and the feminine point of view were regarded by tradition as typically Callimachean.[38]

Just as ancient Alexandria knew its battle of the books, so the modern poet does not hesitate to introduce into his epic comedy some of the literary polemics of the day. For the serious epic, such polemic would have been an outrageous intrusion.[39] It had been quite at home in the Preface to the *Aetia*, and in Roman satire. Once again, the make-up of the amalgam constituting high poetry in the Callimachean tradition is laid bare.

Guinicelli points to another spirit, who turns out to be the Provençal poet Arnaut Daniel, as the *miglio fabbro* ("the better craftsman"). The phrase in itself is redolent of an attitude to poetry which set a high value on that loving attention to technique which distinguished the Alexandrians. Arnaut's subject matter, we learn, was *versi d'amore e prose di romanzi*. Again, the emphasis is on something other than the straightforward narrative of heroic deeds, represented by the Homerizing tradition in antiquity, and by the Latin tradition as it was recommended to Dante by Giovanni del Virgilio.

Arnaut himself was a figure of controversy, who congratulated himself in one of his poems on "swimming against the current."[40]

> Ieu sui Arnautz, q'amas l'aura,
> E chatz la lebre ab lo bou,
> E nadi contra suberna.

I am Arnaut, who gather the breeze, and hunt the hare from the back of the bull, and swim against the current.

His critics, according to Dante, are given to praising instead "him of Limoges," Giraut de Borneil. They urged their favorite's merits by methods with which Callimachus was only too familiar a millennium and a half earlier. They ignore art or reason in their literary judgments, and try to prevail by shouting. They have abandoned any effort to think about what kind of poetry is relevant to the modern

---

[38] Further details are given in "Dante and the Alexandrians," *Neohelicon* V. 2 (1977), 9–36. Cf. *Callimachum fugito, non est inimicus amori, Rem. Am.* 759.

[39] Ennius' polemic with Naevius in the *Annales* is a crude parallel, but even this would have offended Greek taste.

[40] Alan B. Press, *Anthology of Troubadour Lyric Poetry* (Austin 1971), pp. 182 ff., no. III, conclusion.

world, and are content to apply mechanical criteria to its assessment. Only the patient wait for the truth to dawn can answer them.

If however we look back to the *De Vulgari Eloquentia* for Dante's previous views about the work of the troubadours, we find there no mention at all of the quarrel to which the *Purgatorio* now alludes. In the prose treatise, Arnaut and Giraut are cited side by side without any suggestion of rivalry. Arnaut is mentioned as the typical poet of love, and Giraut of *rectitudo*,[41] which appears to mean "moral uprightness." Dante himself is a poet of *rectitudo*, and so by implication a disciple of Giraut.

It must therefore be both fascinating and unexpected to discover that the author of the *Comedy* has, when it comes to the practical problems of writing about his sublime theme, abandoned the claim he made in the *De Vulgari Eloquentia* to be a poet of *rectitudo* and instead thrown in his lot with Arnaut, the poet of love!

We know that Dante (like Aristotle) changed his mind in the course of his development. In the prose treatise he had declared, for example, that Hebrew was the oldest language (*De Vulg. Eloq.* I. 6). But in the *Paradiso* (XXVI. 124 ff.) he goes out of his way to insist that Adam's language had died out *before* the Tower of Babel. The new attitude to a famous quarrel among the troubadours looks like a similar, but of course much more significant, alteration of view.

What in fact were the differences between the poetry of these two troubadours which could have inspired such violent partisanship? Giraut himself appears to have answered some sort of criticism in a *tenso*,[42] where he expresses his own preference for the intelligible style, for the *trobar leu* as opposed to the *trobar clus*. His preference is still hedged around with Alexandrian qualifications: the insistence on hard work, the rejection of any except artistic rewards.

Arnaut is a livelier figure altogether, and a poet of considerable originality, well aware of the virtues of the Aristotelian "gloss," of what the Formalists call "estrangement." Even his Provençal bio-

---

[41] *De Vulg. Eloq.* II. 2. 83 (Moore, p. 392). That the *amicus* is Dante himself follows from the attribution to him at line 94 of *Doglia mi reca* (= Moore, p. 158).

[42] The long history of these literary debates goes at least as far back as the *Certamen Homeri et Hesiodi* (Lesky, *A History of Greek Literature*, p. 93). It is part of the primitive *agōn*, found also in comedy and tragedy. Press gives a text and translation of Giraut's poem (pp. 115–19): cf. H. J. Chaytor, *The Troubadours of Dante* (Oxford 1902), pp. 33–34. The Arabic *naqa'id* of the early Islamic period in which poets assailed one another as well as the enemies of their tribes or masters is mentioned by M. A. Khouri in *The Genius of Arab Civilization* (2nd ed., Cambridge, Mass. 1983), p. 25.

grapher comments on the obscurity of his poems.[43] He uses, for example, Latin words in a Provençal guise, and has a large number of words peculiar to himself. He deploys a certain classical learning, alluding to such famous figures of myth as Paris, Helen, Atalanta, Meleager; to the river Meander and the Lernaean bog. He forces new meanings on his words, much increasing the difficulty of understanding his poems. He pays homage to Alexandrian ideals of poetic toil (*ponos*) in the poem whose conclusion has already been cited:[44]

> To this light and graceful little air I fashion words. I carve and plane them, to make them true and sure, after giving them a touch with the file; for Love soon smooths and gilds my song, which is inspired by her who maintains merit and guides it.

"Light," "graceful," "little," "file"—these are words with a long history behind them, and they betoken a *prise de position* which the literary historian must register.

The classical student in particular in all this is irresistibly reminded of Propertius, the Roman Callimachus. And it is with Arnaut that in the *Purgatorio* Dante goes out of his way to express sympathy. It is *not* true then that the *De Vulgari Eloquentia* represents an early stage in a logical development towards the perfected manner of the *Comedy*. It has important features that were later modified; it blurs distinctions that later became crucial. The treatise was never completed. It may be suggested that the poet's views underwent such transformation as he progressed, that the ultimate finishing of it was the *Comedy*.

Troubadour poetry was musical. In the *De Vulgari Eloquentia* Dante defines poetry as *fictio rhetorica in musica poita* (II. 4: "a rhetorical fiction made in music"), a definition in which the preponderance of Greek words is notable. Part of the modification to which we have referred seems to have been a growing sympathy with Arnaut Daniel,

---

[43] Quoted by Chaytor *The Troubadours of Dante*, p. 46; cf. pp. 152 ff.; and Press, *op. cit.*, pp. 173–75. Ulrich Mölk, *Trobar Clus, Trobar Leu* (Munich 1968), pp. 116 ff., discusses the stylistic quarrels among the troubadours, but not all of his conclusions are acceptable. Modern interpreters (e.g. C. M. Bowra in *Speculum* XXVII [1952], 459–74), mistakenly anxious to play down Dante's debt to the *trobar clus* (which means his feeling for the relevance of Alexandrianism to his task), have decided that Arnaut really used not the *trobar clus* but the *trobar ric*, of which however he says nothing. His biographer says unmistakably "las soas chanssos *non son leus* ad entendre ni ad aprendre" (my italics). The Monk of Montaudon speaks of "us fols motz c'om non enten." Talk about the *trobar ric* then must not be made an excuse for pushing Arnaut into the opposite camp, with the *trobar leu*. Petrarch (*Trionfo d'Amore* III. 43) is still able to refer to Arnaut's *dir strano e bello*. F. Diez, *Leben und Werke der Troubadours* (2nd ed., Leipzig 1882), pp. 279 ff., 285 ff., offers a good example of the embarrassment afforded to conventional scholarship by Arnaut.

[44] Above, note 40. Compare Propertius' *exactus tenui pumice versus eat* (III. 1. 8), and Horace's *limae labor* (*A. P.* 291).

to whom allusions multiply towards the end of the second book. Dante remarks, for example, that Arnaut used, in practically all his poems, a stanza

> sub una oda continua usque ad ultimum progressive, hoc est, sine iteratione modulationis cuiusquam et sine diesi: et diesim dicimus deductionem vergentem de una oda in aliam: hanc voltam vocamus, cum vulgus alloquimur.

> ... with one continuous musical form carried right through to the end, that is, without the repetition of any tune, and without *diesis*; this latter term means a transition passing from one setting to another: the colloquial term is *volta*.

A modern scholar explains:

> Arnaut Daniel thus carried forward the reforms which such poets as Bernart de Ventadorn and Raimbaut d'Aurenga had begun, reforms which had for their object to do away with the monotonous repetition of the same musical phrase. Arnaut abandoned the rimes corresponding within the stanza. ... His ideal was not only to avoid monotony, but to make of his poem an organic whole, and to do this by means of a regular musical development of his thought from the beginning to the end of the poem.[45]

Arnaut has been unsympathetically described as

> ... the most minutely ingenious and metrically resourceful, but at the same time one of the most laborious and tiresome of the Provençal versifiers. His works are a mosaic of odd conceits and rare and difficult forms. ...[46]

In taking sides therefore with him in the *Purgatorio*, Dante, repeating the Virgilian pattern, has found his Callimachus. Just as the Greek poet enriched the failing and incoherent epic of his day by an infusion of lyrical technique, and just as Virgil both quoted Callimachus and borrowed from his techniques (of handling Homer, for example), so Dante turns for inspiration to the Propertian, "learned" Arnaut, to a poet whose aim had been to make his songs *durchkomponiert*—in Aristotelian language, organically whole.

Both poets are exercising criticism of their literary legacy. Academic critics have behaved as if theirs were the only criticism worth talking about, as if critic and poet were two separate entities. Every poet is both, and, except in the rarest instances, it is *poetic* criticism, explicit or implied, which counts. This is the lesson taught by Dante's quarrel with Giovanni del Virgilio.

---

[45] Chaytor, pp. 153–54.
[46] C. H. Grandgent in his edition of the *Commedia* (revised by Charles S. Singleton, Cambridge, Mass. 1972), p. 542; cf. Diez, *Leben und Werke der Troubadours*, p. 285.

The poem that Dante quotes in the *De Vulgari Eloquentia* (II. 2) to illustrate Arnaut's skill as a love-poet is clearly not one of those pretty little pieces content to rework some favorite topos.[47] Controlling—"objectifying"—his emotions, Arnaut is able to write a long meditation on Catullus' *odi et amo* in which, without transgressing for one instant the conventional bounds of courtly love, he can nevertheless give full scope to the negative side of his feelings. The bitter wind silences the birds' song. If the poet sings on in spite of his emotional winter, what must that cost him? A hero of love, he can accept suffering. His passion is so strong that even during the time of snow it needs a kiss to refresh its burning, and no other salve will do. Here, a degree of self-irony is embodied in a conceit that would have appealed to Ovid. The comparison rises to heights that have troubled commentators when we read that the poet loves his mistress more than God did her of Dome (the Virgin Mary). But prudishness is out of place in this tradition, where the poet is not attempting to blaspheme, but to associate his feelings with the most sacred image he can find. Catullus' typically comic *superare divos* is in the same vein.[48]

This poetry, which could not fail to make a striking impression even on a modern audience, is in a deep sense Alexandrian. The poet's thought moves between opposing poles, from the initial image of winter/spring to the final contrast between the lover's fate and the riches of the Aragonese court.[49] Yet the poem is laden with artifice. Its author has a complex audience in mind. Partly he is clarifying his own thoughts (Dante's *isfogar la mente*), partly addressing his mistress, partly thinking of the king, for whose benefit he is writing some sort of apology.

Its careful composition, its slow and deliberate pace, its telling use of rhyme: these are devices which recover for the love lyric that musicality for which the Alexandrians strove. Arnaut shares some features with Pindar. He positions his words where they will have maximum resonance. Musical accompaniment evidently imposes its own discipline.

In later poems, the preoccupation with the lyrical developed and matured to a level that anticipates the tradition culminating in the sonnets of Shakespeare. Abandoning the too intrusive concern with

[47] Chaytor gives a text on pp. 47–48.

[48] Boccaccio borrows from *Paradiso* XXX at *Comedia Ninfe* XLIII (prayer of Venus), perhaps rather more cynically.

[49] The "poor poet" topos in antiquity is illustrated by Callimachus, *Epigram* XXXII, *Iambos* III. Arnaut emphasizes his point by a pun. His mistress not only says to him "Remain!", but suggests that the real riches are with her ("Roma!"). One thinks of Shakespeare's "Rome and room enough."

beauty of technique, the poet reasons about his love in a way that
well illustrates Dante's *intelletto d'amore*. The absolute self-confidence
that marks Shakespeare is seen at the end of poem XXVII:

> Ma chansos prec que no'us sia enois,
> car si voletz grazir lo son e'ls motz
> pauc pretz Arnautz cui que plassa o que tire.

> I pray that my song be no annoyance to you: for if you are willing to
> welcome the air and the words, Arnaut cares little whom else it might
> please or vex.

We note too the classical, and Virgilian, *sphragis*.[50]
Whatever then the outcry raised by the followers of Giraut, who
saw in his simpler and less intellectual style the road ahead, Dante's
poetic instinct taught him a different lesson. Understanding that high
poetry is not written from the heart alone—or perhaps realizing that
the heart has greater depths than are commonly plumbed—Dante
looked for his models, not to the charm and self-content of some of
the Provençal masters, but to the Propertian Arnaut, with his learning,
his "wild words that no one understands." In any case, it is important
that he did not look to the established epic of his day.[51] His glance
flashed beyond the simple narrative of great deeds and courtly love
to the ancient world, and the dark of Virgil's hell.

## III

As it emerged, the *Comedy* was a work that could never have been
forecast from the critical rules, only from the study of what Virgil
had actually done. It was written in the vernacular, a grave affront
to the *genus grande*. It was indeed written in the kind of Italian that
did not even measure up to Dante's own earlier prescriptions. Bembo
would later find (and condemn) there Latin and foreign words;
Tuscan words altered and deformed; low or hard-sounding words.[52]
The poem took, in appearance at least, a very unconventional form,

---

[50] Cf. Press, *op. cit.*, pp. 188–89; Chaytor, p. 53: cf. Shakespeare, Sonnet 29 and,
for the *sphragis*, Virgil, *Georgics* IV. 563; E. Fraenkel, *Horace* (Oxford 1957), p. 362
and notes.

[51] Auerbach, *Mimesis*, pp. 155 ff. Yet in *Literary Language and its Public* (Eng. tr.,
p. 233), Auerbach pushes the novelty of the *Comedy* too far. E. R. Curtius *Europ. Lit.
und lat. Mittelalter*, pp. 364–65, shows that Dante had at least one medieval predecessor
in mind. Cf. J. Oeschger, "Antikes und Mittelalterliches bei Dante," *Zeitschrift für
Romanische Philologie* 64 (1944), 22 ff. This of course leaves completely out of account
the possible debt to al-Ma'arri's prose masterpiece *Risalat al-Ghufran* (*The Epistle of
Forgiveness*): M. A. Khouri, *The Genius of Arab Civilization*, p. 36.

[52] B. Weinberg, *A History of Literary Criticism in the Italian Renaissance*, pp. 820–21.

that of a series of "songs" of relatively short duration. It exhibited a marked tendency to lecture its audience. And it was a *Commedia*!

Virgil had of course written in his vernacular, and been criticized as the inventor of a novel kind of bad style, made up of common words. He had made the comic device of metamorphosis, especially that of a discarded mistress who keeps turning up at the most inconvenient moments, basic to his epic, creating eventually a nightmare world from tricks exploited by the lyric and the mime. He had lectured his audience too, and acknowledged a debt to Lucretian didactic. By reviving the old term *vates* to describe himself in the *Aeneid*, in the book that follows Aeneas' apocalyptic descent to the Underworld, he had set his epic in the service of an ultimately religious purpose.

The *Commedia*'s un-Virgilian form has already been mentioned. Dante's short *canti* are not however anti-Virgilian, any more than his rhymes, or his end-stopped lines. They are pre-Virgilian, a return to the lyric always endemic in this tradition, but which the *Aeneid* had subsumed and transformed. And this provides an important lesson for the whole understanding of the classical epic legacy. Virgil's style was, as has already been remarked, an amalgam. It embraced in its alloy not only the lyric, which in Virgil's case was as close as Catullus, but also the satiric/vatic, the didactic, comedy, tragedy, eulogy, apocalypse, pastoral, to go no further. Great poets who follow Virgil are not being disloyal to his example when they recombine these elements freshly. If we hear the voice of Lucretius, for example, in Dante, that is not infidelity to his master. We hear Lucretius in all three of Virgil's own works.

The same explanation may be applied to the variation in pace between the *Comedy* and the *Aeneid*. Virgil sweeps his reader along with that ocean-roll of rhythm to which Tennyson alludes. Dante proceeds with far more deliberation. It is the difference between Ennius and Catullus 64, the *Peleus and Thetis*, even between Homer and Callimachus' *Hymn 5*, *The Bath of Pallas*. Exactly the same tendency distinguishes the Roman end-stopped elegiac couplet from the Greek freedom to straddle from pentameter to hexameter. The slower pace is a sign of increased lyricism, an Alexandrian option attractive to the Roman genius, as Seneca observes (*Epp.* 40. 11):

> In Graecis hanc licentiam tuleris: nos etiam cum scribimus interpungere assuevimus. Cicero quoque noster, a quo Romana eloquentia exsiluit, gradarius fuit. Romanus sermo magis se circumspicit et aestimat praebetque aestimandum.

> This looseness may be tolerated in the Greeks. We Romans pause between our words even in writing. Even the great Cicero, the

fountainhead of Roman oratory, was a steady trotter. The Roman style is more inclined to look about, to evaluate and offer itself for evaluation.

Shall we separate Dante from Virgil then for his fidelity to *Romanus sermo*?[53]

The analysis may be supported from a single excerpt which must represent the whole. In Canto XII of the *Paradiso* St. Bonaventure pronounces the eulogy of St. Dominic, who had in fact done so much to break the society of which the troubadours were the ornament (1–9):

> Sì tosto come l'ultima parola
> la benedetta fiamma per dir tolse,
> a rotar cominciò la santa mola;
> e nel suo giro tutta non si volse
> prima ch'un'altra di cerchio la chiuse,
> e moto a moto e canto a canto colse;
> canto che tanto vince nostre muse,
> nostre serene in quelle dolci tube,
> quanto primo splendor quel ch'e' refuse.

As soon as the blessed flame took up for utterance its last word, the holy millstone began to revolve, and yet did not turn entirely in its circle before another enclosed it, joining movement to movement and song to song, song which so far outdoes our Muses, our Siren Muses in those sweet pipes, as the first light outdoes its own reflection.

In this introductory passage, the deliberate pace is immediately in evidence. It challenges us to examine carefully every word. Colloquialism and humor are to be found in the description of the circle of dancers as a "holy millstone," and in the use of *moto a moto e canto a canto*.[54] Picking up *canto* by the assonance of *tanto*, the poet shows us that he is entirely at his ease, untroubled by any straining after effect. He is—strange experience for a writer of epic—enjoying himself with the childlike innocence of the blessed spirits. The double anaphora is remarkable (*canto/canto: nostre/nostre*).[55] The expansive allusion to *tube* is another proof that the poet is in no hurry to make his point.

Yet the language, though it may have descended from the stilts of convention, still shows intellectual power. It lies precisely in the refusal

[53] Seneca's remark is amply borne out by the recently discovered Gallus papyrus. See also above, p. 232, on Statius' alcaics and sapphics.

[54] Contrast the elaboration of *Aeneid* V. 580 ff.

[55] The anaphora *canto . . . canto, nostre . . . nostre* is a return to a trick of Hellenistic poetry in particular, discussed by E. Norden in his note to *Aen.* VI. 164 ("epanadiplosis").

to use big words, and in the resulting verbal analyses that recall the similar avoidance of the abstract by the classical Greek orators.[56] Instead of saying that the music of the spirits excels that of earth by as much as light exceeds its reflection,[57] Dante prefers to analyze away a possible "rifletto" by using *quel ch'e' refuse*. So too the lines *e nel suo giro . . . colse* also offer an analysis that conveys a picture rather than employ abstracts that might have lent *grandiloquentia*, but would inevitably have obscured what was happening.

There is indeed the sonority of long words in the continuation (XII. 10–21):

> Come si volgon per tenera nube
> due archi paralelli e concolori,
> quando Iunone a sua ancella iube,
>   nascendo di quel d'entro quel di fori,
> a guisa del parlar di quella vaga
> ch'amor consunse come sol vapori,
>   e fanno qui la gente esser presaga,
> per lo patto che Dio con Noè puose,
> del mondo che già mai più non s'allaga:
>   così di quelle sempiterne rose
> volgiensi circa noi le due ghirlande,
> e sì l'estrema a l'intima rispuose.

As two arches, parallel, and colored alike, sweep through yielding cloud when Juno gives command to her maidservant, the outer springing from the inner, like the speech of that wandering nymph consumed by love as mists are consumed by the sun (here they tell the world that, by the truce which God made with Noah, the earth is never again to be flooded): so the two garlands of those everlasting roses swept around us, and so the outer answered the inner.

Even so, the two adjectives in the magnificent second line here do not destroy the general point we are making about Dante's vocabulary. The verbal analyses that occur in the fourth line, and again in the ninth, are typical of what was noted before. The vigor of the tenth line too lies in its adjective, which is allied with one of the simplest of all nouns, *rose*. Yet this noun, simple though it may be, has a depth that springs, not from an indistinctly conceived romanticism, but from the precisely worked out symbolism which is to recur at the end of the poem.

This *Comedy* has then a firm basis in the *ischnos charactēr*, the plain

---

[56] J. D. Denniston, *Greek Prose Style* (Oxford 1965), discusses these aspects of style in Chapter II. Callimachus had edited Demosthenes (fr. 444 Pf.). Cf. above, p. 147, for Demosthenes and Simonides.

[57] Contrast Seneca, *Epp.* 21. 2, where two nouns are employed.

style.[58] It also exhibits other ancient devices; for example, a type of ring-composition familiar since the days of Homer.[59] It exhibits too an Alexandrian allusiveness. Juno, giving orders to her maidservant, is said to "iube," a strange Latinism in the tradition of Arnaut Daniel, yet one that helps to recall that Dante means by this periphrasis the Iris familiar from the *Aeneid*.

This allusion is simple enough. But who is *quella vaga/ch'amor consunse come sol vapori?* Here we must turn to Ovid.[60] Narcissus spurned the advances of the nymph Echo, who as a consequence wasted away from love. Her *parlar*, the outcome of a curse imposed by Juno, whom Dante has just mentioned as Iris' imperious mistress, was to repeat only the final part of what had been said to her, like the heavenly choruses. But she had her revenge, since eventually Narcissus did fall in love, with his own reflection, and then wasted away in his turn from self-love. It is of this *second* doom that Ovid employs the comparison which Dante borrows, of the effect of the heat of the sun upon the mists.[61] What the poet has done in effect is to give us a cinematic flash-forward (another instance of "vertical time"). Echo's fate already includes that of Narcissus. But this is also the carnival blending encountered in the ancient mime, as later in Shakespeare.[62]

Shakespeare certainly learned from Ovid. The interesting thing is that Ovid could be so useful to the poet of the last things. But the *Metamorphoses* ends with an exposition by Pythagoras of the great flux of existence, which metamorphosis illustrates. One comedy is bound to be in debt to the other, and the critic who does not realize the primacy of comedy in the Roman aesthetic experience will forever be puzzled by Ovid's amazing relevance to so many great—and greater—authors.[63]

The canto proceeds. Bonaventure begins to speak of the dire peril that threatened the church, "Christ's army, which cost so dear to re-arm" (37–38). It is in asides like these that Alexandrian allusiveness is raised to epic heights. To ward off this peril, God, "the emperor

---

[58] Demetrius, *De Eloc.* 190 ff., offers much that illumines what Dante was doing. See above, p. 51.

[59] *Volgon* (10), picked up by *volgiensi* (20). Cf. L. Illig, *Zur Form der Pindarischen Erzählung*, p. 57.

[60] *Met.* III. 346 ff.

[61] *Met.* III. 488.

[62] Lucian had noted the blending of different characters in the mime: above, p. 182. Cf. *The Merchant of Venice* V. 1. 9–12, where Dido is confounded with Ovid's Phyllis (*Heroides* II. 121 ff.), but Virgil had already borrowed from Callimachus' Phyllis for his Dido (fr. 556 Pf.).

[63] One bond between the two is the carnival style: cf. M. Bakhtin, *Tvorchestvo François Rabelais*, pp. 438, 473, for this in Dante. See above, pp. 29 and 196.

who reigns forever" (40), sent two champions. One of them was from Spain (XII. 46–54):

> In quella parte ove surge ad aprire
> Zefiro dolce le novelle fronde
> di che si vede Europa rivestire,
>    non molto lungi al percuoter de l'onde
> dietro a le quali, per la lunga foga,
> lo sol talvolta ad ogne uom si nasconde,
>    siede la fortunata Calaroga
> sotto la protezion del grande scudo
> in che soggiace il leone e soggioga.

In that region where the sweet zephyr rises to open the new leaves by which Europe sees itself reclothed, not very far from the beating of the waves behind which, during its long flight, the sun at times hides itself from every man, sits happy Calaruega, beneath the protection of the great shield on which the lion couches and overcouches.

Who this champion was we are not to know for many lines yet, so that the whole exordium to the tale becomes even more mysterious and impressive.[64]

The poet approaches the eulogy of his hero with an *ekphrasis topou*, exactly as Virgil adorns his eulogy of Augustus in *Aeneid* VI, in which the ancient rules are still observed.[65] He wishes to say: "in the west." He presents us with an elaborate miniature of the beneficent effects of the west wind, opening the new leaves in springtime, a picture clearly symbolic of the renewal in the church brought about by Dominic's efforts. These "Stundenbilder" were a part of the epic apparatus that had been transformed by Callimachus and Apollonius, and further transformed by Virgil.[66] Dante is making a lyrical and Pindaric use of his exordium here. The new leaves of springtime, the waters of the mighty Ocean: these are cosmic anticipations of an imagery that will recur.

Dante's imagination is not confined, like that of some medieval miniaturist, to the pretty. Where the saint was born, the sea is close, "the beating of the waves behind which the sun, in his long flight, sometimes hides himself from every man." The hint of the majesty

---

[64] See Illig, *Zur Form der Pindarischen Erzählung*, pp. 26 ff., who notes Pindar's use of the primitive device of periphrasis ("kenning"), and p. 27 for his holding back of proper names till a decisive moment. Cf. F. Dornseiff, *Pindars Stil*, pp. 28, 32, 92; L. Arbusow, *Colores Rhetorici* (repr. Göttingen 1963), p. 121.

[65] E. Fraenkel, *De media et nova comoedia quaestiones selectae* (Göttingen 1912), pp. 46 ff.

[66] Pollio's remark about Virgil is discussed by R. Heinze, *Virgils epische Technik*, p. 366. See further R. Pfeiffer on Callimachus, fr. 177. 5 ff.: H. Fränkel on *Argonautica* I. 1172–76.

and desolation of the Atlantic lends new dimensions—epic dimensions—to the description.

Here sits blessed Calaruega, beneath the protection of the arms of Castile, which are described by another of those estranging kennings of which Dante, like Pindar, is so fond. This poetry rises far above ordinary discourse, yet it does so, not by the elaboration of vocabulary proposed in the *De Vulgari Eloquentia*, but by using words in a way that makes the reader conscious of the narrow limits we set to their ordinary meanings. It is the doctrine of the *callida iunctura* pushed to its uttermost. Virgil had already striven for the same effects.

Dante imparts a sense of inevitability to his narrative by making Bonaventure describe what was known to be true,[67] and so shows that this epic is able (like the *Aeneid*) to take up into itself the history beloved of the anti-Aristotelian and anti-Callimachean camp. But Dante's history is not aimed at flattering some earthly monarch. From his sublime perspective (a version of carnival height) Bonaventure looks with contempt on what the Franciscans have become. Yet this is not simple satire either. All these manners can find a home within Dante's achievement, but in finding it they are transformed into an amalgam that eludes simplistic analysis.

It was at Calaruega that Dominic was born. His name is approached through a series of approximations and periphrases like those which Pindar employs for "bridle" in *Olympian* 13. Firstly, he is *l'amoroso drudo* (55), where the noun is taken straight from the vocabulary of the troubadours.[68] By an audacious stroke, Dante has elevated this word into heaven itself. Here is where Arnaut's "more than God loved her of Dome" finds its true successor.

Next Dominic becomes the *santo atleta* (56), where once again a noun is being transferred from one sphere to another, this time of course with a tradition going back at least to St. Paul to support the metaphor.[69] The boldness of the Christian propagandists who usurped this word from a culture to which in this aspect at least they were bitterly opposed, and applied it to their own often very unathletic heroes, must not escape notice.

Christians shared this lack of awe towards the Greek ideal with pagan Rome. *Athleta* had already undergone some transformation ("carnivalization") in pre-Christian Latin. When we find Varro re-

[67] What German scholars call "the future style" (*der Zukunftsstil*), which is a variant of "vertical time," making the future available in the present. Cf. L. Adam, *Die aristotelische Theorie vom Epos*, p. 115; H. Herter, *Xenia Bonnensia* (Bonn 1929), p. 67; K. Ziegler, *Das hellenistische Epos*, p. 24, note 1; Illig, *op. cit.*, pp. 24–25.

[68] *Drut* in Provençal: Chaytor, p. 25. Cf. *Inferno* XVIII. 134. It was in Provence that the Dominicans had been especially active.

[69] E.g. I Cor. 9:24; II Tim. 4:7–8.

ferring to *athletae pecuarii* and *athletae comitiorum*[70] we should, if we are true Hellenes, perhaps have something of the same feeling as when we hear of a "marathon sandwich." Dante has followed the author of the Menippean satires in this colloquial evolution.

This use of vocabulary akin to the comic (komic) is not offset by stylistic bombast elsewhere. The refinement of language to epic dignity is made partly by the musical devices of rhythm and rhyme, and partly by the continual kennings. The poet avoids the conventionally picturesque, dismissing quickly, for example, two wonderful dreams associated with Dominic's birth. Instead, we are brusquely introduced into a philosophy seminar (XII. 67–69):

> e perché fosse qual era in costrutto,
> quinci si mosse spirito a nomarlo
> del possessivo di cui era tutto.

And so that he might be what he already was in potency, a spirit went forth from here to inspire his naming by the possessive of Him of whom he was entirely.

The Aristotelian background of this development from potency to act is obvious, and equally obvious is that Dante does not shrink from jargon (we should be comparing all the time Scaliger's demands on epic vocabulary). For the poet, aware of the enormous work done by the Dominicans, in particular by St. Thomas, to systematize theology and to make language capable of subtle thought about the relationship of revelation to reason, there was a peculiar enjoyment to be had from these reminiscences of the schools. But it is also relevant that the ability to take delight in tracking down poetry in prosaic places distinguished Aratus' version of Eudoxus' astronomy, and its defender Callimachus; and distinguished too Dante's greatest and closest predecessor in so many ways, Lucretius.

At line 70 of the canto, Dominic's name at last occurs. A persistent metaphor already prepared for in the exordium runs through the eulogy of the saint's life. It is introduced by another of those transformations (this too borrowed) with which we are familiar. Dominic is an *agricola*, whom Christ chose to help him in his *orto*, his kitchen garden. Here, the poet flouts "Virgil's Wheel" with a vengeance!

The saint's impending vocation is foretold by the fact that his nurse often found the young baby silent and awake on the ground. In these stories, something of the same spirit is at work as that which impelled Horace to relate his own youthful vocation (the divine

[70] *Res Rustica* II. 1. 2; III. 5. 18.

child).[71] In both cases, what at first sight looks inappropriate to epic poetry in the classical tradition is made appropriate by the intense seriousness which animates the context in which it occurs. It is the virtue of the serio-comic style to switch masks in this disconcerting way. On a larger scale, throughout two-thirds of the poem, the figure of Virgil with his "high tragedy" (*Inf.* XX. 113), providing foil to the figure of Dante with his comedy (*Inf.* XVI. 128), generates a similar polarity. So it was that Lucretius had contrasted himself with Epicurus, and Socrates, in Plato's *Symposium*, with Diotima (his Beatrice).

It is characteristic of this poetry that what elsewhere might be dull pedantry can be suffused by its ardor into tragic or ironic meaning. Bonaventure plays with the significance of Dominic's name. This too is serio-comic and Greek.

When the saint becomes a man, he begins to "go round the great vineyard, which soon grows yellow if the vinedresser is at fault" (86–87). The imagery of the opening lines is here negated. The tone of the narrative approaches satire (Lucretius, Lucan), as we are informed of the unworthiness of the pope and high prelates. Satire is part of comedy, and part of lyric, but, in these contexts, it is raised beyond itself.

The switch from this to something more positive is brilliantly and unexpectedly made by the use of an estranging Latin phrase.[72] Dominic did not demand from the papal court all the perquisites for which others contend: *non decimas, quae sunt pauperum Dei* (93), "not for the tithes which belong to God's poor," did he ask, but for leave "to fight with the erring world for the seed of which twenty-four plants encircle thee." This seed (the agricultural metaphor persists) is the Christian faith. *Fascian* (96), here translated "encircle," means literally "bandage," "swaddle." The poet is perhaps being asked by St. Bonaventure to think of God's love as encompassing him like a mother's care. Such an aspect of the divine love had been made peculiarly apparent in the *agricola* Dominic.

Armed with papal authority, Dominic fell upon the heretics of his time like a "torrent driven from a high spring" (99). In this further metamorphosis of the initial image, the farm-laborer has been transformed into the means which brings life to the vineyard. The *vivamente* of his action (101) recalls the *viva virtute* (59) which made itself felt

---

[71] E. Fraenkel, *Horace*, pp. 274 ff.

[72] Compare Shakespeare's *Et tu, Brute*, used by Caesar as he dies and merges (is metamorphosed) into the Caesarism which ultimately defeats his assassins: Eisenstein, *Izbrannye Proizvedeniya*, III, p. 63. It is the famous "leap into another dimension," which in this instance too is a sudden awareness of vertical time.

even when he was still in the womb. The phrase *l'orto catolico* (104)
echoes the *orto* of v. 72.[73]

This careful preservation of komic consistency, although mirrored
in different facets of the poetic glass, resembles the sustained imagery
found in some of Pindar's odes, for example, in *Isthmian* 8, with its
luxuriance of fruit and flowers. The apparent confusion in the passage
which follows therefore is well prepared. It begins with an allusion
to a chariot (106–11):

> Se tal fu l'una rota de la biga
> in che la Santa Chiesa si difese
> e vinse in campo la sua civil briga,
>    ben ti dovrebbe assai esser palese
> l'eccellenza de l'altra, di cui Tomma
> dinanzi al mio venir fu sì cortese.

If such was one wheel of the chariot in which Holy Church defended
herself and conquered on the field her civil strife, the excellence of
the other must be quite plain to you, of which Thomas spoke so
courteously before I came.

The followers of St. Francis, the other wheel of the Church's chariot,
might naturally have been required to follow behind, but they have
failed in their duty (112–14):

> Ma l'orbita che fé la parte somma
> di sua circunferenza, è derelitta,
> sì ch'è la muffa, dov' era la gromma.

But the track made by the topmost part of its rim is abandoned, so
that there is mold where there was crust.

Violently the poet throws his reader back from the warlike image of
the chariot to thoughts of the vineyard. The mixture of metaphors
is lyric, Pindaric. The strikingly colloquial expression of contempt
with which he ends is all the more emphatic.[74]

The degenerating Franciscans are at one moment seen as an army,
which first follows its leader's footsteps and then turns back, or
alternatively, as plowmen who first tread behind and then reverse
their leader's directions. Bonaventure grimly comments that there

---

[73] Sinclair notes (p. 184) more verbal repetition in *Paradiso* XII and symmetry
with canto XI (p. 185). See Grandgent's note on XII. 61–63 (p. 733). Dante is
employing old classical devices, illustrated by Apollonius and Virgil too.

[74] Cf. *Inferno* XVIII. 106. Varro's *bigae cornutae*, quoted by Nonius and Isidore,
may have helped the transition from war to husbandry. It is not for nothing that
Bakhtin (*Problemy Poetiki Dostoevskogo*, pp. 150 ff.) associates Varro with the ancestry
of the carnival style. Perhaps the time has come to reassess his importance as a major
classical poet.

will soon be some harvest of the bad tillage, when the tares shall complain that the bin is refused to them (120). The plowmen have, by an echo of the New Testament, become their own weed-ridden crop.

The poetic mirror has certainly been jerked awry, but there is a logic in the resulting flux,[75] the logic of religion ("through a glass darkly"), comedy, satire. Yet the poet does not need to resort to academic, rhetorical devices of aggrandizement and elevation to enhance the apocalyptic judgment.

The canto moves towards its close. Bonaventure identifies himself (so long have we had to wait for this name!) and some of those with him, early members of Francis' circle, as well as others who can be associated with him only in the most general way, such as Nathan and Chrysostom. The final lines return to the thought of flame with which the canto began (*fiamma*, 2: *fiammeggiarsi*, 23: *infiammata*, 143) and to that combination of courtesy and intellect which, united in St. Thomas, may also be found united in the two saints whom he and Bonaventure have "envied" (*inveggiar*, 142).

The merit of this kind of epic poetry, compared with the dead tradition of grand historical encomium lauded by the critics, is the absence of any attempt to impress with clichés. Because Dante has selected a theme that is able to sustain in an infinite scale the weight of all men's hopes and fears, he can afford not to trouble himself too much about *admiratio* and *ekplēxis*.[76] He has freedom to deploy, against the background of this primeval, komic seriousness, all the resources of language, instead of being irretrievably committed to a shrieking fortissimo, rejected as early as *Donne ch'avete*. He can resort to the colloquial and the satiric. He can move from that resonance of proper names enjoyed alike by Euphorion and Milton (*Natàn profeta, e 'l metropolitano/Crisostomo e Anselmo e quel Donato/ch'a la prim' arte degnò porre mano*, 136–38) to the allusiveness of the *Zukunftsstil*, canonized by Lycophron's *Alexandra*, and the learned reference. He can employ anaphora, chiasmus, ecphrasis, paronomasia, effective word-positioning, symmetry, *Zahlenkomposition*. The rigid framework of his meter lends an incantatory quality of anticipation and recurrence to all he says, and reminds one again of the stately pace of the Latin elegiac couplet. In all this he was the faithful

---

[75] Dornseiff, *Pindars Stil*, pp. 66 ff., remarks on Pindar's "Vergeistigung und Vermischung der Bilder." For other poetic mirrors, see above, pp. 78 and 234.

[76] The aim of epic according to academic critics of both the Latin (e.g. Vida, Pontano) and Greek (e.g. "Longinus" 15. 2) traditions. Of course Dante attains these aims, but not by seeking them in too contrived or single-minded a fashion.

exponent of an epic tradition enriched and extended by lyric that reached back through Virgil to Alexandria and Callimachus. Yet his allegiance to the ancient world rode upon two anchors. One we have described as the instinctive recovery of the Alexandrian literary poetic. The other is revealed by the very title he chose for his masterpiece, not of course *Divine Comedy*, but simply *Comedy*.

Dante's *kōmos*, like that of Pindar in *Olympians* 2 or 14, moves upon three levels.[77] Like Virgil, Ovid and Lucan, it enjoys the carnival "grotesque body," the carnival masking and unmasking. It exploits the tragi-comic figure of the ape/giant who is Satan, with whom we may compare Virgil's Atlas. It illustrates the *monde à l'envers*: popes, even official saints, are in hell, along with the great ones of this world, while troubadours (clowns) are on their way to heaven. There is humor, mockery, vulgarity, comic *mésalliance*, nowhere more evident than in the fate of the poet's old teacher, Brunetto Latini, who taught "how man eternizes himself" (*Inf.* XV. 85), and ended in the seventh circle. The journeys through hell, purgatory and heaven are a typical use of carnival space. In the phantasmagoric world, time itself becomes a spatial dimension, anything but the neutral measurement by a scientific clock.

Yet in this serio-comic style, the last questions are still of overwhelming importance. "The incredible tension of that balance into which the titanic artistic power of the artist drew his world" (Bakhtin) shows how much Dante was determined to impose his own, ordered solutions on the counterworld he evoked. We admire him now for both his faith and his fidelity. We read him still because his rich sensitivity to the long tradition of the carnival/komos shielded him against the tawdry attractions of the univocal eulogy. When he defined his *Comedy* as *quasi villanus cantus* (Letter X to Can Grande), he proved how little he cared for the stilted verse which a John of Virgil, spokesman then for academic orthodoxy, as Scaliger was to be later, would have him write. Which, poet or critic, understood the real Virgil better?

At the very end of the *Commedia*, Dante introduces another old word (*Paradiso* XXXIII. 142):

A l'alta fantasia qui mancò possa.

Here power failed the high fantasy.

It is a word already used (*Par.* XXIV. 24), and one picked up by Michelangelo in a late sonnet addressed to Vasari:[78]

[77] Discussed in *Pindar's Art: Its Tradition and Aims*, pp. 102, 171–72, 219 note 13.
[78] Accessible, for example, in *The Oxford Book of Italian Verse* (2nd ed., repr. Oxford 1952), p. 177.

Onde l'affettüosa fantasia,
Che l'arte mi fece idol e monarca,
Conosco or ben com' era d'error carca,
E quel ch'a mal suo grado ogn' uom desia.

Whence I now know well how laden with error was the capricious fantasy that made art my idol and queen, and that which every man desires in his own despite.

It has already been remarked that "fantasy" was a quality much valued by ancient commentators on Homer.[79]

There has been an extraordinary effort by scholars to draw a sharp distinction between two types of it. On this view, one is merely the mnemonic ability to recall in minute detail a concrete situation, "a photographic memory." The other is a sublime instrument by which the artist of genius penetrates into lofty realms of high truth and knowledge. It is argued that this was only known in late antiquity to philosophers like Plotinus. From there, it was rediscovered by Kant and those aestheticians whom he influenced.[80]

This is all false. Its idealization of late antiquity is of a piece with the idealization of "Longinus". The "fantasy" valued by the scholiasts in Homer certainly includes the power to conjure up more than human scenes, more than ordinary actions. Simonides, who is credited by Cicero with the discovery of the art of mnemonics, is precisely the poet singled out for the sublimity of his imagination by "Longinus" himself. How can we indeed suppose either that ancient artists and poets did not possess fantasy of the highest kind, or that ancient critics were incapable of recognizing this quality?

Dante in fact answers our question in this passage. Will anyone argue that his poem does not show the most amazing power of minute observation (for example, of a burning piece of paper's successively turning brown before it catches alight)? But this kind of fantasy, granted to the ancients by the moderns, is also in him the servant of the Romantic fantasy which can evoke a whole metaphysical and mystical universe of suffering, repentance, triumph. He is of course one of the few authors ever to solve successfully the problem of depicting perfect heroes while avoiding the "goody-goody."

The truth is that "fantasy" is simply a variant of the older *mimēsis* that came to the fore when Plato devalued the earlier term. The poet of genius, bent on imitation, is able, by his close observation of particulars, and subsequent power of "total recall," to select from them the "telling" detail which, when introduced into the artistic

[79] Above, p. 48.
[80] See, for example, J. J. Pollitt, *The Ancient View of Greek Art* (New Haven and London 1974), pp. 52 ff., 201 ff.

construct, will trigger a profound echo in the mind of the listener. But what does this detail actually "tell"? Sometimes perhaps merely what it was like to be there. But sometimes what the metaphysical resonance of a given act or situation was. It is precisely why, to quote Aristotle, poetry is "more philosophical" than history, because it can select the symbolic over the humdrum. No one knows in an abstract way what exactly this "concrete universal" is. Every sensitive listener knows what is meant in practice. Modern scholars, in cheapening the meaning of "imitation," or in divorcing these two types of fantasy, which in reality are one and the same, expose themselves to Blake's criticism: "To Generalize is to be an Idiot. To Particularize is the Alone Distinction of Merit. General Knowledges are those Knowledges that Idiots possess."[81]

T. S. Eliot may be less abrasive:[82]

Dante's is a *visual* imagination. It is a visual imagination in a different sense from that of a modern painter of still life: it is visual in the sense that he lived in an age in which men still saw visions. It was a psychological habit, the trick of which we have forgotten, but as good as any of our own. We have nothing but dreams, and we have forgotten that seeing visions . . . was once a more significant, interesting and disciplined kind of dreaming.

Here, the poet/critic may be thinking of Quintilian on *visiones*,[83] a passage already discussed in a previous chapter.

Whatever therefore the bold assertions of scholars, Dante at least felt that the same word would do for him as had done for the Greeks and Romans. In the *Convivio*, the poet had earlier defined *fantasia* as *la virtù da la quale trae* [*sc. l'intelletto*] *quello ch'el vede* . . . (III. 4: "the power from which the intellect draws what it sees"). "*Intelletto*" in this quotation reminds us of the *Vita Nuova* and its first *canzone*. This is Dante's fidelity to his Alexandrian origins, relevant also to the poet of the *Commedia*, which has already been emphasized. His definition is also Aristotelian, since the role of the understanding provides a basis for poetry's claim to be more philosophical than history. It looks back to Stoic theory of the role of *dianoia* in the creative process.[84] This is profound aesthetic doctrine. Can the poet/critic be regarded as inferior to the critic?

---

[81] Quoted by W. K. Wimsatt, *The Verbal Icon* (Lexington 1954), p. 73.

[82] T. S. Eliot, *Selected Prose*, ed. F. Kermode (New York 1975), p. 209.

[83] *Inst. Or.* VI. 2. 29; see above, p. 67, and below, p. 413 for the development of this theory in Eisenstein.

[84] Diog. Laert. VII. 49: cf. D. A. Russell's note on "Longinus", *De Subl.* XV. 1.

## IV
Dante had the courage of his convictions. What would happen to a poet of genius who was too eager to please the schoolmen? The answer is found in the fate of Petrarch's *Africa*.[85]

That this poem was in its day confidently expected to set the supreme crown on its author's already considerable fame is not now able to find it a sure place—or a place of any kind—in the European canon. It commits too many mistakes for that. The poet took a theme from Roman history, and wished to latch onto the Ennian tradition. He opted against Callimachus because that was what the critics said or implied he should do. His own inmost poetic instincts rebelled against such serfdom, and in the unresolved struggle his epic languished and died.

Since he had decided to be a second Ennius,[86] Petrarch's attitude towards his theme, the Second Punic War and the elder Scipio's role in it, could only be adulatory. With this dismissal of the satiric all hope was lost of a mature commentary on human illusion, greatness and decline, for which the life of Scipio, with its mysticism and eventual end in the obscurity of self-imposed exile, offered ample scope. The poet chose to write about this theme in Latin, guaranteeing the diminution of his potential audience even further. Only scholars can now praise this decision of the "first modern man." Modern men have never heard of the *Africa*.

The tug of war between would-be literary orthodoxy and poetic feel for the true tradition is visible in the continual use of imagery which, in spite of the surface commitment to Ennius, implies a Hesiodic/Callimachean allegiance. The exordium betrays the unrealized dilemma (*Africa* I. 1–6):

> Et mihi conspicuum meritis belloque tremendum,
> Musa, virum referes, Italis cui fracta sub armis
> Nobilis aeternum prius attulit Africa nomen.
> Hunc precor exhausto liceat mihi sugere fontem
> Ex Helicone sacrum, dulcis mea cura, sorores,
> Si vobis miranda cano. . . .

> To me also, Muse, you will speak of a man marked out by merit and terrible in war on whom, broken by Italian arms, famous Africa first bestowed an everlasting name. May it be mine, I pray, to suck this sacred draught from drained Helicon (*or*: May it be mine, drained as

---

[85] E. Suerbaum's valuable essay in *Ennius* (Fondation Hardt, XVII, 1972), pp. 293 ff., fails even so to disentangle the tradition in which the poet wrote from the living (Hesiodic/Callimachean) tradition; cf. especially the confused remarks on Silius, p. 310 and note 1. E. Fraenkel rightly warns against overestimating the poem to compensate for its previous neglect: *Kleine Beiträge* (Rome 1964), II, p. 529.

[86] *Velut Ennius alter, Africa* II. 443.

I am, to suck this sacred draught from Helicon), my sweet favorites, sisters, if my songs earn your admiration. . . .

*Et mihi* at the beginning, followed by the imperatival future, indicates that the poet does not doubt his right to join the company of the Muses. *Virum* and *armis* in the second line suggest a rivalry with the *Aeneid* itself. But in that case the sequel is curious. Petrarch prays that he may be permitted to suck this sacred spring from Helicon that is drained, or alternatively, that he, being drained, may be allowed to suck this sacred spring from Helicon. He could mean that he is barren of inspiration, and so must be allowed to quaff the waters before he can proceed. He may mean rather that Helicon is itself empty of inspiration, and that he, the poet, comes along at a late stage for one last draught from the well before all is dry. The Hesiodic and Callimachean nature of the phraseology is oddly combined with a reminder of Choerilus of Samos.[87]

*Sugere,* "to suck," is a strange word. It was as a matter of fact much too "low" for the normal vocabulary of Latin poetry[88] (and is joined by other low words elsewhere in the *Africa*).[89] The Muses are addressed in a tone of extraordinary intimacy which is far more appropriate to the plain genre than to the high style of conventional epic.[90] Later (21–22) we find the jingle *sede sedere*. Is that expected in the opening of a serious poem?[91] In the same lines, by contrast, Petrarch, unlike Ennius, uses *poeta* and *vates* indifferently. He rides over the essence of the whole Augustan poetic revolution, and by implication over the consequences that had for the role of the poet/ priest.

[87] Choerilus had begun his epic by complaining of not living at a time when the meadow was still unmown (fr. 1, Kinkel). Callimachus may not have drunk from a spring at the start of the *Aetia,* and Hesiod certainly did not at the start of the *Theogony,* but later poets made them both do so, and "water-drinker" is synonymous with "Callimachean," e.g. at *Anth. Pal.* XI. 20. 6; cf. A. Kambylis, *Die Dichterweihe und ihre Symbolik* (Heidelberg 1965), pp. 66 ff., 98 ff.

[88] It is used, for example, by Novius, the writer of Atellan farces; by Varro in his Menippean satires; and by Martial. Petrarch may intend by its use the same poetic humility as Callimachus' παῖς ἅτε (*Aet.-Pref.* 6). This would be another unwitting tribute to the alternative tradition.

[89] E.g. *arra,* V. 155; *lasca,* VI. 549; *furcifer,* VII. 1095; cf. *actum de Hannibale est,* VIII. 36.

[90] Contrast Virgil's solemn *tu vatem, tu, diva, mone* (*Aen.* VII. 41). Petrarch's *dulcis mea cura* on the other hand is the vocabulary of Latin love elegy (e.g. Prop. I. 1. 35) and of the *Eclogues* (*raucae, tua cura, palumbes,* 1. 57; *tua cura, Lycoris,* 10. 22).

[91] Virgil enjoys etymological word-play (Norden on *Aen.* VI. 160 and on 204 ff.), but not in his exordium, unless we take *Musa . . . memora* (8) as such, but this is nothing like *sede . . . sedere.* Cf. W. F. Jackson Knight, *Roman Vergil* (London 1966), pp. 243 ff.; L. R. Palmer, *The Latin Language* (London 1954), pp. 85–86.

Petrarch's prize poem is continually marred by this failure to come to rational terms with the real classical tradition. If the poet was convinced by the theory making the aim of epic *admiratio* (cf. *miranda*, 6), which assigned to epic only the grandest language, how could he possibly use *sugere*, and in such an emphatic place? How could he assume an intimacy of affectionate address to the Muses which might be at home in the *Eclogues*, but is found neither in Homer nor the *Aeneid*? On the other hand, if he disagreed with critical theory, and believed that the epic need not be so grand as was urged, why not go all the way and allow his genius to deploy the full range of the Alexandrian, dramatic and comic epic?

In an earlier chapter, we noted a curious development in which the proem to the third book of Virgil's *Georgics*, with its promise of an epic "one day," was eventually taken up by later poets into epic itself, putting the best the poet had to offer into the category of second best, of something "meanwhile."[92] This was a concession to Callimachean taste, and a way of claiming freedom to write as one wanted by Alexandrian standards, while still acknowledging the legitimate claims of a patron.

Virgil himself had no *recusatio* in the *Aeneid*, since he wanted to meet the Callimachean challenge head on. Dante, who wrote a recusant *ecloga* in answer to Giovanni del Virgilio, again uses the trick at the start of the *Paradiso* (I. 34–36):

> Poca favilla gran fiamma seconda:
> forse di retro a me con miglior voci
> si pregherà perché Cirra risponda.

A mighty flame follows a tiny spark: perhaps after me with better utterance prayer will be made to which Delphi will respond.

But it can be seen that he is not trying to *avoid* commitment to his theme. What is second best is not his poem, but his talent.

Petrarch, the disciple of Ennius, but unlike his master, has two *recusationes* in the exordium to his epic. One is a promise to Christ (*Africa* I. 14–16):

> . . . tibi multa revertens
> Vertice Parnasi referam tibi carmina, si te
> Carmina delectant.

To Thee, returning from Parnassus' top, to Thee I will bring back many songs, if songs are Thy delight.

The other, in debt to Virgil's *Eclogue* 4 (53–54), is a promise to the King of Sicily (*Africa* I. 40–43):

[92] Above, pp. 242–43.

Ipse tuos actus meritis ad sidera tollam
Laudibus, atque alio fortassis carmine quondam
(Mors modo me paulum expectet! Non longa petuntur)
Nomen et alta canam Siculi miracula regis.

I myself will raise your deeds with deserved praises to the stars, and
perhaps one day in another song (let death but wait briefly for me.
Not for much is my request) will sing the name and high wonders of
the King of Sicily.

A fine example of the *recusatio* follows, which is pursued as far as
verse 70. Towards its conclusion we read (65–67):

Nunc teneras frondes humili de stipite vulsi,
Scipiade egregio primos comitante paratus:
Tunc validos carpam ramos.

For the moment I have plucked tender leaves from a lowly stock. It
is the noble Scipio who escorts my first trials. But then I will pull
down mighty branches.

Petrarch is fond of this gambit. In Book II, Hannibal's deeds are left
for a greater poet (183–84):

. . . maiora supersunt
Gesta viri, plectroque aliis maiore canenda.

Greater deeds of the hero are left, deeds to be celebrated by others
with greater quill.

It is all very traditional, but the tradition carried with it certain larger
implications.

One of those implications was the rejection of the historical epic
here and now. After all, this was what was "refused." Petrarch, by
contrast, believes that he is committed now to *historia* (IX. 90–98):

Quicquid labor historiarum est,
Quicquid virtutum cultus documentaque vitae,
Naturae studium quidquid, licuisse poetis
Crede: sub ignoto tamen ut celentur amictu,
Nuda alibi, et tenui frustrentur lumina velo,
Interdumque palam veniant, fugiantque vicissim.
Qui fingit quodcumque refert, non ille poetae
Nomine censendus, nec vatis honore, sed uno
Nomine mendacis.

Whatever history's toil may be, whatever may be devotion to the
virtues and the lessons offered by a life, whatever the study of nature,
all this, believe me, is the proper theme of poets. But it must be
concealed beneath an estranging garb, though sometimes revealed,
and should baffle the eyes with transparent veil. Sometimes these
topics should advance openly, and in their turn retreat. He who invents

all his tale is not to be reckoned by the name of poet, nor given the vatic privilege. He deserves simply the name of liar.

It is true that he allows here for a teasing playfulness with the "truth" which looks like the toying with historical allegory sometimes found in the pastoral (in other words, like a belated concession to the tradition of the "mask"). But how does the *Africa* fulfill its own prescriptions? The poet's flirtation with history is dangerous, if we judge it with the eyes of a theorist like Aristotle, or of practitioners like Virgil and even Lucan. To accommodate his argument, he consigns the poet who makes his story up to the role of liar. The censorship is Platonic. It was Callimachus in Alexandria who had remarked that Plato was incapable of judging poetry.[93]

Silius Italicus had refashioned Ennius in Alexandrian guise. Petrarch does the same. Scipio addresses Ennius (IX. 18–22):

> Si tibi nascenti, quo polles, summus Apollo
> Ingenium caeleste dedit, si turba dearum
> Castalio infantem demersum gurgite lavit
> Ex Helicone sacro, collesque eduxit in altos
> Et calamum et vocem tribuit mentemque poetae . . .

> If, as you were born, great Apollo granted you heavenly genius, if the throng of Muses when you were yet a child bathed you in the Castalian spring that rises from sacred Helicon, and led you to the high hills and gave to you the pipe, the utterance and the mind of a poet . . .

There is here a reference to an ode of Horace (IV. 3) which directly quotes from Callimachus' Preface to the *Aetia* (37–38) in its opening lines. The underlying allusion is to the poetic initiation of Gallus into the Hesiodic succession at the end of the sixth *Eclogue* (64 ff.). The baptism with water is also a traditionally Hesiodic/Callimachean motif. Dante had defended his poetic, comic choice to Giovanni del Virgilio in an eclogue. Petrarch has introduced the bucolic apologia into his epic, but at the same time he wants to use the epic for the historical and eulogistic aims rejected by Callimachus in the Preface to the *Aetia*, and to justify this he is prepared to pretend that Ennius was really a Callimachean after all. There was a long tradition in Roman poetry, going back to Lucretius, of making this pretence. But it is still a sign of typically Roman fuzziness, and in this case of those unresolved questions which would lead the *Africa* into an impasse.

The clear-headed Greek Callimachus agreed with Aristotle in condemning the versification of Herodotus' *History* by Choerilus of Samos. In his fifth book Petrarch, as we shall see, blithely versifies

[93] Fr. 589 Pf.

Book XXX of Livy's *History* while using Callimachean language to describe what he thinks he has done.

Petrarch, accepting that the poet is an historian, also accepts his duty to lay *firmissima veri/fundamenta* (IX. 93–94: "most sturdy foundations of the truth"). But what duties of research does that impose (duties of course which the poet never discharged)! Unless of course *poetic* truth is different from that of history (because it is "more philosophical"). But that is to go back to an Aristotelian insight which Petrarch denies.

We spoke of Lucretius as Dante's greatest predecessor. With some assistance from the *Georgics* (III. 289–93) Petrarch transfers from Lucretius to himself one of his most Alexandrian passages (VII. 500–05):

> Hic mihi, Pierides, quoniam maiora pusillis
> Viribus aggredior, si vos ab origine semper
> Dilexi coluique libens, si rite vocavi,
> Hic praebete animos totoque Elicone favete.
> Avia Castaliae sitiens convexa pererro;
> Urget amor famaeque trahit spes blanda decorae.

> Here, Muses, since I am tackling themes too great for my puny strength, if I have been your willing servant and worshipper from the beginning, if I have duly invoked you, here grant me inspiration, and bless me with all that Helicon can give. Thirsty, I traverse the trackless slopes of Castalia, urged on by love and drawn by the sweet hope of fitting fame.

Once again, the theme of thirst recurs. Like Lucretius[94] (and like Callimachus) Petrarch claims to be ranging where there are no tracks to guide. But that is not the claim of the historical epic poet, since his guide is the truth! And how strange anyway is the sequence Lucretius, the Virgil of the didactic *Georgics*—and the second Ennius of the *Africa*, when we consider the association of the didactic with Callimachus.[95]

If in spite of these confusions we do still read the *Africa*, it is to discover there the continued tension between native brilliance and academic precept. The second Ennius turns out to be indebted to a poet who was not one of Ennius' admirers, Ovid!

Ovid's influence is especially felt in Book V. According to

---

[94] Cf. *Avia Pieridum peragro loca*, I. 926; IV. 1: in general, Robert D. Brown, "Lucretius and Callimachus," *Illinois Classical Studies* VII (1982), 77–97.

[95] Ennius' didactic *Hedyphagetica* (?) translated from a poem by Archestratus which began by *parodying* Herodotus: Lloyd-Jones and Parsons, *Supplementum Hellenisticum*, p. 47, no. 132.

N. Festa,[96] the poet abandoned plans to develop in Book III an episode describing a visit paid by Scipio to the Palace of Truth (i.e. a carnival theme was excised). What is left is a visit to the palace of Syphax. But in this palace are still depicted the signs of the Zodiac and the Seven Planets (111 ff.; 140 ff.). Here, we seem to touch closely on Ovid's description in the second book of the *Metamorphoses* of the Palace of the Sun (*Met.* II. 17–18):

> Haec super imposita est caeli fulgentis imago,
> Signaque sex foribus dextris totidemque sinistris.

Over these was set the picture of the gleaming sky, and six zodiacal signs on the right leaf of the doors, and another six on the left.

The contact with the medieval tradition is also evident (e.g. Chaucer, *Knight's Tale* 1955 ff.).

At the end of Book IV of the *Africa* it is possible to say that nothing has yet happened. A eulogy of Rome has been followed by a eulogy of Scipio. The most successful book is V, the loves and death of Sophonisba, where a lyrical use of rhyme[97] in static and basically anti-epic (because anti-dramatic) description is noticeable (V. 638–39):

> Lumina magnorum mentes tactura deorum,
> Lumina durorum rabiem fractura virorum . . .

Eyes that would touch the hearts of mighty gods, eyes that would tame the madness of cruel men . . .

The speech of Masinissa from which this couplet is taken is a masterpiece strongly reminiscent of Ovidian exploration of the psychology of love. It begins with the first mention of Sophonisba's name (535), something which we have already noted as an old device of lyric, though it has also been claimed as particularly Ovidian.[98] What this seems to imply is that Petrarch is most successful when he treats lyrically of love. But what else does his *Canzoniere* do?

The earlier description of Sophonisba which began at v. 20 and lasted till v. 63 is utterly un-Virgilian (and un-Livian. Livy does not care what Sophonisba looked like). Homer of course had never described Helen at all. Yet it seems to follow closely the prescriptions of medieval *Poetics*, such as that of Matthew of Vendôme, notably in

[96] Pp. LXV ff. See also R. R. Bolgar, *The Classical Heritage* (repr. New York 1964), p. 186, and the epigrams on Santa Sophia in the first book of the *Greek Anthology*.

[97] Here there was Ennian precedent, but significantly in his *dramatic* choruses: cf. Cicero, *Tusc. Disp.* III. 19. 44. See above, p. 57 and note 56. Rhyme of this "leonine" sort had delighted the Middle Ages: Faral, p. 362; Arbusow, *Colores Rhetorici*, p. 78.

[98] Arbusow, above, note 64.

observing the order in which the lady's attractions are mentioned.[99] Petrarch's pun *amans/amens* is also a proof of medieval taste.[100]

There is however one strong link binding Petrarch to the living tradition, and that is formed by his similes. In V. 175, the lovelorn Masinissa is a shipwrecked sailor. The amatory topos is as old as Semonides of Amorgos, and is still vivid to Horace.[101] But it has also internal resonance in the epic. At IV. 184, Rome, assailed by Hannibal, was like a sinking ship. At VI. 377, the Carthaginians were sailors who make vows in a storm, and then cry off once they sail into calmer seas. Later (VIII. 253 ff.) Carthage is shipwrecked, and this image recurs (451). When the Carthaginian fleet burns (VIII. 1070 ff.) it is as if Carthage itself were burning (1082). This shows close kinship with both Virgil and Homer.[102]

When therefore Sophonisba "sinks" Masinissa, the erotic image fits into a pattern. Until he is rescued by Scipio, the king is in danger of manning a doomed vessel.

Virgil had *contrasted* his successive books. Petrarch rides over divisional boundaries, so that Book VI, for example, simply continues the story line of V. It opens with Sophonisba's descent to Hades, and ends with the death of Mago, which has in it something of the *Somnium Scipionis* theme of the epic's early books. There are some fine things here: the Plain of Dead Lovers, who include Achilles, "marking the pale grass with his merciless tread" (58). Sophonisba is like Turnus, "vexed with the gods above and angry with Death" (9), and the transference from hero to heroine shows kinship with Virgil's blend of Dido and Turnus. When she becomes a condemned prisoner suddenly reprieved (27), she reverses the image used of Masinissa in Book V (452), that of a man sentenced to death.

But "operatic" is the word which intrudes itself as the best description of the poet's technique, both in this book and in the poem as a whole. This means that once again, we must invoke from Callimachus our musical analogy. But here lyric has replaced drama, a betrayal of Aristotelian insights into the nature of Homeric epic. The poet does not really care about action at all. The *Africa*'s best passages are deeply Ovidian and Alexandrian, and Petrarch shares with Virgil the elevation of *Invidia* to historical and political impor-

---

[99] Faral, *Les arts poétiques du XIIᵉ et du XIIIᵉ siècle*, pp. 80–81; Bolgar, p. 38, suggests that this doctrine is at least as old as Hermogenes (A.D. 160). This replacement of the dramatic by the static and pictorial is an intrusion which violates the decorum of classical epic (cf. Horace *A. P.* 16 ff.) unless these descriptions serve a structural purpose as in Apollonius (above, p. 77) and Chaucer (below, p. 358).

[100] Faral, p. 94.

[101] Horace, *Odes* I. 5 with Nisbet and Hubbard's notes.

[102] Above, p. 9 and note 9; below, p. 361 and note 50.

tance. The reflections on the poet and Truth however (IX. 90 ff.) already quoted are not a new and brilliant theory of epic, simply an incoherent and never realized attempt to come to grips with a dilemma already resolved by chapter 9 of Aristotle's *Poetics*. The confused literary history on which this magnificent ruin is erected proved in the long term too shaky a foundation for the foot of Pegasus.

The damage which the critical failure inflicted on literature by presenting to Petrarch an inadequate blueprint of his task may be estimated by considering the contrasting subtlety of his other Latin poetry, and of his vernacular writings. How interesting that in the Alexandrian eclogues and Alexandrian sonnets he should have earned the name for which he is still honored! The tenth eclogue treats of Laura's death:[103]

> Forte aberam silvasque ieram spectare vetustas:
> Pestifer hinc eurus, hinc umidus irruit auster,
> Et stratis late arboribus, mea gaudia Laurum
> Extirpant franguntque truces, terraeque cavernis
> Bracchia ramorum frondesque tulere comantes.
> Ei mihi, quo nunc fessus eam? Quibus anxius umbris
> Recreer? Aut ubi iam senior nova carmina cantem?
> Illic notus eram. Quo nunc vagus orbe requirar?
> Quae me terra capit? Potes ad tua damna reverti,
> Infelix, sparsasque solo conquirere frondes
> Et laceros ramos et iam sine cortice truncum
> Amplecti lacrimisque arentia membra rigare?
> Ibis, an ignotas fugies moriturus in oras,
> Infaustum vivaxque caput? Dulcissima rerum
> Spes abiit. Quid vita manens invisa fruenti?
> Quis fragilis lentusque dolor praecordia versas?

It happened that I was away, visiting the ancient forests. From one side rushed in the plague-ridden east wind, from another the rain-laden south. Everywhere the trees were brought low. Savagely they uprooted and broke my joy, the Laurel, and pulled down her branching arms and luxuriant locks to the hollows of earth. Ah me! Where now shall I go in my weariness? In what shades shall my torment find rest? I am too old to find fresh songs. There I was known. In what world shall I now wander where my presence will be needed? What land is to receive me? Unhappy wretch, can you go back to what is lost and seek the foliage scattered on the ground, embrace the torn branches, the trunk now stripped of bark, and bedew with tears the withered limbs? Will you go? Or rather will you flee to find death in some unknown region, unhappy creature, condemned to life? Sweetest of

---

[103] *Le Rime di Francesco Petrarca* ... Commentate da G. Carducci e S. Ferrari (Florence 1946), p. 445.

all the world, hope has vanished. Why does life stay, hateful to its possessor? What brittle, tough sorrow torments my heart?

Like Virgil and Ovid, Petrarch turns to a theme of metamorphosis. If we could see a modern painting in which it was not clear whether a man was mourning a girl or a laurel tree, we should (like the Horace who wrote the opening of the *Ars Poetica*) regard it as another piece of contemporary humbug. But in Petrarch? And what about the Proustian trick of combining paradoxical adjectives into one psychologically convincing whole (*infaustum vivaxque, fragilis lentusque*)? Is this anything except the Horatian *callida iunctura*? But how could such a genius not finish the *Africa*?

The Italian sonnets are of course masterpieces, too successful for their own good. It is quite clear that Shakespeare was inspired by the same tradition. Their tone varies from the most delicately elegiac to the severely masculine. They look back, through the troubadours, to Latin elegy and its manifold sources. They mix religious and Platonic imagery. They combine homage to the heroic and the feminine. Lyrical, euphonious, punning, spoken melodies, they would have delighted the Alexandrian masters of the epigram.

A previous chapter has already noted how in fact Petrarch displaced to his *Song Book*, his *Canzoniere*, the epic device of a calendar found in Apollonius,[104] and used to such effect by Dante. His effort to exploit the gambit in the *Africa* itself (III. 111 ff.) foundered. Yet, at the lyrical level, the poet was brilliantly successful. Only under Callimachean, comic auspices could he have brought the epic and lyrical halves of his genius together.

For the epic style however as it really existed in classical practice, critics had substituted their own dummy. Faithful to this academic tradition, Petrarch had professed to be inspired only by *admiratio rerum* and *amor veri* (II. 441 ff.: "wonder at deeds" and "love of truth"). This acknowledges allegiance both to *ekplēxis* and to the historical epic. But let those who approve of this compare the *Africa* with the *Comedy*!

In a later period, Viperano, in agreement with Vida, remarks in the first sentence of his work on epic theory that the epic *ceteris sublimitate carminis antecellit* ("excels all the rest in the sublimity of its song"). The *carmen heroicum* demands *gravis oratio. Maiestas rerum* requires *sublimis dictio*. The list of ludicrous demands that were made upon the epic by such critics, which eventually included the insistence (borrowed from the *Nicomachean Ethics*) that its perfect hero must

---

[104] Above, pp. 89–94.

show his perfection by practicing distributive justice, could be multiplied.[105]

A poetry so conceived corresponds to the idealization of the ancient
world which is found in Renaissance art and architecture (not to
Renaissance art and architecture itself). Mantegna would have known
what the critics meant, although he would not have painted whole
pictures by their rules. But classical scholars like Scaliger and Muretus
forgot that ideal and reality must always exist in fruitful disharmony.[106]
Certainly an epic poem must treat of heroic action, and *sometimes* it
will use lofty language. But critics had, if nothing else, the serio-
comic Gospel account of Christ's own life before them, written in a
Greek distorted by Aramaic idiom, to act as a reminder that in the
end the really and wholly good man, the solitary hero who withdraws
to the mountainside, is likely, after mockery as a Saturnalian king,
to end on Golgotha, in the company of thieves.[107]

---

[105] Worstbrock, *Elemente einer Poetik der Aeneis*, p. 19; Weinberg has a summary of
the views of the "ancients," *A History of Literary Criticism in the Italian Renaissance*, p.
989. He mentions Campanella's theory that the epic hero must practice distributive
justice on p. 795. It has clearly strayed into the *Poetics* from the *Nicomachean Ethics*
(Book V), but whether Aristotle's megalopsych could ever be the hero of an epic is
another story: cf. his description at *N. E.* 1123 b ff.

[106] "The voice of a past generation": Weinberg, p. 941, on Muretus' letter of
April 27, 1584 about Pagello's *Heraclea*.

[107] Cf. John 6:15. "It is in vain in years of chaos/To seek a good end./It is for
some to execute and repent/And for others to end with a Golgotha": B. Pasternak,
*Lieutenant Schmidt* (1927).

# VII

# THE ITALIAN TRADITION

THE European drive towards Greek has already been observed in Dante, who died in 1321. In Giovanni Boccaccio (1313–1375), it becomes unmistakable.[1]
Boccaccio composed the *Teseida delle nozze di Emilia* expressly to fill a gap noted by Dante in Italian literature. There was no poem which dealt with the theme of arms.[2] Finished probably by 1341, the youthful epic intended to answer this challenge occupies twelve books, and as many lines as the *Aeneid*.

## I

The *Teseida* made such an impression that it was translated into modern Greek and published in Venice in 1529. Even earlier (1387?), Chaucer adapted and abbreviated it for his *Knight's Tale*, and the nature of this adaptation must claim attention in a later chapter. It forms a long meditation, well aware of its Statian model, on the troubled inheritance of the sons of Oedipus.

Two brothers, Arcita and Palemone, are captured at Thebes by Theseus and imprisoned at Athens. There, from a window, they espy Emilia, younger sister of Theseus' Amazon queen, and fall hopelessly in love. Eventually, one of the brothers, Arcita, is released. He visits Thebes, assuming the name of "Penteo." Returning to Athens, he finds employment in Theseus' household as a servant. Only Emilia recognizes him.

---

[1] He secured the appointment of Leonzio Pilato as professor of Greek at Florence about 1360: R. Pfeiffer, *History of Classical Scholarship, 1300–1850* (Oxford 1976), p. 24. As early as the *Teseida* he puns on Greek (VIII. 104. 2, *chesta da due, mentre ch'io son mia* = μία.) But Greek had never been forgotten, even by Dante, who had defined poetry as *fictio rhetorica in musica poita* (*De Vulgari Eloquentia* II. 4), and its survival is discussed by Walter Berschin, *Griechisch-lateinisches Mittelalter* (Bern 1980).

[2] This point is made both in Boccaccio's *Preface* addressed to Fiammetta, and at XII. 84 of the poem. The allusion is to *De Vulgari Eloquentia* II. 2. Unlike Petrarch, Boccaccio maintained the deepest possible admiration for Dante, and nowadays we admire him the more for it. Contrast E. Norden on Petrarch's embarrassing dislike of his great predecessor: *Die Antike Kunstprosa* (5th ed., repr. Stuttgart 1958), p. 771 note 2.

Even though the two brothers have sworn friendship, love proves stronger. The Fury Tisiphone poisons Palemone, still languishing in his cell, against the absent Arcita. When he too manages to give his captors the slip, he seeks out Arcita in the countryside, determined to finish the business by force of arms. A furious duel breaks out. It is interrupted by Emilia, out hunting with her sister and Theseus. When the story is told, it is agreed that the pair will return in a year with a company of knights to settle their differences in a tournament. Before the decisive combat, each hero prays to his chosen patron: Arcita to Mars, and Palemone to Venus. Emilia in her turn sacrifices to Diana. In the tournament, Palemone is captured by an opponent's horse, and Emilia loses no time in ditching him. Arcita is victor in the fray. After all, had he not invoked the aid of Mars?

But Venus must have her hour. A Fury upsets Arcita's horse in the moment of victory. Gravely injured, the hero is conveyed away from the lists in a triumphal chariot. He insists on the completion of the marriage ceremony, even though Emilia has already given a ring to Palemone, which has on it a reminder of the betrayal of Amphiaraus by his wife.

The ailing hero's nuptial night is dismissed in three stanzas. Arcita grows worse. The poet who had little time for his wedding night has a whole book (X) to give to his death. Pathetically, Arcita explains his plight by arguing that "the gods made a mistake." We already know just how wrong he is.

Arcita's corpse will be burned in the very *bosco* where he used to lament his lovelorn fate. It is Emilia who brings the flame for his pyre. Into it she throws the ring which her husband gave her.

The lovely young widow is disfigured by grief. It is time for Theseus to intervene and draw out the moral lesson of the story. He explains that death comes to everyone, and that Arcita has been fortunate in dying young. Mourning has gone on long enough. Arcita's last wish was that Emilia should remarry. That must be respected, and obviously she must marry Palemone. The poet comments that in the excitement Arcita has been forgotten.

The wedding is celebrated in the temple of Venus. At long last, Emilia is described. On the great day, she wears green, exactly the color she was wearing when Arcita and Palemone first fought. The poet informs us that on their wedding night Palemone and his bride coupled seven times, but discreetly draws a veil over the rest.

The outline of the classical epic tradition, musical, ambiguous, learnedly ironic, emotive, unexpected, colloquial, as it began to take shape already in Alexandria under the symbolic patronage of Hesiod, has been traced in Chapter I. To it was added from the Roman side a more vivid sense of carnival metamorphosis, and a satiric/vatic element of public concern about morals (though we must be careful about assuming that these qualities were not also present to Callimachus and Apollonius in due measure). Dante's *Commedia* illustrated the analysis of the literary tradition as it was made by a poet of supreme genius. The study of Cinquecento criticism showed how much that implied poetic set him at odds with academic orthodoxy. These awkward disagreements had already begun in his own day.

Unlike his contemporary Petrarch, Boccaccio was an admirer of Dante, and in later years even gave public readings from and lectures on the *Commedia*. Evidently in fulfilling the call for an epic of arms he read the tradition in just as peculiar a way as his master. He used, for example, an admixture of colloquial vocabulary. His prosey enjambement can at times obscure the verse structure of his poem. Yet his affinity with lyricism is undeniable, and the monologues of his lovelorn hero Arcita have been described as particularly akin to elegy. He borrowed his *ottava* from popular minstrelsy, and shows some liking for *stilnovismo*. The whole poem is dedicated to and controlled by "Fiammetta," a rhetorical fiction comparable to Propertius' Cynthia, or Ovid's Corinna.[3]

The modern editor who detects all this debt to comedy calls attention to even more interesting evidence of Boccaccio's sensitivity to the comic presence in the tradition. The poem hinges on two themes, one of arms and the other of love. But Boccaccio's extraordinary eclecticism, his technique of contamination, his "metamorphosing mind" (*trasformismo*), tend to weaken and confound these two loci, which are continually switching place. Around one of the polar themes—that of Mars and arms—collect reminiscences of epic, of Latin, even certain echoes of Dante: around the other—Venus, Cupid, love—gather and coalesce different allusions from lyric, elegy, with their appropriate sentiment, or sentimentality.[4]

What is happening to the classical epic tradition is once again what the Formalists would call *la dénudation du procédé*. Virgil, as has been repeatedly stressed, created an amalgam. In the hands of others, the constituent elements of his compound tend sometimes to fall apart, and sometimes to be recombined in different and more exposed ways. Boccaccio's use of the elegy is sanctioned by the elegiac spirit of Virgil's *Eclogues*[5] and even certain motifs of the *Aeneid* itself. His

---

[3] These details are taken from Alberto Limentani's "Introduzione" to his edition of the *Teseida: Tutte le opere di Giovanni Boccaccio* (Verona 1964), II, pp. 231 ff.

[4] Limentani, pp. 233 ff.

[5] Cf. E. J. Kenney, "Virgil and the Elegiac Sensibility," *Illinois Classical Studies* VIII (1983), 44–59.

attention to the feminine matches Virgil's concern with Juno, Dido, Penthesilea, Andromache, Camilla, Juturna, Lavinia. . . . His learned *chiose*, appended to his text as the evidence of immense erudition, are his particular version of Alexandrian "learning," in which the normally hidden apparatus of illusion is revealed. One may compare T. S. Eliot's notes to *The Waste Land*, and those modern plays whose producers dispense with backdrops to show us instead the plain brick of the theatre's rear walls. All this might well be called the epic's comic side.

But Boccaccio is serious as well as comic. When he makes the dying Creon recall Dante's Farinata (II. 63), the epic echo is like those which lend resonance to Virgil's symphony. Later, the Fury that upsets Arcita's horse will also recall the same Dantesque figure (IX. 7). Even in Book II, Palemone and Arcita, Thebans like Creon, also evoke Farinata (86). This is not imaginative poverty. It is the use of a commented model to secure dramatic unity and dramatic irony.

Much more than Chaucer (but like Statius), Boccaccio sees the fraternal strife of his heroes as something inherited (V. 57: cf. X. 96 ff.). Even when the two brothers fight "like dragons" (V. 75), we may detect an allusion to the serpent's teeth from which the original inhabitants of Thebes sprang. Emilia, garlanded as a huntress when she comes across the contending pair (V. 79), is like the huntress Venus who meets the hunting Aeneas in Africa in the first book of the *Aeneid*. Virgil's mother and son are well matched, and eventually a hunt will presage Dido's undoing, and drive her to the funeral pyre. But it will be the fair Emilia, garbed in hunting green, who will bring Arcita to his funeral pyre. Boccaccio indeed exploits fire symbolism just as much as Virgil. While Emilia prayed in Diana's temple, "the fires were burning" (VII. 88). She has already "made two funeral pyres" of her offerings to Diana (VII. 74). Her association with greenery, so innocent and "natural," is ominous, since it is the green trees which supply fuel for the flames.[6]

The comic and the tragic meet. Palemone is worsted in the joust and made prisoner by a horse (VIII. 120)! The description is taken from the chariot race in Statius' *Thebaid* (VI. 485–90), where the funeral games of Archemorus are being celebrated. Partly, the poet is thinking of the formal nature of the two contests described by himself and Statius. But, since Lycurgus, still in mourning for Archemorus, had been the first hero to join Arcita (VI. 14), we cannot help reflecting in hindsight that the joust has itself been a sort of funeral games: and of course funeral games for the ostensible victor. The old theme of "the game of life," "all the world's a stage,"

---

[6] Cf. III. 8–9, modified at XI. 77 by the addition of *albori*: cf. XI. 18 ff.

blossoms anew.[7] It will be from the same book of the *Thebaid* that Boccaccio borrows to describe the universal mourning for Arcita's death (XI. 7 ff.), and the Statian analogue for Arcita will be precisely the dead Archemorus.

It is in death that the public and private halves of Boccaccio's theme coalesce. Theseus set out on his conquest of the Amazons at night, a time that "hides all things from us" (I. 19. 3). The poet is thinking of *Paradiso* XXIII. 3, where Beatrice awaits the vision of the Church Triumphant. But in Book X. 89, the same phrase marks Arcita's decisive turn for the worse. The slow-growing seed planted by Theseus, which led to Emilia's coming to Athens, has now borne deadly fruit.

Indeed, Boccaccio is much aware in his epic of the astronomical calendar. An elaborate *Stundenbild* describes the season when the two heroes first see Emilia, and it is the same season that witnesses the burning of those dead in the joust (III. 5; X. 1). Arcita will die soon after.

Theseus had celebrated his wedding after lighting funeral pyres at Thebes. This imagery is again invoked as the wedding of Arcita and Emilia is celebrated after the burning of those dead in the joust which has won her. These particular pyres seem to be kindled in the very theatre (more *dénudation du procédé*) where the combat took place. Arcita's pyre will be lit by Emilia in the *bosco* where he and Palemone first fought. The themes stated separately in the prelude are now fused into an intensely powerful unity when bridegroom and burned are the same, and marriage bed becomes funeral couch. Virgil's Dido taught Boccaccio this skill.[8]

An important aspect of the classical epic was its vatic orientation, the outgrowth of the Roman national weakness for satire. Evidently no Italian lacks this characteristic. It has sometimes been tempting however to believe that satire, particularly in Boccaccio, is all. But the *Teseida* at least exhibits a cool realism about the human condition which is more than satirical. The old curse at work in the Theban line, the futility of expecting providential help from the gods, the vanity of the world, the fickleness of women, the pomposity of an aging Theseus who can only retain his heroic status in the poem by being largely kept in the background: these are moral insights that command attention. When Theseus rises to draw out the lesson of the whole adventure (XII. 6–19) he delivers a *consolatio* that employs

---

[7] On the carnival and Roman theme of life as a game, see above, p. 14, and *Pindar's Art: Its Tradition and Aims*, p. 46 with notes 107 and 108.

[8] *Aen.* IV. 648 ff.: above, p. 177.

many time-honored classical themes.[9] But this is not simple parody. It was all the pagan antique world had to go on. Earlier, Egeo had been ignored when he tried to say something similar (XI. 10, 11, 12, 33). Now the theodicy (if that is what it is) can be heard, but of course now it leaves questions. But so does Book XII of the *Aeneid*. So does Pindar.

It is in these questions that we can see one of the profounder marks of the epic's comic and carnival inspiration. So much of the action has already taken place in a *teatro*, or against a backdrop of ambivalent nature, which pushes towards growth and fruition regardless of death, regardless of conventional morality. There are no final answers in this Roman world of fields and funeral gladiators, so wonderfully recreated by the young poet, only the sting left in the minds of hearers. Arcita and Palemone in their prison and in their theatre are paradigms of us all (Plautus' "Here's our circus!"). Fame compensates, for it means the arrest of time. And fame is aided by the association of the present with the unchangeable, mythical past. It is cruel when Theseus, with an old man's vagueness, keeps talking of Arcita by his assumed name of "Penteo."[10] But as Arcita becomes the legendary king who thought he could resist the power of Dionysus, he rises out of himself into a preserving metamorphosis. His eschatological laughter *in excelsis* (the carnival motif is added to that of height, the dislocation of normal space) is the last we hear from him (XI. 3. 1).

Another famous work of Boccaccio, the *Decameron*, bears, like so many works of the Middle Ages (even, of course, Dante's *Commedia*), a Greek title. Greek influence has been suggested at various points. The Alexander romance has been identified as one of these influences (as it has in Mann's *Doktor Faustus*).

A famous book on the origins and nature of the Greek novel ends with a discussion of the first story of the *Decameron*'s fifth day.[11] The names and setting of this improbable love story are Greek. The author summarizes the plot and then comments:

> The whole narrative seems to me to bear the evident tokens of the Greek novel of late or perhaps even Byzantine times. The action is set in the pagan past. Often "the gods" are at work in its development. The "jealousy of Fortune" has the same unlimited scope as Tyche

[9] Examined by R. Kassel, *Untersuchungen zur griechischen und römischen Konsolationsliteratur*, Zetemata 18, (Munich 1958).

[10] XII. 29. 6; cf. 48. 1–2. Cf. E. R. Dodds on Euripides, *Bacchae* 367. The classical tradition of such names goes right back to Homer. Since it is so primitive, it may be exploited both comically and tragically.

[11] E. Rohde, *Der griechische Roman und seine Vorläufer* (3rd ed., Leipzig 1914).

[Chance] in the novels of the Greek Sophists. The characters' names
are Greek, and not indeed invented by Boccaccio. . . . The unrealistic
elements in the plot, the weak and carelessly realized intrigue, the
cloying excess of the sentiments, the peculiar nature of the adventures
—a sea voyage, the abduction of a bride promised by her father to
someone else, a storm, the magistrate in love, certain unusual scenes
such as the wistful contemplation of the sleeping beloved by the lover,
the long and elaborate speech in which Lisimaco explains to Cimone
his plan for the rape: all this shows the unmistakable signs of the love
novel of the late Sophists. The whole tale reads like an extract from
a romantic story of that period and that genre.[12]

The same scholar is also reminded of Byzantine romance by the
*Teseida*.[13] We saw that Boccaccio shows off some knowledge of Greek
even in this early epic. Is the "romantic" element in Italian literature
of the Trecento, Quattrocento and Cinquecento largely a revival and
continuation of the Greek novel, and what consequences would such
a theory have for the interpretation of the classical epic tradition?

It is certainly true that the Greek novel finds echoes as late as
Thomas Mann. But, as Rohde emphasizes, the Greek novel is itself
a composite genre. It draws together stylistic devices from a number
of predecessors; its episodic narrative, its use of the first person, its
interlacing of themes, its stories of wandering voyages have been
traced to epic. From the stage come its tales of the exposure of
infants and their eventual recognition, and its accounts of partings
and reunions, its reversals of fortune, its use of the *deus ex machina*.
History supplied the mannerism of speech and counterspeech. Ethnography gave material for odd stories about strange tribes, exotic
flora and fauna, travels, journeys, utopian societies. Elegy inspired
the treatment of love. Rhetoric furnished the technique of the
declamatory speech, and the use of the elaborate description or
*ecphrasis*.

Yet even this catalogue of sources is already unfaithful to the
reality of the literature that we know. Both epic and ethnography
are made responsible for "travelers' tales." Rhetoric may have had
something to do with the *ecphrasis*, but the epic *ecphrasis* even so is
as old as the *Iliad*. Again, if rhetoric inspired the declamatory speech,
why does history inspire the balance of speech and counterspeech?
Is not the presence of such pairs of orations in Thucydides used to
prove his interest in contemporary sophistic rhetoric?

Papyrus discoveries in our time have shown that the Greek novel

[12] Pp. 574–75 (my translation).
[13] P. 576 note 2.

is far older than had been supposed.[14] Indeed, the material drawn together in the novel is older still. We cannot use the Greek novel as the explanation of subsequent narrative technique,[15] for the simple reason that the Greek novel is itself a motley, hybrid genre in need of explanation.

In the Middle Eastern countries surrounding the Mediterranean, the fund of tall stories, religious, admonitory, comic, tragic, mystical, semi-scientific, had accrued for centuries. They deserve all these epithets and more because they spring from a primitive consciousness which, in its efforts to make sense of the world, has not yet learned to differentiate what nowadays we so painstakingly and artificially separate. Some of this storehouse is tapped by the epic writer, and the same material later used by the ethnographer and historian. Some of the same resources were used by Callimachus in his *Aetia* and even in his *Iamboi*. Ovid would follow suit in his *Metamorphoses* and *Fasti*. These are simply conscious forays into the amorphous and uncategorized, which betray and distort their prey. The "raid on the inarticulate" of which Eliot speaks is necessary to literature, but of course it is always an act of violence and even of corruption. It is always unsatisfying too, which is why at one end of the scale so many versions exist of Aesop's fables, and why at the other the greatest themes continually attract fresh assaults.

It has already been noted that Ion of Chios, author of travel stories but also of comedies, tragedies and much else besides, had been invoked by Callimachus in Alexandria as an important literary predecessor.[16] Now we can see why. Callimachus was also claiming the right to draw on that oral, floating material of diverse origin which would later be the inspiration of the Greek novel. But what we value in Callimachus, as in every literary artist, is not where he got his material but what he did with it.

If we make the Greek novel the sole origin of the Italian "romantic" epic after Dante, we shall not be able to understand the *literary* debt which that epic owes to Alexandria, evinced, for example, by its use of the *recusatio*. We shall not understand the attention given by these poets to an implied dialogue with classical epic predecessors, notably Virgil, but also Ovid, Statius, Lucan. Even the *Teseida* has exactly as many lines as the *Aeneid*. Chiefly, we shall not be able to do justice to the elements of what eventually became the romance tradition

---

[14] See, for example, B. Perry, *The Ancient Romances* (Berkeley and Los Angeles 1967), pp. 96 ff., 343 ff.

[15] A. Heiserman, *The Novel before the Novel* (Chicago and London 1977), p. 41, notes some problems of methodology.

[16] Above, p. 70.

(Jason and Medea, Aeneas and Dido) which had already been assimilated and intensified by the classical epic long before the late Greek novel as we now study it came on the scene. The vatic dimension will be underplayed, the epic imagination trivialized.

In fact, the most plausible speculation about the Greek sources of the *Teseida* associates the poem, not with the Byzantine novel, but with the great medieval national epic of the Greeks, *Digenes Akritas*, of which a fourteenth-century manuscript was discovered at Grotta Ferrata, near Naples.[17] The names of Akritas and Arcita obviously help this suggestion. But the death of the hero, the Amazon motif, the previous betrothal of the heroine, the encouragement offered by the heroine during the decisive battle, the scene with the physician, the advice given by the dying hero to the heroine to marry again after his death, the siting of the tomb: all these are motifs shared by Boccaccio with the Greek epic which indicate a degree of dependence, if not on the Byzantine poem, at least on some common tradition.

Boccaccio's was therefore an *epic* imagination, and it is as an epic conception that the *Teseida*, like the *Orlando Furioso* and the *Gerusalemme Liberata*, is to be evaluated. Is not this what the poet himself claims? Lyrical, prosey; romantic, realistic; theatrical, rustic; heroic, feminine; holding up a mirror to life's manifold contradictions, the tragi-comic masterpiece intrudes its disturbing questions still on our age, so convinced of its own sophistication.

## II

The historical epic practiced by Petrarch inspired no successors now remembered. Giangiorgio Trissino (1478–1550), who was critic as well as poet, could not carry his *L'Italia Liberata dai Goti* beyond the grave. Boccaccio, who would have made no sense of that poem, would certainly have smiled upon Ariosto's *Orlando Furioso*, and yet even the *Orlando Furioso*, first published in 1516, is no longer required reading. Modern taste has lost its relish for the author who once charmed Europe, so that his poem was passed from hand to hand even in houses of ill fame, according to one of his early critics.[18] This impoverishment is a further sign of failure to grasp the full range of the classical epic, in which the imaginative contact with Alexandria now becomes, as taste matures, even more apparent.

Ariosto has been thought of as a supreme ironist. Yet this quality

---

[17] H. and R. Kahane, "Akritas and Arcita: A Byzantine Source of Boccaccio's *Teseida,*" *Speculum* XX (1945), 415 ff. Boccaccio had spent his youth in Naples, and may have written the *Teseida* there.

[18] Niccolò degli Oddi, quoted by B. Weinberg, *A History of Literary Criticism in the Italian Renaissance*, p. 1035.

stands in need of a redefinition of the kind we already had to undertake for Boccaccio. There is no doubt a corrosive irony, which simply reverses accepted values in order to pour contempt on human failings. But, however much we may admire this acid as mixed by Swift, it has to be remembered that it is only one specimen of its kind, and perhaps not the happiest.

Another, and more fruitful, form stems from the creative, resurrecting laughter of the carnival. It calls for a reader mature enough to understand that to suggest something is not to be taken entirely seriously does not mean that it is not to be taken seriously at all. What the artist does in the case of this second type of irony is to allow his imagination free play. The resulting fantasy may in fact correspond to some facet of reality, but the poet (or composer) does not guarantee this correspondence. He may indeed be doubtful of his own ability to judge what is more or less likely to be true about such large questions as human life and morals. He challenges his audience to see for themselves what elements of truth are caught in his arachnean structures. They may at all times, even if they find the comparison of art with experience tedious, at least admire the structures for their own sake.

In the last analysis, the distinction between a poetry of plain statement and one of allusion and suggestion is forced, since at a certain level great poetry eludes these academic categorizations. But there is something in the distinction, perhaps best summarized by Pascal in his contrast between the *esprit de géométrie* and the *esprit de finesse*. In a mature age, epic too must learn to come to terms with the *esprit de finesse*. Not to do so would be to remain forever backward and behind in the appreciation of refinements which may even have begun to permeate political and legal life. An art that seeks to touch the living experience of contemporaries must take account of contemporary sensibility. The great achievement of Virgil, following Callimachus and Apollonius, was to have created an epic where such sensibility could be at home.

Ariosto understood the Callimachean and Augustan tradition well enough to compose a *recusatio*. In his Latin elegy *De Diversis Amoribus*[19] he catalogues his various loves. Beneath the conventional phraseology something may be detected of the restless and fastidious mind that

[19] Ludovico Ariosto, *Orlando Furioso, Le Satire, I Cinque Canti e Una Scelta Delle Altre Opere Minori*, a cura di Carlo Muscetta e Luca Lamberti, Vol. II (Torino 1962), pp. 1258-60. A more detailed discussion of this poem may be found in "Orazio, Ariosto and Orazio Ariosto," *Acta Conventus Neo-Latini Amstelodamensis* (Munich 1979), pp. 820-34.

was not likely to be pleased with simplistic views of any situation, least of all the heroic.

Coming from a soldier's family, Ariosto (like Horace) had probably seen action. He writes (9–16):

> Hoc olim ingenio vitales hausimus auras,
> Multa cito ut placeant, displicitura brevi.
> Non in amore modo mens haec, sed in omnibus impar;
> Ipsa sibi longa non retinenda mora.
> Saepe eadem Aurorae rosea surgente quadriga
> Non est, quae fuerat sole cadente mihi.
> O quot tentatas illa est versata per artes
> Festivum impatiens rettulit unde pedem!

This was my temperament when I first drank in the breath of life: many things please me quickly, and will just as quickly displease. My mind is not like this in love alone: it is fickle in everything: it cannot hold itself still for any length of time. When Dawn's rosy chariot rises, often it is not the same as it was when the sun set. How many careers has it broached and then, losing patience, withdrawn from them its giddy foot!

He reviews the different careers that have tempted him (17–26):

> Cum primum longos posui de more capillos
> Estque mihi primum tradita pura toga;
> Haec me verbosas suasit perdiscere leges,
> Amplaque clamosi quaerere lucra fori;
> Atque eadem optatam sperantem attingere metam
> Non ultra passa est improba ferre pedem;
> Meque ad Permessum vocat Aoniamque Aganippem,
> Aptaque virgineis mollia prata choris;
> Meque iubet docto vitam producere cantu,
> Per nemora illa, avidis non adeunda viris.

When first I laid aside, as custom dictates, my long hair, and for the first time assumed the dress of a grown man, my mind urged me to study the wordy laws, and to seek the rich rewards of the noisy lawcourt. I hoped to attain the longed-for goal, but her [my mind's] impossible behavior would not allow me to take one step further. She called me to Permessus and to Aonian Aganippe, to soft meadows, fit for girlish dances. I was to spend my life amid learned poetry, in pastures no avaricious man may enter.

He is combining the *Eclogues* with Propertius.[20] The whole passage

---

[20] *Eclogues* 6. 64, 10. 12; Propertius II. 10. 26. On Permessus, see P. J. Enk's notes in his edition of Propertius II (Leiden 1962), vol. II, pp. 165–66. For *mollia* in Ariosto, cf. Enk, p. 13, on Propertius' *mollis liber* (II. 1. 2). See also Tacitus, *Dialogus* 12: *Nemora vero et luci et secretum ipsum* etc.

teems with Alexandrian vocabulary and attitudes, notably in the contrast drawn between the poor poet and the noisy wordiness of the rich lawyer.[21]

When Ariosto first turned away from all this, he thought of epic, the conventional battles and deeds of great generals. He did in fact begin and then give up work on an early poem in *terza rima* on Obizzo d'Este. Just like Virgil, and repeating a pattern traced by Dante and Milton, he found that this type of epic was a dead end.[22]

Ariosto progressed to being a courtier, and even a soldier. We can be sure that this experiment was short-lived, when we recall that the Roman elegists also hated war, even if it promised riches.[23]

Abandoning these false starts, the poet looked again to the Muse. This time, it was not the poetry of war which attracted him:

> Antra mihi placeant potius, montesque supini
> Vividaque irriguis gramina semper aquis;
> Et Satyros inter celebres, Dryadasque puellas
> Plectra mihi digitos, fistula labra terat.

Rather may caves please me, and sloping mountains, and grass kept fresh by ever-flowing streams. Amid the thronging Satyrs and Dryad nymphs may the quill wear down my fingers and the pipe my lips.

Interestingly, this Muse clearly has something to do with the *Eclogues* (and with the *Georgics*), just as it was by also taking refuge with the *Eclogues*, and quoting this same passage, that Dante resisted Giovanni del Virgilio's invitation to the grand, Latin eulogy.[24]

The extraordinary instinct by which a great poet once again manifested his grasp of an ancient dilemma is also evident in the actual form of the poem, not merely in the employment of the elegiac couplet, in contrast to the majestic heroic hexameter, but in the ring-composition which rounds it off. Borrowing another ancient motif,[25] Ariosto wryly comments that there is only one thing where he is constant, and that is in his subjection to love. The beginning and end of the poem merit comparison (1–4):

---

[21] Cf. Propertius IV. 1. 134: *et vetat* [sc. Apollo] *insano verba tonare foro.* Ovid combines an allusion to poetic poverty with one to *verbosi . . . fori* (*Tristia* IV. 10. 18 and 21–22).

[22] Virgil's false start is described by Donatus, *Vit. Verg.*, § 19: *Mox cum res Romanas incohasset, offensus materia ad Bucolica transiit*, where *res Romanae* suggest the Ennian (*Ann.* 472, Warmington), anti-Aristotelian, anti-Callimachean view of epic. Propertius defines his attitude especially in III. 1 and 3; IV. 1. For Milton, see below, p. 373.

[23] Cf. Tibullus I. 10; Propertius III. 5.

[24] Cf. *Geo.* I. 11; II. 485; *Ecl.* 5. 59 and 73; 2. 34 (*trivisse labellum*). This last passage was also imitated by Dante: above, p. 260.

[25] Cf. K. F. Smith on Tibullus IV. 2. 7–14 and Propertius II. 22 with Ovid, *Amores* II. 4.

Est mea nunc Glycere, mea nunc est cura Lycoris,
Lyda modo meus est, est modo Phyllis amor.
Primas Glaura faces renovat, movet Hybla recentes,
Mox cessura igni Glaura vel Hybla novo.

Now Glycere is all my concern, now Lycoris: Lyda is now my love, and now Phyllis. Glaura kindles an old flame, Hybla a new: but shortly Glaura and Hybla will give way before a fresh fire.

The poem ends (67–70):

Et nunc Hybla licet, nunc sit mea cura Lycoris,
Et te, Phylli, modo, te modo, Lyda, velim;
Aut Glauram aut Glyceren, aut unam aut saepe ducentas
Deperiam; igne tamen perpete semper amo.

And though now Hybla, now Lycoris is all my concern, though now I desire you, Phyllis, now you, Lyda: though I faint for Glaura or Glycere, or for one girl or often for two hundred, still I love with a fire that is unquenched.

Glycere began the original list, and Hybla finished it. At the end, Hybla begins, and Glycere finishes. The use of chiasmus also helps to contrast two of the pentameters (*Lyda/Phyllis* in line 2: *Phyllis/ Lyda* in line 68). Glycere, Glaura and Hybla are introduced in that order: when we leave them, they are presented in the order Hybla, Glaura, Glycere. The occurrence of *cura Lycoris* in the same metrical position in two hexameters (3 and 67: cf. *Eclogues* 10. 22) is offset by the chiastic variation of *mea nunc* to *nunc mea*. It seems quite clear that the poet's imagination moved according to precise rules which, even with a different subject-matter, would remind us of Alexandrian taste, Alexandrian control.[26]

Can it be a matter of surprise that a poet with this natural sympathy for Callimachean positions also wrote satires? Such an attention to a *genus humile* would parallel Callimachus' own attention to his *Iamboi*. But, more largely, it would signal an inclination toward the carnival, by demonstrating an interest in a side of life which, with its human foibles and imperfections, its constant revolutions of Fortune's wheel (*la ruota di Fortuna, Sat.* III. 229), is generally ignored by the

---

[26] Some of Pindar's formality may be compared: e.g. in *Nemean* 2 the allusion to the Nemean, Isthmian and Pythian games (vv. 4 and 9) is picked up in the order Pythian, Isthmian, Nemean (vv. 19, 20, 23). In B. Brecht's poem *Kohlen für Mike*, "Ohio/Mike McCoy" is picked up by "Mike McCoy/Ohio."—Ariosto's *modō/modŏ* (vv. 2 and 68) is rare scansion, but good Alexandrianism: cf. Callimachus, fr. 1. 35 Pf.; Virgil, *Eclogues* 6. 44; *Anth. Pal.* VI. 280. 3. For the final long in the adverb, cf. Lucan IX. 766, and Lachmann's note on Lucretius II. 1135.

conventionally heroic.[27] At Rome, such a satirical outlook blended with the concept of the poet as moral reformer particulary emphasized by the Augustans. Horace, the *vates*, had also celebrated *Fortuna saevo laeta negotio* (*Odes* III. 29. 49: "Fortune happy at her ruthless task"). Since this concept was ultimately subsumed into Ariosto's epic, it was not irrelevant to epic beginnings.

Ariosto's *Satire*, which were not published by their author, share with Callimachus and Horace (*nec recito cuiquam nisi amicis, idque coactus*: *Sat.* I. 4. 73: "I read my poems only to friends, and even that against my will"), and with the Dante of "Donne ch'avete intelletto d'amore," the appeal to a limited audience, and the fact that they are not "satirical" in Juvenal's sense. They are not hysterical and ranting denunciations of the ills of the age, abundant in ills though that age was. They are the laying bare of the poet's own thoughts about matters which any man of cultivation and sensibility would find important before the sympathetic eyes of another whom he trusts.[28]

The sixth satire (1523–24) addressed to Pietro Bembo, renowned humanist and churchman, is a case in point.[29] Ariosto speaks of his wishes for the education of his son Virginio (1–3):

> Bembo, io vorrei, come è il commun disio
> de' solliciti padri, veder l'arti
> che essaltan l'uom tutte in Virginio mio.

Bembo, I should like, as anxious fathers generally do, to see all the arts that exalt man in my Virginio.

The reminiscence of a famous sonnet by Dante[30] is striking, and also something else: the use of *terza rima*, allied to the plainest vocabulary, suggests that Ariosto is able to latch onto at least one aspect of Dante's art, that ability to transmute the colloquial and ordinary which is profounder than any theatricality of the high and conventional style. By contrast, the *terza rima* of the fragment on Obizzo d'Este had led nowhere.

The boy is to be taught Greek and goodness. The poet does not regard himself as equipped to teach either, but he knows their worth (16–18):

> Dottrina abbia e bontà, ma principale

[27] Although not wholly by Petrarch in the *Africa*: cf. *Fortuna volubilis*, VII. 324; *instabilem . . . rotam*, 328.

[28] Cf. Lucilius' ideal of the *sermo*, still valid for Castiglione's *Il cortegiano* and even for Racine's tragedies.

[29] Muscetta–Lamberti, *op. cit.*, pp. 1469–77.

[30] No. XXXII, *Guido, vorrei che tu e Lapo ed io. . . .* Dante's escapism contrasts paradoxically with Ariosto's seriousness.

sia la bontà: che, non vi essendo questa,
né molto quella alla mia estima vale.

Let him have learning and goodness, but goodness is to take first
place. Without that, the former has not much value in my scale.

Considerations about virtue naturally lead the poet into some reflections on the vices of his time, particularly homosexuality.[31] The attack
is not made for its own sake. It flows quite logically from a father's
anxieties about what may happen to his son at the hands of unscru-
pulous teachers. The *terza rima* takes on Dantesque overtones of a
more audible kind. They echo round one of the earliest attested
usages of the term *umanista* (22–33):[32]

> O nostra male aventurosa etade,
> che le virtudi che non abbian misti
> vici nefandi si ritrovin rade!
>     Senza quel vizio son pochi umanisti
> che fe' a Dio forza, non che persüase,
> di far Gomorra e i suoi vicini tristi:
>     mandò fuoco da ciel, ch'uomini e case
> tutto consumpse; et ebbe tempe a pena
> Lot a fugir, ma la moglier rimase.
>     Ride il volgo, se sente un ch'abbia vena
> di poesia, e poi dice:—È gran periglio
> a dormir seco e volgierli la schiena.

Alas for our misguided times! How rare are the virtues without
admixture of unspeakable vices! Few humanists are without that vice
which compelled God, not persuaded Him, to punish Gomorrah and
its neighbors. He sent fire from heaven which burned men, houses,
everything. Lot had scarcely time to flee, though his wife remained
behind. The crowd smiles if it hears that a man has a vein of poetry,
and then says: "There is a big risk in sleeping with him and turning
your back!"

This passage is an excellent illustration of Ariosto's irony. It cannot
be supposed that the poet did not take seriously his desire for his
son to have the best possible moral training. But his indignation over
the corrupters of youthful morals still permits him to refer to the
story of Lot's wife in such allusive language that the reader cannot
resist a smile. Yet the smile is misplaced (*ride il volgo*). A popular

[31] E. R. Curtius, *Europäische Literatur und lateinisches Mittelalter*, pp. 121 ff. Again,
one cannot help thinking of Dante (*Inferno* XV).

[32] Cf. A. Campana, "The origin of the word 'humanist'," *Journal of the Warburg
and Courtauld Institutes* 9 (1946), 60–73; D. J. Geanakoplos, *Greek Scholars in Venice*
(Cambridge, Mass. 1962), p. 19 and note 18; R. Pfeiffer, *History of Classical Scholarship*,
*1300–1850*, p. 17 note 2. Evidently for Ariosto "humanist" and "poet" are one.

saying about the ways of poets cannot obscure the underlying earnestness of the whole passage.

This moral concern is emphasized when the poet goes on to mention the heresies of his own time, with which he does not wish his son to become tainted. There is the Averroist refusal to accept the doctrine of the Trinity. Some are moved to doubts merely by the desire to appear original. If Luther errs, there is an excuse for him in the confusions that attend any effort to penetrate too far into the Divine Mysteries. The absence of religious partisanship in a satire addressed to the Secretary of Leo X is amazing. But the humanist and poet can have no such excuses. His themes are the woods and hills, streams, the deeds of old, the softening of harsh minds, the false flattery of princes. How then can he justify an unorthodox theology?

Some poets take their desire to be different to other extremes. They alter their names to make them more like Latin. They forget that what will make them poets is study of many years' duration.[33] They are the sort of poet that Plato excluded from his Republic. Amusingly, here Plato has been enrolled on Callimachus' side.

Ariosto contrasts with these irresponsible practitioners of his art the ancient founders of poetry (70–75):

> ma non fu tal già Febo, né Anfione,
> né gli altri che trovaro i primi versi,
> che col buon stile, e piú con l'opre buone,
> persuasero agli uomini a doversi
> ridurre insieme, e abandonar le giande
> che per le selve li traean dispersi.

Not such a one was Phoebus of old, nor Amphion, nor the others who invented the first verses, who with their good style, and more with their good works, persuaded men that they should come together, and abandon the acorns that kept them scattered throughout the forests.

This civilizing influence exercised by the early poets led to their being credited by the *indotta plebe* (82) with the ability to build cities, or to draw tigers and lions from their lairs. It is clear that Ariosto is thinking directly of that key passage in Horace's *Ars Poetica* (391 ff.) which was earlier noted as of basic importance to the understanding of the Augustan vatic ideal.[34] In it Horace had offered a noble portrait of the past for imitation by Roman writers of the present, following the precedent set by Augustus.

---

[33] Horace's similar contempt for poetic humbug may be compared: *A. P.* 295 ff., 453 ff.; *Epp.* II. 2. 90 ff.

[34] Above, pp. 55, 192.

This is a striking proof of the closeness of the satiric and vatic *personae*. No doubt there is nothing strange in the echoing by a Renaissance poet of a classical predecessor. But to echo this passage in a *satira* not destined for publication, and where the looseness of the genre dictated no one particular mold for thoughts rather than another: this surely demonstrates Ariosto's firm grasp of the epic tradition of which we have spoken, and the error of those who regard the buffoon as *merely* a buffoon.

In lines of biting contempt, the poet goes on to insist that writers like himself have to accept higher moral standards than those of other men.[35] Let judge Cusatro give unjust verdicts, and doctor Battista mix poison in his potions. It matters less than the moral failings of poets like Pandaro, Curio, Pontico or Flavio, the blasphemer. Here, the serio-comic picture of the *vates* painted by Horace in his *Letter to Augustus* is really modified towards the serious!

Ariosto turns back to the question of his son's education. He is to study Greek literature in the original, beginning with the *Iliad* and the *Odyssey*. "Longinus" had depreciated the *Odyssey*. Ariosto sees these two epics as the story of one man (134–35):

> ciò che Ulisse
> sofferse a Troia e poi nel lungo errore.

All that Ulysses endured at Troy, and then on his long wanderings.

Next are to come Apollonius and Euripides, Sophocles, Hesiod, Theocritus, Pindar (136 ff.). The list is one which might be prescribed for any budding poet in the Alexandrian tradition. There is, for example, no mention of Aeschylus, though here one might have expected classicizing influence to have made itself apparent in a topical catalogue of the great.[36] The boy is already acquainted with Latin writers. This list too is instructive: Virgil, Terence (telling

---

[35] Cf. Horace, *A. P.* 330 ff.; *Epp.* II. 1. 119 ff.

[36] Horace, for example, mentions Aeschylus in the context of the history of the drama and style: *A. P.* 279; cf. *Epp.* II. 1. 163.—It is interesting that Ariosto speaks of Hesiod as having "bitten" (*morse*) the laurel. Hesiod makes no such claim in the relevant passage of the *Theogony* (see M. West's note to line 31), but the Greek scholia to line 30 paraphrase his text in this sense, and the story is repeated, for example, (as West remarks) by the Byzantine statesman and scholar Nicephorus Choumnos (1250?–1327) in his treatise on style. Full information about this author is given by J. Verpeaux, *Nicéphore Choumnos* (Paris 1959). But where did Ariosto, who says he knew no Greek, get this information? He could have been thinking of Juvenal 7. 19 (*laurumque momordit*: see J. B. Mayor's note), though there the reference is not specifically to Hesiod at all, or even of Tibullus II. 5. 63–64 (though there the allusion is to the Sibyl). But that would be a remarkable coincidence.

collocation!),[37] Ovid, Horace, Plautus. In assessing its significance, we should remember Ariosto's own composition of comedies (rather than tragedies) for his patrons.

Ariosto regrets that he has neither the energy nor the good fortune to be able to open the temple of Apollo on Delos to his son, as he has been able to open that on the Palatine at Rome. When he himself was younger, he was forced by his father to give up valuable years to the study of law. When eventually he was lucky enough to find a Greek teacher, he was too busy with the study of Latin to take real advantage of the opportunity. He points out that, for an Italian, the study of Latin has to take priority. This at least, especially in its appreciation of the importance of the Palatine Apollo, shows a devotion to and understanding of the tradition in its deepest sense.

The poem concludes with an account of the poet's various misfortunes, especially after the death of his father had left him responsible for the welfare of a large family, in the chequered circumstances of the Italy of his day. It is for these reasons that he is asking Bembo to look after his son's education, so that the boy may have safe guidance to the Parnassus which his father could not reach in time.

If this satire had been written in Augustan Rome, it could only have had one author, Horace (though of course the real Horace had no son). It would be known as one of the most delightful of the master's works. The similarities between the two poets are extraordinary. There is Horace's moral concern, and cool ability to look the facts of secular life in the face. There is the Horatian sense of proportion which avoids the too facile tone of scorn for everyone else, and the assumption that the satirist is the only good man in a world of villains. There is a keen appreciation of the poetic vocation, interpreted in vatic terms as calling for higher standards of morals and greater idealism than are demanded from others.

There is, underlying all this, the instinctive acceptance of the Alexandrian system of poetic beliefs, inspired by the same humility which makes the poet avoid lingering over the shortcomings of his contemporaries. For literary, humanist education, the appeal of straight, eulogistic, pseudo-Homeric epic is dead. If we may interpret Ariosto's prescriptions for his son as expressive of his own deepest literary—and more than literary—beliefs,[38] we may deduce that the modern writer will turn for sustenance and example to comedy, to Apollonius,

---

[37] The references to Virgil and Terence in Racine's Première Préface to *Britannicus* may be compared.

[38] Cf. Horace, *Epp.* II. 2. 65 ff. The autobiographical element in this satire justifies the extension to the poet himself of the prescriptions he offers for the education of his son.

to others whose kinship with and relevance to epic are far from obvious except in the light of an Alexandrian analysis. He is aware all the time that he is really inadequate to his job, because of the distracting political and social circumstances of his life. He refuses for all that to surrender or compromise his vocation by yielding to the temptation to take up law, and law's rewards.

What kind of epic, in the event, had such a poet written? Hardly anything straightforward, as the puzzled efforts to find his exact niche in the literature of the Cinquecento indicate. The paradoxical situation has arisen that, when the *Orlando Furioso* was highly regarded by numerous readers throughout Europe, the critics were not at all sure what to make of it: and now that its popularity, certainly among all except specialists, has faded, it is seen to have been among the greatest masterpieces of epic humanism.[39]

Here we must content ourselves with trying to note the poet's revivification of the tradition which, in the exaggerated fantasy of Boiardo, seemed to have lost all contact with genuine human experience. This is Ariosto's proem (I. 1–2):

> Le donne, i cavallier, l'arme, gli amori,
> le cortesie, l'audaci imprese io canto,
> che fûro al tempo che passaro i Mori
> d'Africa il mare, e in Francia nocquer tanto,
> seguendo l'ire e i giovenil furori
> d'Agramante lor re, che si diè vanto
> di vendicar la morte di Troiano
> sopra re Carlo, imperator romano.
>
> Dirò d'Orlando in un medesmo tratto
> cosa non detta in prosa mai né in rima:
> che per amor venne in furore e matto,
> d'uom che sí saggio era stimato prima;
> se da colei che tal quasi m'ha fatto,
> che 'l poco ingegno ad or ad or mi lima,
> me ne sarà però tanto concesso,
> che mi basti a finir quanto ho promesso.

Ladies, knights, arms, loves, courtesies, bold emprises are my song: things which were at the time when the Moors crossed the sea from Africa and did so much harm in France, following the anger and the

---

[39] Muscetta's introduction to his joint edition with Lamberti (above, note 19) offers particularly stimulating criticism, notably his remarks on Ariosto as musician and film-maker (p. XVIII). A. Borlenghi, *Storia della critica, 9, Ariosto* (Palermo 1961), presents a history of what critics have said about the poem along with an anthology of extracts from their works. See also *Ariosto 1974 in America* (Ravenna 1976), ed. Aldo Scaglione. G. Toffanin, *Storia letteraria d'Italia—Il Cinquecento* (7th ed., Milan 1965), seems to find Ariosto rather more congenial than the devout Tasso.

youthful frenzies of their king Agramante, who boasted of avenging the death of Troiano on King Charlemagne, emperor of Rome. In the same breath I shall tell of Orlando something never yet said in prose or rhyme. For love he became frenzied and mad, after being looked on as so wise before. (All this I shall sing) if by her who has made me almost like him, who files my poor talent all the time, just so much is granted as may suffice me to fulfill my promise.

How it expresses its intentions is of the first importance. It begins with a triple alternation: ladies, knights; arms, loves; courtesies, emprises. The double chiasmus[40] gives priority to the feminine. These things "were at the time when the Moors crossed the sea from Africa and did so much harm to France." The combination of simple vocabulary with rhetorical arrangement removes us quite far from the theory of the *vulgare illustre*, abandoned even by its author, Dante.[41] So little could even the criticism of novice genius illumine the real classical epic tradition. But Ariosto does not lack a certain epic grandeur. The harsh music of his lines, in which the *littera canina* is much in evidence, culminates in the crescendo of *re Carlo, imperator romano*.[42]

The second stanza continues the deliberate simplicity of language, which stands at the opposite remove from Horace's early call for the *os magna sonaturum* in the epic poet, whose scattered remnants would still, as in the case of Ennius, attest their original elevation.[43] Horace himself abandoned this position. In Ariosto's proem, *tratto*, for example, is a strangely lame word to occur in this atmosphere of high romance, yet here it is emphasized by being used as a rhyme. *Che per amor venne in furore e matto* forces the meaning of a common verb.[44] Alternately singing and speaking (*canto/dirò*) the poet places himself even here distantly in the succession of Callimachus.[45]

The choice of a mad hero for an epic has caused surprise. Is this

---

[40] Pindar too makes free use of these rhetorical tricks, combining similarity with variation in a dazzling display of verbal virtuosity. Double chiasmus is found, for example, at *Olympian* 2. 9–10; 4. 14–16. A general appreciation is offered by F. Dornseiff, *Pindars Stil*, pp. 115 ff.

[41] Above, pp. 261–65. Ariosto prefers Horace's *callida iunctura* (*A. P.* 47–48).

[42] Compare Propertius' *vix timeat salvo Caesare Roma Iovem* (III. 11. 66).

[43] *Sat.* I. 4. 43–44. That Horace is here touching upon a vexed question is seen from his contemporary Dionysius of Halicarnassus, who takes exactly the opposite view (*De. Comp.* 26), a view to which Horace was later converted when he wrote the *Odes*. See above, p. 147.

[44] *Venne* is used in zeugma: cf. Dornseiff, *Pindars Stil*, p. 106.

[45] The confusion of *dico* and *cano* by the Latin poets is discussed in my article in *Latinitas* XIII (1965), 86–106. In Greek, Callimachus had written εἶπαν . . . μέλος at *Hymns* IV. 257: εἶπον at fr. 75. 43 Pf. (conjecturally restored). The scholia to Apollonius, *Argonautica* II. 528–29a (Wendel, p. 172), gloss ὑδέονται by ᾄδονται, λέγονται.

another example of that quirky whimsicality that marks the epic of the Cinquecento as something dated, idiosyncratic? But Aristotle himself attributed the comic *Margites*—"The Madman"—to Homer, and at least one Renaissance critic saw that Orlando's amatory frenzy is only quantitatively different from Achilles' pique over Briseis.[46] Madness in fact has been a feature of the heroes of many works which would not at all be regarded as too quirky or too whimsical to survive. The challenge offered by the hero to conventional values, growing sharper as the conventional become more articulate, must make him seem "mad." Even Christ endured this reproach.[47] He has indeed been depicted by artists of our day as a clown.

It is in this choice of hero that Ariosto's epic genius is most apparent. The madman is least trammeled in his response to what he perceives as the real world, least likely to muffle his senses and sensibilities out of narrow calculation or concern for the (to him) unreal world of others. The *furor* of the *Aeneid*, which at the last grips even Aeneas in its fires, is the negative aspect of this terrifying and apocalyptic vision, and another proof of its propriety as a classical theme. The final confrontation is with our own safe and cozy cages. Will we too find the courage to break open their bars, and to face the shadows?

Ariosto's irony forbids extremes. Suavely he professes to be little better than his hero, and in both cases the cause is the same—love.

The language at this point is not entirely clear. How does the poet's mistress "file" his small talent? Commentators understand that she files it away, exhausts it. But it can hardly be forgotten, in so Horatian a poet, that *limae labor et mora* ("the lingering labor of the file," *A. P.* 291) is one of Horace's *positive* ideals.[48] The inspiration that even an epic poet derives from love, the acknowledgment of the small talent he brings to his task and, more important, the ambiguity which he does not scruple to allow even in the proem to his whole work, where organ notes of ambition should swell to a harmonious crescendo: all these tokens point once more to the presence of the Alexandrian qualification.

The poet turns to his patron (I. 3. 1–4):

> Piacciavi, generosa Erculea prole,

---

[46] G. Malatesta notes that Achilles and Odysseus were not perfect heroes: Weinberg, p. 1064; cf. L. Salviati, p. 1018.

[47] NT Mark 3:21; John 10:20.

[48] Arnaut Daniel uses the same word: *Qan n'aurai passat la lima*; and the same appeal to his mistress: above, p. 265. It is another proof of the longevity of these Alexandrian ideals. See further F. Diez, *Die Poesie der Troubadours* (Zwickau 1826), pp. 36–37.

ornamento e splendor del secol nostro,
Ippolito, aggradir questo che vuole
e darvi sol può l'umil servo vostro.

May it please you, noble son of Hercules, ornament and light of our age, Ippolito, to accept what your humble servant wishes to give, and alone can give to you.

The humility has no doubt something of the conventional in it. But it is on a par too with a genuine feeling of incapacity already visible in the poet's attitude. Virgil had spoken of his sense of inadequacy in the *Georgics*, not in the *Aeneid*. This return (which however is far less of a return than is to be seen in Tasso) to the Alexandrian springboard from which Virgil had jumped into the larger world of heroic and national myth must be important in assessing what Ariosto judged to be the epic possibilities, and the nature of the epic tradition.[49]

Ariosto shares something with Lucan which separates him from both Virgil and Homer, and that is his failure to invoke any of the customary Muses. Instead, Lucan had turned to Nero. Ariosto substitutes his mistress, rather as Callimachus had turned to queen Berenice. But the Muses still occupied a powerful place in the conventional apparatus.[50] The deviation from the norm then must be regarded as something significant. They show how much the epic we are to hear is modified, set in parenthesis, by the poet's awareness of the immensity of the challenge.

Cardinal d'Este is asked to listen to the poet's song, because in it he will hear of Ruggiero, the ancient head of his family (I. 4. 5–8):

L'alto valore e' chiari gesti suoi
vi farò udir, se voi mi date orecchio,
e vostri alti pensier cedino un poco,
sí che tra lor miei versi abbiano loco.

His high valor and famous deeds I shall make you hear, if you lend me your ears, and if your lofty thoughts yield a little, so that among them my verses may find a place.

Here, the poet is doing something deeply Alexandrian, and that is civilizing his material. Traditionally, not even the character of Charlemagne himself had been exempt from a certain coarseness.[51] Looking for ideals of behavior in a precarious world that owes its existence

---

[49] Above, pp. 129 ff., on the exordium to Book III of the *Georgics*.

[50] Curtius, *op. cit.*, pp. 233 ff. Ariosto follows Boccaccio: above, p. 295.

[51] Curtius, p. 431. On Boccaccio's *Teseida* I. 57, Limentani notes a similar popular exaggeration in the character of Theseus. So with Philopappos in the epic of Digenis Akritas.

to his own fancy, Ariosto repeats the wistful "if only" which certainly marks the romantic, but is also found on the lips of Virgil himself.[52] The story begins. Orlando has returned from his travels in India, Persia, Tartary. The bacchic theme had already been associated in antiquity with Alexander the Great. He finds Charlemagne ready to teach the kings of Spain and Morocco a lesson for their attack on the fair realm of France ("to make them smite their own faces for their foolish bravado": the calque here of the Latin prose idiom *frontem percutere* is extraordinary in the opening stanzas of an epic). The poet comments (I. 6. 7–8):

> E cosí Orlando arrivò quivi a punto:
> ma tosto si pentí d'esservi giunto.

And so Orlando arrived here just at the right time. But soon he was sorry for coming.

In such a way does he prick the balloon inflated by the expectations he has led us to form.

The reason for Orlando's early regrets about his return is that he loses among friends the lady he has been able to guard among enemies. The whole trouble has been caused by the wise emperor, seeking to put out a damaging fire. We regress to find out what this fire has been. A quarrel had broken out a few days before between Orlando and his cousin Rinaldo, equally smitten by Angelica's beauty. Charlemagne therefore had removed her to the safe-keeping, as he hoped, of the duke of Bavera, and promised that she would be restored to whichever of the two heroes slew more of the enemy in the impending battle. Unhappily, in the course of the battle, the duke of Bavera was worsted and taken prisoner. Angelica, presaging defeat for the Christians, took to flight and entered a wood. Here, she finds a knight coming towards her on foot. It is Rinaldo. She takes to flight again, only to encounter another warrior, Ferraú, a Moor, who has withdrawn from the battle to rest. While Ferraú and Rinaldo fight it out for her hand, she makes off yet again.

Meanwhile, neither of the two champions is able to prevail over the other. Eventually, Rinaldo points out the folly of their continuing to duel when in actual fact neither of them may ever see Angelica again. His opponent in convinced by the argument, and they decide to chase her together. As Rinaldo has lost his own mount, Ferraú

---

[52] Virgil too creates the ideal he is looking for: E. Fraenkel on the end of *Aeneid* VIII, *Kleine Beiträge* (Rome 1964), II, pp. 224–25. The minor key heard in *Eclogue* 4 is an early version of this epic romanticism. "Civilizing" material is an extension of what the ancient commentators describe more prosaically as the avoidance of *tapeinosis*: above, p. 139 and E. Norden's edition of *Aeneid* VI, p. 115 note 1.

takes him onto his horse. At this, Ariosto interrupts his narrative to reflect on the chivalry of the knights of old (I. 22):

> Oh gran bontà de' cavallieri antiqui!
> Eran rivali, eran di fé diversi,
> e si sentian degli aspri colpi iniqui
> per tutta la persona anco dolersi;
> e pur per selve oscure e calli obliqui
> insieme van senza sospetto aversi.[53]
> Da quattro sproni il destrier punto arriva
> ove una strada in due si dispartiva.

Oh the great goodness of those old knights! They were rivals, they were different in their faiths, and each was still smarting all over from the shrewd blows of his opponent: and yet through dark woods and winding paths together they go, without suspicion (back to back?). Pricked by four spurs their steed arrives at a fork in the road.

What can this apostrophe mean? It will not do to make Ariosto merely concerned to poke fun at the naiveté of the knights of old, or at the stories told about them. The poet had enough humanity and realism to know that sympathy between foes, especially between adherents of different religions, was not something to be sneered at in an age when the Reformation was about to tear Europe in pieces. But on the other hand, the humor of the passage, increased if *aversi* implies that they rode the horse back to back, which would certainly give more force to *senza sospetto*, cannot be overlooked either. What we are being asked to do is hold both the serious and the witty intent in our minds at the same time, without letting the one drown out the other. It was exactly what Callimachus had demanded from the audience of the *Hecale*, and what Virgil, in graver tones, had urged about the uncertain ideals of the Augustan age.

To put Ariosto into the classical (which means serio-comic) epic tradition in this way is to discover that a great deal of the debate which has been waged over him loses substance. Is the poet simply concerned to present us with the magical evocation of a vanished world, on which he lavishes all the arts of music and painting, to provide a contrast with the hated reality of everyday? The description is inadequate to the totality of his achievement, and unfair to aspects of the carnival pageantry he knew in contemporary Ferrara. It was from such limitations that Virgil had struggled to free himself right from the days of the *Eclogues* (and Ariosto's own *egloga* of 1505 had masked and confronted serious present concerns). Was he therefore

---

[53] *Aversi* may of course be a reflexive infinitive. But, in so classical an author, can an allusion to the Latin *aversus* be excluded? Cf. Ovid, *Fasti* I. 550, *traxerat aversos* [sc. *boves*] *Cacus in antra*: "Cacus had dragged the oxen by their tails into his cave."

judging that old and vanished world by the standards of the sophisticated present, and holding it up to ridicule and contempt? That would be a silly theme for an epic poet, and its silliness is seen when we recollect just how serious a man the *Satire* showed Ariosto to be. The trouble with both judgments of the poem is that they force us into the dilemma of either/or. The poet himself does not want anything to do with these absolutes. His poetry is able to explore the possibilities of both humor and gravity in its *spoudogeloion*, to fuse them both into an amalgam of art where analysis yields to delight.

Yet such an epic is also "humanist." It is not irresponsibly inimical to moral values, a sublime, geometrical play with abstract patterns which goes on, indifferent to the passing show on earth. Because the poet is not wholly committed to either of the poles which bound his vision of mankind, he can use one to demonstrate the shortcomings of the other. In our particular passage, the *gran bontà* implies a critique of modern *cavallieri*, who know nothing of such generosity.[54] But we would not want to be ancient *cavallieri* for all that. They belong to a world which has vanished, and which it would be futile to try to resurrect. The moral dilemma presented to the reader resembles once more (within its limitations) that presented by Virgil. An epic poetry however which does raise that kind of question is worthy of its name, and this is why, in order to recover Ariosto's claim to be more than an entertainer, it is necessary to understand why clowns and kings have the same horoscopes.

As the story unfolds, a recurrent sameness in the action is observed. The premise is that Angelica's charms are so great that any extravagance is justified by the hope of gaining her favors. Meanwhile, the possibility that any one of her suitors may prevail is removed by her indifference and their mutual rivalries. Common sense may well enquire what such dedicated coyness has to do with the real facts of the relationships between the sexes. Ariosto is well aware of the real facts, and equally aware of human inability to face them. This is hardly a naive romanticism.

"Action" indeed, in the sense of rational progress towards a defined goal, is the last thing which the poem offers. In the canto quoted, Rinaldo and Ferraú, having boldly ridden off together, arrive in no time at a parting of the ways. Here they part themselves, and Ferraú, although as the one with the horse he might be expected to make the greater headway, presently finds himself back where he began. He continues to search for his lost helmet, and is confronted by the specter of a knight rising from the water, holding the very object for which he is looking. It is Angelica's brother, Argalia, whom Ferraú

<hr>

[54] Cf. Ariosto's remarks at the opening of Book XVII, 1–5.

had slain, and to whom he had promised burial in the river with all his armor, excepting his helmet, which the conqueror would borrrow for four days. The four days have long ago gone by and Argalia has now seized for himself the forfeited helmet.

Ferraú is mortified to be reminded of his forgotten pledge. He has no excuse. To extricate himself from his embarrassment, he swears to find another helmet, the one Orlando has taken from Almontes, brother of the Moorish king Troiano. So Ferraú sets off on another quest, this time to find Orlando. We are not to hear of him again until Book XII, when he does in fact acquire Orlando's helmet by default, though his acquisition does him no good at all.

Meanwhile, Rinaldo is wandering alone on foot. His horse crosses his path, but refuses to halt at his master's call. With both heroes engaged in the search for an elusive prize, the poet turns abruptly to Angelica. She is running away, the action being emphasized by the repetition of the verb *fugge*. Her flight is inspired by terror of being overtaken by Rinaldo, though what she fears from him is not entirely clear. The description calls out all the poet's virtuosity (I. 33, 34, 35):

> Fugge tra selve spaventose e scure,
> per lochi inabitati, ermi e selvaggi.
> Il mover de le frondi e di verzure,
> che di cerri sentia, d'olmi e di faggi,
> fatto le avea con subite paure
> trovar di qua di là strani vïaggi;
> ch'ad ogni ombra veduta o in monte o in valle,
> temea Rinaldo aver sempre alle spalle.

> Qual pargoletta o damma o capriuola,
> che tra le fronde del natio boschetto
> alla madre veduta abbia la gola
> stringer dal pardo, o aprirle 'l fianco o 'l petto,
> di selva in selva dal crudel s'invola,
> e di paura triema e di sospetto:
> ad ogni sterpo che passando tocca,
> esser si crede all'empia fera in bocca.

> Quel dí e la notte e mezzo l'altro giorno
> s'andò aggirando, e non sapeva dove:
> trovossi al fine in un boschetto adorno,
> che lievemente la fresca aura muove.
> Duo chiari rivi, mormorando intorno,
> sempre l'erbe vi fan tenere e nuove;
> e rendea ad ascoltar dolce concento,
> rotto tra picciol sassi, il correr lento.

'She flees through forests fearful and dark, through regions, empty, deserted and wild. The movement of the leaves and greenery which she kept hearing from oaks, elms and beeches had made her in sudden alarm find here and there strange paths. For at every shade seen on hillside or in valley she always feared to have Rinaldo at her back.

Like a tiny fawn, or kid, which among the leaves of its native copse has seen its mother's throat squeezed by the leopard or her flank or breast opened, and from wood to wood flies away from the cruel aggressor, trembling with fear and suspicion; with every stump that it touches in passing it thinks it is in the jaws of the merciless beast.

That day and night and half the next day she went in circles without knowing where; finally she found herself in a pretty copse stirred gently by the fresh breeze. Two clear streams, babbling around, always there keep the grasses tender and fresh: and their slow current, broken by little pebbles, made a harmony sweet to hear.

The triptych presents two outer pictures in contrast, that of the dark and fearful forests with which it begins, and that of the delightful copse with its babbling streams with which it ends. But Angelica is not really in two different places. It is the same wood, seen under two different aspects. The poet hints as much when he uses *boschetto* in the central comparison, and in the final stanza again, when Angelica has reached, as she hopes, safety. Actually, we know that while the poem is in progress she is in exactly the same position as before, still liable to be surprised by unknown knights, and she is of course to be overtaken by Rinaldo after all.

It is the central comparison which must control the interpretation of the whole, and prevent any simple equation of Ariosto's landscapes with the mere exploitation of a cliché.[55] The *subita paura* of the first stanza, the *paura* and *sospetto* of the second, show that what looks like action in the sense of physical movement from one place to another is really mental agitation. Angelica does not know where she is wandering, and the poet explains that she was moving in circles (*aggirando*).

Can we take her fears seriously? Superficially, they call for our sympathy. The charming picture of the little fawn or kid is bound to stir protective feelings. But is Angelica a little fawn, or a grown woman? Classical poetry, starting with the komic and sympotic Anacreon, uses that kind of metaphor so often for a girl who is reluctant to face the problem of her own sexuality that, on a deeper reading, we cannot suppose Ariosto's comparison to be entirely flattering. What has frightened this fawn? She has seen her mother's throat squeezed by the leopard, or with her flank or breast opened. The

[55] E. R. Curtius, *op. cit.*, pp. 205 ff.

sexual symbolism is unmistakable. Angelica is afraid of repeating the inevitable pattern of mature femininity.

Horace, with whom Ariosto has such affinities, had explored the same metaphor to the same end (*Odes* I. 23):

Vitas inuleo me similis, Chloe,
quaerenti pavidam montibus aviis
    matrem non sine vano
        aurarum et siluae metu.

nam seu mobilibus veris inhorruit
adventus foliis seu virides rubum
    dimovere lacertae,
        et corde et genibus tremit.

atqui non ego te tigris ut aspera
Gaetulusve leo frangere persequor:
    tandem desine matrem
        tempestiva sequi viro.

You run away from me, Chloe, just like a fawn seeking its fearful mother on the trackless hillsides, filled with empty fear of the breezes and forests. For whether the presage of spring has rustled on the shifting leaves, or green lizards have parted the thorns, it trembles in heart and limbs. Yet I am not pursuing you like a savage tiger or African lion, to break you! At long last stop clinging to your mother, now that you are ripe for a man!

Just as his young fawn was terrified by what was, after all, only the whisper of spring on the leaves, or blaze of green lizards,[56] and had to be reminded that she was not being pursued by a savage tiger or desert lion, so Angelica, we may conclude, is living in a fantasy world, in which the forest reflects her changing moods, and where, by a nervous prolongation of adolescence, the sexual act becomes the tearing of a leopard at her mother. It is this refusal to face reality which explains those interminable wanderings she knows not where.

We can now see why Angelica arrives at the kind of haven she does. It is *adorno*: none of the messy and bloody realism from which she has been running. The fresh breeze moves it gently: no wild tempests of uncontrollable passion. It has two clear streams, that is, two undecided possibilities, whose limpid irresolution is preferable to any muddy commitment. Its grass is always tender and new: no fading of the flower of youth or bloom of maidenhood. There is

---

[56] The sexual symbolism of the advent of spring in this ode is made more explicit by Lucretius, I. 10 ff. Botticelli's *La Primavera* inevitably comes to mind. The Greek *saura* (lizard) is used *sens. obsc.* by Strato: *Anth. Pal.* XII. 3 and 242. Compare J. R. R. Tolkien's "Sauron."

sweet harmony (muzak!). Even the rocks are tiny. The waters run slowly, just like the absence of purposeful movement in her own life. In this delightful grove, Angelica finds flowering thorns and scarlet roses. She also finds a bed (*letto*, 38. 1), happily one hidden from prying eyes. But soon she is disturbed by the arrival of yet another knight. He turns out to be her old suitor and lover, Sacripante, king of Circassia. He has followed her to the west from his distant home and, not knowing how close his beloved is, he halts to muse distractedly on his miserable plight.

This scene too is more complex than it appears. At first, it looks as if there is nothing more than gentle irony. Sacripante lingers over an hour, as if he were turned to stone, lost in his thoughts. He is slowed down by his inability to face the facts of his situation in just the same fashion as Angelica. At length, he breaks out into a soliloquy. He laments in so soft and sweet a tone that he would have bred pity in a tiger (40. 5). He makes of Angelica therefore exactly what she makes of potential husbands. His and her illusion is the same.

After commenting on the fruitlessness of his pangs, the king continues his meditation (I. 42, 43):

> La verginella è simile alla rosa,
> ch'in bel giardin su la native spina
> mentre sola e sicura si riposa,
> né gregge né pastor se le avicina;
> l'aura soave e l'alba rugiadosa,
> l'acqua, la terra al suo favor s'inchina:
> gioveni vaghi e donne inamorate
> amano averne e seni e tempie ornate.

> Ma non sí tosto dal materno stelo
> rimossa viene, e dal suo ceppo verde,
> che quanto avea dagli uomini e dal cielo
> favor, grazia e bellezza, tutto perde.
> La vergine che 'l fior, di che piú zelo
> che de' begli occhi e de la vita aver de',
> lascia altrui côrre, il pregio ch'avea inanti
> perde nel cor di tutti gli altri amanti.

The virgin is like the rose. While in fair garden on its native stock it rests alone and safe neither flock nor shepherd approaches it: the sweet breeze and the dewy dawn, the rain, the earth—all these bend beneath its sway. Fond youths and ladies in love like to have their breasts and brows adorned by it.

But not so as soon as it is plucked from its mothering stem, and from its green stock. All the favor it had from men and from heaven, all the grace and beauty, it loses. The maiden, who allows others to pluck that flower which she should guard more jealously than her eyes and life, loses the value she had before in the heart of all her other lovers.

Sacripante does not set a very good example of believing his own theory, that a girl who has lost her virginity loses with it her attractiveness to other men, as his tormented remarks go on to reveal. It has not escaped commentators that we have in the king's reflections a very beautiful imitation of a Catullan marriage-song. But, given the ironic relationship developed by the Callimachean epic time and again to material borrowed in this way, we must further ask: how does the adaptation compare with the original? In Catullus, the passage forms part of song and countersong performed by two groups, one of youths, the other of maidens, who are waiting at an evening marriage feast for the appearance of the bride. The girls give expression to the bride's natural hesitancy and shyness. The young men rejoin by pointing out that a girl needs a husband, if ever she is to reach full maturity.

The amusing and telling thing here is that the part of the poem that Sacripante quotes is sung by the girls,[57] and describes their reluctance to face the commitment to marriage. In his jealousy of an assumed rival's possible success, the king prefers to see Angelica remain in virginal barrenness. Contributing to the artificiality of the poem's convention, that the loss of virginity is the *summum malum*, he is converted wholly to the feminine point of view.

The cross-reference between this passage and its predecessor about Angelica's flight is helped by the circumstances. The reader is aware that, though the king thinks he is alone, Angelica is eavesdropping on him.[58] It is helped too by the simile of the rose, which reminds us of the flowers by Angelica's bed. But this literary art is more than pretty. Recalling Catullus, and a healthier Roman attitude to the realities of love and marriage, Ariosto implies just how unreal his hero and heroine are. The use of a classical model as a background against which alone the full meaning of a later "imitation" is brought

---

[57] Catullus 62. 39 ff.

[58] Eavesdropping is a good example of the *dénudation du procédé*, since what else are the spectators/congregation doing at ritual performances? So ancient a device is bound to be ambivalent. It is exploited tragically by Aeschylus in the *Choephoroe*, and by Virgil in Books II and III of the *Aeneid* (pp. 168, 176, above): comically by Ovid, *Amores* I. 8. 22; Molière, *Le Tartuffe*, Act III, scenes 2 and 3, Act IV, scene 5; Sheridan, *School for Scandal*, Act IV, scene 3: tragicomically by Shakespeare in the bedroom scene in *Hamlet*, and by Racine in *Britannicus*, where Néron listens to Junie and her lover (II. 6). Fielding, whose *Tom Jones* shows affinities with Ariosto, deliberately associates Square's eavesdropping with that of Polonius: "behind the arras," *Tom Jones* (Everyman edition, London–New York 1962), I, p. 170.

out is exactly the technique illustrated by the relationship of Virgil and Callimachus to Homer.

Angelica, deciding that she needs Sacripante's help, reveals her presence. She has no genuine consideration for him. She knew, the poet remarks, that he was kind and true above all other lovers. Nevertheless, her intention is to use him merely for the moment. Then she can return to her harsh wantonness again.

Her sudden appearance is like that of Diana or Venus on a stage (*scena*, 52. 4). As she emerges, she bids Sacripante "Peace be with you." Here, the irony again depends on a "learned" background. The most familiar appearances of Diana and Venus on a *scena* were in Book I of the *Aeneid*. After Aeneas has landed in Africa, Virgil gives a description of the harbor (*Aen.* I. 164–65):

> tum silvis scaena coruscis
> Desuper, horrentique atrum nemus imminet umbra.

Above was a backdrop of shimmering trees, a dark wood overhanging with bristling shade.

It is on this stage, against this backdrop, that he meets in due course both his mother Venus, disguised as a huntress, and Dido, specifically compared to Diana (and even to Diana armed with a quiver). The powerful symbolism of these Virgilian images is intended to emphasize both the cruelty and the elusiveness of love. The artificiality of carnival art (*scaena/scena*) does not prevent its referring to some grim truths, nor from reinforcing its meaning in either case by clear allusion to an established tradition. Boccaccio, with his huntress Emilia, had already understood this.[59]

When Angelica emerges with these associations clinging to her and then remarks "Pace sia teco"—it was the greeting used by the clergy exchanging the kiss of peace at Mass, or that of Christ suddenly piercing the walls of the Upper Room—the irony is devastating.

Sacripante is already so dominated by the female point of view (an Alexandrian failing, but surely curious in an epic hero), that he has quoted from the girls' chorus in Catullus. It is consistent with this that, as he espies his beloved after so long a separation, he is compared to a mother, recovering the son whom she had feared dead in the war. He has lost his masculine identity to Angelica since, if our invocation of the *Aeneid* is correct, she is the mother, Venus.

---

[59] Above, pp. 296–97. See V. Pöschl, *The Art of Virgil*, Eng. tr., p. 68. G. N. Knauer, *Die Aeneis und Homer*, p. 162, notes that Venus leaves her son in *Aen.* I. 415–17 as Aphrodite leaves her detected amour with Ares in *Odyssey* VIII. 362 ff. Aeneas celebrates his father's funeral games (where also there is reminiscence of the games at Alcinous' court in the *Odyssey*, and therefore of Nausicaa) after *Dido's* death.

Angelica, feeling better, proceeds to reassure the anxious king that she is still a virgin. She has kept her virginal flower just as safe as she brought it with her from her mother's womb. The poet now decides to knock the bottom out of the whole unreal convention of this erotic world (I. 56):

> Forse era ver, ma non però credibile
> a chi del senso suo fosse signore;
> ma parve facilmente a lui possibile,
> ch'era perduto in via più grave errore.
> Quel che l'uom vede, Amor gli fa invisibile,
> e l'invisibil fa vedere Amore.
> Questo creduto fu; che 'l miser suole
> dar facile credenza a quel che vuole.

Perhaps it was true, but not however credible to any man master of his senses. But to him it easily seemed possible, for he was lost in a far greater maze. What a man sees, Love makes invisible to him, and Love makes him see the invisible. This was believed, for an unhappy wretch usually lends easy credence to what he wants.

Sacripante decides that he will not be so foolish as Orlando, and that he will pluck Angelica's rose forthwith, before delay destroys its freshness. Nothing is really so welcome to a woman, in spite of all the pretense of tears and lamentations which it causes at first. But the change in his character is not so great as it seems, and this is clear from the recurrent allusion to the rose (58. 1), where Angelica had merely referred to a *fior virginal*. His attitude to raping Angelica (presumably, beneath all the metaphors, this is the truth about what he hopes to do) is inspired by the false assumption that Angelica's view of the relationship between the sexes is correct, and that the answer is to say that women enjoy what they pretend to fear. When Catullus' young men made a similar point, they made it in the context of a marriage ceremony.

That Sacripante is no man we see in the next stanza, where he prepares for the *dolce assalto* on Angelica. A noise from the wood nearby is enough to put him off his designs. Another knight appears, and a furious combat breaks out between the two of them. No blows actually pierce the combatants' armor, but Sacripante's horse drops dead over him, and his enemy, deeming honor satisfied, makes off, leaving the king pinioned to the ground by the carcass. As he staggers to his feet, he is compared to a plowman, dazed and bewildered by a thunderbolt that destroys his oxen, astonished to observe the pine he used to see in the distance now *senza fronde e senza onore* ("leafless and dishonored").

It is of course the king's own sexual pride which is symbolized by

this pine.[60] His discomfiture is deepened when we find that it is
Angelica who has to heave his dead horse off him, and utter some
palpably false words of encouragement.

Worse is to come. The stranger's groom appears, and enquires
after the knight in shining armor who has just overthrown Sacripante.
The king naturally wishes to know his adversary's name. The reply
is rather unexpected (I. 69. 5–8):

> Et egli a lui:—Di quel che tu mi chiedi,
> io ti satisfarò senza dimora:
> tu déi saper che ti levò di sella
> l'alto valor d'una gentil donzella.

Her answer to him was: "I will satisfy your curiosity without delay.
You must know that what lifted you from your saddle was the high
valor of a gracious girl."

Poor Sacripante is mortified, and Ariosto enjoys his predicament. He
thinks long and to no purpose about his dilemma, and eventually
reaches the conclusion that—he has been worsted by a woman! The
simile in which he was compared to a plowman, *istordito e stupido*,
after his original defeat, seems to regain life, especially when we note
the deliberately colloquial tone of the passage.[61] Climbing onto
Angelica's horse without a word, he takes her up and "postpones"
her to better surroundings. He is echoing her unspoken thought.[62]

Sacripante's troubles are not yet over. Before the pair have gone
far, they are overtaken by Rinaldo's horse, which arrives at an
opportune moment to supply an extra mount. Unhappily, the bold
Circassian's attempts to master Rinaldo's enchanted Bayardo are
rudely frustrated by its restiveness. On the other hand, it answers
submissively to Angelica, who had previously looked after it. Thus
Sacripante, once more dependent on Angelica, is able to climb up.

Rinaldo himself is now espied, approaching on foot. Once Angelica
sighed for him, and he was indifferent. Now their relationship is
reversed. She urges Sacripante to take her away. He is again mortified
to think that she does not trust his protection against the unwelcome
visitor. Rinaldo and Sacripante eye each other threateningly. On this
note of suspense, the book closes.

---

[60] So too Heracles breaks his oar (Apollonius, *Arg.* I. 1168), just before he loses
Hylas to a love-lorn water nymph. Jason had armed himself for his visit to Hypsipyle
(I. 769) with a spear given to him by a warrior maiden.

[61] *Gran pezzo* in stanza 71. 1 seems to introduce a phrase of everyday language.
Callimachus' use of μέγα δή τι may be compared: Pfeiffer's index, vol. II, p. 156,
under δή.

[62] Stanza 54, end. There, Angelica had been hoping "di tosto riveder sua ricca
stanza."

But what has actually happened in the 81 stanzas[63] which it has taken to reach this point? Very little! Wandering in their wood, the knights and Angelica live, it seems, in a world utterly cut off from that of ordinary men. Their irrational and unquestioned assumption is that Angelica is all, and that it is worthwhile to suffer all for her. But is this behavior, on second thoughts, so removed as all that from the *Iliad*'s assumptions about Helen? Is this wood the one in which Dante was lost at the beginning of the *Inferno*? Is there not some paradigm and parable in the pastoral which touches our own senseless pursuit of illusory satisfactions? Ariosto is not, as Hegel thought, poking fun at a vanished world of chivalry. He is offering a model and description of *la condition humaine*.

The poet therefore exercises some of the functions of the *vates*. He is aware of a moral dimension to his narrative (and it is instructive that, like Virgil, he got rid of his *recusatio*—except for the jesting of XXXVII. 20–22—before he wrote his epic). This moral aspect is unmistakable in the delineation of Sacripante. The king, convinced that he is a bold knight, is really Love's fool. These cutting insights into the heroic are shared by Ariosto with the Romans, and by them both with the Alexandrians (Jason).

The error in the critical argument about the status of Ariosto's poem[64] was that neither side understood how the Alexandrian and vatic halves of the epic equation could be reconciled. Those who were content to reduce the poet to the status of entertainer were convinced that he had written a *romanzo*. Those who found in him, or suspected in him, more than "entertainment" were forced to approximate him to an ideal of seriousness which he clearly did not fit. The solution to the dilemma lay in recovering the true nature of the epic tradition, with its carnival masks and metamorphoses, its leaps into other aesthetic dimensions, its serio-comedy, its satirist who is also a *vates*, of which in fact Ariosto's musical, finished verse is so great an ornament.[65]

The poem is not simply a meandering extravaganza. Ariosto clearly

[63] Only one other book has the same number of stanzas, VI, where Ruggiero is taken prisoner by Alcina in spite of Astolfo's warning. The symbolism of the number is perhaps determined by a remark of Dante in the *Convivio* (IV. 24) that, had Christ not been crucified, he would have lived to the same age as Plato, according to Cicero's *De Senectute* 13: *uno et octogesimo anno scribens est mortuus*. These perfect (9x9) lives are travestied in Ariosto's poem.

[64] Weinberg, *op. cit.*, pp. 954 ff. and also Borlenghi's selection of early criticisms, *op. cit.*, pp. 123 ff.

[65] The monster which meets Rinaldo (XLII. 46 ff.) so clearly calls for allegorical interpretation that one wonders if such interpretation is intended for the rest of the poem. In this case the idea that the whole epic is a kind of dream, masking the interplay of deep and tragic forces, gains credibility.

intends two different strands of narrative to unite in contrast. The first is the account of the private lives and loves of his characters. The second is the story of Agramante's siege of Paris, defeat, withdrawal, and eventual death in single combat.

This second story is given explicit epic color and coherence by its obvious imitation of scenes from the latter half of the *Aeneid*, though not quite in the same order as in the original. The interplay of the public and private in this way ("War and Peace") lends a fullness to the creation which would be gravely impaired by the elimination of either element.

The technique of *entrelacement* is meant to contribute to a unified effect, even perhaps to create a spurious air of historical veracity, like the appeals to the authority of "Turpin." Abrupt though the switches from story to story may be, the device is far better than a complete series of separate, episodic narratives. It is a technique quite faithful to Horace's exposition of his matter in the *Ars Poetica*.[66]

In the *Orlando Furioso* we may recognize a broad outline of internal unity in the gradual coming together of the public and private themes. The characters on either side move towards their kings, or at least, in the case of Astolfo, against their kings' enemies. But even before this their stories touch.

Analysis picks on different strands of what is an indivisible fabric. The poet expects us to take his poem as he wrote it, with its motley intertwining of many, even clashing, threads and colors. He demands from his public a sophisticated vision, in which the part unites with the whole to form an iridescent image of the way we live now.

III

In Tasso, graver tones are audible right from the start. It should be possible at this point to read the literary code in which his proem is written with greater comprehension (I. 1–4).

> Canto l'arme pietose e 'l capitano
> che 'l gran sepolcro liberò di Cristo:
> molto egli oprò co 'l senno e con la mano,
> molto soffrí nel glorïoso acquisto:
> e in van l'Inferno vi s'oppose, e in vano
> s'armò d'Asia e di Libia il popol misto;
> il Ciel gli diè favore, e sotto a i santi
> segni ridusse i suoi compagni erranti.

---

[66] Above, pp. 61–64. Ariosto effects a certain unity by the use of *Zahlenkomposition*, audible also in Horace. It is interesting, for example, that Orlando's madness occurs in Canto 23 of the 46. See G. Toffanin, *loc. cit.*, p. 189, and my paper "Orazio, Ariosto and Orazio Ariosto" (above, note 19), pp. 820–34. See also S. Eisenstein, *Izbrannye Proizvedeniya*, III, pp. 302 ff., and below, p. 417.

O Musa, tu che di caduchi allori
non circondi la fronte in Elicona,
ma su nel cielo in fra i beati cori
hai di stelle immortali aurea corona,
tu spira al petto mio celesti ardori,
tu rischiara il mio canto, e tu perdona
s'intesso fregi al ver, s'adorno in parte
d'altri diletti, che de' tuoi, le carte.

Sai che là corre il mondo, ove piú versi
di sue dolcezze il lusinghier Parnaso;
e che 'l vero condito in molli versi,
i piú schivi allettando ha persuaso:
cosí a l'egro fanciul porgiamo aspersi
di soavi licor gli orli del vaso:
succhi amari ingannato intanto ei beve,
e da l'inganno suo vita riceve.

Tu, magnanimo Alfonso, il qual ritogli
al furor di fortuna e guidi in porto
me peregrino errante, e fra gli scogli
e fra l'onde agitato e quasi absorto,
queste mie carte in lieta fronte accogli,
che quasi in voto a te sacrate i' porto.
Forse un dí fia che la presaga penna
osi scriver di te quel ch'or n'accenna.

I sing the pious arms and the captain who freed the great sepulcher of Christ. Much he labored with head and hand, much he suffered in that glorious conquest. Vainly did Hell there struggle against him, vainly did the motley peoples of Asia and Africa arm. Heaven blessed him, and brought back beneath his holy standards his errant knights.

Muse, you do not garland your brow on Helicon with fading laurels; rather, above in heaven, among the blessed choirs, you enjoy a golden crown of immortal stars. Breathe into my heart heavenly ardors, illumine my song, and forgive if I weave ornaments with the truth, if I decorate to some degree with other charms than yours my pages.

You know that the world runs to where playful Parnassus pours out more of its sweetnesses, and that truth, spiced by soft verses, has by allurement won over even the most reluctant. So when a child is ill we give him a cup whose lip is smeared with sweet juices. Deceived, he drinks bitter medicine, and from that deceit recovers life.

You, great Alfonso, take me, wandering pilgrim, from Fortune's fury and guide me to haven, tossed as I am among rocks and waves and almost swallowed up. Welcome these pages of mine with cheerful look, which I bring as it were in fulfillment of a sacred vow. Perhaps one day it will be that my prophetic pen dares to write of you what now it can only hint.

The imitation of the exordium to the *Aeneid* is palpable. Virgil's *arma virumque* becomes *l'arme pietose e 'l capitano* (where *pietose* too is borrowed), his *multum . . . multa* becomes *molto . . . molto*. Even the postponement of the Muse to a second stanza is dictated.

But why, in this new *Aeneid*, must we hear echoes of Lucretius' *De Rerum Natura?*[67] There is a contradiction. Lucretius had been satisfied with Helicon. Anxious to please the theological and literary "experts" of his day, Tasso wishes to make clear that his particular Muse is not the Heliconian (= Hesiodic) goddess whose laurels fade, but one of Christian inspiration.[68] Certainly the Alexandrian poet will reject or rethink the masterpieces of his own tradition if they threaten to stifle originality, and Tasso, in turning to his heavenly Muse, was quite within this tradition of fastidiousness. But he was failing to live up to its standards when he admitted that he would still be forced to borrow something from the rejected style in order to make his new confection palatable. This was a yielding to the taste of the populace (what Tasso himself calls *il mondo* at the opening of his third stanza), which a true Callimachean could not have tolerated.

The terms of Tasso's surrender are instructive. "You know," he says to his Muse, "that the world runs to where playful Parnassus pours out more of its sweetnesses." "Sweetness" and "play" are Alexandrian catchwords.[69] The symbolic sense of the remark is that Alexandrian techniques have been so exploited that they have, in their turn, fallen victim to the very vices they were designed to avoid. They have become, in Formalist language, automated, attractive to the despised "crowd," and so they must now be estranged.

In that case, however, why have anything more to do with them? If Tasso has a new, true and serious theme to propound, why does not the pressure of his vision on his imagination generate a new, true and serious style? In going back to Lucretius, Tasso is returning to a concept of poetry which had served in the days *before* Virgil had finally synthesized for Rome the demands of heroism and art. Torn asunder by the strains of his time, the poet is allowing the Virgilian amalgam to dissolve into its constituent elements. Nothing could more clearly demonstrate the nature of the classical epic compound than this enforced catalysis.

This explains why Tasso's exordium continues in a pattern made

---

[67] I. 936 ff. = IV. 11 ff. The image is embedded in a deeply Alexandrian context. See above, pp. 112–13.

[68] This uneasy compromise is symptomatic of the difficulty inherent in his position: cf. Curtius, *op. cit.*, pp. 247–48. Compare Milton's difficulty with Urania, *P. L.* VII. 5 ff.

[69] "Sweetness": Callimachus, fr. 1. 16 Pf.; *Epigr.* XXVII. 2; "play": *lusimus*, Catullus 50. 2; *Culex* 1 and 3. This last motif goes back to Pindar's παίζομεν, *Olympian* 1. 16.

familiar, no longer by the *Aeneid*, but by the *Georgics*, the didactic poem that had preceded Virgil's final synthesis. The imagery is exploited to flatter Alfonso d' Este. Just as Goffredo led back his wandering followers (*erranti*, 1. 8), so Alfonso leads safely to harbor the wandering pilgrim poet (*me peregrino errante*, 4. 3, where *peregrino* associates Alfonso's action with the Holy Land by implication).[70] This hinted parallel between Goffredo and Alfonso is enough to justify a *recusatio* on Tasso's part, exactly in the manner of the proem to the third book of the *Georgics*.[71] "One day" (4. 7) the poet's pen may summon up the courage to sing of Alfonso what it can now only suggest, for Europe may well choose him as its captain in a renewal of the old Crusades. "Meanwhile" (5. 8) the poem proffered is merely a second-best, which the royal patron will heed only while he is actually arming for the fray. These are the terms of Virgil's promised eulogy of Caesar in the *Georgics*. They find no place in the *Aeneid*.

The hesitancy that prevented Tasso from having full confidence in his own imagination had its roots in his deep sense of the demands of art. But his Alexandrian perplexities were aggravated by the tensions of his age, in which philistinism disguised as piety sought to crush all fancy. He did nevertheless write a masterpiece, remaining faithful to his vocation at the cost of his sanity (like Thomas Mann's Leverkühn).

One of the episodes that came under heaviest attack was that in the second book of the *Gerusalemme Liberata* where the mutual devotion of Sofronia and Olindo is described. Tasso wrote to Luca Scalabrino on May 3, 1576:

> I am in the process of deciding to leave in the episode about Sofronia, with some changes intended to make it clearer to canting critics, while keeping it just as filled with nuances.[72]

On April 9 of the same year he had written to Scalabrino:

> ... love is a theme just as heroic as war, and I shall defend that from reason, with the authority of Aristotle, with passages from Plato which are absolutely and unambiguously clear... and to the devil with the pedants!

"Love" described as a theme just as heroic as war: a treatment which

---

[70] Cf. "pilgrim muses" in Fairfax's translation.

[71] Cf. *modo vita supersit, Georgics* III. 10; *interea, Georgics* III. 40; *Ciris* 44; Propertius III. 2. 1. W. Wimmel, *Kallimachos in Rom*, discusses (pp. 167 ff.) this type of exordium, which became characteristic of post-Virgilian epic (e.g. Valerius Flaccus, above, pp. 220–21; Petrarch, *Africa* I. 38 ff.). See also above, pp. 242–43.

[72] The originals of this and the following passage are given in Luigi De Vendettis' edition of the *Gerusalemme Liberata* (Torino 1961), p. XIX.

is both "clear" and deliberately "nuanced": we are not so far after all from Alexandrian poetics.

Nowadays the episode strikes the reader as a piece of charming, though over-pious, romance, well in the spirit of contemporary Mannerist painting.[73] At the time, it was criticized for being too charming, too soon introduced, and for having an artificial conclusion.[74] All the criticisms turn upon a failure to recognize that artifice was of the essence of the epic convention as it had developed over the centuries.

The episode begins as the first news of the crusade led by Goffredo is reaching the Saracen king Aladino in Jerusalem. Aladino is approached by Ismeno, a renegade and sorcerer. The wizard's powers are detailed in a soberer version of the macabre ("carnival," what used to be called "Grand Guignol") style encountered in Lucan.[75] Since "Ismeno" also suggests "Theban" to the classical ear, we must think too of Statius' *Thebaid* (Teiresias, Manto). He can draw lifeless corpses from beneath the closed marble, and make them breathe and hear. His servants in this impious task are demons.

Ismeno proposes to the king that an image of the Blessed Virgin, which is concealed in a Christian church still surviving in Jerusalem, should be removed to a mosque, where he will guard it by magic. There is evidently some metamorphosis here of the image of the virgin goddess Pallas on which the safety of both Troy and Rome was thought to depend. Ovid had told the story (*Fasti* VI. 421 ff.).

The scheme is carried out but, as next day dawns, it is discovered that the *imagine* has disappeared. The king concludes that some Christian is responsible. Tasso himself is in doubt (II. 9):

> O fu di man fedele opra furtiva,
> o pur il Ciel qui sua potenza adopra;
> che di Colei, ch'è sua regina e diva,
> sdegna che loco vil l'imagin copra:
> ch'incerta fama è ancor, se ciò s'ascriva
> ad arte umana, od a mirabil opra:
> ben è pietà, che, la pietade e 'l zelo
> uman cedendo, autor sen creda il Cielo.

Was it the stealthy deed of some pious hand, was it Heaven employing

---

[73] Vendettis reproduces illustrations made in the first half of the Seicento by a pupil of Battistello Caracciolo, Paolo Finoglio. See also "A Poelenburgh in the National Gallery of Canada" by M. Waddingham, *Bulletin of the National Gallery of Canada* 26 (1975), 3 ff., on the panel now preserved in Ottawa which shows Clorinda saving Olindo and Sofronia from the stake. *Ut pictura poesis*.

[74] Tasso, Letter 31 to Luca Scalabrino: J. Cottaz (below, note 84), pp. 300 and 302.

[75] Above, pp. 211–15.

here its power, disdaining that so mean a place should hide the image
of Her who is its queen and goddess? Fame cannot yet declare if the
event is to be ascribed to human skill or to miracle. It is piety enough
that human piety and zeal should yield, and that the responsibility
should be credited to Heaven.

When the author of the theft cannot be found, the king launches a
general persecution against the Christians. They shall all die. In this
crisis, help appears from an unexpected quarter. Among the Christians
is a beautiful maiden, Sofronia (II. 14):

> Vergine era fra lor di già matura
> verginità, d'alti pensieri e regi,
> d'alta beltà; ma sua beltà non cura,
> o tanto sol quant'onestà sen fregi:
> è il suo pregio maggior, che tra le mura
> d'angusta casa asconde i suoi gran pregi;
> e de' vagheggiatori ella s'invola
> a le lodi, a gli sguardi, inculta e sola.

A maiden there was among them, of maidenhood already ripe, of
lofty, royal thoughts, of lofty beauty. But she cared nothing for her
beauty, or just as much as honor may take adornment from it. Her
greatest excellence is that behind the walls of a confining cottage she
hides her great excellences. She flies from the compliments and looks
of suitors, neglected and alone.

Nevertheless, she is loved, by Olindo, though so far he has either
been unseen, or little noticed, or little rewarded.

Hearing that her people are to be destroyed, Sofronia decides to
go to the king and accuse herself, in the hope that he will spare
them. Modesty fights with courage. Courage wins, and she sets out.
Providing here the greatest possible contrast with Petrarch's Sophonisba, her appearance is not so much described as hinted at (II. 18):

> La vergine tra 'l vulgo uscí soletta,
> non coprí sue bellezze, e non l'espose;
> raccolse gli occhi, andò nel vel ristretta,
> con ischive maniere e generose.
> Non sai ben dir s'adorna, o se negletta;
> se caso od arte il bel volto compose:
> di natura, d'Amor, de' cieli amici
> le negligenze sue son artifici.

All alone, the maiden went out among the crowd. She did not hide
her beauties, and did not expose them. She guarded her gaze, and
walked within a concealing veil. Her demeanor was shy and noble. It
cannot be easily said whether she was adorned or not, whether chance
or art composed her fair features. Her negligence is the artifice of
nature, of Love, of the benevolent Heavens.

She enters the king's presence (like the Biblical Esther) and, had she been so disposed, might have won his heart. She declares first that she knows who took the image, and then, that it was she herself. The king is somewhat incredulous, and demands the names of her partners in crime. She claims sole responsibility. The king wants to know what she has done with the image. She answers that she has burnt it. The king, she hints, is the real thief.

Infuriated, Aladino orders her execution by burning. The pyre stands ready. The people run up. Among them is Olindo who, taking a leaf from Sofronia's book, accuses himself in an effort to save her (Damon and Phintias, Nisus and Euryalus, Dymas and Hopleus, carnival twins!). The king, vexed by the contempt in which his punishments seem to be held, decides to execute them both. They stand back to back on the pyre, face hidden from face.

As the flames take hold, the young hero cannot forbear, and breaks out in a long declaration of unhappy love, in which the old topos fire of passion/real fire[76] is elegantly reworked (II. 33. 5–8; 34. 1–2):

> —Questo dunque è quel laccio, ond'io sperai
> teco accoppiarmi in compagnia di vita?
> Questo e quel foco ch'io credea che i cori
> ne dovesse infiammar d'eguali ardori?
>
> Altre fiamme, altri nodi Amor promise,
> altri ce n'apparecchia iniqua sorte.

This then is that bond, in which I hoped to be united with you in lifelong union? This is the fire that I believed should inflame our hearts with equal blaze? Other flames, other knots were promised by Love than these which unfair doom now makes ready for us.

The lady is more self-controlled. She advises Olindo to remember the high cause for which they are both dying, and the celestial rewards they may expect. Even the pagan onlookers are moved. King Aladino has mixed feelings (another carnival motif) and is forced to withdraw.

But now Clorinda makes her appearance, the warrior maid of unsurpassed renown. Learning the facts of the case, she puts out the fire, goes to see the king, secures the pardon of the victims, and points out that it was wrong in the first place for an image to have been put in a mosque. It was, she suggests, Mahomet himself who brought about its removal, to show that contact with other religions is impermissible.

Released, Sofronia and Olindo are united in marriage. The story does not however end entirely happily. Aladino exiles the pair, believing that such a union of virtues is a dangerous neighbor. Some

---

[76] Above, p. 162 with note 125.

of the other Christians are either banished or imprisoned. Some simply become wanderers. Others turn rebel. In any case, they find the French armies already arrived at Emmaus. With that, the episode ends, and no more is heard of its two leading figures.

That Tasso was puzzled and anxious over the attacks made on this passage cannot surprise us when we think of the easy way in which it fits into the tradition of Alexandrian and carnival epic we have been describing. Callimachus' fifth *Hymn* shows the same technique: the measured, lyrical pace of the narrative where, though technical details are omitted, there is always ample room to note reactions, to apostrophize, to allow the characters to show their emotions in long speeches, to moralize. Even the ambiguously happy ending, which may be compared with Athene's efforts to compensate Teiresias for his blinding, shows some of the refusal to acquiesce in the expected which is most intensely felt at the end of the *Aeneid*. And what did happen to the image? The predominance of the feminine, the hinted description of Sofronia's beauty, the reminiscences of Propertius and Ovid are other Alexandrian elements.[77] Against this background, the intervention of the mannish Clorinda, who has obvious predecessors in Athena, Penthesilea or Camilla, is perfectly intelligible.[78]

The poem also shows an organic use of subtly connected imagery, both Aristotelian and Pindaric. Ismeno steals a statue of the Virgin, hoping to use it as a talisman to frustrate the Christian plan to recover Jerusalem. Since it depends on theft, his scheme is bound to fail, and the king's bloodthirsty plan for mass vengeance, already a moral defeat, is foiled by another Christian virgin. Only Clorinda, a pagan virgin, ultimately however destined to become a Christian, knows how to behave in such a way as to rescue Aladino from total ignominy. The episode, repeating its own beginning in its development, also foreshadows the future development of the poem.[79]

The ground of the attacks made on Tasso was that such borrowing from the tradition of the "romance" was unworthy of the dignity of

[77] The role of nature versus art in feminine beauty was an Alexandrian topos: Callimachus, *Coma Berenices* 110. 77–78 Pf., with Catullus 66. 77–78; *Hymn* 5. 13 ff.; Propertius I. 2; Tibullus I. 8. 15–16; Ovid, *Am.* I. 14. On Cydippe's beauty see Callimachus 67. 11 ff. Pf.

[78] Cf. Callimachus, *Hymns* V. 15 ff.

[79] In the same way Alcibiades' eulogy of Socrates in Plato's *Symposium* concretizes what has been said about Eros; Apuleius' myth of Amor and Psyche encapsulates the symbolism of his *Golden Ass*; Mann's story of Klöpfgeissel and Bärbel in Chapter xiii (!) of *Doktor Faustus* enshrines the theme of German suspicion of the feminine. Virgil's story of Aristaeus in *Georgics* IV has been said to sum up the lesson of the entire poem: C. G. Hardie, *The Georgics: A Transitional Poem* (Abingdon 1971). On p. 12 Hardie describes the episode as "Hellenistic in form and sentiment." But this parable tradition is much older than these literary examples, of course.

religion, or of the high enterprise which the Crusades had been. The answer on the literary level at least could only have been that the romantic tradition was perfectly capable of conveying a serious (vatic) message: Apollonius' Jason and Medea; Virgil's Dido and Aeneas; their forebears Paris and Helen. Ovid jested at the *Aeneid* for retreating to Tyrian couches.[80] He had of course, with his customary acumen, touched on its basic theme.

Tasso saw this truth in the tradition, but he did not cling to it firmly enough. The critics had established an artificial epic, something wholly distinct from the romance. To point out that the epic tradition had in fact been carried by the romance (i.e. the serio-comic *spoudogeloion*), most obviously in the work of Ariosto, but even in Dante, was simply to invite repudiation, by direct or indirect means, of Ariosto and Dante.[81] And even the defenders of the romance never developed a consistent theory of the serio-comic.

Tasso himself was eager to write an "epic," but at least in his theoretical examinations of epic's problems he did not wholly repudiate the romance. He discerned in the mingling of the epic and romance traditions an escape from the narrow pseudo-Aristotelianism of contemporary critics. When later he fell back on the argument that, if Aristotle had not discussed the romance, this meant that it was legitimately exempt from the laws, he was surrendering an earlier insight.[82]

These exclusive categories must deceive no longer. What is the romance except the Callimachean epic, epic which eschews naive eulogy and propaganda bombast because it has deeper truths to communicate? Aristotle had made room for the comic *Margites* and even for the romantic plays of Euripides within the tradition. Apollonius had used a romantic framework to explore the degenerating heroism of a character tested to destruction. Virgil had noted, with Catullus, how closely love borders on hate. How could the Cinquecento critics be so sure that they had understood the tradition better than the poets who had written about mad or lovelorn heroes?

Tasso's tergiversations in the face of critical obloquy are the result of a clash between his poetic insight into the real truth of the position

[80] *Contulit in Tyrios arma virumque toros*, Ovid, *Tristia* II. 534. It is important in determining the kind of epic which Virgil wrote to remember that Dido does not disappear with Book IV: above, pp. 158 ff.

[81] Cf. Castravilla on Dante: Weinberg, pp. 831 ff. Ariosto had been attacked before 1549 for not writing a proper epic (Weinberg, pp. 954–55).

[82] In the early *Discorsi dell' Arte Poetica* Tasso had allowed the epic writer to use "romantic" themes (Spingarn, *La critica letteraria nel Rinascimento*, p. 116). Later he seems to have repudiated this synthesis of the two types of poem, in the face of attacks on his father's *Amadigi* (Weinberg, pp. 1009 ff.).

and his honorable, but mistaken, desire to do justice to those who, without one atom of his genius, had set themselves up as the arbiters of what constituted classical art. Clearly his best course, if circumstances had allowed, would have been not to trouble himself a whit about contemporary criticism, but to leave everything to the judgment of posterity, and to trust his own conscience. It is too late for the madman to enjoy the benefit of this rehabilitation, though not perhaps for his readers.[83]

Literature, and particularly epic, is concerned in the last analysis not with literature, but with life, with the observed moral order of the real world. It is just here that the case against Tasso has been restated in our time.

A French scholar has pointed to the poet's failure to grasp the true historical sense of the events he was describing.[84] In the struggle between Christian and Moslem, Europe was engaged in the long and repeatedly necessary task of reasserting its identity. This reassertion was fraught with destiny. If the Moslems had not been forced onto the defensive, if they had eventually won control of Europe and imposed their ideas and religion, the whole history of the world would have been changed, as anyone may see who walks through the streets of what once was Byzantium. Tasso, it is argued, cared for none of this. His knights and pagans are caught up in a web of unreal fantasy, by which deeper truth is strangled.

This is not entirely fair to Tasso. He does, for example draw a distinction between Christian and Moslem. He does allude at the start of his poem to the plight of Constantinople. But it is certain that he did not write the poem of unambiguous partisanship which the critic demands.

Yet what would this partisan poem of large historical perspective have been like? Would it, for example, have rivaled Ennius' *Annales?* Or those Greek historical epics of which we now hear only whispers? Or Petrarch's *Africa?* Aristotle had already warned against the impropriety of confounding history and poetry, even though the attack on Tasso from this angle is so often made in the guise of a call for adherence to Aristotelian poetics.

A poem that concerned itself more openly with history could nevertheless have done so only by remaining a poem. "Historical" masterpieces from Aeschylus' *Persae* to Tolstoy's *War and Peace* or

---

[83] A sympathetic appreciation of the poet is found in C. P. Brand's *Torquato Tasso* (Cambridge 1965). It is a curious coincidence that mad Tasso should have begun his epic with so striking a quotation from the Lucretius who, according to Jerome's version of his life, also went mad.

[84] J.' Cottaz, *Le Tasse et la Conception Épique* (Paris 1942), pp. 52 ff.

Eisenstein's *Ivan the Terrible* show how much "the facts" must pass through the refining and distorting mesh of the poet's imagination before the work of art emerges.

Even the *Aeneid* makes far-reaching concessions to the romance. There is a kernel of historical truth in that great national epic. But, in raising the bare fact of Rome's struggle with Carthage to the metaphysical and religious plane of a conflict between *furor* and *pietas*, and in surrounding his commitment to a particular vision of the truth with so many reservations (*umbrae*), even the Augustan Virgil must dissatisfy the mind eager for a black and white sketch. He knew that in sober truth Rome's defeat of Carthage, like the Trojan defeat of the Italians, was hardly the simple triumph of the wholly good over the wholly bad.

Virgil shows this by choosing to cast his symbolic explanation of the fight to the death between Rome and Carthage (and between Aeneas and Turnus) in the mold of a love affair, even though he ran the risk of seeming to degrade epic dignity. Here we may gain some insight into Tasso's own position. It is clear, for example, that he did not altogether lack the feel for the grand historical event desiderated by his critic. When he comes to write of the discovery of the New World, reversing Dante's account of Ulysses' blasphemous voyage, he speaks of Columbus' courage (*Ger. Lib.* XV. 31. 1–2):

> Un uom de la Liguria avrà ardimento
> a l'incognito corso esporsi in prima. . . .

A man of Liguria will have the courage first to expose himself to the unknown voyage. . . .

The whole passage is heart-stirring stuff. But why did the poet, who was able to rise to the height of his great argument here, not rise in quite the same way elsewhere?

Two answers are possible. Either the poet lacked genuine historical insight, and so lingered in the foothills when he ought to have been climbing mountains, or he deliberately chose to stay where he did because ultimately he did not share the same vision of things as his critic. At this distance, as we contemplate the chequered history of European freedom, and France's sometimes ambiguous contributions to it, on the one side, and come to appreciate the point of view of the Third World on the other, is it quite so obvious that Tasso's picture of the Crusades is wrong? His use of the Callimachean, romance tradition in epic at least enabled him to avoid too violent a commitment to a truth which, in long perspective, may turn out only to be a half truth. In his age, with its disastrous fanaticisms both of literature and theology, its social and religious corruption, its barbarity and intolerance, the Callimachean legacy may have saved him from Milton's fate.

It is in this light that we must judge the Olindo and Sofronia episode, paradigmatic because it was eliminated by the poet from the *Conquistata* as a concession to his enemies. The story does not lack philosophical insight. The Moslems depend on the black arts of a renegade Christian to provide help. Christian superiority is proved in two ways: by the mysterious disappearance of the image, and by the moral elevation of the maiden and her lover.

The first happening, which Tasso refuses to explain in any more specific fashion, is a good example of the countless occasions when some mysterious force does intervene in affairs to upset the rational calculations of historical agents.[85]

The second is perhaps the very reference to larger perspectives which the critic seeks. Just as the Greek capture of Troy was transformed by the imagination of Virgil, through his remodeling of Sinon, into a moral defeat, so the clever malice of Ismeno is defeated by the moral strength of Sofronia, whose speaking name gives her secret away to anyone with a smattering of Greek. The comedy and carnival of this mime communicates a serious truth, and is matter worthy of an intelligent and even religious reader, if only he will study the conventions of the tradition that includes Pindar's *Nemean* 1 and Cervantes' *Don Quixote*.

To demand from Tasso a poetry which enlarged in naive terms on the differences between black and white is pointless. No such poetry—certainly no such epic—forms part of the classical tradition.[86] At a time when boundaries were tightening and lines of battle being drawn by men who fancied they had this godlike overview of human history, Tasso defended the cause of civilization best by writing still within the less unocular conventions of Alexandria, like Callimachus, and like Virgil.

---

[85] See the second epilogue to *War and Peace*. The "breath of corruption" in Dostoevsky's *Brothers Karamazov* (III. 7. 1) is another aspect of that annoying refusal of reality to correspond with theory which cracks open the human nutshell.

[86] It will be remembered that, even after the tremendous revelations of *Aeneid* VI, Virgil still takes care to dismiss Aeneas from Hades through the gate of false dreams. And Aeneas was an Asian: *desertorem Asiae: Aen.* XII. 15.

# VIII

# THE ENGLISH TRADITION: CHAUCER AND MILTON

I N spite of its geographical isolation across the misty waters of the Channel, England has not been lacking in feeling for the classical tradition. It is nevertheless necessary to understand just how paradoxical this feeling is. Drenched with showers and soot, pushing with his umbrella couchant through driving rain past bleak grey houses, the Englishman, morose, disciplined, classified, with his eighty religions and one sauce, stands at the opposite remove from the inquisitive crowds that throng the sunlit squares of the Mediterranean. But he has grasped something of the classical heritage. Like the Romans, he has civilized—and given his language to—a world. Like the Greeks, he has leapt in imagination from the fall of an apple to the wheeling of the planets. The typical expression of his self-confidence has been, like that of the Athenians, in the theatre. With Aeneas, he has understood the deadly cost of empire.

The classical tradition as it has flourished in England is a peculiarly complex study.[1] There have been the overt imitations, but to concentrate attention on them is to exclude some of the greatest of the English writers, and, worse, to suggest that their greatness is divorced from the classical tradition. The elevation of English to an independent status in the syllabus has confounded matters still further. Now the "classical" elements in English literature are explained in terms of the "unclassical."[2] This can only lead to confused literary history, in which generalization is substituted for precision, especially where that demands the exact reading of the Alexandrian code.

Chaucer and Milton are examples of the European, classical epic

---

[1] Cf. R. M. Ogilvie, *Latin and Greek: A History of the Influence of the Classics on English Life from 1600–1918* (Hamden, Conn. 1964).

[2] "It is almost entirely irrelevant to adduce Latin or Greek epics, or Aristotelian principles, in order to examine the structure of either *Paradise Lost* or *Paradise Regained*": L. A. Cormican in *A Guide to English Literature 3. From Donne to Marvell*, ed. Boris Ford (London 1956), p. 181. *Classical Influences on English Poetry* by J. A. K. Thomson (London 1951) had been so vague as to justify this kind of remark.

tradition which it serves no purpose to isolate. All that can happen is that Chaucer is praised for being other than he is, and Milton altogether misunderstood. If we remember the tradition as we have sought to establish it in these pages, we shall be able to unite the two poets with the living tree from which they sprang.

I

In what sense is the *Canterbury Tales* a classical epic? It is something with which the author of the comic/ironic *Hecale*, and the author of the elegiac *Aetia*, treated as a quarry for epic material already by Apollonius, would have been perfectly at home. A series of narratives, some in verse and some in prose, drawn from the most diverse sources, comic in intent but exhibiting serious knowledge of men and their passions, is tied loosely together to form an embroidered panorama of fourteenth-century England, with its characteristic strengths and weaknesses.[3] The interest which the poem still awakens[4] suggests that the author's Ovidian wit is based on a perennial insight into the human condition.

A critic interested, like Matthew of Vendôme, in seriousness, or in that automatic application of Virgil's Wheel which was still common in sixteenth-century Renaissance criticism,[5] would have been discomfited. Could he have approved instead of the manner displayed in *Piers Plowman*? This noble poem however is far from being the historical epic which is the normal alternative to the Callimachean style. The shifting identity of Piers is shared by him with the shifting identities of the *Aeneid*, both in debt to carnival metamorphosis. The mysticism, the concern for personal salvation, are other elements which prevent us from viewing Langland as a disciple of John of Virgil, or his ancient counterparts, the Telchines. The deadness of that kind of historical epic is seen in its total irrelevance to fourteenth-century English literature. Yet who would doubt that we know a great deal about the feel of fourteenth-century England from its poetry? Who could believe that a versified history of the period would be more revealing than the *Canterbury Tales*, especially if that history had been falsified to flatter the great?

[3] Donald R. Howard, *The Idea of the Canterbury Tales* (Berkeley and Los Angeles 1976) is particularly relevant.

[4] It has even been adapted by Professor Nevill Coghill in our time as a successful musical.

[5] B. Weinberg, *A History of Literary Criticism in the Italian Renaissance*, pp. 804–05. See also above, pp. 249–52.

Chaucer's keen sense of human foibles forbids him to be naively credulous about man's pretensions, but, if he has a positive hero, it is perhaps his Knight.[6] In his day, the knightly ideal had decayed. It is all the more striking therefore that the poet does not call our attention to this decay, as he does, for example (like Dante), to that of the friars. Instead, he allows something of the spirit of the old chivalry to pervade his picture. This admiration for the past no more hampers his critical judgment than it did that of Ariosto after him.

The Knight tells his tale first. It is taken from the twelve-book epic composed by the youthful Boccaccio, the *Teseida delle Nozze d'Emilia*.[7] The continual dependence by poets of the Callimachean tradition on a commented model suggests that the understanding of the *Knight's Tale* is impossible without the study of its predecessor. Here a particularly interesting case is presented, the resonance of two untuned ironies.

Boccaccio's aim, as was previously seen, was to fill a gap in vernacular Italian literature to which Dante had already called attention. He wanted to write an epic of war, to take its place at the side of the poems of *amoris accensio* and *directio voluntatis* which Cino da Pistoia and Dante himself had already composed.[8]

A previous chapter has noted how many concessions to the Alexandrian tradition the poet made in order to bring his ambition to a successful conclusion. Basing his narrative partly upon the popular *cantari* of his time, yet telling a most unusual (Byzantine?) story with a wealth of recondite allusions explained in learned *chiose* (notes) appended to the text, avoiding the solemn *terza rima* for the lyrical and popular *ottava*, descending to the comic in conception and the colloquial in language, professing to find all his inspiration in the invented figure of his mistress Fiammetta, bounding action within lyrical, dramatic, tragic, elegiac monologue and dialogue, Boccaccio offers overwhelming proof of his debt to the poetic defined already so many times in this book.

But, true to that poetic, he does not use technique as an excuse for avoiding thought. Is Theseus a hero? He maintains that status, if he maintains it at all, only by staying well in the background of the poem. Is Emilia a heroine? The poet dips too deeply into the paintpots of convention for her portrait to convince either himself or his

---

[6] So at least F. N. Robinson, *The Complete Works of Geoffrey Chaucer* (Cambridge, Mass. 1933), p. 754. Contrast however T. Jones, *Chaucer's Knight: The Portrait of a Medieval Mercenary* (Baton Rouge 1980).

[7] See the previous discussion of Boccaccio's *Teseida*, above, pp. 293 ff. The reader will also wish to compare the somewhat different account of the relationship between the two poets given by Piero Boitani, *Chaucer and Boccaccio* (Oxford 1977).

[8] Above, p. 293.

readers. The real story, only implicit in the title, concerns the folly of young lovers who take themselves ever so seriously and who, seeking reason in an irrational world, look to the gods for sympathy and help. Their prayers are answered too literally. They fulfill the ancient curse that rests upon the Theban line. One of them, the nobler and more martial, dies and is forgotten. The other, Venus' devotee, lives to copulate seven times on his wedding night with the dead man's widow. This terrifying picture of the way of the world, coloring all the sentiment and protestations, lends piquancy and depth—a "vatic" element preaching acceptance of the biological urge—to what otherwise might seem superficial romance.

Whatever the motives that attracted Chaucer to this tale, they did not lead him to abandon its Alexandrian premises. For the nearly 10,000 lines of the Italian (it is exactly as long as the *Aeneid*), he substituted 2250, hacking away, like Apollonius, at the mass of tradition in order to extract the relevant. A ruthless sense of poetic purpose dictated the removal of the account of Theseus' war with the Amazons which filled the first and part of the second books of the *Teseida*. The Italian had used these episodes, not only to carry out his promise of a martial epic (which could not bind the Englishman), but to prepare the way for an ironic contrast between the successful hero and his victim Creon which would recur in the rest of the poem. The wedding couch and funeral pyre, separate in the proem, would be united in the sequel.

Chaucer prefers to latch directly onto the tradition of Statius' *Thebaid*. In Book XII of that epic, as the poem draws to its conclusion, the aftermath of the bloody civil strife at Thebes is resolved by the arrival of the civilizing Athenian, who has just returned from conquering the Amazons. In twenty lines Statius describes the triumphal procession of the victorious hero, and the critical reaction of the women of Athens to their new queen. This is the scene which Chaucer wants us to recall as the Knight begins his tale. His "as olden stories tellen us" is exactly in the Alexandrian style.[9]

The Alexandrian poetic feigned a naive objectivity while in fact steering the reader's response in a predetermined direction. Milton is an adept at this trick. Chaucer merely actualizes this tendency (another instance of *la dénudation du procédé*) when he employs the device, dear to Plato and Thomas Mann, of the intruded narrator. His Knight, making use of the typical medieval, inherited devices of *occupatio*, which will find later and paradoxically "telling" scope in

---

[9] Cf. C. J. Fordyce's note on Catullus' *dicuntur* at the start of his epic poem 64: *Catullus: A Commentary* (repr. Oxford 1968), p. 276.

the poem, and of *brevitas*,[10] sets Theseus' achievement in a certain perspective (875–92):

> And certes, if it nere to long to heere,
> I wolde have toold yow fully the manere
> How wonnen was the regne of Femenye
> By Theseus and by his chivalrye;
> And of the grete bataille for the nones
> Bitwixen Atthenes and Amazones;
> And how asseged was Ypolita,
> The faire, hardy queene of Scithia;
> And of the feste that was at hir weddynge,
> And of the tempest at hir hoom-comynge;
> But al that thyng I moot as now forbere.
> I have, God woot, a large feeld to ere,
> And wayke been the oxen in my plough.
> The remenant of the tale is long ynough.
> I wol nat letten eek noon of this route;
> Lat every felawe telle his tale aboute,
> And lat se now who shal the soper wynne;
> And ther I lefte, I wol ayeyn bigynne.

This apology, taking 18 lines, is still able to afford 8 lines of personal remarks about the speaker's inability to go into detail because of his own weakness and the largeness of his theme. Courtesy too compels him to think of the rest of the company. These gambits may now be understood within the tradition of the Roman *recusatio*.[11]

The directness with which the Knight vividly expresses his plight seems however to escape behind the formality of Latin to Alexandria itself.[12] We grasp the stylistic trick for what it is. Theseus is not the important center of attention. It is the point that Boccaccio had already made. It is an Alexandrian point. Theseus was not the center of the *Hecale*, and the mature Theseus there was in any case swallowed

---

[10] *Brevitas* is discussed by E. R. Curtius, *Europäische Literatur und lateinisches Mittelalter*, pp. 481 ff. It is the last echo of a doctrine which certainly had some Alexandrian basis (Callimachus, fr. 57. 1 Pf.), whatever its connections with Stoicism. See further, p. 440 below.

[11] See above, pp. 109–10 and notes. There are more protestations by an intruded narrator about his inability to tell his story in the early pages of Dostoevsky's *The Possessed* and Thomas Mann's *Doktor Faustus*. The topos in itself has quite a long history: L. Arbusow, *Colores Rhetorici*, p. 105.

[12] The sharp Greek eye for telling visual detail, shared by Chaucer, is illustrated by Callimachus, fr. 75. 10–11 Pf. The Romans tended to blur their vision. Catullus' translation of Callimachus' *Lock of Berenice* shows this very well: see "Catullus as Translator," by D. E. W. Wormell in *The Classical Tradition*, ed. L. Wallach (Cornell 1966), pp. 187 ff. This may be partially explained by their readiness to let music dominate over painting in their adaptation of the Alexandrian poetic. The same explanation is relevant to the irritating imprecision of which Milton has been accused.

up by the princeling. The difference is that Chaucer exploits more surely than the Italian the Alexandrian love of brevity.

One detail has nevertheless been added by Chaucer in spite of his hurry, and that is the tempest at Hippolyta's home-coming. Editors may be right here to seek an explanation in "real life." When Richard II brought home Ann of Bohemia, there was a storm so violent that it destroyed in harbor the very ship in which she had traveled. But Hoccleve praised Chaucer for treading in Virgil's footsteps,[13] and we are well enough acquainted with the Virgilian manner to expect that this storm, more importantly, will have artistic relevance.[14]

In Statius, Theseus catches sight of the Theban women who have come to appeal to him for help, halts, and asks them their business. He is answered by a long speech of 40 lines, after which his reply and the assembling of troops for the expedition take another 90 lines, which are adorned with a description of Theseus' shield. Boccaccio takes 26 stanzas (208 lines). In him, attention is focused on dramatic speech.

Chaucer takes 52 lines. He too works up his material dramatically. The ladies are clad in black, as in Boccaccio. They make a cry the like of which has never been heard. They seize Theseus' bridle, the duke is taken aback, the woman who speaks first swoons, arousing pity both to see and to hear. All this is the application of Hellenistic narrative technique, such as we now find best exemplified in the Proteus episode at the end of *Georgics* IV, or in the *Aeneid* itself.[15] Chaucer even adds a lyrical touch. Statius identifies his speaker before she begins. Chaucer keeps us waiting 20 lines for her name.[16]

Fired with indignation, Theseus proposes immediately to set out

---

[13] Hoccleve's poem is given in the (old) *New Oxford Book of English Verse*, ed. A. Quiller-Couch (repr. Oxford 1966), no. 17. J. Mitchell, "Hoccleve's Tribute to Chaucer" (in *Chaucer und seine Zeit*, ed. A. Esch [Tübingen 1968]), sees only a debt of rhetoric between the ancient and the medieval poet (pp. 281 ff.). But on p. 283, where he fails to connect Hoccleve's "universal fadir in science" with the long tradition of ascribing omniscience to a favored epic poet (even to Ariosto: Weinberg, p. 1045), he shows that he does not understand the convention of ancient rhetoric: see, for example, [Plutarch], *De Vita et Poesi Homeri* for this in regard to Homer: Macrobius, *Somn. Scip.* II. 8. 1 (Virgil). The primitive assumption that the writer must know all ("clerk"/"cleric") was still an embarrassment to Thomas Mann.

[14] Line 1980, the storm painted in Mars' temple. Storms in the *Aeneid* are discussed by V. Pöschl, *The Art of Vergil* (Eng. tr. G. Seligson), pp. 13 ff. The "Martial serpent" first manifested at Argos in a storm is a leitmotif in Statius' *Thebaid*: above, p. 235.

[15] See above, pp. 142–56, and in general R. Heinze, *Virgils epische Technik* (repr. Stuttgart 1957), pp. 285 ff., 466 ff.

[16] F. Dornseiff, *Pindars Stil*, p. 107; B. L. Gildersleeve's note on *Olympian* 10. 34. See above, p. 275.

for Thebes. Chaucer gives a striking description of his banner and pennant (975–80):

> The rede statue of Mars, with spere and targe,
> So shyneth in his white baner large,
> That alle the feeldes glyteren up and doun;
> And by his baner born is his penoun
> Of gold ful riche, in which ther was ybete
> The Mynotaur, which that he slough in Crete.

Boccaccio has none of this. He gives a plain account of the march and arrival in Thebes. Statius' *ecphrasis* (XII. 665 ff.) has a truly epic swing and romance about it. Inspired by both his predecessors, Chaucer abbreviates, offers vivid color contrasts, and presents a symbol of the god of war which is to be used to powerful effect in his poem.[17]

Yet these are not three different epic traditions. They are three different poets working within the same tradition, and exploiting different facets of it as genius, temperament, and artistic aim dictate. Boccaccio offers the simplicity of the *ischnos charactēr*; Chaucer, the strictly organized lyricism which Callimachus and later Alexandrians such as Moschus had borrowed from the Greek choral poets and, like Euripides, combined with the prosiness of their slender style. Their catalysis of the epic tradition shows both what was in it, and what they considered valuable to themselves in their circumstances.

Theseus' battle with Creon is again abbreviated (985). When it is over, and the ladies have been allowed to bury their dead at the cost of more deaths, the field is given over at night-time to pillagers. Two young knights are found half alive, half dead with their wounds: Arcita and Palamon. Taken to Athens, cured, they are kept in perpetual prison.

One May morning, Hippolyta's sister, Emily, is minded to rise early and go picking flowers in the royal garden. Chaucer enjoys this description of the fair creature in a fair season. She plucks flowers "party white and rede" and sings. Palamon, also awake, hears her, looks out and falls in love with her. He cries out with the pain of his wounded heart. Arcita comforts him, by reminding him that pain must be endured. The stars have willed it so (1084–90):

> For Goddes love, taak al in pacience
> Oure prisoun, for it may noon oother be.

---

[17] Chaucer's red and white is anticipated by Catullus 64, lines 48 and 308, where there is also a contrast between the marriage bed and the fate of Achilles. Virgil uses the same contrast at *Aen.* XII. 67 ff., a simile which prefigures in miniature the action of the entire book: see *Augustus and the New Poetry*, pp. 241–42, and above, p. 87 note 36; below, p. 407 note 22.

Fortune hath yeven us this adversitee.
Som wikke aspect or disposicioun
Of Saturne, by som constellacioun,
Hath yeven us this, although we hadde it sworn;
So stood the hevene whan that we were born.

Palamon explains the situation, and prays to Venus for help. Arcita then looks out, and he too falls in love. He is slain by Emily's fresh beauty. Palamon responds that they have sworn to help each other in love. Arcita is determined to take no notice. Love knows no laws. But, in any case, common sense shows that neither of them is ever likely to win the lady.

Here, Chaucer has made important alterations to his model. In Boccaccio, it is Arcita who sees Emilia first and, when Palemone in his turn falls in love, there is more of kinship than rivalry between the two. But fate is already at work, and Boccaccio innocently brings this out in his description of the heavens. The sun, he remarks (III. 5), was in Taurus, the zodiacal sign which commemorates the rape of Europa. In legend, Europa was the sister of Cadmus, ancestor of the Thebans and first begetter of all their woe. Venus too is rising, while Jupiter lingers in Pisces. The implication seems to be that the gods can get away with their amours. Men, their victims, cannot.[18]

Unlike Boccaccio, Chaucer displays no interest here in the dismal history of the children of Oedipus and the Theban line. For him, Arcita must accept a more direct share of guilt. But this is not the whole story. Chaucer is just as much concerned as Boccaccio to signpost the inevitability of later events. He does it by his imagery of wounds and death (as Virgil does with Dido at the beginning of *Aeneid* IV), of the colors shared by Emily and Mars, by his allusion to "prisoun"[19] and, overwhelmingly, by the introduction of the sinister figure of Saturn, of whom Boccaccio knows nothing.[20]

The lesson of the alterations seems to be that Chaucer and

[18] The "Rape of Europe" theme in Thomas Mann's *Doktor Faustus* is noted below, p. 503, and Apollonius' interest in astronomy is detailed above, pp. 89 ff.

[19] Echoed in *prisoun*, 3061 (speech of Theseus). But the carnival liberates from prison! Cf. Euripides, *Bacchae* 591 ff.; NT Act. Apost. 16:26. Compare . . . *omnes avidi spectant ad carceris oras/Quam mox emittat pictis e faucibus currus*: Ennius, *Ann.* 89–90 (Warmington). The realization of the metaphor of the wound of love (an example of the "Aristophanes effect") recurs in Tolstoy: below, p. 451 note 7.

[20] D. B. Loomis, "Saturn in Chaucer's *Knight's Tale*" (*Chaucer und seine Zeit*, above, note 13, pp. 149 ff.), suggests that of two contrasting characterizations, benign and malevolent, available to him, Chaucer deliberately chose for his story the malevolent, against the "English" tradition, represented, for example, by Walter Map and John Ridewall. The classical background is noted by Klibansky, Panofsky, Saxl, *Saturn and Melancholy* (New York 1964), pp. 193–94, and C. O. Brink, *Horace on Poetry, the 'Ars Poetica'* (Cambridge 1971), p. 334.

Boccaccio are certainly concerned with the moral and philosophical aspects of their story (its "vatic" element), but that Chaucer's concern is less man-of-the-world and accepting, more "gothic" in its horrors. This will be apparent later.

Arcita is unexpectedly freed, thanks to the intervention of Duke Perithous. Once again, the English poet sharpens the note of personal animosity. While in Boccaccio the two brothers part after mutual embraces and protestations, and Palemone's natural jealousy is muted, in Chaucer Arcita already sees his release as a victory for Palamon (1235), exactly as Palamon sees it as a victory for Arcita (1282). Boccaccio offered a touching description of Arcita's departure from Athens, watched by an Emilia who already feels for him a certain sympathy (III. 83). In Chaucer, the two rivals are so locked up in themselves that they meditate more on the vagaries of human life and fortune and on their own personal sufferings than they do on any realistic appreciation of the lady who is their cause. Here, as the two knights reflect on their dilemma, Chaucer ends the first part of his story, addressing the reader directly with the formulation of the unhappy predicament.

Chaucer now makes important modifications to Boccaccio's story-line. His Arcita suffers for a year and more. Then Mercury appears to him in a vision and bids him go to Athens, where he is destined to find an end of his trouble.[21] He disguises himself as a poor laborer. In Athens, he gradually improves his lot until he is appointed by Theseus as squire of his chamber. Meanwhile, Palamon has been languishing in prison. After seven years of it, he succeeds in escaping. On his way back to Thebes, though still in Theseus' territory, he seeks a hiding place in a wood. It is again May. Arcita too is astir betimes, and goes to the very wood in which Palamon is hiding. After a while, he falls to lamenting his unrequited love for Emily (a theme and setting as old as Callimachus' *Acontius and Cydippe*). Outraged, Palamon starts up. Angry words are exchanged. The two rivals agree to fight it out in combat the next day. Arcita goes off to find armor. Next day, they fight long and bloodily in the same wood, but are interrupted by Theseus himself, who has come out to hunt. He hears the whole story from Palamon. His inclination to put the pair to death is balked by the ladies with him, Hippolyta and Emily. He decides to forgive them both, and ordains that whichever of them

---

[21] Mercury is dressed as he was when he brought about the slaying of Argus (1389–90), and the end of Arcita's troubles at Athens will be his death. Yet Mercury tells Arcita to be merry. The ironic contrast between human ignorance and divine malice visible in the figure of Saturn is also evident here, and cannot be overlooked in the assessment of Chaucer's purpose.

wins a tournament to be held in a year's time shall have the lady's hand. Here Chaucer's second part ends.

Boccaccio by contrast takes two books to narrate these events. After leaving Athens, his Arcita changes his name to the speaking "Penteo."[22] He then visits the site of Thebes, wasted by fire, and laments appropriately on the fate of its inhabitants. He goes to Corinth, to Mycenae, to Aegina, all famous examples of vanished greatness, which serve to generalize his personal misfortunes. There, unable to rest, he prays to Apollo to grant him return to Athens. His prayer is heard exactly, and he does return. He is taken into Theseus' service, and is recognized only by Emilia. He falls into the habit of going into the countryside to lament his sorrows in private,[23] but one day there he is overheard by Palemone's servant, Panfilo, who reports to his master that Arcita is back. It is then for the first time that jealousy fills Palemone, and inspires him with thoughts of challenging Arcita to battle. With Panfilo's help, he does at last succeed in escaping from jail, and of course he knows precisely where to go. In the wood, he finds Arcita asleep. They greet each other affectionately, and when Palemone waxes eloquent on the subject of his passion, Boccaccio's Arcita at first tries to reason with him. Palemone will have none of that, and Arcita sees that the old curse of Thebes is at work. They are both armed, and combat breaks out forthwith. It is interrupted by Emilia, who is soon joined by the rest of her hunting party. There then follows the reconciliation with Theseus and agreement to a joust as in Chaucer.

Once again, Boccaccio is interested far more than Chaucer at this point (but like Statius) in the descent of his pair from a cursed lineage. Remarkably, for him Arcita, the devotee of Mars, is the peaceable member of the duo, and Palemone, the servant of Venus, the irascible. Emilia, in hunting garb, is a Virgilian figure.[24]

The Italian is not however concerned with assigning human guilt. Arcita gets from Apollo exactly what he prays for, as he will later when he prays to Mars. The tragedy of the situation lies in the assumption that the gods will either alter the decrees of fate which have from old tormented the Theban line, or that they care enough about men to fit their prayers into some sort of benign and providential scheme. Arcita grasps partially at the truth. He is nevertheless doomed. Palemone has no such self-knowledge. He is to live happily ever after.

---

[22] Above, p. 298.
[23] The motif is Callimachean (fr. 72 Pf.) and was picked up later by the Greek romance.
[24] Above, p. 164: cf. V. Pöschl, op. cit., p. 68.

Chaucer has introduced into his version of the story what looks like an awkward retardation.[25] In Boccaccio, the fight between the pair breaks out on the very morning that they meet again. In Chaucer, there is the strange postponement of one day, during which Arcita fetches armor for them both. The element of deliberate intent is far more prominent in this version of the quarrel. Chaucer's pair are interrupted, not by Emily, but by Theseus. This too gives more masculine and serious tones to his narrative.[26] There is attention to destiny in the English poet. But he lends tension to his story by making it far less of a foregone conclusion that tragedy is to be its end.

Part Three opens with a description of the lists constructed for the tournament. By each gate of the "theatre," which is a mile in circumference, are oratories, at the east of Venus, at the west of Mars, and at the north of Diana. On the description of these shrines the poet has lavished some of his finest writing. Venus is shown in all her power: the cruelty, the false hopes, the pleasures and allurements. Her statue[27] is particularly noteworthy (1955–62):

> The statue of Venus, glorious for to se,
> Was naked, fletynge in the large see,
> And fro the navele doun al covered was
> With wawes grene, and brighte as any glas.
> A citole in hir right hand hadde she,
> And on hir heed, ful semely for to se,
> A rose gerland, fressh and wel smellynge;
> Above hir heed hir dowves flikerynge.

Mars too appears in all his grim might (1975 ff.). In his temple are Felony, Ire, Dread, every kind of murder and deceit, expressed with incomparable vividness (1999–2001):

> The smylere with the knyf under the cloke;
> The shepne brennynge with the blake smoke;
> The tresoun of the mordrynge in the bedde . . .

Conquest is there, with the sword hanging over his own head, and even the deaths of Julius Caesar and "grete Nero" are shown, and of Mark Antony. The use of anachronism is an important indication of the treatment of time in this style, and should be compared with

---

[25] Homer's technique of rest is observed by the scholiasts: L. Adam, *Die aristotelische Theorie vom Epos nach ihrer Entwicklung bei Griechen und Römern* (Wiesbaden 1889), p. 39. The alternation of rest and advance in narrative technique is what the Formalists call "staircase structure."

[26] Yet Theseus too is a huntsman. He may ultimately try to rationalize the cosmic process, but he cannot help exemplifying its cruelty.

[27] Cf. Petrarch, *Africa* III. 212.

the same device in Shakespeare and Milton. Chaucer explains it here in a way familiar to the Middle Ages (2033–38):

> Al be that thilke tyme they were unborn,
> Yet was hir deth depeynted ther-biforn
> By manasynge of Mars, right by figure.
> So was it shewed in that portreiture,
> As is depeynted in the sterres above
> Who shal be slayn or elles deed for love.

The idea that all is predestined is reinforced by Mars' statue. He has two stars over his head (2044–45),

> that been cleped in scriptures,
> That oon Puella, that oother Rubeus.

Puella is also assigned by astrological authorities to Venus.[28] Goddess and god share an eternal principle of order where man must yield to a divine symmetry.

Chaucer's Diana is a powerful and even cruel figure. She hunts, she turns the unfaithful Callisto into a bear; even Daphne's transformation into a tree is associated with her. Actaeon is shown torn to pieces by his hounds. The goddess' statue has its eyes modestly turned down, to the realm of Pluto, god of the underworld, where, in one of her aspects, Diana held sway.

Once again, Chaucer has refreshed tradition by drawing on tradition. Boccaccio had no oratories adjacent to his theatre. He did describe the journey of the prayers offered by Arcita and Palemone to their patrons Mars and Venus in Ovidian language which has clearly influenced the English poet. He did furnish material from which Chaucer was able to construct Diana's oratory. He reserved his descriptions however for his seventh book, just before the tournament was about to begin. Chaucer, reversing the order Mars/Venus for Venus/Mars, and putting the whole passage prominently at the start of his third section, reminds his readers of the terms of the celestial argument in a powerful, even controlling fashion. He had ample precedent in Virgil and Apollonius.[29]

The appointed year has elapsed, and Arcita and Palamon arrive with their company of knights to do battle. This arrival provided Boccaccio with the excuse, not neglected by Statius in Book XII of the *Thebaid*, to introduce a set topos of classical epic, the mustering

---

[28] Robinson on line 2045.

[29] E.g. *Arg.* III. 7 ff. (before Medea); *Aen.* I. 223 ff. (before Dido); *Aen.* XII. 791 ff. (before the death of Turnus). Cf. Homer, *Iliad* XVI. 441–42 = XXII. 179–81: above, p. 13. Chaucer however is not concerned with reconciling divine and human, but with their opposition.

for war. Like Apollonius,[30] the Italian clearly felt the need to modernize this compulsory ritual. He devotes to it 15 stanzas, in which he both manages to summarize and yet to list some absentees. He begins with Lycurgus, king of Nemea, who is still in mourning for the loss of his son Opheltes, and ends with Admetus, king of Thessaly. Neither of these figures occurs by chance. When a funeral pyre is ultimately built for the dead Arcita, it is that of Opheltes with which it is compared.[31] Admetus, to whom Apollo himself became a servant out of love, is a recurring example in the poem of the power of Venus.[32]

Chaucer applies still other Alexandrian techniques to the epic problem. The long epic catalogue, appropriate to the primitive mentality, had already been abbreviated in drama, by Aeschylus as well as Euripides. Similarly, in the lyric of Simonides, a master of the "plain" style, when the Greek fleet set sail home from Troy, the ghost of Achilles was described as rising above his tomb to watch the departure in a way which said more than any tedious roll-call. *Phantasia*, the substitution of the "telling" image for the generalized and silent collectivity, is commended by Aristotle, and practiced by artists as different as Dante and Eisenstein. It was a technique where epic could learn from other genres.[33]

Chaucer conjures up an impression of the assembled magnificence of the knights who join Arcita and Palamon by singling out Lycurgus and Emetreus for close attention. The reader is so taken with their fantastic garb, which does not lack a certain symbolic importance, that he easily fills in, with this stimulus to his imagination, the backcloth of their triumphant train. The muster may then be safely reduced in length without any sense of cheating.

After the welcomes, Palamon rises early and goes to pray to Venus. Here Chaucer takes up again material that he had already introduced from Boccaccio at the beginning of his third section. It is in her hour, so that the astrological significance is being carefully marked. He acknowledges in his prayer that it is Mars who is the god of arms. Yet his service and allegiance are all to Venus, and he begs her either

---

[30] *Arg.* I. 23 ff.

[31] *Tes.* XI. 18. See above, p. 235 and "De Statio epico animadversiones," *Latomus* XXXIV (1975), 80–89.

[32] E.g. Arcita/Penteo invokes the example of Admetus both at the beginning and end of his troubles (IV. 46; X. 25). The alternative title to Boccaccio's *Comedia delle Ninfe fiorentine* is *Ameto*.

[33] Cf. Aeschylus, *Septem* 375 ff.; Euripides, *Phoenissae* 106 ff.; Simonides fr. 52 (Page, *Poetae Melici Graeci*, p. 289); Aristotle, *Rhet.* II. 1386 a 29 ff.; Dante, *Par.* XXXIII. 142 (*fantasia*); above, pp. 42–43 (Aristotle's *Poetics*); p. 280 and note 80; below, p. 422 (Eisenstein).

to unite him with Emily, or to ensure that he dies pierced to the heart on the battlefield, so that he may not see her married to Arcita. The statue shakes, and Palamon departs, convinced that his prayer is answered.

Emily too sets off at an appropriate hour, for the oratory of Diana. She prays that her two lovers may be reconciled, and leave her alone. But, if she must marry one, she prays that it may be the one who loves her more. An omen is granted. One of the fires burning on the altar is quenched and quickened again. Another is quenched and extinguished. As it goes out, it makes a whistling noise, and from its end there run out what look like many bloody drops.

Diana herself then appears, and tells her that she is fated to marry one of the heroes. The goddess is garbed as a huntress,[34] and as she departs, the arrows in her quiver clatter and ring aloud.[35] She tells Emily that the fires on the altar will make destiny clear to her before she leaves the temple.

In this scene, Chaucer appears to have translated from Boccaccio rather carelessly. In the Italian, the omens occur after Diana's messenger has finished speaking, so that it is perfectly proper for the messenger to signal their imminence and symbolism. In Chaucer, the omens have already occurred, and Diana's words come lamely after the event. There is certainly no hint of any further omen, since we pass directly to Arcita and his prayer to Mars. The clumsy displacement of logical sequence by Chaucer seems to be on a par with his mistranslation of Boccaccio at the start of the whole episode. The Italian tells us that the temple was "clean" (*fu mondo il tempio*, VII. 72. 1), as indeed might be expected from a virgin goddess' *sanctum*. Chaucer writes loosely "Smokynge the temple" (2281), a clear misreading, or so it appears, of *fu mondo* as *fumando*.[36]

Chaucer however was not a professional translator but a poet. Awareness of the tradition in which he was working shows on the contrary that it was not carelessness but artistry which dictated the alterations to his model. The first point to be understood is that "smoke" is a symbol of the Divine Presence as old as the Hebrew Scriptures, more familiar perhaps in Chaucer's day than in our own. The second point is that Emily is in a highly wrought state of mind, as any girl would be on such an occasion. In the temple, she is to receive a terrifying omen of death. It is an omen given by fire. With

---

[34] The recurring image again suggests how little Chaucer meant to gloss over the "problem of evil" in his story.

[35] Cf. *Iliad* I. 46; in general, Ovid, *Met.* IX. 782–86.

[36] Robinson, *ad loc.* But textual criticism must always be the handmaid of literary sensibility. The Bible has smoking temples: e.g. Isaiah 6:4; Revelation 15:8.

a woman's intuition, even as she enters the temple, she guesses at what is to come. For her, the temple, normally so neat and tidy, is already smoking, filled with the atmosphere proper to religious revelation. There can be no *poetic* problem here.

But the human heart is a master of disguise, of itself and of unpleasant reality. Emily sees the omens of the quenched brands first, because she does not yet want to see anything else. Only after that does Diana become visible, breaking through material veils. The order is psychologically exact, the lesser phenomenon being followed by the greater. But Emily has had no chance to react intellectually to her situation, to ponder on the significance of these events. That is why it is perfectly correct for Diana to tell her that before she leaves the temple she will be clear over the symbolism of what has occurred. Only when the goddess departs is Emily free to begin to reflect on what is happening to her.[37]

Alexandrian though all this attention to psychological and religious truth may be, it is not to be expected of the Alexandrian poet that he will allow his reaction to tradition to be governed merely by poetic instinct. Some more consciously intellectual exploitation of technique is awaited, and Chaucer has not failed to provide a clue to these literary intentions. He has kept his emphasis on the lineage of the two heroes for this moment, and his alteration to his Italian model is the sign of his new artistic economy. As he refers to Emily's sacrifices in the temple of Diana, the Knight becomes unaccountably reticent and refuses to discuss them in detail, alluding simply to "Stace of Thebes and thise bookes olde" (2294). Of course Statius gives no details of any sacrifice which Emily may be supposed to have made. But he does describe a sacrifice which has some parallel with hers, and we know this because it is the sacrifice of which Boccaccio is thinking in his description of Emilia's offering.[38] In Statius, as the battle for Thebes is about to break out, Eteocles decides to consult the old, blind seer Teiresias concerning the future course of events. Teiresias is aided by his daughter Manto. A gruesome scene is worked up at great length (not without the comic touches always near the surface where primitive laughter has been artistically suppressed). Eventually Laius appears and declares that, though Thebes is to be safe, there are to be Furies and a double crime. The curse of cruel Oedipus is to be fulfilled. What is meant is that both brothers are to be slain, although Laius refuses to disclose the outcome of their combat. So in Chaucer. Two brothers are to meet in battle. The

---

[37] "Anon" (2365) may mean "in due course": cf. *K. T.* 2450.

[38] A. Limentani adduces Statius, *Theb.* IV. 645 on *Tes.* VII. 93. At *Tes.* VII. 106–07, he notes that the simile is taken from *Theb.* IV. 494 ff.

oracle (here Diana) refuses to reveal which of the two is to win. All we know is the cruelty and power of the gods.

Statius' scene involves plenty of smoke (*Thebaid* IV. 467–72):

> . . . nec rapidas cunctatur [*sc.* Manto] frondibus atris
> Subiectare faces. Atque ipse sonantia flammis
> Virgulta et tristis crepuisse ut sensit acervos
> Tiresias (illi nam plurimus ardor anhelat
> Ante genas impletque cavos vapor igneus orbis),
> Exclamat (tremuere rogi et vox terruit ignem).

Without delay, Manto set her torches beneath the dark boughs. Teiresias heard the wood hissing in the flames, and the crackling of the gloomy heaps. Clouds of smoke billowed before his face, and their fiery vapor filled his eyeless sockets. He cried out. The pyres shuddered, and his voice terrified the blaze.

It is to this scene that we may conclude Chaucer, prompted by Boccaccio, turned in imagination as he thought of Emily entering the temple of Diana. Boccaccio had made it clear that his Arcita and Palemone were a twinning metamorphosis of Eteocles and Polynices, whose legendary hostility was the theme of the *Thebaid*. The appalling curse which was worked out in their fate demands that, when this fate re-emerges in Arcita and Palamon, Emily should enter, not a clean temple, but one filled with smoke, the smoke of funeral pyres (*rogi*) as well as that of burnt offerings.

So too in Virgil. When Iarbas enters his temple to pray to Jupiter about Dido's rejection of him for Aeneas, and to begin the process which leads to Aeneas' rejection of Dido, he is greeted by fires (*Aen.* IV. 200–01):

> Centum aras posuit vigilemque sacraverat ignem,
> Excubias divum aeternas. . . .

He set a hundred altars, and had dedicated watchful fire, the everlasting sentinel of the gods.

It is fire which Aeneas carries with him as his last earthly memory of Dido.[39] The storm that Chaucer described at Theseus' homecoming was a double of the storm in the *Aeneid* when Aeneas landed in Africa. Like the first hearing of a musical theme, it hinted at the analogy (not of course an allegory) between Chaucer's action and

---

[39] *Aen.* V. 4. Boccaccio exploits the imagery of smoke and fire in *Tes.* VII. 22–23; 27–28; 40; 42; 75; 78; 82. At 74. 7 and 78. 2 Emilia's "pyres" in the temple anticipate the pyre she is to make for Arcita at XI. 44. The *Teseida* does in fact even have smoking temples (XI. 85). Chaucer was well in touch with the spirit, if not the letter, of his original, in writing "smokynge the temple."

Virgil's which was to be worked out as the English poem developed in intensity.

The next to make his ritual visit and offer prayer is Arcita. The fire symbolism here is unmistakable. Mars too, as Arcita reminds him, has burned in flames, the flames of his passion for Venus, which had once been detected by Venus' husband, the fire-god Vulcan. Boccaccio alludes to this story, but omits all reference to fire. What Chaucer has done, as with Emily's sacrifice to Diana, is to take hints thrown out by the rest of Boccaccio's narrative (VII. 27, 28, 41) and introduce the fire at what he thinks is a more telling point (2382–84):

> Thanne preye I thee to rewe upon my peyne.
> For thilke peyne, and thilke hoote fir
> In which thow whilom brendest for desir.

Arcita goes on to make promises to Mars (2412–13):

> And everemo, unto that day I dye,
> Eterne fir I wol bifore thee fynde.

When he finishes his prayer, more fire appears. The temple doors and their rings clatter aloud, and (2425–29)

> The fyres brenden upon the auter brighte,
> That it gan al the temple for to lighte;
> A sweete smel the ground anon up yaf,
> And Arcita anon his hand up haf,
> And moore encens into the fyr he caste.

Arcita departs with the sound of "Victory" ringing in his ears.

The analogy with the *Aeneid* now becomes insistent. In Chaucer, the strife between the two human rivals has its counterpart in heaven. Jupiter tries to calm the opposing deities, but it is Saturn who settles their differences. Old and cold, he has the timeless wisdom which puts into petty perspective the hot imaginations of youth. Chaucer makes us fully aware of the irony by which this malevolent god of destruction volunteers to appease strife and dread. Saturn, who quiets his (grand-) daughter Venus' fears, is a horrible parody of the benign Jupiter who soothes his daughter Venus in the first book of the *Aeneid* with the prophecy of Rome's coming greatness.[40] The self-description which Chaucer puts into his mouth speaks volumes (2453–60):

> "My deere doghter Venus," quod Saturne,
> "My cours, that hath so wyde for to turne,
> Hath moore power than woot any man.
> Myn is the drenchyng in the see so wan;
> Myn is the prison in the derke cote;

---

[40] *Aen.* I. 223 ff. Cf. above, p. 8 note 8.

> Myn is the stranglyng and hangyng by the throte,
> The murmure and the cherles rebellyng,
> The groynynge, and the pryvee empoysonyng. . . ."

This list of Gothic horrors, advanced in a context where we look for kindly reassurance that daddy can fix everything, is an astonishing example of "suppressed laughter," and in this respect rivals Dante's picture of his hirsute carnival monster, Satan, itself perhaps inspired by Virgil's Atlas. We have, not mere irony, but metaphysics.

In Boccaccio's story, Saturn has no parallel. The contrast between the classical, sunlit clarity of the Italian and the gloomy rainswept chill of the Englishman is the difference between climates and civilizations to which allusion was made at the beginning of this chapter. But Boccaccio, as we saw, has no naively optimistic view of man's relationship to the gods. His Mars and Venus settle their quarrel with as much insouciance as the rich in a Scott Fitzgerald novel. The Italian is concerned too with the lyrical exploitation of emotion, in succession to Euripides and anticipation of Puccini. Chaucer's terrifying awareness of the grim and harsh realities of our earthly plight leaves no room for melodrama.

The fourth and last part of the Knight's story now begins. Once again it is May. A brilliant description of the gathering of people and knights, their costumes, their horses, conveys a swift impression of the scene. Theseus proclaims rules intended to make the combat less bloody. The contestants enter the lists, each from beneath the shrine of his patron deity. In a passage reminiscent of more than the alliterative poetry still flourishing in his day, Chaucer gives a vigorous account of the tournament.[41] Palamon, in Boccaccio captured by Cromis' horse, here is seized by twenty knights and made prisoner. He has lost in spite of his bravery, and Arcita, being told of the capture, comes forward to receive the plaudits of the crowd and the favors of his beloved.

Chaucer avoids, like Apollonius in the *Argonautica*, the direct confrontation of foe with foe. His battle is carefully controlled and stylized. No one is actually killed, as in Boccaccio's Ovidian and serio-comic gladiatorial contest, in which there is death in plenty, and yet one doughty combatant is actually carried to safety by his horse. The poet is meanwhile guiding his epic towards the unexpected and even anti-climactic. He has of course another climax in mind.

---

[41] Boccaccio writes (VIII. 1): *Taceva tutto il teatro aspettando / il terzo cenno del sonar tireno.* This recalls Ennius' *at tuba terribili sonitu tarantara dixit* (Warmington, 143) and Milton's use of the same device for the battle of the angels (*P. L.* VI. 207 ff.). Alliteration was very old in the European epic tradition, but the Alexandrians had given it fresh impulse (e.g. Catullus 64. 262).

Now Boccaccio and Chaucer diverge sharply. In the former, as Book IX of the *Teseida* opens, Venus and Mars have been amicably watching the fray.[42] Venus sees that Palemone's company can make no further resistance and, turning to Mars, she points out that his side of the bargain is fulfilled. Now it is for her to answer Palemone's prayer. Mars cheerfully agrees, and leaves her to work her pleasure. She has already requested a Fury from the god of the Underworld, and this she now deploys against Arcita. There is no celestial argument, no sense of despair, only the completely inhuman, literal granting of prayers made so short-sightedly by humans.

Chaucer is thinking of another passage of the *Aeneid*, inspired in its turn by the *Iliad*. His Venus is completely dispirited by Arcita's victory in the joust, and her streams of tears fill the lists.[43] Once again, it is Saturn who consoles her, reminding her that her turn will come. The Fury which then scares Arcita's horse is sent by him, and it is he who hinders Arcita's recovery from the injury he receives. The whole episode is linked to Saturn's previous intervention by the ghastly parody, common to both, of the benevolent prophecy and intervention of Jupiter at Venus' request in the *Aeneid*. This blends in his imagination with the conversation between Jupiter and Juno in Book XII of Virgil's epic which leads to Aeneas' victory and the death of Turnus.

The Fury in both Boccaccio and Chaucer is owed to Statius, and Statius owed it to the scene from *Aeneid* XII which has just been mentioned. The Callimachean purification of the tradition is well seen in the repeated adaptations. Virgil took 26 lines (*Aen.* XII. 843–68). Statius barely overtopped him with 27 lines (*Theb.* VI. 491–517). The portent (which is not actually described except in terms of its effect), the accident, the reflections on the significance of the death are allotted the usual Statian symmetry of 11, 11 and 5 lines.[44] Boccaccio uses six stanzas (48 lines). He explains carefully that Venus had already visited Dis and obtained the services of a number of Furies, from whom she finally chose Erinis. She shows Erinis what is to be done. A whole stanza describes what Erinis looks like, another her effect on the watching audience. The horse is frightened, Arcita falls and is terribly injured, the horse runs away unharmed.

---

[42] Again an ironic parody of the *Aeneid* (XII. 791 ff.), with malice substituted for benevolence.

[43] At *Aen.* I. 228 Venus is *tristior et lacrimis oculos suffusa nitentis*. There is no parallel to these tears in Boccaccio. Saturn's "deere doghter" may also be compared with *Aen.* I. 256 *oscula libavit natae* and with Zeus' similar address in *Iliad* XXII. 183 (above, p. 8).

[44] Above, pp. 238–39.

Chaucer takes 16 lines. He wastes no time on describing the monster, who is dismissed in three words as "a furie infernal." He wastes no time on the details of the accident. He does give a striking picture of the wounded Arcita (2691–93):

> His brest tobrosten with his sadel-bowe.
> As blak he lay as any cole or crowe,
> So was the blood yronnen in his face.

He has therefore done two things with the treatment he inherited, burdened as it too often was with the descriptive, static *ecphrasis* of physical appearance. He has shortened it, and he has made it relevant to the structure of his poem as a whole, since this kind of close and even homely description was used earlier to impress upon the reader Saturn's power. Chaucer employs the same rhyme to depict the accident as Saturn uses to depict his own nature (*Saturne/turne*: 2453–54 and 2685–86). We are to have more of this ugly detail soon.

Virgil's Fury was introduced at the culmination of his epic to resolve the deadly combat between Aeneas and Turnus. Turnus had up to that moment been protected by his goddess sister, Juturna, until Jupiter sends a spirit from hell to break his and her nerve. Here we see an aspect of Jupiter which reminds us strongly of Chaucer's Saturn. Boccaccio cared nothing for stating the terms of the problem of evil, and perhaps he would have thought it naive to seek any more for sense in the running of the universe. Virgil and Chaucer however are still engaged in the debate.

Virgil's lines may be analyzed as follows:

| 843–44 | Introductory | 2 lines | |
|---|---|---|---|
| 845–52 | The twin Furies | 8 lines | (4+4) |
| 853–54 | Jupiter's orders to one | 2 lines | |
| 855–60 | She makes for earth | 6 lines | (1+4+1) |
| 861–66 | She assails Turnus | 6 lines | (2+2+2) |
| 867–68 | He reacts | 2 lines | |

With this we may compare Chaucer's account:

| 2684–85 | The Fury and the reason for her appearance | 2 lines |
|---|---|---|
| 2686–87 | Arcita's horse reacts | 2 lines |
| 2688–93 | Arcita's injuries | 6 lines |
| 2694–99 | He is taken to the palace and put to bed | 6 lines |

It would be pointless then to attempt to separate Chaucer from Virgil, Statius or Boccaccio on the grounds that he showed less appreciation of careful symmetry than they: and we must of course bear in mind all the time his use of rhyming couplets, which is merely one aspect of ancient lyrical technique pushed to extremes.[45] Virgil devotes a balancing six and six lines to the description of his Fury's leap towards earth and attack on Turnus, in which she is compared to an arrow shot by Rome's most formidable foe, the Parthians. Aeneas, who appeared already in Book I of the epic as a huntsman, and who is to be so described again in Book XII as he closes for the kill, receives in this image the divine and yet damned consecration of his role in history. His opponent becomes Dido, becomes even Aeneas himself at a time when Aeneas was yet human enough to marvel at what the gods wanted of him.[46] This kaleidoscope of identities, passing with nightmarish fever through Turnus' mind, fills the balancing stanzas which catalogue his doom with presage, premonition, relevance.

But is not the same to be said of Chaucer's balancing six and six verses? Arcita's injuries are the fulfillment of Saturn's promise. His being taken to the palace and put to bed "ful faire and blyve" is the mocking parody of a lover's dreams. Chaucer's stark realism may be in some degree more northern than Italian, though Lucan's macabre style and its congeners afford some kind of classical parallel. But its purpose, to bring out the symbolic nature of what has happened, is certainly Virgilian. This explains why Arcita's face is "blak as any cole or crowe." It is as black as the face of a man strangled (cf. 2458), black as the dresses of the ladies who originally appealed to Theseus to intervene at Thebes (cf. 899, 911), black as the bird that beat upon Turnus' shield (*sata nocte*, *Aen.* XII. 860). Beneath all the differences of detail, we recognize the same purpose shaping the same tradition. Statius and Boccaccio had exploited other aspects of this tradition: Statius its irony and interest in psychology, Boccaccio its love of the picturesque as well as these other qualities. When he looked back to Virgil, Chaucer understood where the well of their inspiration lay.

The difference between Chaucer and, on the other side, Statius and Boccaccio in their treatment of the theme is not one of tradition. What the two earlier poets lack is the tragic sympathy needed to lend heroic intensity to their matter. Statius is too pessimistic to do more than play graceful variants upon a borrowed topos. He knows the rules. He leaves his monster largely undescribed, except for the

---

[45] Cf. F. Lapp, *De Callimachi Cyrenaei Tropis et Figuris* (diss. Bonn 1965), pp. 142 ff.; W. Stockert, *Klangfiguren und Wortresponsionen bei Pindar* (diss. Wien 1969); H. Patzer, "Zum Sprachstil des neoterischen Hexameters," *Museum Helveticum* 12 (1955), 77 ff. Above, p. 13 and note 18 (Homer); p. 57 and note 56 (Petrarch and Milton).

[46] Turnus = Dido: cf. *Aen.* XII. 871 = IV. 673. Turnus = Aeneas: XII. 868 = IV. 280. Cf. XII. 863–64 and IV. 461–62.

symbolic hint in *anguicomam*, and concentrates on the psychological effect which it may be supposed to have had. He refuses to indulge in anything so crude as a description of the victim's face. An apostrophe draws out the significance of the death. But the driving force and insight of a Virgil are missing, perhaps deliberately so. The same verdict may be passed on the limpid verses of the neutral Boccaccio. His monster owes more to Ovid than to anyone else.[47]

The important conclusion is not that by this time the Hesiodic/Alexandrian tradition of epic has become so vague that anything can count as part of it. The tradition can do much for an artist, but it cannot do everything. Art is one half of the old equation; *ingenium*, force of genius, is the other. When the best lack all conviction, lack the vatic impulse, rococo prettiness may take over. But from the rococo may spring a Mozart, from *Eine kleine Nachtmusik*, a *Requiem*.

Theseus dismisses the other knights with gifts, but Arcita grows worse. Once again, realistic detail (the "grotesque body" already exploited by Lucan) is not spared (2743-57):

> Swelleth the brest of Arcite, and the soore
> Encreesseth at his herte moore and moore.
> The clothered blood, for any lechecraft,
> Corrupteth, and is in his bouk ylaft,
> That neither veyne-blood, ne ventusynge,
> Ne drynke of herbes may ben his helpynge.
> The vertu expulsif, or animal,
> Fro thilke vertu cleped natural
> Ne may the venym voyden ne expelle.
> The pipes of his longes gonne to swelle,
> And every lacerte in his brest adoun
> Is shent with venym and corrupcioun.
> Hym gayneth neither, for to gete his lif,
> Vomyt upward, ne dounward laxatif.
> Al is tobrosten thilke regioun.

Realizing his predicament, he sends for Emily and Palamon, and declares his love for the one and affection for the other, bidding Emily remember Palamon if ever she thinks again of marriage. It will be noted that, in Chaucer's treatment, Emily comes off far better than she does in Boccaccio.

Arcita dies. His death has not much consolation about it, either for him (2777-79)—

> What is this world? what asketh men to have?
> Now with his love, now in his colde grave
> Allone, withouten any compaignye.

---

[47] *Tes.* IX. 5 with, e.g., Ovid, *Met.* IV. 474 ff.

or from the narrator (2809–15)—

> His spirit chaunged hous and wente ther,
> As I cam nevere, I kan nat tellen wher.
> Therefore I stynte, I nam no divinistre;
> Of soules fynde I nat in this registre,
> Ne me ne list thilke opinions to telle
> Of hem, though that they writen wher they dwelle.
> Arcite is coold, ther Mars his soule gye!

The "retentive virtue" which, according to the medicine of the day, prevented Arcita from expelling the deadly poison of his wound, was under the control of Saturn, so that the malevolent god is still at his work.[48]

Chaucer has deliberately chosen to make Arcita's death more desolate than it is in Boccaccio, who at this point indulges in a description of the soul's journey through the celestial spheres. Arcita's carnival, healing laugh (*rise*, XI. 3) is the last we hear from him. There is no laugh in Chaucer. Perhaps the English poet has sought to relieve his feelings by the rough humor of a colloquial phrase.[49] The devastating absence of any other disguise for the horror of death is important for the interpretation of the whole poem.

The refusal to resort to the clichés of comfort is borne out in the sequel. Emily shrieks and is inconsolable. Chaucer compares the general mourning to that which filled Troy when Hector's freshly slain body was brought home.[50] Aegeus, Theseus' father, attempts to bring the mourning to some sort of issue. Borrowing from Boccaccio's Theseus, he is full of wise saws and modern instances (2837–46):

> No man myghte gladen Theseus,
> Savynge his olde fader Egeus,
> That knew this worldes transmutacioun,
> As he hadde seyn it chaunge bothe up and doun,
> Joye after wo, and wo after gladnesse,
> And shewed hem ensamples and liknesse.
> "Right as ther dyed nevere man," quod he,
> "That he ne lyvede in erthe in som degree,
> Right so ther lyvede never man," he seyde,
> "In al this world, that som tyme he ne deyde. . . ."

---

[48] As he is in the repeated references to "cold," which contrast so pathetically with the images of fire in the poem.

[49] Cf. Robinson's note on 2805 ff.

[50] *Iliad* XXII. 410–11; *Aen.* IV. 669–71. Boccaccio, recalling the imagery of pyres and marriage in *Tes.* X from I, is equally aware of the Theban symbolism of Arcita's death.

The effect is comic, so comic as to appear brutally irrelevant to the sufferings of the dead man. The realism is Callimachean.[51]

Arcita's funeral is magnificently described. The site chosen for the pyre is the very wood where Palamon and Arcita had first met after their release from prison and issued their challenge.[52] The symbolism is again borrowed from Boccaccio, and ultimately from the *Aeneid*. The hot fire of love has kindled the hot fire of death. It is Emily who applies the torch to the pyre, confirming in act what she has already been in fact (the realization of the metaphor).

Descriptions of the construction of funeral pyres were as old as Homer, and scholars have traced their gradual amplification in epic.[53] Chaucer seeks to avoid the pitfalls of topical composition. Theseus gives his orders (2865–69):

> And leet comande anon to hakke and hewe
> The okes olde, and leye hem on a rewe
> In colpons wel arrayed for to brenne.
> His officers with swifte feet they renne
> And ryde anon at his comandement.

This is all we hear at the moment of the tree-felling. Later, when this scene is resumed, the poet puts it in parenthesis, refusing to be drawn into epic cliché (2919–24):

> But how the fyr was maked upon highte,
> Ne eek the names that the trees highte,
> As ook, firre, birch, aspe, alder, holm, popler,
> Wylugh, elm, plane, assh, box, chasteyn, lynde, laurer,
> Mapul, thorn, bech, hasel, ew, whippeltree, —
> How they weren feld, shal nat be toold for me.

This description, which we are "not" hearing from the poet, is actually made so concrete as to arouse the most vivid picture of nature, and the richness of the deciduous forests so much more common in the England of the Middle Ages than now. So it was that

---

[51] Cf. Callimachus' *Epigr.* XXIII Pf., on the man who committed suicide after reading Plato's *Phaedo*. Aegeus is using a topos of the ancient *consolatio* ("Thou know'st 'tis common") which in 52 B.C. Cicero described as *pervulgata maxime*.

[52] So Boccaccio, *Tes.* XI. 13.

[53] Cf. E. Norden on *Aen.* VI. 179 ff., and Robinson on lines 176–82 of *The Parliament of Fowls*. At *Tes.* VI. 14 Ligurgo was the first hero to join Arcita, though still in mourning for the death of his son Opheltes. At XI. 18 Theseus orders a pyre for Arcita like that of Opheltes. Boccaccio drives home his meaning by borrowing from Statius' description of Opheltes' pyre in *Theb.* VI. 96–106, and from Ovid, *Met.* X. 93 ff., where Orpheus too, like Arcita, is the victim of love.

Callimachus had particularized the wood which his comic hero Erysichthon had the rashness to chop down (*Hymn* VI. 25 ff., tr. Mair):[54]

> . . . and unto thyself they made a fair grove abounding in trees; hardly would an arrow have passed through them. Therein was pine, and therein were mighty elms, and therein were pear-trees, and therein were fair sweet-apples; and from the ditches gushed up water as it were of amber.

This is not the view of the countryman, who in some sense comes to take nature for granted. It is that wonderment of the city dweller for whom nature is a romantic world. As the fellers busy themselves, the townee who has unexpectedly accompanied them has time to look about him in the forest, and understand how much greater this life is than his own.

But Chaucer shares more than this with Callimachus. Both poets go on to give dramatic expression to their feelings in a way which may strike the study-bound as grotesque, unless they make an effort to comprehend the underlying insight (2925–30):[55]

> Ne hou the goddes ronnen up and doun,
> Disherited of hire habitacioun,
> In whiche they woneden in reste and pees,
> Nymphes, fawnes and amadrides;
> Ne hou the beestes and the briddes alle
> Fledden for fere, whan the wode was falle.

So when Callimachus' Erysichthon attacked Demeter's sacred wood (*loc. cit.* 33–40):

> He hastened with twenty attendants, all in their prime, all men-giants able to lift a whole city, arming them both with double axes and with hatchets, and they rushed shameless into the grove of Demeter. Now there was a poplar, a great tree reaching to the sky, and thereby the nymphs were wont to sport at noontide. This poplar was smitten first, and cried a woeful cry to the others. Demeter marked that her holy tree was in pain.

Homer's tree-felling knows nothing of this feeling. Ennius appears to have preserved the same remoteness. Virgil, who added at least *stabula alta ferarum* ("the wild creatures' deep lairs") to Ennius' lines, showed that he understood the action of the woodcutters at the Callimachean level. But Chaucer, following Ovid, Statius and Boccaccio in his handling of the topos, has with their aid gone right back

---

[54] Boccaccio refers to the myth at IV. 27 (Arcita/Penteo becomes like Erysichthon) and VI. 63. Ovid, in telling the story (*Met.* VIII. 738 ff.), does not particularize.

[55] Compare the medieval leaf-masks pictured in *Art of the Late Middle Ages* by H. Hofstätter (Eng. tr., New York 1968), p. 98.

to Callimachus himself. His ambiguous tone (we have "not" heard
any of this description), like that of Callimachus, prevents a simple
response to his poetry.

The funeral procession itself is in counterpoint to the arrival of
the knights which opened the fourth part of the story,[56] and a reprise
and combination of themes already heard in its very beginning. Color
contrasts splash vividly: the gold and white of Arcita's funeral garb,
the green laurel wreath upon his head, the black which Palamon
wears and which also decks the streets. The mourners' eyes are red
and white. The symbolism recalls that of Theseus' banner, Emily's
flowers, Diana's shrine and Mars' statue. It is repeated in that of the
vessels of gold, of the white milk, of the red blood and wine which
form the mourners' offerings. The fire symbolism is equally arresting
(2910–12):

> And after that cam woful Emelye,
> With fyr in honde, as was that tyme the gyse,
> To do the office of funeral servyse.

The description develops shortly into a long *occupatio*. The initial
device, which looked so naive and "natural" when it first occurred
(vv. 875 ff.), is taken up yet again. Here, rhetoric brilliantly becomes
the servant of feeling. Ridiculous at first sight, this "refusal" to give
the details of what happened undercuts the whole scene, robbing it
of anything that might distract our minds from its ultimate futility.
Like the musician who modulates into a minor key, Chaucer aims,
by this technique of parenthesis, which is really a technique of
Callimachean *recusatio*,[57] to show that for one person the whole pomp
and circumstance of the occasion was painfully irrelevant—for Arcita.
The finery is devoured by the flames, and among it all lies the corpse,
itself to be burned. When everything is over, and Emily has been led
weeping away, we are left with the reality (2956–57):

> Ne how that lad was homward Emelye;
> Ne how Arcite is brent to asshen colde. . . .

The fire has not warmed him. Saturn too is cold. The fire in Mars'
temple has destroyed its votary.

The cremation is followed by games, an echo of a primitive rite
and, in their origin, a re-assertion of life. But they too are passed

---

[56] Arrival of the knights, 2483–2594 = 112 lines; funeral procession and funeral,
2853–2964 = 112 lines. See below, p. 397.

[57] The Callimachean *recusatio* (see the *Glossary of Critical Terms, s.v.*, p. 528, below)
had already been taken up into epic by the Romans (above, pp. 242–43), but Chaucer's
development of their hint is brilliant. Sidonius Apollinaris (*Carm.* 9. 16 ff.) may have
helped.

over by Chaucer in parenthesis. He is far less open than Boccaccio to the metaphor of "the game of life." At the end, the Greeks go home (2964):

> Hoom til Atthenes, whan the pley is doon. . . .

But it was not play for Arcita, and he does not go home.

Chaucer has ostensibly hurried along his story by his use of *occupatio* in order to bring the events of the tale into philosophical perspective. A council is called at Athens to deal with matters of state, and Palamon is sent for. Theseus tactfully seizes the occasion to make a speech. As formulated by Chaucer, it replaces the well-worn topoi of the ancient *consolatio* developed by Boccaccio's Teseo, which were all Boccaccio could find (and all he wished to find) to sum up the moral of the story. Chaucer has already transferred some of this matter to the lips of Aegeus.[58]

Theseus' seriousness for Chaucer is indicated by the metaphysical embellishments his speech has acquired. Love, Theseus argues, is the chain by which the First Mover intended to bind the whole universe together. Within this general union, everything has its appointed limits and, though God himself is fixed and immovable, creation, sharing to a greater or less degree in imperfection, shares inevitably in instability and change. Our only course is to make a virtue of necessity, to accept transience, and to realize that the particular case of Arcita merely exhibits a universal rule. There is indeed in the circumstances of his death an especial nobility and honor (3058–66):

> Why grucchen we, why have we hevynesse,

[58] See Robinson's note on 2837. However, several qualifications are called for: (1) Egeo is in Boccaccio and does speak (*Tes.* XI. 10, 11, 12, 33), so that Chaucer does not "create" his character. (2) When Chaucer gives Theseus a new speech (*K. T.* 2987 ff.) he retains certain important features of the speech Theseus makes in Boccaccio, notably (a) the idea that it is best to die young and famous (*Tes.* XII. 9 and 12: *K. T.* 3047 ff.); (b) the argument that the manner of death does not matter (*Tes.* XII. 10: *K. T.* 3031 ff.); (c) the analogy with oaks, stones, rivers (in the same order: *Tes.* XII. 7: *K. T.* 3017 ff.); (d) the uselessness of protest against the divine will (*Tes.* XII. 6: *K. T.* 3039–40); (e) the need to make a virtue of necessity (*Tes.* XII. 11: *K. T.* 3042). (3) What Chaucer adds to Boccaccio cannot be dismissed as a borrowing from Boethius' *De Consol. Philosophiae*, in which there is no emphasis on the theory that being becomes corruptible the more it is removed from God: A. O. Lovejoy's standard work on this whole doctrine, *The Great Chain of Being* (Cambridge, Mass. 1936) makes little reference to Boethius. Chaucer's insistence on experience (3000–01) and on God's absolute power (3040) shows some affinity with contemporary fourteenth-century theology (Bacon, Ockham), and its refusal to look for a rational explanation of faith. These are certainly not doctrines of serenity. Playing upon scholastic terms formerly thought to be opposites (*contingenti/necessarie*, XII. 11. 8; 12. 1) Boccaccio showed the way to this treatment, but it took the English poet to travel to the end of the road.

> That goode Arcite, of chivalrie the flour,
> Departed is with duetee and honour
> Out of this foule prisoun of this lyf?
> Why grucchen heere his cosyn and his wyf
> Of his welfare, that loved hem so weel?
> Kan he hem thank? Nay, God woot, never a deel,
> That both his soule and eek hemself offende,
> And yet they mowe hir lustes nat amende.

The pointlessness of sorrowing for Arcita has already underlain the non-description of his funeral rites. Now Theseus shows, without tearing too rudely the veil of illusion thrown by convention over the harsh facts of life, that such pointlessness is part of the very essence of things. Arcita and Palamon in their prison were paradigms of us all, since life itself is a prison. But we have to go on living. The contradiction is patent when Theseus advises Emily and Palamon to marry (3071–72):

> I rede that we make of sorwes two
> O parfit joye, lastynge everemo.

But, on Theseus' own showing, nothing "lasts evermore" in this corrupt world! The philosophy may look more impressive than the commonplaces in Boccaccio. It shares something with them however in its lack of cogency, and in the last analysis it is no more comforting.[59]

Two pictures are therefore presented to us by the *Knight's Tale*. On the surface, it is a romance, in which one knight dies for love, and where ultimately the true love of another knight wins through to perfect happiness. Clothed as it is in the richest and most brilliant colors, this aspect of the narrative cannot fail to attract and hold the reader with its pageantry and display. But, behind all the external show, there lurk certain grim and ineluctable truths. Men are the instruments or, even worse, the playthings of the gods, who have no sense of morality in the human meaning of the word at all. For men, the horrible truth is that they are frail and they putrefy, and their passions are so irrational as to lead them on against their judgment to their own destruction. Beyond all the striking of attitudes, all the glitter, stands the dread principle of necessity. Our destinies are written in the stars, and we fight against them to no purpose.

Chaucer himself clearly felt the cleavage between pious theory and reality which his story illustrates, and this explains why he tried to illuminate the time-honored clichés of Boccaccio with the aid of philosophy. It is often suggested that he was thinking of Boethius.

---

[59] The assertion that the love of Emily and Palamon will outlast the world's corruption depends on the unproved assumption that Arcita was not really in love. In fact, Palamon, Arcita (and the rest of us) are in prison just by being alive.

But what light does Boethius in fact shed? His exalted treatise is based on a deep faith in the ultimate goodness of God, and the belief that all the changes of our earthly existence are ordered towards a beneficent end. As Philosophy points out to him, there is no such thing as bad fortune on this argument.[60] Boethius' sublimity evokes admiration, but where in his view of the world is there any place for Chaucer's Saturn, or indeed for any of Chaucer's gods? His God is the all-wise judge of human actions, whose only motive is love. That is a fine and impressive picture, but it can leave no room for Chaucer's stark vision of the evil malice at work in the world, sanctioned by the gods themselves in furtherance of their own whims.

Is reconciliation possible between the neo-Platonic arguments placed by Chaucer at the end of his story, and the terrifying insights into implacable doom offered in the course of it? The plain answer must be, no.[61] If the two views are to come together, something must yield. Instead of a parody of the scene between Jupiter and Venus found in the *Aeneid*, the scene itself would need to be reinstated. Instead of human love being shown as utterly futile, leading only to the quarrel of two brothers and the death of one of them to satisfy a divine caprice, it would have to be shown to be of the same quality, and as deserving of as much respect, as the love which moves the sun and the other stars. As the story stands, we are left, not with transcendent reconciliation, but with a question mark. The contradiction is already evident in Theseus' speech.

What is important however from the perspective of literary history is not that Chaucer failed to reconcile his contradiction, but that he raised it. There was a visible difference between Chaucer's view of the gods and that exemplified in a particular scene of *Aeneid* I. But this difference must not conceal the fact that Virgil too has no easy notion of how men are to understand the ways of Providence. His epic begins with the question which, in his own way, Chaucer has been amplifying: *Musa mihi causas memora . . . tantaene animis caelestibus irae?* In the course of the divine plan for Rome's eventual foundation,

[60] *De Consol. Philosophiae* III, pr. 12, and IV, pr. 2 imply that there is no such thing as evil. On *fatum* and *providentia* see IV, pr. 6. If a more convincing authority for the "Great Chain of Being" argument is needed, it might be supplied by John Scotus Erigena: cf. G. Leff, *Medieval Thought* (London 1958), pp. 62 ff. But Saturn (like Juno in the *Aeneid*) is always going to remain a difficulty in the way of too much rationalization.

[61] The views of C. Muscatine ("Form, Texture, and Meaning in Chaucer's *Knight's Tale*," *Proc. Mod. Lang. Ass.* 65 [1950], 911–29: see the same author's *Chaucer and the French Tradition* [Berkeley 1960], pp. 175–90), who believes that ". . . the crowning nobility . . . goes . . . to a perception of the order beyond chaos" (p. 190), have been modified by D. B. Loomis (above, note 20), who remarks (p. 161) how little reconciliation there really is in the story.

Aeneas, singled out to be the carrier of this purpose by no wish of his own, becomes the bearer of death and destruction to many whom he loves, many who are innocent. Everywhere he finds that he turns those he encounters into replicas of Dido, *forma pulcherrima*. His blind effort to escape at the very end of the poem by striking out at Turnus in the attempt to avenge Pallas' death merely confirms that he has doomed himself, as Achilles is doomed when he slays Hector.[62] No considerations of ordinary human morality check Virgil's Juno or Jupiter in the pursuit of their ambitions.

Yet it was this same Virgil who, we may suppose, would hardly have had the moral energy to compose his poem without some propelling belief, who also in the last analysis was convinced that the whole enterprise was worthwhile. But he has certainly left us no simple formula of reconciliation between, for example, the malice of the Jupiter who seduces Juturna and presents her by way of reward with a divine status which he must know can only serve to enhance her misery ("lastynge everemo"), and the wisdom of the Jupiter who wills that from the ashes of old Troy a new and purged city should arise to bring peace and moral stability to the world for ever. We have to balance the two halves of the equation in our minds. Their reconciliation can only be on some metaphysical and mystical plane which Virgil leaves in the shadows.[63]

If Virgil however had not raised these problems, if he had taken a naively optimistic view of the workings of Providence and suggested that the opponents crushed by Aeneas really did not matter, he would have offended against the moral feeling of his age so greatly as to rob his poem of all conviction. In fact, what was difficult for him was not to see the point of view of the defeated, but to believe that in all the blood and anguish which Rome cost there was in the end something good at work. It was not an easy affirmation in those days, but the poet was open enough to the potential of the new regime to suggest it. This leap in the dark, which he had to take with full awareness that there was darkness, makes him a *vates*.

It will be seen that at this level we are leaving purely literary considerations behind. "Vatic" poetry is not another genre. It is the fullest exploitation of existing genres, a method of using them to communicate some sort of philosophic and religious truth. When he looked into the literary means available to express his hesitant insights

---

[62] Turnus dies like Camilla (*Aen.* XII. 952 = XI. 831), as Patroclus dies like Hector (*Iliad* XVI. 856–57 = XXII. 362–63). Achilles knows he will be killed in his turn. Can Aeneas, cursed by Dido (IV. 620), alone be exempt from this deadly series?

[63] Even the philosophy of *Aen.* VI is brought back to us through the gate of False Dreams! Cf. VIII. 730, *rerumque ignarus imagine gaudet.*

into divine foreknowledge and human act, Virgil was child enough of his time to realize that in contemporary poetry, written for a learned and ironic audience, there lay ready the instrument which he had to use if he was to speak to his age with any kind of compelling voice. This explains why his epic must be regarded as "Alexandrian" in inspiration. No other sort of poetry could have made sense to the generation which had witnessed the civil wars.

Exactly the same analysis applies to the *Knight's Tale*. As we decipher Chaucer's poem, we infer that fourteenth-century England, far from being happy and gay, made up of overgrown children dancing round the Maypole with flowers in their hair, was a time of grim unrest, social, political, religious.[64] Society was organized into a rigid hierarchy, where obedience was exacted from underlings by cruel means, but where the justification for the hierarchy had too often vanished before the tide of weakness and corruption. In this confusion, who could guarantee that a man's fate would any longer correspond to his deserts? Yet who could abandon the belief that there was some hidden order within the chaos of appearances unless, like Boccaccio, he was prepared to reduce life to a brutal and sentimental game?

Chaucer has presented his readers with these two poles of experience and faith, and left them to bridge the gap. To deny the existence of any gap, or to argue that the poet himself bridged it by Theseus' speech, is at once to remove his poem from the tradition and to negate its sensibility.

Chaucer's greatness is shown by his willingness to confront the Virgilian dilemma. Starting from the learned, Alexandrian epic of Boccaccio, which, like Statius' *Thebaid*, had given up on the human condition, Chaucer faces both the evil and the good in human destiny. In this use of Alexandrian beginnings for vatic ends he was truly the follower and continuer of Virgil. The *Knight's Tale*, reduced in compass and enlarged in scope, is a perfect example of Callimachean epic.

These arguments may be developed in another fashion. The *Knight's Tale*, like Boccaccio's *Teseida*, exhibits many features of Bakhtin's "carnival" style. Its main action takes place in a "theatre." Its heroes are carnival twins, engaged in essentially comic action, sighing for the same lady's charms. It manipulates time. It parodies the trappings of formal rhetoric. It shows a carnival interest in flowers

---

[64] Cf. "the cherles rebellyng," 2459: A. R. Myers, *England in the Late Middle Ages* (London 1953). The opening chapter is entitled "The Tragic Dilemma." Professor Muscatine has some interesting remarks, *Chaucer and the French Tradition*, pp. 246–47. Readers of *Lucky Jim* will contrast Professor Welch's preoccupation with "Merrie England."

and trees and in what these natural phenomena prove, the inevitability of the cycle of life/death/life.

It is here that we may trace a contrast with Ovid's great Augustan epic which outweighs those casual coincidences that prove imitation of the mannerisms of the Roman by the English poet. Ovid ends his *Metamorphoses*, the celebration of the carnival principle, with a long, philosophical speech by Pythagoras is which the poetic insight is given a cosmic grounding. Death must be accepted (XV. 453–57: trans. F. J. Miller):

> Ne tamen oblitis ad metam tendere longe
> Exspatiemur equis, caelum et quodcumque sub illo est,
> Inmutat formas, tellusque et quicquid in illa est,
> Nos quoque, pars mundi, quoniam non corpora solum,
> Verum etiam volucres animae sumus . . .

> But, not to wander too far out of my course, my steeds forgetting meanwhile to speed towards the goal, the heavens and whatever is beneath the heavens change their forms, the earth and all that is within it. We also change, who are a part of creation, since we are not bodies only but also winged souls . . .

It is a corollary of this philosophy that Caesar's soul did not perish, but was caught up by Venus and set among the stars of heaven. Meanwhile, Caesar's son lives on, to surpass his father's glory.

The spirit of this is well seized by Boccaccio, both in the particular instance of the death of Arcita, and in the general emphasis which his poem places on the urge towards life, so that Venus' victory over Mars, certainly not resented by Mars himself, is merely the expression of a creative impulse seen also in the ever-changing life of nature. This is why his Emilia wears green.

Chaucer does not let the spirit of his Arcita visit the stars, and the laughter that follows Arcita's death in his original is suppressed. His figure of Saturn acquires in the light of this a quite definite and negative function. In the carnival style, Saturn, father of the Golden Age, ingests his children and the future because he is trying to replace time with a space in which everything is made available *now*, through the door into the next room.[65] Such a figure is obviously ambivalent, but the ancient world at least was more aware of the good side, of Saturn as the dispenser of blessings to men, displaced by a Jupiter who ordained work and scarcity.[66] Chaucer has chosen to follow the Continental tradition, and to make his Saturn a Satan, giver of evils. He robs the carnival of its bounty. He has taken the

[65] An image developed by Dickens in *A Christmas Carol*, Stave Three, "The Second of the Three Spirits."

[66] Cf. Hesiod, *Works and Days* 47 ff.; Virgil, *Georgics* I. 121 ff.

symbols of comedy and life, and made out of them an icon of melancholy, cold, unredeemed death.

He has therefore set the polarities of his poem in extreme contrast. When Aegeus makes a Pythagorean comment about the cycle of life/death/life, it strikes the reader in that context, not as the comic and Ovidian reassertion of the inevitable, but as jarringly absurd. A corresponding burden is laid upon Theseus, who assumes the role which Pythagoras plays at the end of the *Metamorphoses*, to prove that he has the better part of wisdom.

But, when Theseus suggests that, though decay is inevitable, Palamon and Emily are somehow exempt from it, he raises the possibility of an answer without pursuing it to the point of proof. Marriage is an answer to decay, since it produces children and children's children. Palamon and Emily will escape in this way, but the poet does not let Theseus make the point. Nor does he offer any solace to Arcita. Theseus' "lastynge everemo" thus remains an ungrounded and sententious cliché. His description of life as a "foule prisoun" contradicts the notion of carnival (which is also religious) freedom, and here "whan the pley is doon" is significant. The question of personal survival is raised and left in the dark. Paradoxically, this darkness too is carnival and Virgilian.

## II

What then shall we say of *Paradise Lost* and its darkness visible? Milton sought to justify God's ways to man. Was he more successful at this task of resolution than Chaucer's Theseus? Was his epic's intended finality appropriate to a genre classically formulated by the *Iliad*, the *Argonautica*, and the *Aeneid*? To so many eyes, the late Renaissance poet stands at the opposite remove from Chaucer. But once again, the vital thing is to restore him to the classical tradition of which he was so avid a student.

When we ask what the tradition can do to refresh our image of Milton, answers begin to crowd in upon us. Firstly, we see his beginnings in a far more Virgilian and Alexandrian light. Like Virgil (and Ariosto), the young Milton was attracted by the idea of an historical epic he was never to write. Like Virgil, he found in Alexandrian pastoral an essential stage of his preparation. Like Virgil, he thought of Homer in Callimachean terms, and made a similar modification to Callimachus' rejection of the conventional epic demand.[67]

---

[67] *Elegy* VI. 71, *rivi potor Homerus* contrasts with Horace, *Epp.* I. 19. 6, *vinosus Homerus*. It was the Callimacheans who were "water-drinkers" (Wimmel, *Kallimachos in Rom*, p. 225). At *Lycidas* 76 ff. Phoebus encourages (rather than warns) Milton, just as Virgil's *canerem* (*Eclogues* 6. 3) shows that the poet already felt epic stirrings when Phoebus intervened. Cf. above, pp. 122, 302 ff.

Like Virgil and Homer, he tacitly acknowledged the essentially dramatic nature of high poetry, both by his unfinished sketches at the time when he was still undecided what shape his major work would take, and by his ultimate treatment of epic form.[68]

Yet it is not enough here to refer loosely to "dramatic structure." Chaucer's *Knight's Tale* had in it features of a particular kind of drama, the loose and primitive theatricality of the "carnival" style. Milton had begun with *Comus*, an effort to civilize the spirit of carnival. He would end with *Samson Agonistes*, in which the Philistine carnival, complete with its seductive witch/sorceress, is catastrophically interrupted by the blind, performing, tragi-comic giant. This affinity with the mime makes Milton's *Paradise Lost* unexpectedly akin to the *Dionysiaca* of the Byzantine poet, Nonnus of Panopolis. By yet another carnival thread, he joins in Shakespeare's claim to be the Roman, Neronian Seneca's greatest heir.

The Alexandrians had crossed epic narrative with lyric, and Callimachus, for example, showed a particular debt to Pindar. Selection and dramatic characterization are part of this inheritance. But so also are symmetry and thematic variation. These features too have been detected in both Chaucer and Milton.

Great geniuses raise great challenges. The problem which the understanding of Milton's epic has presented has too often lain in a mistaken balance between the poet's own individuality and his inheritance. It cannot be regarded as original sin on Milton's part if, for example, (*if*), he sacrifices sense to music, since such a bias towards lyric was not only built into the Alexandrian tradition, but had in fact been growing in intensity ever since Statius. It cannot be regarded as original sin if readers are unable to agree on the identity of the hero in *Paradise Lost*. Who is the hero of Callimachus' *Hecale*, or Lucan's *Pharsalia*?[69] Equally, it cannot be regarded as peculiar to Milton that there should be in his poem important elements of drama and lyric on the one side, and of satire and farce on the other. So there are in Dante. They are part of the vatic amalgam. So too, if we look to Virgil and even Chaucer, is a certain obscurity.[70] The

---

[68] This explains both Milton's interest in drama after abandoning the *Arthuriad*, and the dramatic structure which has been discovered in *Paradise Lost*. The poet's early dramatic sketches are described by D. Masson, *Life of Milton* (London and New York 1871), II, pp. 106 ff.; W. R. Parker, *Milton: A Biography* (Oxford 1968), I, pp. 190–92; D. Bush, *A Variorum Commentary on the Poems of John Milton* (New York 1970), pp. 314 ff. Ultimately in *Samson Agonistes* the dramatic principle, which is also an Aristotelian principle, triumphed.

[69] Aristotle was too sensible to believe that what is important in an epic is whether it has a single hero (*Poetics*, ch. 8: cf. D. W. Lucas' note on p. 140 of his edition).

[70] See below, p. 477, on Livy's *skotison*.

history of Miltonic criticism is littered with observations applying to a vast range of epic poetry, yet narrowed to one man and looked upon as plus or minus marks on his report alone.

What might the tradition have suggested to Milton as he approached the composition of *Paradise Lost?* First of all, some negatives. His inclination drew him towards the sublime right from the start, and the sublime was ideally represented by Latin. It was from Ariosto (but of course ultimately from Dante) that he learned to turn away from something now outmoded towards what would speak to plainer men.[71] The sublime was associated with glorification of the great, and the projected *Arthuriad* would have offered scope for the eulogy both of individuals and of a whole people. Milton, like Dante, like Virgil and Callimachus, turned away from that too. As with his use of the vernacular, he chose against the "second Ennius," Petrarch. "Kings and battles" were to be his theme in a very different sense.

The positive lessons that the tradition might have taught Milton were these. Firstly, the knowledge that all great poetry tends towards drama, and that this is true even of the nominally superior epic. Secondly, the readiness to call in other arts to assist the word, but particularly music and painting. Thirdly, the understanding that an epic poem, the projection of human imagination into objective form, must evoke pity and terror if it is to succeed, and that the evocation of these feelings will take precedence over all cold logic. Fourthly, the knowledge that if this evocation is accomplished, the role of any one "hero" does not matter unduly, and that in any case it is necessary to have a hero who displays a *hamartia* if there is to be tragedy. This tempering of the flawlessly heroic may bring with it concessions to the comic. Fifthly, the poem will derive extra resonance from the use of a "classical," ironically commented model or models. Sixthly, the new epic will secure its essential organic unity by the use of linked images, given expression notably in similes and verbal echoes. Finally, the language of the poem, meant to be intelligible, will not purchase this intelligibility by refusing to shock or strain, if the pressure of feeling is great enough. Estrangement always has its legitimate function.[72]

[71] See the Preface to Part 2 of *The Reason of Church Government* (1641: cf. *The Works of John Milton* [New York 1931], III. 1, p. 236) and R. M. Samarin, *John Milton* (Moscow 1964), pp. 109 ff. Milton's admiration for Mazzoni's *Della difesa della commedia di Dante* is significant, since Mazzoni had defined Dante's poem as a "dramatic, epic, monodic comedy" (Weinberg, *A History of Literary Criticism in the Italian Renaissance*, pp. 877–78). It is "monodic" here that gives pause for thought.

[72] The Callimachean poetic outlined above (pp. 20 ff.) may be compared. The Formalist doctrine of "estrangement" is particularly relevant. See the *Glossary of Critical Terms, s.v.*

In the light of this poetic, it is interesting to examine the history of Miltonic criticism to discover where insight has broken through to the real truth of Milton's achievement. If we read his *Preface* to *Paradise Lost*, Milton himself evidently believed that his use of blank verse needed defense, and here he was taking sides in a well-known Renaissance controversy. Even so, it is illuminating in this context to note that, in the year in which *Paradise Lost* was first published, Dryden declared blank verse to be suited to the lighter and more colloquial purposes of comedy.[73] Milton, who speaks in a satirical passage of the "backside of the World" (III. 494), played about by "winds," gravely offended therefore both by meter and language against certain contemporary notions of epic decorum.

Milton had older Renaissance critics on his side. Yet in any case Aristotle had, by assigning the *Margites* to Homer, taken up the comic into the classical epic tradition, and Callimachus had followed him by using comic vocabulary and even motifs in the *Hecale*. Horace had remarked on the proximity of comedy and tragedy in moments of intense emotion, and Servius had called the *stilus* of *Aeneid* IV "paene comicus." Following Callimachus and Virgil, Dante, the author of a *Commedia* eventually called "divine," had used *comica verba* even in the *Paradiso*. Boccaccio had opted for the comic *ottava*. Turning towards drama, turning to a meter which Dryden at least now felt to be suitable for comedy, Milton had grasped the real nature of the classical tradition in a way which stimulates fresh admiration for his genius.

Ancient epic was "oral" long after Homer. "Milton's epic voice" therefore is no more unexpected than Virgil's *vox et os et hypocrisis* referred to by Donatus. Over and above this dramatic emphasis, the classical epic eventually owed a great deal to its crossing with lyric. This implies not only the presence in the poetry of a subjective "mood," coloring and transmuting what is said, but also some sort of precise, quasi-strophic arrangement of lines and paragraphs. It implies further a particular mode of interference with the straight narrative of action which may look like an intrusion, but in fact is essential to the whole tone of the story. The structure of lyrical narrative formed in the Pindaric mold will depend on repetition of word and motif. All this is part of the traditionality of Milton's poem.[74]

[73] *Milton Criticism*, ed. James Thorpe (repr. New York 1969), p. 115: cf. also Thorpe, p. 338.

[74] Cf. E. S. Blanchard, *Structural Patterns in Paradise Lost: Milton's Symmetry and Balance* (diss. Rochester, New York 1966); Anne Ferry, *Milton's Epic Voice* (Cambridge, Mass. 1963). Not only Virgil's (and Ion's) *hypocrisis* (above, p. 184), but also Lucan's epic voice and Eichenbaum's theory of the *skaz* are relevant: above, pp. 207 ff.

In this epic, the language of estranging discourse would be expected to puzzle and even annoy, as it had in the case of Milton's predecessors. (Again, Pindar comes to mind.) Here, the opposed reactions of critics are illuminating. Johnson said that Milton wrote in a "Babylonish dialect," invented by himself. Coleridge rejoined that "The connexion of the sentences and the position of the words are exquisitely artificial; but the position is rather according to the logic of passion or universal logic, than to the logic of grammar."[75] Hazlitt remarked about the "approximation to the severity of impassioned prose which has been made an objection to Milton's poetry" that it was "one of its greatest excellences."[76] Elmer Edgar Stoll speaks of the *leitmotiv* "all our woe," but also tells us that there is in Milton "the true sublime, elevation without inflation. Plain and simple words are not avoided, but all common or mean associations are."[77] Douglas Bush noted "Milton's general movement away from epic grandeur towards plain, undecorated, dramatic speech."[78] Yet Pope had declared that, while Milton borrowed from Homer the "lower sort of narrations," in which "we find not an antiquated, affected, or uncouth word, for some hundred lines together," he was surprised that Milton did not also copy Homer's "plainness and perspicuity in the dramatic parts."[79] Keats remarked laconically that "The Paradise Lost though so fine in itself is a curruption [*sic*] of our language."[80]

The critics cannot agree among themselves, but their comments are still useful. The classical tradition would lead us to expect, for example, that the poet would employ what Macrobius calls in the case of Virgil a *concordia dissonorum*, a mixture of the three styles recognized by antiquity: the low or plain, the middle or smooth, the grand or sublime. It would find prose poetry just as much at home in Milton as in his contemporary Racine. It would lead us to look,

---

[75] Thorpe, p. 95. Cf. P. Harre, *De verborum apud Pindarum conlocatione* (diss. Berlin 1867).

[76] Thorpe, p. 110: cf. the use of prosaic words in Euripides, Callimachus, Virgil, Horace, and the whole ancient doctrine of the *ischnos charactēr*. The epigraph to L. Spitzer's article on Racine ("Die klassische Dämpfung in Racines Stil," *Archivum Romanicum* XII, 4 [1928], 361–472) is "Il rase la prose, mais avec des ailes"; this is partially paraphrased from *De Subl.* 31. 2.

[77] Thorpe, p. 215. O. Schönberger, *Untersuchungen zur Wiederholungstechnik Lucans*, discusses the use of *Leitmotive* in Lucan, though of course significant repetition is widespread in the classical epic tradition. Whether Milton avoids all "common or mean" associations and words is another question ("the backside of the World" ?). "Without inflation" is Alexandrian language: Propertius II. 34b. 32, *non inflati somnia Callimachi*.

[78] Thorpe, p. 308.

[79] *Ibid.*, p. 349.

[80] *Ibid.*, p. 357.

again as in Racine, for a Pindaric impressionism and rhetoric, which crowds out other styles of poetry while making it impossible for this style to be convincingly imitated. If all this could be acknowledged as the deployment by the epic poet of legitimate resources, perhaps it would be possible to assess more calmly the achievement.[81]

What makes this task so awkward is the poet's habit in his exordia to a number of books of *Paradise Lost* of commenting on what he is doing. Here he stands in a well-known ancient rhetorical tradition, in which allegiance to traditional academic rules is professed even by authors who flout them. In these exordia, Milton tends to speak "univocally," as if he had all the answers, and simply needed time to set them out. In the event, he writes/composes polyphonically (again the true child of his age). It is to the achievement, and not the description, that we must attend.

From the angle of strict consistency therefore, Milton does have a weakness, and it is to be discovered by pressing his relation to the classical tradition still further. Virgil had diagnosed and exemplified the likely course of epic development. He had traced his path to the *Aeneid* through the Alexandrian genres of the pastoral and the pastoral/didactic. Even at the site of Rome, we do not escape Arcadia.

But it was logical enough for Virgil to take up into his consciously Alexandrian and unresolved *Aeneid* elements of make-believe, irony and self-questioning, nowhere more plainly evinced than by the similar endings of the *Eclogues* and the epic (*umbrae/umbras*). Could Milton take these same techniques and use them for the unshadowed assertion of a particular religious allegiance? The vatic Alexandrianism of the *Aeneid* allows Virgil to take a pessimistic view of human action, to remind his congregation of mortality and error. The poet's vision of sin extends in the final book to include even Jupiter and Juno, both shown as exploiters of Juturna. Aeneas, "fired by the furies" as he kills Turnus, is re-enacting Dido's despairing suicide. This is an aspect of the *Aeneid* which fascinated Chaucer. For those Augustans who found this hellfire too pessimistic, there was the alternative of carnival mockery, of re-emphasizing the laughter from which it all grew. This explains why Ovid is Virgil's natural successor, turning holy day into holiday in his *Metamorphoses*. Even Virgil himself never strayed too far from his roots. His whole epic is a gigantic metamorphosis of

---

[81] The chorus of blame is particularly audible in Eliot (Thorpe, p. 327), who objects to Milton's *night-foundered* (*P. L.* I. 204). But perhaps the adjective is to be brought into correlation with *nigh-foundered* (*P. L.* II. 940), as another example of Milton's (inherited) tendency to signpost the development of his narrative. Satan becomes in Book II the mariner of Book I, who has involved himself with forces too large for his comprehension (cf. II. 1017 and 1043).

Homer and Apollonius, and the laughter he suppressed always survives in the guise of irony.

Milton too enjoyed the *Metamorphoses*.[82] But, when he wrote his proems, did he wholly understand the ambivalent polyphony of the classical tradition which his artistic genius so freely evokes?

The essence of the poem is to be discovered in Book IX, which tells of Man's disobedience and Fall. The cosmic significance of Adam's act, prompted by that of Eve, is for the believer daunting and horrific. If it did bring death into the world and all our woe, the reader, as he looks out on the contemporary "vision to dizzy and appal" of which Cardinal Newman speaks, may wonder how the poet could ever summon up enough confidence to tackle a theme so terrifying. It is fascinating that Milton, who must have known, for example, what Cromwell did to Ireland, tries to solve his difficulty by conjuring up so Ovidian a vision of the primal sin.

The use of "authorial prefaces" to epic was as old as Hesiod. Choerilus of Samos had used his preface to comment on his difficulties, and there is something of this spirit in the best known of all these proems, that to the third book of Virgil's *Georgics*. They vary in helpfulness. Virgil, whose phrasing is influenced by both Pindar and Callimachus, had been preparing the way for the *Aeneid*, where such a preface is not found. Petrarch had curiously mingled in his preface to the historical epic *Africa* a double *recusatio* of the type used by Callimachus in his Preface to the *Aetia* to reject the historical epic! Ennius had already done something similar, when he adapted Callimachus' Hesiodic dream to a Homeric epiphany at the start of his *Annales*. Tasso had rejected and accepted Alexandrian ideas simultaneously.

Milton's preface to Book IX is of this less helpful variety. The rural repast is over. Tragedy is to come. The tone is deliberately and assertively univocal. All ambiguity is fiercely excluded (IX. 5–19):

> . . . I now must change
> Those Notes to Tragic; foul distrust, and breach
> Disloyal on the part of Man, revolt,
> And disobedience: On the part of Heav'n
> Now alienated, distance and distaste,
> Anger and just rebuke, and judgement giv'n,
> That brought into this World a world of woe,
> Sinne and her shadow Death, and Miserie
> Deaths Harbinger: Sad task, yet argument

[82] Milton's daughter reported her father's pleasure in hearing the *Metamorphoses*: Masson, *Life of Milton* (London 1880), VI, p. 754; Parker, *Milton: A Biography*, II, p. 1098. In general, Davis P. Harding, *Milton and the Renaissance Ovid* (Urbana 1946).

> Not less but more Heroic then the wrauth
> Of stern *Achilles* on his Foe pursu'd
> Thrice Fugitive about *Troy* Wall; or rage
> Of *Turnus* for *Lavinia* disespous'd
> Or *Neptun*'s ire or *Juno*'s, that so long
> Perplex'd the *Greek* and *Cytherea*'s Son.

As it unfolds, this tragic story will be of course Euripidean, even pantomimic, in vein, the tale of the temptation of a naked girl by a talking Serpent, to eat an apple,[83] the effect of which resembles intoxication. Milton's apodictic tone, alien, as the study of Shakespeare shows, to true tragedy, may be instructively contrasted with that of Plato, when he too comes to narrate a myth intended to justify the ways of god to man.

In Book X of Plato's *Republic*, Er relates how souls make choice of their lives before returning to the world. Just like Milton, in his parable Plato uses metamorphosis, as the human souls who have had enough of humanity select animal forms for reincarnation. But Plato, unlike Milton, spells out very clearly the ambiguous status which his religious and metaphysical flight of fancy enjoys (*Rep.* X. 619 e 5–620 a):

> He said that it was indeed a sight worth seeing, how each of the souls set about choosing his life. It was pitiful to behold, and laughable, and marvelous.

The muffling device, typical for this style, of the "intruded narrator" also deserves attention. "Pity" is one of the effects of tragedy, and here Plato and Milton do come together. But "laughter" is comic, and "marvelous" reminds us of the Greek word for a fairground juggler.[84] Plato then is quite content to couch his theodicy in serio-comic terms, and to signal the presence of comedy to his reader. Yet who will deny his passionate commitment to a particular vision of the truth?

Milton is perfectly aware of the role of "mixed feelings" in sudden revelation. At the end of Book I of the epic, he describes how the assembled demons unexpectedly diminish in size, and compares them (I. 781–88) to Pygmies or to

---

[83] Satan himself laughs at this, *P. L.* X. 487. Both Callimachus and Apollonius had modified the epic towards the feminine (Hecale, Medea), the latter with tragic and critical implications: see above, pp. 86 ff.

[84] "Marvel" is also of course the appropriate reaction to a religious manifestation. That the same emotion should occur both in the comic and the religious is proof of the undifferentiated primitive mentality. Contrast θαυματουργός ("wonder-worker") in its pagan and Christian senses.

> Faerie Elves,
> Whose midnight Revels, by a Forrest side
> Or Fountain some belated Peasant sees,
> Or dreams he sees, while over-head the Moon
> Sits Arbitress, and neerer to the Earth
> Wheels her pale course, they on thir mirth and dance
> Intent, with jocond Music charm his ear;
> At once with joy and fear his heart rebounds.

This "belated peasant," in this passage reminiscent of Apollonius (IV. 1479) and Virgil (*Aeneid* VI. 454), feels "joy and fear" "at once," that is, simultaneously. But this admixture of joy, the acknowledgment of the proper role of carnival laughter made even by Plato's Er, does not persist into the exordium to Book IX.

Milton goes on there to declare that his theme is more heroic than that of the *Iliad*, the *Odyssey* and the *Aeneid*. This typically Roman (and Italian) claim is part of the fairground mentality, "the greatest show on earth." The best is always here and now. So it was that Propertius had praised the *Aeneid* as "greater than the *Iliad*." It is a good example of a topos which the reader does well to read with a smile.

Milton's ability to handle his more than heroic theme depends, we learn, not on himself, not even on the Muse, but on his Celestial Patroness. The gambit is familiar from the Italian tradition (20–33):[85]

> If answerable style I can obtaine
> Of my Celestial Patroness, who deignes
> Her nightly visitation unimplor'd
> And dictates to me slumbring, or inspires
> Easie my unpremeditated Verse:
> Since first this Subject for Heroic Song
> Pleas'd me long choosing, and beginning late;
> Not sedulous by Nature to indite
> Warrs, hitherto the onely Argument
> Heroic deem'd, chief maistrie to dissect
> With long and tedious havoc fabl'd Knights
> In Battels feign'd; the better fortitude
> Of Patience and Heroic Martyrdom
> Unsung. . . .

In spite of its poor literary history, this passage preserves much that is Callimachean: the rejection, for example, of the "long and tedious" bloodiness of the traditional epic, the preference for a passive heroism. Nor were poetic slumbers unknown in the ancient world, and the *Aetia* had begun with a famous dream, in which the Alexandrian poet

---

[85] Above, p. 329 (Tasso).

was transported to Mount Helicon, Hesiod's ancient home, where he was able to question the Muses directly about antiquarian topics.

But one phrase must give us pause. When Milton writes "Easie my unpremeditated Verse" he not only contradicts Callimachus' demand for art, and the climb up the steep path, but even his own antithesis in his youthful epitaph on Shakespeare between "slow-endeavouring art" and "Thy easie numbers."[86] Insofar as Milton's lines betray a withdrawal from the intolerable wrestle with words—and with ideas—they signify an ominous abandonment of Callimachean insights. Could Callimachus' technique of half-assertion be adapted to the proclamation of a theodicy, and could this be done by a poet who admits that his verse was "unpremeditated"?

Milton despises the hackneyed themes of past epic. He rejects (like Apollonius) the trivia of our animal existence as material unfit for lofty poetry,[87] and boasts of his higher argument, and the fame it will bring him,[88] provided always he has the right inspiration. The reservations which the poet even so expresses about his powers are the proof of a poetic diffidence which has often appeared in the tradition. With them, another factor comes into play, and that is the author's own awareness of himself. Limited by Aristotle on theoretical grounds, this awareness had become an inevitable part of Callimachean epic, where the consciousness of artifice, the lyrical subjectivity, sometimes broke through even into direct address to the reader.[89] The polyphonic style must occasionally make way for the *phōnē* of the poet. It is in fact an echo of the "presenter" of the primitive mime,[90] the "master of ceremonies" familiar from the *Hymns* of Callimachus.

The confusions of this exordium, in which Callimachean "refusal,"

---

[86] *On Shakespear* (1630), 9–10. Cf. Callimachus' *technē*, *Aet.-Pref.* 17.

[87] Though at V. 331 ff. and 630 ff. he did not mind describing a Hecalean repast. It was Callimachus who had made simple meals famous in epic: fr. 248–52 Pf. Apollonius normally avoided such matters: H. Fränkel, *Noten zu den Argonautika des Apollonios*, p. 142 with note 321. Fielding has some amusing comments: *Tom Jones*, Book IX, ch. 5.

[88] He shares this preoccupation with many ancient writers, including Horace (*Odes* III. 30), Propertius (III. 1. 9), Virgil (*Georgics* IV. 6–7) and Ovid (*Am.* III. 15. 8; *Met.* XV. 871 ff.), but not with the Virgil of the *Aeneid* (IX. 446 ff. really supports this point), nor with Callimachus, unless we count the delicately restrained "many a year" of fr. 7. 14 Pf.

[89] Fränkel, *op. cit.*, pp. 228 and 642 notes Apollonius' readiness to drop the role of mere narrator. What the Alexandrians had done was to understand that, even where the poet appears to be breaking the role of imitator, he is in fact still imitating himself. This is why Callimachus was able to defend the didactic epic of Aratus.

[90] Robert Weimann, *Shakespeare und die Tradition des Volkstheaters* (Berlin 1967), pp. 57, 70–71.

Callimachean subjectivity and literary debate, jostles with un-Callimachean univocity, are a sign of critical and religious confusion in Milton's own time. What we still admire is not the theory implied by some of Milton's statements, but the discourse inspired by his larger and deeper vision of human troubles.

The story begins. An epic *Stundenbild* describes the (symbolic) advent of night, and Satan reappears. His earlier wanderings are recounted musically and learnedly. He decides that he will best succeed in his plans if he disguises himself as a serpent. All this occupies 80 lines. The purpose of the speech, if considered in terms of strict logic, is entirely out of proportion to the space it occupies. Ten lines could have stated Satan's malice, and even some of his thoughts. But the operatic aria we hear instead is not concerned with merely factual communication. A primitive apprehension of time is characteristic of the carnival style, for which the present, past and future suddenly fuse to form a multi-layered space. Satan's speech here therefore is calculated to let us know ahead of "normal" time what the pains of damnation are like from the point of view of the damned, since only then can we have any inkling of what Satan plans to do to man. We have left Adam in total harmony with God and Nature. Satan, in total disharmony, shows what man is likely to (indeed already has) become. Everything that ought to be good makes him more miserable. He is fully aware of his own degradation. His motive is nothing wonderful: it is to repay spite with spite. In this epigrammatic summing-up of his schemes, the irony lies not so much in his complacent satisfaction with spite, as in his utter inability to grasp that God could have had any other motive in the creation of Adam.

His soliloquy over, Satan enters a serpent and waits for morning. When it comes (another *Stundenbild*), Adam and Eve emerge, and after offering their prayers, make ready for the day's toil in their garden. Eve proposes that they should work apart. Adam demurs. He is anxious they should not fall victim to the Tempter of whom Raphael has spoken. Eve replies, nettled by the implication that she is not to be trusted on her own. Adam soothes her offended vanity. Eve persists. Adam responds, and eventually gives reluctant permission.

The comic irony of this domestic tiff, which we remember Milton has claimed as more heroic than the *Iliad*, is not to be appreciated without recourse to the dramatic music that was developing in Milton's own day (Monteverdi's *Orfeo* was first produced in 1607). After Satan's solo aria, Adam and Eve have clearly been engaged in a duet. A close attention to the lyric element of strophic response and balance supplies the deeper resonance which their discourse otherwise so notably lacks.[91]

The analogy that this implies with "Le Nuove Musiche" of contemporary Italy helps to place *Paradise Lost* within its real tradition. Milton lived at a time of musical revolution. The age of polyphony, heard in the work of masters like Palestrina and Byrd, had drawn to a conclusion in his youth. Now dramatic form, fondly believed to be a recovery of the ancient Greek mode, was giving rise to opera. Milton's poem clearly lives in both musical worlds.

As Eve goes off on her own, Milton notes her beauty, though he is far too good a student of the classical tradition to describe it, at least here (IX. 385–96):

> Thus saying, from her Husbands hand her hand
> Soft she withdrew, and like a Wood-Nymph light
> *Oread* or *Dryad*, or of *Delia*'s Traine,
> Betook her to the Groves, but *Delia*'s self
> In gate surpass'd and Goddess-like deport,
> Though not as shee with Bow and Quiver armd,
> But with such Gardning Tools as Art yet rude,
> Guiltless of fire had formd, or Angels brought.
> To *Pales*, or *Pomona*, thus adornd,
> Likeliest she seemd, *Pomona* when she fled
> *Vertumnus*, or to *Ceres* in her Prime,
> Yet Virgin of *Proserpina* from *Jove*.

The expression is brilliant, and its complex pattern of alliteration and assonance clearly compels hesitation before the reader too quickly accepts Milton's argument that rhyme is no necessary adjunct or true ornament of poem or good verse. The poet's imagination moves easily from thoughts of Eve to thoughts of the classical nymphs (he was after all the contemporary of Rubens). The Oreads and their queen Delia (= Diana) recall Virgil. When Dido entered the temple of Juno at Carthage, she too had seemed like the hunting goddess surrounded by the Oreads (*Aen.* I. 498 ff.). But then she had, unknown to herself, been watched by a hidden Aeneas, so soon to tempt her from her vows to Sychaeus, and so soon to destroy her, and in her, her people.

Eve/Dido is overtaken by Eve/Prometheus. "Guiltless of fire" must recall a myth that was the pagan version of both the rebellion of the angels and the Fall. Prometheus had sinned, and been dreadfully punished precisely for imparting to men fire and the knowledge of its use.

Zeus also punished mankind in general, by creating woman. The

[91] Below, pp. 395–96.

first woman, Pandora, was taken to wife by Prometheus' brother, Epimetheus, the "After-thinker." Pandora let out all evils from the stone jar where they were kept. Hesiod, who varyingly narrates this tale both in the *Theogony* and in the *Works and Days*, was in the misogynistic mood that inspires the primitive mentality, and Eve/ Pandora has been already met in Milton's epic.[92]

Here however Milton, after merely hinting at this aspect of the sin Eve is to commit, comes back to Pales or Pomona, or to Ceres. Whatever the exact associations for him of Pales, he tells us plainly what the resemblance was between Eve and Pomona and Ceres. It was (like Dido) to be seduced.[93] What fascinates Milton about Eve's temptation by Satan is its sexuality.

With his reference to Proserpina, Milton has struck again a note which has been insistent throughout the poem. This is more than mere decoration.[94] From the vast web of allusion which Milton spins around his epic, certain references to the myths of pagan antiquity collect tellingly around the garden island of Sicily. Enna was certainly there (IV. 269). But so was Hell (I. 230). So was Satan (II. 1020). So was Sin (II. 660). The angels had rebelled against God like the Titans (I. 197, 510; II. 306: cf. IV. 987) or the Giants (VII. 605), and it was under Etna, in Sicily, that one of their number was crushed (I. 233). Aeschylus' *Prometheus Bound* had described his doom, and it is of Prometheus that Milton has just been thinking in the passage quoted.[95]

United there, Prometheus and Proserpina reveal a complex attitude towards Eve's sin. Was she an innocent victim, like Ceres, like Proserpina? Was she rather a guilty Prometheus, even a Pandora? Was her Sicilian Eden ever safe when such gigantic powers, and their symbol, Etna's hellish volcano, threatened its tranquillity from the

---

[92] Eve is Pandora at *P. L.* IV. 714. There is some ambiguity in the thought. Prometheus, who supported Zeus against the Giants, and who gave fire to men out of pity, thus exposing himself to painful punishment, is a Christ-like figure. Yet Milton thinks he was guilty. Pandora was sent to undo Prometheus' work. Is this Milton's view of woman's role? Cf. X. 867 ff., imitating Euripides, *Hippolytus* 616 ff. and *Medea* 573–75.

[93] Pomona: Ovid, *Met.* XIV. 623; Ceres: Hesiod, *Theogony* 912–13.

[94] What Tasso calls *fregi* (*Ger. Lib.* I. 2. 7, quoted above, p. 328). Cf. Douglas Bush in Thorpe, p. 304.

[95] Cf. Aeschylus, *P. V.* 351 ff.; Pindar, *Pythian* 1. 15 ff. Aeschylus also makes Prometheus refer to the Arimaspians, and perhaps this, rather than Herodotus (III. 116), is the source of the allusion at *P. L.* II. 944. Paradoxically, when the good angels hurl mountains against Satan (VI. 635 ff., anticipated at VI. 195), they are in their turn like the Giants (cf. Nonnus, *Dionysiaca* XLVIII. 15). In all this attention to Sicily, it must not be forgotten that for Milton Sicily was the home of the pastoral. See "Milto in Sicilia et in Partibus Orientalibus," *Hermes Americanus* II (1984), 140–55.

very start? Milton's genius has left these ambiguities in spite of its overt Christian commitment. His epic becomes Callimachean, whether by the evidence of his proems he consciously intended that or no.

The details of Adam and Eve's parting are passed over without direct speech, so that Milton may introduce instead direct speech of his own (404 ff.). Eve is not likely to return as she promised, because the Serpent is lying in wait. He would prefer to find Eve alone, but has not much chance of doing so. The poet expresses this with the virtuosity of an Ovid (421–24):

> He sought them both, but wish'd his hap might find
> Eve separate, he wish'd, but not with hope
> Of what so seldom chanc'd, when to his wish,
> Beyond his hope, Eve separate he spies.

Now, as she is about to lose it (*deflourd*, 901), Eve's beauty is pictured for us, with a suggestive delicacy that recalls Tasso's Sofronia rather than Petrarch's Sophonisba (425–33):

> Veild in a Cloud of Fragrance, where she stood,
> Half spi'd, so thick the Roses bushing round
> About her glowd, oft stooping to support
> Each Flour of slender stalk, whose head though gay
> Carnation, Purple, Azure, or spect with Gold,
> Hung drooping unsustaind, them she upstaies
> Gently with Mirtle band, mindless the while,
> Her self, though fairest unsupported Flour,
> From her best prop so farr, and storm so nigh.

And once again, Alexandrian or Ovidian devices that might be merely pretty are raised to tragic intensity by Alexandrian insights. Gathering her flowers, Eve is so like Proserpina to the cultivated reader that Milton has no need to say so.[96] Simile and reality coalesce. When Adam comes to find her after her Fall, he will be carrying a rose garland for her which withers as he realizes that something is wrong (892–93).[97] What is to be storm for Eve is sunshine after storm for the devils (II. 284).

Satan, drawing nearer, is enjoying the country sights and air of Paradise, like a man who has managed to get out of city pollution, if only for a while. The pastoral theme is dear to the heart of the European tradition,[98] and in Milton's epic imagination serves to break up the heroic construct, so that we already sense the impending sin

[96] Cf. Ovid, *Fasti* IV. 435 ff.; *Met.* V. 391 ff. At Claudian, *De Raptu* II. 140–41, Proserpina's flowers unwittingly anticipate her marriage to Pluto.

[97] Ariosto had exploited the sexual symbolism of roses: above, pp. 321 ff.

[98] Cf. Apollonius II. 655–68: Callimachus, *Hecale* fr. 238. 15 ff. Pf.: Virgil, *Aen.* VIII. 102 ff.

before it is committed. Real time and dramatic time are overlaid, in a way exploited by Shakespeare[99] but familiar to the Greeks, Romans and Dante also. We know the pastoral as make-believe escape from and to a nature that is flawed. Satan knows it this way already. Even so, there is suspense. So deeply is Satan moved by the joys of nature that he almost forgets his purpose. He has to pause and rethink his ambition before he can continue. It is in the ability to enter into this kind of psychological complexity that Milton approaches most closely the Metaphysical poetry of his own age, and even the subtlety of Ovid or Seneca.

Satan rediscovers his bad purpose because life, for him, as it will shortly for mankind, has moved on from the idyllic simplicity of the Golden Age. Milton cunningly reminds us of this by comparing Paradise with some famous examples (439–43):

> Spot more delicious then those Gardens feign'd
> Or of reviv'd *Adonis*, or renownd
> *Alcinous*, host of old *Laertes* Son,
> Or that, not mystic, where the Sapient[100] King
> Held dalliance with his faire *Egyptian* Spouse.

Adonis and Ulysses had unpleasant associations for the attentive reader of the poem,[101] and this is confirmed by the real-life ("not mystic") allusion to Solomon, holding dalliance with his Egyptian queen in his garden. This garden is not mentioned by the Old Testament in the two accounts there presented of the splendors of Solomon's reign. It is alluded to in the description of the destruction of Jerusalem by Nebuchadnezzar, when it provided a means of flight from the ruined city for the defeated Israelites.[102] The Old Testament makes it plain that this destruction was a consequence of Solomon's uxoriousness, and Solomon had precedent in Adam.[103] The healthful escape from the city then turns out to be just another illusion. The Alexandrian pastoral exploits this pathos too.[104]

Rediscovering his ambition, Satan soliloquizes (473–79):

[99] R. Weimann treats this aspect of the poet, *op. cit.*, pp. 409 ff.

[100] "Sapience" is an ill-omened word in this book (797, 1018: cf. the pun *sciential sap*, 837: contrast VII. 195). For Solomon, see I. 400 and 444.

[101] Adonis: I. 446; Ulysses: II. 1019. The allusion to Ulysses was missing at V. 341. The classical references are to Theocritus XV. 113 for Adonis, and to *Odyssey* VII. 112 ff. for Alcinous' gardens.

[102] II Kings 25:4.

[103] Solomon uxorious: I Kings 11:3 (cf. *P. L.* I. 444); Adam uxorious: *P. L.* VIII. 532 ff.

[104] T. G. Rosenmeyer, *The Green Cabinet* (Berkeley and Los Angeles 1969), pp. 224 ff. At IV. 1133–34 Lucretius significantly chooses a garden image to describe the canker at the heart of love's blossoms.

> Thoughts, whither have ye led me, with what sweet
> Compulsion thus transported to forget
> What hither brought us, hate, not love, nor hope
> Of Paradise for Hell, hope here to taste
> Of pleasure, but all pleasure to destroy,
> Save what is in destroying, other joy
> To me is lost.

Playing with his paradoxes, Satan shows all the tortured virtuosity of late Renaissance man.[105] Strangely, so powerful an angel is glad to find that Adam is absent (479–93):

> Then let me not let pass
> Occasion which now smiles, behold alone
> The Woman, opportune to all attempts,
> Her Husband, for I view far round, not nigh,
> Whose higher intellectual more I shun,
> And strength, of courage hautie, and of limb
> Heroic built, though of terrestrial mould,
> Foe not informidable, exempt from wound,
> I not; so much hath Hell debas'd, and paine
> Infeebl'd me, to what I was in Heav'n.
> Shee fair, divinely fair, fit Love for Gods,
> Not terrible, though terrour be in Love
> And beautie, not approacht by stronger hate,
> Hate stronger, under shew of Love well feign'd,
> The way which to her ruin now I tend.

The pathos in Satan's loss, his naive discovery that Eve is not terrible (the very suggestion that she could be is a shock to the reader, after the art which the poet has lavished on making her attractive), his admission of the weakness of hate and its need to disguise itself as its opposite in order to be effective: all this makes excellent theatre, excellent opera.[106]

Yet, when we focus our eyes on the stage, Milton turns out to have written an epic that expressly excludes from its key contest the person who is most intimately involved in its outcome, Adam, who just at this point is described as being of heroic build. The substitute contest is to take place between a devil-serpent and a woman who

---

[105] Cf. S. Gorley Putt's article on Thomas Middleton (*Times Literary Supplement* 3778 [August 2, 1974]), pp. 833–34). But ultimately this is Senecan: cf. G. Braden, *Renaissance Tragedy and the Senecan Tradition: Anger's Privilege* (New Haven 1985). Eve's "Destruction with destruction to destroy" (X. 1006) may be an ironic anticipation of Revelation 11:18.

[106] Euripides had come dangerously close to making a serpent drive an ox-wagon (*Bacchae* 1330, ff.), but since this speech has been uttered (hissed?) by a serpent, the theatre might be rather in Aeschylean vein: cf. Aristophanes, *Frogs* 928 ff. In any case, it is evident how much of the "undifferentiated primitive" there is in all this.

has been presented in terms of the most exquisite sexual attractiveness, who is naked, and with whom her adversary is half in love. He is going to employ the disguise of love. The contest will be a battle of wits. What is there in this tale of Beauty and the Beast with which the Italian "romance" could have quarreled? The names offend. But change them into Greek, and we would have a pleasing fantasy, well in the manner of the ancient mime.

Something further becomes evident as the action unfolds. The Renaissance had been impressed by the theatrical possibilities of the pastoral. Renaissance critics had urged the observance of the rules they deduced from Aristotle's *Poetics*. Had not the *Poetics* also declared that the tragic hero was guilty, not of any villainy, but of a *hamartia*, some kind of miscalculation or misapprehension?[107] Under pressure of the classical imagination, Milton's Eve had already been seen as Proserpina. Now Milton's Adam, the victim of Eve's charms, the passive lover/loser already found in Virgil's *Eclogues* (themselves already staged in ancient Rome), becomes not so much sinner as sinned against; no longer the Old Testament figure known from the book of Genesis, so much as the ancestor (and descendant) of Guarini's *Pastor Fido*.

The language of Satan's soliloquy also deserves attention. Milton has been criticized so often for his Latinate style that this has become a cliché. But what word is there here, except "informidable," whose meaning is apparent to anyone who knows "formidable," that is not common in the English even of today? Yet, undeniably, the passage is hard to follow. The difficulty lies therefore in its arrangement, in those staccato repetitions, of nouns and adjectives in particular, which are forced onto the page with such seeming inconsequentiality.[108] Even so, the speech has psychological mobility, molding to the contours of a disordered mind. "Sweet compulsion," "transported," "forget," all lead to "hate": the deadly monosyllable is kept in reserve until it can make a fuller impression. But Satan's instability is immediately shown by his allusion to the other side of hate: "not love, nor hope." This double aspect (what German scholars call "polare Ausdrucksweise," Eisenstein's "pathetic structure") continues in the paradoxical definition of pleasure, which ends with the doleful "other joy/To me is lost" (another deadly monosyllable). The moment is favorable.

---

[107] 1453 a 15–16: cf. D. W. Lucas' discussion in Appendix IV to his edition of the *Poetics*, pp. 299 ff.

[108] For the predominance of nouns over verbs in Greek lyric and tragedy, see M. Chiappore, "Le chapitre XX de la *Poétique* et le *Logos* de la tragédie," p. 27 note 13, in *Écriture et Théorie Poétiques* (Paris 1976), and for the Aristotelian background, G. Morpurgo-Tagliabue, "La linguistica di Aristotele e il XX capitolo della *Poetica*," *Athenaeum* XLIV (1966), 261–97 and XLV (1967), pp. 119–42 and 356–94.

Eve is exposed to attack, and her husband is absent. Once again, Satan is carried away as, in spite of himself, he eulogizes Adam. His enforced praise again ends with monosyllabic opposites ("I not").

His thoughts turn back to himself. There is another contrast, this time with what he once was. But, what he once was, Eve now is: "fair, divinely fair." The strata of time's rocks are visible in this troubled upheaval. She is what he was: she will be what he is.

Now an ambiguous phrase hints at the moral ambiguity in Satan himself. Eve is "fit Love for Gods"—but what sort of love is this? Is it the providential love of God for his creatures, or the lascivious love that accompanied the fall of the angels, and for which we were prepared by the comparisons evoked for Eve as she tended her flowers? The ambiguity continues. Eve is "not terrible, though terrour be in Love." Satan perhaps passes to this thought because he remembers that, to him, what partakes of divinity is terrible, and that if Eve is still a fit love for God she is guarded against him by the same power that keeps him in such pain.

But of course he does not say "fit love for God," rather "fit love for Gods." The gods are the devils.[109] Nervously dipping his toe in the erotic sea, playing with the twofold loves discussed by Plato in the *Symposium*, and by many Renaissance successors, Satan indulges in the reversal of the roles in love, the attribution of masculine psychology to the woman and female to the male, which was a standard topos.[110] The love and beauty of the female are not to be approached by the "stronger" hate of the male, which can only really become stronger if it assumes a show of love. All this is well enough, but its place in epic is within a tradition enriched by the Medea and Phaedra of Euripides, the Medea of Apollonius and Ovid, and even Seneca. The speech begins and ends with a reference to "hate." The effectiveness of an old device persists.[111]

Satan is now able to proceed. His progress is an extraordinary feat of zoological—and pantomimic—motion (496–503):

> not with indented wave,
> Prone on the ground, as since, but on his reare,
> Circular base of rising foulds, that tour'd
> Fould above fould a surging Maze, his Head
> Crested aloft, and Carbuncle his Eyes;

---

[109] *P. L.* I. 373.

[110] Cf. *Samson Agonistes* 404 ff.: K. F. Smith on Tibullus I. 1. 46. In Greek Isocrates (*Hel. Enc.* 57) and Plato (*Symp.* 183a) both show that similar notions were well understood even in the classical period: cf. Callimachus, *Ia.* III. 37 on Adonis as the servant of Aphrodite. Giraut and Petrarch exploit similar ideas.

[111] Above, p. 272 and note 59.

With burnisht Neck of verdant Gold, erect[112]
Amidst his circling Spires, that on the grass
Floted redundant. . . .

Ovid, Statius and Ariosto would have appreciated the extravagance
of this metamorphosis, which is not the only use of this carnival
procedure in the poem. It must strike the reader as curiously
challenging that a poetry which resorts to such mannerisms is nevertheless regarded by Milton as fit vehicle for a theodicy.

Compared to a ship tacking in a shifting wind,[113] Satan at length
(it has taken 517 lines, of which over half have been talk, for him to
get there) approaches Eve, and attracts her attention by "many a
wanton wreath" and "gentle dumb expression." At this point, the
reminiscence of a Byzantine carnival extravaganza becomes unmistakable. In Nonnus' poem, Zeus, who has taken the shape of a serpent,
seduces Proserpina (*Dion.* VI. 155–62: trans. W. H. D. Rouse: cf. V.
565–70):

> Ah, maiden Persephoneia! You could not find how to escape your
> mating! No, a dragon was your mate, when Zeus changed his face
> and came, rolling in many a loving coil through the dark to the corner
> of the maiden's chamber, and shaking his hairy chaps: he lulled to
> sleep as he crept the eyes of those creatures of his own shape who
> guarded the door. He licked the girl's form gently with wooing lips.

The fruit of this union is to be Bacchus.

The discovery of wine by Bacchus is later reported by Nonnus in
a manner which evokes theological echoes (*Dion.* XII. 319–28: trans.
W. H. D. Rouse):

> A serpent twisted his curving backbone about the tree, and sucked a
> strong draught of nectar trickling from the fruit; when he had milked
> the Bacchic potation with his ugly jaws, the draught of the vine turned
> and trickled out of his throat, reddening the creature's beard with
> purple drops.
>
> The hillranging god marvelled, as he saw the snake and his chin
> dabbled with trickling wine; the speckled snake saw Euios, and went
> coiling away with his spotty scales and plunged into a deep hole in
> the rock hard by.

Already in the third century the roof of the Christian Coemeterium
Maius at Rome displays this picture of the serpent coiled around the
tree, as does the ceiling of the Sistine Chapel painted over a millennium

---

[112] Cf. Shakespeare, *Timon of Athens* IV. iii. 164, *erection*.

[113] The ship image also recurs at II. 636, 927, 1043; IV. 159: cf. I. 204, 292; II.
1017. Its significance for Milton is made plain at *Samson Agonistes* 189 ff. (Samson:
cf. 1044) and 710 ff. (Dalilah). See above, p. 289, for this imagery in Petrarch's
*Africa*.

later. A fourth-century sarcophagus preserved in the Museo Archeologico in Syracuse shows a similar iconography.[114] Nonnus, the paraphrast of St. John's Gospel, with its story of the marriage feast at Cana, may have been imaginatively making a connection already implicit in the sub-Apostolic age between Christ and Bacchus, and certainly visible in the Byzantine drama *Christus Patiens*. It is typical of Milton however that, for him, this connection is negative.

With this recollection of—or convergence towards—Nonnus' epic,[115] the stage has now been set for the temptation on which the fate of the world and "all our woe" is to hang. It is to be nothing except a Miltonic reworking (estrangement) of the countless scenes between Red Riding Hood and the Big Bad Wolf with which fairy stories and romances have charmed the ages. The rustic setting is appropriate to this tradition. It follows that there can be no redoubtable feats of arms at this key moment in the history of mankind; only subtlety, flattery, lies, words, the unheroic, comic and farcical claptrap of a Madison Avenue civilization. How well the poet divined the essence of our modern failings!

After over 100 lines of exchanges, which include the central line of the whole book,[116] Satan is informed that his invitation to eat of the forbidden fruit is fruitless (648). The pun fits perfectly into the carnival style.[117] God has forbidden it. At this, the Serpent waxes indignant on Man's behalf, and the poet cannot forbear a certain irony (667–76):

> and as to passion mov'd
> [Satan] Fluctuats disturbd, yet comely and in act
> Rais'd, as of som great matter to begin.
> As when of old som Orator renound

[114] Christa Schug-Wille, *Art of the Byzantine World*, tr. E. M. Hatt (New York 1969), pp. 13–14. The sarcophagus of Adelphia in Room XIV of the Museo Archeologico in Syracuse may be compared.

[115] For further similarities between Nonnus' imagination and Milton's see *Dion.* II. 170 ff. and *P. L.* IV. 776 ff. (celestial sentries); *Dion.* II. 703 ff. and *P. L.* VI. 880 ff. (return of victorious Zeus/Messiah); *Dion.* XVI. 125 ff. and *P. L.* IX. 388 ff. (comparison with Artemis/Diana); *Dion.* XVI. 270 ff., XXXII. 84 ff. and *P. L.* IV. 690 ff., VIII. 510 ff. (nuptial bowers); *Dion.* XVII. 310 ff., XL. 134 and 137 and *P. L.* IV. 273 (Daphne by Orontes); *Dion.* XLI. 185 ff. and *P. L.* IV. 340 ff. (W. H. D. Rouse: Aphrodite/Eve); possibly also *Dion.* XXVII. 195–96 and *P. L.* VI. 750–51, where the association of a fiery chariot with Sicily may have triggered Milton's imagination.

[116] 595, "Tempting so nigh, to pluck and eat my fill."

[117] Word-play is part of the primitive tradition (above, p. 283 and note 91) and a basic carnival device. It is very doubtful whether Milton thought of it as automatically denoting triviality of mind (as one critic of Eve has suggested). See further R. Pfeiffer, *History of Classical Scholarship* (Oxford 1968), pp. 4–5.

> In Athens or free Rome, where Eloquence
> Flourishd, since mute, to som great cause addrest,
> Stood in himself collected, while each part,
> Motion, each act won audience ere the tongue,
> Sometimes in highth began, as no delay
> Of Preface brooking through his Zeal of Right.

Antiquity has indeed furnished us with just such a representation of Demosthenes. Milton himself showed a similar impatience with rhetoricians' schemes in his prose works.[118] But if we compare either Demosthenes or Milton with this eloquent snake, "so standing, moving, or to highth upgrown"...? And yet this is the most serious moment in world history!

The suggestion by the Serpent of God's jealousy, mingled with flattery, and the argument that proof of the fruit has already been supplied by his eating from it, may be insidious enough. But now a rather more prosaic (and carnival) motive makes itself felt. Noon is drawing on, and Eve is feeling the pangs of hunger anyway. Can the destiny of mankind hang on such an earthy peg as the female digestive processes? Callimachean, Ovidian Milton, who earlier slighted banquets as unworthy of the dignity of modern religious epic, apparently thinks so.[119]

In spite of her pangs, Eve will not eat until she has rehearsed the arguments for and against once more. The 35 lines of her speech (745–79) are matched by the 35 lines (1099–1133) that will be devoted to the making of coverings from fig-leaves, the real, miserable outcome of the Serpent's sophistries. At last, she takes the fruit (780–94):

> So saying, her rash hand in evil hour
> Forth reaching to the fruit, she pluck'd, she eat:
> Earth felt the wound, and Nature from her seat
> Sighing through all her Works gave signs of woe,[120]
> That all was lost. Back to the Thicket slunk
> The guiltie Serpent, and well might, for *Eve*
> Intent now wholly on her taste, naught else
> Regarded, such delight till then, as seemd,
> In Fruit she never tasted, whether true
> Or fansied so, through expectation high

---

[118] R. M. Samarin, *op. cit.*, pp. 198–99, associates Milton's readiness to break the rules of "correct" composition with his epic leanings. The statue of Demosthenes mentioned is reproduced in G. M. A. Richter, *The Sculpture and Sculptors of the Greeks* (New Haven 1957), p. 297 and fig. 757; M. Bieber, *The Sculpture of the Hellenistic Age* (New York 1967), p. 67.

[119] Though cf. Virgil's *mensas consumimus, Aen.* VII. 116.

[120] Contrast VIII. 513–14, where Earth rejoices at Adam and Eve's nuptial bliss.

> Of knowledg, nor was God-head from her thought.
> Greedily she ingorg'd without restraint,
> And knew not eating Death: Satiate at length
> And hight'nd as with Wine, jocond and boon,
> Thus to her self she pleasingly began.

At the height of the action, Milton, contradicting his own prefatory strictures, uses rhyme![121] It has taken just fifteen lines of description before direct speech resumes. But what description? Two lines suffice to sum up the guilty act, and in reality four words: *she pluck'd, she eat.* All the rest is not action, but reaction.

Eve is intoxicated. The result of the primal sin is diagnosed by Milton as the failure to get the world straight which this distortion of the senses implies. The speech which she now makes is the crooked mirror of her sinful state of mind.

Milton is a master at his dramatic task. Eve praises the tree, naively fancying that in future she will be able to tend it each morning, and deal out its fruit to herself. She congratulates herself on eating, and now accepts as true that the tree has been kept from her by envy. She praises the fruit for giving access to Wisdom, in spite of its secretiveness: secretiveness . . . perhaps she will be able to keep all this secret from the great Forbidder. Leaving that unpleasant thought, she debates whether she will share her newly found discovery with Adam or not, that is, whether she will commit the same act of envy of which she has just accused God. If she does not, she will be able to attract more of his love by her superiority in knowledge. But, if she is to die for her offense, and Adam, protected by his innocence, is to live and wed another Eve—the prospect is unthinkable, and because Eve loves him so much, Adam must be induced to commit the sin that will damn him, and all of us.

This piece of logic is worthy of Seneca, Ovid, Apollonius, Euripides. The question is that of the progress of a sin responsible for all the horrors which we, and Milton, see around us in a fallen world. And the sin progresses because of a woman's giddy vanity! Does the punishment fit the crime? Jason had already asked this question, and Medea answered it.[122]

Adam is by definition a perfect man, and how a perfect man may

---

[121] The rhyme in 781–82 *eat/seat* is paralleled in Milton's translation of Psalm 1:3–4 *seat/great* and 86:33–35 *great/seat*. *L'Allegro* 101–02 has *feat/eat*. The lyrical device (cf. W. Stockert on Pindar's "Klangfiguren") is imposed on Milton's artistic sense by the remembering genre. It is also a good example of Eisenstein's "leap into another dimension." See above, p. 57 and note 56, and, for the humanist debate on rhyme, E. Norden, *Die Antike Kunstprosa*, p. 869 note 1, with G. Saintsbury, *A History of Criticism,* II, pp. 156 ff.

[122] Seneca, *Medea* 1008–11.

be shown in literature was, for Renaissance critics, a baffling question. Milton solves his dilemma by the technique he has used in his characterization of Satan. We enjoy Satan, because we too are sinners. Adam is imperfect *before* he commits original sin, because in him the future is already present. Time, once again, is made, not horizontal, but vertical. *Facilis* **descensus** *Averno.*

Adam's inability to think straight even now is shown, for Milton, by his willingness to taste the fruit for the sake of love. It is an absurd act, and Christian theology cannot condemn it, since the sacrifice of Christ on Calvary has been thought by many to be an absurd act committed out of love. Even St. Paul toyed with the idea of accepting damnation for himself, if that would lead to the conversion of his own people.[123] Already, in the sin, there is heard, faintly and suppressed by the poet, the hint of redemption.

St. Paul had also remarked that it was not man who sinned in the first instance, but woman. Man was not deceived.[124] Milton takes up this Pauline theme (997–99):

> he scrupl'd not to eat
> Against his better knowledge, not deceav'd,
> But fondly overcome with Femal charm.

Yet Milton's imagery makes it clear that what Eve had really done was commit adultery with the Serpent.[125] She has become, in the exaggeration of religious fervor, a harlot, and so it is not surprising, that, after her first guilty night with Adam, she is expressly called one (1059–62):

> So rose the Danite strong
> Herculean Samson from the Harlot-lap
> Of Philistean Dalilah, and wak'd
> Shorn of his strength.[126]

Adam's sin is to have been unable to control his appetites ("But fondly overcome with Femal charm").

The story concludes with speeches of mutual reproach, where

---

123 Romans 9:3 ff.

124 I Ti. 2:14.

125 She has been ravished, like Pales, Pomona, Ceres, Proserpina (393, 432); she has played Circe (522) to Satan's Ulysses (II. 1017); she has been Semele, Olympias, Pomponia (505), all seduced by Jove; she has been Solomon's Egyptian queen and the consort of Adonis (= Thammuz: I. 446 ff.) at 439, and Dido at 386. At X. 579 (cf. 868 ff.), in explaining the myth of Ophion and Eurynome (see also Nonnus, *Dion.* II. 573), Milton finds no place for Adam.

126 Cf. Hercules/devils: *P. L.* II. 542. In *Samson Agonistes* Dalilah is both ship (= Satan in *P. L.*: above, note 113) and serpent (997, 1001), thus uniting in herself two diabolical aspects.

there are again ironic symmetries with what has preceded.[127] Its deliberately flat last line ("And of thir vain contest appeer'd no end") is an echo of a technique which Virgil knew, and of which Horace is a master.

For Milton, Italy was more than a visit to the imprisoned Galileo. At an impressionable age, the poet traveled and was feted by kindred spirits among a people still fertile beyond belief in artistic genius. Bernini was working on St. Peter's.[128] Borromini's extraordinary and "chimerical" architecture was just making its appearance. The rich polyphony of Palestrina was rivaled by new theories of operatic, dramatic monody. He attended concerts in Rome. He knew and deeply impressed Tasso's old patron. He read Dante, and learned from Ariosto. How could his imagination not be fired by all these creative flames?

It is as a Renaissance epic then that *Paradise Lost* first parades before us. For the English poet also, as for Boccaccio and Ariosto, love, the relationship between the sexes, occupies the center of the heroic stage. If he claims nevertheless with this *mise-en-scène* to confront in some way the profoundest questions of our human predicament, so did they.

He does this by deploying, like Virgil and Ovid, the primitive tricks of the carnival: his huge, grotesque figures silhouetted against elemental bonfires in his early books; his celestial armies and their maneuvers in the center of the poem where the sardonic humor of the interchange between the opposing leaders is perfectly in keeping with the clownish tug of war; the picnic ambience of the garden of Eden, with its "learned discussions," a survival of the comic *agon*, satisfying the same didactic curiosity as inspired the dinner-table debates of the Alexandrians in their Museum and, at a cruder level, the sympotic wisdom of the *Guinness Book of World Records*. Virgil and Lucan too had indulged this Hellenistic taste. But so had Petronius' Trimalchio, and Seneca's Calvisius Sabinus.

Finally, Beauty confronts the Beast, but this time loses her virtue without being able to reform her lover. Just like Odysseus' crew, she sins by eating the food forbidden by a god. The evocation of these old themes, which recur so ambivalently in Bacchic and Christian worship, is colored by Milton's own experiences: Mary Powell betraying the paradise of his many gardens.

The danger for this style lies in the effort to stereotype response,

---

[127] 1099–1142 (fig-leaves and Adam's speech); 1143–86 (exchange of speeches between Adam and Eve): both 44 lines and echoing the 44 of 226–69.

[128] R. Wittkower is especially instructive: *Gian Lorenzo Bernini* (London 1955); *Art and Architecture in Italy 1600–1750* (Harmondsworth 1958).

to suppress laughter, to freeze movement, for in that ice, as Dante knew, life perishes. Milton comes uncomfortably close to this when he rationalizes his procedures in the proem to Book IX. But his genius rescued him in the event. His sense of time as space, whose convolutions hide and reveal a present truth, lends a prophetic dimension to his narrative, displayed without disguise in the final books as Michael lays bare to Adam the now-past future. The end of the poem is still open. Adam and Eve's "vain contest" (*agon*) leaves them paradoxically solitary. Vain contests have in fact in human life no end. It is why *Paradise Lost*, like the *Aeneid* and the *Knight's Tale*, still challenges interpretation.[129]

The beginning of this chapter made reference to "the English tradition." We can now attach some more precise meaning to this phrase. Obviously, both poets share certain features. Both Chaucer and Milton are "dramatic," to use the adjective that Aristotle perhaps invented to describe Homer. Both take up the pastoral into the epic, but not simply as escapism. Both repeat language and imagery, enjoy irony, satire, "learning," ambiguity. Both pay homage to love and the unexpected predominance of the feminine in the heroic. Both use a language which is not confined to an artificial "sublime."

Yet this is not in itself an English tradition. To find that, paradoxically, we must go behind the English to the British. In the first instance, it is to be sought in a musical complexity strongly reminiscent of the whorls and twists of Celtic ("British") art.

Milton employs, for example, not the recurring *terza rima* or *ottave* of the Italians, but what has been called above "ironic symmetry," in which corresponsive numerical balances offset and counterpoint each other. He signalled early in Book IX to the sensitive ear his intention of using this method by giving 13 lines to Satan's entry into the Serpent (179–91), and another 13 to daybreak, followed by Adam and Eve's emergence (192–204). When Eve speaks for 21 lines (205–225) in making her original proposal to work away from her husband, she is using exactly the number of lines that will be taken by Satan's soliloquy on seeing her alone and exposed to temptation (473–93), by Satan's first speech to Eve and Milton's comment on it

---

[129] Milton's unquiet use of the verb "roll" catches the attention in reading (cf. *P. L.* III. 23, 359, 718; IV. 16, 238, 593; VI. 57, 829; VII. 291, 298; VIII. 19; IX. 183, 631; X. 558, 666; XI. 460, 620, 749; XII. 183). Like Leonardo (K. Clark, *Leonardo* [Cambridge 1952], p. 165), Milton was perhaps fascinated by the universal flux, extending even to the celestial bodies, as in Ariosto's *De diversis amoribus* (61–62) and Donne's *Defence of Women's Inconstancy*. We may contrast both Virgil's *sic volvere Parcas* (*Aen.* I. 22) and Wordsworth's "A motion and a spirit, that impels/. . . And rolls through all things": cf. also "Roll'd round in earth's diurnal course/With rocks and stones and trees."

(532–52), by Adam's speech of reaction when he finds that Eve has eaten the forbidden fruit (896–916), by the guilty aftermath of their now poisoned love-making (1046–66).

Adam's reply of 44 lines (226–69), which is unsuccessful in persuading Eve to stay with him, is just overtopped by Satan's sophistic reply of 46 lines (567–612), when he by contrast successfully persuades Eve to eat. Adam will use another 62 lines (290–317; 342–375) in vainly trying to dissuade Eve from going off on her own. The 61 lines of Satan's triumphant progress through Eden (412–72) will point the futility of his words. Eve will use 32 lines (319–41; 376–84) at the end. It is exactly the number of lines with which Adam rebukes her on first coming to his senses after eating the fruit (1076–98). The 9 lines of her final speech (376–84) on leaving her husband exactly match the 9 lines (1134–42) with which Adam begins the first quarrel in their marriage.

The scene in which Adam finds out what Eve has done is introduced by 30 lines of defensive apology from Eve (856–85). Adam's initial horrified reaction takes 10 lines (886–95). He then speaks for 21 lines (896–916). Four lines of transition (917–20) mean that we have had a block of 35 lines, recalling the 35 lines of Eve's speech before she eats, and the 35 lines which will describe the fig-leaves. When Adam speaks again, he uses 39 lines (921–59), exactly the length of Eve's first speech after eating (795–833). The ironic balance shows what we are to think of the casuistry by which Adam persuades himself to disobey God's command. Eve replies for 30 lines (960–89), repeating the length of her speech after meeting Adam at the start of this scene (856–85). Adam then eats (990–1016): the 27 lines that describe this are half the 54 lines of Satan's last speech before Eve eats (679–732) and half the 54 lines (780–833) occupied by Eve's eating and first speech after eating.

Adam's sin therefore cannot be dissociated from the musical, mathematical symmetry of the rest of the book, and least of all from the sin of Eve. Even his ten lines of revulsion (886–95) are an echo of the ten lines in which Eve first asked the Serpent to guide her to the tree in whose praises he was so lavish (615–24). The rest of the time he has no chance. His 21 lines of first reaction to Eve's eating (896–916) strike a figure of sinister implication in the book: his 39 lines of decision to eat (921–59) are as drunken as Eve's 39 lines (795–833) when she has eaten.

In the *Knight's Tale*, stanzaic composition of a similar kind is quite evident. The third part, for example, opens in Robinson's edition with paragraphs of 12, 21, 4 (= 37) and 37 lines. Here, the second 37, describing the chapel of Venus, are clearly a double of the introduction. Then follow paragraphs of 12, 8 (= 20) and 20 lines: the statue of Venus, a transitional passage, the temple of Mars. The pictures in the temple take 46 lines, and the god's statue 10. The temple of Mars and its statue occupy 76 lines altogether (1975–2050). The paintings in the temple of Diana and her statue take 38 lines (2051–2088), exactly half of Mars' 76.

The following transition to the return of Arcita and Palamon and the actual return with the description of Palamon balance this 38 with 39 (2089–2127). Lycurgus and Emetreus are described in 62 lines (2128–2189). This is exactly the length which will be taken by Palamon's visit to Venus' temple, his prayer and the goddess' answer (2209–2270). The entertainment and transition between Lycurgus/ Emetreus and Palamon's visit to Venus occupy 19 lines (2190–2208), half of 38.

Emily's visit to Diana fills a huge 96 lines (2271–2366). This time therefore Diana weighs as much as Venus and Mars combined (1955–2050 = 96 lines). Arcita's prayer to Mars takes 48 lines (2373–2420), half of 96. Arcita's entire visit to Mars (2367–2437) fills 71 lines. Combined with the report of the turmoil in heaven and Saturn's intervention (2438–2478 = 41 lines), this gives 112 lines, an ironic balance with 2483–2594 and 2853–2964 (arrival of the knights/funeral procession and funeral). The 102 lines of 2095–2196 (return of Arcita and Palamon leading to the entertainment before the tournament) are matched by the 102 of 2271–2372 (Emily's visit to Diana and the start of Arcita's visit to Mars).

The parallels to the technique found in Milton are apparent. There is a sensitivity here to the innermost essence of the classical tradition: the recurrent use of similar numbers of words in Pindar, and the use of balancing numbers of lines even in Attic drama,[130] in Virgil, and particularly, as was seen, in Statius. And yet, when we contrast this subtle patterning, reinforced by the music of alliteration and asso- nance, with the regularity of Italian epic, we find ourselves plunged into a world of knots and mazes, as complex as any devised by the

---

[130] The technique of symmetry in Greek drama is noted, for example, by G. Thomson (Cambridge 1932) on *Prometheus Vinctus* 636–902, 726–27. Similarly in Euripides' *Hippolytus*, Aphrodite's prologue, threatening vengeance, occupies the first 57 lines of the play: Phaedra's speech of resolve to die, the proximate cause of Hippolytus' death, takes 58 lines (373–430). The scene where the nurse leads Phaedra to speak the name of the one she loves (351) fills 95 lines (267–361). Although the later scene where Theseus accuses, and Hippolytus replies, is marred by interpolation, it perhaps showed a symmetry with this earlier 95. There are 100 lines (936–1035), of which however W. S. Barrett (in his edition of the play [repr. Oxford 1969]) suspects 5. Some of Pindar's symmetries are examined in *Pindar's Art: Its Tradition and Aims*. Thus Milton is enriching his epic with borrowings from lyric and drama, exactly what we should expect.

artists of the Book of Kells, or the Welsh virtuosi of *cynghanedd* (alliterative systems), of *y mesurau caeth* ("the strict meters"). It has taken the Greco-Roman tradition to foster the most characteristic features of another literature. This is the best kind of tutelage.

The "Englishness" therefore of the two poets, certainly if we contrast them with Boccaccio, Ariosto and even Tasso, rather than with Dante, lies in the metaphysical awareness of which this older than "English," rather we should say "British," intricacy is both expression and emphasis. We are in a tangled wood, gnarled, uncouth, threatening.[131] Milton associated the "wilde wood" with evil and danger as early as *Comus* and the *Epitaphium Damonis*. It is a powerful theme of *Paradise Lost*, as it had been of certain plays of Shakespeare.

Chaucer confronted the problem of evil in his depiction of Saturn with terrifying effect. Even though he chose the "continental" version of the malevolent Saturn, the Italian poets would have thought him crude and barbarous. Milton's Saturn is Satan. Like Chaucer, he is fascinated by the problem of the evil character: its twisted grandeur, its pettiness, its empty malice, its "paine."[132] The child of a baroque and theatrical age, the heir of Seneca, he tries to explore the psychology directly. Chaucer left us to deduce the cause from the effects. But in both English authors it is loss rather than gain which commands elaboration and scrutiny, which excites the atavistic fantasy.

Chaucer was faithful enough to the serio-comic genre not to impose answers to his questions. Milton no doubt believed he had answers, but in his case too "the genre remembered." His epic ends with a contrast. "Hand in hand"/"solitary": the dividing dilemma of joint sin persists.

---

[131] *Ahi quanto a dir qual era è cosa dura / esta selva selvaggia e aspra e forte* Dante had written at the beginning of the Trecento: but it would be Goethe's Faust who would feel at home there (Part I. 3217 ff.; cf. Mammon's palace, 3941 ff.).

[132] John Bradshaw, *A Concordance to the Poetical Works of John Milton* (repr. Hamden, Conn. 1965), lists 55 examples of the singular of this noun in the epic. When "augmented paine" (VI. 280) is picked up by "A long days dying to augment our paine" (X. 964) the pathos is Shakespearean.

# IX

# THE MODERN EPIC—I:
# EISENSTEIN AND PUDOVKIN

WHAT then of the tradition we have ourselves inherited? Can epic be a concern of modern man at this remove from its first beginnings, and in an age when the attention span is probably shorter than it ever was even in Alexandria? These questions are to be answered by asking another: what is epic about?

As practiced by its greatest masters, epic poetry has been an amalgam. Formal definitions have varied widely over the centuries.[1] There has been a confusion with tragedy, even with comedy. A precise literary form has evidently been less important on occasion than the ambition of the work of art. A Callimachean could accept this looseness without qualm. What he could not accept would be that the epic should be too tied up with history, with the intruding detail. Here, Callimachus and Aristotle come together.[2]

Epic desires its freedom however from constricting insistence on what "really" happened because it is concerned with what really happened. It demands the right to take our imaginations, and with them our minds, away from the external and superficial (What was the victim's "true" name and age? What was her social security number?) to the profound and general (Is it acceptable that daily muggings should take place in the streets of a civilized community? What in man causes him to behave like this?). Just because epic goes further than journalism, its details, when they are used, are not intrusive but "telling." With their aid, it asserts its power to transport us out of the narrow bounds of our own time and age to wider scope and broader sweep, to enhance the possibilities and deepen the failures, to move us from the mental prairies to the Rockies and ask us to contemplate the eternal hills.

---

[1] See S. Koster, *Antike Epostheorien* (Wiesbaden 1970), p. 161, for the ancient world. Sperone Speroni denied that the *Aeneid* was an epic, and Castravilla did the same for Dante's *Comedy* (Weinberg, *History of Literary Criticism in the Italian Renaissance* [Chicago 1961], pp. 689, 831 ff.). Dante himself called the *Aeneid* a tragedy (*Inf.* XX. 113), and cast his *Comedy* in the form of a (tragic) trilogy.

[2] Above, p. 40.

Has Callimachus anything to contribute to the recovery of such an epic in our century? This question at least is wrongly phrased. Callimachus has been in play all the time. Our century, concerned as all centuries and all men must be with the limitations and ideals of its condition, has had no lack of epics, for when such poetry disappears man becomes less than himself. But what we have suffered from is incomprehension. Artists have not understood their tradition, and so have been forced to strike out without the self-confidence which awareness of powerful literary backers could have supplied. More important, for artists are adept at recovering something to use from the unlikeliest sources, audiences have lost the sense of tradition. They have not nourished their imaginations and feelings in such a way as to be able to reject what has no sustenance, to link what they see before them with the achievement of the past, and to judge it by that achievement.

We are asking then for the re-acknowledgment of an old debt. This looks like advocacy for a dangerous and stultifying classicism, by which all that is modern is to be stifled beneath the accumulated debris of a vanished world. But, once we remember that classic art is itself not a uniform thing, the danger lessens. A basic principle of the Callimachean poetic is that it must constantly repudiate its own accomplishments when they stand in the way of rational, human poetry.[3]

The initial demand therefore which a Callimachean poetic would put—has put—to the artist is that he should make an act of humility. He is a man among men. He is not here in the first place to dazzle, to show off, to indulge in pyrotechnics for their own sake, although in their proper place all these activities are consistent with being Callimachean. His primary aim is to show us himself, and the typical part of himself: his weaknesses, doubts and fears as well as his faith, his abilities, his dedication. Because he shows us himself, he shows us ourselves.[4]

But the Callimachean is not naive. He is deeply aware that civilization is a precious creation, and that every moment it must be re-created by a conscious act of volition on the part of those who claim to be its adherents. This will mean two things for his poetry. It will not be open to every fool who blunders into its presence from the bar or the drug orgy. This poet will insist on some corresponding openness from his readers, openness to tradition, to human values,

---

[3] Above, pp. 156, 202, 220, 255, 284, 329, 380; below, p. 437 note 114.

[4] The tone of the Preface to the *Aetia* is particularly noteworthy here: above, p. 27.

human questionings.[5] Like the children of Noah, we must possess the sensitivity to respond without mockery to his nakedness.

Chiefly however, such poetry is not anti-intellectual. True, it will engage the whole man, and there are times when it will use music and color in such a way as to carry the reader forward into realms where cold logic could not be expected to take him. But, though it will expand the reader's mind, it will certainly not burst it. It will always recall that, when men do leave their minds at home, anarchy walks abroad.

In the service of this poetic, rejecting humbug and testing all bland assertion by the reality of observed consequences, the writer of the Callimachean epic will not regard himself as rigidly bound by past precedent. It is not surprising to him, for example, to realize that prose is a perfectly acceptable medium for epic narrative. This development was foreseen by Aristotle, and implicit in the use of "prosaic" vocabulary and idiom by Callimachus.[6] May we not think of it as implicit too in the Virgil who was criticized for inventing a new bad style drawn *ex communibus verbis* ("from common words")?[7]

But epic tended towards more than prose. Aristotle had been among the first to associate such poetry with drama, and there have been many instances where the real epic tradition was best understood, not by its ostensible practitioners, but by writers for the stage.[8] The classical epic must never be thought of as some static, one-dimensional assemblage of thin and printed pages. How could that be true of so Wagnerian an art?

Time and again in this book we have spoken of an "operatic" quality to both classical and more modern epic poetry. The orality of its presentation, most evident in Virgil, but found in many other authors, justified the assumption of a chameleon, Protean narrator, acting out the different roles in the interplay of characters which made up the whole.[9] Only a few measures separate such epic polyphony, vivid, dramatic, musical, intense, unified, from the film, where every conceivable device both of music and painting may be used to enhance the script. Not the use, but the abuse, of such methods is condemned by the Callimachean poetic.

[5] "Apollo does not appear to every man, only to him who is good": *Hymn to Apollo*, v. 9. Cf. below, p. 487 (Thomas Mann).

[6] Aristotle had already foreshadowed the use of prose in imaginative writing: *Poetics* 1447 a 28 f. with D. W. Lucas' note on p. 59 of his edition. Cf. Callimachus' "prose pasture of the Muses," *Aetia* fr. 112. 9 Pf., and Pfeiffer's note on *Hecale*, fr. 233.

[7] Above, p. 245.

[8] Above, p. 15 with note 19.

[9] Above, pp. 207–08.

Highbrows have risen even higher when Hollywood has billed its presentations as "epic," and the claim that a particular specimen of the art contained "a cast of thousands" has been thought amusingly vulgar. There was perhaps a Horatian, even Callimachean, element in the criticism.[10] But what its authors have failed to see is that, in lumping all films together, in allowing no room for experiment, they were in essence taking up exactly the position of the Telchines towards Callimachus. Fixed in a false classicism, in which certain works of the past have been reduced to museum pieces and are no longer comprehended, such critics demand from the modern poet that he should repeat what they judge to have already been done and so, if they are right, cannot be repeated. The failure to accept their wrongheaded challenge is interpreted by them as proof of poetic inability. Too superficial themselves to discern the difficulties of the enterprise, too lazy to live up to their own requirements, they are then entitled to sit back and continue with their trivialities, indifferent to the needs of their age.

It is fortunate that we have lived in a time whose demands were too articulate to be ignored in this naive fashion. There have been artists among us who have realized that the epic poet is not fulfilling his vatic function if he says nothing about the broadest issues of his time, or says it in such a way that people of good will cannot grasp at his meaning. The interesting thing is that such men, no "scholars" in the accepted sense of the term, have nevertheless been sufficiently engaged with the classical tradition to sense its basic premises, even when the official guardians of tradition offered no help at all towards such an undertaking.

I

The paradoxes which these arguments raise may be solved upon the most cursory reflection. The jargon of the film-maker's art is objectively established, and with its aid a practical poetic of the film has been developed.[11] Some of its important terms are:

---

[10] Cf. Horace, *Epp.* II. 1. 180 ff., where E. Fraenkel (*Horace* [Oxford 1957], p. 393 note 3) adduces *inter alia* Call. fr. 282. Cf. also Call. fr. 215, Pf. But we must remember that Callimachus did write dramas, in spite of his strictures.

[11] A simple guide to this cinematic ABC may be found, for example, in *The Filmviewer's Handbook* by Emile G. McAnany, S.J. and Robert Williams, S.J. (Glen Rock, New Jersey 1965), pp. 42 ff. S. M. Eisenstein's views are cited (in my own translation/paraphrase) in this chapter from two Russian sources: *Izbrannye Proizvedeniya* (Moscow 1964), 6 vols.; *Izbrannye Stat'i* (Moscow 1956). A selection and translation of some salient pieces is available to the English reader in *Film Form and The Film Sense* (one volume), tr. J. Leyda (repr. Cleveland and New York 1967). See also the

1. *The shot*: the basic film unit, taken in one uninterrupted photographic process of the motion picture camera. Shots may obviously vary in length, but normally they do not last longer than twenty or thirty seconds.
2. *The scene*: a series of shots, displaying unity of time and place, but generally taken from several different angles and camera positions.
3. *The sequence*: this is the largest unit making up a film, and consists of a collection of scenes arranged to illustrate some theme that the director regards as essential to his story.

The elements made up in this way must be brought together to give an overall unity to the film. Traditional devices include:

1. *Simple juxtaposition*: here, the director may be relying upon an association of ideas easily established by his audience. But he may also be intending deliberately to shock or jolt by the unexpectedness of his juxtapositions. Sometimes, what is odd or bizarre at first sight may turn out to have unity on closer inspection. If the ancients practiced this technique in literature (Pindar, Nonnus), the classical editor (of poems such as those of Propertius, for example, whose elegies continually assume an epic tone) will need to be far less ready to postulate the existence of lacunae. "As an audience becomes more sophisticated in its viewing habits, films can make more demands on its ability to follow complex time sequences and instantaneous flashbacks, joined . . . by simple cuts."[12]
2. *Fade*: in this, one scene disappears gradually as light diminishes, and may then be followed by another in which the light slowly increases.[13] The fade has two variants that were of great value to the Callimachean epic. They are:
3. *The dissolve*, in which a fade-out and a fade-in are superimposed in such a way that there is never complete darkness on the

---

same author's *Eisenstein: Three Films; Battleship Potemkin, October, Alexander Nevsky* (New York 1974). I must express my sincerest thanks to Professor Herbert Marshall, Director of the Center for Soviet and East European Studies at Southern Illinois University at Carbondale, a former student of Eisenstein in Moscow, for reading and criticizing an early draft of this chapter. Its errors of course are my responsibility.

[12] McAnany and Williams, *The Filmviewer's Handbook*, p. 47: a useful principle in the interpretation of the Roman Callimachus, Propertius. An important study remains to be written on "Propertius as an epic poet."

[13] Compare the end of *Odyssey* III. It is perhaps this structural use of chronology which lies behind Pollio's remark, cited by Servius on *Aen.* XI. 183, that Virgil's dawns always have relevance to their contexts. Cf. Heinze, *Virgils epische Technik* (repr. Stuttgart 1957), p. 366.

screen, only the blurring of one image and the clarifying of another,[14] and

4. *Superimposition*, in which the first image is deliberately held so that the two images appear on the screen at the same time.[15]

What the audience sees is conditioned by the instrument at the director's disposal, the camera. It may be used in a number of ways:

1. *Extreme long-shot*, to establish a general view of the surroundings in which the action occurs.
2. *Long-shot*, taken from about fifty yards to twenty feet away.
3. *Medium shot*: this is the shot most often used. It enables the spectator to have a close view of the character(s), while not excluding some awareness of background.
4. *Large close-up*: a shot concentrating upon a particular detail, to the exclusion of any hint of the whole to which it belongs.
5. *Close-up*: a shot concentrating particularly on the face, to emphasize emotion, significance, personal reaction.

What is interesting in this list is the relative infrequency of the two types of long-shot, compared with the three that concentrate on detail. Directors who know their audiences have apparently decided that selection from the mass of detail which the camera could show is essential. The film is not reporting in some impersonal way about all that comes within its view, and it is obvious that such "impersonality" would only be another form of subjective choice (and a choice for chaos). The film aims to make its impact on the emotions more rationally, and to do this it employs a technique found, for example, in Egyptian murals and in Gothic art. What matters is thrown into prominence; what is less important is correspondingly diminished, even to the point of being totally ignored. Of course a great deal of fun is to be had by imposing the standards of the detective's notebook on this kind of narrative technique.[16] The question is: do detectives write epics?

---

[14] Not only Virgil's superimposition of characters (metamorphoses) would illustrate this technique, but also his *interea*: cf. Norden's edition of *Aeneid* VI (repr. Stuttgart 1957), p. 180, and Heinze, *Virgils epische Technik*, p. 388 note 2 and p. 456. *Interea* also occurs in Furius Bibaculus, fr. 7 (Morel–Buechner): cf. *cum interea*, Catullus 64. 305.

[15] Virgil is a master of this, and the interpretations of *Aeneid* II–III offered above (pp. 159 ff.) tried especially to suggest how the ostensibly monotone narrative was colored by being told in a particular place, to a particular listener, and culminated in the double significance of the erupting volcano of passion and punishment, Etna. Verbal reminiscence is a variant of this technique.

[16] Lucian (*Hist. Conscr.* 57) and Elmer Rice (*A Voyage to Purilia*) have both voiced this criticism. M. String is still remarking about Nonnus in 1966: "Es ist erstaunlich,

The viewer's response to a film may be dictated not only by the different shots mentioned here, but also by the angle at which a particular shot or even a whole scene is presented relative to normal, eye-level vision. Sometimes a shot filmed from an unexpected angle, whether from above or below, may convey an ill-defined feeling of awkwardness to the spectator, of something out of true. Sometimes this impression may be more specific. The audience may be made to feel remote from the action, like an eavesdropper on a scene only partially understood. A refusal to allow the audience to grasp the entire implications of a situation may enable it to sense something of the fear and frustration of the mentally deranged, of the neurotic recluse. It may suggest the hopelessness of defining one's adversaries, who are forever hidden behind shadows. Sometimes, unusual camera angles may be repeated ironically, with reversal of their previous implications. Sometimes the camera may concentrate on the unexpected. The sun glinting on the forest trees in *Rashomon* made us aware of nature as the silent witness to man's violence.

The theoretician of the film is confronted in all this with an unexpected paradox. The camera has as its very essence clear, visual presentation, and yet it is being used to obfuscate. It will be open to the Cartesian to protest that the enterprise is self-contradictory. But such a critic will hardly be able to invoke "real life," unless he lives in a world very different from that of the rest of us. The camera is twisted away from mere reportage, because the artist sees more to report. The narrative technique of the Alexandrian poet, and his lyrical predecessors, leaves so many loose ends, because experience is untidy too.[17]

The camera is also mobile, and thus opens a wealth of new dimensions. Now the director can carry a spectator's eye along in

---

wie wenig sich die Ausführlichkeit der Darstellung mit der natürlicherweise anzu-nehmenden Wichtigkeit der dargestellten Ereignisse deckt" (*Untersuchungen zum Stil der Dionysiaka des Nonnos von Panopolis* [Hamburg 1966], p. 8). But suppose Nonnus knew that and meant something by it? See M. Bakhtin's remarks about "carnival time" in *Problemy Poetiki Dostoevskogo* (Moscow 1963), pp. 200, 237. The relation between what Günther Müller has called *Erzählzeit und Erzählte Zeit* has ramifications, too wide to be explored here, in Bergson, the Russian Formalist critics B. Tomashevsky and B. Eichenbaum, Thomas Mann, and must in practice form part of any work of narrative art.

[17] One remembers Maffeo Vegio's Book XIII of the *Aeneid*. But even D. A. Campbell writes of Bacchylides 17: "The ring is not mentioned again; this is *of course* [my italics] a blemish" (*Greek Lyric Poetry* [London 1967], p. 437). And whatever happened to the Golden Fleece? Eisenstein notes (*Izbr. Proiz.*, II, p. 308) that "compositional negligence and inferiority" have been detected in *Hamlet*. Compare Horace on Plautus, *Epp.* II. 1. 170 ff. How refreshing in this context is G. Steiner's assertion (*After Babel* [London 1975]) that one of language's basic functions is concealment!

such a way that he passes rapidly through a whole series of smoothly flowing shots, which completely control his reaction. He sees not only what the director wishes him to see, but in the order in which he is meant to see it, without the possibility of looking away to compare and contrast. The effectiveness of this device was illustrated at the beginning of the post-war French film of the life of the Curé d'Ars. As the saint entered the filthy and derelict village church to which he had been assigned, the camera followed his gaze around the scene of squalor until we were so carried along by our own momentum in this "rubber-necking" (which clearly owed something to Brueghelian realism) that we imagined we were still seeing through the priest's eyes. But suddenly the illusion was broken. The camera swung back to the figure of the priest, who had sunk onto his knees to pray that he might be worthy to enter God's house, and we felt guilty that, unlike him, we had forgotten what a church is. But we were made to commit the offense entirely by the moving camera.[18]

Films have sound-tracks. Most obviously, they allow their characters to speak. But, because our eyes are so attentively engaged by their images, the sound-track of the film will lose all point if it merely tells us what we have already seen for ourselves. A film "dialogue" may admit long pauses, incoherencies, failures to respond, partly because that is how things are in real life, and partly because the gaps are filled up for the audience by other means. If a husband turns his back on a complaining wife, he does not need to spell out his rejection of her nagging. Ultimately, the actors are not talking to each other so much as to the audience, and so long as the audience feels satisfied, nothing else matters: satisfied not logically but emotionally that it could have been so. Scholars are alert to just such a technique in Apollonius and Virgil. But can Nonnus and Pindar, and the tragedians, have meant anything else?[19]

Sound also means music. Here we stand on good Aristotelian ground, since for the *Poetics* music was the most vivid source of

---

[18] This is what the Formalists call "mystification" and classical scholars "misleading retardation." W. Schadewaldt illustrates Homer's use of the trick in his *Iliasstudien* (Leipzig 1938). Compare W. S. Barrett on Euripides, *Hippolytos* 41–50 and 42 (in his edition of the play, Oxford 1964).

[19] See H. Fränkel on *Arg.* I. 327–30, 332–35; R. Heinze, *Virgils epische Technik*, pp. 403 ff. String (*op. cit.*, p. 14) says that Nonnus' characters do not converse and (p. 46) that their speeches are inconsequential. For Pindar, see Wilamowitz, *Pindaros* (Berlin 1922), pp. 388–89. Some of the "inconsistencies of character" detected in Greek tragedy may be traceable to this emotional, "pathetic" manner, which Eisenstein (*Izbr. Proiz.*, III, pp. 136–37) compares with that of Dostoevsky. And do Racine's characters talk to each other, or to the audience?

tragedy's pleasures.[20] But music does more for the film than merely create "atmosphere," or lend itself to the exploitation of the leitmotif. It offers some kind of analogy with the entire art of the film-maker, and this is why background music so often offends by its otiose and distracting presence. Both music and film impose rather than accept a pace or tempo. Both carry their audience forward whether it wants to go or not. Both have this extra power because they are based on something quite unrelated at first glance to emotion, and that is the mathematical calculation of their allotted time.[21]

After sound came color. It would be naive to claim that films were unconcerned with color, even when they were shot only in black and white, since varying intensities of illumination can produce the subtlest harmonies even from so restriced a palette. But color has been welcomed not merely because it is more "realistic." The rich range of European painting has used color sumptuously, parsimoniously, gorgeously, chastely, symbolically, to convey emotion, to speak to levels of the psyche not to be reached by logic. Across the centuries, poets in the lyrical and Callimachean tradition have understood this language.[22]

It is hardly an exaggeration to say that the study of these lists of camera possibilities does more to clarify the history of the European epic tradition from the ancient world to our own than volumes of learned annotations. The parallels with epic technique are striking. The camera, able to switch from angle to angle, to roam about in place and time, to concentrate on the most minute detail and on the broadest panorama, to dictate the viewer's response in the most despotic terms and then to chide him for his obedience, is an instrument that Alexandrian poets would dearly have liked to hold in their hands. How many critics have had the simple idea that the aim of the epic poet is to communicate at eye level, and in full

[20] Cf. *Poetics* 1450 b 16, 1462 a 16–17. On p. 262 of his edition of the *Poetics* D. W. Lucas is interestingly moved to seek an analogy in the silent film and its music to Aristotle's argument.

[21] Cf. Eisenstein's essay "Organichnost' i Pafos" (*Izbr. Proiz.*, III, pp. 44 ff., and pp. 72 ff. in J. Leyda's translation in *Film Form*).

[22] Again, Eisenstein's comments on red and white (*The Film Sense*, p. 143) may be contrasted with the somewhat grudging remarks made by C. J. Fordyce on Catullus 61. 9 f., 187 (with references) and by String on Nonnus (*op. cit.*, p. 55). Racine brilliantly exploits red and white in Phèdre's "Je le vis, je rougis, je pâlis à sa vue" (I. iii. 121). C. G. Jung has pointed out the political/psychological symbolism of the opposition in our time between the White House and the Red Square. Cf. Eisenstein's essay "Tsvetovoe Kino" in *Izbr. Stat'i*, pp. 311 ff., and "Color and Meaning" in *The Film Sense*, pp. 111 ff. See further S. Skard, "The Use of Color in Literature: A Survey of Research," *Proceedings of the American Philosophical Society* XC. 3 (1946), 163–249. Cf. p. 345 and note 17, above.

illumination! The film-makers have taught us the artistic use of angles and shadows to indicate how little we actually discover about people, and how spurious must be the poetry that would claim to tell all.

The camera opens a way into the mind, and shows us there realities of triumph and despair so overwhelming that the invocation of an unfelt and conventional mythology is now worse than pointless. Yet this is not a justification of anti-classicism. The heroes of the past are understood through the experience of the present already in Homer and Virgil. The toil of an obscure priest in a remote village, of a poor worker from a crowded tenement, of an unknown sheriff in a dusty frontier town, is just as moving as that of Achilles or Aeneas,[23] because that is how the classical epic has always proceeded. It is part of the humanist legacy. Myth elevates what is done and suffered here and now. The priest and worker are shown as like Christ, the sheriff is Hector before the walls of Troy. What the Callimachean epic objects to is the uncritical equation of the modern with a past that knew no tears. This is the heart of its quarrel with the Telchines.[24]

The poetic therefore which might be recovered from a manual on film technique would contain at least these principles:

1. The poet's aim, in using a medium that has many parallels with music, is to manipulate feeling. For this, he must control the audience's response by calculated selection of detail. At one moment he will call attention to something of trivial importance in the normal world, but loaded with significance within the closed world he is creating. At another, he will require his spectators to take in an overview of a whole area of time or space which would be utterly beyond their normal receptiveness. In the presentation of these dictated units of sensibility he will not however aim at total clarity or coherence. It will be enough to hint at what is relevant to the overriding emotional impact that the story is intended to make. If, for example, he wishes to show a technical process, he will merely indicate one or two of its stages, since he is not writing a textbook for budding experts.[25] If he wishes to suggest that his character himself

---

[23] As Milton explained: above, p. 378. Compare Eisenstein on the film *Chapaev* (*Izbr. Proiz.*, III, pp. 244 ff.).

[24] See Page's note on pp. 590–91 of *Greek Literary Papyri* (London 1950). Germanus, the hero of this propaganda episode, is compared indirectly to Achilles "breaker of men" (!).

[25] Compare Virgil's plow, *Geo.* I. 169 ff. of which H. H. Huxley remarks: "We have here an impressionist painting, not a blueprint for an agricultural engineer." Eisenstein faced the same problem as Virgil in his own "didactic" *The Old and the*

enjoyed no very clear idea of what was happening, naturally he will leave the spectator in an equal state of doubt.[26]

2. Epic of this kind will not normally intellectualize. There will be little occasion for the direct intervention of the artist calling overt attention to the implications of a given scene (and when he does this, we must be aware of the degree of convention in his behavior). The author's comment will indeed be omnipresent, but it will be in the form of irony, of his choice of incidentals, and then again in the whole way in which the story is presented.[27]

3. Such an epic will be biased towards the relatively short. The reason will be that so rich a technique has no need of the lengthy repetitions dear to primitive narrative.[28] Because this epic is *pathetically* structured[29] from the outset, it will be able to make its effects without undue delay. Long epic would now defeat its own purpose. It would dull the response of the audience, forcing it, in sheer self-defense against the war on its sensibilities, to switch off after a given period. The only justification for length can be art, and for great length, great art.

4. This epic will certainly appeal to the visual, even if not always to the visible. Its use of images will be twofold. Partly, they will help to make particular scenes memorable. But they will also serve to link scene with scene, often in an ironic fashion.[30]

5. In the movement from sequence to sequence,[31] the means

---

*New* (his *Georgics*), where he had to make a cream separator poetic. He did it by deliberate distortion, by lighting, and by allusions to the guns of *The Battleship Potemkin* (*Izbr. Proiz.*, III, pp. 72 ff.). His critics were so overwhelmed that they spoke of his "lyrisme dionysiaque" in this scene. At the back of all this is Aristotle's contempt for the historical particular in poetry.

[26] Hence the ambiguities which attend so much of the *Aeneid*, not least at its end, where the morality of Aeneas' behavior is as controversial as that of Mann's *Doktor Faustus*.

[27] Aristotle, *Poetics* 1460 a 7, is perhaps rightly interpreted (see Lucas) as meaning that the epic poet should, like Homer, be as dramatic as possible, rather than confine himself largely to narration. The element of personal intervention found in Milton or Tolstoy shows the debt of the post-Aristotelian epic to lyric, something Aristotle hardly foresaw. Pindar's *gnomai* provide the model for the cinema's titles, and for Tolstoy's arguments about the meaning of events.

[28] "Relatively short" here means by comparison with folk or Eastern epics. For a Hellenistic argument about brevity, see W. Morel's note on Accius, fr. 10 (*Fragmenta Poetarum Latinorum* [Stuttgart 1963]), p. 36.

[29] The term is Eisenstein's, e.g. *Izbr. Proiz.*, III, pp. 61–62.

[30] Cf. above, pp. 74 ff. (Apollonius' use of the symbolism of the red fleece): below, p. 415 (Eisenstein's use of blending images in *Potemkin*).

[31] Interestingly, Eisenstein insists on remembering the musical origin of this term (*Izbr. Proiz.*, III, p. 97), which also had its importance for the troubadours.

employed will sometimes be deliberately disjointed. The audience will be obliged to supply the connections for itself. Sometimes perhaps there will be no obvious connection, and this will be the final realism. Sometimes the very violence of a dramatic switch, from war to peace or darkness to light, will be superior to all pedestrian logic of explanation.

6. But inattention to "logic" will not mean that this epic has no unity. Yet the unity will be psychological and subjective rather than the objective, rational unity appropriate to a philosopher's discourse. The call for the latter by the critics will thus be seen for the threadbare abstraction which it is. Because the responsive and sensitive reader will be carried forward in this poetry by reasons of the heart, sequences of association which touch his innermost being, he will be able to bridge gaps in the action at an astonishing rate.[32] Because the epic poet will not be doing his job unless he plays the soul's chords, he will pay close attention to the music of his verse, remembering, of course, that music has its jarring dissonances too.

## II

Have we here been creating a new poetic, for the film-director and his imitator in literature, and not rather restating what had already been deduced from a study of the Alexandrian tradition?[33] In one sense perhaps this poetic was novel, if not new. It had been allowed to drop from the consciousness of both the admirers (and official champions) of classical epic and their pupils. Appreciation was impoverished. If a passage still succeeded in communicating some of its force, this was in spite of the commentators.

Comparison of the Alexandrian and film poetics suggests in fact that it is no longer enough to note their similarities. Why are they similar? One reply would be to say that, at whatever stage in his history, Western man—any man—tends to react to like situations in a like way. But he can only react in a like way provided that these poetics have hit upon something essential in his whole ability to apprehend reality. We are necessarily thrown from mere speculation about externals, from mechanically compiled lists of "characteristics of the Alexandrian style," to deeper analysis of human thought and feeling.

This analysis has already been made, notably by Sergei Eisenstein. In an age when the relevance of classical study has been in question,

---

[32] *Semper ad eventum festinat* (Horace on Homer, *A. P.* 148): "This way of looking at poetry is Alexandrian" (C. O. Brink, *ad loc.*).

[33] Above, pp. 20–21, 373, 394–95.

the great Soviet film director and propagandist of revolution began from no other premises than those of the Greeks.[34]

Eisenstein was the rediscoverer of a very simple principle, familiar to Callimachus, that in matters of human thought and judgment two and two do not make four, but four plus.[35] When we are asked to associate two ideas, two images, we cannot help introducing into the sum of our associations a contribution that springs from our own experience and outlook and, at a more primitive level, from our own pre-rational way of reacting to our sensations. It is upon this half-involuntary contribution by the spectator that, according to Eisenstein, the film-maker should play, and the "pathetic" artist in every age has played. His famous "montage" is in the first instance nothing else except the deliberate structuring of a work of art in such a fashion that feeling builds upon feeling to form a bridge into another dimension.

Montage has then, as its very essence, selection. If the author supplies the viewer with every piece of information, what is there left for the recipient of all this detail to do except lose himself in the maze? But if the viewer is called upon to share the work of building up the story, his involvement will raise his level of sympathy, and put him in the mood where the narrator can work his magic.[36] Selection is basic to the Callimachean technique[37] because something has to be left for the audience to do, and something has to be left for the audience to do because without its contribution the whole appeal of the work of art will fall flat.

Selection immediately introduces musical considerations. When the details are selected, how much space will they occupy? The alternation between different or recurring times will itself impinge on the viewer's consciousness and can by no means be left to chance. Hence arises what Eisenstein calls "metric montage."[38] This again is something absolutely basic to the whole method of composition, and not, for example, an extra feature arising only when films acquired sound-tracks. Clearly we are not far here from the recurrences and verse

[34] *Izbr. Stat'i*, pp. 185–86.

[35] Eisenstein, *Izbr. Proiz.*, II, pp. 406 ff.; V, pp. 220–21.

[36] *Magiya*, Eisenstein, *Izbr. Proiz.*, II, p. 381. Cf. Gorgias' *mageia* (*Hel.* 10); *ut magus*, Horace, *Epp.* II. 1. 213. Thomas Mann, the great magician of twentieth-century literature, seems to echo this passage of Horace in his verdict on Goethe: *Ges. Werke* (Berlin–Frankfurt 1960), IX, p. 760. See above, p. 246 note 11.

[37] "Let [the reader] draw his own conclusions, and so cut length off the song": Callimachus, fr. 57. 1 Pf. The poet uses the film-maker's verb, "cut."

[38] See *Film Form*, tr. J. Leyda, pp. 72 ff.

paragraphs so often encountered in our analyses of epics from Homer on.[39]

One of the most difficult aspects of the classical (Platonic/Aristotelian) poetic has been its preoccupation with *mimēsis*, "imitation."[40] Eisenstein finds no problem with the ancient point of view. The creative artist begins from an image or some other type of concrete apprehension which emotionally embodies his universal theme. His job is to transform this image into a few basic partial representations which, by combination and juxtaposition, will recreate in the mind of the spectator the initial image.[41] An art that diverged from imitation would therefore be diverging from human communication, since in real life we talk to one another precisely by means of images, images of ourselves as well as images of language, and, at the simplest level, in the mouths of ordinary people who are actually at grips every day with life's harsh realities, the most poetic images multiply.[42]

Nothing prevents these images and the imitations to which they give rise from expressing the sublimest insights of which the human mind is capable. But to concentrate attention on the sublimity and even to use it as a stick with which to beat the artist is to confuse the end and the means. The critic may find his notion of sublimity either within himself or in the external world. But, when he wants to tell others about it, the artist must resort to the kind of language which others besides critics will understand. This language will inevitably be the language of imitation.

To despise imitation is either to lose oneself in abstractions, which will leave the listener cold, or be forced to withdraw into oneself, thus negating the whole purpose of being an artist. If imitation has a bad name, that may well be deserved, but it is because imitation has been badly used by artists lacking imagination, the ability to make compelling images, and not because imitation is mistaken in itself.

A previous chapter observed that scholars have sometimes argued as if imagination in the modern, Coleridgean sense were something unknown until late antiquity. The classical aesthetic, it is suggested, emphasized simply the ability to reconstruct accurately a remembered scene, and prized the photographic more than the creative. Eisenstein

---

[39] Stanzas, "Zahlenkomposition" (Curtius), recurring paragraphs as in Chaucer and Milton, are all examples of metric montage. They all force the reader to add something, his own heartbeats perhaps, to what he hears.

[40] Above, pp. 42–43, 66–67.

[41] The spectator is not passive during this process, of course. See above, pp. 280–81.

[42] Proverbs, the homely realism of colloquial speech (cf. J. M. Synge's interest in Irish dialects), the Gospel parables, are all relevant here, as is the Callimachean concern with the *ischnos charactēr* and the Ionian tradition of the *ainos*.

enables us to see the falsity of this opposition. Following a method of which both Aristotle and Quintilian would have approved, he conjures up a vivid picture, for example, of the ways in which an actor might recreate in his own mind the feelings of a civil servant who has embezzled public moneys, and now fears that he is on the verge of being found out.[43] It would be useless for the actor to contemplate simply the disembodied, abstract idea of theft and punishment, sublime though such a thought might be. But, if he summons up to his imagination the nervous wait for the telephone call from his superior, the accusing eyes in the courtroom of former colleagues and friends, he will have no difficulty in either entering into the feelings of the character he is to portray, or in communicating those feelings of guilt and shame by his demeanor to his audience. What he will have done in fact is to break down the abstract idea of embezzlement into a series of montage fragments, that is, into a sequence of partial images strong enough in combination with sympathetic imagination to trigger the desired emotional response, both from himself and then from others.

Now it is possible to see why both Aristotle and Horace share a conviction that appears to contradict the modern notion of the necessary distance the writer must keep from his material, and why they both believe that the author, not merely the actor, must be emotionally engaged with his subject if he is to write about it convincingly.[44] The reason is that only such engagement will enable the writer to evoke the appropriate images that will carry his feelings out beyond his own heart. Only the engaged writer will know, in Aristotelian language, how to make a persuasive imitation, persuasive because it evokes the concrete universal which makes poetry more philosophical than history.

Eisenstein shares another insight with Aristotle. Both critics believe that the real test of poetic genius lies in the capacity for seeing resemblances, for the fruitful and imaginative association of the superficially disparate; in other words, in the use of metaphor.[45] For

---

[43] *The Film Sense*, pp. 38 ff. This kind of analysis makes sense of a great deal in the ancient theory of poetic creation: cf. *De Subl.* 15. 1 with D. A. Russell's notes; Quintilian VI. 6. 35; L. Friedlaender, *Darstellungen aus der Sittengeschichte Roms,* II (10th ed., Leipzig 1922), p. 132 note 3; and above, note 40.

[44] Cf. Euripides ("the most tragic of the poets," *Poetics* 1453 a 29) in Aristophanes, *Ach.* 412 ff. and Agathon at *Thesm.* 148–49. See further *Poetics* 1455 a 29 ff. and Horace, *A. P.* 101 ff. Horace's context is Callimachean: Porphyrion on *A. P.* 97. Is it possible that some such rhetorical theory and method lie behind the "subjectivity" of Roman elegy?

[45] *Poetics* 1459 a 5. Eisenstein notes that there is no prescription for making successful films: *Izbr. Proiz.*, III, pp. 70–71; cf. Aristotle's *euphuïa*. See further Eisenstein, *op. cit.*, II, pp. 342 ff., 409 ff.

Eisenstein, a metaphor is the image that conveys the relationship of the writer to his subject. "He loves her" is interesting, but cold. "He loves her as the sun loves the flowers" immediately offers the chance of communication, since the comparison touches on an experience we can all share, and also tells us what attitude the writer wants us to take to his message. Change the metaphor—"He loves her as the murderer loves his victim"—and the whole ethos of the statement is changed. Imagery therefore is the means by which the writer will express a whole gamut of relationships to his narrative, whether straightforward or in that varying complexity which we call, perhaps rather indeterminately at times, "ironical." It is evident that a mature poetry, one aware of the ambivalences that attend our most ordinary feelings, will rarely maintain the simple relation of image to imaged offered by our first example here. Eisenstein's subtle analysis[46] allows us to look for the full resonance of ancient poetry, without the uneasy feeling that this simple relationship is somehow superior or paradigmatic. Primitive "mixed feelings" must be given their due.

Tragic irony can come dangerously close to comedy. The well-known passage at the end of the *Symposium* where Socrates argues that artistic writers of tragedy must also know how to write comedy is more than a *jeu d'esprit*. If we possessed the second volume of the *Poetics* we might have been struck by a definition of comedy closely modeled on the definition of tragedy given in the first.[47]

Eisenstein accepts Plato's point of view. The pathos of comedy is not the same as that of tragedy, but there is an astonishing nearness and even identity in their methods of composition.[48] Moreover, pathetic structure, the constant switching between opposites, always permits of its reversal, the choice of the other pole, while still retaining its effectiveness. The hero may be identified with the masses rather than raised on a pedestal. His language may be that of ordinary prose rather than that of poetry.[49]

Again, the modern film-maker's theorizings help to elucidate a great deal in the ancient tradition, whether we think of the "anti-heroic" in the *Hecale*, the *Argonautica* and the *Aeneid*, of the prosaic vocabulary found in so many classical epics, or of their sometimes unexpected kinship with comedy, already licensed in the ancient world

---

[46] Cf. Eisenstein, *Izbr. Proiz.*, II, pp. 364, 366 on irony and pp. 376 ff. on "conflict."

[47] The definition found in the *Tractatus Coislinianus* (of which G. M. A. Grube makes such needlessly heavy weather in *The Greek and Roman Critics* [London 1965], p. 146) deserves the closest attention just because it resembles the definition of tragedy offered by the *Poetics*. See below, p. 421.

[48] *Izbr. Proiz.*, III, pp. 230–31.

[49] *Loc. cit.*, pp. 242 ff.

by Aristotle's acceptance of the *Margites* into the Homeric canon,[50] and by certain features of the *Iliad* and *Odyssey* themselves.

The pathetic structure characterizing an emotionally effective work of art will, according to Eisenstein, continually move between antitheses. He seeks an example from his own work. In *The Battleship Potemkin* the mutinous crew put in at Odessa harbor after the death of one of their comrades. The harbor is wrapped in mist. The camera plays lovingly over the muffled outlines of familiar, but now "estranged," objects, over the grey surface of the sea. Gradually, these soft outlines begin to harden and polarize. Shades of grey part, and separate into black and white. The body is brought ashore, shrouded in white canvas, and laid on the black, dripping stones of the quay. There is black and white among the mourning townsfolk.

Then a candle is placed in the corpse's hands. The primeval elements, earth, air, water, have been completed by fire. From now on, this leap towards the opposite, already foreshadowed in the black and white polarity which developed out of grey, gains in intensity. The literal fire of the candle is metamorphosed into the fiery anger of the witnesses standing over the body, and this anger spreads like wildfire throughout the city. Emboldened and strengthened, the mutineers raise over their vessel the fiery red flag of defiance. The fire of their cannon echoes over Odessa. It provokes the counterfire of the Czar's soldiers when, in the famous scene of the "Odessa steps," the crowd of unarmed civilians is driven headlong down, trampled under the black jackboots of the white uniformed militia.[51] How much is illumined in ancient poetry by this kind of analysis! Eisenstein picked up an old phrase when he defined the pathetic style as the "unity of opposites." Cannot the same phrase be used of Pindar, Virgil, Horace, Propertius?[52]

One of the most unexpected, and in some ways irritating, developments of the epic tradition was its early romanticization. The *Iliad*

---

[50] Eisenstein notes the turning of a metaphor into a reality as the "Aristophanes effect": e.g. the "King's Eye" in *Acharnians* 92 (cf. Herod. I. 114; Aesch., *Persae* 979, and, in general, E. Fraenkel, *Elementi plautini in Plauto* [Florence 1960], pp. 21 ff.). But he was able to exploit the embodied image of the "Czar's eye" in *Ivan the Terrible* for tragic purposes. And Virgil was able to take the topos "my love is like the fires of Etna" and raise it to the terrifying symbolism of *Aeneid* III and IV.

[51] See Eisenstein's own analysis, *Izbr. Proiz.*, III, pp. 64 ff.

[52] For the unity of opposites see, for example, *Izbr. Proiz.*, II, p. 381. Cf. Pindar's "polare Ausdrucksweise" (Franz Dornseiff), and for Thomas Mann, below, p. 509. Virgil, according to an ancient critic, *sententias suas . . . velut contraria sentiendo dissolvat* (quoted in Schanz–Hosius, *Römische Literaturgeschichte* [4th ed., Munich 1959], vol. II, p. 97). Horace and Propertius alike baffle the search for a strictly logical unity in a number of their poems (cf. C. O. Brink's discussion of the *Odes* and the *Ars Poetica* in *Horace on Poetry*, II, pp. 445 ff.).

and the *Odyssey* had of course their galaxy of women characters. But Apollonius saw love as the indispensable condition of heroism, and perhaps he simply viewed Homer with clearer eyes than we. Virgil was a great Roman, but Ovid was able to joke about him for so soon bringing arms and the man to Dido's couch.[53] In Dante, Boccaccio, Ariosto, Milton, love and sexuality play as great a part as they do in Apollonius. Is this simply degeneracy, or is it recognition of one of the inescapable facts of life?

Eisenstein suggests that it is the latter. Soviet Russia, inheriting a rather grim Puritanism from its high-minded nineteenth-century forebears, is not likely to favor romanticism for its own sake in its official epics. How interesting then that Eisenstein describes the basic imagery of *Potemkin* as that of a frustrated love-affair![54] The battleship and its crew are the gallant hero, wishing to rescue the fair maiden Odessa from the clutches of the villainous Czar. They fail, though there is promise for the future (the "not yet" of the carnival, the "one day" of the epic tradition). Eisenstein goes on to say that he still has some old notes for an unrealized film that would have been made between *Strike* (1924) and *Potemkin* (1925):

> At that time I wanted to make an epic about the First Cavalry Army. And in the notes relating to the planned dramatic structure of this film I find the following remark: "Construct the fates and mutual interactions of the collectives and social groupings after the model of the *peripeteiai* within a triangle!"[55]

"Triangle" here refers of course to the "eternal triangle" beloved of the writers of romantic comedies and bedroom farces. But this was to have been an epic about the First Cavalry Army!

The same method went into *Potemkin*, which probably explains, according to Eisenstein, the film's humanity. The thudding engines of the battleship are the thudding heart of the crew. The same imprint, he declares, is to be found on all his so-called "impersonal" films, e.g. *October* (1927). *The Old and the New* (1926–29) may look as if it is about the Party's policy of collectivization of agriculture, but really it is in the line of Zola's *La Terre* or Laclos' *Les Liaisons Dangereuses*.

---

[53] *Tristia* II. 533–34: for the suggestive pun on *arma* cf. Propertius I. 3. 16. Arnaut Daniel uses the same trick in his poem *Lo ferm voler*: G. Toja, *Arnaut Daniel, Canzoni* (repr. Florence 1961), no. 18.

[54] *Izbr. Proiz.*, III, pp. 296 ff.

[55] *Loc. cit.*, p. 296. Eisenstein readily employs ancient critical terminology for his modern art: *pathos, peripeteia*; cf. *pars pro toto* (*synecdoche*), *Izbr. Proiz.*, II, pp. 408, 425, 433. Another remarkable revival is *amplificatio* (*Izbr. Proiz.*, III, editors' note to p. 90): cf. E. R. Curtius, *Europ. Lit. und lateinisches Mittelalter*, pp. 483 ff.; Russell on *De Subl.* 11 – 12. 2.

If Eisenstein greets across the centuries Ariosto among others in his feeling for the romantic, he understands too Ariosto's complex manner of narration. The montage method of selection raised immediately the question of musical balance, of the time which each selected detail was to occupy by comparison with its fellows. These details therefore could not help being drawn into some sort of mathematical, musical proportion and, if the author was free to impose one musical pattern, why not another? If event A and event C are related in direct sequence, with the happenings of event B supplied at some later stage, not only may such a narrative be truer to experience, but the contrast, ironical or otherwise, between A and C becomes more obvious. Eisenstein points to the use of "knot" language (*dénouement*) in dramaturgy, found in Aristotle too.[56] But it is when events are told in other than their chronological sequence, when pattern and psychological impact become the determining factor in their presentation, that such knots are found. This is also the way in which Time becomes active in the story, the carnival C(h)ronus restored to his role as King of the Revels.

This is also the circumstance when narrative comes closest to the musical technique of polyphonic counterpoint. Here Ariosto's complicated story-line may be made to fit into a development characteristic of much twentieth-century art.[57] Classical scholars note the rule that prevents Homer from describing two events as simultaneous.[58] But

[56] Aristotle speaks of *lysis* and *desis* (*Poetics* 1455 b 24: cf. *plokē* 1456 a 9). Using a quotation from Hogarth's *Analysis of Beauty* (Chapter V, "Of Intricacy"), Eisenstein develops a theory in which non-unilinear narrative may be diagrammed as a knot. If events ABCDE are told in the order AEBDC, we have:

$$A \ B \ C \ D \ E \qquad becoming \qquad A \ B \ C \ D \ E$$

$$x\text{-}x\text{-}x\text{-}x\text{-}> \qquad\qquad\qquad\qquad x \ x \ x \ x \ x$$

Interestingly (and Eisenstein draws this analogy too) we also have something which may be described as polyphony/counterpoint in the tradition of, for example, Josquin des Prés, who was in Ferrara in 1504, just when Ariosto was reflecting on his epic-to-be. Eisenstein's own, loose, wide-ranging, recapitulatory style of exposition, like that of Horace's *Ars Poetica*, may be an illustration of the same manner. Compare also Sterne, *Tristram Shandy*, p. 347.

[57] Eisenstein notes Conrad's *Lord Jim* in particular. But this was also the method used by A. J. A. Symons for his biography of Frederick Corvo (*The Quest for Corvo* [London 1934]), just because of its greater fidelity to experience. Such a method of exposition is however by no means confined to our century, as Eisenstein shows. He has an enlightening quotation from Maupassant.

[58] Cf. T. Zielinski, *Philologus, Supp. VIII* (1901), 405 ff. But Hesiod violates this rule in the *Theogony* (West on 617, 711) and on the *Odyssey* see now the arguments of R. Friedrich, *Stilwandel im Homerischen Epos* (Heidelberg 1975). L. Adam has some relevant quotations from the Homeric scholia: *Die aristotelische Theorie vom Epos nach ihrer Entwicklung bei Griechen und Römern* (Wiesbaden 1889), pp. 24, 38, 58.

ancient critics were right to be more impressed by his plunge into the middle of his story, imitated by Pindar[59] when so much else from traditional epic is jettisoned in *Pythian* 4. Such emotionally governed ("pathetic") conditioning of narrative order is an ever-present resource of the classical tradition.

Eisenstein's early training was as an engineer, and so it is appropriate that, in spite of his preoccupation with the emotional impact of his art, he should also have had an equal interest in its mathematics. He believed that his film *Potemkin* owed some of its effect to its use of the "golden section."[60] The spiral of growth formed by the graph of this proportion (the Fibonacci series) seemed to him to show its intimate connection with the biological processes of life itself. Five acts were established as the norm for classical drama—and it is as such a drama that, for all its revolutionary intent, *Potemkin* is offered to us—because they contain the balance $2/3$. In the scene already mentioned of the harbor mists even and odd numbers alternate as they do in the *commedia dell'arte*.[61] Of the film as a whole Eisenstein writes (*Izbr. Proiz.*, III, p. 48):

> Its five acts, connected though they are by the general theme of revolutionary brotherhood, display on the whole little mutual resemblance. But in one respect they are absolutely uniform. Each part clearly falls into two almost equal halves. This is especially noticeable from the second act on.

Each of these halves is marked by sharp opposition to its predecessor.

Later, defining his terms more exactly, Eisenstein remarks that the divisions of each act into two and of the film as a whole are as a matter of fact closer to the proportion $2/3$. It is between the end of the second and beginning of the third act, for example, that the basic caesura is encountered, the point of complete inaction. This is where the theme of the dead sailor and the tent erected over his body are found at a place determined by the golden section.[62] The reaction to his death, the raising of the red flag, is also at another point marked by this proportion, this time looking at the film from the other end, the conclusion of part three, overlapping into part four.

"The raising of the red flag"—but how can a flag be red in a black and white medium? Partly perhaps because the audience makes allowances for the medium's conventions. But convention cannot be the whole story. Eisenstein suggests that, at its moment of greatest

---

[59] See, for example, L. Illig, *Zur Form der Pindarischen Erzählung* (Berlin 1932), pp. 55 ff. See above, p. 96, and note 57.

[60] *Izbr. Proiz.*, III, pp. 46 ff.

[61] *Izbr. Proiz.*, II, p. 88.

[62] *Izbr. Proiz.*, II, p. 477.

psychological involvement, the audience is ready to take off into another dimension of apprehension, provided only that the artist offers a suitable route along which this flight can take place. A red flag raised at any old time might just as well be green, even if the director is using a color camera. But a red flag raised as the culmination of an imagery of fire, after the careful preparation of the audience, and even after the deliberate witholding of fire in earlier scenes, is perceived as red even though its "real" color is dirty grey. The black and white film, by its pathetic structure, tended towards color from its very inception.

Similarly, the silent film tended towards sound.[63] A machine gun dragged across a parquet floor at a tense moment, a chandelier swaying as a warship's guns fire upon Petrograd: these are phenomena which become aural, however physically silent the film which holds them. No one could deny the possibility of the reverse process. The incidental music of a film becomes visual when, as a musical theme changes, a scene takes on a fresh dimension, "looks different."

Eisenstein touches here on the topic of synaesthesia.[64] The Greek word betrays the likelihood that this too is part of an ancient poetic, as indeed it is.[65] It is notable that it was Virgil who went further than other Latin poets in the use of this trick (Leo).

Care is needed in the interpretation of a device that has puzzled critics. No words need be wasted on the assertion that we have in it a proof of the exhaustion of language.[66] But it is too simple on the other hand to argue that, since sight is the paradigm sense, it is naturally used on occasion as a substitute for the other senses, so that "to see a sound" is merely a loose way of saying "to perceive a sound." The pathetic contexts in which the poets jump from one dimension to another rather suggest that, in the intensity of experience, the tragic victim leaps from one way of apprehension to another, not loosely, but in a momentary elevation into total sentience. So the tortured Prometheus, when about to be visited by the daughters of Ocean: so the defeated Etruscans and Carthaginians, when "their battle-cry saw that their insolence was ship-groaning": so Hippolytus, exiled by his unjust father, and having "a song of tears."[67]

---

[63] *Izbr. Proiz.*, II, pp. 455–56.

[64] Cf. *Izbr. Proiz.*, III, p. 336; "Synchronization of the Senses," in *The Film Sense*, tr. J. Leyda, pp. 67 ff.

[65] Cf. E. Norden's note to *Aen.* VI. 256 ff., who cites St. Augustine, *Confessions* X. 35. 54, and E. Lobeck, "De confusione vocabulorum sensum significantium" (1846). See further W. B. Stanford, *Greek Metaphor* (Oxford 1936), pp. 47 ff., and I. Waern, "Zur Synästhesie in griechischer Dichtung," *Eranos* 50 (1952), 14 ff.

[66] J. M. Cohen, *Poetry of this Age* (London 1959), p. 19.

[67] Aeschylus, *Prometheus Vinctus* 115; Pindar, *Pythian* 1. 72; Euripides, *Hippolytus*

It is this leap, for which the innate Greek tendency towards polar expression provides such an obvious springboard, which may also help us to understand Aristotle's *catharsis tōn pathēmatōn*, one of the most baffling features of his theory of tragic effect. If we accept with Eisenstein that the whole purpose of the pathetic style is to lead the audience into a higher mode of consciousness, we would expect this purpose to form part of the definition of tragedy. Without it, after all, however clever a given work of art might be, it would be in the end a futile, and impotent, exercise in technique. The catharsis wrought by listening to enthusiastic music, if it effects a cure in the emotionally disturbed, must do so because it provokes some sort of crisis or resolution in their sickness. Can this resolution be anything except the sudden realization that the turbulent, feverish fragments of the disordered imagination are reducible to an intelligible order after all, by music, which takes those same excited elements and yet encloses them within a framing harmony?[68]

So with tragedy. The wild, deranged ("dislocated" in Formalist language) events of the tragic experience, upsetting and destructive when encountered in raw and brutal fact, are there organized into the controlled structure of a formal and musically organized work of art.[69] But to serve its purpose tragedy has to work, according to Aristotle, through pity and fear. These are not reactions reserved for one culminating moment alone. They are aroused at every step of the tragic development, just as music builds its ultimate crescendo from its opening bars. When that ultimate crescendo occurs, pity and fear purify pity and fear and similar emotions because the spectator breaks through (to use Mann's term), by a process which transcends normal thought, to a perception of truth, to some sort of vision, of inexplicable conviction of the final rightness of things which acts as a release. This catharsis is Eisenstein's leap into another dimension, for him the synthesis produced by the continuous switch between thesis and antithesis which denotes pathetic structure.[70]

---

1178; see F. Dornseiff, *Pindars Stil*, p. 57, who notes *inter alia* Eur., *Phoen*. 1377. The phenomenon is discussed further by D. Sansone, *Aeschylean Metaphors for Intellectual Activity* (Wiesbaden 1975), pp. 14 ff.

[68] Cf. Aristotle, *Politics* VIII. 1341 b 32 ff. Pindar paid notable tribute to music as the ordering principle of the universe (*Pythian* 1), but of course it was an idea at least as old as Pythagoras (and Pindar was writing for a Sicilian audience), and one with a long life before it throughout antiquity. Eisenstein notes its occurrence in Dostoevsky (*Izbr. Proiz.*, III, p. 392) and it forms the theme of Mann's *Doktor Faustus*.

[69] The *Bacchae*, for example, is remarkable for its formal structure (cf. Dodds, preface, p. xxxvi). The *Tractatus Coislinianus* appropriately speaks of tragedy's *symmetria phobou*.

[70] Cf. Aristotle's "*ekstasis* into opposites," *De Gen. Animal.* 768 a 27–28. The life-

The cathartic effect of comedy would be the same. Eisenstein defines comedy as vaudeville (carnival) raised to the monumental plane.[71] He is never tired of invoking the *commedia dell'arte*, and his own theories of montage first began to crystallize in an early production of his which united comedy and circus. He would return to the Bacchic in his final film.

Polarizing ordinary experience in such a way that its conventions and irrationalities are thrown into relief, comedy eventually provokes its own cathartic laughter, the cleansing experience of universal absurdity which makes our own absurdities no longer morbid and frightening, but the honest expression of the way things are.[72]

Eisenstein believed that his particular analyses of film technique were only the application to a modern art-form of criteria universally valid for all art-forms.[73] His work abounds in illustrations drawn from the most diverse sources. We must be especially interested here by what he has to say concerning literary narrative.

Eisenstein begins a discussion of Pushkin's merits as a *montageur*[74] by quarreling with Lessing's criticism of Virgil's depiction of a cow in the *Georgics*.[75] He argues that Lessing's sharp distinctions between the methods of poetry and painting are wrong. Both the method of static representation and of representational establishment have their place in every art, and neither must usurp the functions of the other. Virgil has the right to show his cow as being rather than becoming if he wants. *Ut pictura poesis*. The artists of the tradition would agree with this, provided that description is structurally integrated into the dramatic and moving whole.

He turns from this to the battle with the Pechenegs in Pushkin's *Ruslan and Ludmila*. Like Leonardo, Pushkin knows how to select details, not at random, but in such a way that, by the law of *pars pro toto*, they evoke the wholes from which they are taken. "A detail

---

affirming language of Eisenstein's theory of pathetic effect has some analogies with parturition, and perhaps this is the best way to understand Aristotle's *catharsis* too, certainly a medical "purge," but one with the deepest psychic interaction and consequences.

[71] *Izbr. Proiz.*, III, p. 364: cf. pp. 219, 230–31. It is here that Eisenstein touches most closely the ground covered by M. Bakhtin in his theory of carnival literature.

[72] The emotions by which comedy works, according to the *Tractatus Coislinianus*, are pleasure and laughter. This seems preferable to Lucas' "scorn and over-confidence" (ed. of the *Poetics*, p. 287).

[73] Though, like Aristotle, he thought that all great (literary) art tends towards drama, or in his case film.

[74] *Izbr. Proiz.*, II, pp. 433 ff.

[75] *Geo.* III. 51 ff.: *Laokoon*, ch. xvii.

correctly chosen in this sense offers a colossal economy of the means of expression. Here is where it is truly possible with six fishes to feed six thousand men, with six correctly chosen details to give the feeling of an event grandiose in scale."[76]

Pushkin's alternations of "shots" between panoramas and close-ups are made in such a way as to preserve clarity. The poem reads:

1. They meet—and the battle is joined.
2. Scenting death, the horses rear.
3. Swords begin to beat on armor;
4. With a whistle, a cloud of arrows flies,
5. The plain is awash with blood;
6. Headlong the riders dart forward,
7. The squadrons of cavalry are mingled;
8. In a closed, serried wall
9. Line there clashes with line;
10. With a rider there a footsoldier struggles;
11. There a frightened horse runs along;
12. There fell a Russian, there a Pecheneg;
13. There are battle-cries, there flight;
14. One is toppled by a mace:
15. One is struck by a light arrow;
16. Another, crushed by a shield,
17. Is trampled by a maddened horse . . .[77]

Line 1 here, comments Eisenstein, is a typical cinematic title. Line 2 moves to close-ups of the horses: it is as it were a *Vorschlag* to the rhythm and action of the picture.[78] Line 3 gives the basic sound for the whole scene, the clash of swords on armor. Line 4 gives more sound, and a panoramic view. Line 5 moves from sound to sight, and narrows the scene. Line 6 presents a sharp reaction and gives a general view of the cavalry. In line 7, the two cavalries meet. In line 8 we see the battle front, and in 9 the ensuing melee. Thus lines 1–9 show defined groups closely bound, both thematically and by the logic of events. Taken together, they give an introductory general picture of the fight.

In lines 10–17 they are followed by eight close-ups, which are interrupted by two panoramic views, one of sound and the other of

[76] *Izbr. Proiz.*, II, p. 433.

[77] A. S. Pushkin, *Polnoe Sobranie Sochinenii v Shesti Tomakh* (Moscow 1949), II, p. 327. It should be noted that Eisenstein quotes lines 12 and 13 in reverse order. Such slips were inevitable in the conditions under which he worked, and do not affect his argument.

[78] A note to the text explains that *Vorschlag* is a musical term, indicating a preparatory tone. Cf. Illig's *kephalaion, anabolē* in *Zur Form der Pindarischen Erzählung*, pp. 33, 62.

sight, in line 13. This line thus serves to unite the details. Lines 10–17 are at one and the same time a single fight and an image of the whole battle. The same soldiers could be at work in lines 10 and 17.

The play of forces in lines 14–17 demands attention. We do not meet ABC in increasing intensity, but BAC, where A is the weakest ("with a light arrow"). This technique corresponds to Meyerhold's "refusal before a favorite movement" or "movement of refusal." Eisenstein is hinting at the technique which classical scholars call "misleading retardation."[79] The riderless horse of line 11 hardly prepares us for the horse's victory in line 17. Eisenstein is aware too of ring-composition. The trampling of the maddened horse in line 17 looks back to the rearing horses of line 2. He concludes: "The composition of these lines, examined *solely* with regard to their interplay of images, is developed by montage methods with all the refinement of an entire drama."

Eisenstein turns for further examples to Pushkin's narrative poem *Poltava*:

1. Like a heavy cloud
2. The ranks of flying cavalry
3. With their bridles, their sabres echoing,
4. Clashing, cut each other down from the shoulder.
5. Hurling heaps of corpses on heap
6. The iron cannonballs everywhere
7. Among them leap, strike,
8. Dig up the dust and hiss in blood.
9. Swede, Russian, pierces, slashes, cuts.
10. Drum noise, cries, gnashing,
11. Roar of cannon, trampling, neighing, groan,
12. And death and hell from every side.[80]

Here, the verbs are especially noteworthy.[81] By contrast with the earlier extract from *Ruslan*, the sound elements receive greater emphasis. Pushkin had evidently moved on from the silent cinema! More sound, according to Eisenstein, means more drama. It is the leap into another dimension of which he is always speaking.

Directing our attention particularly to lines 5–8, Eisenstein observes firstly that the cannonballs are personified.[82] The order of presen-

---

[79] Cf. W. Schadewaldt, *Iliasstudien*, pp. 15, 54–55, and above, p. 406 note 18.

[80] Pushkin, *Polnoe Sobranie Sochinenii*, II, p. 468.

[81] Cf. W. S. Maguinness' note on *Aeneid* XII. 327. Evidently Pushkin's effective verbs do not exclude equally effective nouns (lines 10–12). Dornseiff's "farblose Zeitwörter" (*Pindars Stil*, pp. 94 ff.) for this lyric style is not quite fair.

[82] Cf. Dornseiff, *op. cit.*, pp. 50 ff. for this phenomenon in Pindar, and Illig, *op. cit.*, p. 22 for a particular example in *Nemean* 1.

tation is also important. First the action is given, and only then its subject. Line 8 unites the separate ideas (corpses, cannonballs) of lines 5 and 6. A long analysis of how Pushkin's description might be filmed begins with Eisenstein's counting of the relative numbers of syllables used in the Russian of the different phrases. He is delighted to note that, by their position, the lines about the cannonballs fall into the area of the golden section of the extract, and that there is the echoing of two passages (ring-composition) when the hissing of the cannonballs recalls a line that has occurred earlier.[83]

Elsewhere in *Poltava* there is found the scene in which Kochubei is executed:

> In this scene the theme of Kochubei's end is expressed with particular sharpness through the image of "the end of Kochubei's execution." The actual image however of the end of the execution arises and grows out of the juxtaposition of three documentarily taken impressions of three details denoting the end of the execution:
>> "It is already too late," someone said to them
>> And in the field pointed with his finger.
>> There they were breaking up the fateful gallows,
>> In his black robes a priest was praying,
>> And onto a cart were lifting
>> Two cossacks an oak coffin.
>
> It would be difficult to find a more powerful selection of details to convey the feeling of the image of death in all its horror than is done in the finale of the execution scene.[84]

*Poltava* also supplies material for a striking analysis of the counterpoint in which sense and music may be found. The poet is describing the appearance of Peter the Great (*Poltava*, p. 467):

I. Just then from on high inspired
II. There echoed the sonorous voice of Peter:
III. "To work, with God's aid!" From the tent
IV. By a crowd of courtiers surrounded
V. There emerges Peter. His eyes
VI. Are shining. His face is terrifying.
VII. His movements are quick. He is handsome.
VIII. From head to foot he is like a god-sent storm.
IX. He walks. To him they bring a horse.

---

[83] "Beneath a burning hail," not quoted above. The visual image is picked up by the auditory "hiss" of line 8 (pathetic structure).

[84] *Izbr. Stat'i*, p. 275. English readers will find a translation in J. Leyda, *The Flim Sense*, pp. 46 ff., including an important extension of the analysis to a passage of Milton, *Paradise Lost* VI (see below, p. 429). The translation here however is my own.

    X. Mettlesome and humble is the faithful horse.
   XI. Sensing the fateful fire
  XII. It trembles. With its eyes it looks askance
 XIII. And gallops in the dust of battle
 XIV. Proud of its mighty rider.

Eisenstein has allotted Roman numerals to the lines in this way in order to contrast the musical recurrences of the poetic presentation, its line-by-line verbal structure, with the images that are suggested to the reader's eye. An enumeration from this latter point of view would lead to a rather different division of the same material:

1. Just then, from on high inspired, there echoed the sonorous voice of Peter: "To work, with God's aid!"
2. From the tent, by a crowd of courtiers surrounded,
3. There emerges Peter.
4. His eyes are shining.
5. His face is terrifying.
6. His movements are quick.
7. He is handsome.
8. From head to foot he is like a god-sent storm.
9. He walks.
10. To him they bring a horse.
11. Mettlesome and humble is the faithful horse.
12. Sensing the fateful fire it trembles.
13. With its eyes it looks askance.
14. And gallops in the dust of battle, proud of its mighty rider.

The number of lines and shots has turned out to be the same, fourteen in either case. But, at the same time, there is practically no internal correspondence of line-division and shot-division. In all fourteen cases they coincide only twice (VIII = 8 and X = 11). Moreover, the content of the shots varies from two complete lines (I + II = 1: XIII + XIV = 14) right down to one single word (9).

This is very instructive, Eisenstein continues, for students of the cinema, especially of the sound cinema. Peter the Great is presented by Pushkin in his poem by no other than the montage method. The poet's first three images (1, 2, 3) are a fine example of the significant portrayal of character. Three stages in the Czar's appearance are completely clear:

(a) Peter is not yet actually shown, but presented only by the sound of his voice.
(b) Peter has emerged from the tent, but cannot yet be seen. All that is visible is the group of courtiers who have come out of the tent with him.

(c) Finally, only in the third shot, is it revealed that the person coming out of the tent is Peter.[85]

The shining eyes on which the fourth shot concentrates are chosen as a fundamental feature in the impression made by the Czar. After that, we are given his entire face (5). Only then do we get his whole figure, probably from the knees up, showing his movements with their rapidity and decisiveness. Here, the rhythm of the poem is jerkily contained in clashing, short sentences. A full-length view of the figure is at last offered in shot 7, and then not literally, but in an idealized image: "He is handsome." In the following shot this general description is strengthened by a concrete comparison: "From head to foot he is like a god-sent storm."[86] Thus only in the eighth shot is Peter revealed in all his sculpturally expressed might. This eighth shot obviously gives Peter's figure at full length, marked out by all the means of expressive imagery in the frame, with a corresponding arrangement of a crowning heaven of storm clouds above him and of people around him and at his feet. It is after this broad, stationary shot[87] that the poet immediately returns us to the sphere of movement and action with the single word *idyot* ("He walks"—9). Nothing could seize and drive home more decisively a second determining characteristic, after the "shining eyes" of 4. This short, terse "He walks" communicates completely the feeling of that massive, elemental, spasmodic pace of Peter, with whom his whole suite finds it difficult to keep up.

Defending his application of such an analysis to Pushkin's poem, Eisenstein goes on to point to the poet's own order of words, which imposes the sequence in which we see the images he is creating. Rearrange the words, and the effect would be different, if not lost. Here, Eisenstein adapts a phrase used by Tolstoy in his essay *What is Art*: "The only possible order of the only possible words."[88]

But Pushkin teaches something more. The film director will learn from him how to avoid the mechanical coincidence of image and music. His frequent enjambement prevents a monotonous regularity which might lead to the noisy overdoing of the total effect.[89] In the

---

[85] In *Izbr. Proiz.*, II, p. 450, Eisenstein comments on the way in which Peter's name is held back in this passage. This is a well-known trick of Greek choral poetry: Dornseiff, *op. cit.*, pp. 107 ff.; Illig, *op. cit.*, pp. 27, 30, 34 note 6; E. Fraenkel on *Agamemnon* 681 ff.; above, pp. 143, 344.

[86] Eisenstein returns to this line in *Izbr. Proiz.*, II, pp. 355–56.

[87] Cf. H. Fränkel's "Stillstehen der Zeit," quoted by Illig, *op. cit.*, p. 70.

[88] Something which should make us chary then of the scholiast's "ordo est": E. Fraenkel, *Horace*, p. 304.

[89] Cf. Milton's *Preface* to *Paradise Lost*. How much we should avoid then the

passage quoted, image and line coincide in actual numerical order only once (VIII = 8). This is no accident. The meeting of music and image in VIII/8 underlines the most significant moment of the whole montage composition. It is exactly the moment when, in all its fullness, there is revealed the sight of Peter. It is this verse too which contains the only simile in the whole passage ("like a god-sent storm"). Pushkin chooses this coincidence between rhythm and image to make his most powerful impact and, with his metaphor, to leap into another dimension. This is exactly the behavior of the skilled user of montage, the real composer working with units of sight and sound.[90]

At a later stage in the same essay, Eisenstein speaks of the importance of punctuation in the proper understanding of an author's intentions. Taking a famous comedy of the early nineteenth century, Griboedov's *Woe from Wit*, he shows how subsequent editions had departed from the original text in favor of greater smoothness, but at the cost of surrendering the author's meaning. The modern text had come to read:

> . . . When will the Creator rescue us
> From their hats, their caps, their hair-pins, their straight-pins,
> Their book-shops, their confectionery shops . . .

But Griboedov had printed:

> . . . When will the Creator rescue us
> From their hats! Caps! And hair-pins!! And straight-pins!!!
> And book-shops and confectionery shops!!! . . .

It is evident that the enunciation of the text is different in the two cases. The flattened, modernized punctuation offers a general picture of one large confused mass. But the author's intention was to present a series of pictures, one reinforcing the other, in which, were the speech to be recast for the screen, the exclamation marks might be replaced by increasing emphasis on detail as the shots progressed. Eisenstein supports his case by further examples, which are not without importance for the student of the classics.[91]

---

temptation to see in Catullus' end-stopped lines in poems 63 and 64 anything except a device of extreme, almost violent art! The enjambement at lines 51–52 of poem 63, for example, ironically anticipating Attis' real position (90, *famula*) gains in intensity from being set amid all the other pauses.

[90] Eisenstein's biographer, the Formalist critic V. Shklovsky (fittingly, since Eisenstein was probably the Formalists' greatest disciple), was also interested in his subject's view of Pushkin: cf. pp. 146–49 of his book *Eisenstein* (Moscow 1973).

[91] *In Graecis hanc licentiam tuleris: nos etiam cum scribimus interpungere assuevimus*, Seneca, *Epp.* XL. 11. Quite apart from the vexed, but not therefore to be ignored, question of "Kolon und Satz," one thinks of the "Worthäufung" discussed by Curtius, *Europäische Literatur und lateinisches Mittelalter*, pp. 287 ff.

In another article dedicated to a long appreciation of the American film-producer D. W. Griffith, Eisenstein turns his attention to the origins of the montage method practiced by Griffith in some of his most famous films.[92] Griffith had claimed, in an interview with the London *Times*, to be a particular disciple of Dickens, and Eisenstein enjoys supporting this thesis up to the hilt with a brilliant analysis of chapters from *Oliver Twist*. But then the question arises: is the montage method only the invention of Dickens, or had Dickens himself predecessors? It was of course Eisenstein's profoundest conviction that montage had the deepest roots in the past, even in Chinese scroll painting, but here he fixes upon Shakespeare, drawing an illustration from the fifth act of *Macbeth*.

The act opens with Lady Macbeth's sleepwalking. Then comes a series of dual scenes, which passes into the two final duel scenes. A table clarifies the analysis:

*Macbeth Act V*

Scene 1: A room in Dunsinane Castle. Lady Macbeth sleepwalks.
Scene 2: The countryside near Dunsinane.
Scene 3: A room in Dunsinane Castle. Macbeth. Seyton.
Scene 4: Countryside near Dunsinane. Birnam Wood.
Scene 5: Inside Dunsinane Castle. Macbeth. Seyton. Lady Macbeth dies.
Scene 6: A field before Dunsinane Castle. Old Siward.
Scene 7: A field before Dunsinane Castle. Macbeth kills young Siward in a duel.
Scene 8: A field before Dunsinane Castle. Macbeth duels with Macduff. Old Siward hears the news of his son's death. Macduff enters carrying Macbeth's head. Finale.

The action switches three times in succession between the poles of castle and countryside, until, in scenes 7 and 8, it settles outside the castle. Now the dualities become duels. The warring sides confront each other. Macbeth's duels lead him from the pole of victory to the opposite pole of defeat. The last ironic (Dionysiac) contrast is between the headless usurper and his successor. It is aided by a retardation during the news of young Siward's death.

Cutting one sequence into another like this, Shakespeare not only solves the difficult problem of showing simultaneous action on the stage, but increases emotional tension by continually alternating between opposites. He treats of conflict by means which depend on conflict, and reveals his fidelity to a stylistic principle also acknowl-

---

[92] *Izbr. Stat'i*, pp. 153 ff.

edged by Virgil and Goethe. It is a principle cherished by Eisenstein too.[93]

Eisenstein finds further support for his analyses in the structure of *Richard the Third* and Webster's *The White Devil*. Some remarks added to the English version of his Russian lectures[94] are particularly illuminating for the student of Milton.

There, in the course of a discussion of the approach of Satan's army in Book VI of *Paradise Lost*, he notes how in v. 81 Milton introduces a hint for the camera-man (78–86):

> . . . at last
> Farr in th'Horizon to the North appeer'd
> From skirt to skirt a fierie Region, stretcht
> In battailous aspect, and neerer view
> Bristl'd with upright beams innumerable
> Of rigid Spears, and Helmets throng'd, and Shields
> Various, with boastful Arguments portraid,
> The banded Powers of *Satan* hasting on
> With furious expedition . . .

The infernal host is seen first as fire, and then in closer and closer detail, until in v. 85 Satan himself is named.

The structure of this passage is musical in itself, but within the total economy of the book, the classical student will note that it is a further development of imagery already presented in the opening lines (6–7),

> Where light and darkness in perpetual round
> Lodge and dislodge by turns. . . .

"Dislodge" will recur in the book. When the first day's fighting is over, Satan retires discomfited (413–15):

> . . . on th'other part
> *Satan* with his rebellious disappeerd,
> Far in the dark dislodg'd. . . .

The "dislodge" of the proem, and the "Farr . . . appeer'd" of v. 79 were fragmentary preparations for this later union of effect ("dislodg'd," "disappeerd"). The technique is at least as old as Pindar.[95]

---

[93] It is the principle that the image of the whole should also be reflected in the parts of a work of art. Cf. V. Pöschl, *The Art of Vergil*, Eng. tr., p. 172 (who also cites Goethe): Eisenstein, *The Film Sense*, tr. Leyda, p. 86 and *Izbr. Proiz.*, II, p. 367.

[94] *The Film Sense*, pp. 58 ff.

[95] Boccaccio's funeral pyres/wedding in Book I eventually coalesce into Arcita's wedding/funeral pyre at the end of the *Teseida*: above, p. 297. The technique of verbal reminiscence in Pindar and Apollonius is discussed above, pp. 99–100. See also pp. 159 ff. (Virgil).

When Eisenstein comes to examine his own films, he shows some striking affinities with the classical epic tradition as these pages have attempted to define it. The very circumstances surrounding the making of *The Battleship Potemkin* bear testimony to Aristotelian insights. Plans for celebrating the twentieth anniversary of the 1905 Revolution in film had reached grandiose proportions, and, because of that, were at a standstill. Eventually, efforts to tell the whole story were scrapped, and instead a single incident was selected which, if treated universally, would do duty for the whole. This single incident was *Potemkin*.

Eisenstein's feeling about the relation between poetry and history is exactly that of Aristotle, or rather, that which Aristotle discovers in Homer.[96] It becomes even more Aristotelian when we read his assurance that, although the film may look like a chronicle, it is in reality organized as a five act tragedy along classical lines. In the original print, each act was titled to separate it from its fellows. Soviet critics affirm that Eisenstein's analogy with the five acts of a tragedy has not much to do with the reality of his film.[97] But epic and drama have such close connections in the tradition that this is one occasion when we may suppose the author knew best what he was doing.

The emotional impact of *Potemkin*, enhanced by its concern with the golden section[98] already noted, is what Eisenstein calls by the Greek name of "pathos." This pathos depends, according to him, on the continual jumps which the action of all artistic narrative makes into opposites. These jumps are most effective when their increasing intensity offers the spectator a model for his own reactions. A classic example of such increasing intensity would be the storm in *King Lear*.

The mention of artistically convenient storms brings us close to the *Odyssey* and the *Aeneid*. But Eisenstein seeks instead an analogy with Greek painting. Cicero and other ancient writers tell of a lost picture by Timanthes, *The Sacrifice of Iphigenia*.[99] Sadness pervaded the scene. The priest Calchas could be observed at the altar, perhaps reflecting that after all this was the will of the gods. Ulysses watched, hardened warrior, and yet, even so, sadder than the priest. Menelaus mourned: what could have been his feelings for his innocent niece, offered up to secure the return of an adulterous wife?

---

[96] *Poetics* 1459 a 30: see ch. 9 on the difference between poetry and history, and Eisenstein, *Izbr. Proiz.*, III, pp. 94 ff., on the allegedly realistic novels of Zola. Sir Charles Chaplin makes Aristotle's point with greater urgency: *Autobiography*, p. 321, quoted by Shklovsky, *Eisenstein*, p. 271.

[97] So R. N. Yurenev on p. 429 of Eisenstein's *Izbr. Stat'i*.

[98] Cf. *Izbr. Proiz.*, III, pp. 55–56.

[99] *Orator* 22. 74: cf. *Aetna* 596–97; Pliny, *N. H.* XXXV. 73; Quintilian II. 13. 13; Val. Maximus VIII. 11. 6; Eustathius 1343. 62 ff. (on *Iliad* XXIV. 162–63).

The last witness was Agamemnon, the doomed girl's father. How could the artist do justice to this last stage in the crescendo of grief? He solved his problem by ignoring it. Agamemnon had turned away and muffled his head. Each spectator was forced to supply the missing features for himself, which meant that he would supply them to his own satisfaction. This last master stroke of pathetic structure is precisely the leap into the opposite which Eisenstein preaches. By involving the viewer of the picture in its creation in this way, Timanthes exploited the technique of montage.[100]

In *Potemkin* too the Odessa steps sequence is designed as a trigger for the audience's emotional response.[101] Not only are the participants in it seen in extreme emotion, but the movement of the various stages of the action is rhythmically organized back and forth, up and down, from mass to individual, from fast to slow, so as to sweep the spectator along with it into an ecstasy of pathos.[102]

There is indeed a level at which pathos leaps beyond itself, lifts the consciousness of the patient to a new height qualitatively different from anything to be attained by the merely mechanical collocation of disturbing contrasts of imagery or action. Eisenstein associates this leap with Hegelian ideas of the dialectical process at work in history, where thesis and antithesis suddenly coalesce into a novel synthesis. But of course we are not far here from Greek thought, from Aristotle in particular. Can this sudden attainment of a new degree of consciousness, accompanied as it must be by the most intense emotional and physical sensations, be anything except an experience of catharsis? To suggest that we are in some way different for having been worked upon by a great artist seems credible enough.[103] It is the Dionysiac in the Apolline.

---

[100] Compare Homer's refusal to describe Helen, *Iliad* III. 156 ff. So Sterne refuses to describe the Widow Wadman, *Tristram Shandy* (repr. London 1961), p. 345. His blank page is a fine example of the *dénudation du procédé*. See below, p. 503, for Mann's imitation of this trick.

[101] Cf. the ancient *psychagogia*, a notion which Horace, in a rhymed couplet which practices what it preaches (*A. P.* 99–100), associates with the Alexandrian *dulcia*. Perhaps this accounts for Plato's opposition to "pathetic" scenes (e.g. *Rep.* X. 605c). He saw the poets deliberately, not incidentally, triggering these emotions as some sort of revelation of truth. Eisenstein views the leaps in *Potemkin* as illustrating society's leap towards revolution.

[102] Compare Eisenstein's own account, *Izbr. Proiz.*, III, pp. 64 ff.; *Film Form*, tr. J. Leyda, pp. 115 ff.

[103] Lucas' interesting appendix II to his edition of the *Poetics* seems to indicate that the whole discussion has been bedeviled by the failure to see that an emotional experience can also give intellectual insight ("intelletto d'amore": Dante would have understood Aristotle).

III

Montage is also a favorite theme of the theoretical writings of Eisenstein's contemporary and countryman, V. Pudovkin. At the side of the expansive richness of the one, the laconic tones of the other make an expressive contrast.

Callimachus had urged his reader to draw his own conclusions, and so cut length from the song. This is pure film technique. Pudovkin describes montage as the equivalent of what English-speaking film-makers call "cutting."[104] He is not well satisfied with either term, but we can at least understand what the process is. When a film has been shot, after the actors have departed, the director will want to review the footage recorded by his camera-men. Often he will find that he has amassed more material than he needs to convey the particular story-line of his film. He will then resort, quite literally, to cutting and subsequent splicing, so that what he has to say is presented in the most effective manner possible, without excessive emphasis or overload. A really skillful director will have ensured even before shooting starts that there is a minimum of superfluous footage. But, whenever the cutting takes place, whether in the pre-shooting conferences or in the cutting room afterwards, Pudovkin insists that it is by no means to be looked upon as a merely mechanical task. Rather, it offers the director an opportunity to show his particular insights into the world of his story, to display his own artistic gifts and his general culture in what he determines to leave to the imagination of his audience.

The tension between immediacy and generalization (once again, the problem of the concrete universal) will be resolved differently by different artists. The cinema approaches literature in uniting external description with inner feeling. But the full reflection of reality demands montage.

Pudovkin has high claims to make for this process of montage. It is by its use that the inner connection of events may be laid bare, as when a scene of feverish activity on the Stock Exchange is coupled with one of soldiers dying at the battle front (*The End of St. Petersburg*, 1927). By contrast, if the camera is employed merely as a passive instrument, if the director has no truth to communicate, whatever the superficial tricks to which he may resort in order to relieve monotony, the result of his efforts is bound to be unconvincing and flat.[105] The idea that it is the camera's purpose to give a clear and

---

[104] V. Pudovkin, *Izbrannye Stat'i* (Moscow 1955), pp. 103 ff. See also pp. 80–81. Compare Callimachus, fr. 57. 1 Pf. (above, note 37).

[105] So Illig explains Pindar's method of narration by his moral convictions: *op. cit.*, pp. 12 ff. *Pectus est enim, quod disertos facit, et vis mentis*: Quintilian X. 7. 15.

complete account of events looks reasonable, but in fact is entirely mistaken. The director uses photography to control the spectator's reactions. So it was that the American D. W. Griffith used to shoot all his sad scenes in a deliberately foggy fashion. He wanted them to be seen as it were through a veil of tears. Ancient rhetoric, which knew its "Obscure!" as well as "Clarify!" (Livy's teacher), would have understood this painterly *chiaroscuro*.[106]

"Montage is a new method, invented and developed by the art of the cinema, by which all really existing things may be clearly and totally revealed from their superficial to their most essential relationships." In this regard, it is capable of serving as the instrument of thought in any realm whatsoever. Eisenstein is therefore correct, argues Pudovkin, when he extends montage analysis to artists like Leonardo and Pushkin.

The artist who employs montage is interested in having an audience. He is interested too in speech, since for him the sequence speech—thought—montage is peculiarly significant. But montage here cannot be left as an undeveloped concept. Examination of the notion of dialectical thought shows how important to it is the idea of relationships, of what the connections are between the object we see before us, what it was, what it will be. It is exactly this network of interconnections (what elsewhere in this book has been called "vertical time") that montage is fitted to explore.[107]

The revelation of the relations and meanings of individual phenomena depends on analysis, upon what has already been defined as "cutting." Pudovkin immediately thinks of other arts to illustrate his meaning. Music in particular, especially in its more complex forms, employs division and separation. So too a novel has parts, which are themselves made up of the smaller parts called chapters.[108] But it should be noted that in no case is cutting used to maim our apprehension of reality. Only this analytical approach allows the full understanding of what "reality" is.

The cinema possesses the power of analysis by means of cutting

---

[106] Above, p. 302; below, p. 477.

[107] Cf. Tolstoy's phrase "that endless labyrinth of connexions which is the essence of art" in his letter to N. N. Strakhov of 23 and 26 April 1876 (quoted by R. F. Christian, *Tolstoy's 'War and Peace'* [Oxford 1962], p. 124). Cf. Pudovkin, *Izbr. Stat'i*, p. 278, on dialogue. Polyvalent speech is not to be judged by the simple criterion of logical coherence (above, p. 406 and note 19). Pudovkin also comes close here to the notion of "polyphony" developed by M. Bakhtin in his *Problemy Poetiki Dostoevskogo* (Moscow 1963), that dialectically structured, open style, which in Chapter IV he traces back to the Menippean satire and its ancestors in antiquity.

[108] One thinks of the Alexandrian concern with "Gedichtbücher," their own or Homer's. It is interesting that Pudovkin associates such concern with music.

and selection in its most perfect form. Wherever the artist uncovers a relationship he can, by cutting, show it directly to the spectator. He can take an event happening today in Paris, and another that occurred ten years ago in Washington and, by bringing them into immediate proximity, reveal their internal connection. By the same token, he can take a whole phenomenon, select from it what most accurately indicates the internal law of its development, and then by uniting the pieces he has hacked out in this way, present the thought to the spectator.[109]

"This method of division and union, developed by the technical resources of the cinema to its highest point of perfection, is precisely what is called 'cinema montage'."[110]

Although the most striking achievements of the montage method have so far been effected with visual images, the same method must be applied to sound also. Unhappily, the discovery of the sound-track has meant retrogression even in the visual use of montage.[111] The explanation is that, with the introduction of sound, the screen has been invaded by the theatre with all its existing traditions worked out for a different medium. Pudovkin is particularly scathing about the exploitation of stereotyped ("automated") theatrical techniques to ensure box-office success. His Alexandrian demand for reform in art passes easily over to the Alexandrian rejection of money (the "poor poet" topos), and from there to a vatic program, the culmination of Alexandrian ideas at Rome, for the true cinema. In this vatic program, the satirical element is well in evidence.

The summary which Pudovkin gives in another article[112] of his principles of composition seems also to show Alexandrian affinities. He points out, as Kuleshov had already demonstrated, that the film-maker controls space and time. He is able to expel all irrelevance, and to concentrate his spectators' attention on what is important and characteristic. The mathematical procedures of differentiation and integration will offer an analogy with what the artist does. He analyzes the object into its smallest parts, from which it may then be reconstructed. The calculation of the dimensions of those parts in space and time is essential. Otherwise, all sense of their relative importance would be lost. The director must intervene in the pace of his film. Retardation and repetition are required. He deforms and subordinates reality to his needs. Rhythm helps him to establish emotion. The

---

[109] Cf. H. Fränkel on Apollonius' approach to the Argonaut legend (*Noten zu den Argonautika des Apollonios*, p. 21).

[110] Pudovkin, *Izbr. Stat'i*, p. 115.

[111] A view shared by Evelyn Waugh, *When the Going was Good* (Harmondsworth 1951), p. 11.

[112] *Izbr. Stat'i*, pp. 49 ff.

cinema needs simile, comparison, figures, just like literature. Its method is that of free imagistic exposition, and its aim is to force the spectator out beyond the normal limits of human perception. The kinship with the Formalist language of estrangement here is apparent.

There can be no such thing as indifferent choice of backgrounds in this hard task, or indifferent evocation of nights and days and other external phenomena. Even though the camera lens cannot "see" as much as a man of normal vision, the director will sometimes narrow its scope even further. Conversely, he will sometimes enhance its view by special technical tricks. There may be a thousand different angles on each scene to be shot. The selection of the one to be used cannot be left to chance here either.

Montage, the art of reconstructing a coherent story from the bits into which the scenario falls, depends on juxtaposition. This takes various forms. There is contrast, in which individual scenes or even individual parts of a scene are so arranged as to compel the viewer continually to compare two actions, one of which reinforces the other. There is parallelism, in which two thematically disconnected actions may be connected by some symbolic object recurring in them. There is simile. There is simultaneity, in which two actions going on at the same time are cut into each other. There is the use of leitmotif or reminiscence. Time may be slowed or speeded to lend fresh emphasis to the action.

What kind of epic film would in fact result from these prescriptions? Pudovkin has already illustrated a point about cutting by referring to his film *The End of St. Petersburg* (1927). A recurring sequence of images in this film showed the classically imposing Cathedral of St. Isaac in the former capital, inscribed on its architrave with a quotation from the Psalms: "The Czar rejoices in thy might, O God." The stability and religiously sanctioned strength of the old regime were powerfully emphasized by this massive building. But then we saw the columns of the architecture reflected in the waters of the river Neva, with its rippling current, rather as Monet saw the façade of the cathedral of Rouen in the ever-changing light. Suddenly, the solid looked impermanent, weak, caught up in the flow of the elements. The camera's concentration later on the fast-moving clouds in the sky at one point of the action was of a piece with this evocation of the mutable, metamorphosing life of nature, with its portent of political change.

This was supposedly a "historical" film, but sometimes the action became sheer farce, as when grandees were photographed minus their heads, or a procession demonstrating loyalty to the Czar included an ostentatiously large poster carried by a dwarf. The brutal realism of the fighting in the front line, cross-cut with scenes from the Stock Exchange, where fortunes were being made out of suffering, raised satire to vatic levels. Even the titles were given a didactic function. They were not just baldly informative. They varied in size, depending on the degree of urgency which they were meant to convey.

The film was attentive to ring-composition. At the beginning, the sun was glimpsed through the smoke of the Petersburg factories, where workers toiled for little reward. At the end, the same sun was seen through the smoke from the stacks of the battleship *Aurora*, which had joined the side of the revolution. The abrupt ending left a great deal to the spectator's reflections.

Pudovkin's revolutionary epic showed off therefore some ploys familiar to the student of the classical tradition. His concept of the artist as actor was equally traditional. He believed indeed in the paradigmatic nature for all art of acting. His mentor here was Stanislavsky. The actor has two tasks, to summon up emotion, and then to combine it with the logic of the play in which he has a part. He can never treat his art as a mere trade, a statement that Callimachus (fr. 222 Pf.) and Pindar (*Isth.* 2. 9) would have wholeheartedly applauded. He has to experience his role and then to represent it. The intensity of this experience is the same as that of any artist seeking the appropriate images in which to represent his ideas.

The cinema has the power to offer a very close picture of reality, and to indulge in formal abstractions. The clarity and sharpness of the rhythmical construction of a motion picture, which includes within itself the actors' performances, may be compared only with the accuracy and rhythmical structure of a musical composition. Two rhythms may in fact be at work in a film: speech and pauses, and the images. Turning to his own film *The Deserter* (1933) for an example, Pudovkin points out how the accompanying music, composed by Shaporin, grew steadily in intensity from beginning to end of the final scene, in contrast to the ups and downs of the action. The music gave a "subjective" interpretation (that "one day" victory would come) to the "objective" images. In contradiction at first, the two met in triumphant accord at the end.

Stanislavsky inspires a number of terms dear to Pudovkin. There is the "as if" of the actor's attitude. The actor says to himself: "All this is false," but his task is to behave as if it were real. There is "stamp!", the wearisome resort to cliché which threatens the living response at every moment. "Stamp" used to provoke the characteristic outburst "I don't believe it!" When the actor strayed during rehearsals from the human feel of his role into rhetorical emptiness, however much he might be impressed with his own prowess at the time, this was the agonized cry which was liable to interrupt him from the great director. Like Blake in an earlier age,[113] Stanislavsky considered the generalized to be the enemy of art. Each play must have an aim. The separate images must be subject to an overall unity of action. The actor must experience what he acts. His properly developed subjectivity will then work objectively on the spectator, giving clarity and expressiveness to the image, with sincerity, the absence of all false notes, the rejection of all formal tricks.[114]

Pudovkin evidently believes that it is possible for the artist to experience, not directly, but through the imagination. He compares Stanislavsky's feeling for the vividly realized detail with Tolstoy's procedures in his novels. Both select, without losing sight of the whole. Both use their powerful imaginations. "The presence of the gift of imagination defines by itself the man of art, and the development of this gift is the foundation of every artist's education."[115]

In this regard, Pudovkin emphasizes the importance of gesture. Analyzing the scene in *Anna Karenina* in which Dolly attempts to intercede with Karenin on behalf of his erring wife, he remarks on the difficulties of filming he encountered. Eventually he decided that Dolly, the mother of a large family, more used by this time to the company of children than that of adults, would probably talk to Karenin as if he were a little boy, wanting all the time to punctuate her remarks with a kiss or a pat, and yet realizing, as a lady brought up in high society, that she could hardly behave like this to the cold and dignified civil servant. He explained all this to the actress who was to play the role, asking her to restrict her gestures, to feel them but to suppress them. During the filming he noticed that the actress kept beginning a gesture of endearment with one hand, and then checking it with the other. It seemed unexpectedly convincing. Later, Pudovkin saw that Tolstoy himself had written of Dolly during this scene that she was "squeezing on her lap her bony hands." It was exactly what the actress had done, but only now did the director understand the sense of a passage he had read many times. Gesture in fact precedes speech. There can be the "mean" gesture, the barely hinted movement. There can be the significant absence of gesture. All this springs from the deeply felt experience or appropriation of the given role.[116]

---

[113] Above, p. 281.

[114] Pudovkin writes elsewhere (*Izbr. Stat'i*, p. 362): "Advancing to each new work, the genuine artist more than anything else fears the danger of falling captive to the models he himself worked out in his previous creations." Here is evidence both of the Alexandrian readiness to repudiate the past when it threatens deadness, and of the dangers of "topical" criticism.

[115] *Op. cit.*, p. 226: cf. *euplastos*, *Poetics* 1455 a 33.

[116] Cf. *Poetics* 1455 a 29–30, *schēmasin*. The rich language of ancient gesture has

Aristotle objected to the confusion of history and poetry. Criticizing certain Russian documentary films, Pudovkin notes that their plan and text were devoid of the necessary brevity and symmetry, and were crammed with commonplaces (topoi!). The theme could have been related more clearly and more expressively. The documentary should be short, without repetition of identical frames, without commonplaces, stereotypes or frills, full of the spirit of emotionally charged thought.

The creative process in a great artist is a complex phenomenon. The birth of such a work of art takes place as it were in a white-hot atmosphere, which reaches a critical temperature, after which there follows a sudden leap or explosion into a new quality. Here, Pudovkin is impelled to think of *Potemkin*.

> The whole extremely broad theme of the year 1905 was concentrated in a single episode. . . . But this episode was not chosen at random. It was precisely the epic of the *Potemkin* mutiny which allowed the most poetic interpretation of the basic task. . . . The film has indeed a poetic sweep. . . . This gives it its amazing musicality, the perfection of the correspondence of all its parts.[117]

As *Potemkin* shows, the upheavals of revolution and civil war have roused in the Russian people the desire to come to fresh terms with its past, in literature as well as in the film. This interest is not at all in the anecdotal type of history, but in knowledge, in the didactic. Russians are looking for what makes intelligible the people's past in the light of its present, the present in the light of the past. The classical scholar will perhaps reflect that this would not be a bad prescription for defining the function of the *Aeneid*, itself written after a revolution and a civil war, and its preparation in the didactic *Georgics*.

These thoughts naturally lead Pudovkin on to Eisenstein's *Ivan the Terrible*, the most striking of all these historical reconstructions. Elsewhere, he has not spared Eisenstein some criticism, accusing him, for example, of an excessive fondness for irony.[118] He sees the characters in this film as the deliberately simplified bearers of a single feeling. They become pieces in a gigantic game of chess, right down

---

been investigated by G. Neumann, *Gesten und Gebärden in der griechischen Kunst* (Berlin 1965), following the pioneering work of C. Sittl, *Die Gebärden der Griechen und Römer* (Leipzig 1890): cf. also Quintilian XI. 3. 63; H. Fränkel, *Noten* etc., p. 455 note 7.

[117] *Izbr. Stat'i*, pp. 306–07.

[118] *Op. cit.*, p. 271. Cf. Eisenstein himself, *Izbr. Proiz.*, II, pp. 364, 366.

to the limitations imposed on the moves they are able to make.[119] "The whole film is constructed in the form of the precise solution of a problem in chess."

> For me, the manner of Eisenstein's film is just as stylized as the tragedies of Aeschylus. And it is remarkable that in the film are to be found all the attributes of Greek tragedy, cothurni, masks, and even a chorus in its most modern guise.[120]

## IV

The theoretical observations excerpted here, along with a number of technical terms of the cinematic art, may at first hearing repel. Not only are they unusual in the literary criticism of the classical poets, but they are couched in language which smacks strongly of an ideology we have been taught to regard as foreign to our own. But all these ideas have their roots in the ancient world, and Hegel has done more than influence Marx. Perhaps the time has come to take Russia (and Byzantium) back into the European community, from which Russians themselves believe they have never departed.

Secondly, it may be recalled that the moral flavor distinguishing some of the remarks, though it may be unpalatable in certain modern mouths, would not have been so distasteful to the ancients, whose debates about the moral value and purpose of art were hardly ended with the philosophers of the fourth century. The compromise eventually reached by Peripatetic critics, and echoed by Horace, is not alien to the Alexandrian Greeks.[121]

There are in fact striking resemblances between the arguments of Pudovkin and Eisenstein, and what we may suppose to have been the practical poetic with which Callimachus and his sympathizers worked. Although the film is a "short" art-form, viewable in two or three hours and sometimes far less, neither of the Russian directors has the slightest hesitation about describing it as a fit vehicle for epic.

The cinema is a short art-form, not because film-makers have no

---

[119] The spectator will recall that, for example, the floor of the Polish court is marked out with the black and white squares of a chess board, and that it is a chess set which Ivan presents to Queen Elizabeth of England. It is amusing to see the revolutionary Eisenstein revive the old Apollonian and Virgilian trick of the offering of symbolic gifts. So also Valerius Flaccus, above, pp. 224–25.

[120] Pudovkin, *op. cit.*, p. 349. Actually, the classical scholar will be even more struck with the parallel to Euripides' *Bacchae* (below, p. 442). For analysis of this scene in terms of Bakhtin's theory of carnival literature see V. V. Ivanov in *Problemy Poetiki i Istorii Literatury*, ed. S. S. Konkin (Saransk 1973), pp. 37–53.

[121] See C. O. Brink's notes on Horace, *Ars Poetica* 333 ff., and above, pp. 52 ff. It was after all Callimachus who defended the didactic poetry of Aratus by reference to Hesiod.

inspiration to compose at length,[122] but because cutting is of the very essence in the communication of their ideas. The whole technique may now be seen as something far more creative than negative. To "cut" a poem is not to have as one's ideal a long poem which is then shortened for mechanical reasons, as a journalist shortens his copy to match the space on the page. A "cut" poem exists as a completely separate and independent concept from the start. Length in itself becomes irrelevant. It is the method of composition that matters, what Callimachus called "art."[123]

As the artist reflects on the story he is to tell, its implications and moral resonances, he finds that the most effective way to convey his meaning is to make his audience conscious from the outset of the depth and ramifications of his narrative. For this purpose he will need to impose on events a cinematic time and space.[124] What is important in a merely quantitative sense must yield to what counts qualitatively. The occurrences of a lifetime may have to be passed over in a couple of scenes, if that life has been largely lived at a level irrelevant to the story. Conversely, the details of a room, its flapping blind, its carved ceiling, its dripping tap, may be something which for the hero takes on a cosmic significance, and requires correspondingly close attention in the presentation.[125] If these details are leitmotifs of the plot, we are with Pindar, Virgil and Thomas Mann.

The Russian directors make it clear that the film's superiority resides, among other things, in the vastness of its range. For Pudovkin, the film is the art towards which all the other arts, with varying success, aspire. For Eisenstein, it is an art-form which does again what writers and artists have been doing over the centuries by poetic instinct. The film-maker who takes lessons from Shakespeare and Milton, from Euripides, Aeschylus and Timanthes, is acknowledging his place within a tradition. His theories in their turn help us to understand why Aristotle pays attention to music, and is concerned with assimilating the creative writer to the actor. Eventually, Apollonius took music, painting and pathetically structured character into epic. This Hellenistic sensibility is already anticipated by the lyric

[122] According to the scholiast on *Hymn* 2. 106, Callimachus' critics sneered at him on the grounds that "he was not able to write a big poem." He responded by writing the *Hecale*.

[123] Above, p. 27.

[124] The "Kuleshov effect": cf. Pudovkin, *op. cit.*, p. 53.

[125] The technique of the French "nouvelle vague" then is not so nouvelle. The modern movement too will have its Euphorion, its Eratosthenes, even (dare one suggest it?) its Lycophron.

poet and master of the *ischnos charactēr*, Simonides.[126] And shall we deny this kind of genius to the "leader of tragedy," Homer?

These technical similarities are clues to deeper resemblances between modern film and Alexandrian attitudes. Technique is inspired here by questions of outlook which it is not wrong to term philosophical, even though Callimachus is so often thought to have been no philosopher. What are ancients and moderns doing, in the last analysis, with their stylistic tricks? They might have used them for the crudest propaganda, and have reaped agreeable rewards from gratified patrons.[127] But anyone acquainted with Eisenstein's films, though he will admit that they are by no means uncommitted works, will refuse to believe that "propaganda" exhausts their significance. They have been too widely admired for that, by the most diverse audiences. And *Potemkin*, after all, was, according to its maker, a love story!

Eisenstein's brilliance reached its zenith in *Ivan the Terrible* (1943, 1946), planned as a trilogy, although the second part of the trilogy was at first banned, and the third never completed (the scenario survives for all three parts).[128] Once again, in seeking to interpret to the Russian people its own present, Eisenstein turned to a historical theme. Once again, this theme was treated with cavalier disregard for "the facts," so that instead the facts of Russian experience of brutality and despotic cruelty might emerge. Eisenstein's aim is to enter imaginatively into the mind of the maniacal ruler of whom everyone normally thinks when Ivan's name is heard, and to suggest how, like Nero, he might have been a complex, intuitive artist of government,[129] burdened by his own talent and the backwardness of his contemporaries, reacting with angry violence to their opposition, but ultimately with some sort of truth in him. That this sympathy for the Czar did not mean the abandonment of ordinary moral criteria is shown by the displeasure with which the second and third parts of the project were greeted.

The film's techniques were based on simplification, repetition,

---

[126] Plutarch, *Glor. Ath.* 3: "Simonides calls painting silent poetry and poetry painting that speaks." Rilke's 1919 essay on "Primal Sound" is relevant here. See also [Plutarch], *De Vita et Poesi Homeri* 216–17.

[127] *Praemia*, Horace, *Sat.* II. 1. 12; *nummum*, *Epp.* II. 1. 175; *Philippos*, *ibid.*, 234. For the contrasting Alexandrian ideal of the "poor poet," see Callimachus, *Iamboi* III, *Epigr.* XXXII.

[128] Kristina Thompson, *Ivan the Terrible: a Neoformalist Analysis* (Princeton 1981), is especially illuminating.

[129] *Qualis artifex pereo!* Nero, quoted by Suetonius, *Vit. Ner.* XLIX. 1: "A poet of the idea of the state," K. D. Kavelin about Ivan, quoted by Eisenstein, *Izbr. Proiz.*, VI, p. 506.

symmetry. Eisenstein singled out three points in Ivan's career, none of them historically true. They were: the murder in the cathedral of Vladimir Staritzsky, Ivan's dull-witted rival for the throne; the deaths of the two Basmanovs, father and son, who betrayed their oaths of office as members of Ivan's personal army, the Oprichnina; the unmasking of Ivan's own chaplain as the young brother of his enemy, the Metropolitan Philip, and as a traitor to the Czar's plans.

It is apparent in what a paranoiac atmosphere Ivan moves. At every step he finds treachery and self-seeking. His most intimate relatives and friends have to be crushed as he makes his way towards that sole power which, by an ambivalence not wholly translatable into English, will also be solitary.[130]

Eisenstein admitted his borrowings from the most diverse sources.[131] The episode of Vladimir's murder, for example, is traced to Victor Hugo's *Le roi s'amuse*, best known from Verdi's *Rigoletto*, where a distraught father finds that his hired assassin has killed his own daughter rather than her royal seducer. Dumas provided material for the scene in which the oprichnik Malyuta is crushed by the collapsing walls of the castle of Weissenstein. Piranesi inspired the imaginative architecture. A Cambridge Grace before Dinner was transmuted into the antiphon which echoes around the coffin of the deceased Anastasia. Lear's relationship to Edgar and Edmund colored Ivan's relationship to young Basmanov and to his chaplain Evstaphy. Pushkin's *Boris Godunov* contributed to the picture of the aging Czar prostrate before the fresco of the Last Judgment while the names of his victims are recited.

The "frenzied sound of bells" for which Eisenstein's scenario calls on a number of occasions, the constant resort to music, both orchestral and vocal, the leap into color[132] at the feast preceding Vladimir's murder, suggest that these operatic, comic, melodramatic, medieval and classical parallels are not accidental. The whole work is overlaid with richly emotional associations. In Eisenstein's original concept, the first film began with the "traumas" (Eisenstein's own word)

---

[130] See Shklovsky's biography of Eisenstein, p. 289, which quotes a letter on this point from Eisenstein to the Formalist critic Yu. Tynianov. Shklovsky's general discussion of the film is found on pp. 250 ff. He notes its autobiographical element (Eisenstein's own unhappy childhood), but on p. 251 curiously objects to the romantic feeling which Prince Kurbsky shows for Ivan's wife.

[131] Compare Mann's *Entstehung des Doktor Faustus* for similar revelations. The reader must always be wary of course of falling victim to the "intentional fallacy." And a work of art is more than a collection of sources. The most surprising thing is that Eisenstein says so little about the *Bacchae*, where also a mother kills her transvestite son.

[132] Discussed by Shklovsky, *op. cit.*, pp. 280 ff. This is the scene that attracts Ivanov's attention (above, note 120).

inflicted on the eight-year-old Ivan: the poisoning of his mother and the murder of her lover by Shuisky. It was Shuisky who uttered the fateful order "Seize him!" which was later to become Ivan's characteristic reaction to opposition, and Shuisky is Ivan's first victim when the boy prince discovers his own power, and what Eisenstein calls the automatism of the imperial machine.

As Ivan's mother was poisoned, so is his wife. Chalices develop an evocative symbolism. Like Christ in Gethsemane, Ivan prays "that this chalice may pass from me." It is then that young Basmanov first inspires him with the suspicion that his wife was actually poisoned, a suspicion which leads to the sending of an empty chalice to Vladimir's doomed mother, and to the chalice which makes her son so drunk that he betrays himself and her. Vladimir's last supper is a parody of the Last Supper, and a parody of Ivan's own wedding feast. Young Basmanov, wearing women's clothes, and a mask which makes him look like the dead Tsaritsa, dances. He is Balzac's hermaphrodite Séraphîta, as well as the apostle John, and Salome. When Vladimir is dressed in the Czar's own coveted robes in preparation for his death, he is a carnival king, a Pentheus, a mocked Christ.[133]

Ivan himself is tragically divided. The Metropolitan Philip and his young monk brother Evstaphy represent one possibility, and the head of his oprichniki, Malyuta, another. Racine had already exploited this trick, in giving two confidants and advisers to his Néron in Britannicus. Malyuta is the elemental force of the drive towards power at any cost, even if, like a Titan, he has to bear the falling world on his own shoulders. Philip and Evstaphy symbolize both a blind attachment to the past and a chaste, virginally barren horror at the ruthless bloodiness of Ivan's career. There is no resolution of these two opposites. Vladimir's mother quotes from Machiavelli, just as she is about to fall victim to her own precepts. Ivan himself is acting out the patterns imprinted on him by his childhood. His nurse sang of Russia's great rivers and their access to the sea, cut off by foreign usurpers. The third part of the trilogy was to end with Ivan standing alone on the shore, his aim, however fleetingly, achieved, his last friend dead in the moment of achievement.

Eisenstein's drawing for the unmade film at this point bears the legend "The Apotheosis of Ivan," and the script tells us that, as the Czar stood by the stormy Baltic, he was to command it to be still, and it was still. Eisenstein has perhaps christened[134] the figure of

---

[133] Compare Virgil's shifting identities, his metamorphoses. Ivan is Nebuchadnezzar and perhaps Herod as he arrests Metropolitan Philip.

[134] Compare the Czar's habit of prefacing his sentences with *Istinno, istinno,* "Verily, verily."

Oedipus at Colonus, passing through horror towards some kind of ultimate peace. His hesitations about how the film was to end show how difficult he found it to make sense of Ivan's life and work.

Nowhere do we read in Eisenstein's published notes about the analogy with chess which has struck more observers than Pudovkin, though his sketch of the Polish court clearly shows the chessboard squares of its floor.[135] The film obviously has its castles; its bishops, with their diagonal movement of conspiracy; its knights, limited and bizarre; its opposing king, Sigismund of Poland, ineffectual and sly; its black queen, Vladimir's mother, an energetic and determined opponent, able to move both by the diagonal of treachery and the direct line of violence (she beats off the attack of the elder Basmanov). Ivan's wife is the white queen, fighting for her son as much as her rival fights for Vladimir, and in the person of young Basmanov even surviving death.

But who then is the king opposed to Sigismund? Can it possibly be Ivan? Can Ivan, tireless, cruel, ambitious, busy at Moscow, Kazan, Alexandrov, Novgorod, busy in Livonia, be the piece on the chessboard which makes the fewest moves on its own side, whose importance is that of symbol rather than agent? Eisenstein does not say so, though he was worried about Ivan's real-life cowardice at Kazan, and at the final assault Malyuta deflects his intention to lead the charge with some interesting words. But should we remember here his phrase about "the automatism of the imperial machine"? Tolstoy, an author never far from Eisenstein's mind, had in his depiction of Napoleon made the classic formulation of imperial irrelevance. What was irrelevant in Ivan was perhaps his illusion of freedom. He could only walk the course predetermined by history, and by his memories of childhood. The Last Judgment, the Forty Martyrs, the painted frescoes of the saints and angels, stare down at the living everywhere in the film in sardonic mockery of their little dilemmas, and as a reminder that the essence of things does not change, in spite of all our strutting.[136]

Such a film is not to be dismissed as propaganda in any ordinary sense of that word. It does not glorify the deeds of kings and heroes in many thousands of verses, as demanded by Callimachus' enemies, the Telchines. Neither does the *Aeneid*, which itself has not escaped misinterpretation as the statement of a propaganda theme. Here we

---

[135] On chess symbolism cf. Bakhtin, *Tvorchestvo François Rabelais*, pp. 255 ff. He refers to Francesco Colonna's *Hypnerotomachia Poliphili*, but also remarks (p. 256) that Rabelais and all the Renaissance humanists were still aware of the ancient view of games as more than empty pastimes. One hears a distant echo of Pindar.

[136] *Aut ante ora deum pinguis spatiatur ad aras*, Aen. IV. 62.

come to the very heart of that deeper philosophy of which we spoke above. The Alexandrian technique is, after all, merely a technique, a series of unrealized possibilities, waiting to be called into life by the individual genius of the artist. The artist with a more optimistic temperament will call these potentialities into play at another level from the artist who is profoundly burdened by the mysteries of the human condition. Mendelssohn will write a different music from Brahms. They are nevertheless exponents of the same musical tradition. Ovid will write differently from Virgil. For him, painting, music, the ambivalence of irony will certainly enlarge the word, but they will not raise any too insoluble problems. Everything will be set in the clear sunlight of an Italian spring, amid the boisterous humor of an Italian carnival.

Ovid's amoralism is more akin to the primitive and careless spirit. When Virgil addresses himself to the problem of the hope left for Rome after more than a century of civil strife, he will be unable to give clear and sunlit answers. His moral ambivalences will often confuse his reader, rather than induce easy oblivion. His presentation of issues will often be dark and obscure (*fugit indignata sub umbras*). His cross-references and use of sources will demand the most minute attention as the clue to his awareness of moral complexity. For him, mathematics, music, allusion, imagery, will all blend into one sweeping, forward-pressing composition which will forever baffle the enquiries of its admirers.

The same is true of Eisenstein. The different "books" (as they have been called) of the first part of his unfinished trilogy present a hero who is as isolated from others as Aeneas, and who, like Aeneas, is pushed by what he conceives to be his mission into behavior that is plainly wrong in the accepted sense. The suggestion of the film is that Ivan, in a blind and muddled way, is acting in the name of the people and for an abstraction which is yet more important than any trivial reality, Russia. The suggestion of the *Aeneid* is that Aeneas is acting in the name of the people (he bears the relics of Priam's old authority) and for an abstraction which is yet more important than any trivial reality, such as his own or Dido's personal happiness— Rome, the Rome which he would never live to see.

Yet the difference between these two epics and, say, the *Metamorphoses*, is not primarily that between an Alexandrian *Metamorphoses* and a new, Roman,[137] imperial poetry. All these poems use the same

---

[137] Moscow had been proclaimed as the "Third Rome" early in the sixteenth century, and Ivan the Terrible claimed descent from "a mythical Prus, own brother to Caesar Augustus himself" (B. H. Sumner, *Survey of Russian History* [2nd ed., London 1947], p. 90). The agnomina *Augustus* and *Grozny* also have something in common: cf. the Renaissance concept of *terribilità* and Horace, *Odes* III. 1. 5.

literary, carnival devices. It is the difference between two sisters sprung from the same mother, tragedy and comedy.

To force a distinction between Alexandrian and Roman epic would indeed obscure the far more important distinction between the epic favored by the Telchines, in their ancient or modern guise, and that advocated by Callimachus, with whom Virgil and Eisenstein—and Ovid—ultimately stand. The philosophical question again demands attention. Callimachus rejected the long epic, couched in eulogistic terms and destined for the easy market of lucrative flattery. There must have been moments when the temptation to seek an easier path was pressing. Only the firm conviction that his poetic principles demanded fidelity to a stern vocation could have enabled the poet to continue for so many years the steep climb. This accounts for the vehemence of tone in the Preface to the *Aetia*.

The epic therefore propounded by Callimachus was based upon moral insights that he refused to betray even at the cost of denying himself the kind of attention and popularity of which we catch some glimpses in other men's poetry.[138] If the poet would not be content to play the role of a Choerilus, to exalt the exploits of some second (and often second-rate) Achilles and hope that this would qualify him as a second Homer, it was because his artistic conscience rebelled against the false picture of life which such naiveté encouraged. This explains the critique of the heroic ideal found in Callimachus' disciple, Apollonius, and in Callimachus' disciple, Virgil.

The Alexandrian "playfulness" of art does not mean a license to manipulate moral truths unscrupulously. By contrast, the Telchines' epic cares very little for truth. Its aim is to please and to flatter, and in the course of achieving its effects it will find innumerable occasions when awkward and unhappy facts require whitewash. It will describe an Ivan the Terrible as a "progressive statesman" (Stalin's phrase in conversation with Eisenstein), and a Scipio, a Johannes or a Germanus as forever *sans peur et sans reproche*. But it will not produce the sort of poetry to which we shall look for illumination of our human plight. It will in the end not turn out to be very satisfactory even to its patrons; for its poets, carried away by their own achievements as liars, will eventually assert their ability to "sell" anyone who pays them, regardless of the historical record.[139] Such are the dangers of ignoring Aristotle's distinction between poetry and history. The knowledge of this lie in the soul will obscure the greatness even of

---

[138] See Theocritus XVI. Callimachus himself beautifully parodies the topos "my poetry will bring you fame [and therefore you should pay me well]" in *Iambos* XII, dedicated to a seven-day-old baby girl!

[139] See *Augustus and the New Poetry*, pp. 412–17.

those who do deserve praise, and all the vaunted preoccupation with the Truth will lead, not to Helicon, but to Madison Avenue.[140]

Given this enormous difference between the two types of epic, where it is hardly an exaggeration to say that the future of civilization is at stake, it seems pointless to elevate subsidiary differences *within* the Callimachean tradition to a level where they confuse rather than clarify. Of course Callimachus could not explore all the new horizons he opened up. This was immediately apparent in the *Argonautica*. As the Callimachean spring was enriched, particularly by its contact with the deep and primitive wells of the Roman aesthetic, there arose the continual danger that accretion would muddy the original clear insight. There were new circumstances, new challenges, new personalities, new languages. In their refracting medium, old doctrines take on unexpected forms. Who, for example, could expect to find Callimachus' artistic principles relevant to Dante? But who would have expected to find Ovid or Lucan or even Lucretius relevant to the poet of Christian eschatology, and shall we say there is no Callimachus in them? Our preconceived, familiar notions of literary history must not be allocated undue importance.

The delicate, Callimachean stream of epic potential has become broader and more opaque over the centuries. The Telchines have impudently attempted to borrow from its fertility. Its principles have been modified to suit pioneer ages when complexity was out of place. It has been left in our own age to film-directors to restate its essence, its manifold promise, its stern moral injunctions, yet deep concern with human values. From their shadows we return with fresh eyes and cleaner palates to Aganippe.

[140] Petrarch's *Africa* is better than this, but better only because it compromises with Callimachean ideals: above, pp. 287 ff.

# X

# THE MODERN EPIC—II:
# TOLSTOY AND THOMAS MANN

THE poetic that unites such diverse figures as Apollonius
Rhodius and Eisenstein runs the risk of losing all cogency. If
its principles are so loose as to accommodate such strange
bedfellows, can it have any critical fidelity?

There are two advantages however in seeking to extend our
analysis to modern epic. We have the possibility, denied to us so often
in the case of older authors, of actually studying the process of
composition, the author's comments, the rejection or acceptance of
alternatives through long hours of toil, as well as the finished
masterpiece; and we have too the services of a criticism which,
precisely because it has freed itself from "classicism," touches in fact
the most intimate springs of classical practice. If both these sources
of information still offer evidence of what has been called here the
classical epic tradition, perhaps the danger of looseness and infidelity
vanishes.

The scope for critical enquiry thus opened in modern literature
is vast. In this context it must be limited to two authors. The first
of them is Leo Tolstoy, and the epic is therefore *War and Peace*.

I

After an early success with *Sebastopol Stories* (1855–56), based on his
experiences in the Crimean War, Tolstoy's position among the writers
and thinkers of the late fifties and early sixties in nineteenth-century
Russia was isolated.[1] This may have inspired his decision to withdraw
to his estate and open a village school.

Only with his marriage (1862) did the plan of composing a large-
scale work begin to take shape in his mind. Among a number of
experiments, he toyed with the idea of a novel about the Decembrist
conspirators against Nicholas I. Prince Labazov, a condemned con-

---

[1] B. M. Eichenbaum, *Lev Tolstoi*, 2 vols. (Leningrad 1928–31, repr. Munich 1968),
I, pp. 261 ff.; II, pp. 5 ff.

spirator exiled to Siberia, was to be shown returning to Russia thirty years later, after the pardon granted to the Decembrists by Alexander II. Through his estranged eyes—those of an aristocrat who yet knew what it was to do a job of hard physical work—contemporary Russia was to be judged and, by Labazov's Christian standards, found wanting.

Then the technique of parallelism came to the fore. The novel was now to be called *Three Moments* (*Tri Pory*), and the Decembrist revolt of 1825 was to be contrasted with 1856 (Russia's defeat in the Crimean War) on the one side, and 1812 (the triumph over Napoleon) on the other. Eventually, this scheme dropped away, and Tolstoy decided to concentrate on the year 1805. The momentous events of that period would be reduced to the status of mere background, and the real happiness of domesticity would be shown to be all that mattered. The novel would be a deliberately old-fashioned revival of a genre which contemporaries believed played out, a slap in the face for public taste.

But slowly, under the influence both of Western writers like Proudhon and extreme Slavophiles like Prince Urusov, the ideological content of the novel was expanded. There emerged, to quote Boris Eichenbaum, no longer an *Odyssey* but an *Iliad*.[2] *Nescio quid maius nascitur Iliade.*

Readers of *War and Peace* find it hard to believe that the existing novel, long though it is, represents less than half the material surviving in Tolstoy's manuscripts. The process of refinement and selection that went into the composition of the final version—a process which the classical scholar will see as a growing approximation to the Aristotelian and Callimachean model outlined so many times in these pages—has been followed by a number of critics.[3] Such critics have noted, for example, that it took Tolstoy time to grasp the need to

---

[2] *Lev Tolstoi*, II, p. 280. See below, note 52. Tolstoy himself said that, like the *Iliad* and *Odyssey*, his novel contained portraits of morals founded on a historical happening (*Diary* for September 30, 1865, quoted by E. Wedel [below, note 3], p. 169 note 168). "Without false modesty, *War and Peace* is like the *Iliad*": Tolstoy to Gorky, quoted by R. F. Christian (below, note 19), p. 117.

[3] E.g. E. Wedel, *Die Entstehungsgeschichte von L. N. Tolstojs "Krieg und Frieden"* (Wiesbaden 1961); R. F. Christian, *Tolstoy's 'War and Peace': A Study* (Oxford 1962); E. Zaidenschnur, *"Voina i Mir" L. N. Tolstogo: Sozdanie velikoi knigi* (Moscow 1966). This last book was written to controvert, by reference to Tolstoy's manuscripts, Eichenbaum's view of the gradual expansion of the novel's scope during its writing. It should be remembered however that Eichenbaum, a leading Formalist, was also a noted textual scholar, who himself collaborated on the authoritative edition of Tolstoy's works. Here Wedel has been largely followed, and cross-reference to Zaidenschnur, who makes many of the same points, avoided except in special cases.

plunge with his story *in medias res*, and that he himself traced this lesson to his study of Pushkin. In the final version, brevity and the softening of any too coarse traits in the earlier presentation are evident. Personal comments are limited. Long descriptions are eliminated. The final version pays less attention to the physical appearance of the characters. A few essential features are noted, and the rest is brought out by means of dialogue and action. Milder language replaces the frankness of the original. Eroticism is toned down. Sometimes dialogue is substituted for action even at the cost of depending on the reader's imagination to fill the gap. But contrast (polarity) remains one of the author's typical devices.

Tolstoy makes it his aim to "demythologize" his heroes. Both the episode of Berg's ostentatious wearing of his sword[4] and the contrast between parade-ground splendor and the realities of battle serve this purpose. In the rearrangement of events that marks the final version Tolstoy wished to effect a more dynamic change of scenes as well as to underscore the multiple lines of the plot.

Amazingly for an "historian," Tolstoy was careless about chronology, most grossly in the disappearance of an entire year from the time-scheme. He is uncertain even about the ages of his characters. His similes are important, and sometimes they are linked to intimate personal reminiscences of the author.[5]

The story evidently treats of the most grandiose themes of public enterprise and martial pomp. But Tolstoy designated as the "knot" of his entire novel the attempted abduction of Natasha by Anatol:

> In fact, with this conflict in the lives of the central figures affected, the culmination—insofar as one may speak of culmination—is passed, and the remaining part of the work (volumes III and IV), regardless of its wide sweep, which is a consequence of its broad picture of the war of 1812, forms only a pendant to the private strand of the action.[6]

*Contulit in Tyrios arma virumque toros* indeed!

This epic is never therefore long on stilts. Tolstoy's debt to the humbler genres is seen in his borrowings from Krylov's fables for his comparison of abandoned Moscow to an empty beehive. The student of the epic tradition notes without surprise that this compar-

---

[4] Book VI, chapter 11. In this guying of military pretensions, Tolstoy comes close to Apollonius. Jason too arms himself to no purpose: see H. Fränkel, *Noten zu den Argonautika des Apollonios* (Munich 1968), pp. 468 ff.

[5] Wedel, pp. 189–90.

[6] Wedel, pp. 203–04: cf. Zaidenschnur, pp. 82–83 and 240. This admission of the central importance of the domestic side to the story seems rather to concede Eichenbaum's point about its origins.

ison has been used before in the novel.[7] Tolstoy's description of
Pierre's behavior on the day of his attempt to assassinate Napoleon
is not free from burlesque details, for example, when the would-be
assassin is so excited that he forgets to load his pistol. What Tolstoy
thought of such behavior had already been signposted by the scene
in which a lunatic tries to murder the French Captain Ramball and
is foiled by Pierre.

A comparison with the variants shows that greater discretion and
nobility mark the final version. Remarks about Kutuzov's private life
are deleted. The French army's camp-followers are depicted less
harshly. The classical reader will think here of the tone of the New
Comedy, and of Apollonius Rhodius. The death of Prince Andrei,
who, in one version, after resigning Natasha to Pierre, had continued
his military career, deepens what might have been merely the happy
ending of a family story. Here, the reader will think of Turnus.

Tolstoy made great use of his own family in drawing the characters
of his novel, sometimes by the technique of fusing two originals into
one. Conversely, one prototype may be divided into several fictional
personages. Here we seem to find an echo of Virgil's dealings with
his heroic exemplars.

Contrary to the skepticism of the Formalists, he did have a concern
with the architectonics of his novel, not only in the use of contrast,
but in the shortening and concentrating of the first part of the work
in its final version, and balancing extension of the concluding parts.[8]
In the course of these revisions, a continuous style of narrative was
replaced by one of interruptions, which underlines the simultaneity
of the happenings. Thus the novel repeatedly postpones the imminent
dénouement of its "knot."

Yet although Tolstoy sets his private heroes over against the heroes
of official history, he never spares their human weaknesses.

The answer therefore to the question—what can *War and Peace*
possibly have to do with Alexandria?—now becomes clearer. The

---

[7] Book IV, chapter iii *ad init.* (the English Club in Moscow): cf. *Aen.* XII. 587 ff.
Other repeated images which deserve investigation are the transferences of military
and hunting terminology to domestic life: e.g. when Anna Pavlovna becomes a general
at her soirées (Zaidenschnur, p. 73), or Prince Andrei is killed and wounded by
Natasha's betrayal (Zaidenschnur, p. 206), we have the oldest amatory tradition
(reversal of roles by the male and female). On Tolstoy's similes see G. Steiner, *Tolstoy
or Dostoevsky* (London 1960), pp. 85 ff. On ironical similes in epic see W. B. Stanford's
note on *Odyssey* X. 215.

[8] Wedel, p. 265. Zaidenschnur (p. 50) gives a provisional compositional scheme
drawn up by Tolstoy himself, in which the author's attention to what Hellenistic
historians called "symmetry" is quite evident. See below, p. 500, for the same in
Thomas Mann.

basic quarrel, it will be recalled, between Callimachus and his critics the Telchines, as set out in the Preface to the *Aetia*, was that the critics favored long historical epic written to honor kings and mighty heroes. From such activities, lucrative rewards might be expected by the author. Callimachus evidently did not favor this kind of poetry, and he expected to remain a "poor" poet. He is particularly scathing by implication about putting the history of Herodotus into verse. Since Aristotle had already declared that versifying Herodotus still did not make one a poet, the two theories, Athenian and Alexandrian, seem here to coalesce.[9]

Tolstoy clearly wrote a long epic. But is it a history, and is it a eulogy of the mighty? He himself answered this question quite decidedly. In a planned conclusion to the novel, later suppressed on technical grounds, he had both apologized for his historical analyses and explained why he had been unable to glorify his characters (i.e. to write a Telchines epic). The historical analyses, he stated, were there purely for the benefit of readers unable to read between the lines. Those who objected to the unvarnished presentation of heroic figures were reminded that art is not gold leaf, to be applied at whim. It has its own laws. "That is why there are many admirers of Napoleon, and yet no poet has made an image of him, and none ever will." So much for the example of Choerilus of Iasos, who wanted to be "the second Homer of the second Achilles," and whose money-grubbing efforts at epic are sarcastically dismissed by Horace.[10]

One of the most pervasive features of the Callimachean tradition, reinforced by the Roman propensity towards carnival humor, was its irony. Sometimes this may burst out into open mockery. Sometimes it may be attenuated or suppressed, even though the comedian's apparatus remains on the stage. Sometimes it may be exploited for tragic ends. Tolstoy is a master of irony but, although this quality might seem at home in a novel of contemporary life like *Anna Karenina*, it is unexpected to find it displayed on such a broad scale in the epic of Russia's triumph. The author particularly likes to deploy his ironic tone with the help of a device which may be called that of the "intruded spectator," the uncomprehending witness best compared with the child in Hans Andersen's story who blurted out that the emperor had no clothes.[11]

---

[9] Above, p. 44.

[10] Above, p. 59; Wedel, pp. 254–55. Wedel also notes a much more virulent attack on conventional historians, p. 211 and note 37.

[11] This is what V. Shklovsky calls "estrangement": cf. his article "Iskusstvo, kak Priyom" (Petrograd 1917), reprinted in his *O Teorii Prozy* (Moscow–Leningrad 1925), pp. 7–20, a part of which is translated into French in *Théorie de la Littérature*, ed.

A famous example in *War and Peace* is that of Natasha at the Moscow opera. Everything turns on a refusal by the author to make the normal "willing suspension of disbelief":

> The floor of the stage consisted of smooth boards, at the sides was some painted cardboard representing trees, and at the back was a cloth stretched over boards. In the centre of the stage sat some girls in red bodices and white skirts. One very fat girl in a white silk dress sat apart on a low bench, to the back of which a piece of green cardboard was glued. They all sang something. When they had finished their song the girl in white went up to the prompter's box, and a man with tight silk trousers over his stout legs, and holding a plume and a dagger, went up to her and began singing, waving his arms about.
>
> First the man in the tight trousers sang alone, then she sang, then they both paused while the orchestra played and the man fingered the hand of the girl in white, obviously awaiting the beat to start singing with her. They sang together and every one in the theatre began clapping and shouting, while the man and woman on the stage—who represented lovers—began smiling, spreading out their arms, and bowing.[12]

But, even on this minor scale, the artistic trick (which eventually touches pure farce) is not just an instance of boorish insensitivity. The artificial world of the theatre is just the place where Natasha's innocent and natural values will be corrupted, and Tolstoy hates opera, not because he has no feelings, but because his feelings are outraged by the false mold into which the performance would force them.[13]

Tolstoy's more indulgent comedy is visible in his description of Prince Bagration's reception at the English Club in Moscow after the defeat at Austerlitz. Paradoxically (polar structure) the atmosphere is entirely one of triumphant celebration. Tolstoy alters his source to include details verging on farce, as when the prince, offered a congratulatory ode on a silver tray, fails to notice the ode and instead

---

Tzvetan Todorov (Paris 1965), pp. 76 ff.; cf. also pp. 83 and 290–92. V. Erlich, *Russian Formalism, History—Doctrine* (3rd ed., The Hague 1969), pp. 176 ff., offers general information. See further below, note 35.

[12] Book VIII, chapter ix, translated by L. and A. Maude (repr. London 1970), p. 199. Translations below are taken from this work (with occasional minor modifications) unless stated otherwise.

[13] The throw-away irony of "who represented lovers" recalls Tacitus' *spectato munere Caecinae* (below, p. 462). Tolstoy's preoccupation with the artificiality of opera recurs in *What is Art?*, chapter 1, and reminds the classical reader of Lucretius' *vitae poscaenia* (*De Rer. Nat.* IV. 1186) and Callimachus' "bombastic Muse" of tragedy (fr. 215 Pf.): cf. Horace, *A. P.* 97, *Epp.* I. 3. 14. But he did of course himself write for the stage (including a comedy during the work on *War and Peace*).

grasps the tray, thus immobilizing both his hands until he is rescued by his embarrassed hosts. Meanwhile, the estranging presence of Pierre, tormented by the thought of the duel he is to fight next day with one of his wife's lovers, lends to the whole occasion a note of disharmony, exactly as later at Borodino.

But the duel too is treated comically. Pierre has never held a pistol in his hands before, and is facing a crack shot. He blunders off the trodden path through the snow towards his adversary, fires at random into the morning mist, and scores a hit. His enemy insists on mustering his ebbing strength for his shot but, though the naive Pierre presents an ample target, he misses. It turns out that "Dolokhov the brawler, Dolokhov the bully, lived in Moscow with an old mother and a hunchback sister, and was the most affectionate of sons and brothers." Here the eighteenth-century combination of satire and sentiment is particularly in evidence.

How much more powerful must be his ironic contempt when he comes to speak of Napoleon! An example is Tolstoy's treatment of Napoleon's interview with Balashev, the emissary of Alexander I in 1812.[14] The novelist's whole aim is to show the futility of every effort to prevent what is predestined. The Russian emissary cannot in fact deliver the message he has been given, and Napoleon is so demented that he cannot control either his own words or the course of events. His quivering calf (a wonderful example of the carnival grotesque body) plays an unexpected role in the negotiations (IX. vi, pp. 277–78, slightly altered):

> Napoleon noted Balashev's embarrassment when uttering these last words: his face twitched and the calf of his left leg began to quiver rhythmically. Without moving from where he stood he began speaking in a louder tone and more hurriedly than before. During the speech that followed, Balashev, who more than once lowered his eyes, involuntarily noticed the quivering of Napoleon's left leg, which increased the more, the more Napoleon raised his voice.

What Napoleon is unable to take in during his harangue is that the earlier Russian demand for a French withdrawal from Pomerania has been replaced by the much more conciliatory request for a withdrawal over the river Niemen:

> 'You say that the demand now is that I am to withdraw beyond the Niemen before commencing negotiations, but in just the same

---

[14] See V. Shklovsky, *Mater'yal* [sic] *i Stil' v Romane L'va Tolstogo 'Voina i Mir'* (Moscow n.d. [1928]), p. 170. The treatment of the novel in this chapter is particularly indebted to this book, since it offers quite independent confirmation of Tolstoy's preference for the Alexandrian option in epic.

way two months ago the demand was that I should withdraw beyond the Vistula and the Oder, and yet you are willing to negotiate.'

He went in silence from one corner of the room to the other and again stopped in front of Balashev. Balashev noticed that his left leg was quivering faster than before and his face seemed petrified in its stern expression. This quivering of his left leg was a thing Napoleon was conscious of. 'La vibration de mon mollet gauche est un grand signe chez moi,' he remarked at a later date.

'Such demands as to retreat beyond the Vistula and Oder may be made to a Prince of Baden, but not to me!' Napoleon almost screamed, quite to his own surprise. 'If you gave me Petersburg and Moscow, I could not accept such conditions.'

Not only Callimachus, but even Ovid, might have enjoyed himself with this quivering calf. A comic device has been raised to epic intensity.

Boris Eichenbaum's critical elucidations are of particular relevance, since they seem to show that Tolstoy was in touch with a tradition of narrative, both satirical and hortatory, reaching all the way back to Byzantium.

Eichenbaum's *The Young Tolstoy*[15] starts by considering the character revealed in Tolstoy's diaries, with their constant concern for rules of behavior on the one hand, and detailed observations of the diarist's failure to live up to these rules on the other. From these polarized beginnings Tolstoy developed a mature artistic style depending on the continual juxtaposition of what Tolstoy himself called generalization and minuteness.[16] What Romantic writers had swept together into one maelstrom of feeling, where a dominating rhapsodic tone was all, was here scrupulously separated. If detail was introduced, it was used with precise accuracy. If generalization occurred, it was something apart. It is on the alternation of these contrasts that Tolstoy's work depends.

In his refusal to be carried away by Romanticism, Tolstoy looks back, in the first instance at least, to the eighteenth century. His method, because it is one of interruption, one in which all details

[15] *The Young Tolstoy*, translated and edited by G. Kern (Ann Arbor 1972).

[16] See also "Lev Tolstoi," in Eichenbaum's *Literatura* (Leningrad 1927), pp. 19–76. Compare M. String on Gregory Nazianzen, *Or.* VII (Migne); String remarks (*Untersuchungen zum Stil der Dionysiaka des Nonnos von Panopolis* [Hamburg 1966]) that Gregory has no idea of a middle course in narration. Either everything must be related, or the narrative must turn to metaphysical generalization. The Byzantine epic poet Nonnus follows Gregory, according to String (p. 90), only with even less sense of restraint. K. Lindemann, *Beobachtungen zur livianischen Periodenkunst* (Marburg 1964), observes (p. 163) that the juxtaposition of concrete and more general expressions is a constant feature of Livy's style.

mentioned have equal importance, can dispense with the unifying figure of a central hero. Tolstoy is in essence a nihilist. To every effort at romantic idealism he replies "Not so!" But the giving of this answer is all. He has no interest in telling a story for its own sake. What he offers is a series of vignettes. The unity of his work is secured, not by inner development, but by external devices such as ring-composition, parallelism, the well-marked lapse of time.[17]

In developing these essentially parasitic techniques (they all presuppose an existing body of romantic conventions from which they draw their life of ironic parody) Tolstoy refuses to impose any order. Everything that passes through the mind of the character is equally important. Nothing is suppressed for the sake of decorum. Trivialities condition great events. Conventional heroics are utterly irrelevant to the real business of war. The man who thinks he has been grazed is killed. The man who thinks he must be dead has got off with a flesh wound. Characters do not so much act as react, and their method of self-revelation is often conversation, or that other form of conversation, the interior monologue.

For the interior monologue, Tolstoy likes to cast his characters into some sort of sleep or drowsy state.[18] This gives him the chance to develop the free play of random details at which he is such a master. Meanwhile, the author himself refuses to narrate, but he is always available with an annihilating comment, undercutting the pretensions of his characters. His rational tone easily passes over into that of the orator or preacher in long set pieces. The classical observer notes that these display all the time-honored tricks of Gorgianic— and Byzantine—rhetoric.[19]

As he matured, Tolstoy gradually began to perfect the style which would shape *War and Peace*. He came to understand that he could hold a large work together by alternations of generalization and

---

[17] The epic model here had been set by Apollonius Rhodius. Whereas Callimachus turned to a dream to motivate the narratives of the first two books of the *Aetia*, Ovid, in the *Fasti*, though imitating the *Aetia*, turned to an Apollonian chronological sequence. Both techniques found a disciple in Tolstoy, and both spring from an artistic impatience with the long and formless *hen aeisma diēnekes* (Aet.-Pref. 3).

[18] Compare the opening of Proust's *À la recherche du temps perdu*. Proust looks so different from Tolstoy, until one remembers Tolstoy's *Dyetstvo* ("Childhood"), and notes the degree of nostalgia for *temps perdu* in *War and Peace*.

[19] Cf. the remarks of R. F. Christian, *Tolstoy's 'War and Peace'*, pp. 49 ff., 152 ff. Christian says (p. 153): "Running through the syntax of Tolstoy's narrative passages is every device of arrangement and balance known to Cicero and Demosthenes (excluding the rhetorical question)." The passages of argument have rhetorical questions too! But the influence of later Greek rhetoric must always be remembered in Orthodox lands: cf. K. Krumbacher, *Geschichte der Byzantinischen Litteratur* (repr. New York 1970), I, pp. 160–63.

minuteness, provided that the generalizations conveyed in themselves some sense of an ongoing process, and provided that the minuteness was organized in parallel. The historical background of the novel was ideal for the first requirement, and the parallelism of the characters was entailed by the second.

Given this mold, which was found only after long search, Tolstoy had something into which to pour out his "Not so!", his nihilistic feeling of mistrust towards intellectuals, towards all the apparatus of civilization, and his mystical longing for some kind of consolation, whether in union with "the people," or with God.

What kind of *Iliad* then was this? Certainly not that univocal glorification of the mighty favored by the Telchines.[20] Already we seem to sense, as we read Eichenbaum, and as we study the history of the manuscript changes, that, like so many of his predecessors in the tradition, Tolstoy had recovered by instinct the outlines of the epic genre as it had been modified in Alexandria, and then again in Rome: the mistrust of public faces, the irony about human pretensions, the sense of life's tragi-comedy, even farce, the firm belief in family values, in the superiority of the country to the town, the willingness to use rhetorical devices in the service of moral declarations, the indifference to mere "facts," the interest in emotional effect, in drama. The novel is not the equivalent of a versification of Herodotus. It is the projection into objective form of the deeply subjective feelings of a great artist.

One of the high points of the action is the battle outside Moscow which Napoleon ostensibly won, but which, according to Tolstoy, actually marked the beginning of the end for his ambitions. At the outset, the opposing systems of values are set in sharp contrast. Napoleon, in an edict to his troops, would appeal to them to fight for comfortable quarters and a speedy return to their country. Nothing could more arouse Tolstoy's contempt. Napoleon is *not* the hero of his work!

The Russians meanwhile were invoking the blessing of heaven. The icon of Our Lady of Smolensk was carried in solemn procession around the lines (X. xxi, pp. 470–72):

> At the summit of the hill they stopped with the icon; the men who had been holding it up by the linen bands attached to it were relieved by others, the chanters relit their censers and the service began. The hot rays of the sun beat down vertically, and a fresh soft wind played

[20] "The ancients have left us model heroic poems in which the heroes furnish the whole interest of the story, and we are still unable to accustom ourselves to the fact that for our epoch histories of that kind are meaningless" (X. xix, p. 459 in the Maudes' translation). But Callimachus might have said this.

with the hair of the bared heads and with the ribbons decorating the icon. The singing did not sound loud under the open sky. An immense crowd of bareheaded officers, soldiers and militiamen, surrounded the icon. Behind the priest and a chanter stood the notabilities, on a spot reserved for them. A bald general with a St. George's Cross on his neck stood just behind the priest's back, and without crossing himself (he was evidently a German) patiently awaited the end of the service, which he considered it necessary to hear to the end, probably to arouse the patriotism of the Russian people. Another general stood in a martial pose, crossing himself by shaking his hand in front of his chest while looking about him. Standing among the crowd of peasants, Pierre recognized several acquaintances among these notables, but did not look at them—his whole attention was absorbed in watching the serious expression on the faces of the crowd of soldiers and militiamen who were all gazing eagerly at the icon. As soon as the tired chanters, who were singing the service for the twentieth time that day, began lazily and mechanically to sing: 'Save from calamity Thy servants, O Mother of God,' and the priest and deacon chimed in: 'For to Thee under God we all flee as to an inviolable bulwark and protection,' there again kindled in all those faces the same expression of consciousness of the solemnity of the impending moment that Pierre had seen on the faces at the foot of the hill at Mozhaysk, and momentarily on many, many faces he had met that morning; and heads were bowed more frequently and hair tossed back, and sighs and the sound men made as they crossed themselves were heard.

Eventually the worshippers are joined by the commander-in-chief, Prince Kutuzov:

With a long overcoat on his exceedingly stout, round-shouldered body, with uncovered white head and puffy face showing the white ball of the eye he had lost, Kutuzov walked with plunging, swaying gait into the crowd and stopped behind the priest. . . .

When the service was over Kutuzov stepped up to the icon, sank heavily to his knees, bowed to the ground, and for a long time tried vainly to rise, but could not do so on account of his weakness and weight. His white head twitched with the effort. At last he rose, kissed the icon as a child does with naïvely pouting lips, and again bowed till he touched the ground with his hand. The other generals followed his example, then the officers, and after them with excited faces, pressing on one another, crowding, panting, and pushing, scrambled the soldiers and militiamen.

The Russian army is invincible in the long run, whatever its temporary vicissitudes may be, because it has *pietas* and ultimately *fatum* on its side. The age-old gesture of touching the ground with the hand[21] evokes primitive folk-memories far more deeply rooted than French

---

[21] Cf. *Iliad* IX. 568; *Hom. Hymn. Ap.* 333, 340; Bacchylides 5. 42, 8. 3.

cleverness. Because these are the terms of the debate, Tolstoy feels no more need than Lucan to glamorize his Caesar/Czar, or his surrogate here, Kutuzov.

The battle itself is described impressionistically, and with the aid of an uncomprehending witness. This trick was already used in the procession scene, where the "intruded and naive spectator" was played by the German general with the Order of St. George. There, the spectator was himself satirized. Elsewhere, he gives the author an opportunity to satirize the events he witnesses. Natasha's visit to the opera has already been quoted.

A supreme example of this comic procedure is found at Borodino. Pierre, wandering over the battlefield, has often been excused as part of a world where class distinction was so strong that a gentleman civilian's right to wander in frock coat and tall hat around a scene of bloody carnage could go unchallenged. But Tolstoy's contemporaries, who presumably knew about class distinction, objected strongly to this piece of improbability. Tolstoy answered by referring to the case of Prince Vyazemsky, who had, though a civilian, been present at the battle. Unfortunately for this defense, Prince Vyazemsky was alive when *War and Peace* was published, and he was one of the objectors. It was true that he was present as a civilian (i.e. as a non-professional soldier), but he was in charge of local peasant militia, and by no means a superfluous observer on the scene. V. Shklovsky comments that what has happened is the peculiar realization of a metaphor.[22] A civilian present among the military has become a civilian present only as a civilian. A particular historical fact has been exploited by Tolstoy for his own estranging purposes, and so has been turned into a stylistic device.

Tolstoy's use of stylized devices is particularly evident in his description not only of Borodino, but also of Austerlitz. The contemporary satirical periodical *Iskra* remarked in 1868 that no one could paint a picture of Austerlitz from the description given by Count Tolstoy, since all he offers is sun, smoke, two running soldiers and Napoleon's white, small hand. The criticism is excellent. Its only weakness is that it reveals a total ignorance of how the classical epic tradition in fact has always described battles.[23]

Of the descriptions of Austerlitz and Borodino Shklovsky remarks that, what his source gives in points, Tolstoy extends to a linear

[22] Once again, the "Aristophanes effect." See above, p. 415 note 50.

[23] Above, pp. 421 ff. Cf. P. Scheller, *De hellenistica historiae conscribendae arte* (Leipzig 1911), pp. 57 ff., "De evidentia atque affectibus": E. Fraenkel on Aeschylus, *Agamemnon* 65. On Livy's battles, see K. Witte, "Ueber die Form der Darstellung in Livius' Geschichtswerk," *Rheinisches Museum* 65 (1910), 381 ff.; on Virgil's, R. Heinze, *Virgils epische Technik* (4th ed., Stuttgart 1957), pp. 193 ff.

treatment in his artistic prose. Even the symbolic emphasis on the
sun at the beginning of the battle may have been caused by the fact
that "the sun of Austerlitz" was a proverbial expression, one lending
itself to emphasis. It has already been seen that contemporary critics
disliked his whole approach to his account of Borodino.

At Borodino, Shklovsky remarks, Napoleon becomes a puppet
dancing without music. Details are heaped up, but shifted from the
setting where they would have made sense. Motives are passed over
in silence.[24] Napoleon's toilet before the battle, his rubbing down
and sprinkling with eau-de-cologne, are carefully described. But in
fact these details are taken from the journal kept by Napoleon's
doctor on St. Helena, where the emperor was living in a hot climate,
and had very little to occupy his time. There is no evidence that they
were his routine on campaign.[25]

Once again, images are employed to enhance the meaning of this
eve of battle scene. The allusion to chess, for example, is developed
from an incidental mention in the histories until it becomes a refrain
in the novel.

Tolstoy's sketch-plan of Borodino and analysis of Napoleon's tactics
may have been approved by military specialists but, as found in the
book, Borodino still remains a literary battle because its military
features are pushed to one side in the treatment, and the center is
occupied by Napoleon's fruitless wait for news of decisive victory.
The most glorious moment of eulogistic epic is replaced by a deliberate
let-down, a non-event.

The author's moral bias comes particularly to the fore in what he
writes of the end of Borodino:

> Several tens of thousands of human beings lay dead in varying
> positions and uniforms on the fields and meadows which belonged to

---

[24] Cf. Polybius on Phylarchus (II. 56. 13); he accuses the exponent of "tragic"
history of not ascribing a cause to events. See further E. Burck, *Die Erzählungskunst
des T. Livius* (Berlin 1934), p. 212 note 3. K. Lindemann remarks (*Beobachtungen zur
livianischen Periodenkunst*, pp. 163–64) that the discrepancy between thinking and
action in an individual can at first be so great as to baffle the effort to connect them.
This feature is especially found where Livy is concerned about vividness. See
B. Walker, *The Annals of Tacitus* (Manchester 1952), p. 67, on Tacitus' exploitation
of this device to discredit Tiberius at *Ann.* III. 60.

[25] It is strange that Shklovsky, who believed that in poetry "L'objet est perçu non
pas comme une partie de l'espace, mais pour ainsi dire dans sa continuité" (*Théorie
de la littérature*, ed. Todorov, pp. 94–95), who wrote on *Literature and the Cinema*
(Berlin 1923) and was Eisenstein's biographer (Moscow 1973), does not see that this
technique of "flash forward" in time was already exploited by Virgil (e.g. *Aen.* IV.
669–71) and even by Homer (in the parting of Hector and Andromache:
W. Schadewaldt, *Iliasstudien* [Leipzig 1938], p. 21). It is a fine example of "vertical
time." Napoleon is already in exile before the battle begins.

the Davydovs and to the Crown serfs, on those fields and meadows, on which for hundreds of years at the same season the peasants of the villages of Borodino, Gorki, Shevardin and Semonovsk had gathered their harvests and pastured their cattle. At the field dressing stations over a space of three acres the grass and earth were drenched with blood. Crowds of wounded and unwounded men from different commands, with frightened faces, from one side were toiling back to Mozhaysk, from the other, back to Valuevo. Other crowds, weary and hungry, led by their officers, were going forward. A third group stood in their positions and continued to fire.[26]

Over the whole field, previously so gaily beautiful, with the flashes of the bayonets and smoke clouds in the morning sun, now hung a mist of damp and smoke, and there was a strange sour smell of gunpowder and blood. Clouds gathered, and a shower began to drizzle on the killed, on the wounded, on the frightened, and on the exhausted and doubting men. It was as if it were saying: "Enough, enough, you men. Stop! Come to your senses! What are you doing?"[27]

Compare this with Vitellius' visit to the field of Bedriacum (Tacitus, *Histories* II. 70):

Then Vitellius bent his steps towards Cremona. After viewing Caecina's show he was seized by the desire to set foot on the fields of Bedriacum and to survey with his own eyes the traces of his recent victory. It was a horrible and shocking sight. Less than forty days had elapsed since the battle; and maimed bodies, lopped off limbs, decaying shapes of men and horses, the ground tainted and foul, the trampled trees and crops presented a scene of dreadful desolation. No less grisly was that part of the road which the inhabitants of Cremona had strewn with laurel and roses, after raising altars and slaying victims in truly royal style; optimistic for the moment, these acts were in due course their authors' undoing. Valens and Caecina were on hand, and pointed out the combat areas. Here the legionaries' column had broken through, from here the cavalry had charged, there the reserves had performed their outflanking maneuver. By this time the tribunes and commanders, each extolling his own merits, were confounding falsehood, truth and exaggeration. The common soldiers too left the road with shouts of triumph as they recognized the field of conflict, as they contemplated with astonishment the mound of arms, the heaps of corpses. Some were moved by thoughts of fickle fortune to tears of compassion. But not so Vitellius: he averted his gaze, and did not shudder at all those thousands of his fellow citizens, left without a

---

[26] Livy's trick of imposing (a sometimes spurious) clarity on the narrative should be noted here: Witte, pp. 383 ff.

[27] *Voina i Mir*, Tom tretiy, chast' vtoraya, gl. xxxix (Moscow 1957), pp. 276–77: my translation.

grave. Indeed his joy was so great, and his ignorance of approaching doom so profound, that he began a sacrifice to the gods of the locality.

Like Tacitus, the Hellenistic and yet unmistakably Roman historian, Tolstoy too is impressed by the horror of battle, and by the contrast between peaceful rustic toil and bloody war. Like Tacitus, he sets the usual steely inhumanity of the commander (Napoleon) against the more human reaction of others. Tolstoy enhances his picture by turning to other perceptions than sight: the sense of smell, the feel of the rain. Tacitus suggests this same contrast: decaying corpses, the tainted ground, and yet a part of the road strewn with sweet-smelling laurel and roses. Vitellius is ignorant that his triumph is to be short-lived. But so is Napoleon. Tolstoy preaches more explicitly. But in both writers the description is conditioned, not by a sober effort to communicate plain facts, but by the emotion-laden, artistic drive towards that "second truth" of which a modern critic has written so finely.[28]

The Roman historian anticipates the Russian novelist in a number of other ways. *Spectato munere Caecinae* ("after viewing Caecina's show"), ostensibly factual, but implying a comparison in Vitellius' mind between the combats of hired gladiators and the carnage of civil strife, is in Tolstoy's best manner of oblique irony. In his description, Tacitus is savagely parodying the "old soldier" topos, found for example in Virgil and Ovid, but reversing its effect.[29] Tacitus' *flexit . . . flexit* (*Vitellius Cremonam flexit/at non Vitellius flexit oculos*) illustrates a form of ring-composition as old as Homer,[30] and Tolstoy, with his parallelism between sun and mist, smoke and smoke at the beginning and end of his battle, is using a similar device. Both Tacitus and Tolstoy are interested in locating their battles in time. In both authors, military values are judged by humane standards, and found wanting.

What then *is* the subject of *War and Peace*? An unenlightened reader might be tempted to answer this question by giving some sort of summary of the story, although even he would find it difficult to assert that this historical epic is a glorification of the mighty. The Formalists however would have none of this. The story of *War and Peace* is what they call its *fabula*, what classical scholars would call its

---

[28] B. Walker, *The Annals of Tacitus*, p. 196.

[29] Cf. *Aen.* II. 27 ff.; Ovid, *Heroides* I. 31 ff. For the reversal of the effect see Lucan VII. 786 ff., which itself goes on to parody a motif familiar from Psalm 23:5: "Thou preparest a table before me in the presence of mine enemies." Compare Shklovsky on Tolstoy's use of the "reversed detail" and Lucan's "Let me say the opposite!" (below, p. 468; above, p. 217).

[30] Above, p. 13 notes 17 and 18; p. 272 note 59.

myth. The "subject" (*syuzhet*) is what the author does with his myth, the treatment, the system of devices in their mutual interaction.[31] The working of this system on the material offered by the *fabula* deforms it. The author selects what is relevant to his literary purpose and throws away the rest.[32]

Tolstoy's deformations are important because he was rebuilding the epic style against a background that was unfavorable. His efforts drew some familiar criticisms. The novel, he was told, lacked unity. Shklovsky finds a parallel here between Tolstoy's procedures and those of Thackeray's *Vanity Fair* (1847–48), not in the sense of direct borrowings, but in a shared tendency to parody the conventional trappings of the family novel. What Tolstoy has really done is to take this kind of novel, with its romantic warmheartedness, and to exploit its positions ironically. Pierre marries his Natasha in the end—and Tolstoy undercuts the romance by remarking on his toothlessness.

At the same time, in exploiting this family genre, Tolstoy renews it by some unexpected omissions. For example, though the whole domestic side of the story has been working towards the final marriage of Pierre and Natasha, Tolstoy simply omits any description of the proposal scene. The affair culminates during one of the novel's intervals.

In general, the extraordinary mass of material which Tolstoy had to deploy compels him to make great use of the technique of interruptions. The characters are moved in fits and starts. Transitions are left out.[33] The heroes are often, at moments of extreme tension, just abandoned.

Tolstoy liked to claim that his book was the product of long and exacting historical researches. Shklovsky asserts the obvious contrary, that it is the work of an artist, recasting material relatively easily accessible, not the dispassionate study of a scholar and "realist." The protests by contemporary reviewers, some of whom still remembered the events described, are proof of this.

Shklovsky therefore views Tolstoy as, like every other artist, "deforming" his material. Locked in his humdrum world of everyday,

---

[31] Cf. Shklovsky, *O Teorii Prozy*, index, s.v. "Syuzhet," and particularly the article on Sterne, pp. 139 ff. The detailed application of his theories to *War and Peace* is made by Shklovsky in *Mater'yal i Stil'* (above, note 14).

[32] Horace says this of Homer, *A. P.* 149–50. Thucydides has been accused of doing the same thing.

[33] Compare Eisenstein's theory of "play without transitions" described by Shklovsky in his biography of Eisenstein, p. 25. L. Illig notes this interrupted manner as characteristic of Pindar: *Zur Form der Pindarischen Erzählung* (Berlin 1932), p. 22. Pindar's *gnomai* ultimately become Tolstoy's chapters of moralizing reflection. See further Heinze, *Virgils epische Technik*, pp. 405 ff.

the average man is concerned to automate his responses. He does not want an agonizing epistemological debate every time he reaches for the coffee pot, or dully observes his wife at the kitchen sink. The artist tries to reverse this process, to stop his audience from recognizing things and compel it instead to see them. He uses any trick he can think of to dislocate our experience of the world, to prevent us from imposing our normal standards and prejudices on our perceptions and force us to observe things as if they had just been newly created. This explains why art advances, not in smooth transitions, but in violence and repudiation.[34] Once the tricks of the previous generation lose their novelty and are automated in their turn, they must be cast aside and replaced by something more novel, more shocking. This process is called by Shklovsky "estrangement,"[35] and it is upon Tolstoy's mastery of it that his fame depends.

Tolstoy's estrangement or deformation of the historical material he had available for *War and Peace* is not however a matter of simply recovering for his readers an innocent eye. It is fueled by his Swiftian irony, his cold and "horsy" contempt for human pretensions. But this irony is not just metaphysical, directed at all human affairs indifferently. An aristocrat,[36] hating the changes occurring in contemporary Russia, and the emergence of the meritocracy, those enabled by education to rise above their proper stations, Tolstoy saw in Napoleon, and to a lesser extent in the Russian reforming statesman Speransky, the type of the new intellectual, the rootless, classless *raznochinets*, who fancied that, because he had passed an examination, he could fathom the workings of God's universe. These men had to be shown that their sophistries were worthless. *War and Peace* therefore, opposing the soul-searching profundities of blue-blooded Russian nobles, whose only teachers paradoxically could be the uneducated, natural peasantry, to the trivialities of French and frenchified smart

[34] See above, p. 70. Shklovsky's view of art is quite literally life-enhancing. It makes us live more intensely.

[35] Cf. the ancient *deinosis*, a species of *auxesis*: D. A. Russell on *De Subl.* 11–12.2 (pp. 107 ff. of his edition). Eisenstein was interested in *amplificatio* (the Latin name for *auxesis*): above, p. 416 and note 55. See further B. Eichenbaum, *Lev Tolstoi*, II, p. 339, "magnification."

[36] E. Wedel (*op. cit.*, pp. 146–47) quotes an amazing fragment from the rough draft of *War and Peace* beginning "I am an aristocrat." On p. 183 Wedel notes Tolstoy's declaration "I am an aristocrat because I cannot believe in the profound intellect, refined taste and great honor of a man who picks his nose and whose soul converses with God." That Pierre, who incorporated certain features of his creator (Wedel, p. 140 note 30), should have had this unfortunate mannerism in an early version can only be the sign of a deep-seated ambivalence in Tolstoy himself. See further Christian, pp. 102–03.

alecks, is a deeply tendentious piece of writing, as tendentious, the classical scholar will add, as Pindar or Thucydides.

Once Tolstoy had perfected his method of estrangement, the actual material was no longer of prime importance. Naive readers were impressed with the historical reconstruction of a vanished period. But Turgenev had other thoughts:

> Tolstoy amazes his reader with the tongue of Alexander's shoe, with Speransky's laugh, and compels him to think that he must know all about it if he has even penetrated as far as these trivialities. . . . But the trivialities are all he knows. . . . And so far as Tolstoy's alleged psychology is concerned, there is much to be said: there is no genuine development in any character, only the old trick of giving us hesitations, the trillings of the same feeling, attitude. . . . I love, says he, but really I hate, and so on. . . . Tolstoy does not know any other psychology, or else he intentionally ignores it.[37]

Eisenstein was later to note and imitate this use of the telling detail, which forces the audience to work out the rest of the picture. It was a Greek ploy already recommended by Aristotle's successor Theophrastus in his discussion of the plain style:

> These, then, are the main essentials of persuasiveness; to which may be added that indicated by Theophrastus when he says that not all possible points should be punctiliously and tediously elaborated, but some should be left to the comprehension and inference of the hearer, who when he perceives what you have left unsaid becomes not only your hearer but your witness, and a very friendly witness too. For he thinks himself intelligent because you have afforded him the means of showing his intelligence. It seems like a slur on your hearer to tell him everything as though he were a simpleton.[38]

It was also Callimachean, and Tolstoy's favorite writer, Sterne, had been well aware of it in the "classical" eighteenth century:

> Writing, when properly managed (as you may be sure I think mine is) is but a different name for conversation. As no one, who knows what he is about in good company, would venture to talk all;—so no author, who understands the just boundaries of decorum and good-breeding, would presume to think all: The truest respect which you can pay to the reader's understanding, is to halve this matter amicably, and leave him something to imagine, in his turn, as well as yourself.

---

[37] Letter of Turgenev from Baden-Baden, Feb. 2, 1868, quoted by Shklovsky, *Mater'yal i Stil'*, pp. 86–87.

[38] Theophrastus is cited here from Demetrius, *De Eloc.* 222, tr. W. Rhys Roberts. See above, p. 411 note 37 and p. 430 with note 99 (Timanthes). Cf. Tolstoy's letter of Sept. 5, 1909, to V. G. Chertkov on the casually thrown out artistic detail (quoted by Christian, p. 138).

For my own part, I am eternally paying him compliments of this kind, and do all that lies in my power to keep his imagination as busy as my own.[39]

Turgenev's error lay in not recognizing the antiquity of the device. But on the other hand his assessment of Tolstoy's *odi et amo* is extremely shrewd. This ambivalence was layered deep within the writer's whole attitude to life. It cannot be our task here to do more than note its kinship with Callimachean, and Virgilian, ambivalences.

Tolstoy was fond of using "non-specific epithets," adjectives which, instead of describing concretely, evoke emotions. Early in the novel, for example, Hippolyte appears at a fashionable St. Petersburg soirée wearing pants that are "the color of the thigh of a frightened nymph" (I. iii, p. 15):

He was dressed in a dark-green dress coat, knee-breeches of the colour of *cuisse de nymphe effrayée*, as he called it, shoes and silk stockings.

"Perhaps this expression characterizes Hippolyte," comments Shklovsky severely,[40] "but it by no means characterizes a color." But of course it characterizes Hippolyte, since comedy is primarily concerned with character, *ethopoïïa*! By inserting "as he called it" Tolstoy makes it quite clear that he is looking through Hippolyte's eyes. The irony of the proper name, which recalls both Racine and Euripides, stands in biting contrast with the foppish, self-indulgent young wastrel who bears it.[41]

Tolstoy commits further sins of this kind. He has the habit of throwing into his descriptions adjectives like "massively tall," "huge," "massive," "big," "high," which substitute impressionism for detail. In other words, although Shklovsky does not realize it, Tolstoy behaves just like Virgil, Dante, Tasso, Milton . . . and Tacitus.[42]

In the course of exploiting these emotion-laden adjectives, Tolstoy is led to use another ancient device, and that is repetition.[43] Shklovsky

---

[39] *Tristram Shandy*, II, ch. XI (Everyman edition, London 1961), p. 79. For Callimachus, see above, p. 20.

[40] Shklovsky, p. 91.

[41] The use of "speaking names" in epic is as old as Homer. The device is used with varying degrees of intensity. That Tolstoy was not excluding a certain allusion to classical myth is suggested by the use of *Hélène* for Hippolyte's seductive (and even incestuous?) sister.

[42] Cf. F. J. Worstbrock, *Elemente einer Poetik der Aeneis* (Münster 1963), pp. 193 ff., 245 ff., 256 ff. For Tacitus, B. Walker, *The Annals of Tacitus*, p. 192.

[43] Two types must be distinguished: (1) Repetition where the author merely means the same thing, which was not a stylistic fault in classical antiquity (see E. Norden on *Aen.* VI. 423, R. G. Austin on *Aen.* II. 505); (2) Significant repetition, of which, for example, anaphora is simply a special case. For (2) cf. Demetrius, *De Eloc.* 212 (the "poetic" historian Ctesias, who is interestingly discussed under the rubric of the plain style).

compares Tolstoy's account of the execution of Vereshchagin, the scape-goat held responsible for setting fire to Moscow just before its abandonment to the French, with the source from which it is drawn, to show how in the novel the phrase "a young fellow in a sheepskin coat trimmed with fox fur" is repeated eight times. "Cut him down!" is repeated four times. This is not to be dismissed as "rhetorical repetition" (although it is that). By taking the story out of its normal boundaries with this trick the novelist estranges it. He makes us attend to the details and, since he has a powerful tale to tell, with their help he compels our imaginations and feelings to work.

The same trick may be used for comic irony. In the course of his mission to Napoleon, the Russian emissary Balashev encounters Marshal Murat, elevated by his master to the throne of Naples. Carried away by his senseless title (he is another *raznochinets!*), Murat is wearing a gold-embroidered uniform. Tolstoy insists on mentioning it no less than four times, and the title, or some allusion to it, nineteen times.

But symbolic details may be used rather differently. Shklovsky singles out Tolstoy's habit of dwelling on the "little princess's" (Princess Bolkonskaya's) short upper lip.[44] This particular is repeated throughout the novel. It becomes a leitmotif. In reducing the princess to such sketchy proportions that a reference to her lip is enough to conjure up memories of her previous appearances, Tolstoy is working with his customary technique of the "minimum device." Just one sign out of a whole system is used if it is enough to do the trick.

A similar technique is found in the characterization of both Napoleon and Speransky by their white hands. But the lip and the hands work differently. The lip works by the principle of inequality (the princess is after all more than her lip). The white hands work by the principle of equivalence (there is no more to Napoleon and Speransky than their mutual reluctance to dirty their hands with a job of real work). Both these devices may be employed together in the structure of the novel because they are, in the last analysis, both devices of emphasis, and of course devices of comic distortion (the "grotesque body"). Thus it becomes necessary to explain the differences between Tolstoy's characters by *métrage* ("footage"), as the film director would say or, as the student of the classical epic tradition may say, by the total of lines devoted to them. The stock epithet, already prominent in Homer, and adapted by Virgil, is an early version of Tolstoy's "minimum device."

Tolstoy's indifference to the facts of history is proved by his re-use of details occurring in his *Sebastopol Stories* to enhance the vividness

[44] Shklovsky, pp. 96 ff.

of *War and Peace*. The details introduced fall into two categories, indifferent and reversed. The final text of the novel had been criticized as lacking clarity by comparison with the earlier version because of omissions made by the author. Shklovsky calls such criticisms naive. It was Tolstoy's deliberate policy in his work to make use of contradictory details. The whole psychology of his heroes is founded on the contradiction between the real cause of their behavior and their pretext for acting.[45] Their psychology consists in their selection of grounds for decisions already made. So although the critic Pokrovsky found it odd that Prince Andrei should still smile even after Tolstoy had changed his thoughts from cheerful in the first version to gloomy in the second, Shklovsky remarks that the author himself found it necessary that a man should smile while talking about something sad.

Examples of reversed detail in Tolstoy are these.[46] The historical record of Napoleon's retreat from Moscow stated that the French troops, reduced to eating horse meat, were even more distressed by their lack of salt, which they were forced to make up by using gunpowder. The taste was horrible. Tolstoy reverses the detail, and makes the taste palatable. Elsewhere he offers a description of a soldier being flogged for pilfering. The officer witnessing the scene is said to be suffering, while the victim's groans are referred to as "forced." For those present at the death of Prince Andrei, the sight of the capital city of Moscow burning on the horizon is of secondary importance.

Since the hero is serving as a means of deforming and estranging the material, it follows that he exists for the sake of the narrative, and not the narrative for him. This recovery of an Aristotelian position (that the "soul" of tragedy is the myth, and not the soul of the protagonist) is one of a number of parallels between Formalist and ancient criticism.[47]

Tolstoy's indifference to his heroes is shown, for example, by his vagueness over Pierre's title and surname until it came to the moment when, for the sake of the plot, he had to make the surname add up to the number of the Beast in the Book of Revelation. Then and only then was the surname fixed. So with Prince Andrei. Tolstoy explained in a letter that originally he needed a dashing young officer

---

[45] K. Lindemann, *op. cit.*, p. 163, finds the same thing in Livy, as does M. String in Nonnus, *op. cit.*, pp. 16 ff.

[46] For this device in Callimachus we may note the triumphant *phyllobolia* which nevertheless recalls autumn (*Hecale*, fr. 260. 12). At *Hecale*, fr. 238. 29 the north wind brought on a storm.

[47] See Erlich, *op. cit.*, p. 189; E. M. Thompson, *Russian Formalism and Anglo-American New Criticism* (The Hague–Paris 1971), p. 53; Guido Morpurgo-Tagliabue, "La stilistica di Aristotele e lo strutturalismo," *Lingua e Stile* 2 (1967), 1–18.

to be killed at Austerlitz. Later he found this officer useful in the rest of the story, and so let him off with a severe wound (his fatal wound was now reserved for Borodino). Because it was inconvenient to have a random character, Tolstoy made him the son of old Prince Bolkonsky.

Tolstoy passed for a representative of Russian "Realism," but for a realist he had an extraordinary preoccupation with states of mind removed from the normal. His interest in details rather than in persons is shown by the fragments of a dream which he had written up, and which he tried to fit into the story of both Pierre and Nicholas Rostov. This detachment from individual character again confirms the pre-eminence for him of the myth. But when we find him using a fact taken from the biography of the detested Speransky for Prince Andrei,[48] into whom has gone a great deal of his author, we are confronted with something more than mere indifference to character. The author's deeply contradictory view of himself now comes into play. His corrosive irony about others was, in the last resort, the product of his dissatisfaction with himself.[49]

A literary device does not fulfill in every instance the original role it had when it was first introduced. The function of a device is not the same as its genesis. It may even happen that a device, like the coloring on a cheap print, will smudge its outline and acquire in the course of use an opposite tendency.[50] In Tolstoy's case, the result of his tricks was that the very society he wanted to rehabilitate (the landed nobility) ended up as estranged.

Tolstoy wrote like a *raznochinets*, whatever his view of them may have been. He had the same "debunking" mistrust of the established order, and the same interest in psychological motivation. His novel, instead of a glorification, became an attack on the society he was describing.

Literary devices are deployed in language, and Shklovsky begins his discussion of Tolstoy's language by emphasizing the survival of the genres, with their different linguistic levels.[51] This is certainly ancient terrain. Tolstoy was in trouble with the critics for his characteristic use of language because they judged him by the standards

---

[48] Shklovsky, *op. cit.*, pp. 121–22: cf. however Christian, p. 85.

[49] It is interesting that the elegant Prince Andrei can think of himself in a famous scene (Book VI, chapter 1 in the Maudes' translation) as a gnarled and twisted oak. Tolstoy's disintegrated personality (Andrei/Pierre: cf. Vronsky/Levin in *Anna Karenina*) is ultimately at the basis of his disintegrated style. Eichenbaum well compares Tolstoy's dissolution of love in marriage into "the need for sexual intercourse and the rational desire for a lifelong companion" (*The Young Tolstoy*, p. 42).

[50] Shklovsky, *Mater'yal i Stil'*, p. 111.

[51] Shklovsky, pp. 198 ff.

of Turgenev.[52] His repetitions were particularly vexing. "His style piles up periods with repeated words like medieval Latin," wrote one reviewer in 1870. What Tolstoy had done was to abandon Turgenev's elegant smoothness for the style of memoirs and war books, of commentaries and official histories. In all this, he was showing some concern for the "transrational" aspect of language, which played so important a part in Formalist doctrine.[53] Whenever *how* a thing is said attracts attention, extra-semantic associations give rise to trans-rational echoes and reverberations. In using a peculiar, "difficult" style Tolstoy was calling attention to the "how," and therefore invoking the transrational. The use of French in the novel deserves especial study here.[54] It helps the estrangement, as, for example, when Napoleon lards his speech with words like "les popes," "la mosquée" (the Cathedral of St. Basil!), and so becomes that phenomenon which always irritates Russians so much, the Westerner who finds their country picturesque, odd, and in the last resort, barbaric, because he has forgotten that the Roman Empire had an eastern half. The funny lingo of the foreigner is already a comic trick in Aristophanes.

Contemporary critics could not decide to what genre *War and Peace* belonged. It was not a novel, and it had no unity of action. The material had not been mastered. There was too little about the heroes, and the intrusion of quasi-philosophical arguments was out of order. In fact, the novel was unfinished. On the literary scene of its day it was like some huge sivatherium, or an Indian idol with six arms.[55]

---

[52] "The man who needs a novel in the epic sense of the word will find me no use": letter of Turgenev to Goncharov, cited by Shklovsky, *Mater'yal i Stil'*, p. 222. Contrast Tolstoy's diary for January 3, 1863: "The epic genre is becoming for me the only natural one" (Wedel, *op. cit.*, p. 15). The fact that Thomas Mann nevertheless found Turgenev useful for the writing of his epic *Buddenbrooks* is an example of that alternation of genres which, according to B. Tomashevsky, was one of the Formalists' most important discoveries. It certainly has its relevance to the understanding of ancient Alexandrian poetry.

[53] The transrational element (*zaum'*) is what makes "five" better poetry than "six" in Shakespeare's "Full fathom five thy father lies." The experiments of the twentieth-century Futurist poets Kruchënykh and Khlebnikov have their ancient counterparts in those of Heracleodorus and the *kritikoi* (see, for example, J. F. D'Alton, *Roman Literary Theory and Criticism* [repr. New York 1962], p. 397), but also in all Alexandrian poets, notably Euphorion. This makes chapters 20–22 of Aristotle's *Poetics* probably the most basic of the whole treatise. See further B. A. van Groningen, *La poésie verbale grecque*, Koninklijke Nederlandse Akademie van Wetenschappen, Letterkunde, N. R. 16 (1953), pp. 169–272: I. Ambrogio, *Formalismo e Avanguardia in Russia* (Rome 1968), pp. 81 ff.: G. Morpurgo-Tagliabue (above, note 47).

[54] Shklovsky, pp. 206 ff. Compare M. Friedberg, "The Comic Element in *War and Peace*," *Indiana Slavic Studies* 4 (1967), 101 ff.

[55] One hears echoes of the misapprehensions which have greeted so many epics in the tradition, e.g. the *Aeneid*, the *Divine Comedy*, the *Orlando Furioso*, the *Gerusalemme Liberata*.

Shklovsky ends by remarking that Tolstoy intended to write a novel of the traditional type, but that his creation burst the bounds set for it. Perhaps the incompatibility of the genre with the content, about which the critics so frequently complain, is one of the genre's most essential phenomena. The remark is acute. This is because the novel always has, when exploited by an artist of sufficient imagination, epic potential.

The features of Tolstoy's practice in *War and Peace* which make him particularly akin to the classical epic tradition as it was "deformed" by Callimachus and his successors are these:

1. In spite of its glorious theme, his epic is not a stilted and monotonous eulogy of the mighty. Its shows affinities with humbler genres, such as satire, romance, fable, comedy. It avoids or parodies conventional heroics. It uses the country to judge, and condemn, the town.[56]
2. It is dramatic, based in the final version on dialogue rather than description, and on a technique of rapidly changing scenes.
3. It is "subjective" and selective. It psychologizes. It undercuts *all* its heroes with the aid of an omnipresent irony.
4. Because the author has an ambiguous attitude towards his characters, the total impression produced by his work was such that readers could not decide whether it had eulogized or denigrated.[57]
5. It permits long digressions which reinforce its structure.[58]
6. It abandons the accepted and trite manner (of Turgenev) in favor of a complex and difficult style intended to estrange the narrative. Yet this complex style is traditional enough to recall "medieval Latin."

[56] Shklovsky notes this technique in the ancient Greek romance: cf. "La construction de la nouvelle et du roman" in Todorov, *Théorie de la littérature* (above, note 25), p. 186. At the same time that he was working on his epic *War and Peace* Tolstoy wrote his comedy of manners *An Infected Family* (1863): cf. Eichenbaum, *Lev Tolstoi*, II, pp. 212 ff. Again, one detects a pattern familiar in the tradition, e.g. Homer's *Margites*, the comedies of Callimachus, Ariosto, Racine.

[57] Compare the conflicting views on the morality of Aeneas' killing of Turnus at the end of the *Aeneid*, and on what Mann's *Doktor Faustus* did. See above, p. 415 for *sententias suas Vergilius velut contraria sentiendo dissolvat* in Virgil.

[58] Cf. the digressions in the *Hecale*. But the fact that the old crow proses on (fr. 260) as Hecale does to Theseus hints that this digression at least may have been linked to the main narrative by the Tolstoyan method of parallelism. On the structural relevance of the Archemorus episode in Statius' *Thebaid*, cf. "De Statio Epico Animadversiones," *Latomus* 34 (1975), 86 ff.

7. The carefully selected, telling detail and the "non-specific," emotionally charged epithet (like Virgil's *ingens*) demand the reader's collaboration and therefore involvement.[59]

8. The novel is "learned." It depends on an existing genre, the family novel, and uses the reader's knowledge of and expectations about this traditional type of story both to supplement gaps and, at times, to create an ironic reversal. Study of the manuscripts also shows that a great deal of material drawn from Tolstoy's wide acquaintance with literature in many European languages helped to form the often deceptively simple final statement.

9. Tolstoy makes great use of repetition (parallelism) of image, metaphor and actual words. Here, his debt to and interest in music is evident.

10. The work is didactic, yet it plays with the normal themes of didacticism (strict attention to facts) in favor of an overriding moral conviction.[60]

A deeply personal, anti-heroic, comic epic written by an author indebted to so classical a period as the eighteenth century (Rousseau, Sterne, Stendhal) about the national struggle against the French invaders is perhaps not so far removed from the classical tradition as might have appeared. We are confronted by a recurring phenomenon. Classicism, as defined by the critics, had obscured the classical achievement. A Greek hero meant for Tolstoy a museum piece. Turning to literature rather than scholarship for his inspiration, he discovered what the real classical tradition was in spite of its official custodians.

Inattention to the tradition has prevented a proper emphasis on certain important questions in the understanding of *War and Peace*. Even Shklovsky's brilliance is ultimately inadequate. Yet the answers to these questions might both illumine what Tolstoy did and make his novel's kinship with Callimachean art even more apparent.

In the first place, it is well known that Tolstoy was ardently fond of music. The study of Dostoevsky's poetic in musical terms has been

---

[59] Tolstoy shared the ancient (Aristotelian/Horatian) belief in the need for emotional engagement by the writer with his material: cf. *What is Art?*, tr. A. Maude (repr. London 1969), p. 229, and Maude's introduction, pp. vi ff. See further Eichenbaum, "Lev Tolstoi" (in *Literatura*: above, note 16), p. 72; and above, pp. 42–43 and 413 note 44.

[60] Tolstoy was anxious that Russia's future soldiers should not be demoralized by a false picture of war: Zaidenschnur, pp. 139, 349, 370.

extremely fruitful.[61] The statement by the youthful Eichenbaum that Tolstoy's alternations of generalization and minuteness in *War and Peace* display a complete contempt for architectonics[62] is contradicted by the proof of his concern with rearrangement and length in the manuscripts, and by Shklovsky's remark that Tolstoy's works are "formalisées comme des pièces musicales."[63] Repetition, so common in Tolstoy, has been called music's most characteristic procedure. A full-length examination of the novel and its many voices in these terms would be instructive.[64]

It is proper therefore to ask about the role of the lyrical element in the novel.[65] The alternation of lyricism and prosaic flatness is exploited by Eliot, for example, in *Four Quartets*. What is the effect of Tolstoy's alternations between exalted emotion and prosaic argumentation?

In this regard, it is also proper to ask what is the nature of the authorial "I." In particular, who is the "I" who makes all those sweeping statements about the historical process, rightly compared with the (Byzantine) preacher or the orator rather than the dispassionate philosopher? Can we urge that the "I" of ordinary narrative is never to be confused with the "I" of real life, while assuming that the "I" of argument *in this context* is the "real" Tolstoy? At a guess one would say that the so-called historico-philosophical parts of the novel are just as much—and just as little—fiction as the rest. They are certainly emotionally loaded. If their status could be determined, the dogmatism might dissolve into assertive self-consolation, a whistling in the dark by a man afraid.

What is the relation of Tolstoy's "estranged" perception to that of the child,[66] and to the naive tone so popular with Alexandrianizing writers?

[61] M. Bakhtin, *Problemy Poetiki Dostoevskogo* (Moscow 1963), is careful to insist (e.g. pp. 29–30) that his reference to Dostoevsky's "polyphony" is only metaphorical. But the term must point to something shared with music, and it was a favorite analogy with Eisenstein, a practicing artist. See further N. S. Trubetzkoy, *Dostoevskij als Künstler* (The Hague 1964), pp. 145, 154.

[62] *The Young Tolstoy*, p. 32.

[63] "La construction de la nouvelle et du roman" (above, note 56), p. 185 (= *O Teorii Prozy*, p. 62).

[64] Christian, who is sure (*op. cit.*, p. 147) that Thomas Mann saw in Tolstoy only a sprawling richness, is nevertheless impelled on p. 149 to speak of Tolstoy's repetitions as musical leitmotifs. When Mann wrote his Wagnerian *Buddenbrooks* with Tolstoy's bust on his desk, had he, the artist, failed to observe what the critic sees?

[65] Wedel, p. 15: "A return or an effort at a return to lyricism" (Tolstoy's diary for Feb. 23, 1863). This was in spite of his rejection of Turgenev, and shows how deeply the lyrical impulse is contained within Alexandrian epic.

[66] Eichenbaum, *Lev Tolstoi*, II, p. 111, notes the importance of Tolstoy's article of 1862, "Who ought to learn to write from whom—peasant children from us or we

What use does the novel make of literary models, not as collections of devices, but as sounding boards to secure ironic or reinforcing resonance? The original title, *All's Well that Ends Well*, must evoke for the English ear Shakespeare's comedy.[67] Some of the characters recall Greek myth: Hélène, with her seductive charms; Hippolyte, with his "thin and weak body," perhaps ironically contrasted with his robust and chaste Greek namesake.[68] Hélène is suspected in popular gossip of incest with her brother Anatol, and it is in her drawing room that a French (!) actress entertains the company with a recitation from Racine's *Phèdre*. When Tolstoy deliberately suppressed a great deal of literary allusion between the early and final versions of certain scenes,[69] was this simply dispensable ballast, or is it rather something which the author, in Callimachean fashion, still expects us to supply because it adds another layer of meaning to the text?

What part in fact is played in the novel by sex?[70] The Alexandrian epic of Apollonius, like that of Virgil or Ariosto, and for that matter like the *Iliad*, looked these facts, with their tendency to obscure the heroic ideal, straight in the face. Tolstoy, himself deeply sexual, was clearly exploring certain facets of sexuality in his portrayal of Natasha. He makes enough concessions to Prince Andrei's "feminine" side to satisfy Jung. It cannot be enough, if he purged some overtly sexual references from the final version, to acquiesce in this stylistic tactic as if it affected the substance of his work. The New Comedy is certainly less coarse than the old. But it is precisely the place where sexual infatuations are scrutinized.

---

from peasant children?" in his return to literature which culminated in *War and Peace*.

[67] Itself indebted to Painter's *Palace of Pleasure*. The story of the energetic and capable Helena, determined to get her rather reluctant man, has perhaps an archetypal similarity to that of the life-affirming Natasha, denied by the cold Andrei. In general, the affinity of the classical epic tradition for comedy and romance (found in Thomas Mann too) demands that we should redefine its antecedents if we are not to be continually scolding great authors for their inexplicable backslidings.

[68] Above, note 41. And is not "Ramball" for a military man pure New Comedy?

[69] E.g. Wedel, p. 223. One thinks of the concealed literary allusions in the New Comedy: see, for example, E. W. Handley's edition of the *Dyskolos* (London 1965), index, s.v. *tragedy*. On the incidental relationship of great events to ordinary life, which Tolstoy said he learned from Stendhal, see E. Fraenkel, *Elementi plautini in Plauto* (Florence 1960), pp. 355 ff.

[70] Shklovsky in fact begins his *Mater'yal i Stil'* with some remarks about Tolstoy's sexuality (pp. 8–9). Tolstoy's own feminine side (Eichenbaum, *Lev Tolstoi*, II, p. 108) has clear parallels with Prince Andrei's femininity (Zaidenschnur, pp. 159, 162, 164 ff., 177). The intensely feminine Natasha, who yearns for a husband and enjoys the messy part of motherhood, is musical and interested in "comme il faut," again like Tolstoy. Cf. R. C. Benson, *Women in Tolstoy: the Ideal and the Erotic* (Urbana, Illinois 1973).

Can we dismiss Tolstoy's ambivalences, basic to the whole Calli-machean tradition, with some airy remark about his "deeply contra-dictory nature"?[71] This question again touches the nature of the Tolstoyan "I." But we must dissociate the psychological "I" from the literary, and ask whether the ambivalences are part of the intended literary effect. The characters, even when they are contrasted in Tolstoy's favorite polar or pathetic manner, sometimes share unex-pected features. This technique, developed by Virgil, must be ex-amined in Tolstoy.

What aspects of the novel's structure are determined by "carnival" vestiges? The closed and opening door plays a powerful role in the scene of Prince Andrei's death, which is greeted with mixed emotions by his family. The story begins with a party, at which Prince Andrei arrives late. Birth alternates with death. Time is freely manipulated. Evidently there is plenty of humor and even farce which yet serves a serious civic purpose in this narrative of great events.

These questions are by no means meant to form an exhaustive list. One important problem has been completely ignored, and yet it is one where classical scholarship ought to be uniquely qualified to supply the answer. If Aristotle influenced Callimachus,[72] and if he also influenced ancient historical and narrative prose of the post-classical, Hellenistic period, it ought to be true that Callimachean epic and Hellenistic history-writing have some things in common. This analogy seems in fact justified by the resemblances which scholars detect, for example, between Virgil's narrative technique and that of both Callimachus and ancient historians of the so-called Peripatetic school.[73] The question inevitably arises: is Tolstoy, who also, as we have seen, shares some features with Callimachean epic as it developed over the centuries, a Hellenistic historian?

Several considerations suggest that he is. Hellenistic history was based on a conscious effort to answer Aristotle's criticisms of tragedy by assimilating the writing of history to the writing of tragedy.[74]

---

[71] Zaidenschnur, p. 39. Tolstoy exhibits Alexandrian symptoms. His refusal to follow the crowd is the Callimachean *odi profanum vulgus*. His headaches are like Virgil's (and Leverkühn's).

[72] Above, pp. 44 ff.

[73] Cf. Heinze, *Virgils epische Technik*, pp. 263–64, 471 ff. Ralph C. Williams points out (*The Theory of the Heroic Epic in Italian Criticism of the 16th Century*, diss. Johns Hopkins 1917, p. 17) that Castelvetro, in an effort to recapture some kind of freedom for epic poetry, had declared it to be a *rassomiglianza d'historia*—meaning that the epic poet should be allowed to write like Livy. He evidently sensed where the tradition lay.

[74] Cf. P. Scheller, *De hellenistica historiae conscribendae arte*, pp. 41 ff. B. L. Ullman, "History and Tragedy," *Trans. Am. Philol. Assn.* 73 (1942), 25–53, while making many acute observations, misses the point that the theoretical arguments about their métier

Within this broad theoretical framework, different historians made very different adjustments to their facts in order to secure the desiderated artistic effect. A particular importance attaches in all this to the adaptation of Hellenistic techniques made by the Romans, since this transference of Greek ideas to foreign soil offers the fairest comparison with *War and Peace*.

Of course Tolstoy is not to be identified with any one Roman or Greek historian, any more than one ancient historian is to be identified with another, but he does use their devices. Like Livy and Tacitus, he writes with a moral, patriotic purpose, to serve which he distorts his material.[75] He has a philosophy of history dominated by the idea of predestination, which makes much play with reversals of fortune and other paradoxes.[76] He denigrates Napoleon, just as Livy denigrates Hannibal.[77] Like Tacitus, he employs savage irony. Again like Livy and Tacitus, he suppresses personal comment in favor of letting the reader deduce what is happening.[78] His preoccupation with individual psychology, dreams, large questions of personal destiny, was shared by the Hellenistic world, where it induced a dramatic, emotional style.[79] Tolstoy's use of minuteness leads him to write in separate scenes, again like Livy and Tacitus.[80] Yet the total effect of his novel is compared to music by E. M. Forster, as is that of Livy's orations by E. Burck and of Tacitus by B. Walker.[81] The "difficult" style of which he is accused runs back through the rhetorical tradition of Byzantium to the ancient world, displaying as it does long sentences,

---

conducted by the Hellenistic historians are all nevertheless couched in Aristotelian terms.

[75] As permitted by ancient rules where one's own country was concerned: Scheller, pp. 34–36.

[76] E. Burck, *Erzählungskunst*, remarks on p. 221 that a belief in human impotence in the hands of God led the Hellenistic historians to develop a loose, excited narrative style. Compare Tolstoy's apparently disordered clumsiness.

[77] See Burck in *Livy*, ed. T. A. Dorey (London–Toronto 1971), pp. 29 ff. Moscow is Napoleon's Capua: cf. Livy XXIII. 45. 4.

[78] See K. Witte's article, "Ueber die Form der Darstellung in Livius' Geschichtswerk," p. 407; Burck, *Erzählungskunst*, pp. 239–40; Walker, *The Annals of Tacitus*, p. 45.

[79] Cf. R. Reitzenstein, *Hellenistische Wundererzählungen* (repr. Stuttgart 1963), pp. 84 ff. We many compare the romance which grew up around Alexander the Great (still influencing Thomas Mann: H. J. Mette, "Doktor Faustus und Alexander," *Deutsche Vierteljahrschrift* 25 [1951], 27–39), the mysticism cultivated by the elder Scipio, the general tendency of a self-conscious age to put personal psychology in the forefront of interest. Polybius accuses the historian Timaeus of resorting, *inter alia*, to dreams, ignoble superstitions and womanish fantasy (XII. 24. 5).

[80] *Einzelerzählungen* in Livy: Witte, p. 273; in Tacitus: Walker, pp. 13 ff.

[81] Forster is quoted in the Maudes' translation of *War and Peace*, p. xvi. For Burck, see *Livy*, ed. Dorey, p. 41. For Walker, see her *The Annals of Tacitus*, p. 5.

anaphora and other hallowed tricks.[82] It is in fact a brilliant recovery from unpromising sources of the time-honored medium for historical narrative, and its difficulty vanishes when set beside that of the average passage of Thucydides. Its use of digressions is traditional. Even the famous estrangement has ancient parallels.[83]

Some similarities of approach between Tolstoy's description of the end of Borodino, and Tacitus' account of the visit to the field of Bedriacum, were already remarked. It would not be difficult to multiply general resemblances between the two authors. Tacitus too has been called a novelist of genius.[84] Drama, parallelism, digression, an interest in character amounting to a psychological bias in narrative, allusiveness, the avoidance of physical description unless it reveals inner qualities, impressionism in battle scenes, attention to actions and gestures—these are all procedures detected in the ancient historian by Miss Walker, and by modern critics in Tolstoy. Tacitus too was aristocratically inclined (it is part of the satirical *persona* even in democratic Athens). He too hated the *raznochintsy*, the Opportunists, of his time. He too was ever ready with the annihilating comment on his characters' pretensions. If the *Annales* are a "reinterpretation of the past, coloured and animated by a great artist's experience of the present,"[85] what else is *War and Peace?*

With Livy, Tolstoy shares a belief in "the spirit of the army" as the deciding factor in history. Both historians have a liking for reversals of fortune, for describing scenes of confusion, for contrasts, for delicate cross-references,[86] for a vividness which yet economizes in its use of detail, for psychological insight. The aftermath of Cannae is described by Livy in terms which seem outrageously gruesome,

---

[82] See above, note 19. Compare the rhetorician of whom Livy spoke (Quint. VIII. 2. 18) who advised his pupils to obscure their work, *Graeco verbo utens skotison.* He was not quite so absurd as he seems, and neither Livy himself nor Tacitus failed to follow his advice. Demetrius (*De Eloc.* 254) says that obscurity contributes to *deinotēs*, "forcefulness." But we should remember that *deinos* also means "strange."

[83] When Laocoon in Virgil calls the Wooden Horse *lignum* ("a piece of firewood," *Aen.* II. 45) he is doing what Tolstoy does when he calls a military banner "a piece of cloth on a stick." Virgil is of course doing more, since the Horse is precisely what will burn Troy down. But it is interesting that a device which in the ancient world had two sides (*tapeinōsis/auxēsis*, "playing down" and "playing up") is employed habitually by Tolstoy in the aspect (*tapeinōsis*) appropriate to comedy and satire. The bombast noted in the historians Callisthenes and Cleitarchus by "Longinus", *De Subl.* 3. 2, was presumably their form of estrangement. Dionysius actually uses *epi to xenon* of Thucydides: *De Thuc.* 50.

[84] By E. Bacha, quoted by Walker, *op. cit.,* p. 6.

[85] Walker, p. 257.

[86] Burck, *Erzählungskunst*, p. 191: compare the "labyrinth of interconnexions" which Tolstoy found in *Anna Karenina* (Christian, p. 124), and Wedel's *Mehrsträngigkeit* (p. 186) of *War and Peace.*

until we consult the pages of Tolstoy's *Sebastopol Stories*.[87] In both cases, the moral desire to communicate the second truth, and the carnival sense of the grotesque body, prevail over niceness. Tolstoy is not Livy any more than he is Tacitus. But he does stand in their company.

Tolstoy was deeply affected by the death from tuberculosis in 1860 of his older brother Nicholas. Descriptions of the last agony form one of his most powerful themes, as readers of *The Death of Ivan Ilyich* are aware. The death of Prince Andrei is another climactic moment in *War and Peace* (XII. xvi, pp. 219–20):

> He dreamt that he was lying in the room he really was in, but that he was quite well and unwounded. Many various indifferent and insignificant people appeared before him. He talked to them and discussed something trivial. They were preparing to go away somewhere. Prince Andrei dimly realized that all this was trivial and that he had more important cares, but he continued to speak, surprising them by his empty witticisms. Gradually, unnoticed, all these persons began to disappear, and a single question, that of the closed door, superseded all else. He rose and went to the door to bolt and lock it. Everything depended on whether he was, or was not, in time to lock it. He went, and tried to hurry, but his legs refused to move and he knew he would not be in time to lock the door though he painfully strained all his powers. He was seized by an agonizing fear. And that fear was the fear of death. *It* stood behind the door. But just when he was clumsily creeping towards the door, that dreadful something on the other side was already pressing against it and forcing its way in. Something not human—death—was breaking in through that door and had to be kept out. He seized the door, making a final effort to hold it back—to lock it was no longer possible—but his efforts were weak and clumsy and the door, pushed from behind by that terror, opened and closed again.
>
> Once again, *it* pushed from outside. His last superhuman efforts were vain and both halves of the door noiselessly opened. *It* entered, and it was *death*, and Prince Andrei died.

This dream precedes the hero's physical death, which is then all the more easily borne. But the terror behind the opening door is a phenomenon exploited by Greek tragedy with its *ekkuklēma*, and by Shakespeare in *Macbeth*.[88] It is in fact a primitive experience of suprahuman reality, which can be comic, even farcical in one aspect, and horrifying in another, according to the degree of intensity with

[87] XXII. 51. 5 ff. See, for example, *Sevastopol'* (repr. Geneva, Éditions du Rhône, 1945), pp. 11–12, 40–41, 56.

[88] O. Freudenberg has particularly discussed this phenomenon in *Poetika Syuzheta i Zhanra* (Leningrad 1936), *passim*.

which it is realised. But it evidently has little to do with the historical epic which is written for pay to glorify kings and heroes by imitators of Homer.

There are moments in the epic tradition when the vatic impulse raises ingenuity and charm to tragic intensity. This new impulse does not entail the abandonment of Alexandrian techniques, only their exploitation at new levels, as when Aeneas quotes to the dead Dido from Catullus' translation of Callimachus' *Lock of Berenice*.

The national self-awareness of nineteenth-century Russia fostered another such moment. A vast country, imperial in intent, formed by visions of Roman and Byzantine pomp, of classical and baroque splendor in its public palaces and buildings, racked by social problems, was bound to torment by the disharmony between possibility and achievement. A great writer, himself the epitome of the contradictions of his age, flung before his countrymen an apocalyptic scroll of fate, majesty, resignation, death. He could not chain the dragon. But, while his book was opened, he could make a silence in heaven for the space of about half an hour.

## II

No constellation of twentieth-century writers of epic could fail to contain the names of Joyce, Proust and Thomas Mann. The relevance of the Callimachean poetic to the interpretation of their musically structured, learned, ironic masterpieces is evident. Here we may single out the story of the hero of our own time, *Doktor Faustus*.

When *Doktor Faustus* was first published in 1947, the world was filled with horror and contempt for the revelations made at Nuremberg and elsewhere of Nazi barbarism. The book was a long, complex composition making great demands on the foreign reader, and its title seemed to confirm, from the lips of Germany's greatest living author, happily a man of unblemished anti-Nazi record, what everyone already knew: Germany had sold its soul to the devil, and must now pay the price. Was there really such need to labor the point?

But Mann's own novel, with its rich web of allusion to German music and literature, showed that Germany has been, and is, more than Nazism! Absurdly one-sided as this first interpretation of what Mann had written now looks, it was in fact shared even by German critics.[89] Indeed, Mann's own career lent plausibility to their views. He had long been an "engaged" writer. His wartime broadcasts to Germany had been listened to widely, and in them he had spared no word of condemnation for Hitler and his brood of devils. The novel

[89] See especially *Die Welt ohne Transzendenz* by H. E. Holthusen (Hamburg 1949).

looked like the artistic restatement of well-known and established beliefs, a sadistic, unneeded "I told you so!"

Nevertheless, this apparently committed novel, ostensibly dealing with clear-cut issues of black versus white, good versus evil, intended as a big, epic, historical narrative,[90] is Alexandrian through and through, and constitutes in itself the vivid proof of the survival of the classical epic tradition in our age.

Mann felt some obligation to comment on his own work, already a sign that its meaning could hardly be so obvious as it had at first seemed, already a concession to Alexandrian notions of the *poeta doctus*. In the *Entstehung des Doktor Faustus: der Roman eines Romans*[91] he gave evidence of the wide reading on which the book was based. Certain old ideas begin to emerge. Life is the re-enactment of myth, and the only difference is between those who know this, as Leverkühn knows it when, using Shakespearean language, he sends Schwerdtfeger off to woo Marie Godeau for himself, and those who do not, like Schwerdtfeger and even like the intruded narrator of the story, Zeitblom, when he unwittingly quotes Shakespeare back to Leverkühn, who has learned of his plan's miscarriage.[92] The central figure of the novel, the German composer Adrian Leverkühn, was largely modeled on Mann himself (the blameless anti-Nazi) and on Nietzsche— but Nietzsche was one of Mann's cultural heroes, and in a letter written in the year of his death Mann stated quite simply: "I am Nietzsche's heir."[93] The theme of artistic inspiration and intoxication bought at the cost of a pact with the devil had, it turned out, occupied the author as early as 1901, and in 1905 he had surprised a fatherly Munich bookseller by purchasing a number of reference works on syphilis.[94] Leverkühn's homosexual attraction for Schwerdtfeger, em-

[90] For *Doktor Faustus* as big, see *Entstehung* (below, note 91), p. 169, where also the comic admixture should be noted; as epic, *Entstehung*, p. 205; as historical, G. Bergsten, *Thomas Manns Doktor Faustus* (Lund 1963), pp. 173 ff.

[91] *Thomas Mann, Gesammelte Werke* (Berlin–Frankfurt 1960), vol. XI, pp. 145–301.

[92] *Entstehung*, pp. 166 ff. It is interesting that Mann looks to Shakespeare's comedies for his tragic motif. On life as myth see Mann's remark: "Denn wir wandeln in Spuren, und alles Leben ist Ausfüllung mythischer Formen mit Gegenwart" (*Joseph in Aegypten, Ges. Werke*, IV, p. 819). The provenance of these ideas in Schopenhauer and Nietzsche is discussed by Bergsten, *Thomas Manns Doktor Faustus*, pp. 187 ff. See also G. Schmidt, *Zum Formgesetz des Doktor Faustus von Thomas Mann* (Wiesbaden–Frankfurt 1972), pp. 44 ff. Leverkühn only gradually discovers his destiny. His tragedy—and Germany's—is that he discovers it in the wrong terms.

[93] Quoted in *Thomas Mann und die Tradition*, ed. Peter Pütz (Frankfurt 1971), p. 227.

[94] *Entstehung*, pp. 155–56, 186. The allusion to 1901 is queried by some scholars: see T. J. Reed, *Thomas Mann: The Uses of Tradition* (Oxford 1974), p. 361 and note 4. But in any case all this was before Nazism was ever heard of.

phasized in the novel by a certain parallelism between his life and those of both Tchaikovsky and Ludwig II of Bavaria, echoed the theme of a powerful story, with perhaps personal resonance, from the writer's early period, the famous *Der Tod in Venedig* (1912). Leverkühn's youthful music lessons from the local church organist, even the picture of Meyerbeer at the piano surrounded by characters from his operas (which include *Robert le Diable!*), in his Munich room, could not help but recall Hanno's lessons and nursery in *Buddenbrooks* (1901), and Mann himself drew attention to the connection of the later novel with his early masterpiece.[95] The notion of strict, musical composition (*der strenge Satz*) was found in both books. Speaking of *Faustus* as his *Parsifal* (is Parsifal damned?), Mann made it clear that this new novel was the product of old preoccupations.[96]

But there is more to be said. *Doktor Faustus* is an Alexandrian epic firstly because it presupposes a knowledge of the classics, surprisingly often the Greek and Latin classics.[97]

Classical echoes are particularly loud, for example, in the scene where Leverkühn decides to take up residence on the Schweigestill farm outside Munich where he can compose undisturbed, while at the same time having occasional access to the city by train.[98] He is fetched from the station by the farmer's son Gereon, a rather surly cattleman.

For the modern Faust, about to enter his personal hell, evidently this Gereon is the double of Dante's Gerion, the monster of fraud who in the *Inferno* transports Dante and Virgil to Malebolge. But can we be meant to ignore the celebrated Geryon of Greek myth, who also kept cattle?[99] The stealing of these cattle by Heracles formed a

---

[95] *Entstehung*, pp. 189–90. Hanno's music-making before his illness and death is another anticipation of *Faustus*.

[96] What the young Mann learned from Wagner, all of it relevant to the Alexandrian poetic, is summed up on p. 840 of vol. X of his *Gesammelte Werke. Die Kunst des Romans* (*Ges. Werke*, X, pp. 348 ff.) contains more interesting reflections on the novel as epic, on irony and on other Alexandrian topics.

[97] See "Thomas Mann und die Antike Literatur" by Willy R. Berger in *Thomas Mann und die Tradition*, ed. Peter Pütz, pp. 52 ff. Berger concludes a fascinating, though incomplete, essay with a list of features of Mann's art, including *Mosaiktechnik* and *Sinn für Totalität und Polyphonie*, which "bear throughout the stamp of Alexandrianism" (p. 99).

[98] *Doktor Faustus*, pp. 337 ff. References to the German text of the novel are always to the pages of the 1956 edition (*Stockholmer Gesamtausgabe der Werke von Thomas Mann*).

[99] He is the cowboy son of a *Seejungfrau* and "Golden Sword," while his uncle is Pegasus: so Hesiod, *Theogony* 281 ff. Dante depicts him as a serpent monster with a scorpion's tail (*Inferno* XVII. 27). In medieval legend, he enticed strangers to be his guests and then killed them. Dante's allusion to Icarus here (*loc. cit.* 109) connects Geryon with the imagery of Mann's *Gesang vom Kindchen* (below, p. 499). Mann's

famous theme of Greek lyric. Stesichorus had described how the hero had traveled to perform this task in the golden cup which carried the chariot and horses of the sun by night across Ocean.[100] With yet more relevance, Pindar had meditated on the morality of Heracles' action:

> Law, which is king of all, both mortal men and immortals, conducts the uttermost violence with the hand of power, making it just. I judge from the deeds of Heracles, since he drove the oxen of Geryon to the Cyclopean porch of Eurystheus without asking and without buying.[101]

Pindar alluded to the same story in the second *Dithyramb*, evidently puzzled by the morality of Heracles' behavior:

> I praise you, Geryon, beyond him [Heracles], but I must keep silent altogether about what is not pleasing to Zeus.

Geryon was right to resist, Pindar argues, but God was against him (and on the side of Heracles), and so we must pass over his fate in silence.

Music first comes to the young Leverkühn while he is still on his father's farm, from the cowgirl Hanne. As he begins his long vigil among the herds of another farm, he is not only Faustus then. He is also the famous Greek hero, invoking the Apolline principles of order and control over a dark, distant world. The relevance of these echoes to his hero's determination to impose law on what he calls the "cow warmth" of music, even at the cost of breaking (like Heracles, who however was subsequently deified) normal moral restraints, suggests that Mann did indeed intend something classical in the bass of his orchestra.[102]

The farmyard dog at the Schweigestills' is surly and snappish,[103]

---

"auf dem Bock eines Char à bancs" (p. 340) in this scene of *Faustus* uses a pun to convey a world of tragic meaning. So also "auf zwei Böcken" of Dr. Erasmi's coffin (*Faustus*, p. 209).

[100] *Poetae Melici Graeci*, ed. D. Page (Oxford 1962), p. 100.

[101] See Pindar, fr. 169 Snell; and Plato, *Gorgias* 484 b 1–c 3 with E. R. Dodds' notes in his edition (repr. Oxford 1966). Wilamowitz translates the second passage about Geryon from Pindar here (fr. 81 Snell): "ich will von dem ganz schweigen, was Zeus minder genehm ist" (*Pindaros*, p. 462): "Schweigestill"!

[102] Cf. *Doktor Faustus*, p. 94 (*Gesetz/Kuhwärme*).

[103] Geryon's dog, Orth(r)os (Hesiod, *Theogony* 293), was the brother of Cerberus, who guarded the gates of hell (Hesiod, 309 ff.), and father of the Sphinx, who was often depicted as a winged, woman-headed lion (i.e. partly as Mann's butterfly, and partly as another embodiment of his lion motif: below, p. 502). But this dog also has a mythical analogue in Maera, the hound of Erigone (identified with Virgo), a maiden who hanged herself, like Mann's sister Julia, before being translated to heaven as a star. There is an old classical motif here: "Der Heilige und die Tiere": cf. O. Weinreich, *Studien zu Martial* (Stuttgart 1928), pp. 74 ff.

yet Leverkühn knows how to calm it on this first occasion with a simple gesture. He is re-enacting "the coaxing of Cerberus by Heracles,"[104] a painting from a red-figure amphora by Andocides in the Louvre [Figure 10-1]. Arias and Hirmer comment:

> On the left Athena with helmet, spear and snake-bordered aegis. She makes a gesture of encouragement towards Herakles. . . . With his right he makes a soothing gesture towards the dog, in his left he holds a chain. A spreading tree with purple leaves grows in front of the house guarded by Cerberus whose dog's body has a lion's mane and a snake-headed tail.

This illustrates why, in the courtyard of the Schweigestills' farm, as described by Mann, there stands an elm, whose leaves are dropping.[105]

On later occasions Adrian soothes the animal with the aid of a special pipe, which only it can hear. The classical allusions show clearly that we are at the entrance to hell, and Leverkühn is now Orpheus as well as Heracles, just as later he will be Aeneas.[106] All three of these heroes visited hell, but all three were the champions of civilization.

Like the Greek sage and first philosopher Pythagoras, whose discourse concludes Ovid's *Metamorphoses*, Leverkühn is mathematician/musician/abbot. One of the rooms allotted to him in the old, formerly monastic building is dominated by a plaster cast of the Winged Victory of Samothrace. This second famous treasure of the Louvre (the first being the Andocides amphora) was the figurehead of a stone ship which once stood in the shrine of the Cabeiroi, deities

---

[104] See Figure 10–1. Mann could easily have seen this Greek amphora in Paris. For photographs and commentary see *A History of Greek Vase Painting* by P. E. Arias and M. Hirmer (London 1962), nos. 88 and XXIX with p. 317: K. Schefold, *Götter- und Heldensagen der Griechen in der spätarchaischen Kunst* (Munich 1978), pp. 120–23. On Geryon in general, see also Schefold, pp. 113–20. On the important motif of Heracles as musician, Schefold, p. 276.

[105] Cf. E. Norden's note on *Aen.* VI. 282–84, the entrance to hell. H. W. Bates says of the butterfly *Hetaera esmeralda* that it "flies low over dead leaves in the gloomy shades where alone it is found" (*The Naturalist on the River Amazon* [2nd ed., London 1864], p. 63). The elm finds its pictorial counterpart on the amphora mentioned in the previous note. For Virgil, the elm's leaves represent dead dreams. At *Entstehung*, p. 202, Mann refers to Germany from his Californian perspective as "Vergangenheit und Traum."

[106] Heracles (also a mystical musician) is particularly important because in XXX. 1 of the *Problemata* attributed to Aristotle he is chosen as the type of melancholic genius, and the author especially mentions ulcerating sores as symptoms of such genius: Leverkühn's syphilis is as it were his shirt of Nessus. Cf. C. O. Brink's note on Horace, *Ars Poetica* 302; E. Panofsky and F. Saxl, *Dürers Melencolia I: Eine Quellen- und Typengeschichtliche Untersuchung*, Studien der Bibliothek Warburg II (Leipzig— Berlin 1923); R. Klibansky, E. Panofsky, F. Saxl, *Saturn and Melancholy* (New York 1964). For Faust/Aeneas see *Doktor Faustus*, p. 473: for Faust/Orpheus, p. 647.

# Figure 10-1. Heracles Coaxing Cerberus

Several themes from the novel (the tree, the lion, the arrow, the encouragement of a patroness, here Athena, seen on the far left, the snaky locks of Professor Kumpf's daughters) are placed in a less damning perspective. Heracles, selected as a type of the melancholy genius by [Aristotle's] *Problemata*, certainly entered hell, but did not lose his soul there. As Leverkühn's projected visit to Paris never materialized, he was unable to see his own problems in this classical light.

of the underworld who came to be the particular patrons of seafarers.[107]

In his Nike room Leverkühn occasionally receives his friends. At one of his evening suppers, the idea is advanced that comedy and tragedy really spring from the same tree. We are at Plato's *Symposium*, and Leverkühn is Socrates, condemned to death for principle, who was also in his way a *Tonsetzer*.[108]

The year is 1914. Germany's guilt in attacking Belgium is discussed in terms of the *Durchbruch*, the "breakthrough," which plays so large a part in the novel's dilemmas. Can evil be committed to secure a greater good? Leverkühn argues that a genuine breakthrough is worth the price of doing something the world may consider a crime. But how does one break open the chrysalis to become a butterfly? He is touching on one of the novel's major symbols, but he is doing it in language which, through Dante, reaches back into Greek religion.[109]

Like a second Christ, Leverkühn has no difficulty about rejecting the kingdoms of the world and the glory thereof, offered to him in

[107] See M. Nilsson, *Geschichte der griechischen Religion* (Munich 1961), II, pp. 101 ff., and Apollonius, *Argonautica* I. 915 ff. For Adrian's sea-faring see *Doktor Faustus*, pp. 354 ff. According to G. Gullini, "La datazione e l'inquadramento stilistico del santuario della Fortuna Primigenia a Palestrina" in *Aufstieg und Niedergang der römischen Welt* (Berlin–New York 1973), IV, p. 776, the main cult statue of the goddess (not the one mentioned below, note 144, for which see Gullini, *loc. cit.*, p. 767) immediately recalls "lo schema famoso della Nike di Samotracia." Mann may have seen the remains, perhaps uncovered as long ago as the late seventeenth century, during his residence in Palestrina. See below, pp. 493–94. The image of the Heavenly Twins represented by the Cabeiroi (Gemini) is of far-reaching importance in the novel: see below, pp. 503 ff.

[108] Cf. *Doktor Faustus*, p. 406 and Plato, *Symp.* 223 d. Like Socrates in his cell (*Phaedo* 60 b ff.), Mann's novel adapts to music "Aesopian fables" (= Apuleius' *Golden Ass*) and a "prelude to Apollo" (= Callimachus' *Hymn to Apollo*). The theme of the *Phaedo* also provides a link with the little sea-nymph's longing for a soul (*Doktor Faustus*, p. 501). For more kinship between Plato's and Mann's imaginations see *Republic* X. 611 c ff. (and Dante, *Paradiso* I. 68). T. J. Reed (*op. cit.*, pp. 8, 56 ff.) interestingly quotes the *Symposium* as the model of the irony typical of Mann, but does not draw the conclusions from this ancestry for Mann's artistic inheritance and method which are so brilliantly suggested by M. Bakhtin, *Problemy Poetiki Dostoevskogo*, pp. 224 note 1, 300 note 1.

[109] *Purgatorio* X. 121 (the purgation of pride): cf. *non v'accorgete voi che noi siam vermi / nati a formar l'angelica farfalla, / che vola a la giustizia sanza schermi?* (*ibid.* 124–26). The amatory topos of the butterfly/moth which prefers to die in love's flame was at least as old as the troubadours: see the commentators on Petrarch, *Sonnets* XIX and CXLI: and for the amatory *schermo de la veritade*, Dante, *Vita Nuova* V. 3. For soul (*psyche*)/butterfly see M. Nilsson, *Geschichte der gr. Religion*, I, p. 198. The ambiguous French *papillon*, both "butterfly" and "prostitute," must also be remembered. See below, p. 488.

a richly comic scene by the impresario Saul Fitelberg.[110] But the violinist Schwerdtfeger asks him for a concerto to be written "auf den Leib"—for life and on life, on body. It would be a Platonic child between them. Here, the reminiscence of the *Symposium* is unmistakable.[111] Yet Socrates resisted the advances of Alcibiades. Did Leverkühn resist those of Schwerdtfeger? He made a solitary trip with him to Hungary, like Brahms with Joachim—but were they lovers? It was in Hungary that he had embraced, and been infected by *Hetaera esmeralda*. Did he later send him away because he was a distraction from the hemlock of cold and paralysis which he accepted as his destiny, the piano/cross of a musical Calvary?

Leverkühn's mysterious, invisible patroness, the Hungarian noblewoman Madame de Tolna,[112] modeled on Tchaikovsky's Frau von Meck, presents him on one occasion with a Renaissance ring, naturally with an emerald stone (*Hetaera esmeralda*), which, Zeitblom sagely comments, might have belonged to a prince of the Church—as of course it does still, since Pythagoras/Leverkühn works in the Abbot's room of a monastery. The composer wears it on his left hand while writing his cantata *Apocalipsis cum Figuris*, a musical interpretation of Dürer's woodcarvings of that title. The emerald is engraved. Below, there is a winged, snakelike monster, its flickering tongue resembling an arrow. Zeitblom is reminded by it of Philoctetes' wound, received in the precinct of Chryses. He thinks also of the name given by Aeschylus to the arrow, "hissing, winged snake," and of the relation

---

[110] Pp. 526 ff. The treatment has a carnival ambiguity. Fitelberg's speaking name (*Fittich*, "wing or pinion," *Berg*, "mountain") evidently chimes with an interpretation of him as Satan tempting Christ on the mountain top. On the other hand, he comes from Lyublin (= "Love-town"), and the first part of his name may also recall both the Winged Victory and Madame de Tolna (cf. Hungarian *toll*, "quill, feather, pinion"). Leverkühn should perhaps have yielded to the temptation to visit Paris, where he might have understood his problems more classically by visiting the Louvre. It is not for nothing that Paris is also Marie Godeau's home. Yet when Fitelberg refers to Leverkühn's *Viereckigkeit* (*Faustus*, p. 533), who will not think of Simonides' good man, "foursquare without blame" (Page, *PMG*, pp. 282–83)? If Leverkühn is guilty, what is he guilty of?

[111] *Faustus*, pp. 466–67; *Symposium* 209.

[112] According to V. A. Oswald, Jr., "The Enigma of Frau von Tolna," *Germanic Review* 23 (1948), 249 ff., to be identified with *Hetaera esmeralda*. Compare the *Symposium*'s theme of Aphrodite as both heavenly and earthly. One Renaissance author, Valeriano, asserted that the emerald is characteristic of of virginity and the pure and heavenly Venus: see Florence M. Weinberg, "Platonic and Pauline Ideals in Comic Dress: 'Comment on Vestit Gargantua'," *Illinois Classical Studies* IX (1984), 184–85. This is why Rabelais used this stone for the buckles of Gargantua's codpiece. Mann and Rabelais cross paths again: below, note 145.

between Phoebus' arrows and the rays of the sun.[113] Over this picture are inscribed two lines from the opening of Callimachus' *Hymn to Apollo*:

> What a rustling shakes the laurel bush of Apollo! Shakes the whole temple! Flee, yield, unholy ones!

It is the quotation which the Sibyl makes at the sacrifice before Aeneas' descent into hell.[114]

Aeneas was not damned. Philoctetes may have been wounded, but he atoned by suffering for his impiety, and without him Troy could not have been taken, nor Helen ever recovered. The hissing, winged snake of Aeschylus' *Eumenides* was Apollo's own threat, used to drive off the Furies tormenting Orestes for the murder of his mother.[115] Can the childless Madame de Tolna then be anyone other, in one aspect at least, than the virgin goddess Athena, who also in Aeschylus' play protects Orestes? The Louvre amphora makes this identification especially tempting.[116] Athena was the guardian of the arts; of the seafaring, necromancing Odysseus; of Heracles. Neither symbol on the ring sets Leverkühn in an unrelievedly bad light. And the emerald ring stone, for the Renaissance, was the symbol of virginity, and of the pure and heavenly Venus.

Did Mann therefore never read further in Callimachus' *Hymn to Apollo*? (v. 9)—

> Not to every man doth Apollo show himself, but to him who is good.

Leverkühn spent his whole life imposing an Apolline discipline on his inspiration. At the end, like Beethoven, he had mastered technique to such a degree that it became the transparent expression of feeling.[117]

---

[113] *Faustus*, pp. 521–22: cf. *Eumenides* 181. According to Berger (*op. cit.*, pp. 95–96) Mann was indebted for his information here to Karl Kerényi. "Chryses" (Greek χρυσός, "gold") recalls Adrian's setting of Blake's poem about the serpent in the golden temple which forces the poet to lie down among the pigs (*Faustus*, pp. 220–22). There is sociological criticism here of the corrupting influence of money. It is another version of the Callimachean theme of the "poor poet" (above, pp. 70 and note 86; 304, notes 21 and 23).

[114] *Aen.* VI. 258. Mann adapts another Callimachean motif in renaming the Munich numismatist called in real life Georg Habich, who represents a cold and self-centered scholarship (*gestit enin nummum in loculos demittere*, Hor. *Epp.* II. 1. 175), Dr. Kranich (= "crane": cf. Callimachus' *geranos*, *Aet.-Pref.* 14): see also Bergsten, *op. cit.*, p. 36.

[115] Cf. "Das Mutter-Motiv," *Entstehung*, p. 191. Like Orestes, the insane Leverkühn attacks his mother (*Doktor Faustus*, p. 673).

[116] "On the left Athena with helmet, spear and snake-bordered aegis. She makes a gesture of encouragement towards Herakles . . ." (Arias and Hirmer, *op. cit.*, p. 317).

[117] Cf. *Faustus*, pp. 73, 643, 647.

Did Apollo never appear to such an artist? The use of a quotation from Callimachus himself to invest the figure of damned Faustus with Callimachean ambiguity confirms the thesis of this chapter.

Germany's classical scholarship is so firmly a part of its culture that so rich a novel must come to terms with it. Friedrich Nietzsche, Professor of Greek at Basle at age 24, stands in the center of the story. The devil tempts Leverkühn with quotations from *Ecce Homo* about the absence of genuine inspiration in modern art. Only Leverkühn himself is normally allowed to cite Nietzsche directly in this way. Zeitblom, the narrator—and classical scholar—is merely permitted to quote from works *about* Nietzsche.[118] Erwin Rohde, the author of *Psyche*, whose own youthful relationship to Nietzsche was so warm, lends some tragic words to Zeitblom's description of Leverkühn's ultimate condition.[119]

Another Greek vase painting, a false but fruitful interpretation, may have set Mann's artistic imagination working in all this, so that reality took on a symbolic garb, the fate of Nietzsche and the title of his friend Rohde's book combining to transmute sordid fact into poetry. The motifs of music, sexual intercourse and *psyche* come together on a black-figure vase described by M. P. Nilsson.[120] The scene shows a man with an erect phallus blowing a double flute, while drops of his semen fall onto a fluttering butterfly. Here is the musical, and syphilitic, Nietzsche; here is the composer Leverkühn in the company of his *Hetaera esmeralda*, the butterfly/prostitute who infects him! Nilsson reminds his readers that the butterfly has been identified with the soul at least from the days of Aristotle right down to the modern Greek ψυχή/ψυχάρι. It was then possible to think of Nietzsche as seeking more than sexual gratification when he contracted the illness that was to destroy him, as seeking *psyche*, soul; and this is exactly what the musician Leverkühn is doing—looking for *Beseelung* (his word) for an art in danger of dying, at whatever cost to himself.

What kind of hero for a mythical epic is Nietzsche? It is no longer quite so necessary as it once was to defend the great genius against accusations of being a jack-booted storm-trooper in disguise. Mann did not like that side of Nietzschean influence at all. To him, Nietzsche

---

[118] Bergsten, p. 73. Evidently Zeitblom "knows the literature" but not the author, a common failing among scholars.

[119] On Rohde and Nietzsche see *Entstehung*, pp. 212–13 (*Unverhältnis*).

[120] *Geschichte der gr. Religion*, I, p. 198. Here again, it is hard to believe that Mann had not been collecting the material which was ultimately used in *Faustus* for many years. The works cited by Nilsson (*loc. cit.*, p. 198, notes 5 and 6) date from 1902, 1911, 1913, 1915. Rohde's *Psyche* may have acted as stimulus (Eng. tr. by W. B. Hillis [repr. New York 1966], p. 170).

rather seemed to be the confirmation of another favorite idea, that illness is the price which genius pays for its accomplishments:

> I regard people like Heracles or Siegfried as popular champions, but not as heroes. Heroism is for me an "in spite of it all," weakness overcome, tenderness belongs to it. . . . Physical suffering seems to me historically speaking to be a pretty well indispensable accompaniment of greatness, and that has psychological plausibility. I do not believe that Caesar would have been Caesar without his weakness and his falling sickness, and if he had been, in my eyes he would have been less a hero. Lastly, is there not in the tough façade presented by the exhausted Thomas Buddenbrooks a whole host of heroism?[121]

It is a theme to which Mann returns time and again. The remote ancestor of this kind of heroism is Apollonius' Jason, with his "helplessness," or Virgil's Aeneas, his limbs paralyzed with cold.

Leverkühn notes with much satisfaction at one point that it was an astronomer and mathematician from Upper Egypt, who lived in Alexandria, Claudius Ptolemaeus, who propounded the best of all known musical scales, the "natural" or correct one.[122] "Satisfaction" (*Gefallen*) here is an interesting word. Leverkühn himself has shown no particular interest in either Egypt or Alexandria. His Callimachean ring is a later gift which he gladly accepts, but has not sought. The satisfaction is evidently Mann's own. Elsewhere he relates how, though so poor a pupil at school, he was once able to discomfit a master with a recondite Egyptian name,[123] and his largest work is precisely a critical exploration of the wisdom of the Egyptians. Mann understood in a way not always given to specialists the mediating importance of Greece *and* Alexandria in the creation of European civilization. Ptolemy's musical contribution was merely the further proof of a long held theory, the conscious acceptance of a place within the tradition this book has sought to elucidate.[124]

The Alexandrian nature of *Doktor Faustus* is already discernible. It is indeed the work of a *poeta doctus*, displaying all the features we have so often noted. It exemplifies, as Mann himself remarks,[125] what it describes, "constructive music," and in this regard both looks back

---

[121] *Briefe* (Frankfurt 1961), I, p. 63. Evidently Mann did not always think so badly of Heracles!

[122] *Faustus*, p. 213.

[123] *Entstehung*, p. 138.

[124] Mann's kinship with Theodore Adorno and Joyce is the proof of his adherence to the modern Alexandrian tradition: cf. his reflections on Joyce (*Entstehung*, pp. 204–05) and Bergsten's quotations from Adorno (*op. cit.*, p. 142).

[125] *Entstehung*, p. 187.

to the technique of Apollonius' *Argonautica*[126] and forms an excellent introduction to the study of the *Aeneid*. Like the *Aeneid*, it deploys both internal and external references.

External reference is made to innumerable sources, most obviously (and misleadingly) to the late medieval popular account of the life and death of Doctor Faustus. The use of the source shows the typically Alexandrian displacement of structure.[127]

The popular story tells of Faust's signing a pact with the devil in his own blood, of the devil's appearance in different shapes, of Faust's journeys to hell and the stars in the eighth year of the pact, of his pilgrimage in the sixteenth year, his second pact with the devil in the seventeenth year, in which he also becomes a procurer, his amorous adventures in the nineteenth and twentieth years, his fathering, by Helen, of a beloved son in the twenty-third year, and concludes with his farewell speech to his friends in the twenty-fourth year, when his time runs out.

Confident that the reader will do his work for him, in his reworking of this tale, Mann omits any description of the pact, which one would have thought to be the essence of the whole story. Instead, he offers a letter to Zeitblom from Leipzig,[128] describing how as a young student the naive and innocent Leverkühn is led to a brothel by his guide at the end of a tour round the town, and flees precipitately as soon as he realizes where he is. The demonic overtones of what would normally be thought of as an embarrassing, but essentially comic, misadventure are conveyed by allusion. The letter is written by Leverkühn in old German, evoking the medieval atmosphere in which Faust is at home. The guide looks like the cousin of a Halle theology lecturer, the sinister Schleppfuss.[129] The wording of the letter is modeled on Nietzsche's letter to Paul Deussen about a real-life experience of a similar kind in Cologne. The important difference is that, while Nietzsche does not specify what chords he struck up on the piano to relieve his nervous discomfiture, Mann makes Leverkühn play something from Weber's *Der Freischütz*, the story of a

---

[126] Above, pp. 88–89.

[127] Bergsten (*op. cit.*, pp. 57–58) sets out the old and new accounts in parallel columns. "Displacement of structure" is the technique that leads Callimachus to call a story about Theseus' capture of the Marathonian bull—*Hecale*.

[128] There is an important allusion here to the scene in Goethe's *Faust*, Part I, "Auerbachs Keller in Leipzig," where Mephistopheles produces wine. This suggests the Dionysiac theme of the novel: cf. T. J. Reed, *op. cit.*, pp. 364, 396.

[129] A speaking name ("Dragfoot") which also recalls the Greek epic epithet *eilipous*, used of Geryon's cows by Hesiod (*Theogony* 290).

pact with the devil.[130] The ladies of the establishment resemble butterflies in their garb. A motif which looked like a mixture of homespun science and Faustian curiosity in the hands of Leverkühn's father at the opening of the novel now starts to take on more deadly coloring.

But is coloring always a reflection of reality? Is Leverkühn's *Hetaera esmeralda* a poisonous butterfly,[131] and what in fact would that mean? There is of course no such creature as a "poisonous butterfly" which actually goes out aggressively to poison its prey. Some butterflies are chemically protected against predators. But probably *Hetaera esmeralda* is not even that, whatever the loose and misleading sequence of thought suggested in the early pages of the novel. The readiness of readers to fob off guilt onto another Eve has prevented them from realizing just how innocent and passive this poor butterfly is!

Leverkühn's real fault is quite different and much more profound. It is not his quixotic union with a diseased girl in a brothel (not sought by the girl), but his failure to seek appropriate, continuing treatment for his sickness, just then becoming available in the shape of the "magic bullet," the drug salvarsan. When Adrian played chords from *Der Freischütz* in Leipzig, his apparently random choice of music had already made plain his road to salvation. His tragedy (and Germany's) is that he resolutely refuses to follow it. His romantic hostility to rationality and science is what his countrymen will pervert into Nazism.

If the sin is not the visit to the brothel,[132] but the failure to seek medical treatment, the novel's chronology becomes more intelligible. Interpreters have been puzzled by the author's choice of narrative sequence. Why does Mann place Leverkühn's formal sealing of his

---

[130] Cf. Bergsten, pp. 277–78. Dr. Paul Ehrlich's *salvarsan*, the remedy which in 1909–10 began to replace the old-fashioned and dangerous mercury treatment of syphilis, was popularly known as "the magic bullet" (used by Max in Weber's opera). The story is told in Paul de Kruif's *Microbe Hunters* (New York 1926), pp. 334–58 (German translation, *Mikrobenjäger*, Zürich 1927). I owe this information to Dr. P. Bogue, whom I should like to thank most warmly for her many helpful comments during the writing of this section on Mann.

[131] H. W. Bates, *The Naturalist on the River Amazon*, p. 63, makes no such suggestion. Mr. R. I. Vane-Wright of the Department of Entomology, British Museum, informs me by letter that "*Haetera esmeralda* [sic] Doubleday is a Brazilian butterfly of the family Satyridae. . . . From . . . the general biological innocuousness of Satyrid butterflies, I conclude that it is very unlikely that the *esmeralda* is chemically protected (poisonous)." Contrast C. S. Brown, "The Entomological Source of Mann's Poisonous Butterfly," *Germanic Review* 37 (1962), 116–20. "Satyridae" once again picks up the Dionysiac theme.

[132] See V. A. Oswald, Jr., "The Enigma of Frau von Tolna" (above, note 112), 250.

pact with the devil *after*, rather than before, the episode in the brothel with *Hetaera esmeralda?*

> It weakens the development of Leverkühn's personality to have him commit himself resolutely to his fate in the shape of an infected prostitute's embrace, and then only afterwards allow him to wrestle with the hazards of doing so in a lengthy dispute between his godly and demonic selves. . . . Fortunately the dialogue, with its idea of a freely, but most painfully, chosen pact, is such a superbly worked out invention that it eclipses the Hetaera episode.[133]

The solution to this difficulty lies, not in accusing a great artist of incompetence, but in attending closely to the calendar. Mann states that Leverkühn's second, consummated visit to *Hetaera esmeralda* occurred at the time of the Austrian première of Strauss' *Salome*, in May 1906.[134] We are also told that the conversation with the devil took place sometime during the composer's stay in Palestrina, that is, not before the end of June 1911, and not after his return to Munich in the autumn of 1912. The winter of 1911–1912 is also ruled out, since Leverkühn spent that in Rome.[135]

During the conversation, the devil (Sammael) notes how long the unspoken pact has already been in existence (my italics):

> "Still? But we have been still *for nigh five years.*"

Compare the later remark:

> "I tell you, we have been silent *more than four years.*"

And again:

> "*More than four years* after you got it."[136]

Mann hammers home the dates. But from May 1906 until any time in June or after in 1911 would be *over* five years. Only if the conversation had occurred before May 1911, when Leverkühn was not yet in Palestrina, could the devil be alluding to the visit to the brothel. Since Leverkühn however does not complain about the arithmetic, the conclusion follows that he understands the devil to be talking not about the visit at all, but about something else which had occurred more than four but not quite five years ago.

This something else is Leverkühn's decision not to persevere with treatment for the local infection which broke out five weeks after his encounter with *Hetaera esmeralda*, even though she had warned him

[133] P. Carnegy, *Faust as Musician* (New York 1973), p. 73.
[134] *Doktor Faustus*, p. 205.
[135] For the dates, see pp. 280–81 of the novel.
[136] *Doktor Faustus*, pp. 305, 308, 312: Eng. tr. by H. T. Lowe-Porter (New York 1948), pp. 229, 231, 234.

of her condition. He did in fact consult two physicians, one of whom died unexpectedly, while the other was arrested for some mysterious reason. After this, he let matters alone. If we think of the fatal resolution as slowly taking shape between July and autumn of 1906, this would explain the devil's allusion, probably in summer 1911, to "nigh five years," "more than four years." Attention to the calendar alters the whole symbolism of the novel.[137]

Mann himself remarked that he sympathized with his hero because of his conviction that he was damned.[138] But one may be convinced of a lie! This is where the whole misery of Leverkühn's plight is to be found. He is too easily carried away into romantic, irrational and ultimately self-destructive behavior by a compelling national myth, that of Faust, and has too much reluctance to interpret his problems on a larger, more human, more rational and more classical scale.

Within the structure of the novel this means that a second myth is at work, something which both Adrian Leverkühn and Zeitblom fail to see, and yet a myth which is both widely enjoyed and was a favorite with Mann himself.[139]

To uncover this second myth, we need to consider the importance accorded by the story to Palestrina. It is here that the devil's visit to Adrian occurs, and of course the *musical* significance of the place is clear.

But Palestrina (Praeneste, as Mann explains)[140] was famous in antiquity too. It was in fact the site of what was probably pagan Italy's largest religious shrine, the temple of Fortuna Primigenia. Princes and potentates were among those who flocked to consult the *sortes* there for guidance. One potentate, the Roman dictator Sulla, whose twin children were named Faustus and Fausta in honor of their father's special patroness Aphrodite/Venus,[141] had adorned the temple with two striking mosaics, for which the finest Alexandrian techniques were employed.

These mosaics have partially survived to our own day. One of them is adduced by a modern scholar to illustrate his view of the

---

[137] M. Klare, *Studien zu Thomas Manns "Doktor Faustus"* (diss. Bonn 1973), p. 114, sees the chronological problem well enough, and suggests that Zeitblom has misleadingly postdated the conversation for personal reasons. Zeitblom's sinister influence on the framework of the narrative is noted below, p. 501. But here we have rather an example of montage, the technique of offering the reader two and two and allowing him to make five.

[138] *Entstehung*, p. 204.

[139] *Ges. Werke*, X, pp. 350, 831.

[140] *Doktor Faustus*, p. 281.

[141] Plutarch, *Life of Sulla* 34. Appian says (*Bell. Civ.* I. 97) that Sulla actually received the name of Faustus himself.

technique of Apollonius' *Argonautica*.[142] It shows a panorama of the course of the Nile, flowing past exotic animals and birds of every kind. The other is a seascape, in which the waters gradually darken as they recede further from the shore, and where fish and sea creatures of many varieties move. Flecks of white against this watery darkness remind the reader that Adrian's first, and symbolically titled, orchestral work is *Meerleuchten*.[143]

Praeneste is not a seaside resort. What can the dictator Sulla, who always thought of himself as peculiarly the favorite of Fortune, have meant by installing in her temple a seascape? The offering, a recurrence of the carnival sea-on-land motif, hints at the goddess' universal power. In ancient thought she takes many forms. At Praeneste she took a form which must recall nowadays the Christian Madonna.[144] The surviving omnipresence of the eternal feminine could not find more evident confirmation.

Fortune then might be Our Lady. She might also be Athena and Isis. What Adrian and his friends could not see during their sojourn in Palestrina was that the presiding daemon of their lives, and their governing myth, could be one which acknowledges the truth proclaimed in antiquity by the massive temple at the top of their hill. It need not always be a question of Mephistopheles and Faust. Why may we not instead think in terms of Fortune and Faustus/Fausta? It is a kindlier destiny which controls men's lives, if they will but see them from this classical, Italian perspective. Adrian does not see this, and he gets no aid from the classical scholar, Zeitblom. He is tempted by his German upbringing to believe that he is condemned to hell, when even at the worst he is no more than Lucius, the golden ass.[145]

---

[142] A. Hurst, *Apollonios de Rhodes: Manière et Cohérence* (Rome 1967), Figure 1.

[143] *Doktor Faustus*, pp. 201–02. Cf. G. Gullini, *I Mosaici di Palestrina* (Rome 1956), who remarks (p. 30) on the "note di bianco" in the fish mosaic, and (p. 24) speaks of the darker depths of the sea ("il mare dove non giunge la luce"). Stesichorus had spoken of Heracles' sea voyage in the sun's cup: above, p. 482; below, notes 151, 152, 181.

[144] Cicero, *De Div.* II. 41. 85; cf. K. Latte, *Römische Religionsgeschichte* (Munich 1960), p. 176. For Isis/Tyche Protogeneia see Nilsson, *Geschichte der gr. Religion*, II, p. 126. Plutarch, *De Is. et Os.* 354 c, speaks of a veiled Athena, "whom they believe to be Isis." For the gesture, cf. Timanthes' Agamemnon, and Electra in Euripides, *Orestes* 280. Compare the veiled female stranger at Adrian's funeral: see below, p. 510.

[145] V. A. Oswald had already pointed out, "Full Fathom Five: Notes on Some Devices in Thomas Mann's *Doktor Faustus*" (*Germanic Review* 24 [1949], 275), that the Manardi family, with which Adrian lodges in Palestrina, bears the name of a pioneer Renaissance student of syphilis. Bakhtin notes (*Tvorchestvo François Rabelais*, p. 393) that Rabelais, himself a doctor, translated Manardi's medical letters into French, as indeed the theme of syphilis plays a large role in his great comic literary work. Panurge, for example, is vastly reassured to find out that those who never caught

Mann had already used Apuleius' romance in *Joseph*.[146] With its technique of a story within a story the work employed devices familiar from Catullus and Virgil,[147] and itself sanctioned the contrapuntal interplay of two different versions of the same events, found in *Doktor Faustus*. In Apuleius, the Virgin Goddess, Isis of many names, becomes Lucius' enemy because, like an early Faust,[148] he pries into forbidden magic, even though he has been warned by a revelation of the goddess' power in the shape of statues of the Winged Victory (the very statue which Adrian has in his Nike room). His lust, which he uses to gratify his curiosity, reduces him to the level of an ass, the lewdest, most diabolical and ugliest of animals in one aspect, the most intelligent and patient of beasts of burden in another (and either way the typically carnival animal).[149] He must pass through a year-long punishment, beginning and ending in the season of roses,[150] before eventually his repentance secures his restoration to human form and initiation into the Virgin's mysteries.

The terms of his initiation are interesting (*Metamorphoses* XI. 23):

Accessi confinium mortis et calcato Proserpinae limine per omnia vectus elementa remeavi. Nocte media vidi solem candido coruscantem lumine: deos inferos et deos superos accessi coram et adoravi de proxumo.

I approached the bound of death and trampled on Proserpina's threshold, yet returned, carried through all the elements. At midnight I saw the sun shining with clear light. I entered the presence of the

---

syphilis in this world catch it in the other! As with the playing of a theme from *Der Freischütz* in the Leipzig brothel, there is the hinted possibility of salvation in all this which the actors in the melodrama resolutely insist on ignoring.

[146] Berger, *op. cit.*, pp. 83 ff. In a letter to Kerényi of March 23, 1934 (cited by A. Hofman, *Thomas Mann und die Welt der russischen Literatur* [Berlin 1967], pp. 9–10, who makes valuable comments on the nature of literary influence) Mann noted with keen amusement the debt of *Joseph* to the late Greek novel. As Bakhtin remarks (*Problemy Poetiki Dostoevskogo*, p. 162), the author may not remember, but the genre in which he works remembers.

[147] Above, p. 152 and note 98. See further, H. Riefstahl, *Der Roman des Apuleius* (diss. Frankfurt 1938); P. Junghanns, *Die Erzählungstechnik von Apuleius' Metamorphosen und ihrer Vorlage* (*Philologus Suppl.* XXIV [1932]); R. Heine, *Untersuchungen zur Romanform der Metamorphosen des Apuleius von Madaura* (diss. Göttingen 1962).

[148] Cf. H. Ruediger, "*Curiositas* und Magie: Apuleius und Lucius als literarische Archetypen der Faustgestalt," *Wort und Text, Festschrift für F. Schalk*, edd. H. Meier and H. Sckommodau (Frankfurt 1963), pp. 57–82.

[149] Bakhtin discusses the symbolism of the ass: *Rabelais*, pp. 87–88.

[150] Mediterranean roses are already in bloom in late April and early May, and this would put Lucius' adventures at their start and finish in the sign of Taurus, the astrological house of Venus, to whom roses were sacred: [Ausonius], *De Rosis Nascentibus* 18 and 21.

gods of the underworld and those of the upper world, stood near and worshipped them.[151]

How much of this applies to the novel! When Adrian came to the Schweigestills' farm, with its dropping elm, he was approaching the bound of death, and Frau Schweigestill's young daughter, with whom he strikes up such a friendship, is his Proserpina (and her mother, the farmer's wife, therefore Demeter, goddess of the grain that must die). "Elements" is a word of repeated importance in the story, whether we think of "die elementa spekulieren" or of Adrian's alleged journeys to the heights and depths of sea and sky. The "clear sun at midnight" picks up Stesichorus' description of Heracles' voyage at night in the Sun's golden cup to steal Geryon's cattle and is another leitmotif of the novel.[152]

"I entered the presence of the gods of the underworld." We can see how Adrian does that. But Lucius, like so many of the classical heroes found in the novel's background, went on to enter the presence of the gods of the upper world; he was redeemed from his sin.

His fate is poetically interpreted and elevated in the myth of Amor and Psyche. Psyche's sin is to offend Venus. Even so, all might have been well, since her beauty disarms Amor, who is sent to punish her. But she gives way to curiosity. Amor has to leave her and, like Adrian, take to his sickbed. Loaded with hard tasks by her mistress Venus, which include a descent to hell, Psyche wins acceptance of her marriage by patient suffering. Amor is healed and reunited with his bride. Only then can she bear her child.

Apuleius' story lends to Mann's *Faustus* its basic symbols and its basic *Problematik*. Psyche, the soul of man, but also the butterfly, *Hetaera esmeralda*, is disordered, and does not understand her proper relationship to Venus. But Amor/Adrian, Venus' child, the artist seeking *Beseelung*, cannot reject such beauty. He pursues its possessor, identifying himself with her, becoming winged and serpentine (his ring). He can only be with her at night.

Psyche's gift of herself to disobedient Amor can only be the wriggling worm of the spirochaete. But, blessed in the end by Venus, Amor can be made whole, and the worm become an immortal butterfly.[153] This is the lesson which Adrian slowly learns. Amor can

---

[151] See further M. Nilsson, *Geschichte der gr. Religion*, II, pp. 632 ff.; F. Cumont, *Lux Perpetua* (Paris 1949), pp. 265–66.

[152] See below, note 181 and the "steht als ein Licht in der Nacht" of the end of "Dr. Fausti Weheklag."

[153] See above, note 109. When at a Munich soirée Adrian accompanies the *diva* Orlanda in a song from *Tristan und Isolde*—"Die Fackel, und wär's meines Lebens Licht, lachend sie zu löschen zag' ich nicht"—we seem to find Petrarch's butterfly/moth motif combined with the theme of light/darkness (*Doktor Faustus*, p. 368).

find Psyche, Love can gain a soul, music can break through its coldness to intimacy with mankind. But the price is great, and it is the mark of Adrian's dedication that he pays it.

It is characteristic of Alexandrian poets that, aware of the immense difficulties of their task, they should always seek refuge in a human modesty. So it was that, for example, Ariosto, like Horace, like Callimachus, revealed some of his deepest thoughts in his occasional poems. Again, it was characteristic that, like the Virgil of the *Eclogues* or the Dante of *Donne ch'avete*, they should approach the epic through Alexandrian foothills.[154] Mann repeats the pattern. His youngest child was born in 1919, at a time of great stress for Germany and for her father, convinced German patriot as he was. He celebrated the event in a hexameter poem, whose nine parts are crowned by a description of the baby's christening in Munich.

Hexameters, nine parts like the nine Muses, an Alexandrian baptism with water,[155] an Alexandrian preoccupation with domesticity (a whole section is taken up with reflections on the baby's morning bath and feed): can we be far from Callimachus, whose own *Iamboi* include a delightful *Genethliakon* for a baby girl? Callimachus' poem contained an ironic comment on the claims made by "big" poetry. Mann's mock-heroic *Gesang vom Kindchen* opens with a meditation on its author's own vocation:

> Am I a poet? Was I one from time to time? I cannot say. . . .

He goes on to declare that his chosen field is that of prose, whose sense and substance are awareness, the awareness of the heart and that of the refined ear. It was prose that seemed to him both morals and music. Yes, he is a poet! He shows that through his love of language. But what about the old embarrassment, the secret defeat of a never admitted surrender? But even this defeat was turned into virtue, and led to a harvest of admiration. Yet a bitter taste was left in the mouth:

> Do you still remember? An exalted intoxication, an extraordinary feeling came once I think over you and threw you down, so that you lay, your forehead buried in your hands. In hymn then rose your soul, the wrestling spirit pressed towards song amidst tears. But alas! All

---

[154] Above, pp. 115 ff., 256 ff. Horace had actually meditated on the heroic ideal at Praeneste (*Epp.* I. 2). Mann's poem particularly reminds one of Callimachus' *Iamboi* XII.

[155] Cf. A. Kambylis, *Die Dichterweihe und ihre Symbolik* (Heidelberg 1965), pp. 110 ff., 125 ff.: Propertius III. 3. 51–52. Mann's poem is translated and paraphrased here from *Ges. Werke*, VIII, pp. 1068 ff. T. J. Reed has some pertinent comments: *op. cit.*, pp. 152 ff.

remained as it had been. For an objectifying toil began there, a cold effort at mastery. The drunken song became a moral fable. Is that not true? And why? It seems you did not dare to make the flight? What was proper for you, what was not, you knew in your inmost heart and behaved with quiet restraint. But the deeper failure still gave pain.

The hexameter, he continues, joyful and sober at the same time, remains an acceptable compromise, not poetry of the highest kind, but certainly not prose. It is a meter familiar to the author ever since he took more interest in the battles of Cronion[156] than in those of the Indians. It has often occurred, unmarked, in his prose writings:

Grant me then once, Muse, the gaily measured step openly!

This *Vorsatz*, whatever its poetic modesty, touches the deepest springs of Mann's own creativity.[157] The immediate allusion is to *Der Tod in Venedig*. The poetic impulse is given by Eros. But this inspiration is worked upon and objectified by a cold mastery. The Alexandrian implications are obvious. A poet who nevertheless normally dwells in the prose pastures of the Muses, who finds that he needs as qualifications a conscience, which is also consciousness, both of the heart and of the ear,[158] would have found a brother in Callimachus. But, as the epic theme of *Doktor Faustus* matured in its author's mind, he would also find a brother (twin) in Adrian Leverkühn. What else is Adrian's lifelong struggle except the grueling, self-destroying effort to impose a cold order on inspiration, intoxication, which will however not betray that inspiration, as Mann accuses himself of betraying it at an earlier period in his career? And what are the weapons Adrian uses, except those with which Zeus Cronion fought the monsters who would rob him of his throne, those with which Greek civilization resisted the barbarian hordes—measure, joyful and yet sober, inspired and yet controlled? This was already the theme developed by Pindar in his first *Pythian*.

Mann describes his refusal to yield to intoxication as the refusal of a flight. Later in the poem he takes up this theme again. He tells us that he has been particularly careful in selecting godparents for his daughter. One of them is a young scholar/poet —

full of childlike gaiety, yet acquainted with suffering, more closely bound to the spirit by illness, which is his life-long bride and in cycles

[156] An interesting affinity with Hesiod (*Theogony* 617 ff.).

[157] See Reed's remarks in the *Times Literary Supplement* no. 3839 (Oct. 10, 1975), p. 1206.

[158] On the Callimachean ear see "Pushkin and Horace," *Neohelicon* 3, numbers 1–2 (1975), 333 note 5, to which may be added Propertius' *purae aures* (II. 13. 12).

tortures him. Lovingly his piety dared to describe the legend and myth of the last child of Icarus and his deadly lot. He, truly also a son of Faust and Helen, stamped by Wittenberg and Eleusis, stormed up the dizzying steps in noblest blasphemy, nursing the command of death in his dangerously doubled soul which, in fearful equilibrium hangs between all that is unlike, between yesterday and tomorrow, music and goal-pointing will, between secret and utterance, German-ness and French logic, and then fell (sorrow enough!) into uttermost night. Yet his radiance rose up to heaven, to men a most holy spectacle. Yes, he wrote it, treated of it in twenty chapters, changed it about I should rather say, for these are variations on the theme of the fatally balanced scale. He ennobled with deep feeling the philological han-diwork, and in each of the parts he distilled all the inexpressible charm of his theme.

So in 1919, over a quarter of a century before *Doktor Faustus* saw the light of day, and at a time when the Nazis were hardly known, Mann is captivated by the thought of an Icarus flight which is to be made by a son of Faust and Helen, whose ambivalence will poise momentarily between all contradictions. The Goethean and Nietz-schean ancestry of this *Umwertung aller Werte* is clear. What must fascinate the reader of the novel is that Mann saw the paradigm of his own earlier artistic failure ("It seems you did not dare to make the flight?"), and of his friend's experiment, in these Faustian terms. *Doktor Faustus* becomes therefore a fresh attempt to solve an old problem. It makes sense as a mirror of contemporary Germany only because it reflects a deeply personal dilemma. Yet there is a change. In the novel, Eleusis/Demeter is suppressed, and only Wittenberg remains.

Adrian had no son, yet in his final confession to his friends, the *oratio Fausti ad studiosos*, he accuses himself of fornication with a sea nymph, Hans Andersen's little mermaid, who was brought to his bed by the devil.[159] The fruit of this lust has been a holy child, pretty beyond all wont, as if of a distant and older stamp. But since the

---

[159] *Doktor Faustus*, pp. 663–64. The longing of the little sea-nymph for legs, which is also a longing for a soul, finds a parallel in a fragment of the Menippean satires of Varro. For him, the legs are stilts, which can only be set in motion by the soul. The same satire illustrates the closeness of body and soul by the homely image of *mutuum muli scabunt* ("Ein Esel reibt den anderen": cf. Mann's debt to the *Golden Ass*). See further E. Norden, *In Varronis Saturas Menippeas Observationes Selectae* (Leipzig 1891), pp. 290–93. Incidentally, in *Die Geburt des Kindes* (Leipzig–Berlin 1924), p. 71, Norden notes that even the emperor Augustus was presented with the possibility of a sea-nymph for a bride (*Georgics* I. 31). All this suggests the cheerful normality of ideas which, when carried across the Alps from their classical homeland, become in a German atmosphere distorted and perverse.

devil had forbidden him to love anything human, the child was taken away, and to do that the devil used Adrian's own evil eye.

The sick fancy here reweaves to its own liking, but on predetermined patterns, the fate of little Nepomuk Schneidewein, Adrian's nephew, who had died of meningitis while staying with his uncle on the farm. Nepomuk, an innocent and graceful angel, accustomed to refer to himself as "Echo," is the symbolic possibility of redemption for Adrian, the proof that his music "echoes" in heavenly spheres. In a musical, mystical and "Platonic" sense he is Adrian's child, the reason and the future for which he has endured so much.

But how can he be the son of Helen? Only because the sea nymph/mermaid represents the willingness to take a chance in the service of love which Helen of Troy showed. We have a choice. We may prefer the safety of Zeitblom's staid wife, the *former* Helen Ölbaum, placid, sandwich-making, faded, with a daugher Helen married to a bank-manager.[160] Or we may go after the real Helen, lost now in the depths of ocean, with all the attendant risks. But the artist must precede us. Like Rilke, Mann believed that only the poet-musician could mediate between the two realms of life and death, only Orpheus hope to return from the shades with a message of reconciliation and peace.

An Alexandrian hexameter poem, a *Kleinepos*,[161] foreshadowed the problem and mystery which lay at the heart of *Doktor Faustus*. This clinging to the classical tradition permits further insights into the book's structure. Adrian, we remember, was pleased that the best and natural scale had been discovered by an Alexandrian astronomer and mathematician. Mann's well-known preoccupation with *Zahlen-mystik* may now be seen in perspective. Like his ancient and medieval predecessors, like Eisenstein, he calculates the space and position to be allotted to his themes.

The pagination of the original edition[162] shows a characteristic attention to symmetry. The novel falls into six sections:

| | | | |
|---|---|---|---|
| I | 49 pages | | chapters 1–4 |
| II | 217 pages | 386 | chapters 5–20 |
| III | 120 pages | | chapters 21–25 |
| IV | 128 pages | | chapters 26–32 |
| V | 213 pages | 387 | chapters 33–45 |
| VI | 46 pages | | chapters 46–end |

[160] Cf. Theocritus XVIII. 45–48, "The Bridal Song of Helen," where twelve maidens let drip smooth oil on "Helen's tree." This ancient Helen Oelbaum stands then in ironic contrast with her modern counterpart, married nevertheless to a classicist! Twelve is a number important to Leverkühn.

[161] *Ges. Werke*, XI, pp. 587–89.

[162] Stockholm 1947.

Yet the detailed anatomy of the novel has rather more sinister implications. The 47 chapters divide into 34 and 13, 34 being the number produced by Dürer's magic square, of which a replica hangs in Adrian's room in Leipzig. It is the number of cantos in Dante's *Inferno*, from which *cantica* of the *Divine Comedy* the epigraph for the whole work is drawn. Chapter 34 itself has three parts, the blasphemous repetition of the Holy Trinity, as in canto 34 of the *Inferno*, where Satan has three faces, and eternally devours three traitors.

The conversation with the devil in Palestrina occupies Chapter 25, which is in the middle of the book's pagination, and even in the middle of the chapters, since Chapter 34 has two extra divisions, giving 49 in all (7x7).

These calculations, of which we have here the briefest illustration, are solemnly accompanied by Zeitblom's assurance that, in pausing, his tale takes no account of anything except the reader's convenience.[163] In fact, the intervention of the intruded narrator is decisive. Zeitblom is all the time slanting his story towards a particular interpretation. To behave as if Zeitblom and Mann were the same is to commit as grave a fault of interpretation as to ignore the presence of narrating Aeneas and listening Dido in the second and third books of the *Aeneid*. Mann has created Zeitblom and made him act as he does in order to tell us something about the failure of German humanism, which had of course similarly misunderstood Nietzsche. Yet, as we trace the methods by which he characterizes his intruded narrator, how much confirmation of numerical symbolism in the tradition is gained from a study of the conscious manipulations of the twentieth-century magician, which no skeptic can overlook!

But Ptolemy, and Faust, were also astronomers. A simple example of the astronomical/astrological symbolism of the book may be drawn from the beginning of Echo's illness. The author has described how Adrian and his nephew "Echo" loved to take country walks, through fields of grain that were ripe for cutting.[164] The *Vordeutung* is too clear, and sure enough, at the start of the next chapter, as the young boy falls ill, Zeitblom remarks that the harvest was then in full swing on the farm, Gereon being assisted by "additional workforces." Can we guess that these "workforces" are more than extra farmhands?

It is the middle of August. But the middle of August stands in the sign of Leo. We recall that when Adrian, never a popular student,

---

[163] *Doktor Faustus*, pp. 149, 235; contrast p. 207 (Adrian). See further Bergsten, *op. cit.*, pp. 217 ff. on the novel's "strenger Satz," and M. Henning, *Die Ich-Form und ihre Funktion in Thomas Manns "Doktor Faustus"* (Tübingen 1966), p. 51.

[164] *Doktor Faustus*, pp. 621–22, 627. The famous story (Herodotus V. 92. ς – η; Aristotle, *Politics* III. 13. 1284 a 26 ff., V. 10. 1311 a 20; Livy I. 54; Ovid, *Fasti* II. 706) was apparently preferred by Mann in its Greek version.

left school, his headmaster had taken occasion, in a last interview, to remind him of the First Epistle of Peter: "The devil as a roaring lion walketh about, seeking whom he may devour" (5:8). The passage has already recurred, when Adrian seizes the opportunity of his sister's wedding to theorize about the paradox of Christian matrimony, and the dangers of driving love along with pleasure out of marriage by too much regulation. Now the astronomical coincidence of the Sun (Apollo) in Leo as Echo begins to suffer unites the themes of pride and sensuality at a demonic and metaphysical level.[165]

Attention to Leo even lets us see Mann as a political commentator. Adrian's fatal encounter with *Hetaera esmeralda* is, as we have noted, not the one in Leipzig, but later, in Pressburg, in May 1906, and Mann is careful to add in parenthesis that this is the Hungarian Poszony.[166] The town is historically important. In 1491 the Treaty of Pressburg united Austria and Hungary, and in 1805 another Treaty of Pressburg dissolved the Holy Roman Empire. Pressburg is then "the ashing of Caesar," "Kaisersaschern" (the town where Adrian received his first schooling, and where the church contained the body of an early Emperor), in a historically transfigured sense.

Eventually, when the Austro-Hungarian Empire was broken up in the twentieth century, Pressburg, the former capital city of Hungary, was ceded to Czechoslovakia, and the Czech coat of arms bears in its middle a lion. Both Adrian and the city where he committed himself to his *Hetaera* would therefore feel the domination of that symbolic beast.

It is no accident that Mann tells us he started thinking about the theme of *Faustus* on the Ides of March, the day of Caesar's assassination and cremation.[167] He saw in Austria, and in Switzerland (Marie Godeau's home, and old Habsburg territory), an openness to the outside world, a *Durchbruch* which Germany itself, for all its Bismarckian imperial pretensions, lacked.[168] Adrian, like Mann, chose to live in Munich. But it had been Ludwig II of Bavaria who invited the King of Prussia to found a new, and disastrous, German Empire in 1870. Ludwig, in spite of his brilliance, ended in tragic madness.

The devil himself explicitly confirms the significance of astronomical dating when he remarks that it was under the sign of Scorpio

---

[165] Cf. *Doktor Faustus*, pp. 114, 251, 544 ff. The scriptural passage used to form part of the Church's Office of Compline, marking the end of the day. The lion is also Nietzschean; it occurs in *Also sprach Zarathustra*, e.g. in the section "Unter Töchtern der Wüste" in part III. Cf. *Libera eas* (sc. *mortuorum animas*) *de ore leonis, ne absorbeat eas tartarus* in the Offertory of the (old) Requiem Mass.

[166] *Doktor Faustus*, p. 205.

[167] *Entstehung*, p. 155.

[168] Cf. *Ges. Werke* X, p. 919.

that the spirochaetes of syphilitic infection were let loose on Europe.[169] The spirochaetes, in the devil's fancy, are like medieval flagellants. The resemblance to the scorpion, which was said to poison itself with the whip of its own tail, is apparent. Now we understand why Adrian takes up residence on his farm at Pfeiffering, to which he is transported by Gereon, at the end of October. That time too is under the sign of Scorpio, and in Dante Gerion, "he that infects all the world," has a scorpion's tail.[170]

An extraordinary amount of the action occurs in May. Zeitblom begins to write on May 23, 1943. In May 1906 Adrian makes his fatal visit in Pressburg to *Hetaera esmeralda*. Clarissa Rodde commits suicide by taking "enough cyanide to poison a whole regiment" at Pfeiffering in May 1922. Nepomuk Schneidewein catches measles in May 1928. Adrian summons his friends for a last farewell in May 1930. Can it be coincidence that the sun stands in the sign of Taurus, the Bull (commemorating the Rape of Europe), and Gemini, the Twins, during this month?[171] Mann's Christian name, Thomas, means of course "twin," and Gemini was Dante's zodiacal sign.[172]

In his *Entstehung*, explaining how much of himself he had put into his novel, Mann innocently remarks that he made Zeitblom start writing on the very day (May 23) when he himself wrote the first pages of his new story.[173] So he and Zeitblom are in this respect "twins," and interestingly enough, in 1943 the sun (Apollo, god of music, medicine, poetry and prophecy) entered Gemini exactly on May 23.

But Mann explains also that one reason why he refused all invitations to describe either Zeitblom or Adrian in the course of the story was that they both have too much to conceal, namely, the secret of their identity.[174] This is in one respect their identity with each other, and in that case Adrian/Zeitblom form another set of twins, the A and Z, the touching extremes, of a biographical alphabet. They could also be the classical Amphion and Zethus, models of the contemplative (musical) and active life.[175]

---

[169] *Doktor Faustus*, p. 309.

[170] *Doktor Faustus*, p. 340: *Inferno* XVII. 26–27.

[171] May is also important to Boccaccio and Chaucer: above, pp. 346, 356.

[172] NT John 11:16; 20:24; 21:2; *Paradiso* XXII. 152.

[173] P. 164. Mann was then conscious of Zeitblom's separate existence.

[174] *Entstehung*, p. 204. To allow the reader to make his own image of the characters is montage in the most exact sense: above, pp. 430–31 with notes 99 and 100. Cf. *Doktor Faustus*, p. 502: "das tiefste Geheimnis der Musik, welches ein Geheimnis der Identität ist." See also M. Klare, *op. cit.*, pp. 111 ff.

[175] The long resonance of their debate in musical history is noted by E. K. Borthwick, "The Riddle of the Tortoise and the Lyre," *Music and Letters* LI (October

When Clarissa Rodde poisons herself, she is re-enacting the suicide of Mann's own sister, and the identification is made clear by the precise repetition about her of language used by Mann about his sister already in the sketch of his life which he drew up in 1930.[176] More twins here then. But Clarissa is also anticipating the cyanide deaths of the Nazi bosses,[177] since Nazism is the outgrowth of the degenerate society in which she has moved. This is why she takes "enough cyanide to poison a whole regiment." The callous-sounding cliché has symbolic and twinning sense. When, by contrast, young Echo catches the measles, which will weaken him enough to make him an easy victim for meningitis, in the same month as his uncle contracts syphilis, he is indeed "echoing," reducing and redeeming Adrian's plight. Adrian's last farewell is addressed to more of his twins (including Zeitblom), to those who will in so short a time follow him into night, the spiritual night of Nazism.

Twins are important in yet another sense. Among all the authors and books so carefully noted in the *Entstehung*, which include Voltaire's *Mahomet*, one author and one book in particular is missing,[178] Baudelaire's *Fleurs du Mal*, the work of another syphilitic genius, another secular Christ. Baudelaire would in fact provide interesting parallels to Adrian's art and life: the belief in "correspondences," the association of music and the word, the readiness to confront and explore moral evil in an age of sham, the *Abtrünnigkeit* (Satanism) which is still an apostasy in God, the sensuality of religion and the religion of sensuality.[179] Like Mann, Baudelaire invoked for himself the figure of the doomed Icarus, and like Mann he was fascinated by the themes both of the sea and of alchemistic magic.[180] But fleetingly in the novel we do have a hint of Baudelaire's presence. Adrian has been explaining to an embarrassed Zeitblom

---

1970), 373–87. One suspects that Adrian's name also has something to do with the dying Hadrian's *animula vagula blandula* ("Kaisersaschern" motif).

[176] *Ges. Werke*, XI, p. 120: cf. Bergsten, *op. cit.*, pp. 23–24.

[177] *Doktor Faustus*, p. 668. Mann's word for them, "Matadore," seems to point directly to the Taurus/Rape of Europe symbolism already mentioned.

[178] The *Entstehung* is "ein hochliterarisches Werk" (H. Petriconi), concealing as much as it reveals, and in this playing with the autobiographical "facts" deeply Alexandrian. See further L. Voss, *Die Entstehung von Thomas Manns Roman "Doktor Faustus"* (Tübingen 1975), pp. 241 ff. Baudelaire had in fact anticipated, for example, Mann's view of Wagner: see *Thomas Mann und die Tradition* (above, p. 480 note 93), p. 207.

[179] Cf. *Doktor Faustus*, pp. 85 (sensuality, correspondences); 176 (*Abtrünnigkeit*); 215 (*Wort*).

[180] See C. Baudelaire, *Les Fleurs du Mal*, ed. E. Starkie (Oxford 1947), pp. 180–81 (*Icare*); 76–77 (*Alchimie de la Douleur*); 15 (*L'Homme et la Mer*).

his alleged voyages in space in the company of the American Professor Capercailzie,[181] and the terrifying distances there which annihilate human claims to greatness. Zeitblom makes Pascal's reply, that all this inhuman vastness is in itself mere pointless and irreligious size.[182] Adrian argues that man and his spirituality are nevertheless rooted in this vastness of physical nature:

> Physical nature, this monstrous universe which so vexes you, is unquestionably the presupposition for morality. Without it, morality would have no ground, and perhaps we must call goodness the bloom of evil—une fleur du mal. (*Doktor Faustus*, p. 363)

This image of the "flower of evil" looks back inside the novel to the ice flowers whose right to be called flowers was defended by Adrian's speculative father, and by the devil, earlier in the book.[183] But its external reference must surely be to Baudelaire's own poem in *Les Fleurs du Mal*, "Le Gouffre."[184] There Baudelaire takes up Pascal's thought about *le silence des espaces* of which Zeitblom has been thinking, and sees in it the image of Pascal's own awareness of emptiness, which he shares. Baudelaire's anguished cry:

> —Ah! Ne jamais sortir des Nombres et des Êtres!

might well be that of Adrian himself. But of course, like Pascal and Baudelaire, he labored not to let that be the whole story.

The overwhelmingly German tone of the novel does not encourage sallies into French literature by its exegetes, although Adrian himself was less exclusive.[185] This is a deliberately misleading tactic by the author, illustrating the neurotically closed world which has been

---

[181] *Doktor Faustus*, pp. 359 ff. Zeitblom does not make the connection with Alexander the Great made by H. J. Mette: above note 79. The name Capercailzie provides an excellent example of Mann's complexity. At one level it is a play on *caper*, "goat," as is appropriate for one of the devil's henchman (see V. A. Oswald, "Full Fathom Five: Notes on Some Devices in Thomas Mann's *Doktor Faustus*," *Germanic Review* 24 (1949), 274–78). But "capercailzie" as a common noun is a synonym for "woodcock," and when, at p. 608 of the novel, Adrian assures Zeitblom that his string trio was dictated to him by his "Geist und Auerhahn," we have to know that *Auerhahn* = "woodcock" = "capercailzie" to see that Adrian's description of the piece as "eine Nacht, in der es vor Blitzen nicht dunkel wird" is intended to recall the mysterious lights of the deep ocean where Adrian had allegedly traveled with Capercailzie 250 pages previously. This is the *strenger Satz*. It is also Apollonian and Virgilian.

[182] *Pensées*, ed. L. Lafuma (Paris 1947), I, p. 209.

[183] Pp. 28–29, 323.

[184] Starkie, p. 180.

[185] E.g. he sets to music poems by Verlaine (*Doktor Faustus*, p. 220): not, of course, by Baudelaire, since that would mean he had begun to obtain a perspective on his own predicament.

Germany's prison and doom. Adrian planned a trip to Paris, which never came off, just as the German armies failed in their drive on Paris in 1914. If he had been able to marry Marie Godeau, who worked in Paris, he might have seen in the Louvre the Greek vase paintings which would have given him another myth to explain his dilemmas. If he had yielded to the impresario Fitelberg's invitation, he might have found among ladies of high society in Parisian salons a conversation more stimulating than that of Baron Riedesel in Munich. But if, in spite of these failures of contact, we may make a parallel between him and Baudelaire, we may look further. The French poet dedicated his 1857 edition of *Les Fleurs du Mal* to Théophile Gautier, calling him the "parfait magicien ès lettres françaises," and this figure of the magician, so dear to Mann, was taken up in the poem which in the posthumous 1868 edition became the Preface:

> Sur l'oreiller du mal c'est Satan Trismégiste
> Qui berce longuement notre esprit enchanté,
> Et le riche métal de notre volonté
> Est tout vaporisé par ce savant chimiste.

The devil's most potent weapon, and horror, in the alchemistic evaporation of the human will is exactly Adrian's greatest temptation: ennui, boredom.[186] But it is not something unique to either Baudelaire or Leverkühn:

> Tu le connais, lecteur, ce monstre délicat,
> — Hypocrite lecteur,—mon semblable,—mon frère!

When all is said and done *we* are Adrian's, and Zeitblom's, twins too. The careful astronomical dating of the start of the work to May 23, 1943, in the sign of Gemini, becomes, in the light of tradition, a clue to the understanding of the meaning of the whole.

That the sympathetic collaboration, even *Zerknirschtheit*, of the reader is demanded in this way before the book can make its full moral impact explains why, in the *Entstehung*, Mann declares that he had made an almost reckless use of montage.[187] Eisenstein is another name missing from that volume however and, less excusably, from that of the novelist's critics, and this in spite of the fact that among Mann's most dangerous romanticisms was a weakness for the Russian

---

[186] E.g. *Doktor Faustus*, pp. 62–63, 65. The motif is associated with his laugh, which is not necessarily proof of a potential for evil, as Zeitblom (*Doktor Faustus*, p. 116) seems to assume. A smiling baby can hold divine promise, as Virgil knew. Dr. Zeitblom should have consulted E. Norden, *Die Geburt des Kindes*, p. 65.

[187] P. 166. Cf. the allusion to the "panoramas" of his youth on p. 165.

Revolution, among his most fruitful fascinations one with Russian literature.

Mann himself notes the way in which, through montage, reality and fiction are blended into a dreamlike consistency. It is in these dreams that we are most open to suggestion. Therefore it *is* important (in spite of certain critics) to know that Adrian is in some degree Nietzsche, as he is Beethoven, Tchaikovsky, Hugo Wolf, Brahms (whose early apprenticeship was as a brothel pianist), as well as Faustus, Orpheus, Aeneas, Pythagoras, Christ, since this is precisely the metamorphosing technique sanctioned by Virgil. But the union of these bits of information into a whole is, in the final analysis, the work of the reader, not of the author.[188] He can only offer a score, which each must perform on the instrument he has with the talent he has.

In attaining his musical synthesis, his *Durchbruch*, one of the most striking examples of Eisensteinian montage and the "leap into another dimension" which literature offers, Adrian traverses some characteristically Alexandrian terrain. He has, for example, to come to terms with Wagner. He does it by the Formalist method of the *dénudation du procédé*, which is also the Euripidean (and comic) method of "reduction"[189]—quite literally. Wagner's full-blown heroes and heroines become puppets, their adventures are now drawn from the *Gesta Romanorum*, a popular medieval collection of folktales whose earthy wisdom, not devoid of romance, nevertheless does not take itself too seriously.[190] When Adrian sets to music poems by Brentano, Zeitblom remarks that they are a proof of his leaning towards the "small and lyrical form of the song." But they are also *recht umfangreich*, "quite ambitious in scope," and Adrian forbids any performance of the thirteen (!) songs except as a cycle, even though that militates against their becoming widely known. The artificiality of the cycle does not prevent it from carrying a deeply "subjective" meaning.[191] Important Alexandrian concepts seem to be at work here, useful for the appreciation of Horace and Propertius as well as Leverkühn.

The basic tendency of the Callimachean poetic was towards music, both in general structure and in individual treatment. Mann's debt

<hr>

[188] Well brought out by Margrit Henning, *op. cit.*, pp. 103, 125 ff., 153.

[189] Cf. Aristophanes, *Frogs* 941, and Mann's "im Kleinen und Leisen," *Ges. Werke*, X, p. 840. For the Formalist *dénudation du procédé (obnazhenie priyoma)* see Shklovsky, *O Teorii Prozy*, pp. 139, 141, 173 ff., and B. Tomashevsky in *Théorie de la Littérature* (ed. Todorov), pp. 289, 300.

[190] *Doktor Faustus*, pp. 420 ff. Busoni's puppet operas (including *Doktor Faust*, 1925) may have been in Mann's mind.

[191] *Doktor Faustus*, pp. 243 ff.

to musical procedures has been investigated at length.[192] His acknowledgment of Turgenev's influence, with its "lyrische Exaktheit," is
particularly interesting in the context of the present chapter, since it
was Turgenev whom Tolstoy had to repudiate when he was creating
the epic style afresh.[193] But even Tolstoy had not repudiated lyricism,
and secure in the possession of Tolstoy's achievements, confronted
with the need to renew the epic manner in his turn, Mann could
now find room even for Turgenev's lyric, and room within the
evolution of German prose for his highly polished, cosmopolitan
style.

Mann in fact exploited language at every level. He was of course,
like Virgil, a public reader of his own works, and by this acknowledged
the orality and dramatic polyphony of epic. The virtuosity of *Joseph*[194]
has a graver counterpart in the recapitulation of Lutheran and even
older German in *Faustus*. When we read at the end of a chapter:

> auf die Dauer erwies sich die Wehrlosigkeit der Einsamkeit gegen
> solche Werbung allerdings zu des Werbers Verderben. (*Doktor Faustus*,
> p. 467)

what have we except the delight in verbal echo and word play which
goes right back to Gorgias, to Pindar, and beyond them to Homer,
and which was certainly welcomed by the Alexandrians? Gorgias
would have further reason to be delighted with this sentence:

| | |
|---|---|
| auf die Dauer . . . Einsamkeit | 16 syllables |
| gegen solche Werbung | 6 syllables |
| allerdings . . . Verderben | 10 syllables |

Mann himself speaks of the "versartige Schlusskadenz"[195] of his
description of the end of *Dr. Fausti Weheklag*. Repetitions like "Dann
ist nichts mehr," "der nicht mehr ist," "ist es nicht mehr" perform
in prose (if this is prose) what Leverkühn performed in music. They
render the technique transparent, like the wings of *Hetaera esmeralda*,
to expression. Only the veins with their beating blood show through.

The entire artistic dilemma in which Adrian finds himself, to solve

---

[192] By H. Grandi, *Die Musik im Roman Thomas Manns* (diss. Berlin 1952); K. Heim,
*Thomas Mann und die Musik* (diss. Freiburg im Breisgau 1952); and see now P. Carnegy,
*Faust as Musician* (London and New York 1973).

[193] *Ges. Werke*, X, p. 592. Contrast Tolstoy, above, p. 473 note 65.

[194] See O. Seidlin, "Ironische Brüderschaft: Thomas Manns 'Joseph der Ernährer'
und Laurence Sternes 'Tristram Shandy,'" in *Thomas Mann und die Tradition*, pp. 130
ff. The affinity between Sterne and Mann, like that between Sterne and Tolstoy
(above, p. 465), is particularly noteworthy in view of the prominence accorded to
Sterne in Formalist criticism (e.g. by Shklovsky, *op. cit.*, pp. 139 ff.).

[195] *Entstehung*, p. 294. The quotations from the novel are from p. 651.

which he becomes a martyr to art, has Alexandrian implications.[196] The bourgeois art of harmonious, romantic, complacent self-expression has exhausted its possibilities. It has become too easy, too obvious. It slides, under the eyes of a penetrating intelligence, into parody (Ovid). It is threatened by sterility. What can its relationship be now to genuine experience? How can the new and coming world be absorbed by it?

Only by a return to origins (*Aetia*), by a re-examination of first principles which involves a great deal of parodistic negation and "barbarism" (really, "carnivalization") before a fresh start can be made. And when this fresh start is made, when art does look the world and nature again in the face, how can there be a human reaction to the horrors of our particular time, which the artist also finds within himself, since he too, like Christ, is a Son of Man, other than the pure scream of pain or shriek of despairing laughter?

Exploring the worst the devil has to offer; recklessly exposing himself to destruction for the sake of those who will come after;[197] imposing the Apolline sternness of the *strenger Satz* on the intoxicating poison of his new apocalypse, the modern Alexandrian drives the old poetic to extremes which could hardly have been thought possible. But it is recognizably the same Pegasus[198] he rides, the same chariot he mounts.

One of the most powerful of its moving forces is irony, as it was one of Callimachus' most typical urges. But irony, as we can now see, is not so much the denial as the assertion of possibility. It can be a loving acceptance of what cold reason might be inclined to reject.[199] It can be the union of opposites in that art for art's sake which is paradoxically our only hope of the needed *Durchbruch* to salvation.[200] The modern Virgil, the modern *vates*, brings back from hell a message very like that of his ancient predecessor.

---

[196] Especially explored by G. Schmidt (above, p. 480 note 92), following T. W. Adorno.

[197] Mann evokes here the language of Statius to Virgil in Dante: *Doktor Faustus*, p. 217; *Purgatorio* XXII, 67 ff. Later Zeitblom "deliberately exposes himself" (*Doktor Faustus*, p. 493) to the proto-Nazi ideas of the Kridwiss circle. Once again we have to remember that, though Virgil may have entered hell, he was certainly not damned.

[198] Geryon's uncle: above, p. 481 note 99.

[199] Cf. *Die Kunst des Romans*, *Ges. Werke*, X, pp. 352–53. The classic discussion is that of E. Heller, *The Ironic German* (Boston–Toronto 1958). See above, p. 302 (Ariosto).

[200] Cf. "Identität entgegengesetzter Pole" (Bergsten, p. 244): "coincidentia oppositorum" (cited from Nicholas of Cusa and applied to Mann by O. Seidlin, *loc. cit.*, p. 146). This is a favorite formula of Eisenstein (above, p. 415 and note 52). For "art for art's sake" see *Doktor Faustus*, p. 290. For the *Durchbruch* to salvation, *Doktor Faustus*, p. 428.

When Adrian dies, after ten years of vegetation, on the 25th of August 1940 (the day and month of Nietzsche's death, and the day and month of Leopold II's birth), the sun, Apollo, is just entering Virgo, and has just escaped from Leo's clutches. Exactly twelve[201] years have elapsed since Echo's death. At Adrian's graveside appears a veiled female stranger, who disappears again as the first clods begin to fall on his coffin.

It is tempting to suppose that this lady is Madame de Tolna, whose invisible and encouraging presence has been felt in the composer's life in so many ways. But Madame de Tolna was herself a symbolic figure, the pledge of a kindly interest by ultimately gracious powers in Adrian's earthly travail. And perhaps all the time in the composer's Nike room Madame de Tolna's image stood as the guarantee of his final triumph. The Winged Victory[202] of Samothrace has been robbed by time of her human features, but this accidental "veiling" has, by a *felix culpa*, served to strengthen her resemblance to the faceless Virgo whom Eratosthenes and Hyginus find now in heaven, to the "veiled Isis" whom Plutarch saw in Sais,[203] as surely as Mann saw the Winged Victory in Paris. Adrian dies under the sign of Virgo. Only the reader can restore the appropriate expression of joy or sorrow to her face, and thus decide where the soul of Faustus burns.[204]

On a memorable evening in his Nike room Adrian had re-enacted Plato's *Symposium*. The principal theme of that dialogue (which also has its "intruded narrator") is the difference between the earthly and the heavenly Venus.[205] A few days after the death of the modern Faustus, perhaps on the day of his burial, Venus reached her greatest western elongation in the decan of the Fishes and, as the morning

---

[201] Again the significant number: cf. the 12 syllables of "Denn ich sterbe als ein böser und guter Christ" (*Doktor Faustus*, p. 646). Unity of opposites indeed!

[202] It is the apotheosis of the butterfly motif. For its occurrence in Apuleius' *Golden Ass* see p. 496 above, and, for the suggestion that Tolna is a speaking name connected with the Hungarian *toll* ("quill, feather, pinion"), note 110. Mann's debt to Hungarian sources needs further investigation: see, for example, Lörinc Szabó's *A Sátán müremekei* ("Satan's Works of Art"), 1926.

[203] The evidence of Eratosthenes/Hyginus on the faceless constellation Virgo is found in *Eratosthenis Catasterismorum Reliquiae*, ed. Carolus Robert (Berlin 1878), pp. 82–85. Mann has taken a powerfully ambivalent symbol from the ancient world to illustrate the many-sided nature of the artist's quest, which includes even the search for Justice. For Plutarch, see above, p. 494, note 144. When we read in Virgil *extrema per illos* [farmers]/*Iustitia* [= Virgo: cf. Aratus, *Phaenomena* 96 ff.] *excedens terris vestigia fecit* (*Geo.* II. 473–74) we realize why Adrian had to begin his search on a farm.

[204] Again Timanthes: see above, pp. 431, and 503 note 174.

[205] Also a Pythagorean doctrine (and Adrian is Pythagoras, with his mathematics and his music): K. Kerényi, *Töchter der Sonne* (Zürich 1944), p. 170. Rohde, *Psyche* (Eng. tr. by W. B. Hillis [repr. New York 1966], II, Appendix X), notes Pythagoras' legendary descent into hell.

star, began the climb back towards the sun. It is Venus the morning star who shines on Dante as he leaves hell, and begins his slow ascent to Purgatory and redemption.[206]

Adrian was not a Nazi, any more than Mann, for whose artistic career this novel is a long apologia. But he had qualities of romantic pessimism and death-wish which were to foster Nazism in his compatriots. Their delusion is not less horrible for being based on error and emptiness, and on a preoccupation with a wrong mythology.

In leaving the reader to resolve these allusive ambiguities, Mann has done more than bequeath to his novel a dying fall. The long tradition which we have been investigating in these pages, and which has led from the walls of Troy to the bewildering confusions of our own century, implies something for life as well as for letters. The devils have assailed more hearts and minds than those of Faustus. Literary criticism, literary scholarship, which ought to have been the guardian of pure and inspiring wells, have too often become an apothecary's aspirin, seeking to deaden the sea nymph's agonies of transformation as she searches, out of love, for a human soul. The "third humanism" ended in the Third Reich. Or did it?

[206] Dante's description of Venus in this passage: *velando i Pesci ch'erano in sua scorta* (*Purg.* I. 21), when applied to the interpretation of Mann's novel, shows that the *kleine Seejungfrau* has at last lost her fish tail, and broken through to immortality.

# Glossary of Critical Terms
## Select Bibliography
## Index

# GLOSSARY OF CRITICAL TERMS

**Acting:** According to (among others) Aristophanes, Aristotle, Horace, Tolstoy, Eisenstein, Pudovkin, the paradigm art for the major writer of epic/drama. Emotionally involved and even temporarily identified with each of his characters, the author is able to project into his work the fragments he selects from his imagination (see EIDOLOPOEIA), which are then reconstructed by his sympathetic audience. The work of art conceived in this way will, like a Shakespearean play, convey a totality of polyphonic ("many-voiced") meaning, and be incapable of carrying a univocal eulogistic or propaganda message. See also DRAMATIC, HERO, HYPOCRISIS, MONTAGE, POLYPHONY, PROSOPOPOEIA, RECITATIO, SKAZ.

**Admiratio:** Combining the meanings of "admiration" and "astonishment," this is the sole aim of great writing, according to a long tradition beginning after Aristotle and continuing at least until J. C. Scaliger. *Admiratio* implies high principles and high vocabulary. This partial view of the classical epic tradition, which ignores the comic admixture in both vocabulary and characterization found from Homer to Mann, should be recognized as a critic's bloodless abstraction which has damaged appreciation of the full range of many epics, notably the *Aeneid*. See also EKPLEXIS, CARNIVAL, COMIC EPIC, SUBLIME, THREE STYLES, VIRGIL'S WHEEL.

**Aetia (Aitia)** and **Aetia-Preface:** The *Aetia* is a major work in four books of elegiacs by the Greek Alexandrian poet of the third century B.C. Callimachus. It began with a reminiscence of Hesiod's *Theogony*, the poet as dreaming shepherd to whom the Muses appear. Its diverse narrative scheme anticipates, in later epic, works as different as Chaucer's *Canterbury Tales* and V. Hugo's *La Légende des Siècles*. Its account of Greek "origins," annihilating time (*q.v.*), has appealed to artistic imaginations at different levels, triggering both Virgil's *Aeneid* (*Musa, mihi causas memora*) and Ovid's *Fasti* (*Tempora cum causis*). The verse Preface prefixed by Callimachus in his old age, though preserved only fragmentarily, is a major document of the European poetic tradition, and has been often imitated. For a summary of its contents see above, pp. 24 ff.

**Alexandrian Code:** The complex of ideas denoting the Alexandrian intervention in epic. See ASCRA, BREVITY, CROWD, ENVY, HELICON,

HESIOD, HESIODIC EPIC, IRONY, PASTORAL, PLAY, POOR POET, PRIMUS LANGUAGE, RECUSATIO, SWEETNESS, WATER DRINKERS.

**Alexandrianism:** Narrowly defined, the spirit of the poetry written by Callimachus and his disciples. More largely, the poetry resulting from conscious calculation by artists uneasy with their world and profoundly aware of the past, and therefore a recurring phenomenon in the European tradition. For a statement of its poetic, see pages 20–21, 294–95, 394–95 above. It should be noted that nothing in Alexandrianism forbids the writing of epic, though clearly such poetic reflection on the heroic ideal will not readily yield all its meaning.

**Amplificatio:** See AUXESIS.

**Anaphora:** Emphatic verbal repetition (*q.v.*) at the beginning of successive clauses, a variety of the repetition (*q.v.*) which is so marked a feature of classical style. By "deforming" the narrative (i.e. departing from the norm of cool, abstract disclosure), it helps to convey emotion.

**Anti-hero:** An epic/dramatic character who to a greater or less degree flouts the conventional ideals of heroic behavior (see ADMIRATIO above). Since pathetic structure (*q.v.*) moves between polar antitheses, the anti-hero must occur, and has a legitimate place, in classical epic. See also HERO, MARGITES.

**Antithesis:** Contrast, the basic element of emotionally loaded pathetic structure (*q.v.*). It can occur on the small (red/white: see COLOR CONTRASTS) or the large scale (*War and Peace*). In its absence, the work of art falls flat.

**Aristophanes Effect:** Eisenstein's term for the unexpected realization of a metaphor: e.g. in Aristophanes' *Acharnians* the "King's Eye" turns out to be an actual Persian official, who literally "keeps an eye" on things. This comic (carnival) device has often been exploited for tragic ends, e.g. when Virgil turns the cliché "My love burns like the fires of Etna" into the real Etna of the end of *Aeneid* III. See also METAMORPHOSIS.

**Ars/Ingenium:** Sensitive to emotion, the Greeks, followed by the Romans, enjoyed antithesis (*q.v.*) even at the cost of logic. Art/genius, one of these antitheses, has some small critical value, which has been greatly exaggerated by the unthinking, especially since the Romantic Movement. It is evident that in fact great art demands great genius, and that great genius generates great art.

**Ascra:** Hesiod's birthplace, on the slopes of Mount Helicon (*q.v.*) in Boeotia. Hence *Ascraeum carmen* signifies Hesiodic/Callimachean poetry, and *Ascraeus senex*, Hesiod (*q.v.*).

**Autobiographical Fallacy:** The mistaken belief that Shakespeare must have murdered Duncan in order to write *Macbeth*; the naive failure to allow scope for powerful artistic imagination; the notion that a poet's "I" commits him to a binding affidavit.

**Automatism:** The development of the routine response which it is the artist's job to prevent, whether in himself or in his audience. See DISLOCATION, ESTRANGEMENT.

**Auxesis:** The use of rhetorical devices to enhance meaning, usually intended to excite the serious passions. A type of estrangement (*q.v.*).

**Brevity:** A basic device of pathetic structure (*q.v.*), which offers only fragments to the imagination of the auditor so that, by reconstructing the wholes from which the artist began, he becomes emotionally involved with the work of art, which he is as it were co-creating. See Callimachus fr. 57. 1 Pf. It should be noted that in this sense even a long work may be brief: cf. Quintilian's *brevis* of Thucydides, *I. O.* X. 1. 73. Stylized and taken to absurd length in the Middle Ages, and reduced nowadays to a subeditor's catchword. See EIDOLOPOEIA, MONTAGE, PARS PRO TOTO, PHANTASIA, TELLING DETAIL.

**Callida Iunctura:** "Cunning join," Horace's term (*A. P.* 47–48) for the unexpected juxtaposition ("montage," *q.v.*) of two ordinary words, which builds a bridge into fresh vistas. A method of avoiding pretentious vocabulary, while still effecting estrangement (*q.v.*).

**Carmen Perpetuum:** "One continuous song" (*hen aeisma diēnekes*) was what the Telchines (*q.v.*) missed in Callimachus, as he explains at the start of the *Aetia-Preface* (*q.v.*). This was the monotonous (i.e. devoid of polyphony, *q.v.*), wearisome epic harping on propaganda themes by pseudo-Homeric poets in return for pay. See also CYCLIC EPIC. Ovid employs the Latin equivalent of Callimachus' term with the conscious paradox of which he is fond to describe his *Metamorphoses* (I. 4), and Horace more soberly illustrates the real meaning of the term in his *Odes* (I. 7. 6).

**Carnival:** The popular, public feast at which all the normal values of staid, workaday life are reversed (dislocated). Characterized by the mixture of opposites, doubles, parody, puns, profanities, drunkenness, sex, masking, unmasking, laughter; by a special space (the public square, street, corridor, threshold, height, depth); and by a special, emotionally measured time (*q.v.*). The age-old tradition of such celebrations goes back to the ancient world (see KOMIC), and has left many traces in ostensibly more serious literature. See also METAMOR-PHOSIS, REDUCED LAUGHTER.

**Catharsis:** The purge/purification of the feelings which, in one form, is the aim of tragedy, according to Aristotle's famous definition (*Poetics* 1449 b 28). Often found puzzling by scholars, the doctrine of catharsis acquires new relevance from Eisenstein's insistence on the "leap into another dimension" (see ECSTASY OF PATHOS) produced by pathetic structure (*q.v.*). Perhaps the best analogy for both writers' meaning would be parturition, at once physical and psychological in effect. Compare the "Platonic child," *Symp.* 206 b.

**Character:** A person represented in narrative or drama. Since the "soul" of such literature is the myth (Aristotle, *Poetics* 1450 a 38) and not the individual soul of the hero (a term Aristotle does not use in this sense), the characters must serve the overriding, antithetical economy of the whole, and may therefore be inconsistently drawn, especially since their integration is a matter for the individual listener/spectator. It is enough for them to carry conviction in individual scenes. See also ANTI-HERO, ETHOS, HERO, VERISIMILITUDE.

**Chiasmus:** An ABBA structure.

**Clarity** (Greek *enargeia*): Not so much the dominie's prescription for uniform illumination (and therefore uniform monotony), as the stage-director's use of the spotlight for heightening effect. Obviously light on some things implies a corresponding obscurity for others (the painter's *chiaroscuro*), and this is why classical epics are no less clear, by their own standards, for leaving some things in the dark. See also GRAPHIC, VIVIDNESS.

**Color Contrasts:** Since both contrast (antithesis, *q.v.*), and the analogy with the other arts are basic to pathetic structure (*q.v.*), color contrasts in classical epic must be judged in relation to their emotional effect and structural function. Red/white in particular forms a basic psychological polarity still dominant in our day (Red Square/White House) which must be understood for what it is.

**Comic Epic:** Already attributed by Aristotle to Homer (the *Margites*, *q.v.*). Yet comedy is a feature even of more serious epics, from the *Iliad* (Andromache's "laughing through her tears," VI. 484) to Tolstoy and Thomas Mann. See also CARNIVAL.

**Counterpoint:** In literature, the musical harmony of recurring discords which compels us to integrate the individual part within a larger whole rather than single any one voice out for special attention. See POLYPHONY.

**Cross-reference:** Significant repetition (*q.v.*) of words and images at a distance, usually within the literary work, but sometimes intended to evoke a commented model. Often ignored or misunderstood as "carelessness," "lack of revision" or "learned affectation," this technique contributes powerfully to the unity and emotional impact of classical epic. See EXTERNAL REFERENCE, INTERNAL REFERENCE, LEIT-MOTIF, PARALLELISM, REPETITION, STRENGER SATZ, UNITY.

**Crowd:** The Alexandrian antithesis to the poet and his select audience. A perennial literary symbol ("O sprich mir nicht von jener bunten Menge . . ."), alive and well even in modern Russia (Blok). Its synonyms include *populus, vulgus* in Latin, and in Italian *plebe, volgo, mondo.*

**Cyclic Epic:** Originally a generic term for heroic epic believed not to be by Homer, and then applied by Callimachus to the trite Telchines' (*q.v.*) *carmen perpetuum* (*q.v.*), written to serve a propaganda aim. Since Greek *kyklos* = Latin *orbis*, the latter word acquired the meaning of "dull round of mediocre poetry" from the former: cf. Horace, *A. P.* 132; Prop. III. 2. 1.

**Deformation:** The manipulation of style or narrative away from the normal or expected to secure emotional effect. See DISLOCATION, ESTRANGEMENT, FABULA, SUBJECT.

**Deinosis:** "Making terrible," a species of auxesis (*q.v.*). Both are types of estrangement (*q.v.*), since the Greek adjective *deinos* means both "terrible" and "strange."

**Dénudation du Procédé:** The French translation of the Russian Formalist term *obnazhenie priyoma*, the "laying bare of the device." A technique by which the self-conscious artist exposes the artificiality of his art. Its uses range from the comic aside directed at the audience to a deliberate simplicity and even apparent naiveté of expression intended to be transparent to the profoundest feeling.

**Didactic:** An ancient stylistic polarity (see ARS/INGENIUM) revolved around the aim of poetry: was it entertainment (see PSYCHAGOGIA) or instruction? The ancients answered this question generically (i.e., without creating a separate subgenre of "didactic"): if poetry's aim was instruction, that was the aim of all poetry, including Homer's epics; if entertainment, that included the *Georgics* too. The greatest poetry, as some ancient critics saw, in fact serves both ends. Aristotle had wondered whether the expository didactic could be poetry at all. In affirming that it could, and championing Aratus' *Phaenomena*, Callimachus was reasserting the right to approach the problem of epic differently from the pseudo-Homeric pastiche (see CYCLIC EPIC) which had become fashionable. See also TELCHINES. Hence the importance to this Alexandrian alternative of Hesiod (*q.v.*). But Callimachus would have said that Hesiod wrote epic, not "didactic."

**Dislocation** (Russian *sdvig*): The carnival jolt given to stereotyped responses by the artist, the shift of perception which compels us to see rather than recognize things. See also AUTOMATISM, DEFORMATION, ESTRANGEMENT.

**Displacement of Structure:** Manipulation of the details of a story away from the trite and expected towards the emotionally gripping: often marked by lacunae (*q.v.*), or simple omission of the familiar and obvious in favor of some new perspective. See also DEFORMATION, SUBJECT.

**Dissolve:** A cinematic term for the retention of some outline or reminiscence of a departing scene as its successor takes shape: e.g. *Aeneid* III. 589 is repeated at IV. 7.

**Distancing:** Diderot's paradox, that the consummate actor impresses by his sincerity in the very moment that he is himself aware of artificiality, remains true of all art. Modern criticism has tended to emphasize the second part of the paradox (naturally enough in our Alexandrian age) to the detriment of the first. But this must not provoke a reaction that falls victim to the autobiographical fallacy (*q.v.*). Paradox requires two poles. See PHANTASIA, SINCERITY.

**Door:** The characteristic locale of religious and dramatic action. The terror behind the door may reveal itself as God, death, or, at another level, an eavesdropping slave. See THRESHOLD.

**Doubles:** The ambivalence basic to carnival (*q.v.*) art is often projected into twin or schizophrenic (internally twinned) characters. Virgil gives us Dido/Camilla, Dido/Turnus; Apollonius has Hypsipyle/Medea, Medea maiden/Medea witch.

**Double Chiasmus:** An ABBAAB structure.

**Dramatic:** This adjective was perhaps invented by Aristotle (*Poetics* 1448 b 35) and is certainly used by him to describe the technical qualities which he felt made the *Iliad* and *Odyssey* superior. Hence the fruitful interaction between the epic and tragic/comic genius so marked in the classical tradition. See ACTING.

**Durchbruch:** "Breakthrough"—the escape from the banality of tradition gone sour or trivial sought by Thomas Mann's hero Leverkühn in an archetypically Alexandrian dilemma: akin to Eisenstein's "leap into another dimension," "ecstasy of pathos" (*q.v.*).

**Ecphrasis:** A description introduced into the narrative, whether of scenery (*ekphrasis topou, locus amoenus*), architecture, or some material object or gift. Although such *ecphraseis* may at times be made for their own sake, poets of the classical tradition usually employ them as extended metaphors or symbols of the epic action. The most famous example of this is perhaps Aeneas' viewing of the paintings in Dido's temple of Juno (*Aeneid* I. 456 ff.). They are a film strip of the future course of the poem.

**Ecstasy of Pathos:** Eisenstein's term for the "leap into another dimension" which occurs after the spectator, hurled by the pathetically structured work of art from thesis to antithesis and back again, suddenly breaks through to a novel synthesis. See also CATHARSIS, DURCHBRUCH.

**Eidolopoeia:** "The formation of images." Under pressure of emotion, the imaginatively gifted artist bodies forth his feelings in visual images or other sensuous structures. He then breaks these down into fragments, which his work of art offers to his audience. Working from these fragments, the audience reconstitutes them (if they are compelling enough) into the wholes from which they came, experiencing in the process the same emotions as inspired the artist. See also ACTING, BREVITY, PARS PRO TOTO, PHANTASIA, TELLING DETAIL.

**Ekplexis:** "Consternation," "knockout." One of the effects of great art, erroneously regarded by some critics as its only effect. The error is compounded when such critics exclude from the artist's repertoire anything except the serious and sublime (*q.v.*), supposed to produce *ekplexis* without fail. They will not allow Beethoven to write his Sixth Symphony. See also ADMIRATIO.

**Enargeia:** See CLARITY, VIVIDNESS.

**Entrelacement:** "Interlacing." See KNOTS.

**Envy:** The reaction which the Alexandrian poet expects from the crowd (*q.v.*). The term had larger theological connotations ("the jealousy of the gods") in both Greek (Pindar, Herodotus) and Latin (Lucan), and the admixture of the two meanings seems important in the understanding of Petrarch's *Africa*.

**Epanadiplosis:** See ANAPHORA. In this form of rhetorical repetition, the plain narrative is deformed by intrusive initial and final recurrences, whether of proper names or a whole phrase. See E. Norden's note on *Aeneid* VI. 164.

**Epanaphora:** Another term for anaphora (*q.v.*), the repetition (*q.v.*) of the same word at the beginning of successive clauses. A device of estrangement and deformation (*qq.v*).

**Epyllion:** A small epic. The word is not used in this sense until late antiquity. An Alexandrian experiment in techniques to refresh the failing epic of the day. NOT a genre separate from or intended to replace the large-scale epic, except insofar as all attempts at novelty and originality must oppose the trite and stale. Eventually the techniques of the epyllion were subsumed into the larger epic, notably by Virgil.

**Estrangement** (Russian *ostranenie*): The dislocation (*q.v.*) of routine perceptions made by the artist in order to compel his audience to pay attention. V. Shklovsky's word, "a cumbersome coinage of his own" (R. F. Christian), uses the old rhetorical trick of practicing what it preaches.

**Ethos:** "Character" (*q.v.*), felt by the ancients to be appropriately explored for its own sake in comedy. This suggests in tragedy the primacy for them of the myth (Aristotle). The myth, not the soul of the hero, is the soul of the play.

**External Reference:** An allusion to another work of art, whether by the same author or someone else, intended to enhance and/or unify the narrative. See CROSS-REFERENCE.

**Fabula:** In Formalist doctrine, the myth on which a story is based: the normal or logical statement of what happens as opposed to the "subject" (*q.v.*), how the author in fact allows his audience to apprehend his tale. The distinction is valuable, since it forces us among other things to attend to what the author does not say. See also LACUNA.

**Fantasy:** See PHANTASIA.

**Gloss:** A rare or difficult word, intended to estrange the poetic narrative. May be combined with prosaic vocabulary, equally intended to estrange by deviating in the opposite direction from the poetic norm.

**Golden Section:** Divide the line AB unequally at C in such a way that AB : AC :: AC : CB. The Fibonacci series represented by 2/3, 3/5, 5/8, 8/13 etc. gives a rough approximation to the resulting proportion, which has had wide application in classical art and literature.

**Graphic:** "Painterly." Although the analogy between literature and painting was common in ancient criticism, it should be noted that a literary artist is not irrevocably committed to painting all the time, and much less to clarity (*q.v.*) in its Cartesian sense. Uniform clarity would be uniformly flat, and not visual but acoustic imagination is primary in the classical epic tradition, because its first analogy is with music. See Callimachus, fr. 282 Pf.

**Grotesque Body:** M. Bakhtin's term for the carnival exaggeration of physical characteristics seen in the wearing of ugly masks, long noses, etc. In general, metamorphosis (*q.v.*) of the smooth and well-proportioned into the rough and misshapen (*Iam iam residunt cruribus asperae/Pelles* . . . , Horace, *Odes* II. 20. 9). See MACABRE.

**Helicon:** The Boeotian mountain where Hesiod (*Theogony* 23) says he met the Muses while tending his sheep, and hence often a symbol of Hesiodic (and Alexandrian) poetic allegiance, since it was this scene from the *Theogony* which Callimachus recalled at the opening of his own *Aetia* (*q.v.*). The Homerizing, anti-Aristotelian Ennius significantly invoked at the start of his un-Callimachean epic the Muses of Olympus. See also HESIOD, HESIODIC EPIC.

**Hero:** A term not used by Aristotle in the sense of "leading character," and evidently alien to polyphonic (*q.v.*) art. Classical epic, since it is dramatic (*q.v.*) in structure, imitates *people* in action, and not ideal people at that.

**Hesiod:** An ancient Greek epic poet, variously dated, but possibly even older than Homer: author of *Works and Days, Theogony, Eoae* (*Catalogue of Women*), and supposedly of *The Shield, Astronomy*, etc. Used by Callimachus as the patron of the new Alexandrian epic, since Homer was pre-empted as a patron by the authors of the Telchines (*q.v.*) school. See ASCRA, HELICON.

**Hesiodic Epic:** The epic sanctioned by Callimachus, with Hesiod as its ancient patron or figurehead. Not opposed to Homer, since Callimachus' own *Hecale* imitates the *Odyssey*, but to imitations of Homer's mannerisms which miss his essence (see CYCLIC EPIC). Often denoted by allusions to Helicon, Ascra, water-drinking (*qq.v.*), the poet as dreaming shepherd (see PASTORAL), as receiving a garland or staff from the Muses.

**Hypocrisis:** "Acting ability," attributed to Virgil in a supreme degree (*Vit. Verg. Donati* 28–29), but latent in all classical epic authors, since their art, as Aristotle noted, always tends towards the dramatic. See ACTING.

**Imitation:** See MIMESIS.

**Intentional Fallacy:** The mistaken belief that an author is the best commentator on his own work, already rejected by Kant. If in fact a work of art engages levels of consciousness not accessible to ordinary, blinkered reason, the artist speaking in less intense moments may easily fail to comprehend what he has done.

**Interference:** The intervention by a powerful influence, whether that of an artist or a culture or both, which produces an unexpected development in a particular line of literary inheritance. Especially applied in this book to the twist given by Callimachus to the epic tradition. See DISLOCATION.

**Internal Reference:** An allusion within the work of art to another part of itself. See CROSS-REFERENCE, LEITMOTIF, STRENGER SATZ.

**Intruded Narrator:** A *persona* put by the author between the reader and the events of the story. A stage messenger is one version of this device, but so is any narrator who calls attention to his presence. A method of estranging the *fabula* (*q.v.*).

**Irony:** A commented relationship of the narrator to his narrative, indicated by devices of estrangement (*q.v.*). May exist at various levels, from amusing to profoundly tragic.

**Ischnos Character:** The "plain style" of ancient rhetoricians. Its use of ordinary language, repetition, triple structure (cf. Dante's *terza rima*), explains much in the epic tradition obscured by critical adherents of the grandiose sublime (*q.v.*).

**Kenning:** An allusive periphrasis intended to estrange familiar objects, already exploited by Hesiod.

**Knots:** Deviations from logical sequence. The complications of narrative intended to produce antithesis (*q.v.*) of action and character. See also COUNTERPOINT, POLYPHONY, SUBJECT.

**Komic:** More than comic, although both are the same word: having to do with the ancient *kōmos*, the Greek carnival (*q.v.*) procession in honor of Dionysus, characterized by masks, garlands, fancy dress, singing, punning, frankness, clowning, drunkenness, obscenity, scurrilous abuse, sexual license. For some stylized survivals of all these features, compare Alcibiades' intervention at the end of Plato's *Symposium*.

**Kuleshov Effect:** The camera's ability to create its own world and its own space and time by the most basic use of montage, simple juxtaposition.

**Lacuna:** A gap in narrative. Since such gaps are basic to pathetic structure (*q.v.*), the assumption that they are textual potholes disturbing the ideally smooth path of narrative should be scrutinized with some care. See also BREVITY, MONTAGE, SELECTION.

**Leap into Another Dimension:** See ECSTASY OF PATHOS.

**Learning:** The Alexandrian poet's awareness of vertical time (*q.v.*) leads him to enlarge and estrange the narrow horizons of the present by evoking obscure memories. Can produce resentment in readers who prefer automatism (*q.v.*).

**Leitmotif:** In literature, significantly repeated word(s) or images(s), intended to secure antithesis, irony, unity (*qq.v.*).

**Macabre:** The serio-comic exploitation of the "grotesque body" (*q.v.*). A type of estrangement (*q.v.*), often found in epic descriptions of battle scenes, corpses, necromancy and so on. See also CARNIVAL.

**Mannerism:** Exaggeration of normal characteristics: a mild and usually rather "downbeat" carnivalization of the classical.

**Margites:** "The Madman." A comic epic in mixed meter with a bumpkin hero attributed by Aristotle and Callimachus to Homer:

welcome evidence that the sterotyped sublime is not the real classical epic tradition.

**Metalepsis Aestheseos:** "Sharing of perception" (Greek). See SYN-AESTHESIA.

**Metamorphosis:** Transformation, a basic carnival device exploited by classical epic at many levels: Aristophanes effect, *callida iunctura*, doubles, grotesque body, leitmotif, metaphor, pun (*qq.v.*).

**Metaphor:** The seeing of one thing in terms of another. The sudden, fruitful association of the superficially disparate, the basic and un-teachable poetic gift.

**Metric Montage:** Presentation of narrative in measured and calculated units, from which the audience will reconstruct a whole conditioned by its emotional reaction to these mathematical and musical symmetries (*q.v.*).

**Mimesis:** Imitation, communication by means of sensuous images or structures intended to evoke emotionally compelling wholes. Brought into bad repute by Plato, but since the human organism depends for its life on sensory stimulation, without mimesis there cannot be art. Because the human mind is at work in the selection of the aspects of nature to be imitated, imitation is also a part of the process by which the particular is made a clue to the universal. See also TELLING DETAIL, PHANTASIA.

**Montage:** The presentation of narrative in juxtaposed fragments, to each of which the listener adds his own contribution, thus producing for himself an emotionally and intellectually satisfying whole. See EIDOLOPOEIA, PARS PRO TOTO, PHANTASIA, TELLING DETAIL.

**Musa Lecythizousa:** "Bombastic Muse": Callimachus' term (fr. 215 Pf.) for the overblown tragedy of his day. See also REDUCTION.

**Neoteric Simplification:** The "Neoterics" were the Roman first century B.C. poetic disciples of Callimachus. As befitted pioneers, they simplified some of his doctrines. In particular, his insistence on the irrelevance of length to poetic merit, intended to re-assert the primacy of artistic control, was blurred at times to suggest that *only* the short poem mattered. Neotericism is a version of Alexandrianism, but must not be taken too hastily to be a central definition of it.

**Non-linear Narration:** Linear narration is the logical/chronological statement of what happened. Artistically it is replaced by non-linear narrative, intended to secure antithesis and hence emotion. See DISPLACEMENT OF STRUCTURE, KNOTS, LACUNA.

**Occupatio:** "Anticipation": the medieval rhetorical term for the classical *praeteritio*, "passing over," in which the speaker affects to ignore a topic while actually mentioning it. Evidently in addressing an audience avid for brevity (*q.v.*), the speaker "anticipated" their objections to his long-windedness by promising to pass over a particular theme. This awareness of telling on borrowed time is brilliantly exploited by Chaucer's intruded narrator in the *Knight's Tale*.

**Opposites, Unity of:** The collocation of thesis and antithesis (*q.v.*) with the aim of their ultimate fusion into a novel synthesis. The basic form of pathetic structure (*q.v.*). See also UNITY.

**Parallelism:** Repetition (*q.v.*) of similar character(s), object(s), scene(s), motif(s), to secure unity and/or irony.

**Paronomasia:** Word play, punning (*q.v.*). By frustrating the pedestrian desire to make words mean what they say, this carnival device forces us to fresh visions of understanding. A good example of a comic trick with tragic possibilities.

**Pars Pro Toto (synecdoche):** The montage fragment from which our sympathetic imagination reconstructs the whole to which it belongs. *Ex pede Herculem.* See BREVITY, SELECTION.

**Pastoral:** Sanctioned as part of the Hesiodic epic tradition by the *Theogony* (23), but already the *Theogony* is far more than pastoral, so that inability to escape from that level must suggest a failure to explore the full range of the genre.

**Pathetic Structure:** The organization of a work of art in antithetical fragments. Demanding the collaboration of the audience for their interpretation, they continually force it into novel syntheses, ultimately with aesthetically shattering effect. See also ANTITHESIS, BREVITY, ECSTASY OF PATHOS, MONTAGE, OPPOSITES, UNITY OF.

**Pathos:** Emotion or feeling of any sort. An essential part of the desired aesthetic response to classical epic.

**Phantasia:** Artistically gifted imagination, ability to select emotionally stimulating images to convey meaning. See BREVITY, CLARITY, EIDOLOPOEIA, MIMESIS, PARS PRO TOTO, TELLING DETAIL.

**Play:** An Alexandrian term for art and artistic creativity, intended as a counterblast to serious and pompous notions of the grave sublime (*q.v.*). Not however always to be taken seriously.

**Play Without Transitions:** The relentless collocation of unexplained, jolting antitheses, favored by Eisenstein in his early period.

**Polarity:** The use of antithesis (*q.v.*). See also PATHETIC STRUCTURE.

**Polyphony:** As applied to literature, a narrative with many voices, all important and all ultimately absorbed into a harmony of the whole (*concordia dissonorum*). See COUNTERPOINT, OPPOSITES, UNITY OF, SKAZ.

**Polyptoton:** Use of the same word in different cases in the same context.

**Poor Poet:** A basic Alexandrian antithesis is between the creative artist, who remains true to his artistic conscience in writing what is aesthetically satisfying while ignoring material rewards, and the rich panderer to popular taste, whether as author of propaganda epic or wordy lawyer. See also CROWD, ENVY.

**Praeteritio:** See OCCUPATIO.

**Primus Language:** The claim to have been "first" with a particular poetic development, especially common in the classical Latin poets. A descendant of the Greek Alexandrian insistence on freshness and novelty, itself a variation of estrangement, (*q.v.*), but in its forthright crudeness smacking of the "neoteric simplification" (*q.v.*).

**Prose Poetry:** The concept of "imaginative" prose is already sanctioned by Aristotle, and indeed his teacher Plato had been a master of it. The continual exploitation of prosaic vocabulary by ancient poets, and the corresponding poeticization of prose (both forms of estrangement), inevitably meant that one day the prose epic would become a possibility, without entailing the repudiation of the classical inheritance. The epic ambition is already visible in historians like Herodotus, Thucydides, Livy and Tacitus.

**Prosopopoeia:** The vivid attribution of a particular speech to a character summoned up for the purpose of delivering it. Evidently a basic technique of the dramatist, later given wider scope in rhetorical theory. The "I" of such a character is not to be confounded with the real-life "I" of the author. See AUTOBIOGRAPHICAL FALLACY.

**Psychagogia:** "Soul enticement," an ancient name for the effect of powerful writing, evidently in Horace's mind when he thinks of rhyme as a species of "sweetness" (*q.v.*) at *A. P.* 99–100. Eratosthenes, third head of the Alexandrian Library, said that this, rather than instruction, was the aim of all poetry.

**Pun:** Komic (*q.v.*) double-entendre, dislocating (*q.v.*) safe and ordinary meanings. See PARONOMASIA.

**Recitatio:** The reading aloud by a poet of his own works, offering much scope for acting, drama, polyphony, sound gesture (*qq.v.*). Poetry so intended cannot be criticized in terms of selective quotation or simplifying outlines, any more than a Shakespearean play. The "evil effects of the *recitatio*" is a critical cliché of little value. Why did the *recitatio* have no evil effects on Herodotus, Virgil, Gogol, Dickens, Thomas Mann?

**Recurrence:** Significant repetition. Compare the musical "reprise."

**Recusatio:** The conventional "refusal" of the Alexandrian poet to sing of trite and hackneyed epic themes, sometimes disguised as the confession of his inability to do so. This poetic humility must not however be taken seriously. In a variation of the gambit, the poet may promise an epic eulogy "one day"; "meanwhile" he offers his present poem as a second best. This language too must not deceive. The discussion of the traditional features of the *recusatio* (e.g. the epiphany of the warning Apollo, as in Milton's *Lycidas*) by W. Wimmel, *Kallimachos in Rom*, is essential to the understanding of the classical epic tradition.

**Reduced Laughter:** In the counterpoise of the serio-comic style, a tip of the balance in one direction by the author may lead to an intended preponderance of the serious, even while basically komic (*q.v.*) devices and situations are still being exploited. Lucan and Milton, with their metamorphoses and paradoxes, are good illustrations of this lopsided type of poetry, which must always make the reader uneasy.

**Reduction:** A term put into Euripides' mouth to describe his approach to art by Aristophanes (*Frogs* 941). It signifies the removal of accumulated bombast by the reforming artist, an attempt to reduce the overblown affectations of a moribund tradition to a manageable and human scale. Since Euripides' actual word is *ischnana*, we may compare the rhetoricians' *ischnos charactēr* (*q.v.*).

**Repetition:** Music's most characteristic procedure. Hence to be both expected and closely scrutinized for its meaning in an art so deeply influenced by music as the classical epic tradition. See also CROSS-REFERENCE, LEITMOTIF, RECURRENCE, RING-COMPOSITION, STRENGER SATZ.

**Retardation:** Slowing down of the epic action to build suspense. See STAIRCASE STRUCTURE.

**Ring-composition:** A form of recurrence (*q.v.*), often a repeated word or words, used to mark the beginning and end of a larger or smaller section of narrative.

**Satire:** An unexpectedly frequent feature of the classical epic tradition (Lucretius, Lucan, Dante, Ariosto, Milton: compare Homer on Thersites), but to be understood as part of the whole complex of the *spoudogeloion* or serio-comic and of the carnival (*qq.v.*), not isolated and narrowed to the modern sense of "satirical," i.e. the negatively critical.

**Sdvig:** See DISLOCATION.

**Selection:** A basic principle of narrative technique in classical epic. The author highlights the emotionally compelling, and obscures or ignores the rest of his story (see Horace on Homer, *A. P.* 148 ff.). What he chooses to highlight may form his critique of the traditional tale. See also BREVITY, CLARITY, LACUNA, MONTAGE, SUBJECT, VIVIDNESS.

**Serio-comic:** The ambivalence of the carnival (*q.v.*), using fun for the serious purpose of refreshment and renewal, generates an ambiguous, motley style, half-poetry, half-prose, characterized by puns, metamorphosis, surprises, frankness, innuendo, anecdotes, satire, which can never quite take itself seriously, yet plays a larger role in epic than has been recognized.

**Signpost:** An anticipation, often verbal, of something to come: a preparation for a major development in the action. Of interest to the musician rather than the tourist.

**Simile:** An extended comparison, obviously a species of antithesis or unity of opposites, and of montage (*qq.v.*). Repeated similes are a favorite means in classical epic of securing unity and ironic contrast.

**Sincerity:** If it means "moral honesty," a necessary but not sufficient condition for great art. A sincere fool remains a fool, but a genius who implies, for example, that killing is enjoyable sins against the humanity of the classical epic tradition, and will find no place there.

**Skaz:** The oral narrative style, dominated by the changing voices of the actor/author, in which no one speaker has the final word. See ACTING, HYPOCRISIS, POLYPHONY, RECITATIO, SOUND GESTURE.

**Sophia/Technē:** Poetic wisdom/art: Callimachus' version (*Aetia-Preface* 17–18) of the Latin *ars/ingenium* (*q.v.*) antithesis, in which he declares that art is the final test of genius. This is right. The classical genius at least proves itself by its controlled response to creative stimulus.

**Sound Gesture:** The telling use of language by the *skaz* (*q.v.*), which with the aid of alliteration, assonance, puns, comic compounds, unexpected juxtapositions (a version of the *callida iunctura, q.v.*) allows the speaker's/actor's voice to convey a rich gamut of inflections, his comments in sound on the sense of what he is saying. See also PARONOMASIA, RECITATIO, TRANSRATIONAL LANGUAGE.

**Sphragis:** The "seal" set by an author on his work, when at the beginning or end he names himself. An old trick, perhaps inspired by Hesiod, *Theog.* 22.

**Spoudogeloion:** The Greek name for the serio-comic style (*q.v.*).

Developed at Rome under the name "satire" (*q.v.*) and already taken into epic by Lucretius, but not to be confused with the narrowly negative sense often given to modern satire. See also CARNIVAL.

**Staircase Structure:** The rise and rest of tension in the epic narrative, obviously a good example of antithesis (*q.v.*) and of pathetic structure (*q.v.*). Already noted by the ancient commentators in Homer. See RETARDATION.

**Strenger Satz:** The "strict style" explored by Thomas Mann in both *Buddenbrooks* and *Doktor Faustus*. The epic/musical themes are stated in order, and then each is taken up and developed in relation to the general unity of the story, never at random or without structural significance. The method of composition to which all classical epic aspires, notably the *Aeneid*.

**Stundenbild:** A more or less elaborate epic way of indicating the passage of time, often overdone, but effective when well handled and made part of the total structure. Shakespeare's satire of the topos (*q.v.*) in the Player King's speech in *Hamlet* (III. 2) contrasts with Horatio's "But, look, the morn, in russet mantle clad,/Walks o'er the dew of yon high eastern hill" in the same play (I. 1).

**Subject (Syuzhet, Sujet):** What the author does with the *fabula* (*q.v.*), his artistic deviations from the norms of cool, logical narrative. See DEFORMATION, DISPLACEMENT OF STRUCTURE.

**Sublime:** Emotional height, rightly regarded as one of epic's main ends, but not necessarily to be attained by following restrictive rules about vocabulary and heroic behavior. Such rules have in fact been frequently violated by the sublimest authors (Dante), and are basically anti-poetic, because they overlook the antithetical nature of pathetic structure (*q.v.*).

**Superimposition:** The (cinematic) blending of images in which memories of the old persist in the new amalgam. See DISSOLVE. A version of metamorphosis (*q.v.*) especially liked by Virgil.

**Sweetness:** A misleading translation of ancient terms for the powerful, piquant fascination aimed at by the Alexandrian poet. A Mozartian rather than "Sugar Plum Fairy" quality.

**Symmetry:** Balance, always latent in classical epic, and made patent by e.g. the Italian *ottava*. Since ancient rules prescribed that topics of equal importance should have equal space, by telling us what the author thought of the relative importance of his themes, it may imply an ironic commentary on the action. See also METRIC MONTAGE.

**Synaesthesia:** The interaction of senses which reveals the heightened awareness of the epic agonist under stress. Not to be flaccidly described as the "use of one sense instead of another."

**Synecdoche:** See PARS PRO TOTO, TELLING DETAIL.

**Tapeinosis:** "Making humble." The deliberate cheapening of some person, object or quality, intended to estrange. A comic and carnival device.

**Telchines:** Callimachus' name for his literary enemies, the advocates of the "one continuous poem in many thousands of verses" (see CARMEN PERPETUUM), intended to honor kings and heroes, i.e. of the pseudo-Homeric propaganda pastiche which passed for epic in his day. See CYCLIC EPIC.

**Telling Detail:** A narrative fragment which sets the audience's imagination working to reconstruct the larger whole from which it came. Not simply "a corroborative detail intended to lend artistic verisimilitude (*q.v.*) to an otherwise bald and unconvincing narrative" (W. S. Gilbert, *The Mikado*), but a particular clue to the universal. See BREVITY, CLARITY, MONTAGE, PARS PRO TOTO, VIVIDNESS.

**Tenuis (Genus Tenue):** "Thin," "slender," the Latin name for the *ischnos charactēr* (*q.v.*), a code word indicating the presence of Alexandrian influence. Opposed to *pinguis* "fat, rich."

**Three Styles:** At least from the time of Cicero's youth on, ancient rhetoricians distinguished the high or sublime style, the middle style, and the plain or low style. This schematism has its uses, but it had a disastrous consequence when certain genres were assigned to particular categories of it, and as a result the appreciation of the changing subtleties and range of genuinely classical epic was lost. See VIRGIL'S WHEEL.

**Threshold:** The religious point at which both sides of the door (*q.v.*) meet. Often a place of contest (*agon*), judgment or decision.

**Time:** Manipulated by the epic writer (see CARNIVAL, KULESHOV EFFECT) for emotional purposes, in a way which makes it as different from clock time as Bergson's *durée vécue* is from ordinary *temps*. Time in this mechanical sense may either be ignored (Ovid's *Metamorphoses*, Tolstoy's *War and Peace*), or given new elevation by being associated with sidereal phenomena, even with astrology (Apollonius, Dante, Petrarch, Boccaccio, Chaucer, Thomas Mann: cf. Ovid's *Fasti*). See also VERTICAL TIME.

**Topos:** A traditional theme or complex of themes. Certainly it is important to recognize them and guard against their too literal interpretation (see AUTOBIOGRAPHICAL FALLACY), but a great work of art uses its old material freshly, and it is the freshness which should interest the critic.

**Transrational Language:** Language whose sound and extraneous associations (see CALLIDA IUNCTURA, PARONOMASIA, SOUND GESTURE) convey as much meaning as or more than its literal sense. "Musical" language would be one variety of it.

**Unity:** The essential condition for a work of great art in the classical tradition: the combination of its parts into an aesthetically satisfying, organic (the metaphor is already used in Aristotle's *Poetics*) whole. Not to be obtained by simple logical or external criteria, but by such musical devices as repetition, parallelism, recurrence, leitmotif, external and internal reference, pathetic structure leading to ecstasy of pathos (*qq.v.*). See also STRENGER SATZ.

**Univocal:** "One-voiced," not displaying polyphony (*q.v.*).

**Vates:** An old word for "seer," revived at Rome under the influence of Posidonius and Varro Reatinus by Virgil and Horace in particular to denote the responsible public poet (following the example of his emperor) of the Augustan renewal. Mocked by Ovid in the *Metamorphoses*, the ideal is nevertheless of great importance in interpreting the intent of later poetry.

**Verbal Repetition:** A basic device of classical epic, intended to secure emotional, ironic and unifying effect.

**Verisimilitude:** Plausibility in epic narrative, evidently variable from audience to audience and reader to reader. Not objectivity but persuasion is its aim, because it is concerned with the particular only as a clue to the universal.

**Vertical Time:** The apprehension of time (*q.v.*) as a space in which past and future are here now. Evidently implied by those languages which find difficulty with Western tenses in the verb (although the "historic present" occurs even in Sanskrit) and often used by artists of every tradition.

**Virgil's Wheel:** See illustration facing p. 251. The misleading medieval diagram assigning different styles, vocabularies and topics to Virgil's *Eclogues, Georgics* and *Aeneid*. The notion that the *Aeneid* excludes (rather than subsumes) the plain and middle styles in favor of a monotonous sublime is utterly mistaken.

**Vividness:** The emotionally compelling description or narration of particular scenes, with evocation of telling detail (*q.v.*). See also BREVITY, CLARITY, MONTAGE, PARS PRO TOTO, PHANTASIA.

**Water Drinkers:** The old Greek antithesis water-drinker/wine-bibber, already used in the fifth century B.C. to contrast what Nietzsche was

ENNIUS, *Remains of Old Latin*, I (Ennius and Caecilius), tr. E. H. Warmington, reprinted London 1967.

ERATOSTHENES, *Eratosthenis Catasterismorum Reliquiae*, ed. Carolus Robert, Berlin 1878.

EURIPIDES, *Bacchae*, ed. E. R. Dodds, reprinted Oxford 1953.

————*Bacchae*, ed. J. E. Sandys, 4th edn., Cambridge 1900.

————*Euripides. Herakles*, ed. U. von Wilamowitz-Moellendorff, 3 vols., reprinted Darmstadt 1959.

————*Hippolytos*, ed. W. S. Barrett, reprinted Oxford 1969.

FARAL, E., ed., *Les arts poétiques du XIIᵉ et du XIIIᵉ siècle*, Paris 1924.

FIELDING, HENRY, *Tom Jones*, 2 vols., reprinted London 1962.

GALLUS, "Elegiacs by Gallus from Qaṣr Ibrîm," R. D. Anderson, P. J. Parsons, R. G. M. Nisbet, *Journal of Roman Studies* 69 (1979), 125–55.

GOW, A. S. F., ed., *Bucolici Graeci*, reprinted Oxford 1966.

————and PAGE, D. L., edd., *The Greek Anthology. Hellenistic Epigrams*, 2 vols., Cambridge 1965.

HESIOD, *Hesiodi Theogonia, Opera et Dies, Scutum*, ed. F. Solmsen, *Fragmenta Selecta*, edd. R. Merkelbach and M. L. West, Oxford 1970.

————*Hesiod. Theogony*, ed. with Prolegomena and Commentary by M. L. West, Oxford 1966.

HOMER, *Homeri Opera*, edd. David B. Monro and Thomas W. Allen, 5 vols., reprinted Oxford 1962–66.

————*Homer, Iliad XXIV*, ed. C. W. Macleod, Cambridge 1982.

————*Homer. Odyssey*, ed. W. B. Stanford, 2 vols., London and New York 1965.

HORACE, *Q. Horati Flacci Opera*, ed. E. C. Wickham, 2nd edn. by H. W. Garrod, reprinted Oxford 1941.

————*Horace on Poetry. The 'Ars Poetica'*, ed. with commentary by C. O. Brink, Cambridge 1971.

————*Q. Horatius Flaccus. Briefe*, edd. A. Kiessling and R. Heinze, 5th edn., Berlin 1957.

————*Q. Horatius Flaccus. Oden und Epoden*, edd. A. Kiessling and R. Heinze, 10th edn., Berlin 1960.

————*Q. Horatius Flaccus. Satiren*, edd. A. Kiessling and R. Heinze, 6th edn., Berlin 1957.

JUVENAL, *Juvenal and Persius*, ed. W. V. Clausen, reprinted Oxford 1966.

————*Juvenal: 13 Satires*, ed. J. E. B. Mayor, reprinted London 1966.

KINKEL, G., ed., *Epicorum graecorum fragmenta*, Vol. I, Leipzig 1877.

LLOYD-JONES, H. and PARSONS, P., edd., *Supplementum Hellenisticum*, Berlin–New York 1983.

LOMMATZSCH, E., ed., *Provenzalisches Liederbuch*, Berlin 1917.

"LONGINUS", *'Longinus' On the Sublime*, ed. D. A. Russell, Oxford 1964.

————See *Aristotle, The Poetics* etc., tr. W. H. Fyfe.

LUCAN, *M. Annaei Lucani Belli Civilis Libri Decem*, ed. A. E. Housman, reprinted Oxford 1958.

————*Lucan. De Bello Civili VII*, ed. J. P. Postgate, revised O. A. W. Dilke, Cambridge 1965.

LUCAS, ST. JOHN, *The Oxford Book of Italian Verse*, 2nd edn. revised by C. Dionisotti, Oxford 1952.

LUCRETIUS, *Lucretius. De Rerum Natura*, ed. C. Bailey, reprinted Oxford 1922.

———*Lucretius. De Rerum Natura III*, ed. E. J. Kenney, Cambridge 1971.

MACROBIUS, *Macrobius*, ed. J. Willis, 2 vols., reprinted Leipzig 1970.

MANN, THOMAS, *Gesang vom Kindchen. Ges. Werke*, Vol. VIII, pp. 1068 ff., Berlin–Frankfurt 1960.

———*Die Kunst des Romans. Ges. Werke*, Vol. X, pp. 348 ff., Berlin–Frankfurt 1960.

———*Briefe 1889–1936*, ed. Erika Mann, Frankfurt 1961.

———*Doctor Faustus*, tr. H. T. Lowe-Porter, New York 1948.

———*Doktor Faustus*, Stockholmer Gesamtausgabe der Werke von Thomas Mann, Frankfurt 1956.

———*Die Entstehung des Doktor Faustus: der Roman eines Romans. Ges. Werke*, Vol. XI, pp. 145–301, Berlin–Frankfurt 1960.

———*Über die Kunst Richard Wagners. Ges. Werke*, Vol. X, pp. 840 ff., Berlin–Frankfurt 1960.

MARTIAL, *M. Val. Martialis Epigrammata*, ed. W. M. Lindsay, 2nd edn., Oxford 1929.

MENANDER, *Dyskolos of Menander*, ed. E. W. Handley, London 1965.

MILTON, JOHN, *Works of John Milton*, New York 1931.

———*Milton's Complete Poems*, revised edition by F. A. Patterson, New York 1961.

———*The English Poems of John Milton*, ed. Walter Skeat, reprinted London 1948.

———*University of Illinois Edition of John Milton's Complete Poetical Works*, Vol. III, ed. H. F. Fletcher, 4 vols., Urbana 1948.

MOORE, G., ed., *The Penguin Book of Modern American Verse*, London 1954.

MOREL, W., ed., *Fragmenta Poetarum Latinorum*, Stuttgart 1963.

MOSCHUS, *Moschus. Europa*, ed. W. Bühler, Wiesbaden 1960.

———See Edmonds (tr.).

NONNUS, *Nonnus. Dionysiaca*, tr. W. H. D. Rouse, introduction and notes by H. J. Rose, textual notes by L. R. Lind, 3 vols., London 1962.

OVID, *P. Ovidi Nasonis Fastorum Libri VI*, ed. C. Landi, 2nd edn., L. Castiglioni, Turin 1950.

———*Metamorphoses*, tr. F. J. Miller, 2 vols., reprinted London 1960.

PAGE, D. L., ed., *Poetae Melici Graeci*, Oxford 1962.

———tr., *Select Papyri III. Literary Papyri. Poetry*, London 1950.

PERSIUS, See *Juvenal and Persius*.

PETRARCH, *L'Africa* per cura di Nicola Festa, Florence 1926.

———*Le rime di Francesco Petrarca* commentate da G. Carducci e S. Ferrari, Florence 1946.

PETRONIUS, *Pétrone, Apulée, Aulu-Gelle*, ed. M. Nisard, Paris n.d.

PHILODEMUS, *Philodemos: Über die Gedichte*, ed. C. Jensen, Berlin 1923.

PINDAR, *Pindar: Olympian and Pythian Odes*, ed. B. L. Gildersleeve, reprinted Amsterdam 1965.

_____*Pindari Carmina*, ed. L. Dissen, 2 vols. (esp. Vol. I, pp. XLVI ff.: "De tractatione fabularum"), Gothae et Erfordiae 1830.

_____*Pindari carmina cum fragmentis*, ed. A. Turyn, Oxford 1952.

_____*Pindarus*, ed. H. Maehler post B. Snell, Vol. I, 5th edn., Leipzig 1971, Vol. II, 4th edn., 1975.

_____*Scholia Vetera in Pindari Carmina*, ed. A. B. Drachmann, 3 vols., reprinted Amsterdam 1966.

PLATO, *Gorgias*, ed. E. R. Dodds, Oxford 1959.

_____*The Symposium of Plato*, ed. R. G. Bury, 2nd edn., Cambridge 1932.

PLUTARCH, *De Vita et Poesi Homeri* in *Plutarchi Chaeronensis Moralia*, ed. G. N. Bernardakis, Vol. VII, pp. 329–462, Leipzig 1896.

POWELL, J. U., ed., *Collectanea Alexandrina*, reprinted Oxford 1970.

PRESS, ALAN R., ed., *Anthology of Troubadour Lyric Poetry*, Austin 1971.

PROPERTIUS, *Propertius*, ed. E. A. Barber, 2nd edn., Oxford 1960.

_____*Sex. Propertii Elegiarum Liber I*, ed. P. J. Enk, 2 vols., Leiden 1946.

_____*Sex. Propertii Elegiarum Liber II*, ed. P. J. Enk, 2 vols., Leiden 1962.

PUDOVKIN, V., *Izbrannye Stat'i*, Moscow 1955.

PUSHKIN, A. S., *Polnoe Sobranie sochinenii v shesti tomakh*, Moscow 1949.

QUINTILIAN, *Institutio Oratoria*, ed. M. Winterbottom, 2 vols., Oxford 1970.

_____*Quintiliani Institutionis Oratoriae Liber XII*, ed. R. G. Austin, reprinted Oxford 1954.

QUINTUS SMYRNAEUS, *Quintus Smyrnaeus. Posthomericorum libri XIV*, ed. A. Zimmermann, reprinted Leipzig 1969.

RACINE, *Théâtre Complet de Racine*, Paris 1948.

_____*Les Plaideurs, Britannicus, Bérénice par Jean Racine*, ed. V.-L. Saulnier, Paris 1950.

SILIUS ITALICUS, *Punica*, tr. J. D. Duff, reprinted London 1961.

SMYTH, H. W., ed., *Greek Melic Poets*, reprinted New York 1963.

STATIUS, *Silvae*, ed. A. Marastoni, Leipzig 1970.

_____*Thebais*, revised ed. by Th. C. Klinert, Leipzig 1973.

_____*P. Papini Stati Thebais et Achilleis*, ed. H. W. Garrod, reprinted Oxford 1965.

_____*A Concordance to Statius* (computer based list of occurrences of all unique words in Statius taken from the Teubner editions of Klinert and Marastoni), ed. J. A. Klecka, Library of the University of Illinois 1977.

STERNE, L., *Tristram Shandy*, reprinted London 1961.

TACITUS, *Cornelii Taciti Annalium . . . Libri*, ed. C. D. Fisher, reprinted Oxford 1946.

_____*Cornelii Taciti Dialogus de Oratoribus*, ed. M. L. de Gubernatis, Turin 1949.

_____*Histories I and II*, ed. A. L. Irvine, reprinted London 1961.

_____*Cornelii Taciti Opera Minora*, ed. H. Furneaux, reprinted Oxford 1949.

TASSO, T., *Gerusalemme Liberata, Aminta, Rime Scelte* etc. a cura di Luigi De Vendettis, Turin 1961.

_____*Jerusalem Delivered*, tr. E. Fairfax, introduced by R. Weiss, Carbondale, Ill. 1962.

THEOCRITUS, *Theocritus*, ed. A. S. F. Gow, 2 vols., Cambridge 1965.

TIBULLUS, *The Elegies of Albius Tibullus*, ed. K. F. Smith, reprinted Darmstadt 1964.

TOLSTOY, LEO, *Voina i Mir*, 2 vols., reprinted Moscow 1957.

_____*War and Peace*, tr. L. and A. Maude, reprinted London 1970.

_____*What is Art?*, tr. A. Maude, reprinted London 1969.

TRYPANIS, C. A., *Medieval and Modern Greek Poetry: An Anthology*, reprinted Oxford 1968.

VALERIUS, C. *Valeri Flacci Setini Balbi Argonauticon libri octo*, ed. P. Langen, reprinted Hildesheim 1964.

_____*Valerius Flaccus. Argonautica*, ed. J. A. Wagner, Göttingen 1805.

VIRGIL, *The Aeneid*, ed. J. W. Mackail, Oxford 1930.

_____*P. Vergili Maronis Opera*, ed. R. A. B. Mynors, Oxford 1969.

_____*Virgil. Aeneid I*, ed. R. G. Austin, Oxford 1971.

_____*Virgil. Aeneid II*, ed. R. G. Austin, Oxford 1964.

_____*Virgil. Aeneid III*, ed. R. D. Williams, Oxford 1962.

_____*Virgil. Aeneid IV*, ed. R. G. Austin, Oxford 1955.

_____*Virgil. Aeneid V*, ed. R. D. Williams, Oxford 1960.

_____*Vergilius. Aeneis VI*, ed. E. Norden, reprinted Stuttgart 1957.

_____*Virgil. Aeneid XII*, ed. W. S. Maguinness, London 1953.

_____*Vitae Vergilianae*, ed. J. Brummer, Leipzig 1912.

_____*Vitae Vergilianae Antiquae*, ed. C. Hardie, Oxford 1967.

## II. Select Secondary Works

ADAM, L., *Die aristotelische Theorie vom Epos nach ihrer Entwicklung bei Griechen und Römern*, Wiesbaden 1889.

AHL, F., *Lucan, An Introduction*, Ithaca 1976.

ALLEN, DON CAMERON and ROWELL HENRY T., edd., *The Poetic Tradition. Essays on Greek, Latin, and English Poetry* (esp. "The Uniqueness of Spenser's Epithalamion" by W. Clemen, pp. 81 ff.), Baltimore 1968.

ALLEN, W., Jr., "The Epyllion: A Chapter in the History of Literary Criticism," *Transactions and Proceedings of the American Philological Association* 71 (1940), 1–26.

ALLOTT, K., ed., *The Penguin Poets: Contemporary Verse* (esp. p. 16), London 1951.

AMBROGIO, I., *Formalismo e Avanguardia in Russia*, Rome 1968.

ARBUSOW, L. *Colores Rhetorici*, reprinted Göttingen 1963.

AREND, W., *Die typischen Szenen bei Homer. Problemata 7*, Berlin 1933.

ARIAS, P. E. and HIRMER, M., *A History of Greek Vase Painting*, London 1962.

AUERBACH, E., *Literary Language and its Public*, tr. R. Manheim, London 1965.

_____*Mimesis*, tr. W. Trask, New York 1957.

AXELSON, B., *Unpoetische Wörter*, Lund 1945.

BAKHTIN, M., "Epos i Roman," *Voprosy Literatury* 14. 1 (1970), 95–122.

_____*Problemy Poetiki Dostoevskogo*, Moscow 1963.

_____*Tvorchestvo François Rabelais i Narodnaya Kul'tura Srednevekov'ya i Renessansa*, Moscow 1965.

BARDON, H., *La littérature latine inconnue*, 2 vols., Paris 1952, 1956.

―――――*Les Empereurs et les lettres latines d'Auguste à Hadrien*, Paris 1940.

BAROOSHIAN, VAHAN D., *Russian Cubo-Futurism 1910–1930*, The Hague–Paris 1974.

BATES, H. W., *The Naturalist on the River Amazon*, 2nd edn., London 1864.

BAYLEY, J., *Tolstoy and the Novel*, New York 1967.

BENGTSON, H., *Griechische Geschichte*, Munich 1950.

BENSON, R. C., *Women in Tolstoy: The Ideal and the Erotic*, Urbana 1973.

BERGSTEN, G., *Thomas Manns Doktor Faustus*, Lund 1963.

BERSCHIN, WALTER, *Griechisch-Lateinisches Mittelalter*, Bern 1980.

BEYE, C., *The Iliad, the Odyssey and the Epic Tradition*, Garden City, N. Y. 1966.

BIEBER, M., *The Sculpture of the Hellenistic Age*, 2nd edn., New York 1967.

BLAIKLOCK, E. M., "The Nautical Imagery of Euripides' *Medea*," *Classical Philology* 50 (1955), 233 ff.

BLANCHARD, E. S., *Structural Patterns in Paradise Lost. Milton's Symmetry and Balance*, diss. microfilm, Rochester, N. Y. 1966.

BLOCH, G. and CARCOPINO, J., *Histoire Romaine*, 3rd edn., Paris 1952.

BOGUE, P., *Astronomy in the Argonautica of Apollonius Rhodius*, diss. Urbana 1977.

BOITANI, PIERO, *Chaucer and Boccaccio*, Oxford 1977.

BOLGAR, R. R., *The Classical Heritage*, reprinted New York 1964.

BORINSKI, K., *Die Antike in Poetik und Kunsttheorie vom Ausgang des klassischen Altertums bis auf Goethe und Wilhelm von Humboldt*, Bd. 1–2, Leipzig 1914–24.

BORLENGHI, A., *Storia della critica, 9. Ariosto*, Palermo 1961.

BORTHWICK, E. K., "The Riddle of the Tortoise and the Lyre," *Music and Letters* LI (1970), 373–87.

BOSC, ROBERT, "Le Théâtre épique de Berthold Brecht," *Études* 89, t. 288 (1956), 79–93 (esp. 84–87).

BOWRA, C. M., "Dante and Arnaut Daniel," *Speculum* XXVII (1952), 459–74.

―――――*From Virgil to Milton*, London 1945.

―――――*Heroic Poetry*, reprinted London 1964.

―――――*The Simplicity of Racine*, Oxford 1956.

―――――*Tradition and Design in the Iliad*, reprinted Oxford 1963.

BOYDE, P., *Dante's Style in his Lyric Poetry*, Cambridge 1971.

BRAND, C. P., *Torquato Tasso*, Cambridge 1965.

BRADEN, GORDON, *Renaissance Tragedy and the Senecan Tradition: Anger's Privilege*, New Haven 1985.

BRINK, C. O., *Horace on Poetry. Prolegomena to the Literary Epistles*, Cambridge 1963.

―――――*Horace on Poetry. The 'Ars Poetica'*, Cambridge 1971.

―――――(K. O.), "Callimachus and Aristotle," *Classical Quarterly* XL (1946), 11 ff.

BROOKS, DOUGLAS, *Number and Pattern in the Eighteenth-Century Novel*, London 1973.

BROWN, E. L., *Numeri Vergiliani*, Brussels 1963.

BROWN, ROBERT D., "Lucretius and Callimachus," *Illinois Classical Studies* VII (1982), 77–97.

BÜCHNER, K., *Lukrez und Vorklassik*, Wiesbaden 1964.

BURCK, E., *Die Erzählungskunst des T. Livius. Problemata 11*, Berlin 1934.

BURCKHARDT, J., *The Civilization of the Renaissance in Italy*, tr. S. G. C. Middlemore, reprinted Oxford and London 1945 (Phaidon).

BUSH, D., *A Variorum Commentary on the Poems of John Milton*, New York 1970.

BUTLER, H. E., *Post-Augustan Poetry from Seneca to Juvenal*, Oxford 1909.

CAHEN, J.-G., *Le vocabulaire de Racine*, Paris 1946.

CAIRNS, F. J., *Generic Composition in Greek and Roman Poetry*, Edinburgh 1972.

CAMERON, ALAN, *Claudian: Poetry and Propaganda at the Court of Honorius* (esp. pp. 253 ff., "Techniques of the Poet"), Oxford 1970.

CAMPANA, A., "The origin of the word 'humanist'," *Journal of the Warburg and Courtauld Institutes* 9 (1946), 60–73.

CAMPBELL, M., *Studies in the Third Book of Apollonius Rhodius' Argonautica*, Hildesheim 1983.

CANCIK, H., *Untersuchungen zur lyrischen Kunst des P. Papinius Statius*, Hildesheim 1965.

CARNEGY, P., *Faust as Musician*, London and New York 1973.

CHIAPPORE, M., "Le Chapitre XX de la *Poétique* et le *Logos* de la tragédie," in *Écriture et Théorie Poétiques*, Paris 1976.

CHRISTIAN, R. F., *Tolstoy's 'War and Peace': A Study*, Oxford 1962.

CLARKE, H., *Homer's Readers*, Newark–London–Toronto 1981.

COHEN, J. M., *Poetry of this Age*, London 1959.

COLLINGE, N. E., *The Structure of Horace's Odes*, Oxford 1961.

COMBELLACK, F. M., "Contemporary Homeric Scholarship," *Classical World* XLIX (1955), 29.

————"Contemporary Unitarians and Homeric Scholarship," *American Journal of Philology* LXXI (1950), 337.

————"Milman Parry and Homeric Artistry," *Comparative Literature* XI (1959), 193.

COMPARETTI, D., *Virgilio nel medio evo*, Florence 1896.

————tr. E. F. M. Benecke, reprinted Hamden, Conn. 1966.

CORMICAN, L. A., "Milton's Religious Verse," *A Guide to English Literature 3: From Donne to Marvell*, ed. Boris Ford, pp. 173 ff., London 1956.

COTTAZ, J., *Le Tasse et la Conception Épique*, Paris 1942.

CULLEN, JONATHAN D., *Structuralist Poetics*, Ithaca 1975.

CURTIUS, E. R., *Europäische Literatur und lateinisches Mittelalter*, Bern 1948.

————*Kritische Essays zur europäischen Literatur*, 2nd edn., Bern 1954.

D'ALTON, J., *Roman Literary Theory and Criticism*, reprinted New York 1962.

DEMETZ, P., ed., *Brecht: A Collection of Critical Essays*, Englewood Cliffs 1962.

DENNISTON, J. D., *Greek Prose Style*, Oxford 1965.

DICKIE, M. W., "Ovid Metamorphoses 2. 760–64," *American Journal of Philology* 96 (1975), 378–90.

DIEZ, F., *Die Poesie der Troubadours*, Zwickau 1826.

————*Leben und Werke der Troubadours*, 2nd edn., Leipzig 1882.

DOREY, T. A., ed., *Livy*, London–Toronto 1971.

DÖRING, A., *Die Kunstlehre des Aristoteles*, Jena 1876.

DORNSEIFF, F., *Pindars Stil*, Berlin 1921.

DRAEGER, A., *Syntax und Stil des Tacitus*, reprinted Amsterdam 1967.

DRONKE, P., *Medieval Latin and the Rise of European Love-Lyric*: Vol. I, *Problems and Interpretations*; Vol. II, *Medieval Latin Love Poetry*, 2nd edn., Oxford 1968.

DUCKWORTH, G. E., *Foreshadowing and Suspense in the Epics of Homer, Apollonius and Vergil*, Princeton 1933.

_____*Structural Patterns and Proportions in Vergil's Aeneid: A Study in Mathematical Composition*, Ann Arbor 1962.

DUPONT-ROC, R. and LALLOT, J., "La Syrinx," *Poétique* 18 (1974), 176 ff.

EICHENBAUM, B. M., *Lev Tolstoi*, 2 vols., Leningrad 1928–31, reprinted Munich 1968.

_____*Literatura*, Leningrad 1927.

_____*Skvoz' Literaturu*, The Hague 1962.

_____*The Young Tolstoy*, tr. and ed. G. Kern, Ann Arbor 1972.

ELSE, G. F., *Aristotle's Poetics: The Argument*, Cambridge, Mass. 1957.

ERBSE, H., "Aristoteles über Tragödie und Geschichtsschreibung," *Bonner Festgabe Johannes Straub*, pp. 127–36, Bonn 1977.

ERLICH, V., *Russian Formalism, History–Doctrine*, 3rd edn., The Hague 1969.

ESCH, A. ed., *Chaucer und Seine Zeit*, Tübingen 1968.

FERRY, ANNE, *Milton's Epic Voice*, Cambridge, Mass. 1963.

FRAENKEL, E., *De media et nova comoedia quaestiones selectae*, Göttingen 1912.

_____*Elementi plautini in Plauto*, Florence 1960.

_____*Horace*, Oxford 1957.

_____*Kleine Beiträge zur Klassischen Philologie*, Vol. II, Rome 1964.

_____*Leseproben aus Reden Ciceros und Catos*, Rome 1968.

FRÄNKEL, H., *Die homerischen Gleichnisse*, Göttingen 1921.

_____*Noten zu den Argonautika des Apollonios*, Munich 1968.

VON FRANZ, M.-L., *Die aesthetischen Anschauungen der Iliasscholien*, Zürich 1943.

FRASER, P. M., *Ptolemaic Alexandria*, Oxford 1972.

FREUDENBERG, O., *Poetika Syuzheta i Zhanra*, Leningrad 1936.

FRIEDLAENDER, L., *Darstellungen aus der Sittengeschichte Roms*, Vol. I, 10th edn., Leipzig 1922.

FRIEDRICH, HUGO, "Ueber die Silvae des Statius (insbesondere V, 4, Somnus) und die Frage des literarischen Manierismus," *Wort und Text: Festschrift für Fritz Schalk*, edd. H. Meier and H. Sckommodau, pp. 34–56, Frankfurt 1963.

FRIEDRICH, R., *Stilwandel im homerischen Epos*, Heidelberg 1975.

GEANAKOPLOS, D. J., *Greek Scholars in Venice*, Cambridge, Mass. 1962.

GELZER, M., *Caesar*, 6th edn., Wiesbaden 1960.

GRANDI, H., *Die Musik im Roman Thomas Manns*, diss. Berlin 1952.

GRANT, M., "Nero: The Two Versions," *History Today* 4 (1954), 319–25.

GRIFFIN, J., *Homer on Life and Death*, Oxford 1980.

GRIMM, R., *Berthold Brecht: Die Struktur seines Werkes*, 3rd edn., Nürnberg 1962.

_____*Episches Theater*, Köln–Berlin 1966.

VAN GRONINGEN, B. A., *La composition littéraire archaïque grecque*, 2nd edn., Amsterdam 1960.

————*La poésie verbale grecque*, Koninklijke Nederlandse Akademie van Wetenschappen, Letterkunde, N. R. 16 (1953), pp. 169 ff.

GRUBE, G. M. A., *The Greek and Roman Critics*, London 1965.

GULLINI, G. M., *I Mosaici di Palestrina*, Rome 1956.

————"La datazione e l'inquadramento stilistico del santuario della Fortuna Primigenia a Palestrina," *Aufstieg und Niedergang der römischen Welt*, Vol. IV, Berlin–New York 1973, 767 ff.

HÄNDEL, P., "Vergils Aristaeus-Geschichte," *Rheinisches Museum* 105 (1962), 66 ff.

HALTER, T., *Form und Gehalt in Vergils Aeneis*, Munich 1963.

HARDING, DAVIS P., *Milton and the Renaissance Ovid*, Urbana 1946.

HARRE, P., *De verborum apud Pindarum conlocatione*, diss. Berlin 1867.

HÄUSSLER, R., *Das historische Epos der Griechen und Römer bis Vergil*, Heidelberg 1976.

————*Das historische Epos von Lucan bis Silius und seine Theorie*, Heidelberg 1978.

HEIM, K., *Thomas Mann und die Musik*, diss. Freiburg im Breisgau 1952.

HEINE, R., *Untersuchungen zur Romanform der Metamorphosen des Apuleius von Madaura*, diss. Göttingen 1962.

HEINZE, R., *Virgils epische Technik*, 4th edn., Stuttgart 1957.

HEISERMAN, A., *The Novel before the Novel*, Chicago and London 1977.

HELLER, E., *The Ironic German*, Boston–Toronto 1958.

HELLER, J. L. with the assistance of J. K. NEWMAN, edd., *Serta Turyniana. Studies in Greek Literature and Palaeography in honor of Alexander Turyn*, Urbana–Chicago–London 1974.

HENNING, M., *Die Ich-Form und ihre Funktion in Thomas Manns "Doktor Faustus" und in der deutschen Literatur der Gegenwart*, Tübingen 1966.

HERRICK, MARVIN T., *The Fusion of Horatian and Aristotelian Literary Criticism 1531–1555*, Urbana 1946.

HERTER, H., "Kallimachos und Homer," reprinted in *Kallimachos*, ed. A. D. Skiadas, pp. 354 ff., Darmstadt 1975.

HOFMAN, A., *Thomas Mann und die Welt der russischen Literatur*, Berlin 1967.

HOFMANN, J. B., *Lateinische Umgangssprache*, 3rd edn., Heidelberg 1951.

HOFSTÄTTER, H., *Art of the Late Middle Ages*, tr. R. E. Wolf, New York 1968.

HOLTHUSEN, H. E., *Die Welt ohne Transzendenz*, Hamburg 1949.

HOUSE, H., *Aristotle's Poetics*, London 1967.

HOWARD, DONALD R., *The Idea of the Canterbury Tales*, Berkeley 1976.

HURST, A., *Apollonios de Rhodes: Manière et Cohérence*, Rome 1967.

ILLIG, L., *Zur Form der pindarischen Erzählung*, Berlin 1932.

JANKO, RICHARD, *Aristotle on Comedy: Towards a Reconstruction of Poetics II*, London 1984.

JENSEN, J. J., "An Outline of Vergil's Mathematical Technique," *Symbolae Osloenses* XLV (1970), 113–17.

JUNGHANNS, P., *Die Erzählungstechnik von Apuleius' Metamorphosen und ihrer Vorlage. Philologus Supplementband* XXIV, 1932.

KAHANE, H. and R., "Akritas and Arcita: A Byzantine Source of Boccaccio's *Teseida*," *Speculum* XX (1945), 475 ff.

KAKRIDIS, JOHANNES TH., *Homeric Researches*, Lund 1949.

KAMBYLIS, A., *Die Dichterweihe und ihre Symbolik*, Heidelberg 1965.

KASSEL, R., *Untersuchungen zur griechischen und römischen Konsolationsliteratur*, *Zetemata* 18, Munich 1958.

KENNEDY, JUDITH M. and REITHER, JAMES A., edd., *A Theatre for Spenserians*, Manchester 1973.

KENNEY, E. J., "Virgil and the Elegiac Sensibility," *Illinois Classical Studies* VIII (1982), 44–59.

KERÉNYI, K., *Töchter der Sonne*, Zürich 1944.

KHOURI, M. A., "Literature," in *The Genius of Arab Civilization*, ed. J. R. Hayes, 2nd edn., Cambridge, Mass. 1983.

KIERKEGAARD, S., *The Concept of Irony*, tr. Lee M. Capel, London 1966.

KIRK, G. S., *Homer and the Oral Tradition* (esp. pp. 69 ff.), Cambridge 1976.

————*The Songs of Homer*, Cambridge 1962.

KLARE, M., *Studien zu Thomas Manns "Doktor Faustus,"* Bonn 1973.

KLIBANSKY, R., PANOFSKY, E. and SAXL, F., *Saturn and Melancholy*, New York 1964.

KLINGNER, F., *Römische Geisteswelt*, 4th edn., Munich 1961.

————*Virgils Georgica*, Zürich–Stuttgart 1963.

KNAUER, G. N., *Die Aeneis und Homer*, Göttingen 1964.

————"Vergil's Aeneid and Homer," *Greek, Roman and Byzantine Studies* 5 (1964), 61–84.

KNIGHT, R.-C., *Racine et la Grèce*, Paris n.d.

KÖHNKEN, A., *Apollonios Rhodios und Theokrit*, *Hypomnemata* 12, Göttingen 1965.

KÖRTE, A. and HÄNDEL, P., *Die hellenistische Dichtung*, Stuttgart 1960.

KONKIN, S. S., ed., *Problemy Poetiki i Istorii Literatury* (esp. the article by V. V. Ivanov, "Iz zametok o stroenii i funktsiyakh karnaval'nogo obraza," pp. 37–53), Saransk 1973.

KORNEMANN, E., *Römische Geschichte*, II, 4th edn., Stuttgart 1954.

KOSTER, S., *Antike Epostheorien*, Wiesbaden 1970.

KRAUSSE, O., *De Euripide Aeschyli instauratore*, diss. Jena 1905.

KREMERS, D., *Der "Rasende Roland" des Ludovico Ariosto*, Stuttgart 1973.

KREUZER, H. and GUNZENHÄUSER, R., *Mathematik und Dichtung*, 2nd edn., Munich 1967.

KROLL, W., "Rhetorik," *RE Supplement VII*, cols. 1039–1138.

————*Studien zum Verständnis der römischen Literatur*, Stuttgart 1924.

KRUIF, PAUL H. DE, *Microbe Hunters*, New York 1926, German tr. *Mikrobenjäger*, Zürich–Leipzig 1927.

KRUMBACHER, K., *Geschichte der Byzantinischen Litteratur*, 2 vols., reprinted New York 1970.

LALLOT, J and BOULLUEC, A. LE, edd., *Écriture et Théorie Poétiques. Lectures d'Homère, Eschyle, Platon, Aristote*, Presses de l'école normale supérieure, Paris 1976.

LANGERBECK, H., "Margites," *Harvard Studies in Classical Philology* 63 (1958), 33 ff.

LAPP, F., *De Callimachi Cyrenaei Tropis et Figuris*, Bonn 1965.

LAQUEUR, R., "Ephoros," *Hermes* 46 (1911), 161 ff.; 321 ff.

LATTE, K., *Römische Religionsgeschichte*, Munich 1960.

LEBEK, W. D., *Lucans Pharsalia*, Göttingen 1976.

LEFF, G., *Medieval Thought*, London 1968.

LE GRELLE, G., S. J., "Le premier livre des Géorgiques; poème pythagoricien," *Les Études Classiques* 17 (1949), 139–235.

LESKY, A., *A History of Greek Literature*, tr. J. Willis and C. de Heer, London 1966.

————"Homeros," *RE Supplement XI*, cols. 687–846.

LEVIN, D. N., *Apollonius' Argonautica Reexamined I. Mnemosyne Supplement 13*, Leyden 1971.

LINDEMANN, K., *Beobachtungen zur livianischen Periodenkunst*, Marburg 1964.

*L'Influence grecque sur la poésie latine de Catulle à Ovide* (Entretiens Hardt, II), Vandoeuvres–Genève 1953.

LLOYD, G. E. R., *Polarity and Analogy*, Cambridge 1966.

LLOYD-JONES, HUGH and REA, JOHN, "Callimachus, Fragments 260–261," *Harvard Studies in Classical Philology* 72 (1967), 125 ff.

LOVEJOY, A. O., *The Great Chain of Being*, Cambridge, Mass. 1936.

MASSON, D., *Life of Milton*, II, London and New York 1871.

MCANANY, E. J. and WILLIAMS, R., *The Filmviewer's Handbook*, Glen Rock, New Jersey 1965.

MARESCA, T. E., *Epic to Novel*, Columbus, Ohio 1974.

MAYER, H., *B. Brecht und die Tradition*, Pfullingen 1961.

MEHMEL, F., *Valerius Flaccus*, Hamburg 1934.

MEIER, H. and SCKOMMODAU, H., edd., *Wort und Text: Festschrift für Fritz Schalk* (esp. H. Ruediger, "Curiositas und Magie: Apuleius und Lucius als literarische Archetypen der Faustgestalt," pp. 57–82), Frankfurt 1963.

METTE, H. J., "Doktor Faustus und Alexander," *Deutsche Vierteljahrsschrift* 25 (1951), 27–39.

METZLER, I., *Dämonie und Humanismus. Funktion und Bedeutung der Zeitblomgestalt in Thomas Manns Doktor Faustus*, Munich 1960.

MEYER, E., *Caesars Monarchie und das Principat des Pompejus*, 3rd edn., Stuttgart–Berlin 1922.

MEZGER, F., *Pindars Siegeslieder*, Leipzig 1880.

MÖLK, U., *Trobar clus, trobar leu*, Munich 1968.

MORPURGO-TAGLIABUE, G., "La linguistica di Aristotele e il XX capitolo della *Poetica*," *Athenaeum* XLIV (1966), 261–97 and XLV (1967), 119–42 and 356–94.

————"La stilistica di Aristotele e lo strutturalismo," *Lingua e Stile* 2 (1967), 1–18.

MUSCATINE, C., *Chaucer and the French Tradition*, Berkeley 1960.

————"Form, Texture and Meaning in Chaucer's Knight's Tale," *Proceedings of the Modern Language Association* 65 (1950), 911–29.

MYERS, A. R., *England in the Late Middle Ages*, London 1953.

NEUMANN, G., *Gesten und Gebärden in der griechischen Kunst*, Berlin 1965.

NEWMAN, F. S. and NEWMAN, J. K., "L'unité musicale dans les odes de Pindare: la deuxième néméenne," *Les Études Classiques* XLII (1974), 3–12.

NEWMAN, F. S. and NEWMAN, J. K., *Pindar's Art: Its Tradition and Aims*, Hildesheim–Munich–Zurich 1984.

NEWMAN, J. K., *Augustus and the New Poetry*, Brussels 1967.

―――――"Callimachus and the Epic," *Serta Turyniana*, ed. J. L. Heller and J. K. Newman, pp. 342 ff., Urbana–Chicago–London 1974.

―――――"The Classical Background to Thomas Mann's *Doktor Faustus*," *Neohelicon* VIII (1980), 35–42.

―――――*The Concept of Vates in Augustan Poetry*, Brussels 1967.

―――――"Dante and the Alexandrians," *Neohelicon* V, 2 (1977), 9–36.

―――――"De Novo Galli Fragmento in Nubia Eruto," *Latinitas* XXVIII (1980), 83–94.

―――――"De Statio epico animadversiones," *Latomus* XXXIV (1975), 80–89.

―――――"De verbis *canere* et *dicere* eorumque apud poetas Latinos ab Ennio usque ad aetatem Augusti usu," *Latinitas* XIII (1965), 86–106.

―――――"Ennius the Mystic–I," *Greece and Rome* X (1963), 132–39.

―――――"Ennius the Mystic–II," *Greece and Rome* XII (1965), 42–49.

―――――"Ennius the Mystic–III," *Greece and Rome* XIV (1967), 44–51.

―――――"*Memini me Fiere Pavum*: Ennius and the Quality of the Roman Aesthetic Imagination," *Illinois Classical Studies* VIII (1983), 173–93.

―――――"Milto in Sicilia et in Partibus Orientalibus," *Hermes Americanus* II (1984), 140–55.

―――――"The New Gallus and the Origins of Latin Love Elegy," *Illinois Classical Studies* IX (1984), 19–29.

―――――"Orazio, Ariosto and Orazio Ariosto," *Acta Conventus Neo-Latini Amstelodamensis*, pp. 820–34, Munich 1979.

―――――"Pushkin and Horace," *Neohelicon* III (1975), 331–42.

―――――"Pushkin's *Bronze Horseman* and the Epic Tradition," *Comparative Literature Studies* IX (1972), 173–95.

―――――Review of D. Vessey, "Statius and the Thebaid," *The Classical World* 69 (1975), 83–84.

―――――"Small Latine and Lesse Greeke? Shakespeare and the Classical Tradition," *Illinois Classical Studies* IX (1984), 309–30.

―――――"*War and Peace* and the Greco-Roman Historiographical Tradition," *Neohelicon* XI (1984), 261–76.

NILSSON, M., *Geschichte der griechischen Religion*, 2 vols., Munich 1955, 1961.

NISBET, R. G. M. and HUBBARD, MARGARET, *A Commentary on Horace's Odes, Book I*, Oxford 1970.

NORDEN, E., *Agnostos Theos*, Leipzig–Berlin 1913.

―――――*Die Antike Kunstprosa*, 2 vols., 5th edn., Stuttgart 1958.

―――――*Die Geburt des Kindes. Studien der Bibliothek Warburg 3*, Leipzig–Berlin 1924.

―――――*Die römische Literatur*, reprinted Leipzig 1954.

―――――*In Varronis Saturas Menippeas Observationes Selectae*, Leipzig 1891.

NOTOPOULOS, J. A., "Studies in Early Greek Oral Poetry," *Harvard Studies in Classical Philology* 68 (1964), 45 ff.

OESCHGER, J., "Antikes und Mittelalterliches bei Dante," *Zeitschrift für Romanische Philologie* 64 (1944), 22 ff.

OGILVIE, R. M., *Latin and Greek. A History of the Influence of the Classics on English Life from 1600–1918*, Hamden, Conn. 1964.

OLSON, E., ed., *Aristotle's Poetics and English Literature*, Chicago 1965.

OSWALD, V. A., Jr., "Thomas Mann's *Doktor Faustus*: The Enigma of Frau von Tolna," *Germanic Review* 23 (1948), 249–53, esp. pp. 250 ff.

————"Full Fathom Five: Notes on Some Devices in Thomas Mann's *Doktor Faustus*," *Germanic Review* 24 (1949), 274–78.

————"Thomas Mann and the Mermaid. A note on Constructivist Music," *Modern Language Notes* 65 (1950), 171–75.

PARKER, W. R., *Milton: A Biography*, 2 vols., Oxford 1968.

PATZER, H., "Zum Sprachstil des neoterischen Hexameters," *Museum Helveticum* 12 (1955), 77 ff.

PAVESE, CARLO, "The New Heracles Poem of Pindar," *Harvard Studies in Classical Philology* 72 (1967), 47–88.

PERRY, B., *The Ancient Romances*, Berkeley and Los Angeles 1967.

PETERSON, R. G., "Critical Calculations: Measure and Symmetry in Literature," *Proceedings of the Modern Language Association* 91 (1976), 367–75.

PFEIFFER, R., *History of Classical Scholarship. From the Beginnings to the end of the Hellenistic Age*, Oxford 1968.

————*History of Classical Scholarship. 1300–1850*, Oxford 1976.

PIGANIOL, A., *Histoire de Rome*, Paris 1962.

PÖSCHL, V., *The Art of Vergil*, tr. G. Seligson, Ann Arbor 1962.

POLITZER, H., "How epic is Berthold Brecht's epic theater?" *Modern Languages Quarterly* XXIII (1962), 99–114.

POLLITT, J. J., *The Ancient View of Greek Art*, New Haven and London 1974.

POMORSKA, K., *Russian Formalist Theory and its Poetic Ambiance*, The Hague–Paris 1968.

PROPP, V., *Morfologiya Skazki*, Leningrad 1928, Eng. tr. Bloomington, Indiana 1958.

PUCKETT, L. C., *Milton's Theories of the Epic as exemplified in Paradise Regained*, diss. Urbana 1938.

PUELMA PIWONKA, M., *Lucilius und Kallimachos*, Frankfurt 1949.

PÜTZ, P., ed., *Thomas Mann und die Tradition*, Frankfurt 1971.

QUADLBAUER, F., "Die genera dicendi bis Plinius d. j.," *Wiener Studien* 71 (1958), 55–111.

REED, T. J., *Thomas Mann: The Uses of Tradition*, Oxford 1974.

REICH, H., *Der Mimus*, Berlin 1903.

REINHARDT, K., *Die Ilias und ihr Dichter*, Göttingen 1961.

REINMUTH, O. W., "Vergil's use of *interea*: a study of the treatment of contemporaneous events in Roman epics," *American Journal of Philology* 54 (1933), 323–39.

REITZENSTEIN, E., "Zur Stiltheorie des Kallimachos," in *Festschrift Richard Reitzenstein*, pp. 23–69; esp. 41 ff., "Hesiod als Vorbild des Epikers," Leipzig and Berlin 1931.

REITZENSTEIN, R., *Hellenistische Wundererzählungen*, reprinted Stuttgart 1963.

RICE, E. E., *The Grand Procession of Ptolemy Philadelphus*, Oxford 1983.

RICHTER, G. M. A., *The Sculpture and Sculptors of the Greeks*, New Haven 1957.

RIEFSTAHL, H., *Der Roman des Apuleius*, diss. Frankfurt 1938.

ROCHE, THOMAS P., JR., "The Calendrical Structure of Petrarch's *Canzoniere*," *Studies in Philology* LXXI (1974), 152 ff.

ROHDE, E., *Der griechische Roman und seine Vorläufer*, 3rd edn., Leipzig 1914.

―――*Psyche*, tr. W. B. Hillis, reprinted New York 1966.

ROSENMEYER, T. G., *The Green Cabinet*, Berkeley and Los Angeles 1969.

ROSS, D. O., *Backgrounds to Augustan Poetry*, Cambridge 1975.

ROSTAGNI, A., *Storia della letteratura latina*, *II*, Turin 1955.

ROSTOVTZEFF, M., *Rome*, New York 1960.

RUEDIGER, H., See Meier.

SAINTSBURY, G., *A History of Criticism*, 3 vols., London and New York 1900–04.

SAMARIN, R. M., *John Milton*, Moscow 1964.

SANSONE, D., *Aeschylean Metaphors for Intellectual Activity*, Wiesbaden 1975.

SCAGLIONE, ALDO, ed., *Ariosto 1974 in America*, Atti del Congresso Ariostesco–Dicembre 1974. Casa Italiana della Columbia University, Ravenna 1976.

SCHADEWALDT, W., *Der Aufbau des Pindarischen Epinikion*, Halle 1928.

―――*Iliasstudien*, des XLIII Bandes der Abhandlugen der philol.-hist. Klasse der sächsischen Akademie der Wissenschaften, nr. VI, Leipzig 1938.

―――*Von Homers Welt und Werk*, 2nd edn., Leipzig 1944.

SCHANZ, M. and HOSIUS, C., *Geschichte der Römischen Literatur*, 2 vols., reprinted Munich 1959.

SCHEFOLD, K., *Götter- und Heldensagen der Griechen in der spätarchaischen Kunst*, Munich 1978.

SCHELLER, P., *De hellenistica historiae conscribendae arte*, Leipzig 1911.

SCHLUNK, R. R., *The Homeric Scholia and the Aeneid*, Ann Arbor 1974.

SCHMIDT, G., *Zum Formgesetz des Doktor Faustus von Thomas Mann*, Wiesbaden–Frankfurt 1972.

SCHÖNBERGER, O., *Untersuchungen zur Wiederholungstechnik Lucans*, 2nd edn., Munich 1968.

SCHOLES, R. E., *Structuralism in Literature. An Introduction*, New Haven–London 1974.

SCHUG-WILLE, CHRISTA, *Art of the Byzantine World*, tr. E. M. Hatt, New York 1969.

SCHÜRCH, P., *Zur Wortresponsion bei Pindar*, Bern and Frankfurt 1971.

SCHWABL, H., "Beispiele zur poetischen Technik des Hesiod," *Hesiod*, ed. Ernst Heitsch, Darmstadt 1966.

SEIDEL, M. and MENDELSON, E., edd., *Homer to Brecht. The European Epic and Dramatic Tradition*, New Haven 1976.

SEVERYNS, A., *Homère II. Le Poète et son oeuvre*, Brussels 1946.

―――*Homère l'artiste*, Brussels 1948.

SHKLOVSKY, V., *Eisenstein*, Moscow 1973.

―――*Materyal i Stil' v Romane L'va Tolstogo 'Voina i Mir'*, Moscow n.d. [1928].

―――*O Teorii prozy*, Moscow–Leningrad 1925.

SIRLUCK, E., *Paradise Lost: A Deliberate Epic*, Cambridge 1967.

SITTL, C., *Die Gebärden der Griechen und Römer*, Leipzig 1890.

SKARD, S., "The Use of Color in Literature. A Survey of Research," *Proceedings of the American Philosophical Society* XL, 3 (1946), 163–249.

SKIADAS, A. D., ed., *Kallimachos*, Darmstadt 1975.

SKUTSCH, OTTO, ed., *Ennius*, Fondation Hardt, tome XVII, Vandoeuvre–Genève 1972.

SMEED, J. W., *Faust in Literature*, London 1975.

SNELL, B., *Die Entdeckung des Geistes*, 3rd edn., Hamburg 1955.

———"Die Klangfiguren im 2. Epigramm des Kallimachos," *Glotta* 37 (1958), 1 ff.

SPALTER, M., *Brecht's Tradition*, Baltimore 1967.

SPINGARN, J. E., *La critica letteraria nel Rinascimento*, tr. A. Fusco, Bari 1905.

———*A History of Literary Criticism in the Renaissance*, reprinted Westport, Conn. 1976.

SPITZER, L., "Die klassische Dämpfung in Racines Stil," *Archivum Romanicum* XII (1928), 361 ff.

STANFORD, W. B., *Greek Metaphor*, Oxford 1936.

STEAD, C. K., *The New Poetic*, London 1967.

STEINER, G., *After Babel*, London 1975.

———*Tolstoy or Dostoevsky*, London 1960.

STOCKERT, W., *Klangfiguren und Wortresponsionen bei Pindar*, Vienna 1969.

STRING, M., *Untersuchungen zum Stil der Dionysiaka des Nonnos von Panopolis*, diss. Hamburg 1966.

STROUX, J., *De Theophrasti Virtutibus Dicendi*, Leipzig 1912.

SUSEMIHL, F., *Geschichte der griechischen Literatur in der Alexandrinerzeit*, 2 vols., reprinted Hildesheim 1965.

THOMPSON, KRISTINA, *Ivan the Terrible: A Neoformalist Analysis*, Princeton 1981.

THOMPSON, E. M., *Russian Formalism and Anglo-American New Criticism*, The Hague–Paris 1971.

THOMSON, J. A. K., *Classical Influences on English Poetry*, London 1951.

THORNTON, H. and A., *Time and Style*, London 1962.

THORPE, JAMES, ed., *Milton Criticism*, reprinted New York 1969.

TODOROV, T., ed., *Théorie de la littérature*, Paris 1965.

TOFFANIN, G., *Storia letteraria d'Italia—Il Cinquecento*, 7th edn., Milan 1965.

TRUBETZKOY, N. F., *Dostoevsky als Künstler*, The Hague 1964.

VELZ, J., *Shakespeare and the Classical Tradition*, Minneapolis 1968.

VERPEAUX, J., *Nicéphore Choumnos. Homme d'État et Humaniste Byzantin*, Paris 1959.

VESSEY, D., *Statius and the Thebaid*, Cambridge 1973.

VOIGT, G., *Die Wiederbelebung des Classischen Altertums oder das erste Jahrhundert des Humanismus*, 2 vols., 3rd edn., Berlin 1893.

VOSS, L., *Die Entstehung von Thomas Manns Doktor Faustus*, Tübingen 1975.

WACE, J. B. and STUBBINGS, FRANK H., *A Companion to Homer*, London 1967.

WADDINGHAM, M., "A Poelenburgh in the National Gallery of Canada," *Bulletin of the National Gallery of Canada*, Ottawa 26 (1975), 3 ff.

WAERN, I., "Zur Synästhesie in griechischer Dichtung," *Eranos* 50 (1952), 14 ff.

WAHL, F., ed., *Qu'est-ce que le structuralisme?* Paris 1968.

WALKER, B., *The Annals of Tacitus*, Manchester 1952.

WARMINGTON, B. H., *Carthage*, London 1960.

WEBSTER, T. B. L., *Hellenistic Poetry and Art*, London 1964.

WEDEL, E., *Die Entstehungsgeschichte von L. N. Tolstojs "Krieg und Frieden,"* Wiesbaden 1961.

WEHRLI, F., "Der erhabene und der schlichte Stil in der poetisch-rhetorischen Theorie der Antike," *Phyllobolia für P. von der Mühll*, pp. 9–34, Basel 1946.

WEIMANN, R., *Shakespeare und die Tradition des Volkstheaters*, Berlin 1967. Eng. tr. *Shakespeare and the Popular Tradition in the Theater*, ed. Robert Schwartz, Baltimore 1978.

WEINBERG, B., "From Aristotle to Pseudo-Aristotle," *Aristotle's Poetics and English Literature*, ed. E. Olson, pp. 192 ff., Chicago 1965.

_____*History of Literary Criticism in the Italian Renaissance*, 2 vols., Chicago 1961.

WELLEK, R., *A History of Modern Criticism 1750–1950*, 4 vols., New Haven 1955–.

WHITMAN, C. H., *Homer and the Heroic Tradition*, Cambridge, Mass. 1958.

WILAMOWITZ, U. VON, *Hellenistische Dichtung*, 2 vols. in 1, reprinted Berlin 1962.

_____*Pindaros*, Berlin 1922.

WILKINSON, L. P., "Pindar and the Proem to the Third Georgic," *Forschungen zur römischen Literatur. Festschrift zum 60 Geburtstag von Karl Büchner*, pp. 286–90, ed. W. Wimmel, Wiesbaden 1970.

WILLIAMS, GORDON, *Tradition and Originality in Roman Poetry*, Oxford 1968.

_____*Change and Decline*, Berkeley 1978.

WILLIAMS, R. C., *The Theory of the Heroic Epic in Italian Criticism of the 16th Century*, diss. Johns Hopkins 1917.

WIMMEL, W., *Kallimachos in Rom*, Wiesbaden 1960.

WIMSATT, W. K., *The Verbal Icon*, Lexington 1974.

WITTE, K., "Ueber die Form der Darstellung in Livius' Geschichtswerk," *Rheinisches Museum* 65 (1910), 270–305; 359–419.

WITTKOWER, R., *Gian Lorenzo Bernini: the Sculptor of the Roman Baroque*, London 1955.

_____*Art and Architecture in Italy 1600–1750*, Harmondsworth 1958.

WÖLFFLIN, H., *Classic Art*, tr. P. and L. Murray, London 1952.

WOLF-KESTING, M., *Das epische Theater*, Stuttgart 1959.

WORSTBROCK, F. J., *Elemente einer Poetik der Aeneis*, Münster 1963.

ZAIDENSCHNUR, E., *"Voina i Mir" L. N. Tolstogo: Sozdanie velikoy knigi*, Moscow 1966.

ZIEGLER, K., *Das hellenistische Epos*, 2nd edn., Leipzig 1966.

# INDEX